C000185479

OXFORD WORLD'S CLASSICS

THE LITERARY DETECTIVE

OXFORD WORLD'S CLASSICS

JOHN SUTHERLAND

The Literary Detective
100 Puzzles in Classic Fiction

With cartoons by
MARTIN ROWSON

OXFORD
UNIVERSITY PRESS

OXFORD
UNIVERSITY PRESS

Great Clarendon Street, Oxford OX2 6DP

Oxford University Press is a department of the University of Oxford.
It furthers the University's objective of excellence in research, scholarship,
and education by publishing worldwide in

Oxford New York

Athens Auckland Bangkok Bogotá Buenos Aires Calcutta
Cape Town Chennai Dar es Salaam Delhi Florence Hong Kong Istanbul
Karachi Kuala Lumpur Madrid Melbourne Mexico City Mumbai
Nairobi Paris São Paulo Shanghai Singapore Taipei Tokyo Toronto Warsaw

with associated companies in Berlin Ibadan

Oxford is a registered trade mark of Oxford University Press
in the UK and in certain other countries

Published in the United States
by Oxford University Press Inc., New York

British Library Cataloguing in Publication Data

Data available

Library of Congress Cataloging in Publication Data

Sutherland, John, 1938–
The literary detective: 100 puzzles in classic fiction/John Sutherland;
with cartoons by Martin Rowson.
(Oxford world's classics)
1. English fiction—Miscellanea. 2. American fiction—Miscellanea. 3. Literary
recreations. 4. Puzzles. I. Title. II. Oxford world's classics (Oxford University Press)
PR821 .S885 2000   823.009–dc21   00–037498

ISBN 0–19–210036–X

1 3 5 7 9 10 8 6 4 2

Typeset in ITC New Century Schoolbook
by RefineCatch Limited, Bungay, Suffolk
Printed in Great Britain by
Cox & Wyman Ltd., Reading

Contents

Can Jane Eyre be Happy?

Contents

Who Betrays Elizabeth Bennet?

Contents

Introduction and Acknowledgements

This omnibus volume comprises three earlier collections of literary puzzles: *Is Heathcliff a Murderer?* (1996), *Can Jane Eyre Be Happy?* (1997), *Who Betrays Elizabeth Bennet?* (1999). As the publication dates indicate these books are not the fruit of deep or new research. They are more in the nature of a relaxed conversation with other readers of classic (principally Victorian) fiction—many of whom I discover, as a salutary correction to any authorial vanity, are sharper readers than I.

Most critical discourse on the subject of classic fiction is unrelaxed: regimented by the exam-driven discipline of the classroom or the theoretical cut-and-thrust of the academic conference. I have served my time (four life-sentences, as it happens) in both these arenas. Fancifully, I like to imagine these puzzle-books, and the responses they have elicited, as inhabiting somewhere like the East-Enders' 'Queen Vic' pub. An informal place, where lovers of good fiction exchange views—and sometimes bicker— as enjoyably, pointlessly, and amateur-expertly about 'VicLit' as do lovers of soccer.

None the less, I am gratified by some evidence that these puzzles have had an effect in the real world. At the end of his admirable and revisionary adaptation of *Oliver Twist* for ITV in late 1999, Alan Bleasdale concluded (in defiance of Dickens's text) by having the young hero ask the question raised in the second of my volumes, 'Why is Fagin hanged?' Bleasdale's Mr Brownlow, I am glad to report, was stumped as to how to answer (as was I, until Mr Andrew Lewis—an expert on the history of British law—came to my aid; see 'Does Dickens lynch Fagin?').

Is Heathcliff a Murderer?, the first in the series, grew

out of 'Explanatory Notes' which I supplied for the
dozen or so volumes of Oxford World's Classics texts
that I have edited. An OWC editor should, of course, be
omniscient; able to supply answers to any and all queries
arising out of the narrative. Few of us, alas, are omniscient. Over the years I would occasionally insert a note
confessing editorial perplexity—a kind of 'help please'.
In Trollope's *The Way We Live Now* (1982), for example, I
wondered how it was that, in Chapter 91, Hetta knows
where her rival in love, Mrs Hurtle, lives. A hawk-eyed
reader, Ann Totterdell (now a good friend) wrote in
pointing out that for any *careful* reader, the information
was obvious. Anthony Trollope supplied it fourteen
chapters earlier. In those days the Library of Congress
habitually confused me with the venerable Professor Sir
James Sutherland, and my date of birth on the copyright
page of *The Way We Live Now* was listed anachron-
istically (by thirty years) as '1909'. Ms Totterdell, who
is as hawk-eyed about prelims as the texts of the novels
she devours, deduced that I must be far gone into the
vale of years. Tactfully, she suggested to the editors at
OUP that they make the necessary emendation silently
lest the shock of being faulted be too much for my
superannuated frame.

Both the annotation to *The Way We Live Now* and the
Library of Congress data are now corrected. More importantly, it was to tap into this kind of reader expertise that
the puzzle books were written. There was a more personal
motive. I wanted to recover some of the childhood pleasures I had experienced in my first encounters with fiction.
In my experience children typically ask good questions
about narrative. Often, too, they are the most puzzling
questions—critically primitive as they may seem.

The point is made by James Sutherland himself, in his
Daniel Defoe: A Critical Study (Harvard, 1971):

Daniel Defoe almost certainly wrote his various narratives in much the same way as an adult tells a serial bedtime story to a child, making up most of it as he went along. Anyone who has ever told such a story has probably made some slips which are instantly pounced on by the vigilant young listener, who would be the first to object that Crusoe couldn't possibly have taken his parrot with him on board the ship that rescued him since he had already said that he had left it on the island and that 'poor Poll may be alive there still, calling after *Poor Robin Crusoe* to this day'. (pp. 127–8)

Who is reading *Robinson Crusoe* more intelligently here, the child or the professor? One would like to see them in a condition of fruitful collaboration. All of us, that is, have a child-reader within asking shrewd and impertinent questions.

I have received scores of letters arising out of these books. Most open with a statement of how much they have enjoyed the puzzles. Then they go on to take me to task. I have reviewed some of these good-natured objections in the introductions to *Can Jane Eyre Be Happy?* and *Who Betrays Elizabeth Bennet?* The latest crop, arising from the third of the volumes, is, as usual, stimulating and corrective.

An earlier correspondence which I particularly relished was that arising from how the Cratchit family contrives to cook the turkey Scrooge sends them late on Christmas Day (see pp. 521–6). The puzzle was initially suggested by the 11-year-old 'Sleuths of 7E, St Christopher's School, Bahrain' who calculated 'By our estimation, to prepare a turkey it takes at least 1 hour to clean and stuff and in the case of a very large turkey, 8 hours to cook—a total of 10 hours. In any case, would they have a big enough oven to cook it in?' (see p. 524).

My suggested solutions to the Sleuths of 7E will be found on pages 525–6. An alternative answer is offered by

Dr Tig Lang. I quote at length, since Dr Lang's reasoning is fiendishly close:

The HOW is quite clear—the Cratchits take the turkey to the local baker, as they had done their Christmas goose in the vision of Christmas Present. The WHEN raises some interesting questions. In Arnold Palmer's book *Moveable Feasts* I found that at the time *A Christmas Carol* was written, Londoners 'might be found dining at any hour between one and eight' . . . The Cratchits, though not in fashionable society, may also have dined late—I don't suppose that Scrooge gave Bob a long mid-day break, nor that he ever went home on time. (They do, however, appear to be dining early in the vision of Christmas Present.) It is notable in this vision that shops remain open before morning service on Christmas Day, and then mingling with the crowds on their way *to* church Scrooge sees 'innumerable people carrying their dinners *to* the bakers' shops' (my emphasis). So the geese were only reaching the ovens before eleven o'clock. On the day he buys the turkey, Scrooge has time to get it sent to Cratchit's, to dress (in his best, and not quickly) and to join the crowds flooding to church; the bells must have rung for a long while before the service, as he is not too late to attend in spite of stopping to talk on the way. So, if the Cratchits had all helped and if they were quick about it, they might just possibly have had time to get their turkey into the baker's oven before church.

It is my firm belief, however, that they did NO SUCH THING. Mrs Cratchit would hardly have arrived at Christmas morning with no goose ready for the baker's oven. And if she had a goose ready, would she, the prudent housewife of a needy family, have said 'Ooh! some kind soul has sent us a turkey, let's have that instead'? Of course not. It is clear that the weather was cold enough for there to be no problem keeping the turkey for a day or so longer, and I am sure that it was plucked and dressed on Boxing Day, and provided the family with some well-deserved meals for the rest of the week!

Should I fall ill in St Andrews, Fife, I trust that I will be referred to Dr Lang, a worthy successor to his gimlet-eyed countryman, Dr Joseph Bell—the original of Sherlock Holmes.

Oxford World's Classics readers are, in my experience, mustard-hot on fine points of etiquette. Mark Attwood-Wood, for example, wrote to chide that:

> In the postscript to 'Is Betsey Trotwood a Spinster?' in *Who Betrays Elizabeth Bennet?* you twice refer to the wife of Sir Percival Glyde as 'Lady Laura Glyde'. Being married to a baronet, Laura's correct style is 'Lady Glyde'. 'Lady Laura Glyde' would make her the daughter of either a duke, a marquess or an earl.

But then, to salve my shattered *amour propre*, Mr Attwood-Wood goes on to note that 'Dickens and Jane Austen make the same mistake in *Little Dorrit* and *Pride and Prejudice* respectively.' Good company. I have corrected my errors; those of the great writers must stand.

Daisy Hay took time off from revising for her A levels in English to contest the contention made by one of my earlier correspondents that Mr Bingley's fortune cannot be derived from trade, which I discussed in the Introduction to *Who Betrays Elizabeth Bennet?* (not reprinted here). Ms Hay reminds me that:

> in Chapter Four of *Pride and Prejudice*, we are informed that the Bingleys 'were of a respectable family in the north of England; a circumstance more deeply impressed on [Miss Bingley's and Mrs Hurst's] memories than that their brother's fortune and their own had been acquired by *trade*.' From this one can only assume that Mr Darcy, who after all marries a woman whose uncle lives in Cheapside, is not as snobbish as his forbidding exterior might suggest.

I do not know what grade Ms Hay got for her English A level papers. Anything less than 'A' would be an injustice, if *Pride and Prejudice* were one of her set books.

The title essay in *Who Betrays Elizabeth Bennet?* provoked a barrage of defences of Charlotte Lucas, whom I indict as the snitch. Roz Earthy agrees that Mrs Collins (née Lucas) may well be the covert informant, but offers a different and 'more plausible motivation':

Charlotte probably decided to invent the 'rumours' knowing that Mr Collins would pass them on to Lady Catherine. If the relationship should develop Lady Catherine cannot accuse the Collinses of keeping her in the dark while if Darcy speedily removes himself from Netherfield Lady C. will attribute what was said to Mr Collins's silliness. I doubt if Charlotte would really want to jeopardise any possible Darcy–Elizabeth marriage as she would certainly see the sense of Mr Bennet's advice: 'stand by the nephew. He has more to give.' Indeed, I wonder if she considered the possibility that opposition might make Elizabeth look on Darcy with more interest. At any rate while she would certainly not want to risk antagonizing Lady Catherine my guess is that she would be delighted to further a marriage between Elizabeth and Darcy if it could be done without incurring Lady C.'s wrath. The invented rumours would be her 'safety net' but I like to imagine that Darcy might soon install the Collinses in some profitable but difficult living which required careful handling. Careful handling? Mr Collins? Well, no, but Darcy would be well aware that there are six weekdays to one Sunday and Darcy clearly recognizes Charlotte's qualities ('Mr Collins appears very fortunate in his choice of a wife'). Her intelligence and diplomacy might then be rewarded.

Contrary as they are to my own, I find Ms Earthy's suppositions delightful.

Joan Aiken was, similarly, in half-agreement:

Of course you are right that it was Charlotte Lucas who told Lady Catherine that Elizabeth was in a fair way to marry Darcy, but I don't think it was in a spirit of meanness and revenge— Charlotte was not mean-natured, but she was practical and knew the news was bound to get round sooner or later, so it might as well be sooner.

Ms Aiken has turned her gift for speculation to more

creative ends than I have. She kindly sent me a copy of her *Mansfield Park* 'prequel' *The Youngest Miss Ward* (1999) 'as a token of fraternal respect'. It narrates how 'Frances Ward happens to find herself in Portsmouth'.

Janeites are, I discover, formidably knowledgeable about their author and read with a forensic attention to detail. Mr Christopher Jessel, writing as a 'solicitor who still has to deal with entails' (a nightmare subject for annotators of nineteenth-century fiction) thinks I am on the right track in 'Who betrays . . . ?' but have entirely the wrong target. The traitor is quite other. 'The clue', he writes, 'is in Chapter 45 where Miss Austen says of Caroline Bingley "for jealousy had not yet made her desperate".' There follows an extended investigation leading to the acquittal of Charlotte and the indictment of Caroline.

Catriona Graham is minded towards a less malevolent interpretation: 'As to the betrayal, is it not possible that the report which reached Lady Catherine's ears might just as easily have come inadvertently from the lips or pen of Georgiana, or from Colonel Fitzwilliam?' Ms Graham raises an associated point arising from the highly successful television adaptation of *Pride and Prejudice*:

As usual, Colin Firth played Darcy with a 'Received Pronounciation' accent. But historical linguists have argued that RP would not necessarily have been the accent of all in Darcy's class. Darcy was educated at home, until he went to University. It is perfectly possible that his accent would be what is now called North Midland—Darcy sounding like D. H. Lawrence!

Andrew Davies and other adapters, take note.

I do not suppose that any final solution will be found for the 'who betrayed?' enigma. Niall Litton, in a virtuoso survey, puts the case (with voluminous circumstantial evidence) against no less than eight suspects including Mr Bennet—'a longshot!', as he sportingly confesses. Mr

Litton evidently likes to let his imagination soar, and he also comes up with an ultra-ingenious explanation for the 'apple-blossom in June' puzzle in *Emma*:

During the course of the book Emma sees what she wants to see until stress induces clarity. Emma is idling away at a picnic. It is a gorgeous bucolic scene. She sees apple-blossom, smoke and herding sheep. Unfortunately the details do not accord with reality, but that is what she wants to see, so that is what she sees . . . Jane Austen may have been an amateur meteorologist but she also liked jokes, and would enjoy having Emma see smoke when there is no fire. As a joke it fits.

Indeed it does.

A 'betrayal' suspect Mr Litton does not arraign in his round-up is pointed to by Dr M. J. T. Robinson (of Magdalen College, Oxford) in a long and learned letter. He 'cannot swallow' the idea of Charlotte acting maliciously, but goes on:

There is one other Lucas in a position to speculate about Elizabeth and Darcy and that is Maria, the eldest of Charlotte's sisters. She had many opportunities to watch Elizabeth and Darcy at Hunsford and to discuss what she had seen with her elder sister, who had herself observed Darcy's interest in Elizabeth. If, as seems plausible, she was Charlotte's regular correspondent she may have exchanged several letters with Charlotte including speculation about Elizabeth and Darcy, *without* always telling the rest of the family. It would then require only that Charlotte spoke of Jane's coming marriage and a possibility of something similar for Elizabeth for Mr Collins to jump to a premature conclusion and self-importantly blab about it.

To my chagrin, I did not acknowledge in 'Who betrays Elizabeth Bennet?' the letter and draft article Kim Damstra sent me while the book was in preparation. It anticipates my main point. I have added a postscript to the chapter in question (see p. 494) and apologize to Dr Damstra here.

Nigel Davis, QC—'a fully paid-up member of the "Jane Austen can do no wrong" club', concluded his mock-serious review of the variable sexuality of Lady Bertram's pug with the observation that:

I would like to think that this reflects the contemporary skill (well known to Miss Austen, surely) of early 19th century veterinary surgeons in performing *totally* successful canine sex change operations—a fact inexplicably overlooked by modern historians.

R. W. Farrington, who writes from one of the London Inns of Court, offers a letter which—were I one of his clients—would doubtless cost me. In the republic of fiction-lovers, however, I have his expert opinion on the portions of the Ward sisters in *Mansfield Park* gratis and pass it on in the same spirit:

I would have thought it highly probable that Mrs Price's £7,000 (if she had such) was protected by being kept in trust. It would not have been taken into a marriage settlement only because of the near-clandestine circumstances of the marriage. But I doubt if a deceased father would have left £7,000 entirely within a young woman's own control. A trust established by a will seems most likely. Income from this sum, within the range £200–£250, plus Mr Price's half-pay would have been not as poor an income as all that. JA's point is surely that the family was too large and Mrs Price too hopeless as a manager. And though the Price family is hard-up it does not seem insecure, i.e. its income is quite reliable.

I find this a concise and convincing speculation.

William Wates (surely a retired admiral) wrote to thank me for 'another well-written and entertaining set of literary puzzles'. But he could not pass over 'your animadversions on the Royal Navy and the (not yet Royal) Marines in the chapter on *Mansfield Park*. The view that the Royal Navy in the eighteenth century was a sort of floating concentration camp' has been 'torpedoed (or should I say

"forced to strike its colours"?) by modern scholarship.'
Nor is it the case that 'the marines had earned great credit
for their part in putting down the 1796 mutinies at the
Nore and Spithead':

So if Lieutenant Price's job had nothing to do with imposing
discipline, why does Jane Austen make him a Marine at all? The
answer is that the Marines were then, even more than now, the
Royal Navy's poor relations. Not only had the sale of commissions been abolished, thus preventing people like Lieutenant
Price being the object of patronage by the wealthy; but the senior
ranks in the Corps were reserved as sinecures for successful
naval officers. The fictional Hornblower, for example, was
appointed a Colonel of Marines, and he had many counterparts
in reality. To accept a permanent commission in the Marines at
that time was publicly to embrace mediocrity. Certainly Jane
Austen, who (very unusually) had two brothers with the talent to
reach Admiral's rank, would have been well aware of all this, as
would many of her readers.

There is a final touch of the lash. 'And by the way,'
Admiral Wates concludes, 'if George Osborne lost his
teeth on the field of Quatre Bras (on Friday 16th June
1815), they must have been yanked from a still-living
mouth. He got killed at Waterloo, which was fought on
Sunday 18th June.' I have put this last straight, but keep
the original form of the *Mansfield Park* essay, with
the nautical observations sticking to it like limpet mines.
The main points, I think, are still seaworthy—just.

Michael Grosvenor Myer has pursued my various suppositions with the relentlessness of an amiable Hound of
the Baskervilles. Among the wittily quibbling issues he
raises are: where does Pumblechook live? ('I suspect you
have the local topography of *Gt Expects* slightly awry');
the nineteenth-century age of sexual consent (crucial to
the plot of *Tess of the D'Urbervilles*); where, exactly, Lt.
Price drinks ('since he is no longer on active service, so

not a member of a mess'); why does Tenniel give Alice a summer dress in the illustrations to *Through the Looking Glass* ('the date is early November and snowing')? I could go on—and so, as I know to my cost and constant instruction, can Mr Myer. I am thankful that he did not examine my Ph.D. thesis.

John Bramley takes practical issue with my hypothesis that the dead leaves fluttering on Alice's face at the end of Carroll's story indicate that, within the space of a few hours, the season has changed from high summer to early autumn. Mr Bramley writes on 25 July 1999, from Allesley Village, in Coventry:

You assume the dead leaves are autumn leaves—brown, sere and yellow. Firstly, Carroll does not so describe them. Secondly, leaves falling in high summer is not unusual, even in the sheltered Christ Church gardens, the University Parks, Meadows or wherever. In my garden at the moment there are many leaves lying on the ground. They have fluttered down at various times in the last weeks. They are dead, but they are green on arrival, only turning yellow, brown or sere later. This happens every summer. Carroll was describing an ordinary natural phenomenon, and you perhaps were being carried (blown?) away.

Perhaps. Mr Bramley is good enough to conclude, 'anyway I find your whole approach in the three books both refreshing and intriguing.' As I do his letter and his habit, shared by so few critics of literature, of looking up from his books to the world outside his window.

I had a number of interesting communications on the question of 'name games' (see pp. 611–20). Philip Gaskell expressed doubt about 'the connection of *servetur ad imum* with Johnny Eames's name'. Trollope 'must have learned and used the "English" pronounciation of Latin, and would have said "serveeter ad eyemum", not "servay-tur ad eemoom" as we do.' Harry Lesser was similarly sceptical about a Dickensian name game. He doubted

xxvi   *Introduction and Acknowledgements*

whether we should think of urine with regard to Uriah Heep, or whether Victorians, steeped in the Bible, would not think much more automatically 'David–Uriah', with the inversion that Uriah, not David is the villain. Should we be so lavatorial with Dickens? Some people I know think that 'Merdle' has more to do with 'muddle' than *merde*.

The David–Uriah opposition had not occurred to me. But I suppose Dickens (a lifelong campaigner for sanitary reform) would point out that Victorian London was as steeped in urine as its inhabitants were in the Bible.

Mr Lesser throws in a tantalizing query of his own, about *The Old Curiosity Shop*:

Are Sampson and Sally Brass Jewish, though presumably estranged from the community? (I'm Jewish myself—this isn't anti-Semitism!)—they live in Bevis Marks, and have Biblical names. More interestingly, who are the Marchioness's parents?— a sister of Sampson and Sally who had an illegitimate child and died in childhood, or disappeared leaving the child? Or was there incest between this sinister couple? We know Quilp noticed some resemblance, but not to whom. Do you have any thoughts on this?

I must reserve my response on the origins of Sampson and Sally until a re-reading of the novel. But the invaluable *Oxford Reader's Companion to Dickens* (Oxford, 1999) informs us that: 'Dickens found the space available for weekly instalments constricting, but composed the story quickly and easily, with few manuscript corrections— notably, the suppression at proof stage of a passage from Chapter 66 which indicated that the Marchioness was the illegitimate child of Sally Brass and Quilp' (p. 422).

On the related question of why Dickens gave Fagin an Irish name (as I note) Alan Myers writes:

Fagan is certainly an Irish name, but Feigin (or Feigen), so translated from the Cyrillic, is a Jewish name in Russia, though not so widespread as Kogan (Kagan). L. Feigin is a long-time promoter of Russian jazz and has appeared on Radio 3. He's certainly Jewish. There are Feigens in the London telephone directory.

As always, Dickens is more likely to be right than carping commentators like myself.

If Janeites tend towards punctiliousness, Dickensians have a penchant for the jocose. Clive W. Porter (editor of the the *Journal of the Cricket Society*) notes that Dickens and his illustrators are chronically uncertain in *Dombey and Son* about which of Captain Cuttle's arms has a hook. 'Could Cuttle,' Mr Porter muses, sometimes be 'the odious Bagstock in disguise? I think not . . . Was, then, old Cuttle a professional beggar and his hook but one of the tools of his trade? Sound in wind and limb was he, however, absent minded and simply forgot which hand was supposed to be missing?' I think not. Nor, I suspect, does Mr Porter.

Less jocosely, Eveline Coker writes to

share with you an anomaly or an inconsistency which I have stumbled upon while reading *Bleak House*. It is only a trivial incident but it has stuck in my mind and I cannot get rid of it. It concerns the differing outcomes of the smallpox illness sustained by both Charley and Esther. In particular, the fact that Esther's face suffers from the ravages of smallpox whereas Charley's does not.

Now, of course, the anomaly sticks in my mind.

Eleanor Melville proposed a puzzle in *Barnaby Rudge* for which, at the moment, I have no solution:

Why does Mrs Rudge accept an annuity from Geoffrey Haredale when she knows her husband is probably still alive, and was her brother's murderer? She is presented as an upright, hard-working woman—surely she would change her name and remove herself and her son from any connection which might allow her husband to find her again?

More light-heartedly, Ms Melville asks of *The Wind in the Willows*:

How does Toad avoid being dragged back to jail after defeating the stoats and weasels? He is sentenced to 20 years in prison, but escapes after approximately one month. He adds the crimes of jail-breaking, horse theft, car theft and riding the footplate of an engine (trespass?) to his previous misdemeanours. He returns to his own home, and lives under his own name. What are the police and justice system up to? Does he buy them off?

Crooked cops? Perish the thought.

Mr Colin Tapner (who I suspect may be in the legal profession) points to a tricky side issue in *The Woman in White*:

What happens to Blackwater Park? In the third volume Walter Hartright mentions that the rightful heir to the estate was a distant cousin of Sir Percival who was at sea. With the evidence of the original untampered register at the lawyer's office he could have helped restore the property to him, yet no mention is made ever again of the real heir. Could it be that, as with his reluctance to have Laura tell her story, Walter wants to keep some things, in this case, such as the nature of how Sir Percival came to die, covered up to protect her from scandal?

I think it could. But not everyone will.

One of the most usefully informative letters I received on my *Mill on the Floss* 'hydraulic' puzzle was from Mr Mark Tatam, 'writing to you not as a literary critic but as a farmer living close to "St Ogg's" [i.e. Gainsborough]' (see pp. 647–53). The Eliot scholar, Beryl Gray, wrote to me in July 1999, having read *Who Betrays Elizabeth Bennet?*, to say that:

I thought you might be interested to know that earlier this month, I gave a talk to the (very friendly) Friends of Gainsborough Old Hall about the connection between St Ogg's and Gainsborough. In the course of the talk I drew (friendly) attention to 'Should we change the end of *The Mill on the Floss?*', and quoted your quotations from Mr Tatam's letter. It turned out that lots of those present knew Mr Tatam (I was sorry he wasn't there himself), and several people came up to me at the end of the evening with their own flood stories. One woman told me that, when she had been trapped in her aunt's house during a flood (in the 1980s, I think), she had actually witnessed items travelling at different speeds in the water. (She also told me that the water had risen very rapidly, and that the experience was extremely frightening.)

Dr Gray adds that 'although I tell myself you're kidding' the Postscript 'Is Maggie Tulliver a murderer?' makes her very 'twitchy'. She writes, of course, as a distinguished editor of the novel.

Barry Fletcher also wrote to confirm the historical fact of flash floods at Gainsborough. He recalls a severe inundation in 1947 and adds 'The Trent Aegir is mild now but fifty years ago it was much more powerful and the cry of "Ware Aegir" would be be shouted along the banks to warn those on boats, mainly barges, to hold on to something. In the time of George Eliot it was no doubt still more powerful.'

Dr David Zuck wrote me a letter of such formidable expertise on the subject of chloroform that I hesitate to summarize it. He suggests, gently, that I may have picked up the idea that ether is a gas from Graham Greene ('who should have known better') in *The Power and the Glory*. A well-read scientist, Dr Zuck despairs of the scientific ignorance of novelists (and, as he is too polite to stress, most literary critics).

Deirdre Le Faye, the most wide-rangingly well-read and courteous of nineteenth-century literary historians offers a 'small comment' on

Heathcliff's bright white teeth—yes, this reinforces my opinion as to his Asian ancestry—look at any Asian you see in the London tube ... Africans and Asians have beautiful regular white teeth; and English have smallish usually rather discoloured teeth. Good teeth are un-English!

'Is Heathcliff an Asian murderer?' Perhaps not.

Mrs Anne Louise Bormann writes from Denmark, where she has just finished reading *Around the World in Eighty Days* to her children. She notes that:

Phileas Fogg crosses the date line on his way from Japan to America, and from this point his calculations must be off by one day. When he arrives in San Francisco at the end of Chapter 24 on what he thinks is December 3rd, it must actually be December 2nd. After his arrival in San Francisco, he goes to the British Consulate to have his passport stamped (Chapter 25), but apparently does not notice the date.

I wonder whether it was Mrs Bormann or her children who noticed the anomaly?

Tom Barnes points to a detail in *Frankenstein* which has not, I think, been generally noticed. Namely that in Chapter 21 we are told that after his fever, Victor evidently addicts himself to laudanum. 'Could it be', Mr Barnes asks, 'that the creature is merely a product of a diseased imagination, and not a physical creation at all?' It's beguiling. But who in the nineteenth century *didn't* take laudaunum?

The authoritative study on 'Opium and the Romantic Imagination' has been written by Alethea Hayter. Ms Hayter is also an active member of the Charlotte M. Yonge fellowship. If Janeites are precise and Dickensians jolly, Yongeians are terriers in defence of their (woefully neglected) author. In the original version of the essay 'What English novel is Anna reading?' I perpetrated, as Ms Hayter 'indignantly' pointed out, a 'sad libel on Guy Morville', confusing him with the scapegrace Philip Morville:

You run the risk of having a demonstration outside your door of the elderly writers of the élite Charlotte M. Yonge Society and the middle-aged academics and housewives of the Charlotte M. Yonge Fellowship, parading with banners reading UNFAIR TO GUY MORVILLE.

Charming thought. I have repaired the unfairness and apologize to both groups.

Miss Jean Elliott makes what I think is an interesting point about my essay 'How many siblings has Dobbin?' where

you deduce that William is the eldest son because he is named for his father. Quite often, however, the eldest is named for the paternal grandfather and the second for the father. In this case the smart Mr Dobbin who appears at Denmark Hill may be the eldest—not necessarily a scapegrace, but enjoying the privileges of seniority. The existence of a dashing and no doubt indulged elder brother might account for William's shyness and awkwardness and also for his father's failure to buy him a lieutenant-colonelcy.

Finally, I cannot forebear from finishing with what I think is the most satisfyingly piddling correction I have received. 'You are too dismissive,' Mr Paul McQuail tells me,

in the *Middlemarch* essay, 'Elms, limes, or does it matter?' about lime having 'apparently, some use for sculpting or carving.' See, for example, Michael Baxandall's classic *Limewood Sculptors of Renaissance Germany*. Closer to home, I saw a few years ago a sign on a shop in Marylebone Lane advertising 'Limewood as used by Grinling Gibbons'.

As always, I stand corrected and grateful.

I could protract this review into book-length. I will conclude by thanking all those, named and unnamed, who have taken the trouble to write to me and my patient and infinitely helpful editor at OUP, Judith Luna, to whom I would like—without ceremony—to dedicate this volume.

Is Heathcliff a Murderer?

Jane Austen · *Mansfield Park*

Where does Sir Thomas's wealth come from?

Edward Said's book *Culture and Imperialism*[1] was well received in the United States, but provoked some bad-tempered responses in the United Kingdom (notably in the *TLS*). The reason for the bad temper, one might suspect, was that as the imperial power principally targeted in his book's historical discussions there remained a legacy of colonists' guilt in Britain. Particular exception was taken by British commentators to Said's chapter 'Jane Austen and Empire', and its triumphant conclusion: 'Yes, Austen belonged to a slave-owning society' (p. 115). The central piece of evidence for a meaningful conjunction between the author of *Mansfield Park* and black men sweating under some sadistic overseer's whip is Sir Thomas Bertram's absence for the early stages of the novel in his estate in Antigua, during which period his unsupervised offspring put on a domestic production of Kotzebue's scandalous (for the time) play, *Lovers' Vows*.[2] Fanny Price, the waif who has been brought as a penniless young dependant to Mansfield Park, strenuously declines to participate in this godless activity. After various trials of her goodness she eventually wins the heart of the second son (and, given his elder brother's ruined health, prospective heir to the estate) Edmund, correcting in the process his wayward sense of vocation. (Edmund's 'ordination' as a clergyman was given by Austen in a cryptic remark in a letter as her novel's principal subject-matter, although there is critical dispute about just what she meant; see p. xv). Finally, after a symbolic rejection of her sordid family home at Portsmouth, Fanny is adopted by Sir Thomas as the presiding spirit of Mansfield Park. Said sees her apotheosis as an installation of world-historical significance:

Like many other novels, *Mansfield Park* is very precisely about a series of both small and large dislocations and relocations in space that occur before, at the end of the novel, Fanny Price becomes the spiritual mistress of Mansfield Park. And that place itself is located by Austen at the centre of an arc of interests and concerns spanning the hemisphere, two major seas, and four continents. (p. 112)

Miss Fanny Price—one of the most retiring heroines in the history of English fiction—emerges transformed from Said's analysis as a pre-Victoria, empress (and oppressor) of a dominion over which the sun never sets.

According to Said: 'The Bertrams could not have been possible without the slave trade, sugar, and the colonial planter class' (p. 112). But, 'Sir Thomas's infrequent trips to Antigua as an absentee plantation owner reflect the diminishment of his class's power' (p. 113). Said is here building on two brief comments early in the novel's action. On page 20 the narrator records that Sir Thomas's circumstances 'were rendered less fair than heretofore, by some recent losses on his West India Estate, in addition to his eldest son's [Tom's] extravagance'. A little later, on page 26, Mrs Norris observes to Lady Bertram that Sir Thomas's means 'will be rather straitened, if the Antigua estate is to make such poor returns'. It is clear, however, that on her part Lady Bertram does not anticipate any serious 'diminishment' of her family's position. 'Oh! *that* will soon be settled', she tells Mrs Norris. And indeed, on his unexpected return, Sir Thomas confirms that he has been able to leave the West Indies early because 'His business in Antigua had latterly been prosperously rapid'. At the end of the novel, the Bertram estate—with Tom chastened and sober—seems on a sounder footing than ever.

Anyone attempting a historical reading should note that the period in which *Mansfield Park's* action is set (between 1805 and February 1811, when Jane Austen began writing) was not the period in which the British Empire fell, but the prelude to its extraordinary rise.[3] The year following the novel's publication, 1815 (Waterloo year), marked the beginning of imperial Britain's century. If we follow Said, this imperial achievement was a bourgeois rather than an aristocratic thing. The co-opting of middle-class Fanny Price into the previously exclusively aristocratic enclave of Mansfield Park predicts the new bourgeois energies of nineteenth-century British imperialism. The patrician absentee landlord like Sir Thomas will yield to the earnest (and essentially middle-class) district commissioner, missionary, and colonial educator (the class represented most spectacularly by the Arnolds). Fanny Price leads on, inexorably, to that wonderful apostrophe to the battalions of British 'Tom Browns' at the opening of Hughes's novel—ordinary young men and women from ordinary backgrounds, who have helped colour the bulk of the globe red.[4]

Said's insights are coolly argued and persuasive. They also supply an attractive way of teaching the novel, and will be adopted in any number of courses on post-coloniality and literature of oppression. Inevitably they will surface as orthodoxy in A level answers ('"Austen belonged to a slave-owning society": Discuss.') There are, however, a number of problems. One obvious objection is that Jane Austen seems to take the Antigua business much less seriously than does Edward Said. Like the French wars (which get only the most incidental references in

Persuasion), Austen seems to regard affairs of empire as
something well over the horizon of her novel's interests.
So vague is her allusion to what Sir Thomas is actually
doing abroad that Said is forced into the awkward speculation, 'Sir Thomas's property in the Caribbean *would have
had to be* a sugar plantation maintained by slave labour
(not abolished until the 1830s)' (my italics). Not necessarily. Since Jane Austen says nothing specific on the subject,
the Bertrams could have had a farm supplying produce
and timber to other plantations. And if, as Said claims, Sir
Thomas is doing badly, it could be because he ill-advisedly
chose to raise some other crop than sugar, or because he
declines to use slave labour as heartlessly as his fellow
plantation owners (there is, as we shall see, some evidence
for this hypothesis).

There is one rather tantalizing reference to slavery in
Volume 2, Chapter 3 of *Mansfield Park*. Fanny tells
Edmund that 'I love to hear my uncle talk of the West
Indies. I could listen to him for an hour together' (p. 177).
She continues:

'I do talk to him more than I used. I am sure I do. Did not you hear
me ask him about the slave trade last night?'

'I did—and was in hopes the question would be followed up by
others. It would have pleased your uncle to be inquired of farther.'

'And I longed to do it—but there was such a dead silence!'
(p. 178)

Dead silence pretty well describes *Mansfield Park's* deal-
ing with Antigua generally. Edward Said gets round this
absence of reference by a familiar critical move. Texts, just
like their readers, have their repressed memories and their
'unconscious'. Austen's not mentioning colonial exploitation betrays neurotic anxiety on the subject. In his
stressing absent presences, Said is following a trail flam-
boyantly blazed by Warren Roberts's monograph *Jane
Austen and the French Revolution* (London, 1979), a work

written at the high tide of theoretic 're-reading' of classic texts. Roberts's line goes thus: as is well known, Jane Austen never mentions the French Revolution. Therefore it must be a central preoccupation, and its silent pressure can be detected at almost every point of her narratives. In *Mansfield Park*, Roberts argued for a quite specific time setting of 1805–7, when the French blockade had disastrous implications for the British sugar trade, forcing down the price to the growers from 55s. to 32s. a quintal. It is deduced that this 1805–7 crisis accounts for Sir Thomas's urgent trip to Antigua.

There is, however, nothing in the novel to confirm this historically significant date. If anything, the date markers which the narrative contains rather contradict 1805–7. There are clear references, for instance, to the *Quarterly Review* (which was not founded until 1809), Crabbe's *Tales* (not published until September 1812), and the imminent 1812 war with America. (See notes to pp. 94, 141.) These suggest a setting exactly contemporaneous with Jane Austen's writing the novel, 1811–13. On the other hand, references to *The Lay of the Last Minstrel* (published in 1805) but none of Scott's subsequent poems, could he thought to confirm a setting of 1805–7. It remains a moot point.[5] The strongest argument against an 1805–7 setting is, of course, the Crabbe reference. His *Tales* were published in September 1812 (by Hatchard, in two volumes). But, if one examines the relevant passage carefully, there is some warrant for thinking that Austen may not have had this specific 1812 publication in mind. Edmund, at the end of Volume 1, Chapter 16, asks Fanny: 'How does Lord Macartney go on?' Without waiting for answer he opens up some other volumes on the table which Fanny has apparently been reading: 'And here are Crabbe's *Tales*, and the Idler, at hand to relieve you, if you tire of your great book' (p. 141). The 'great book' is identified as Lord

Macartney's *Journal of the Embassy to China* (1807),
which Fanny is dutifully reading since Sir Thomas is currently also on a trip abroad. It would make sense (from
Edmund's ironic use of the term 'great') to assume it is a
new book. And if one lower-cased the first letter of the
Crabbe reference, so that it read 'and here are Crabbe's
tales', it could as well refer to the much-reprinted *The
Borough* or the verse stories in *Poems* (1807). Austen's
manuscript, as R. W. Chapman reminds us, was not always
precise on such details. There is at least sufficient
uncertainty in the matter for one to consider carefully
Roberts's 1805–7 hypothesis, and the elaborate super-
structure he erects on it.

It remains, however, hypothetical in the extreme, and in
passing one may note that Roberts's book marked a new
gulf which had opened between the advanced literary
critics of the academic world and the intelligent lay reader for whom, if Jane Austen or any other novelist did not
mention something, it was because they did not think that
something worth mentioning. *Jane Austen and the French
Revolution* provoked one of the most amusing of *New
Statesman* competitions, asking sportive readers of the
magazine to come up with the most unlikely titles for literary critical works they could think of. The winner was
the delightful: '*My Struggle*, by Martin Amis.'

It will not, of course, do to laugh Edward Said's carefully laid arguments out of court. But one can question
certain aspects of his reading of *Mansfield Park*. On historical grounds one can question Said's contention that
Sir Thomas's wealth comes primarily from his colonial
possessions and that his social eminence in Britain is
entirely dependent on revenues from Antigua. During the
Napoleonic War large landholders (as Sir Thomas clearly
is) made windfall fortunes from agriculture, sheep-
farming, and cattle-farming. (Although, as Marilyn Butler

points out, agricultural wages fell during the period, and southern England became 'a relatively depressed area', p. xiii.) Walter Scott—who had toyed with the idea of emigrating to the West Indies in 1797—discovered when he took over a farm at Ashestiel in 1805 that he could enrich himself by raising sheep, and by subletting portions of his rented agricultural land. It was the euphoria engendered by this bonanza that inspired him to go on a farm-buying spree around his 'cottage' (later a baronial mansion) at Abbotsford.[6] It led to disaster when the value of agricultural land and produce slumped in the postwar period, after 1815. If *Mansfield Park* is set at some point around 1805—13 (taking the most relaxed line on the question), Sir Thomas may conceivably have been coining it from rented and agent-managed farms on his estate. If so, Mansfield Park itself would have been the main source of his income, and would have compensated for any Caribbean shortfall.

According to Said, the fact that Fanny Price shows so little concern about what goes on Antigua is a measure of how successful the imperialist ideology was in neutralizing 'significant opposition or deterrence at home' (p. 97). This most artificial of economic arrangements—a small, northern island sucking wealth from a Caribbean island by means of workers forcibly expatriated from Africa— was rendered a fact of nature. Something so natural, in fact, that it provoked no more comment than the sun's rising in morning and setting at night. It is a beguiling argument. But it can be objected that there was indeed 'significant opposition' to the colonial exploitation of slaves in England in the early nineteenth century, and that Fanny Price—particularly as elevated by Sir Thomas's favour after his return from Antigua—would have been in the forefront of it. It is useful, in making this point, to look at an earlier critical commentary. Interest in the

Antigua dimension of *Mansfield Park* is, as it happens, of fairly long standing. The first detailed reference I have come across is by Stephen Fender (a critic specializing in immigration studies) in 1974, in a conversation recorded for a publisher of educational tapes for British sixth-formers. Fender asked:

Can it be said that Jane Austen is concerned with the 'real' social life of her time? The answer is yes. The house, Mansfield Park, no longer fills its 'ideal' role, its members no longer fulfil their functions. Tom Bertram's relationship with the land is occasional and predatory—he only comes home to hunt—and the land no longer supports the house. Its wealth is from Antigua which produced sugar which had been worked by slaves. The Wilberforce anti-slavery movement was at its height when *Mansfield Park* was written and its contemporary readers would see that the house was, in a sense, 'alienated' from its environment. Perhaps in this context it is significant that the moral inheritor of the true values of 'Mansfield Park' is Fanny Price, the outsider.[7]

Fender's point is that *Mansfield Park* is as much a novel about the English class system and its resilient modes of regeneration as it is about British imperialism. One should also note that the novel contains clear indications that Fanny Price belongs to the Clapham Sect of evangelical Christianity, which hated plays and light morality only slightly less than it loathed slavery. Her prejudices are centrally aligned with those of the sect's 'Reform of Manners' campaign. These evangelicals were mobilized politically by William Wilberforce, who allied them with the British abolitionist movement. It may well have been Wilberforce's successful bill for the abolition of slavery in 1807 which inspired Fanny's artless question to Sir Thomas about slaves. Wilberforce's bill remained a dead letter until, five years after his death in 1838, slavery in the West Indies was finally abolished. But, it is safe to say,

Fanny would have been on the side of the abolitionists from the first—as much a hater of human slavery in 1811 as she was a distruster of domestic theatricals, and from the same evangelical motives.[8]

If we take the Antigua dimension of *Mansfield Park* seriously, reading more into it than the slightness of textual references seem to warrant, it is clear that far from buttressing the crumbling imperial edifice Fanny will, once she has power over the estate, join her Clapham brethren in the abolitionist fight. Jane Austen (in 1814) may well, as Edward Said reminds us, have belonged to a slave-owning society. Fanny Price's creator died in 1817, while slave owning was still a fact of British imperial rule, whatever the Westminster law-books said. Fanny Price, we apprehend, will survive to the 1850s, before dying as Lady Bertram, surrounded with loving grandchildren and a devoted husband, now a bishop with distinctly 'low', Proudie-like tendencies. Both of them will take pride in the fact that there is no taint of slave-riches in their wealth—and that England has rid herself of the shameful practice of human bondage a full decade before the French, and no less than thirty years before the Americans. Fanny Price, and her docile husband, will certainly have done their bit to bringing this happy end about.[9]

The Oxford World's Classics *Mansfield Park* is edited by James Kinsley, with an introduction by Marilyn Butler.

Walter Scott · *Waverley*

═══

How much English blood (if any) does Waverley spill?

═══

Scott, in a much-quoted comment to his friend J. B. S. Morritt, expressed a low opinion of the hero of his first novel. Edward Waverley, the author of *Waverley* declared, was 'a sneaking piece of imbecility'.[1] One of the more extraordinary aspects of Waverley's imbecility is that— as far as one can make out from the account given in the narrative—he wanders through the battlefields of the great 1745 Rebellion offering as little danger to his English foe as a dormouse in a tiger's cage. Take, for instance, the highpoint in Chapter 24 of the second volume ('The Conflict'), which describes the Battle of Prestonpans in which the Scottish forces (under whose flag Waverley now fights, although he is still technically an officer of the English crown) won a famous victory, suggesting that they might indeed overrun England and restore the Stuarts to the throne. For the English military, Prestonpans was a chilling reminder of how formidable highlanders were in hand-to-hand engagement. The English commanders fondly thought that the bare-legged barbarians would be so overwhelmed by the novelty of artillery, that they would turn tail in fear when the first shells and cannon-balls exploded among them. Instead, the Scots flanked their static English foe and fell on them with cold steel. As Burton's *History of Scotland* records:

A slaughter of a frightful kind thus commenced, for the latent ferocity of the victors was roused, and grew hotter and hotter the more they pursued the bloody work. To men accustomed to the war of the musket and bayonet, the sword-cut slaughter was a restoration of the more savage-looking fields of old, which made even the victorious leaders shudder.[2]

Waverley's conduct on the field at Prestonpans is less than bloodthirsty. Observing among the mêlée an English officer 'of high rank', he is so struck by 'his tall martial figure' that he decides 'to save him from instant destruction' (p. 225), going so far as to turn the battle-axe of Dugald Mahoney, which is about to descend on Colonel Talbot's head. Waverley, who evidently has a keen eye for insignia of rank, then perceives another English colonel in trouble. 'To save this good and brave man, became the instant object of Edward's anxious exertions' (p. 226). But try as he does, again apparently impeding his own sworn comrades from their business of killing Englishmen, he can only witness the death of his former commander Colonel Gardiner and suffer his withering *et tu, Brute?* look.

What on earth, one wonders, is Waverley doing on this battlefield, scurrying around trying to save enemy *officers* from being killed? The reader is not helped by Scott's account of the battle which is remarkably patchy and vague (the event is 'well known', the narrator says by way of excuse: p. 225). Yet, we later learn, the Chevalier 'paid [Edward] many compliments on his distinguished bravery' (p. 238). After the battle Fergus informs Edward that 'your behaviour is praised by every mortal, to the skies, and the Prince is eager to thank you in person; and all our beauties of the White Rose are pulling caps for you' (p. 237). Captain Waverley is a Scottish hero—what does this mean but that he did great slaughter among the enemy? After the battle, we are told, the field is 'cumbered with carcases' (p. 230). Fergus, who is a fire-eater and a merciless warrior; would hardly praise Edward for saving his former

English comrades from destruction. 'You know how he
fought' (p. 249), Rose later reminds Flora. Would that we
did.

From the lustre which attaches to him after the battle,
we have to assume Edward did at least a fair share of killing. But Scott's evasive narrative begs the question: did
Waverley kill any Englishmen? Did his sword pierce and
skewer English guts? Did he cut English throats or cave in
English skulls? Did he so much as draw a drop of English
blood? Soldiers on battlefields have only one mission—to
kill the enemy. Either Edward Waverley is the most
incompetent warrior who ever lived or—still bearing the
English king's commission—he killed the English king's
men.

Scott was clearly in a personal dilemma in this, all-
important, aspect of his hero's military exploits. The
king's commission which he himself held as a captain in
the Edinburgh Light Cavalry was the most treasured possession of Scott's manhood, more dear to him by far than
his being laird of Abbotsford or 'the author of *Waverley*'.[3]
When, a few months after his novel's triumph, he visited
Brussels and the field at Waterloo, it was in his cavalry
officer's uniform that Captain Scott chose to be presented
to the Tsar of Russia (it led to an unfortunate misunder-
standing when the potentate assumed the novelist had
been wounded in the recent battle—Scott had, in fact,
been lamed from childhood by polio). Scott, the serving
officer, would have been nauseated by the idea of Edward's
killing fellow holders of the king's commission—it would
have been a treachery deeper than Judas's. Other ranks—
'erks', 'PBI' ('poor bloody infantry'), 'grunts': they have
always attracted names testifying to their subhumanity—
were something else altogether. What Scott intimates
by highlighting Edward's stout protection of his fellow
(English-Hanoverian) officers in their extremities of

danger on the battlefield is that his killing (for which he had his due of fame among the Stuart ladies) was reserved for the English other ranks—those uncommissioned, unregarded, private soldiers and NCOs who have always been treated by their commissioned betters as expendable battle-fodder. In *Waverley* they are of no more account than the horses who die on the battlefield or the crows who peck at the corpses. Yes, the perceptive reader apprehends, Waverley did indeed spill English blood and a lot of it—but it was not blue blood. Had it been, his head might well have joined Fergus's on the pikes at Carlisle.

The Oxford World's Classics *Waverley is* edited by Claire Lamont.

Jane Austen · *Emma*

====

Apple-blossom in June?

====

The early nineteenth-century novelists inherited from their Gothic predecessors a sense that, where landscape was concerned, lies were more beautiful than truth and, for that reason, often preferable. In his essay on Mrs Radcliffe in *The Lives of the Novelists*, Scott notes the pervasive vagueness of her scene-painting, a quality which at its best aligns her word-drawn settings with the imaginary landscapes of Claude:

Some artists are distinguished by precision and correctness of outline, others by the force and vividness of their colouring; and it is to the latter class that this author belongs. The landscapes of Mrs Radcliffe are far from equal in accuracy and truth to those of her contemporary, Mrs Charlotte Smith, whose sketches are so very graphical, that an artist would find little difficulty in actually painting from them. Those of Mrs Radcliffe, on the contrary, while they would supply the most noble and vigorous ideas, for producing a general effect, would leave the task of tracing a distinct and accurate outline to the imagination of the painter. As her story is usually enveloped in mystery, so there is, as it were, a haze over her landscapes, softening indeed the whole, and adding interest and dignity to particular parts, and thereby producing every effect which the author desired, but without communicating any absolutely precise or individual image to the reader. (pp. 118–19)[1]

For all the realism of his historical analysis and characterization, Scott often found a similar 'haze' very useful in his own higher-flying landscape descriptions. It was pointed out to him when embarking on *Anne of Geierstein*

(1829) that it might be a handicap never to have visited the Swiss Alps, where the action is set. Nonsense, Scott replied, he had seen the paintings of Salvator Rosa, and that would do very well, thank-you.[2] Radcliffian haze was also very useful to Scott in what remains the most famous anomaly in his fiction, the 'reversed sunset' in *The Antiquary* (1816). In an early big scene in that novel, Sir Arthur Wardour and his daughter Isabella are trapped between the onrushing tide and unscaleable cliffs. The location is identifiably Newport-on-Tay (called in the novel 'Fairport'), near Dundee, on the east coast of Scotland. Scott highlights the scene by having it occur while the great disc of the sun sinks into the North Sea—a lurid panorama on which two paragraphs of fine writing is lavished.

The problem is, of course, that in our cosmos the sun does not sink in the east, it sinks in the west, in the Irish Sea. Given the haste with which he wrote his novel it is not surprising, perhaps, that Scott should have perpetrated the error. What is surprising is that he should have retained it in his 1829 revised edition of *The Antiquary*. The mistake was certainly pointed out to him. Evidently he felt that where land and seascapes were concerned, the novelist's artistic licence extended to changing the course of the planets through the heavens. Novelists later in the century were more fastidious. Rider Haggard, for instance, rewrote large sections of *King Solomon's Mines* in order to correct an error about the eclipse of the sun which is so technical as to be beyond all but the most astronomically expert readers.[3] Haggard mistakenly had the solar eclipse occur while the moon was full. In all editions of *King Solomon's Mines* after the '37th thousand' he changed it to a lunar eclipse.

This fetishism about scenic detail develops in the 1830s and 1840s. It may well have coincided with more sophistication about the authenticity of theatrical sets, a greater awareness of what foreign parts looked like with the growth of the British tourism industry, and the diffusion of encyclopaedias among the novel-reading classes. Captain Frederick Marryat wrote *Masterman Ready, or the Wreck of the Pacific* (1841) specifically to correct the travesty of life on a South Seas desert island perpetrated by Johann Wyss's *The Swiss Family Robinson* (1812, 1826). Marryat, who as a sailor had felt the brine of the seven seas on his cheek, was appalled by such freaks of nature as flying penguins and man-eating boa-constrictors.[4]

Jane Austen's most lamentable landscape-painting error occurs in the Donwell picnic scene in *Emma*. The date of the picnic is given to us very precisely 'It was now the middle of June, and the weather fine', we are told on page 319. And again, on page 323, the excursion is described as taking place 'under a bright mid-day sun, at almost Midsummer' (i.e. around 21 June). Strawberries are in prospect, which confirms the June date. During the course of the picnic, Austen indulges (unusually for her) in an extended passage describing a distant view— specifically Abbey-Mill Farm, which lies some half-a-mile distant, 'with meadows in front, and the river making a close and handsome curve around it'. The narrative continues, weaving the idyllic view into Emma's tireless matchmaking activities:

It was a sweet view—sweet to the eye and the mind. English verdure, English culture, English comfort, seen under a sun bright, without being oppressive.

In this walk Emma and Mr Weston found all the others assembled; and towards this view she immediately perceived Mr Knightley and Harriet distinct from the rest, quietly leading the way. Mr Knightley and Harriet!—It was an odd tête-à-tête; but she was glad to see it.—There had been a time when he would have scorned her as a companion, and turned from her with little ceremony. Now they seemed in pleasant conversation. There had been a time also when Emma would have been sorry to see Harriet in a spot so favourable for the Abbey-Mill Farm; but now she feared it not. It might be safely viewed with all its appendages of prosperity and beauty, its rich pastures, spreading flocks, orchard in blossom, and light column of smoke ascending. (pp. 325–6)

James Kinsley offers a note to 'in blossom':

The anomaly of an orchard blossoming in the strawberry season was noticed by some of the novel's first readers. Jane Austen's niece Caroline wrote to a friend as follows: 'There is a tradition in the family respecting the apple-blossom as seen from Donwell Abbey on the occasion of the strawberry party and it runs thus— That the first time my uncle . . . saw his sister after the publication of *Emma* he said, "Jane, I wish you would tell me where you get those apple-trees of yours that come into bloom in July." In truth she did make a mistake—there is no denying it—and she was speedily apprised of it by her brother—but I suppose it was not thought of sufficient consequence to call for correction in a later edition.' (p. 444)

One could defend the anachronistic apple-blossom in the same way that one defends the anastronomical sunset in that other novel of 1816, *The Antiquary*. Both represent a hangover from the free-and-easy ways of the Gothic novel of the 1790s when such liberties could be taken with artistic impunity. But this is not entirely satisfactory with the author of *Northanger Abbey*, a novel which hilariously castigates Gothic fiction's offences against common sense. And, as R. W. Chapman notes (apropos of the apple blossom), such mistakes are 'very rare' in Miss Austen's fiction.[5]

It was evidently assumed by Jane Austen's family that no correction was made because the error was 'not thought of sufficient consequence'. This is unlikely; elsewhere one can find Jane Austen going to some length to

authenticate detail in her fiction (she put herself to
trouble, for instance, to verify details as to whether there
was a governor's house in Gibraltar, for *Mansfield Park*).

If the 'apple-blossom in June' error were pointed out to
her, why then did Jane Austen not change it? 'Orchards in
leaf' would have been an economical means of doing so,
requiring no major resetting of type. One explanation is
that she did not have time—some eighteen months after
the publication of *Emma* Jane Austen died, in July 1817. A
more appealing explanation is that it is not an error at all.
It was not changed because the author did not believe it
was wrong. In order to make this second case one should
note that there is not one 'error' in the description (blossom in June), but two, and possibly three. Surely, on a
sweltering afternoon in June, there would not be smoke
rising from the chimney of Abbey-Mill Farm? Why have a
fire? And if one were needed for the baking of bread, or
the heating of water in a copper for the weekly wash, the
boiler would surely be lit before dawn, and extinguished
by mid-morning, so as not to make the kitchen (which
would also be the family's dining-room) unbearably hot.
The reference to the ascending smoke would seem to be
more appropriate to late autumn. And the reference to
'spreading flocks' would more plausibly refer to the lambing season, in early spring, when flocks enlarge dramatically. It will help at this point to quote the relevant part of
the passage again: 'It might be safely viewed with all its
appendages of prosperity and beauty, its rich pastures,
spreading flocks, orchard in blossom, and light column of
smoke ascending.' What this would seem to mean is that
now Harriet is so effectively separated from Mr Robert
Martin, the occupant of Abbey-Mill Farm, she is immune
to its varying attractions over the course of the year—
whether in spring, early summer, midsummer or autumn.
What Austen offers us in this sentence is not Radcliffian

haze, but a precise depiction, in the form of a miniature montage, of the turning seasons.[6] Months may come and months may go, but Harriet will not again succumb to a mere farmer.

The Oxford World's Classics *Emma* is edited by James Kinsley with an introduction by Terry Castle.

=====

Effie Deans's phantom pregnancy

=====

The wonderful plot of *The Heart of Midlothian*—Jeanie
Deans's refusing to perjure herself in court to save her
sister's life, and her tramp down to London to beg mercy
from the queen—originate in the misfortune of Effie's
pregnancy. Yet that misfortune, closely examined, is an
extremely problematic thing. Certain improbabilities in it
force us to assume either, (1) that Scott found himself
trapped in a narrative difficulty which he could not easily
write himself out of, or (2) that there is more to the episode
than meets the casual reader's eye.

I prefer the second of these assumptions, although in
support of the first it should be said that the law by which
Effie is condemned contains some very dubious propositions. Scott outlines the 1690 law (which was repealed in
the early nineteenth century) in a note to Chapter 15. A
woman was liable to execution for infanticide on the circumstantial grounds 'that she should have concealed her
situation during the whole period of pregnancy; that she
should not have called for help at her delivery; and that,
combined with these grounds of suspicion, the child
should be either found dead or be altogether missing'
(p. 528). What is unlikely is that a woman, in any normal
social situation, should be able to disguise her altered
physical shape in the last months of pregnancy, or that
she should be able to deliver her own child without the
assistance of a midwife. Common sense suggests that the
ordinance must have been most effective, not against
infanticide, but abortion. A woman might well conceal her

condition for four or five months and procure an abortion, at the actual climax of which the abortionist might be prudently absent. Women likely to fall foul of the law would not anyway be reliable as to when menstruation stopped, and 'the whole period of pregnancy' would be very hard to establish.

In Chapter 10 of *The Heart of Midlothian* we are told, in a rapid summary way, how Effie is sent to work in the Saddletrees' shop, by the Tolbooth Kirk, in the High Street. Her half-sister (who is some years older, less beautiful, and more religious by nature) is pleased, since there have been signs of lightness in Effie's conduct—most worryingly a propensity to dancing and unidentified 'idle acquaintances' which the young girl has formed around St Leonard's Crags, at the south side of the city, where her father keeps his small dairy herd.

At first things go well with Effie, who lodges with Mr and Mrs Saddletree (something of a termagant). The young woman does her work cheerfully and well. They are relatives, and kind employers. But:

Ere many months had passed, Effie became almost wedded to her duties, though she no longer discharged them with the laughing cheek and light step, which at first had attracted every customer. Her mistress sometimes observed her in tears, but they were signs of secret sorrow, which she concealed as often as she saw them attract notice. (pp. 103–4)

Her 'disfigured shape, loose dress, and pale cheeks' inevitably attract the 'malicious curiosity' and the 'degrading pity' of neighbours and fellow-servants. But she confesses nothing, returning all taunts with bitter sarcasm. Why, one wonders, do not her master and mistress (who are living alongside her) note their kinswoman's alteration as readily as casual customers in the shop? Bartoline Saddletree, we are told, is 'too dull at drawing inferences from the occurrences of common life'. Scott concedes that

Effie's changed shape and demeanour 'could not have escaped the matronly eye of Mrs Saddletree, but she was chiefly confined by indisposition to her bedroom for a considerable time during the latter part of Effie's service' (p. 104). What this indisposition is, we are not told. But it would seem to have kept her in total quarantine, even from talkative servants (who would surely have observed Effie's interestingly changed shape). Mrs Saddletree is lively enough in subsequent sections of the narrative, suggesting a wonderfully quick recovery.

A more troubling question is why Effie's pregnancy escaped the notice of her half-sister. Jeanie, as a cow-feeder and an older woman (old enough, indeed, to remember Effie's birth) would certainly have known what a pregnant young girl looked like. Scott, rather fuzzily, suggests they never met. Mrs Saddletree's illness gave Effie a pretext for never coming to St Leonard's Crags. And 'Jeanie was so much occupied, during the same period, with the concerns of her father's household, that she had rarely found leisure for a walk into the city, and a brief and hurried visit to her sister' (pp. 104–5).

There are two problems here. The first is that—despite what readers who do not know Edinburgh may be led to think—the Deans's farm at St Leonard's Crags, on the common land beneath Arthur's Seat—is about twelve minutes walk from the High Street. For a healthy young body like Jeanie Deans (who would be bringing her produce to the High Street anyway), the excuse that she was too busy to walk a mile to visit her sister is highly unconvincing. Moreover, under oath in court Jeanie testifies that she did indeed visit her sister during the latter months of her pregnancy, noticed that she looked unwell, and questioned her as to 'what ailed her' (p. 231). No answer was given by the unfortunate young woman. None the less, when Effie returns, minus baby, to St Leonard's

Crags, Jeanie immediately deduces (without being told) what the problem is, even though Effie's shape is now more like its old self. Her half-sister has been 'ruined', Jeanie realizes—just by looking at her. This percipience, following on earlier impercipience, is very odd.

The Saddletrees' ignorance of Effie's swollen belly and desperately changed appearance is barely credible. But one would have liked a little more detail about the strange illness that kept the lady of the house (an inveterate busybody) so completely out of the affairs of her household for so many months. What is not believable is that Jeanie, having observed Effie's condition, did not make the obvious deduction, based on her knowledge of what might happen to young girls with light morals in the city. There are two possible explanations: (1) Jeanie saw, and suspected, but said nothing—in the hope that she was wrong or that some act of God might put all right; (2) that, out of anger against her sister, Jeanie deliberately kept out of Effie's way, thus leaving her exposed to danger. Guilt at having abandoned Effie at this most precarious moment of her existence may be thought to have strengthened Jeanie's determination to walk, barefoot, like some medieval self-flagellant, the length of the kingdom to win a reprieve.

The Oxford World's Classics *The Heart of Midlothian* is edited by Claire Lamont.

Mary Shelley · *Frankenstein*

How does Victor make his monsters?

Answering from one's visual recollections of the films, the answer to the question in the title is easy. Colin Clive (in James Whale's and Universal Pictures' 1931 modern-dress classic), Peter Cushing (in a string of Hammer-produced, Terence Fisher-directed gothics from 1957 onwards), James Mason (in the 1973 TV-movie, scripted by Christopher Isherwood), Gene Wilder (in Mel Brooks's hilarious 1974 spoof *Young Frankenstein*), Kenneth Branagh (in the 1994 blockbuster, *Mary Shelley's Frankenstein*), and even the heroes in such delightfully zany send-ups as *Frankenhooker* (a story based on monstrous exploding prostitutes) and *Frankenstein, the College Years* are—all of them— half surgeons of genius, half mad scientists. In this dual capacity these cinematic Frankensteins dispatch goblin-like henchmen to scour the local graveyards, gibbets, morgues, and anatomy schools for human parts. This ana-tomical junk is assembled by the surgeon's art like some carnal jigsaw ('can we use this brain?'), and the final inert, composite cadaver is raised on a platform to be struck— like Benjamin Franklin's kite—by lightning, harnessed into life-giving energy by the scientist's brilliant technology.

This episode has been repeated so often on the screen as to be folkloric. It is, however, wholly unfaithful to what Mary Shelley wrote and published in 1818.[1] The spare-parts, galvano-animated Frankenstein's monster derives from a number of sources well outside the source narra-tive. Whale's mad scientist—which has been formative—

is an elision of Frankenstein and a range of popular misconceptions about the wild-haired Nobel Prizewinning German with the same-sounding name, Albert Einstein. Hence the bizarre fact that, in the classic 1931 film, Shelley's early-nineteenth-century tale is transposed into an alien, early-twentieth-century setting. Shelley's Frankenstein is no 'scientist', whether mad or sane, but an Enlightenment *philosophe*. As the *OED* records, the word 'scientist' was not even coined until 1840.

The main distortion of Shelley's original conception of Frankenstein can be laid at the door of the novelist herself. Writing in her 1831 preface ('to the Third Edition'), the author muses about how the great experiment *might* have been achieved: 'Perhaps a corpse would be reanimated; galvanism had given token of such things: perhaps the component parts of a creature might be manufactured, brought together, and endued with vital warmth.' Shelley enlarges on this idea, picturing some 'pale student of unhallowed arts kneeling beside the thing he had put together. I saw the hideous phantasm of a man stretched out, and then, on the working of some powerful engine, show signs of life, and stir with an uneasy, half-vital motion' (p. 196).

This scenario is given precise detail (fleshed out, one might say) by graphic accounts of Percy Shelley at Oxford University showing off a small model dynamo to his friends. According to Thomas Jefferson Hogg, while they were both students at Oxford, Shelley:

proceeded, with much eagerness and enthusiasm, to show me the various instruments, especially the electrical apparatus: turning round the handle very rapidly so that the fierce, crackling sparks flew forth; and presently standing on the stool with glass feet, he begged me to work the machine until he was filled with the fluid [i.e. electrical current], so that his long wild locks bristled and stood on end. Afterwards he charged a powerful battery of several large jars; labouring with vast energy and discoursing with increasing vehemence of the marvellous powers of electricity, of thunder and lightning; describing an electrical kite that he had made at home, and projecting another and an enormous one, or rather a combination of many kites, that would draw down from the sky an immense volume of electricity, the whole ammunition of a mighty thunderstorm; and this being directed to some point would there produce the most stupendous results.[2]

As Maurice Hindle observes, in his Penguin Classics edition *of Frankenstein*, 'it is almost as if Shelley were providing film-makers of the future with that "thunder and sparks" image of electrical reanimation of the Creature which has become so standard a feature of Frankenstein films'.[3] Film-makers, as we shall see, were certainly grateful for the cue. But before moving-films arrived, *Frankenstein* had established itself as an immensely popular melodrama in the theatre in the nineteenth century, and had seeped from the stage into proverbial currency (it was, for instance, commonplace for Victorian cartoonists to depict rampaging working-class or Irish mobs as 'Frankensteins'). There were, as Steven Forry calculates, over ninety different dramatizations of Mary Shelley's novel in the nineteenth century—almost as many, in fact, as there have been films in the twentieth century.[4] All these nineteenth-century theatrical versions, lacking a complex stage machinery with which to simulate 'creation', presented a monster manufactured by alchemy or some *elixir vitae*.

The possibilities of Shelley's story were quickly apprehended by the fledgling American movie industry of the early twentieth century. The first serious film version of *Frankenstein* was produced by Thomas A. Edison's company, in 1910.[5] Although Edison was the arch-apostle of 'electricity', this pioneer film of *Frankenstein* retained the alchemically generated monster of nineteenth-century melodrama. It was actually a 1915 Broadway stage adaptation, called *The Last Laugh*, which picked up on Mary Shelley's afterthought about galvanism by introducing electrical machinery into the creation scene.[6] And this motif was taken over and enlarged in the 1931 Universal Pictures production, with its massive laboratory set, dominated by huge electro-galvanic generators, designed by Kenneth Strickfadden. As has been observed, there are clear analogies between Frankenstein's laboratory and the cavernous studio in which the film was shot (also powered by electrical generators). But James Whale was more directly influenced by an elaborately staged scene in Fritz Lang's dystopian epic *Metropolis* (1926), where a robot is electrically activated. Whale carried over into his lumbering Karloff-creation of Frankenstein's 'monster' a robotic clumsiness and total inarticulacy (not to mention a metallic bolt attaching its head to its body) which is wholly alien to Shelley's highly literate and athletically lithe monster, who trains himself in human emotion by reading Goethe's *Sorrows of Young Werther* and is an expert rock-climber.

The electro-robotic-Karloffian stereotype of Frankenstein dominated popular reproductions until virtually the present day. By the 1990s, however, bio-genetics had taken over from physics as the cutting-edge science. What Relativity was in the 1920s, the Genome Project now is. As Kenneth Branagh notes in his afterword to the 'novelization' of *Mary Shelley's Frankenstein*: 'we hope audiences [of the 1994 film] today may find parallels with Victor today in some amazing scientist who might be an inch away from curing AIDS or cancer and needs to make some difficult decisions.'[7]

This is clearly a new turn in the *Frankenstein* industry, and reflects the state of things at the end of the twentieth century. What Branagh's film shares with its predecessors,

however, is a morbid fascination with the scientific details
of the creation process, even if it disagrees on the precise
scientific bases of that process. In the novelization's text
(reflecting the space devoted to the episode in the film), no
less than three chapters are expended on mechanical
description of the great life-giving experiment. We are
taken painstakingly through the manufacture of the
gigantic copper sarcophagus in which the embryonic monster is suspended, the collection of body parts (including
the *de rigeur* genius's brain), the pooling of many buckets
of amniotic fluid into a sufficient placenta, the construction of the electrical generating apparatus (with a tankful
of electric eels as back-up—a fine surreal touch).

What happens in Mary Shelley's source narrative is very
different from what we recall from film treatments of her
novel (even that latest version, which proclaims itself
Mary Shelley's). Victor Frankenstein's initial researches
are into alchemy via the ancient wisdom of Cornelius
Agrippa, Albertus Magnus, and Paracelsus (p. 23). He
progresses beyond the limits of this sterile and antique
book-learning on witnessing the effects of a thunderstorm:

As I stood at the door, on a sudden I beheld a stream of fire issue
from an old and beautiful oak, which stood about twenty yards
from our house; and so soon as the dazzling light vanished, the
oak had disappeared, and nothing remained but a blasted stump
. . . I never beheld any thing so utterly destroyed. (p. 24)

This demonstration of the awesome power of lightning
turns Victor's attention away from the learning of the past
towards the contemplation of 'electricity and galvanism'
and the study of mathematics.[8] He subsequently leaves the
schools of Geneva for those of Ingolstadt where he is
exposed to the scientific puritanism of Monsieur Krempe,
'professor of natural philosophy'. Under Krempe and his
colleague Monsieur Waldman, Victor principally studies

chemistry. Through the revelations of modern chemical science, the young man has a blinding vision of how the old dreams of the alchemists can at last be realized. He duly moves on into biology, where he investigates 'the principle of life' (p. 33). Victor now turns his mind to the mysterious processes of decay and degeneration in animal tissue. His arduous studies bear fruit: 'After days and nights of incredible labour and fatigue, I succeeded in discovering the cause of generation and life; nay, more, I became myself capable of bestowing animation upon lifeless matter' (p. 34).

The stage is now set for the novel's great scene— creation. But, Victor warns his correspondent, he will be 'reserved upon the subject', and reserved he certainly is. Evidently, he collects and arranges various materials for his experiment: but what precisely these materials might be is not divulged. There follows a piece of magnificent Gothic fuzz:

One secret which I alone possessed was the hope to which I had dedicated myself; and the moon gazed on my midnight labours, while, with unrelaxed and breathless eagerness, I pursued nature to her hiding places. Who shall conceive the horrors of my secret toil, as I dabbled among the unhallowed damps of the grave, or tortured the living animal to animate the lifeless clay? My limbs now tremble, and my eyes swim with the remembrance; but then a resistless, and almost frantic impulse, urged me forward; I seemed to have lost all soul or sensation but for this one pursuit. It was indeed but a passing trance, that only made me feel with renewed acuteness so soon as, the unnatural stimulus ceasing to operate, I had returned to my old habits. I collected bones from charnel houses; and disturbed, with profane fingers, the tremendous secrets of the human frame. In a solitary chamber, or rather cell, at the top of the house, and separated from all the other apart- ments by a gallery and staircase, I kept my workshop of filthy creation; my eyeballs were starting from their sockets in attend- ing to the details of my employment. The dissecting room and the

slaughter-house furnished many of my materials; and often did
my human nature turn with loathing from my occupation, whilst,
still urged on by an eagerness which perpetually increased, I
brought my work near to a conclusion. (pp. 36-7)

A number of interesting features stand out from the
swirling rhetoric. Clearly Victor Frankenstein has undertaken field-work which would get him disbarred from most
self-respecting medical associations: in morgues ('charnel
houses'), graveyards, the vivisectionist's bench, the anatomy theatre, and—interestingly—the animal abattoir
('slaughter-house'). It remains unclear whether his motive
has been research into primal tissue, or the kleptomaniac
filching of limbs and organs with which Fritz's midnight
forays in the films have made us familiar.[9] The most urgent
feature of Victor's description is the emetic disgust and
the narrator's irresistible urge to avert his eyes from his
'workshop of filthy creation'.

Finally, on the fateful, dreary night in November (five
months later), the monster comes to life—not under the
stimulus of some immense bolt of meteorological energy,
but simply by opening his eyes and shuddering, like any
other newborn human. A veritable convulsion of nauseated disgust follows Victor's first sight of his animated
'creation':

How can I describe my emotions at this catastrophe, or how
delineate the wretch whom with such infinite pains and care I
had endeavoured to form? His limbs were in proportion, and I
had selected his features as beautiful. Beautiful!—Great God!
His yellow skin scarcely covered the work of muscles and
arteries beneath; his hair was of a lustrous black, and flowing;
his teeth of a pearly whiteness; but these luxuriances only
formed a more horrid contrast with his watery eyes, that
seemed almost of the same colour as the dun white sockets in
which they were set, his shrivelled complexion, and straight
black lips. (p. 39)

The mysterious animating operation is repeated later in the narrative, when Victor is induced to 'create' a mate for his monster. He does so (surreally enough) in the Orkneys' wilderness. There are, apparently, no graveyards, anatomy theatres, or slaughterhouses for him to prey on in this northern wasteland. The island has only three huts, into one of which Victor moves himself and his laboratory equipment. Again we are told it is 'a filthy process', and virtually nothing more other than that the operation is even more loathsome than before:

During my first experiment, a kind of enthusiastic frenzy had blinded me to the horror of my employment; my mind was intently fixed on the sequel of my labour, and my eyes were shut to the horror of my proceedings. But now I went to it in cold blood, and my heart often sickened at the work of my hands. (p. 137)

As far as one can make out, the 1818 text, stripped of the 1831 preface, gives no warrant for the surgery, transplants, and electrical apparatus of cinematic folklore.[10] In literary terms the creation of Victor's monster is closer to the mythical clay beast of Judaic folklore, the Golem, traditionally animated by charms (or *shems*) uttered by profane medieval rabbis. But the key to understanding what is implied in Mary Shelley's genesis passages is the physical, eye-averting revulsion—far in excess of what is actually described. It is a reflex and a rhetoric associated traditionally in Anglo-Saxon cultural discourse with two activities: sexual intercourse (and its variant, self-abuse), and childbirth (and its variant, abortion). Both of these are conventionally 'filthy'.

Mary, unlike Percy, did not have the advantage of an Oxford education where she might acquaint herself with the latest discoveries in Natural Philosophy. But she did know about making babies—too much, as it happened. The author of *Frankenstein* had good warrant for mixed feelings about sex and the 'labour' of childbirth. A strikingly original analysis of the novel along these lines was outlined by Ellen Moers in 1974. Moers read the 'creation' episode not as some alchemical transmutation, nor as a scientific experiment, but as an expression of the 'trauma of the afterbirth'. Moers traced the experiences which, over Mary's short lifetime, might have conduced to a jaundiced view of motherhood.[11] Mary Wollstonecraft Godwin was born on 30 August 1797, five months after her parents' marriage (as the Creature is born, after a mysterious five months' gestation). Mary's mother, Mary Wollstonecraft, died ten days after Mary's birth in August 1797, of puerperal fever. Mary, in a sense, killed the woman who gave her life—or, as the young child may have thought, her mother could not bear to live, having looked on her child. Barely past puberty, Mary eloped to France with Percy Shelley in July 1814. Sexual intercourse began early for her. And her devirgination was unhallowed. In February 1815 Mary (aged 17) gave premature birth to a daughter who died a few days later. In January 1816 she gave birth to a son, William. Mary and Shelley did not marry until December 1816 (a few days after the suicide of Percy's first wife, Harriet, who was pregnant by another man). While she was completing *Frankenstein* in May 1817, Mary was pregnant with her third child, Clara, who was born in September. She was just 20.

Despite her free-thinking, rationalist background, Mary may well have been ashamed of her irregular and busy sexual career. Her first unhappy experience of motherhood—which must surely have occurred before she was emotionally ready for it—was horrific. Mary's distaste for the business of procreation spills over, Moers plausibly argues, into the plot of her novel. One can enlarge on this insight, and see the trauma extending beyond the 'afterbirth' into disgust at the whole 'filthy' mechanics of sex.

Reading between the lines, the strong implication is that Victor creates his monster not by surgical manufacture, but by a process analogous to fertilization and *in vitro* culture. The initial work 'of his hands' which Victor refers to is, presumably, masturbatory, The resulting seed is mixed with a tissue, or soup composed of various tissues. The mixture is grown *ex utero* until, like the child cut from the umbilical cord, it is released into life. Victor Frankenstein, that is, is less the mad scientist than the reluctant parent, or semen donor. He does not make his monster, as one might manufacture a robot—he gives birth to him, as one might to an unwanted child, the sight of whom fills one with disgust. His revulsion for his 'Creation' may well, as Moers suggests, reflect aspects of Mary's own postnatal depressions and her distaste for the nasty business by which babies are made. The principal warrant for this speculation is, of course, the flavour of the rhetoric. Had Victor Frankenstein been the scientist of later film fame, his creation would have been 'blasphemous', 'vile', 'outrageous', or 'an offence against nature'. It would not have been, as Shelley repeatedly labels it, 'filthy'.

Over the last century-and-a-half one can see an interesting evolution in answers to the 'making Frankenstein' question. The early stage versions, because of the limitations of theatre machinery, fell back on the standby of the 'elixir of life' device (flasks are easier to come by as props than the paraphernalia of laboratories). The electrico-robotic Frankenstein comes in with the growth of the movie industry in the 1930s, and the Hollywood studio's no cost-spared attitude to special effects. In the 1970s, as a consequence of feminist rereadings of classic literary texts, a 'gynocritical' explanation is asserted by academics, and *Frankenstein* becomes the central work in the formation of a canon of feminist literary criticism.[12]

Kenneth Branagh's latest reproduction awkwardly combines in its filmic imagery the masculinist 'electric' and the feminist 'obstetric' interpretations. The monster, 1994-style, is gestated in a gigantic copper womb, suspended in gallons of amniotic fluid. Like Venus, he is born from the waves. But, come delivery time, he is animated by the traditional phallic jolt of electricity. Branagh's conciliatory imagery is, however, doomed by contradictions inherent in the source text. Victor is ineradicably male and, like bright middle-class males of the early nineteenth century, he has the privilege of a university education—something entirely denied young women of the period, however bright. Given his sex, Victor can 'invent' but he cannot plausibly 'mother' his monster. Yet many of the emotions ascribed to him in the highly charged description of his creature's creation are clearly maternal—and seem to be directed as shared experience to other women. The dilemma this raises can only be solved by a science-fiction scenario as daring as Shelley's in her novel. Were the author to be resurrected to rewrite her novel today, she might well devise a 'Victoria Frankenstein, Ph.D (Biology, MIT)'. Failing that, the reader and film-goer can look forward to many other contorted answers to the question: 'How does Victor make his monster?'

There are two Oxford World's Classics editions of *Frankenstein*. That by James Kinsley and M. K. Joseph reproduces the 1831 text. *Frankenstein (1818 Text)* is edited by Marilyn Butler, and reproduces the first version of the novel.

Charles Dickens · *Oliver Twist*

===

Is Oliver dreaming?

===

The mysterious apparition of Fagin and Monks at the window outside the room where Oliver is dozing in the supposed safety of his country retreat with the Maylie family furnishes one of Cruikshank's memorable illustrations to *Oliver Twist:*

Monks and the Jew

The circumstances surrounding this episode have been much worried over by commentators on the novel. The convalescent Oliver is described as being in his own little room, on the ground-floor; at the back of the house. The situation is Edenic:

It was quite a cottage-room, with a lattice-window: around which were clusters of jessamine and honeysuckle, that crept over the casement, and filled the place with their delicious perfume. It looked into a garden, whence a wicket-gate opened into a small paddock; all beyond was fine meadow-land and wood. There was no other dwelling near, in that direction; and the prospect it commanded was very extensive.

One beautiful evening, when the first shades of twilight were beginning to settle upon the earth, Oliver sat at this window, intent upon his books. He had been pouring over them for some time; and as the day had been uncommonly sultry, and he had exerted himself a great deal; it is no disparagement to the authors: whoever they may have been: to say, that gradually and by slow degrees, he fell asleep.

There is a kind of sleep that steals upon us sometimes, which, while it holds the body prisoner, does not free the mind from a sense of things about it, and enable it to ramble at its pleasure. So far as an overpowering heaviness, a prostration of strength, and an utter inability to control our thoughts or power of motion, can be called sleep, this is it; and yet we have a consciousness of all that is going on about us; and if we dream at such a time, words which are really spoken, or sounds which really exist at the moment, accommodate themselves with surprising readiness to our visions, until reality and imagination become so strangely blended that it is afterwards almost a matter of impossibility to separate the two. Nor is this, the most striking phenomenon incidental to such a state. It is an undoubted fact, that although our senses of touch and sight be for the time dead, yet our sleeping thoughts, and the visionary scenes that pass before us, will be influenced, and materially influenced, by the *mere silent presence* of some external object: which may not have been near us when we closed our eyes: and of whose vicinity we have had no waking consciousness.

Oliver knew, perfectly well, that he was in his own little room; that his books were lying on the table before him; and that the sweet air was stirring among the creeping plants outside. And yet he was asleep. Suddenly, the scene changed; the air became close and confined; and he thought, with a glow of terror, that he was in the Jew's house again. There sat the hideous old man, in his accustomed corner: pointing at him: and whispering to another man, with his face averted, who sat beside him.

'Hush, my dear!' he thought he heard the Jew say; 'it is he, sure enough. Come away'

'He!' the other man seemed to answer; 'could I mistake him, think you? If a crowd of devils were to put themselves into his exact shape, and he stood amongst them, there is something that would tell me how to point him out. If you buried him fifty feet deep, and took me across his grave, I should know, if there wasn't a mark above it, that he lay buried there. I should!'

The man seemed to say this, with such dreadful hatred, that Oliver awoke with the fear, and started up.

Good Heaven! what was that, which sent the blood tingling to his heart, and deprived him of his voice, and of power to move! There—there—at the window; close before him; so close, that he could have almost touched him before he started back: with his eyes peering into the room, and meeting his: there stood the Jew! And beside him, white with rage, or fear, or both, were the scowling features of the very man who had accosted him at the inn-yard.

It was but an instant, a glance, a flash, before his eyes; and they were gone. But they had recognised him, and he them; and their look was as firmly impressed upon his memory, as if it had been deeply carved in stone, and set before him from his birth. He stood transfixed for a moment; and then, leaping from the window into the garden, called loudly for help. (pp. 271–2)

Chapter 34 breaks off at this point. The next chapter opens with a general alarm at Oliver's cry ('The Jew! The Jew!').[1] Oliver points out the 'course the men had taken'.

But, despite everyone's vigorous efforts, 'the search was all in vain. There were not even the traces of recent foot-steps, to be seen' (p. 275). The physical improbability of the two men having been in the area is pondered:

They stood, now, on the summit of a little hill, commanding the open fields in every direction for three or four miles. There was the village in the hollow on the left; but, in order to gain that, after pursuing the track Oliver had pointed out, the men must have made a circuit of open ground, which it was impossible they could have accomplished in so short a time. A thick wood skirted the meadow-land in another direction; but they could not have gained that covert for the same reason. (p. 275)

But when Harry Maylie tells Oliver 'it must have been a dream', the boy protests: 'Oh no . . . I saw him too plainly for that. I saw them both, as plainly as I see you now' (p. 275). Inquiries are pursued, servants are dispatched to ask questions at all the ale-houses in the area, but nothing is turned up. Monks and Fagin have not been seen by another human eye in the neighbourhood, going or com-ing, although the appearance of two such low-life aliens would surely have attracted the notice of suspicious locals (as Monks immediately attracted Oliver's attention when he earlier ran into him at the nearby market town). Nor is the fact that the two men were actually at Oliver's window confirmed later in the story. Has Oliver imagined the whole thing? Was it a dream? By commissioning an illus-tration of the scene by Cruikshank, Dickens seems to sup-port Oliver's insisted declaration—that it visibly and actually happened. The men *were* there at the window. Moreover, the conversation (particularly Monks's charac-teristically melodramatic expressions of hatred) rings very true in the reader's ear.

But, if one accepts the actuality of what Oliver saw, three problems follow: (1) How did Fagin and Monks dis-cover where Oliver was staying? (2) How did the two men, neither of whom is notably agile, disappear so suddenly — before Oliver, who *is* agile and has jumped out of the window, can see where they have made off to? (3) Why did the interlopers leave no physical trace of their presence?

A number of explanations have been put forward. That Dickens was less careful in writing the novel than we are in reading it is the most primitive. Humphry House, in his introduction to the 1949 Oxford Illustrated edition of *Oliver Twist*, notes that Dickens wrote and published the work in a huge hurry, and that it 'was Dickens's first attempt at a novel proper. The sequence of the external events which befall Oliver [are] complicated and careless.' John Bayley elsewhere notes that Dickens repeats in this window scene material which is to be found earlier in the novel, at the beginning of Chapter 9 ('There is a drowsy state, between sleeping and waking . . .', see p. 64). This recycling of material would support the view that Dickens was under severe pressure.[2] Another primitive explanation is that in the window episode Dickens is resorting to the crude tricks of the Gothic ghost story. There is, for instance, a parallel instance earlier when, as he conspires at midnight with Fagin, Monks sees 'the shadow of a woman, in a cloak and bonnet, pass along the wainscot like a breath!' (p. 206). The two men search the whole house and find nothing—the woman, we apprehend, is the wraith of Oliver's mother, his protective angel.

Many critics prefer more ingenious readings. Steven Marcus, for example, in *Dickens: From Pickwick to Dombey* (London, 1965) examines the scene and its 'hypnagogic' references for Freudian clues that can be tracked back to Dickens's primal experiences in the blacking factory. J. Hillis Miller reads the scene for its demonstration of 'the total insecurity of Oliver's precarious happy state'. The vision of evil at the window is proof that his 'past is permanently part of him'. The absence of prints suggests that Fagin is to be equated with the similarly lightfooted devil (p. 73).[3]

Colin Williamson, reviewing these and other hypotheses, offers what he calls a more 'mundane' explanation.[4] He advocates reading *Oliver Twist* as one would a detective story or crime thriller. Williamson notes as significant a perplexing earlier episode in Chapter 32 in which Oliver is travelling to London with Mr Losberne to find the house of Mr Brownlow (Oliver can recall the street and the general aspect of the building, but not the number). Suddenly, at Chertsey Bridge, the excited boy turns very pale when he 'recognises' another house—that in which he and Sikes's gang hid before the attempted burglary (p. 249). They stop the carriage and the impulsive Losberne bursts his way in. They encounter 'a little, ugly hump-backed man', who is understandably furious at the invasion of his property by these two strangers and vociferates horrific but comically impotent threats. There is, as it turns out, absolutely nothing to prove that the burglars were ever in the house. The furniture and interior decoration are entirely different from what Oliver remembers and has told his friends about: 'not even the position of the cupboards; answered Oliver's description!' (p. 250). Oliver and the doctor leave with the little man's curses ringing in their ears. Losberne is embarrassed by the whole episode, and evidently sees it as evidence of Oliver's extraordinary nervousness. None the less, the good-hearted doctor trusts the boy sufficiently to go looking for Brownlow's house, which they discover after a little trial and error. Oliver remembers the way to the street and recognizes the house immediately by its white colour.

As Williamson points out, the odd thing about the business with the little ugly hump-backed man's house 'is its apparent pointlessness' (p. 226). But, Williamson suggests, if we approach *Oliver Twist* as a crime thriller, the obvious explanation of the confusion over the house is that the hunchback is an associate of Sikes who allows him the use of the house for his nefarious purposes, and that Dickens had planned that Losberne's action in entering the house should give its occupant a chance to see and identify Oliver ... All the members of the gang would doubtless have been alerted to Oliver's disappearance in the district and the threat he constituted to their safety; and it would be easy enough for an astute hunchback to track Oliver down through his companion and the carriage he occupied. (pp. 227–8)

It is an attractive hypothesis—except that a bona fide thriller-writer would surely have alerted the reader to the significance of the event later in the story. Williamson implies that pressure of serialization may have prevented Dickens from working out this detail of the plot satisfactorily.

There are other logical objections. It would hardly be necessary for the gang to use accidental sources of information and all the complicated business of trailing carriages many miles into the countryside—assuming that the little man could set the operation up before Losberne's carriage was on its way into the maelstrom of the London streets. Since the wounded Oliver was taken into the same house that was set up for the burglary (an establishment that had been thoroughly 'cased' in advance), and had remained there several weeks convalescing from his bullet-wound, he could have been effortlessly tracked by Sikes, who could have found his way to the scene of the crime blindfolded. It is true that the Maylies have moved for the summer to the country; but they have left servants in the house who know the other address and have no reason for keeping it secret. It would be the work of minutes for the Artful Dodger to invent some ruse for being told where the Maylie household and their little invalid guest are now residing. If there is a larger significance in the episode of the little hump-backed man it is, surely, that despite this evidence of Oliver's unreliability (and his whole story strains credulity to breaking-point) the good doctor and his friends persist in believing him. Although he clearly is in error about the gang's house, they trust that he can locate Brownlow's house. And, by implication, they believe his whole incredible story.

Yet another explanation of the window episode is offered by Fred Kaplan in *Dickens and Mesmerism* (Princeton, 1975). Kaplan notes that *Oliver Twist* was written at the height of 'The Mesmeric Mania', when Dickens was closely associated with the arch apostle of this new science, Dr John Elliotson. The long disquisition about Oliver's half-sleeping sensory awareness seems a clear pointer to the author's current fascination with mesmerism and 'animal magnetism'. As Kaplan records, it was one of Elliotson's claims that 'the mesmerized subject can see with his eyes closed' (p. 152). This would seem to be how Oliver becomes aware of the criminals at the window before he has woken from his sleep—which may more truly be described as a trance, or what the mesmerists called 'sleepwaking'. One could go one step further (as Kaplan does not) and suggest that the whole episode is a mesmeric phenomenon. This would explain the lack of any footprints or visible signs of Fagin's and Monks's preternaturally sudden disappearance ('It was but an instant, a glance, a flash, before his eyes; and they were gone').

There is, as it happens, strong supporting evidence for the hypothesis that the whole episode is an example of what the practitioners of mesmerism called 'mental travelling'. It is not the case that Monks and Fagin visit Oliver; he visits *them*, borne on the wings of mesmeric trance. As Alison Winter has recorded, from August 1837 to May 1838 Elliotson carried out private experiments on many of his patients, and in particular the domestic

servant, Elizabeth O'Key, in the wards of University
College Hospital. In the spring and summer of 1838 he put
on a series of public demonstrations at UCH. According to
Kaplan, Dickens attended the first O'Key demonstration
on 10 May 1838, or the second on 2 June, or 'perhaps even
both' (p. 36). As Winter describes the experiments:
'Elliotson did things such as mesmerizing her through
walls from various distances; she had visions in which she
represented herself as if she felt that various personages
were around her—these individuals told her things which
became personal prophecies.'[5] There is also a notable simi-
larity between the language of Dickens's remarks about
Oliver's tranced sensitivity to absent personages, and what
commentators were saying about O'Key in 1838.

Probably no explanation of this episode will convince
everyone and some will convince no one. I would like,
however; to offer an explanation of my own. *Oliver Twist*
was first published as a serial in *Bentley's Miscellany*, from
February 1837 to April 1839. It was an amazingly busy
period in Dickens's early career. He had outstanding contracts for new novels and editorial commitments to no less
than three different publishers, and felt that he was in
danger of 'busting the boiler'.

One of the problems for the serialist working at full
stretch was providing early enough copy for his illustrator,
particularly if his partner (like George Cruikshank) needed to have his designs engraved on steel—a long and
difficult procedure. When he had time in hand, Dickens
preferred to supply manuscript or proofs to Cruikshank,
so that he could portray narrative details accurately. But,
as Kathleen Tillotson notes, 'although Dickens originally
promised to let Cruikshank have the manuscript by the
fifth of the month, the evidence suggests that after the
first month he was always later, sometimes sending an
instalment of manuscript, and sometimes conveying

instructions for the illustration by a note or by word of mouth'.[6]

'Monks and the Jew' appeared in the *Bentley's* instalment for June 1838. Dickens felt himself particularly pressured at this point, because he thought copy was needed early, on account of the Coronation on the 28th of the month. My speculation is that before actually writing this section of the narrative Dickens foresaw an abduction or murder attempt on Oliver; and duly instructed Cruikshank to go ahead with the villains-at-the-window illustration, preparatory to that scenario. But, while writing the episode, Dickens settled on something more complex, bringing the Bumbles, Noah Claypole, and Bill Sikes back into the centre of things. It remains uncertain, *if* they are real, and not figments of Oliver's superheated imagination, what Fagin and Monks intend to do with the intelligence that Oliver is now lodged with the Maylies. But once Cruikshank had supplied the illustration, it was impossible, at this short notice, to procure another and Dickens suddenly realized that he could elegantly write himself out of the dilemma by means of the 'mesmeric enigma' device, using material gathered at the O'Key demonstrations.[7]

It would seem that Dickens's more scientific contemporaries registered the interesting overtones of the window scene in Chapter 34. G. H. Lewes wrote a letter (which has not survived) evidently enquiring exactly what Dickens had intended, and on what scientific authority the scene was devised. Towards the end of November 1838 Elliotson himself responded. Dickens wrote the following note to his illustrator:

My Dear Cruikshank,

Elliotson has written to me to go and see some experiments on Okey [*sic*] at his house at 3 o'clock tomorrow afternoon. He begs me to invite you. Will you come? Let me know.

Ever Faithfully Yrs.[8]

Why, one may go on to wonder, did Dickens in later prefaces to the novel not alert the reader to the scientific plausibility of Oliver's clairvoyance as, for instance, he ferociously defended the 'spontaneous combustion' in *Bleak House*, when G. H. Lewes questioned it? There is a likely explanation. In September 1838 O'Key was denounced as an impostor by Thomas Wakley in the *Lancet*. In the squabble that followed, Elliotson was forced to resign his position at UCH in late December of the same year. In the judgement of most intelligent lay persons (even those like Dickens who were friendly with Elliotson) the O'Key experiments, if not wholly discredited, had been rendered extremely dubious. In these circumstances, although he saw no reason to change his text, neither did Dickens see any good reason for drawing the reader's attention to the 'science' on which the window scene is based.

The Oxford World's Classics *Oliver Twist* is edited by Kathleen Tillotson with an introduction by Stephen Gill.

Charles Dickens · *Martin Chuzzlewit*

═══

Mysteries of the Dickensian year

═══

Novelists like George Eliot, Thackeray, and Trollope make it easy for the pedantic reader to work out a monthly calendar of events in their major fictions. In *Middlemarch*, for example, we can set down the following chronology for the novel's main events:

1829 early summer: Dorothea and Casaubon meet
1829 September: Dorothea and Casaubon marry
1829 Christmas: Dorothea and Casaubon in Rome
1830 May: Peter Featherstone dies
1830 July–August: Lydgate and Rosamond marry
1831 March: Casaubon dies
1832 March: Raffles dies
1832 May: Will and Dorothea marry
1832 June: the Reform Bill[1]

Vanity Fair, although it covers a much longer tract of history (1813–32) than *Middlemarch* (1828–32), is meticulous about calendar time-markings, particularly in its early, tight-knit sections covering the period from summer 1813 to summer 1815. Thackeray's narrative opens with ostentatious chronological exactitude: 'While the present century was in its teens, and on one sunshiny morning in June . . .' In the next hundred pages we learn that Rebecca is to stay ten days with the Sedleys, that the year coyly given as the 'teens' of the century must be 1813, and the 'sunshiny morning in June' is the fifteenth of that month.[2] Thackeray's chronometer continues its exact calendric beat throughout the subsequent narrative. As did George Eliot for *Middlemarch*, Trollope drew up a detailed

monthly time-line for *The Way We Live Now*.[3] George Eliot
made fine changes to her schedule. And it has been argued
that Trollope used an actual 1872 calendar to get even
greater precision for his layout of *The Way We Live Now*.[4]

Dickens is much less precise about monthly and seasonal references, particularly in his early novels.[5] Anyone
attempting to draw up a calendric schedule for the central
events of *Martin Chuzzlewit* will run into some perplexing
and thought-provoking anomalies. These anomalies witness less to any carelessness on Dickens's part, than to his
Shakespearian confidence in making the elements do
whatever it is that the current mood and dramatic needs of
his narrative require them to do. Dickens is no slave to the
calendar.

To demonstrate this, one may start with Martin's break
with Pecksniff. We are told the hero leaves on 'a dark winter's morning' (p. 179). There is supporting evidence as to
the wintriness in Dickens's description of the bleak skies,
cold rain, and mud that accompanies Martin's tumbril-
like journey by cart from Salisbury to London. In Chapter
14, preparatory to his departure for the New World,
Martin has his farewell meeting with Mary Graham in
St James's Park. Dickens gives another wintry picture of
the dawn assignation between the lovers:

He was up before day-break, and came upon the Park with the
morning, which was clad in the least engaging of the three hundred and sixty-five dresses in the wardrobe of the year. It was raw,
damp, dark, and dismal; the clouds were as muddy as the ground;
and the short perspective of every street and avenue, was closed
up by the mist as by a filthy curtain.

'Fine weather indeed', Martin bitterly soliloquized. (p. 202)

The theme of funereal winter darkness is reiterated in the
description of England, as Martin and Mark set sail for
America (Chapter 15):

A dark and dreary night; people nestling in their beds or circling late about the fire; Want, colder than Charity, shivering at the street corners; church-towers humming with the faint vibration of their own tongues, but newly resting from the ghostly preachment 'One!' The earth covered with a sable pall as for the burial of yesterday; the clumps of dark trees, its giant plumes of funeral feathers, waving sadly to and fro: all hushed, all noiseless, and in deep repose, save the swift clouds that skim across the moon, and the cautious wind, as, creeping after them upon the ground, it stops to listen, and goes rustling on, and stops again, and follows, like a savage on the trail. (p. 211)

Dickens does not give any precise monthly reference, but it would seem self-evident from the bitter cold that Martin's embarkation occurs at deep midwinter, January or early February at the latest.

At one early point in New York, Martin tells the obnoxious Jefferson Brick that it is 'five weeks' (p. 225) since he left England. He and Mark cool their heels (although there are no precise references to seasonal temperature) for a few weeks more in the big city before setting off for Eden. No date reference is given. Meanwhile, back in Britain, old Anthony Chuzzlewit in Chapter 18 complains at 'What a cold spring it is!' (p. 255). Presumably a couple of months have passed and we are now to understand that it is early April. The same spring season is subsequently described as 'lovely', as Mr Pecksniff and Jonas return from Anthony's funeral (p. 285). The day of that ceremony is 'fine and warm'—late April, presumably Chapter 20 (in which this description occurs) ends Number 8 in the novel's original serialization, and Number 9 switches to America where, at exactly the same moment, it is implied, Mark and Martin are setting out on their journey to the interior. When the young men arrive in Eden (i.e. Cairo, Illinois, at the junction of the Ohio and Mississippi rivers), it seems to be high summer: 'A fetid vapour, hot and sickening as the breath of an oven, rose up from the earth, and hung on everything around' (p. 328). Illinois does not get baking hot until June and July.

Back in England, in what is now evidently midsummer, Pecksniff makes his wooer's assault on Mary. Dickens expatiates on the seasonal warmth and fecundity which matches Pecksniff's own bounding libido:

The summer weather in [Pecksniff's] bosom was reflected in the breast of Nature. Through deep green vistas where the boughs arched over-head, and showed the sunlight flashing in the beautiful perspective; through dewy fern from which the startled hares leaped up, and fled at his approach; by mantled pools, and fallen trees, and down in hollow places, rustling among last year's leaves whose scent was Memory; the placid Pecksniff strolled. By meadow gates and hedges fragrant with wild roses ... (p. 413)

Pecksniff's subsequent failure to win Mary's heart leads to Tom Pinch's dismissal, the crisis coming 'one sultry afternoon, about a week after Miss Charity's departure for London' (p. 419). Banished forever from his patron's favour, Tom also makes his way to London, by stage-coach. The panorama of pre-railway rural England that accompanies his trip lingers lovingly on the summery landscape which Tom sees from his seat on the driver's box:

Yoho, among the gathering shades; making of no account the deep reflections of the trees, but scampering on through light and darkness, all the same, as if the light of London fifty miles away, were quite enough to travel by, and some to spare. Yoho, beside the village-green, where cricket-players linger yet, and every little indentation made in the fresh grass by bat or wicket, ball or player's foot, sheds out its perfume on the night. (p. 482)

Meanwhile, Martin and Mark undergo their regeneration in Eden. No precise time references are given, other than that after some weeks Martin falls ill, and

it is thereafter 'many weeks' before he recovers from his
'long and lingering illness' (p. 455) sufficiently 'to move
about with the help of a stick and Mark's arm' (p. 451).
After they have resolved to leave Eden it is a further
'three crawling weeks' before the steamboat arrives to
pick up the reluctant immigrants. On the voyage back
along the river, it is clearly high summer: the first person
Martin and Mark see on board the paddle-boat is 'a faint
gentleman sitting on a low camp-stool . . . under the shade
of a large green cotton umbrella' (p. 457). There is little
delay, apparently, in their embarkation from New York, on
the *Screw* again. The description of their arrival back in
England in Chapter 35 is euphoric, with weather to match.
They left at gloomy midnight; they return at joyous
midday:

It was mid-day, and high water in the English port for which the
Screw was bound, when, borne in gallantly upon the fulness of
the tide, she let go her anchor in the river.

Bright as the scene was; fresh and full of motion; airy, free, and
sparkling; it was nothing to the life and exultation in the breasts
of the two travellers, at sight of the old churches, roofs and
darkened chimney-stacks of Home. (p. 471)

The narrative goes on to inform us: 'A year had passed,
since those same spires and roofs had faded from their
eyes.' We feel, of course, that a year *must* have passed, for
all this travelling, new experience, chronic illness, and
moral regeneration to have taken place (apart from anything else, Martin on his return is clearly recovered in
health). Adding up all the casual references to 'months',
'weeks', and 'days', a year might even seem too short.
Primitive calculation, however, reveals that this twelve-
month duration means that Martin and Mark must return
in winter, not summer. Nor, on the other hand, can it be
eighteen months (which might bring them to the next

summer), since that would create a missing year in the
convergent Pinch—Chuzzlewit sector of the narrative.

From the lack of any clear date-markers, we are given to
understand that the travellers' return from the New World
is coincidental with Tom Pinch's arrival in London, his
reunion with Westlock and Ruth, and his installation with
Mr Fips. Tom is well established in his new employment at
the Temple while it is still summer. In Chapter 40, for
instance, he is described going down to the London docks
at seven in the morning, with Ruth, to enjoy 'the summer
air' (p. 532).

The fact that these two strands of the narrative (the
Martin strand and the Tom strand) have merged in summer (of whatever year it may be) is clinched by the great
summer storm of Chapter 42. The prelude to this cata-
clysm, which will bring the melodrama to the boil, is
described as coming at the climax of a heatwave:

It was one of those hot, silent nights, when people sit at windows,
listening for the thunder which they know will shortly break;
when they recall dismal tales of hurricanes and earthquakes;
and of lonely travellers on open plains, and lonely ships at sea
struck by lightning. Lightning flashed and quivered on the black
horizon even now; and hollow murmurings were in the wind, as
though it had been blowing where the thunder rolled, and still
was charged with its exhausted echoes. But the storm, though
gathering swiftly, had not yet come up; and the prevailing stillness was the more solemn, from the dull intelligence that seemed
to hover in the air, of noise and conflict afar off. (p. 550)

On the night of the storm Mark and Martin come to the
Blue Dragon. This picks up a comment made by Mark
immediately on returning, as they sit in the tavern by the
docks: 'My opinion is, sir . . . that what we've got to do, is
to travel straight to the Dragon' (p. 472).

This, then is the problem: some six hectic months have
passed in Tom Pinch's life, bringing him from February

to August. 'A year' has passed in Mark and Martin's life
bringing them from February to the same August. Clearly,
if Dickens had been precise about his chronology, Martin
and Mark would have missed the great summer storm by
six months, arriving back in gloomy, wintry January or
February following. Nor could their stay in America be
abbreviated to half-a-year, given all the events and long
experiences it had to contain. 'There are some happy
creeturs', Mrs Gamp observes to Mr Mould, 'as time runs
back'ards with' (p. 347). Martin Chuzzlewit would seem to
be just such a happy creetur.

Dickens eludes any charge of error by a kind of prophylactic vagueness—he never names a month, only seasons.
But the missing six months in his hero's career also
relates to the Great Inimitable's masterful way with background.[6] Clearly, for the purposes of mood, Dickens wanted black, depressive winter for Martin's departure for the
New World. It matched the low point his career had
reached. As clearly, Dickens wanted high summer for his
hero's return. In its turn, the summer season chimed with
Martin's spiritual rebirth and his happier relationship
with life, society, and his friends and sweetheart. Coinci-
dentally, one may note that Martin's trip to America
matches Dickens's exactly: the novelist left Liverpool on
2 January 1842, and returned in June the same year.

The Oxford World's Classics *Martin Chuzzlewit* is edited by
Margaret Cardwell.

Emily Brontë · *Wuthering Heights*

Is Heathcliff a murderer?

When he returns to Wuthering Heights after his mysterious three-year period of exile Heathcliff has become someone very cruel. He left an uncouth but essentially humane stable-lad. He returns a gentleman psychopath. His subsequent brutalities are graphically recorded. They are many and very unpleasant. He humiliates Edgar Linton who has married Cathy during his absence. 'I wish you joy of the milk-blooded coward' (p. 115), he tells Cathy in her husband's presence. The taunt is the more brutal since Edgar is clearly the weaker man and in no position to exact physical reparation. Heathcliff goes on to torment Edgar by hinting that he has cuckolded him. Subsequently Heathcliff beats his wife Isabella, as he has gruesomely promised to do in earlier conversation with Cathy: 'You'd hear of odd things, if I lived alone with that mawkish, waxen face; the most ordinary would be painting on its white the colours of the rainbow, and turning the blue eyes black, every day or two; they detestably resemble Linton's' (p. 106).

When Nelly sees Isabella, after she has fled from Heathcliff, she does indeed describe 'a white face scratched and bruised' (p. 170). Isabella goes on to describe her husband's 'murderous violence' (p. 172) to Nelly in some detail. Heathcliff has shaken her till her teeth rattle (p. 170). He has thrown a kitchen knife at her head which 'struck beneath my ear'; she has a wound which will probably scar her for life (p. 181). Had she not run away, who knows how far he would have gone in his cold brutality towards her.

In later life Heathcliff would certainly have beaten his son as savagely as he beat the boy's mother, were it not that he needs the degenerate brat whole and unmarked for his long-term scheme of revenge against Thrushcross Grange. He has no compunction about punching young Catherine. Young Heathcliff tells Nelly about his father's violent reaction on learning that the girl has tried to keep for herself two miniatures of her dead parents:

'I said *they* were mine, too; and tried to get them from her. The spiteful thing wouldn't let me; she pushed me off, and hurt me. I shrieked out—that frightens her—she heard papa coming, and she broke the hinges, and divided the case and gave me her mother's portrait; the other she attempted to hide; but papa asked what was the matter and I explained it. He took the one I had away, and ordered her to resign hers to me; she refused, and he—he struck her down, and wrenched it off the chain, and crushed it with his foot.'

'And were you pleased to see her struck?' I asked: having my designs in encouraging his talk.

'I winked,' he answered. 'I wink to see my father strike a dog, or a horse, he does it so hard.' (p. 281)

Or a woman, one may add. It is not just four-footed victims who feel the weight of Heathcliff's fist.

Heathcliff is capable of more cold-blooded and calculating cruelty. He abducts young Catherine and keeps her from her dying father's bedside, accelerating Edgar's death and ensuring that it shall be an extremely miserable one. He urges Hindley towards self-destruction by encouraging his fatal mania for drink and cards. On a casual level, Heathcliff is given to killing household pets (he strangles his wife's favourite dog by way of wedding present) and desecrates graves.

Mr Heathcliff; we may assume, is not a nice man. And in a later age his violence and lawlessness would have earned him a prison sentence—or at the very least a string of restraining orders and court injunctions. But does Heathcliff commit the cruellest crime of all, murder?

To answer this question we must examine the suspicious circumstances of the death of Hindley Earnshaw, master of Wuthering Heights. 'The end of Earnshaw was what might have been expected,' Nelly recalls in her long narrative to Lockwood, 'it followed fast on his sister's, there was scarcely six months between them. We, at the Grange, never got a very succinct account of his state preceding it.' Nelly learns of the death, after the event, from the local apothecary, Mr Kenneth. 'He died true to his character;' Kenneth cheerfully adds, 'drunk as a lord' (p. 184). Hindley was just 27. Evidently Kenneth has witnessed the death and signed the necessary certificate.

Nelly's suspicions are immediately aroused. 'Had he fair play?' she ponders. The anxiety 'bothers' her and she makes a trip to Wuthering Heights to discover what she can of the truth of the case. Before going she learns from Earnshaw's lawyer (who also acts for Mr Linton, Nelly's employer) that the 'whole property [of Wuthering Heights] is mortgaged'—to Heathcliff.[1] At the Heights, Nelly meets Heathcliff who, rather shiftily, as we may think, gives his eyewitness account of Hindley's death:

'That fool's body should be buried at the cross-roads, without ceremony of any kind [i.e. Hindley committed suicide]—I happened to leave him ten minutes, yesterday afternoon; and, in that interval, he fastened the two doors of the house against me, and he has spent the night in drinking himself to death deliberately! We broke in this morning, for we heard him snorting like a horse; and there he was, laid over a settle—flaying and scalping would not have wakened him—I sent for Kenneth, and he came; but not till the beast had changed into carrion—he was both dead and cold, and stark; and so you'll allow, it was useless making more stir about him!' (p. 185)

By the last enigmatic remark, Heathcliff means that it

would have been 'useless' calling in the coroner, on the grounds that the death was suspicious.

Heathcliff's account is 'confirmed' to Nelly by Joseph, the misanthropic (but wholly reliable) old manservant at the Heights. Joseph, however, is by no means happy about his former master's last hours:

Aw'd rayther he'd goan hisseln fur t'doctor! Aw sud uh taen tent uh t'maister better nur him—un' he warn't deead when Aw left, nowt uh t'soart' ['I would rather that Heathcliff had gone himself for the doctor! I should have taken care of the master better than him—and he wasn't dead when I left, nothing of the sort!'] (pp. 185–6).

Joseph is invincibly honest. And one concurs in his 'muttered' doubts (he dare not voice them out loud, in case Heathcliff hears, and gives him the back of his hand). It is most improbable that a 27-year-old man, in otherwise robust health, should be able to 'drink himself to death' in a single night. Young men do, of course, kill themselves by excessive drinking, but usually by driving cars drunk, or by inhaling their own vomit while sleeping. It is clear that—although he is 'snorting'—Hindley is breathing efficiently when he is left alone with Heathcliff. Did he show signs of being about to suffocate, it would be an easy thing for Heathcliff to lift him up and bang him on the back, thus clearing his throat. And, as Joseph recalls, although dead drunk, Hindley did not appear to be dying. He was, however, insensible and incapable of resisting anyone stifling him with a cushion. Kenneth is a somewhat elusive figure, but it is likely that as a mere apothecary ('Mr' Kenneth) he would not have been able to conduct any expert medical examination of the body. It may even be that Heathcliff bribed him to sign the certificate and obviate any embarrassing coroner's inquest.

It is nicely poised and every reader must make his or her own judgement. If Heathcliff did stifle Hindley (albeit that Hindley has earlier tried to shoot and stab Heathcliff) we have to see him as a sociopathic monster. If he watched the man die, and declined to prevent his death (by clearing Hindley's throat, for example) he is scarcely better. These plausible reconstructions of what happened at Wuthering Heights while Heathcliff and the incapable Hindley were alone together render absurd such rosy adaptations as the Samuel Goldwyn 1939 film (the Goldwyn screenplay, by Ben Hecht and Charles MacArthur, ends with Heathcliff, played by Laurence Olivier, and Cathy, played by Merle Oberon, reunited as carefree ghosts skipping merrily over Penistone Crags). If we believe that Heathcliff was simply an innocent bystander at Hindley's self-destruction, then we can credit the sympathetic reading of his character suggested by the exclamation Nelly overhears him make, in the intensity of his wretchedness: 'I have no pity! I have no pity! The [more the] worms writhe, the more I yearn to crush out their entrails! It is a moral teething, and I grind with greater energy, in proportion to the increase of pain' (p. 152).

When a baby savagely bites its teething ring, it is because it (the baby) is experiencing excruciating pain from the teeth tearing their way through its gums. So Heathcliff may be seen to inflict pain on others (hurling knives at his wife, taunting Edgar, striking young Catherine, lashing his horse) only because he feels greater inward pain himself. But one cannot so justify the furtive smothering, in cold blood, of someone whose death will mean considerable financial gain to the murderer.

There are no clear answers to this puzzle. As Ian Jack has noted, '*Wuthering Heights* is one of the most enigmatic of English novels'. Whether or not Heathcliff is guilty of capital crime remains a fascinating but ultimately inscrutable enigma at the very heart of the narrative. For what it is worth, I believe he *did* kill Hindley, although for any unprejudiced jury it is likely that enough 'reasonable doubt' would remain to acquit him.

The Oxford World's Classics *Wuthering Heights* is edited by Ian Jack with an introduction by Patsy Stoneman.

——

Rochester's celestial telegram

——

On the face of it, Rochester's astral communication with
the heroine at the conclusion of Jane Eyre ('Jane! Jane!
Jane!', p. 419) is the most un-Brontëan thing in Charlotte
Brontë's mature fiction. This was the author who declared
in the preface to one of her novels that it should be as
unromantic as a Monday morning. The Jane—Rochester
exchange across the ether would seem to be the stuff of
Walpurgisnacht. It is the more surprising since Brontë is
a novelist who firmly eschews supernatural agency and
intervention in her narratives.

It will help to summarize the events which precede
Rochester's celestial telegram. Jane is at St John Rivers's
home, where she is detained after evening prayers. It is
around nine o'clock on a Monday evening. The family and
servants go to bed. St John renews his proposal of marriage. Jane wavers: 'I could decide if I were but certain,'
she says, 'were I but convinced that it is God's will I
should marry you' (p. 419). She wants a sign. There are
only a few minutes-worth of conversation recorded, but
evidently St John Rivers and Jane are together for a
period of some hours, she staring intently at the 'one candle' which illuminates the room (the Rivers' household is
frugal):

All the house was still; for I believe all, except St John and
myself, were now retired to rest. The one candle was dying out:
the room was full of moonlight. My heart beat fast and thick: I
heard its throb. Suddenly it stood still to an inexpressible feeling that thrilled it through, and passed at once to my head and

extremities. The feeling was *not like an electric shock*; but it was quite as sharp, as strange, as startling: it acted on my senses as if their utmost activity hitherto had been but torpor; from which they were now summoned, and forced to wake. They rose expectant: eye and ear waited, while the flesh quivered on my bones.

'What have you heard? What do you see?' asked St John. I saw nothing: but I heard a voice somewhere cry—

'Jane! Jane! Jane!' Nothing more. (p. 419, my italics)

Jane recognizes the 'known, loved, well-remembered voice' of Edward Fairfax Rochester. She rushes into the garden and calls back, 'I am coming! Wait for me! Oh, I will come!'

Brontë moves quickly to forestall any 'Gothic' interpretations by her readers. 'Down superstition!', Jane is made to command: 'This is not thy deception, nor thy witchcraft: it is the work of nature. She was roused, and did—no miracle—but her best' (p. 420). That Rochester's communication was not hallucinatory is confirmed after Jane makes her trip to Ferndean four days later. Rochester tells her that on the Monday night in question he sat for some hours in his room gazing at the moon (as Jane was simultaneously gazing at the candle). Involuntarily, 'near midnight' he came out with the exclamation 'Jane! Jane! Jane!' Then, to his consternation, he heard her voice reply, 'I am coming: wait for me!' (p. 447). He does not, at this point, know that she heard his call and used in reply the very words which at his end he reports hearing.

What is going on here? Margaret Smith's note to the previous World's Classics edition puts the problem clearly, if inconclusively:

Charlotte Brontë defended this incident by saying 'But it is a true thing; it really happened.' (See *Life*, ii. 149) A similar incident occurs in the Angrian story *of Albion and Marina* (1830) as Miss Ratchford points out: see *B.S.T*, 1920, p. 13 f., and Ratchford 212. Charlotte Brontë's fear of being accused of plagiarism when,

after she had written *Jane Eyre*, she read of the midnight voice in
Mrs Marsh's *Two Old Men's Tales*, certainly rules out any conscious literary indebtedness. See *Life*. ii. 311. Parallels have been
noted in Defoe's *Moll Flanders* and George Sand's *Jacques* (by
Mrs Humphry Ward, Haworth edition, 1899).

It is not hard to come up with other literary analogies,
some of which Brontë might have been more likely to
know than Defoe (the voice which St Augustine in his
Confessions recalls hearing; the visionary communication
between the tragic lovers in Keats's *Isabella*). But what is
problematic is the author's insistence, reiterated in the
text and in commentary on the text, that 'it is a true thing;
it really happened'; 'no miracle.' Brontë does not, as would
seem tempting for someone perpetrating an episode so
fantastic, take refuge in the traditional licence of the
romancer.

Some early reviewers apprehended that Brontë was
alluding to the newly discovered invention of telegraphy.[1]
But 1847 is too early for this. It is true that the Electric
Telegraph Company was formed in 1846, but it was not
until the 1850s that full commercial exploitation occurred.
What seems more likely is that Brontë was drawing on her
knowledge of the science of mesmerism. She was, as is well
recorded by her biographers, fascinated by 'animal magnetism' (as mesmerism was sometimes termed in the 1840s)
and the related field of phrenology. She attended lectures
on the subject in the early 1840s and communicated with
mesmeric investigators and phrenologists. Her novels are
peppered with incidental allusions to her knowledge of
the field.

In her defiant assertion, 'it is a true thing', Charlotte
Brontë was probably thinking of two specific authorities
on the subject of mesmerism and clairvoyant communication. Catherine Crowe, a novelist and popularizer of
spiritualism, had recently attempted a historico-scientific

vindication of psychic phenomena in her translation of the German *Die Seherin von Prevorst* (*The Seeress of Prevorst*, translated from the German of Justinus Kerner, London, 1845). The 'seeress' was Frederica Hauffe, born in 1801, whose life was a long succession of witnessed and confirmed acts of clairvoyance, prevoyance, 'sleep-seeing', and prophecy—all justified by Crowe on the basis of 'magnetism' (the explanatory source of mesmerism). In 1848 Crowe published *The Night Side of Nature*, an assortment of weird tales, haunted houses, supernatural happenings, and apparitions—all vouched for as genuine by the author.[2]

Crowe, who was to become a full-time propagandist for spiritualism in the 1850s (and a social acquaintance of Brontë's, after the success of *Jane Eyre*), was probably congenial to Brontë but less than convincing as a scientific authority. In making her claim for the 'truth' of the etherial exchange between Jane and Rochester, Brontë was more likely drawing on another popular treatise on mesmeric phenomena, the Revd Chauncy Hare Townshend's *Facts in Mesmerism, with Reasons for a dispassionate Inquiry into it* (London, 1840). Townshend's book, which was put out by the very respectable publisher Longman and Green, offered a huge array of 'facts' testifying to the validity of the pseudo-science. Many of these facts dealt with remote communication between mesmerically sensitized subjects. Townshend was quite dogmatic that this was a scientifically authenticated truth and cited chapter-and-verse cases to support his theories:

It has been said that persons in certain states either mesmeric or akin to the mesmeric can become aware of the thoughts of others without the usual communication of speech . . . But is there, it may still be asked, any one acknowledged instance in nature by which the possibility of receiving actual experiences, other than by the normal inlets of sense can be demonstrated? There is. (pp. 365, 460)

Townshend gives a number of historically recorded instances of messages received 'other than by the normal inlets of sense'. The 'Testimony to a curious Fact by Dr Filippi of Milan' in July 1839, for example: 'Mr Valdrighi, advocate, had his sense of hearing so exquisitely exalted that he could hear words pronounced at the distance of two rooms, the doors of which were shut, although pronounced in a weak and low voice' (p. 473).

More significantly, Townshend, who was himself a practising mesmerist, describes experiments along these lines which he conducted with a subject called 'Anna M.' He discovered that it was possible to 'magnetize' her from a distance—and communicate with her, suggesting objects and messages which she could pick up far beyond the range of the human ear. Over the course of his experiments with Anna M., Townshend successfully extended the distance between himself and his magnetized subject to a quarter of a mile, transmitting his 'influence' electrically (as he assumed) and communicating information to her,

There were other sensational displays of mesmeric clairvoyance and 'mental travelling' which might have inspired Brontë's protestation that the 'Jane! Jane! Jane!' episode was a 'true thing'. In the early 1840s Alexis Didier (previously a clerk in a Parisian haulage firm) toured extensively in France, Belgium, and England, giving shows. As Alison Winter records: 'His routine included playing cards and reading books whilst blindfolded, identifying the contents of envelopes, and "travelling clairvoyance"— viewing objects at a great distance.'[3] Even more likely to have been in Brontë's mind was the public quarrel over clairvoyance and mental travelling that Harriet Martineau became involved with in late 1844 and early

1845. The Martineaus (the woman of letters, Harriet, and
her Unitarian brother, James) were the most powerful
literary figures with whom the young Brontës could claim
connection before the success of *Jane Eyre* made Charlotte
nationally famous.[4] In late November 1844 Harriet
Martineau sent the London review; the *Athenaeum*, a long
letter describing the clairvoyant feats of a young maid-
servant called Jane Arrowsmith (the echo of this name
in 'Jane Eyre' may not be accidental). Sensationally,
Martineau claimed that her Jane had, while in a mesmeric
trance, witnessed a shipwreck occurring some dozen miles
distant at sea. Jane also gave proof of being able to hear
at great distances, without the aid of her physical ears.
Martineau followed up with three more pieces, describing
and analysing Jane's powers of 'mental travelling' as a
demonstration of the truth of mesmeric science.[5]

These reports of Jane Arrowsmith's clairvoyance provoked a huge controversy, including pamphlets and a
series of savagely denunciatory pieces by an irate London
doctor, who visited the town where Jane Arrowsmith lived
and claimed to have discovered that she had been told
about the shipwreck just before the crucial session with
the mesmerist. Martineau stuck to her guns, insisting on
the 'truth' of Jane's clairvoyance. It is extremely likely
that, one way or another, Charlotte would have caught
wind of the Jane Arrowsmith affair; it is equally likely
that she would have stood firmly with Harriet Martineau
in asserting its 'truth'.

How then should we read the critical scene in *Jane
Eyre*? Accidentally, it would seem, both Jane and Rochester
put themselves simultaneously into a mesmeric state of
'sleepwaking'. Jane does it by staring for a long period at the
single candle (this, incidentally, was the standard parlour-
game technique for putting someone under the influence;
it is possible that Brontë had used it successfully on

herself). Rochester produces the same effect on himself by staring at the moon. He, as the stronger will, has Jane under his influence, which she feels as something akin to, but not quite like, an electric shock (one of Townshend's favourite tricks at lectures on mesmerism was to give members of his audience mild electrical shocks, to demonstrate the nature of mesmeric energy). Like Anna M. and Townshend, in this condition of nervous 'exaltation' the exchange of messages can take place. It is, as Jane protests, no 'miracle', but an accident produced by their fortuitously mesmerizing themselves at the same critical moment.

The Oxford World's Classics *Jane Eyre* is edited by Margaret Smith with an introduction by Sally Shuttleworth.

W. M. Thackeray · *Vanity Fair*

Does Becky kill Jos?

Students of literature are routinely told that Thackeray is an 'omniscient' novelist; indeed, that with Fielding he is probably the perfect specimen of the type. He himself tells us, repeatedly and with apparently complacency in *Vanity Fair*, that 'the novelist knows everything'. But this omniscience has its holes. The reader is teased by what this allegedly all-knowing narrator would seem not to know, will not acquaint himself with, or declines to impart. Omniscient he may be; omnidictive he is not.

Most provoking of the text's silences is that concerning Jos's death. He dies in mysterious circumstances on the continent, sometime in the early 1830s, while in the dangerous company of Becky Crawley. From his first encounter with her, some twenty years before, Jos has been in danger from this fatal woman. In 1813 she almost netted him; but George Osborne, unwilling to have a governess marry into the family ('low enough already, without *her*', p. 71) frightened the fat man off. At Pumpernickel, despite Dobbin's efforts, she finally lands her prey. Becky cannot marry Jos (Rawdon, her estranged husband, is still staving off the fevers of Coventry Island). But she lives with her victim until he dies—prematurely. She is his insurance beneficiary; the rest of the nabob's once substantial wealth has mysteriously evaporated. And in later life Becky is a *very* prosperous lady, we are told. When she was first setting her hat at Jos in Russell Square she was netting a purse; now, at last, it would seem that the purse is comfortably full.

How does Jos die? The insurance people are suspicious. Their solicitor swears it is 'the blackest case that ever had come before him' (p. 877). Thackerayan innuendo confirms our sense that Becky helped Jos out of the world. *Her* solicitors are ominously named Messrs. Burke, Thurtell and Hayes. Burke, with Hare, was the Edinburgh body-snatcher who killed and sold corpses to the university school of medicine. John Thurtell was a murderer, hanged in 1824. Catherine Hayes was a husband killer, celebrated by Thackeray in his anti-Newgate satire, *Catherine* (1839).

There is another broad hint in the penultimate full-plate illustration to the novel, 'Becky's second appearance in the character of Clytemnestra' (p. 875).

Becky's second appearance in the character of Clytemnestra

Becky's first appearance as the Greek husband-killer was in the charade at Gaunt House, just before she betrayed Rawdon into the hands of the bailiffs. Here we feel that she will use the knife that, somewhat melodramatically, Thackeray shows her holding. (An ironic Hogarthian print of the good Samaritan is behind Jos, who vainly implores an implacable Dobbin to help him.)

It all points one way. But why does Thackeray not tell us straight out? It is a mote that he seems deliberately to have left to trouble generations of readers. And when asked in later life by just one such troubled reader; 'did Becky kill Jos?' the novelist is reported to have merely smiled and answered, 'I don't know'.

'Was she guilty?' The narrative asks that question of Becky (but gives no direct answer) at two crucial junctures: first, in the liaison with Steyne; secondly, after Jos's death. It is, of course, odds on that Becky was thoroughly guilty of both these and many other like offences. Would the notoriously lecherous Marquess of Steyne have given Becky a cheque for over a thousand pounds, provided for her son and companion Briggs, and given her diamonds (which she feels obliged to hide from her husband) if he were not enjoying with her what he more flagrantly enjoys with the Countess of Belladonna? So too with Jos's untimely decease; any open-minded reader concurs with the insurance office's suspicion.

If we accept the hint that Becky indeed killed Jos, then the last illustration 'Virtue rewarded: a booth in Vanity Fair' (with its ironic echo of Fielding's *Amelia, or Virtue Rewarded*) is one of the most un-Victorian endings in Victorian fiction. I can only think of one other Victorian novel in which a main character escapes punishment for murder (Mrs Archer Clive's eccentric romance, *Paul Ferroll*, 1855). To have left Becky unpunished for her capital offence would also have been radically out of character for Thackeray, who had been one of the main castigators of the so-called Newgate Novel—more particularly the 'arsenical' variety recently made notorious by Bulwer-Lytton's *Lucretia* (1846), a novel which *The Times* called 'a disgrace to the writer, a shame to us all'—on the grounds that it glorified wives who poisoned husbands for gain. Thackeray had built his early career around attacks on the immoralities of Bulwer-Lytton's fiction and its depictions of vice rewarded.

Virtue rewarded. A booth in Vanity Fair

Would Thackeray, one wonders, have emulated a writer whom he loathed? More significantly, as has been pointed out by a number of commentators on *Vanity Fair*, murder seems entirely out of character in Becky—an adventuress who might well stoop to some well-paid adultery but is, we feel, no homicidal psychopath capable of the premeditated crime of slow poisoning by arsenic.

To return to the text which surrounds the Clytemnestra illustration. In the last years of his life the 'infatuated man', Joseph Sedley, is reported to be entirely Becky's 'slave'. Colonel Dobbin's lawyers (who have clearly been undertaking some discreet spying on their client's behalf) inform him that Jos has taken out a heavy insurance upon his life. Moreover; 'his infirmities were daily increasing' (p. 873). What, one may well ask, are these 'infirmities'—the physical decrepitude consequent on a lifetime's gluttony? Or the slow effects of criminally administered toxins?

Dobbin, at his wife's alarmed request, goes to visit his brother-in-law in Brussels, where he is staying in an adjoining apartment to Mrs Crawley. She is living in great style, presumably on Jos's dwindling store of money. A mysteriously terrified Jos tells Dobbin that Mrs Crawley has 'tended him through a series of unheard-of illnesses, with a fidelity most admirable. She had been a daughter to him' (p. 873). He, despite these daughterly attentions, is perceived by the Colonel to be in 'a condition of pitiable infirmity'. Mrs Crawley, Jos further insists to a disbelieving Colonel, 'is as innocent as a child'. The Colonel leaves, sternly indicating that he and Mrs Dobbin can never visit such as Mrs Crawley and her consort again. Before doing so, he urges Jos 'to break off a connexion which might have the most fatal consequences to him' (p. 874). Three months later Jos duly dies at Aix-la-Chapelle, a watering place, whither he and Mrs Crawley have repaired in a vain attempt to recover his health.

There follows the coded business about the lawyers, Burke, Thurtell and Hayes, and the insurance company's dark suspicions.

If Becky killed Jos, how was it done? By poison? Or is he, as it seems in his last interview with Dobbin, terminally ill and terrified of dying alone? Someone, that is, who is going to depart the world without the assistance of arsenic. The Clytemnestra picture is, on close inspection, baffling. It is made clear in the text that Becky is not, in fact, hiding behind the screen. (Jos is morbidly careful to arrange the meeting 'when Mrs Crawley would be at a *soirée*, and when they could meet *alone*', p. 873.) Nor, if Becky actually does kill Jos, is the deed done with a knife. Whatever else, Becky is no Lizzie Borden.

What the picture would seem to allegorize are the exaggerated fears and suspicions of the respectable world ('I warrant the heartless slut was behind the screen all the time, just biding her time to kill the poor man!'). And Thackeray casts those suspicions in their most lurid form. So lurid, in fact, that the discriminating reader must dismiss them as preposterous. Of course—if we weigh up all the prior evidence Becky is no cutthroat. There is no question but that she is an unscrupulous woman, taking monetary advantage of a dying man, treating him doubtless with the same careless kindness which characterizes her last acts towards Amelia (whose path to a happy marriage she clears, with some well-placed malicious information about George Osborne).

In short, in this last section of the novel Thackeray is playing a game with his readers. He lures them—by flattering their responsiveness to authorial nods and winks—into thinking themselves cleverer than they in fact are. Complacently we readers, priding ourselves on being sophisticated enough to decode the Burke, Thurtell, Hayes, and Clytemnestra allusions, fall into the same

vulgar prejudice as does the 'world' that condemns
Becky. Does Becky kill Jos? Of course she doesn't—but
maliciously wagging respectable tongues will never
believe otherwise.

The Oxford World's Classics *Vanity Fair* is edited by John
Sutherland.

===

Who is Helen Graham?

===

Shortly after her arrival, the hero's irrepressibly cheeky young brother, Fergus, tells the fascinating new tenant of Wildfell Hall: 'It amazes me, Mrs Graham, how you could choose such a dilapidated, rickety old place as this to live in. If you couldn't afford to occupy the whole house, and have it mended up, why couldn't you take a neat little cottage?' (p. 57). The lady gives an unsatisfactory answer— perhaps, she lightly tells the young man, she was too proud or too 'romantic'.

Fergus's observation opens up another question which neither Helen nor Anne Brontë's text answers for us. Helen Huntingdon wishes to escape her brutally alcoholic husband, Arthur. Given the date (and until 1857, well after the novel's publication), Mr Huntingdon would be quite entitled, should he find his errant wife in England, to repossess his conjugal rights (i.e. rape her at will), to repossess whatever personal things she has taken with her as his stolen property, and to reassume sole parental responsibility for his son, little Arthur. It is clear (since he has adamantly refused her permission to leave his house, has alienated their child's affections, and has removed her from all access to money) that Mr Huntingdon is in no mood to give up the chattels which the marriage laws of England have made over to him. Helen has every reason for going to ground and for throwing her vindictive spouse off her scent with every ingenious ruse available to her. To this end, she has changed her name to 'Mrs Graham', and has taken refuge in the broken-down

mansion, Wildfell Hall. In her farewell letter to her closest
friend, Esther Hargrave (whom she does not inform of her
future whereabouts), Helen stresses that it is 'of the last
importance that our future abode should be unknown to
him [her husband] and his acquaintance'. She will disclose
it to 'no one but my brother', she tells Esther (pp. 369–70).
At one point, Helen seriously contemplates emigration to
America to escape her husband's clutches.

With this in mind, it is very odd indeed that Helen
chooses Wildfell Hall as her asylum. The house belongs to
her brother, Frederick Lawrence, 'the young squire whose
family had formerly occupied Wildfell Hall, but had deserted it, some fifteen years ago, for a more modern but
commodious mansion in the neighbouring parish'. It
would not take a moderately curious husband (or his
lawyers) a week to discover a runaway wife and child (she
masquerading as a widow, but going into local society
with no other cover than an assumed name) in such an
obvious hiding place as her parental home. It is clear that
Mr Huntingdon does indeed institute a vigorous search
for Helen and Arthur—why then does he not find her?

This goes together with other odd features in Helen's
background. Although, as it emerges, her parents have
just the two children, and clearly have lived as local digni-
taries in Gilbert Markham's district of England (we are
never precisely told where it is), it emerges that Helen has
only seen her father once in her adult life and—until her
flight from Grassdale—her brother is a virtual stranger to
her. We learn this, obliquely, in one of the early marital
quarrels with Arthur, when Helen dresses in black in recognition of her father's death, and indicates an intention
to attend his funeral. 'I hate black', Arthur says:

'I hope, Helen, you won't think it your bounden duty to compose
your face and manners into conformity with your funereal garb.
Why should you sigh and groan, and I be made uncomfortable

because an old gentleman in —shire, a perfect stranger to us both, has thought proper to drink himself to death?—There now I declare you're crying! Well, it must be affectation.'

He would not hear of my attending the funeral, or going for a day or two, to cheer poor Frederick's solitude. It was quite unnecessary, he said, and I was unreasonable to wish it. What was my father to me? I had never seen him, but once since I was a baby, and I well knew he had never cared a stiver about me;—and my brother too, was little better than a stranger. (pp. 256–7)

That brother has, apparently, been brought up in the bosom of his family as the future squire. Helen, however, is quite unknown to anyone in the district. Although the Lawrence family inhabited Wildfell Hall until fifteen years ago (well within the memory of Gilbert's parents and the local vicar, the Revd Milward)—she has never, before reappearing as 'Mrs Graham', set foot in Wildfell Hall, nor, apparently, in the nearby commodious mansion.

There are some curious features here, which correspond with other curious features. Helen's mother is never mentioned in the text—she is simply not there (her funeral may be the 'one' occasion on which Helen has met her father in adult life). Helen's 'wedding to Arthur is only described summarily in passing and the ceremony, we apprehend, was not graced with the presence of either her father or brother. Although her family is demonstrably well off (they left Wildfell Hall not because of financial difficulties, but to take up a more luxurious residence), she has brought no dowry with her to the wedding, and only a tiny portion of family jewels (p. 337)—on the face of it, the only daughter of such a prosperous family, marrying with full parental consent, should come to her husband laden with treasure. Helen inherits nothing on her father's death, although her brother Frederick comes into considerable wealth. Helen was brought up by her uncle and aunt Maxwell (Mrs

Maxwell was her father's sister, apparently; see p. 456). It is they who bring her into society, vet her suitors, and make all necessary parental choices. When Mr Maxwell dies, he leaves—on his wife's instruction—the bulk of his fortune not to his widow (as, being childless, would he natural), but to Helen. We are told that Mrs Maxwell (as the former Miss Lawrence) brought a fine fortune—the bulk of her husband's subsequent wealth—to the marriage with her. It has apparently not always been the practice of the Lawrence family to send their daughters penniless to the altar.

It is singular that we are not informed by the text what Mrs Graham/Huntingdon's maiden name was. The narrative of Helen's premarital life (which is given through her own journal) goes to considerable contortions to avoid divulging this information in any clear way (see, for instance, Mr Boarham's laborious use of the 'My dear young lady' formulation, to avoid using the 'Miss Lawrence' address, which would be natural; pp. 132–4). The only way we can work out Helen's maiden surname is by speculation and the text (her text) gives us no firm evidence that she is, indeed, Miss Lawrence, the only daughter of Squire Lawrence (senior) the resident of Wildfell Hall, and the sister of Squire Lawrence (junior), the landlord of Wildfell Hall.

There are two hypotheses which the reader can advance to account for these anomalies. The first is that, the old Squire Lawrence being a dipsomaniac (see Huntingdon's comment about his drinking himself to death, and Frederick's enigmatic comments about congenital alcoholism on p. 38), his young daughter was removed as a baby from the house, to save her from its corrupting influence. But this would not explain her subsequent estrangement from her brother Frederick (who is clearly not a toper nor misanthropic), nor her apparent disinheritance from what would seem to be an only daughter's normal portion of family wealth.

The second hypothesis, which is more plausible, is that Helen is illegitimate—one of her debauched father's by-blows. As the central narrative makes clear, in the world of Brontë's novel a weakness for drink goes together with the grossest sexual delinquency. Helen, we surmise, is not Squire Lawrence's legal daughter but his bastard daughter, not Frederick's sister, but his half-sister. This would explain her total alienation from 'her' family and her being brought up well away from Wildfell Hall, and never once returning even for such family festivals as Christmas. It would also explain why Mrs Maxwell is at such pains to instill a high level of sexual morality into her ward. As a bastard, Helen would, in English law, take not her father's but her mother's surname which was, significantly, 'Graham'—the name by which she chooses to be known at Wildfell Hall. Illegitimacy (and the disowning that goes with it) would explain why her family does not attend her wedding, why her husband has met none of her family (other than the Maxwells), and why it is he cannot easily trace her back to Wildfell Hall.

The Oxford World's Classics *The Tenant of Wildfell Hall* is edited by Herbert Rosengarten, with an introduction by Margaret Smith.

Mrs Gaskell · *Mary Barton*

<hr>

What kind of murderer is John Barton?

<hr>

As Edgar Wright points out, Mrs Gaskell 'originally meant her novel to be called "John Barton". She mentions to two or three correspondents that she had envisaged the novel as a tragic poem with John Barton as the hero' (p. xv). This ur-narrative would have concentrated in detail on the working-class hero's suffering, his alienation and seduction by the 'vile' doctrines of Chartism and Communism, his lapse into homicidal crime, and his redemption. Unfortunately, as many modern critics feel, Gaskell succumbed to the preferences of her readers and publishers by recasting her plot as *Mary Barton*, the story of a virtuous working-class girl who resists the blandishments of a rich seducer and heroically saves her true love from the gallows. John Barton's melancholy story is relegated to the status of sub-plot.

One of the consequences of Mrs Gaskell's decision (which was entirely justified if she wished to reach a mass readership) was that details of John Barton's capital crime are left forever enigmatic. To summarize: driven to despair by the masters' lock-out, the trades union of which Barton is a conspiratorial ringleader resolves on an act of terror, specifically the assassination of Harry Carson, the haughty son of their chief tormentor among the employers. (Barton does not know that Harry is also the would-be seducer of his seamstress daughter, Mary.) Lots are drawn by flaring gaslight, and Barton is selected as the assassin.

The dreadful pact of the trades union occurs in chapter

16 ('Masters and Workmen'). The next chapter ('Barton's Night-Errand') is set two days later. The nature of the night-errand is ambiguous. Superficially it refers to John's being sent as a union envoy by rail to Glasgow (with a sovereign's expenses, which suggests a relatively short stay) to negotiate support from sympathetic fellow workers in the northern city. The other night-errand is, of course, the murder. In preparation John has borrowed a 'gun' from Mary's working-class suitor, Jem Wilson. A model of Smilesian self-improvement, the virtuous Wilson has nothing to do with horrible trades unions. But his deceased father and John Barton were friends, and liked to go target shooting with each other. He gives Barton the weapon (from later references to its 'stock' and the small wound it makes we apprehend that the weapon is some kind of small-bore rifle, although Mrs Gaskell is resolutely ignorant about such essentially masculine matters). Since Barton has been unemployed for some months, is starving, and addicted to opium, a sudden whim to improve his marksmanship might seem strange. But Jem is unsuspicious.

Barton, as we deduce, lays in wait for Carson in a hedge as the young man returns from his day's work in town to his father's house. One well-aimed shot to the temple does the awful deed. John Barton then disappears—possibly to Glasgow as he claimed. Although there were no witnesses, and no evident need to hurry himself, Barton leaves two clues behind at the scene of the crime. The gun is thrown down where the police can easily find it; since it has distinctive markings on it, tracing the weapon back to Wilson is the work of a few hours. John Barton also leaves behind some paper 'wadding', which he evidently removes and throws down before firing the weapon. This piece of paper has written on it the words '—ry Barton'. It was presumably placed in the barrel by Barton after cleaning the gun and hiding it in the hedgerow, prior to the murder, to protect the weapon from rusting in the dew. Although the handwriting of '—ry Barton' is distinctively Jem's, the document (a copy of Samuel Bamford's poem, 'God help the poor'; see pp. 128–9) from which the paper was torn belonged to Barton. The police, whose examination of the crime scene is perfunctory, miss this crucial piece of evidence. The paper is discovered by Mary's aunt Esther, who gives it to her niece, who destroys it. The tell-tale piece of paper persuades Mary of the dreadful fact that it must he her father who has shot Carson.

Gaskell seems to have been extraordinarily nervous of the subject of murder, and her narrative of this episode is remote and infuriatingly vague. Crucially, she does not inform us as to whether John Barton's leaving the gun and the wadding with his name on it was the consequence of panic or a deep-laid plan. Assuming the second, Barton's motives would seem to be as follows: the weapon would quickly be traced back through Jem to him, and the wadding—with the murderer's name on it—would clinch the matter. The '—ry Barton' inscription suggests a man leaving a deliberate trail for his pursuers. The chance of the premeditating, cold-blooded murderer 'accidentally' leaving a scrap of paper with his own surname by his victim exceeds even Mrs Gaskell's penchant for providential coincidence. Speculating further, we may suppose that in Glasgow—where it will cause least trauma for his daughter—Barton intends to kill himself (one of Mrs Gaskell's notes for this section mentions that Barton's 'temptation was suicide'; p. 469). Alternatively, if his nerve fails him, he may emigrate to the United States from the Scottish port under a false name, never to be seen again by his friends and family.

Barton does not know that Jem (having been informed by Esther of the other young man's evil intentions) has

quarrelled publicly with Harry over Mary, and has threatened the mill-owner with dreadful consequences if he does
not leave her alone. The threats are on record with the
police, who—having traced the gun—arrest Jem and look
no further for the assassin. On his part, Jem knows that
John Barton must be the killer, since he borrowed the
murder weapon a couple of days before, but out of love for
Mary (whom he supposes not to know about her father's
guilt) says nothing to the police or his defence lawyers,
prepared as he is to go to the gallows to spare her shame.
As it happens, thanks to Esther's giving her the wadding,
Mary *does* know that her father is the killer. In her notes
for the novel, Mrs Gaskell initially intended that Mary
should visit Jem in prison; this scene was never written,
presumably so that the two young people should remain at
cross-purposes during the trial. Clearly, if Jem knew that
Mary knew, his supreme self-sacrifice would be unnecessary. And if she knew that he knew, the sensible thing
would be to instruct him to inform on John Barton rather
than going, as she does, to frantic lengths to procure him
an alibi.

What, meanwhile, is John Barton doing? The novel does
not tell us. In a note, Gaskell wrote 'he had not heard of
Jem's arrest and trial till it was over' (p. 469). This is very
unconvincing. Political assassination was a sensational
event (Mrs Gaskell was aware of the murder of a mill-
owner; Thomas Ashton, during a strike in 1831, and admitted that it may have 'unconsciously' inspired her novel;
p. ix). The *Manchester Guardian* would have been full of
the matter. It is incredible that, having murdered someone,
Barton would not, if he were in Glasgow, examine the
papers for reports of the event. One assumes that he was
not in Glasgow, nor in any city, but somewhere in the
countryside trying, unsuccessfully, to screw himself up to
suicide.

There is another plausible possibility, namely, that
Barton intended to frame Jem. In the novel, as written,
this is rendered improbable by his not knowing that Harry
was the putative seducer of his daughter, and that Jem had
made death-threats to his rival. In Gaskell's notes for the
novel, however, Esther tells not Jem about Harry's evil
plans but her brother-in-law, John. In the author's mind,
then, was a pre-existing narrative in which John Barton
was fully aware of how suspicious it would be if a gun
belonging to Jem and a piece of paper with the words
'[Ma]ry Barton' were found near the corpse. Naturally,
the police would assume lover's jealousy. Suspicion would
be averted from the trades union, who would have committed the perfect crime. In this version of the plot, John
Barton would be many times more culpable than in the
novel as written. And this second scenario would make
more sense of John Barton's not hurrying back to prevent
an innocent man going to the gallows in his stead (as
would seem logical in the novel as written). That Jem
should hang in his place was what John Barton intended
from the first.

Mrs Gaskell never enlightens us. John Barton returns
after the trial. Where he has been, and what he knew
while he was away, we are not told. On his return we are
informed that he does appear strangely crushed—'beaten
down by some inward storm, he seemed to grovel along,
all self-respect lost and gone.' This seems something other
than assassin's remorse. It is plausible that he hates
himself for having framed an innocent man; this it is
that gnaws at his self-respect, and reduces him to a
grovelling thing. But, as far as one can make out, Gaskell
leaves the point unclear. John Barton's actions and
motives are clouded in the tremendous religiosity of his
final reconciliation with Carson senior and his euthanasia, forgiven by the man he has so horribly wronged.

Dives and Lazarus, man and master, are united in Christ. Nevertheless, in our speculations about the unwritten novel, 'John Barton', one is left wondering just how guilty a felon Mrs Gaskell originally had in mind.

The Oxford World's Classics *Mary Barton* is edited by Edgar Wright.

W. M. Thackeray · *Henry Esmond*

═══

On a gross anachronism

═══

No one much liked the ending of *Esmond* when it was published in 1852. George Eliot's comment is typical: 'the most uncomfortable book you can imagine . . . the hero is in love with the daughter all through the book, and marries the mother at the end.'[1] Eliot's discomfort has been shared by many—perhaps most—readers. It is troubling that a woman whom the orphaned hero clearly regards for much of the narrative as his mother should end up the mother of his own child. But Eliot is wrong, or impercipient, in her implication that there is something unexpected, or unprepared for, in Esmond's eventual union with Rachel. For one thing, her name, with its allusion to the long-waited-for biblical bride (Genesis 29), is a clear hint sown in the earliest pages of the narrative. At other points Thackeray is at elaborate pains to predict the final marriage, and cue the reader that Harry's ultimate happiness will lie not with the flighty Beatrix, but with her serene mother.

One such cue is found in Volume 3, Chapter 4, 'Beatrix's New Suitor' (i.e., the Duke of Hamilton), where the young heroine upbraids her discomfited 'knight of the rueful countenance' (i.e., Esmond):

'I intend to live to be a hundred, and to go to ten thousand routs and balls, and to play cards every night of my life till the year eighteen hundred [it is currently 1712]. And I like to be the first of my company, sir; and I like flattery and compliments, and you give me none; and I like to be made to laugh, sir, and who's to laugh at *your* dismal face, I should like to know; and I like a

coach-and-six or a coach-and-eight; and I like diamonds, and a
new gown every week; and people to say—"That's the duchess—
How well her grace looks—Make way for Madame l'Ambas-
sadrice d'Angleterre—Call her excellency's people"—that's what
I like. And as for you, you want a woman to bring your slippers
and cap, and to sit at your feet, and cry "0 caro! 0 bravo!" whilst
you read your Shakespeares, and Miltons, and stuff. Mamma
would have been the wife for you, had you been a little older,
though you look ten years older than she does—you do, you glum-
faced, blue-bearded; little old man! You might have sat, like
Darby and Joan, and flattered each other; and billed and cooed
like a pair of old pigeons on a perch. I want my wings and to use
them, sir.' And she spread out her beautiful arms, as if indeed she
could fly off like the pretty 'Gawrie', whom the man in the story
was enamoured of.

'And what will your Peter Wilkins say to your flight?' says
Esmond, who never admired this fair creature more than when
she rebelled and laughed at him. (pp. 363–4)

This banter ('Mamma would have been the wife for you')
is a clear premonition of the final outcome, couched as it
is in the elaborate games of literary allusion through
which Esmond and Beatrix conduct their sexual relationship. Beatrix's mock contempt for 'your Shakespeares and
Miltons' (she is, in fact, a highly civilized woman) and
Harry's graceful allusion to the 'Gawries' perfectly catch
the tension under its veneer of badinage. Esmond's specific reference at the end of the exchange (which may
elude the modern reader, but would have been picked up by
every Victorian) is to Robert Paltock's fantasia, *The Life
and Adventures of Peter Wilkins*. The Gawries whom he
alludes to were flying women and—significantly—the
pedestrian Peter finally marries one. Henry Esmond still
hopes he may one day capture the high-flying Beatrix.

It's an elegant exchange, and in keeping with the
highly wrought literary quality of this section of *Esmond's*
narrative. The preceding chapter, 'A Paper out of the

Spectator', is universally acclaimed as one of the most brilliant *tours de force* in Thackeray's prose, containing as it
does a brilliant pastiche of Addison. Like the Peter
Wilkins' allusion, Henry's mock *Spectator* essay is loaded
with clever and coded messages. It follows on from his sentimental comedy *The Faithful Fool*, with its representation of the hero as Eugenio (the name is a hint to
Beatrix—if she could but catch it—that Esmond is, in fact,
not illegitimate but well-born, and the true Marquis;
something that she will discover later to her astonishment.) The *Spectator* paper is pseudonymously addressed
by 'Oedipus' to 'Jocasta', signalling that Thackeray was
well aware of what knowing post-Freudian readers would
find in his novel, a hundred years later. Has Esmond
chosen these names unconsciously, or is he aware of certain unusual sexual desires in himself?

There is, however, a big problem with the 'Gawrie' reference in the following chapter. *The Life and Adventures of
Peter Wilkins* was first published in 1751. Paltock's fable
was hugely popular all through the late eighteenth and
nineteenth centuries.[2] Its date (or rough period) of publication would have been familiar to any of *Esmond's* early
readers capable of enjoying the *Spectator* joke. And any
reader incapable of picking up that literary joke would
have been beneath the narrator's notice. The 1751 date of
Peter Wilkins's publication is, however, wholly irreconcilable with the date at which the exchange between Harry
and Beatrix takes place. Thackeray is insistent about the
precise year (1712) and even the month and day on which
the conversation occurs. (1 April—April Fool's Day—is
the date carried by the spoof *Spectator* paper). The nobleman Beatrix is about to marry (her 'new suitor', the
fourth Duke of Hamilton, a historical figure) was killed
in a duel in November 1712—an episode which is used
climactically soon afterwards in the novel. Queen Anne

enters the novel in person, further clinching the 1712–14 date of action. The third volume of *Esmond's* narrative is locked into precise, obtrusive, chronological markers which Thackeray seems intent on hammering home. In the final chapters, Esmond and Rachel emigrate to Virginia in 1718. She dies in 1736, and he is dead (presumably in the 1740s, around the period of the Scottish Rebellion) well before the publication of Paltock's work from which he is supposed to quote in 1712.

Thackeray often makes small errors of chronology But the 'Gawrie' lapse is gross—suspiciously so. It is equivalent to Hardy's Jude quoting at length from *The Waste Land*, or Emma Woodhouse comparing Harriet Smith's plight to that of Jane Eyre. It jars. And it occurs at a section in the novel where Thackeray is so exact and virtuosic in his play with eighteenth-century comic literature (a subject on which he was currently lecturing to British and American audiences, and on which he was the leading authority)[3] as to render it wholly incredible that he did not register the error. And—if by some blindspot he did not register it—why did he not remove the reference in the revised edition of *Esmond* (as he dropped other embarrassing material)?

Readers certainly registered the lapse. Thackeray's 'Peter Wilkins' solecism was gleefully seized on by early contributors to *Notes and Queries*, and every edited text of the novel ruefully notes it as a damaging anachronism. Rather than join the querists and annotators in gloating over or lamenting what looks like a monumental blooper, it makes better sense to assume that Thackeray put this anachronism into his text, and kept it there in revised editions, for an artistic purpose. That purpose can be deduced from the intricate narrative framework of the novel. The story is 'edited' by the daughter of Rachel and Esmond, Rachel Esmond Warrington ('REW'), who has

had the written 'Memoirs' (i.e. the text of the novel) from
Esmond's own pen. Her garrulous and frequently vulgar
preface is dated 3 November 1778.

'REW' is an unequivocally ridiculous figure as she
appears on the edges of the story: vain and jealous of her
mother's claim on her father's affections, vengeful against
'Mrs Tusher' (i.e. Beatrix—who has to descend a long way
from her 'Duchess' aspirations), headstrong, and rather
stupid. And in the last volume REW loses editorial control
over her material, inserting a series of increasingly fatu-
ous footnotes, culminating in a bizarre footnoted disserta-
tion in Volume 3, Chapter 10 on her father's Christian
gentleness of manners to all and sundry, not excluding
'the humblest negresses on his estate' (p. 431).

What we are led to assume is that REW's spoiling pen
has also intervened in the text of the 'Memoirs', as well as
at its prefatory and marginal edges. The passages which
speckle the third volume, predicting the eventual 'Darby
and Joan' happiness of Esmond and Rachel have been
inserted by REW we may plausibly deduce, at some point
after 1751 and her parents' death. Like other pious biographers, she wants to project a whitewashed image of
her parents to the world. Thackeray himself was morbidly
aware of the dangers of such loyal filial impulses, and the
kind of pious absurdities they might lead to. He frequently instructed his daughters over the last years of his
life, 'No biography!'—an instruction which his daughter
Anne religiously observed (there was no family-
authorized biography of Thackeray until the 1950s, when
Gordon Ray was finally given permission).[4] REW is not
restrained as strictly as Thackeray's daughters on the
question of paternal biography—indeed, Esmond seems to
have consciously charged his daughter with the care of
his 'Memoirs' and a *nihil obstat* on their eventual
publication. REW as we can see, habitually exceeds her

strict editorial remit, adding her own 'improvements' which go well beyond the signed footnotes into the actual text of Esmond's memoirs. But, impulsive and unscholarly as she is, REW betrays her interference by a gross solecism—a solecism so gross, indeed, that no one who knows the author(s) can picture Thackeray or Esmond making it. It is only too easy, however, to imagine Rachel Esmond Warrington perpetrating the blunder.

The Oxford World's Classics *The History of Henry Esmond* is edited by Donald Hawes.

Charles Dickens · *Bleak House*

═══

What is Jo Sweeping?

═══

In Philadelphia, in the winter of 1994-5, the pedestrian waiting at any of the cross-streets at Center City (as the heart of the metropolis is called) would find a helpful person with a broom sweeping an already spotless and carefully built-up gutter. Since the winter was the warmest since the thermometer was invented and the crossings no dirtier than the pavements, many tourists must have wondered why the governors of a city in financial crisis should have supplied this service. The reason for the army of crossing sweepers was the series of devastating ice-storms which had raged through the city in 1993-4, and the crop of lawsuits brought against Philadelphia by injured pedestrians.

Why, one may go on to wonder, did the Victorians need crossing-sweepers of the kind who furnish main characters in at least three novels of the period? (Thackeray's *The Yellowplush Papers*, 1841; Bulwer-Lytton's *Lucretia*, 1846; and—most famously—*Bleak House*, 1853.) If Dickens's Jo is a sweeper, what precisely does he sweep? An answer is given in the first paragraph of the novel:

London. Michaelmas Term lately over, and the Lord Chancellor sitting in Lincoln's Inn Hall. Implacable November weather. As much mud in the streets, as if the waters had but newly retired from the face of the earth, and it would not be wonderful to meet a Megalosaurus, forty feet long or so, waddling like an elephantine lizard up Holborn Hill.

'Mud', it would seem, is what the mid-Victorian sweepers swept.[1] Here Dickens pictures it as the primal soup from which the post-diluvian, fallen world, has evolved. But, as he must have pronounced it, the word 'mud' had overtones of another of Dickens's favourite words, *merde*—shit. *Merde* was memorably compounded elsewhere into two of the author's most biting names, Merdle and Murdstone. The anglicized form of the word is picked up by T. S. Eliot, in *Gerontion*, in one of his more Dickensian visions of urban life:

> The goat coughs at night in the field overhead;
> Rocks, moss, stonecrop, iron, merds.

As Fred Schwarzbach points out, in his book *Dickens and the City*, mud and *merde* had much in common in 1853:

The mud of mid-century London was, after all, quite different from the harmless if messy stuff children today make into pies. It was compounded of loose soil to be sure, but also of a great deal more, including soot and ashes and street litter, and the fecal matter of the legion horses on whom all transport in London depended. In addition, many sewers (such as they were) were completely open, and in rainy weather would simply overflow into the streets. Dogs, cattle in transit either to Smithfield or through the town (many dairies were still inside the city), and many people as well used the public streets as a privy, but then even most privies were simply holes in the ground with drainage into ditches or another part of the street. (London was still a good fifteen years away from having an effective drainage system.) The mud must at times have been nothing less than liquid ordure.[2]

Norman Gash, in *Robert Surtees and Early Victorian Society* is more analytic, if no less disgusted:

Everyone agreed that London was the dirtiest of English cities. The central streets were covered with a thick layer of filth, the principal ingredients of which were horse manure, stonedust from the constant grinding of iron tyres on the paving stones, and soot descending from the forest of London chimneys. The resultant compound resembled a black paste, which clung glutinously to everything it touched and emitted a characteristic odour reminiscent of a cattle-market. Though contractors were employed to clean the streets, the work was hard and ill-paid; it could only be done at night; and the filth carried away had little commercial value. London produced in fact such a vast amount of excrement, both animal and human, that the surrounding agricultural districts were unable to absorb it. As a result the streets seemed to remain permanently foul. To get across busy streets, especially in wet weather, was a hazardous business except at the regular paths—'isthmuses of comparative dry land', as one observer called them—kept clean by the unremitting work of crossing-sweepers.[3]

Henry Mayhew devotes a fairly long section of *London Labour and the London Poor* (1851) to crossing-sweepers— 'a large class of the Metropolitian poor', as he terms them. Mayhew noted: 'We can scarcely walk along a street of any extent, or pass through a square of the least pretensions to "gentility", without meeting one or more of these private scavengers.'[4] As Mayhew observed, for most of these broom-wielders sweeping was an excuse for begging. Using this cover was attractive because: (1) it required very little capital to commence the business; (2) the pseudo-occupation enabled the sweeper to solicit gratuities without being considered in the light of a street beggar; (3) being seen in the same place constantly excited the sympathy of the neighbouring householders, encouraging the donations of small weekly allowances or 'pensions'. The Victorian crossing-sweeper was exactly analogous to the ubiquitous windscreen cleaner to be found importuning motorists at London and New York traffic-lights in the 1980s and 1990s. As is often observed, one of the finest achievements of Reagonomics and Thatcherism was to reinvent the able-bodied pauper and the Victorian street beggar. Dickens would have been amazed.

As is his wont, Mayhew anatomizes the different classes

of crossing-sweeper in great factual detail. The average income is, he reckons, a shilling a-day. The sweepers, he judges, constitute 'the most honest of the London poor' (p. 466). They vary from the well-known London landmarks, who have occupied the same pitch for years, to the 'irregular' bands of young girl and boy crossing-sweepers. Mayhew makes the chilling point that the children sweepers can only survive for any length of time in the streets by forming themselves into organized gangs, living and working together co-operatively. As he notes:

The irregular sweepers mostly consist of boys and girls who have formed themselves into a kind of company, and come to an agreement to work together on the same crossings. The principal resort of these is about Trafalgar Square, where they have seized upon some three or four crossings, which they visit from time to time in the course of the day. (ii. 466)

Jo, one recalls from Chapter 11, has his pitch by St Martin-in-the-Fields Church, in Trafalgar Square. And the reason that he is 'moved on', so calamitously, is because he is alone—he has not, that is, acquired sufficient street smarts to realize that he can only survive if he throws in his lot with others who hunt in packs.

One of the modern reader's principal problems in visualizing the world of *Bleak House* is not being sure of how far one should let one's imagination rip. Should we accept Fred Schwarzbach's Dantean vision of a London swimming in 'liquid ordure'? Or were the urchins around Trafalgar Square simply going through the motions (like windscreen cleaners at modern crossroads), the more conveniently to beg a penny or two from passers-by? And even if there were a lot of droppings in the street, would they necessarily be so obnoxious? George Orwell (in his essay on Swift) makes the point that horse dung—given the beast's graminivorous diet and fast metabolism—is not, as dung goes, physically nauseating (compared to, say, the tons of dog-mess dropped daily on London parks today). The streets of the West End in 1852 might not have been more unpleasant than, say, the stretch of Oxford Street outside McDonalds with its detritus of French-fry packets, milk-shake cartons, and hamburger grease. A modern-day Jo would be rather welcome sweeping the crossroads at Tottenham Court Road and Oxford Street.

This question relates to another quarrel in recent Dickens studies—namely, what constitutes the 'dust' in the dust heaps in *Our Mutual Friend* (1865). Humphry House, in his influential study *The Dickens World* (1941), announced to a less squeamish age than the Victorians that 'dust' was a euphemism for 'human excrement'. The revelation gave a new *frisson* to such descriptions as that of Silas Wegg, stumping triumphantly over the mounds, his wooden leg puncturing the surface crust, leaving a trail of mephitic vapours behind him.

It is true that the English habitually use the word 'dust' euphemistically—as in 'dustman' and 'dustbin'. But in his 1971 Penguin Classics edition of *Our Mutual Friend*, Stephen Gill disputes House's garish vision of a mountain of decaying human turd lowering over the love-making of Bella and Harmon. Drawing on Mayhew, Gill argues that human excrement was too liquid to form into heaps and too valuable to dispose of as garbage. The dust heaps, as Mayhew pointed out, were composed of seven elements, all of them valuable as salvage, but none so valuable as human excrement (which was used as manure). They were: (1) fine dust, sold to brickmakers; (2) cinders, or brieze, sold to brickmakers for breeze-blocks; (3) rags, bones, and old metal; (4) old tin and iron; (5) old bricks and oyster shells, sold to builders for footings; (6) old boots and shoes; (7) money and jewellery. It has been pointed out elsewhere, however, that Mayhew does indicate that another main constituent of the heaps was manure—

which would suggest that animal (as opposed to human) excrement formed a large part of the substance.[5] The question is still somewhat open.

Decoding Dickens on the mud/*merde*, dust/shit question is difficult, because in general the Victorian novelists (excluding the pornographers) are extraordinarily fastidious about mentioning human or animal waste—excretion, like sex, is a rigorously tabooed subject. In the whole of Surtees, for instance, one detects few clear references to horse dung, although a moment's reflection reveals that the Jorrocks narratives must be ankle-deep in the odoriferous substance (but then, how many horse droppings does one see in John Wayne cowboy movies?). Of course, one can often supply what the novelist carefully omits to name directly. In the following passage by Mrs Gaskell from *Mary Barton* describing the utter squalor of a Manchester slum dwelling it is not hard to fill in the lexical blank of 'slops of *every* description':

[The street] was unpaved; and down the middle a gutter forced its way, every now and then forming pools in the holes with which the street abounded. Never was the old Edinburgh cry of 'Gardez l'eau!' more necessary than in this street. As they passed, women from their doors tossed household slops of *every* description into the gutter; they ran into the next pool, which overflowed and stagnated. Heaps of ashes were the stepping-stones, on which the passer-by, who cared in the least for cleanliness, took care not to put his foot. (p. 66)

As the World's Classics editor, Edgar Wright, points out, the Edinburgh reference is to the emptying of chamberpots, and 'ashes' is to be read 'as a euphemism for excrement'. The experienced reader of Victorian fiction becomes adept in filling in such blanks and picking up such hints. It is, for instance, a commonplace that characters in Victorian fiction do not go to the lavatory. Yet, if we are moderately sensitive, we apprehend that when Casaubon asks Dorothea and Celia twice during their first visit to his house at Lowick if they are 'tired' he is politely inquiring if they wish his maid-servant to conduct them to the ladies' room.[6]

It is also the case that a writer like Dickens did not have to specify what London street mud was like for the reader of his time, any more than he was obliged to record that the same streets were cobbled or that the carriages were pulled by horses. Everybody already knew. On his part Mayhew, despite the most pedantic anatomization of the condition and variety of street-sweepers, rarely feels obliged to allude to what is actually being swept. He did not have to. The reader would only have to look from the page to the sole of his shoe. In a hundred years' time students may wonder exactly what kind of slime, grime, grit, or filth accumulated on the windscreens of late-twentieth-century cars that needed to be cleaned off so frequently. No one, writing today in newspapers, would feel obliged to describe the exact composition of the grime thrown up on our roads (sprayed mud, squashed insects, a patina of oil and rubber). It may well require a footnote a century hence. And casual readers, a century hence, might well surmise that city streets in the 1990s were exceptionally dirty—otherwise why was there any need for that army of windscreen cleaners?

With Dickens, however, there is a peculiarly Dickensian problem. His disinclination to specify mud/*merde*, dust/shit, makes it difficult for the historically alienated modern reader to know whether or not the writer is indulging in his characteristic hyperbole, and to what degree. Clearly the megalosaurus in the opening passage of *Bleak House* is a flight of hyperbolic fancy (inspired, I would guess, by the papier-mâché dinosaurs constructed for the Crystal Palace Exhibition, a couple of years earlier). But, if we follow Schwarzbach, Dickens's description of the street mire in Holborn is, if anything, understated—'mud' is not hyperbole, but litotes.

The point is clearer if one goes on to the parallel scene in Chesney Wold, in the opening of the second chapter. Here the elemental excess is not earth/mud, but water/rain:

The waters are out in Lincolnshire. An arch of the bridge in the park has been sapped and sopped away. The adjacent low-lying ground, for half a mile in breadth, is a stagnant river, with melancholy trees for islands in it, and a surface punctured all over, all day long, with falling rain. My Lady Dedlock's 'place' has been extremely dreary. The weather, for many a day and night, has been so wet that the trees seem wet through, and the soft loppings and prunings of the woodman's axe can make no crash or crackle as they fall. The deer, looking soaked, leave quagmires, where they pass. The shot of a rifle loses its sharpness in the moist air, and its smoke moves in a tardy little cloud towards the green rise, coppice-topped, that makes a background for the falling rain.

Unlike London mud, English rain has not altered in composition over the last hundred years, and one can precisely gauge how far Dickens is over-writing here, in his description of the unnaturally silent landscape. But is the description of the excess of mud in Holborn hyperbolic? And for mud, should we read *merde*? One is driven to surmise. My guess is that the crossing Jo superintends at Trafalgar Square is not all that bestrewn with muck, and although by no means wholesome is no more filthy than the same streets today at the end of a busy week-day. What, one may ask oneself could an undersized boy, with a worn-out broom (such as is described by Dickens and pictured below by Frank Beard) be expected to clean? Not much. Is the gentleman depicted complacently handing over his coin really worried about getting his shoes and understrapped trousers dirty? Or is discreet charity his main motive? Certainly the artist is careful to sketch in two carriages in the background to the picture, and there will be droppings. But not, one apprehends, the ankle-deep tide of filth which recent commentary has pictured swirling around the public places of Victorian London.

The Oxford World's Classics *Bleak House* is edited by Stephen Gill. The Oxford World's Classics *Mary Barton* is edited by Edgar Wright.

The Boy Crossing-Sweepers

Villette's double ending

Critics have traditionally been fascinated by the enigmatic ending of *Villette*—particularly hyper-modern
critics who see in the novel an anticipation of the 'prob-
lematized text', so beloved of deconstructionists and of
theorists generally.[1] To summarize: at the end of the narrative, Lucy Snowe has her virtuous pluck rewarded by the
declared love and marriage proposals of her stern 'professor', Paul Emanuel. But before he can make Lucy his wife,
Paul must spend three years working in the French pro-
tectorate Guadaloupe. The reasons for his exile to this far-
off place are vaguely communicated to the reader by Lucy,
in Chapter 39: 'its alpha is Mammon, and its omega
Interest' (p. 576), she declares. Madame Walravens, we are
informed, has earlier inherited by marriage a large estate
at Basseterre, on the West Indian island: 'if duly looked
after by a competent agent of integrity' for 'a few years',
the estate will be 'largely productive'. Madame Walravens
asks Paul to be her 'competent agent'. As Lucy observes,
such a wish is a command: 'No living being ever humbly
laid his advantage at M. Emanuel's feet, or confidingly put
it into his hands, that he spurned the trust, or repulsed the
repository' (p. 577). Whatever might be Paul's 'private pain
or inward reluctance to leave Europe', he accedes.

It is, on the face of it, strange that Paul should accede.
The claims of Lucy and his own happiness would seem to
be stronger than the financial convenience of Madame
Walravens. He is not, in any case, a businessman, but a
schoolteacher and a very good one—if a little too fond

of 'discipline'. But it is not hard to deduce what duties Paul Emanuel is required for. The date of *Villette's* action is the early 1840s (the period of Charlotte Brontë's own residence in Brussels, 1842–4). Slavery had finally been abolished in the British West Indies in 1833, precipitating a disastrous collapse in the sugar industry, with the widespread defection of pressed labour. In neighbouring Guadaloupe, under the unenlightened French imperial regime, the institution of slavery (and the profitability of the sugar plantations) was to limp along until its eventual, long-overdue abolition in 1848. The stern and dictatorial Professor Emanuel—the bully of Madame Beck's classroom—has been recruited to rally the increasingly dissident slave labourers of Madame Walravens's estate, with whips and scorpions, if necessary. For 'competent', read 'brutal'. There is another putative factor in the virtuous lady's choosing Monsieur Emanuel as her overseer. He has shown himself, in his attendance at Madame Beck's establishment, remarkably capable of restraining himself sexually in the presence of nubile young women. All nineteenth-century accounts of Guadaloupe stress that it is a place of almost irresistible temptation for European males. As the *Encyclopaedia Britannica* (14th edition, 1929) records:

Guadaloupe has a few white officials and planters, a few East Indian immigrants from the French possessions in India, and the rest negroes and mulattoes. These mulattoes are famous for their grace and beauty of both form and feature. Women greatly outnumber men, and illegitimate births are very numerous. (x. 927)

Clearly only a man of iron self-discipline can be trusted in such a Sodom.

One assumes that Paul's motives for exiling himself from Lucy are at least partly to test his bride-to-be, to try her ability to survive without him. Is she worthy to be

Madame Emanuel? He is fond of imposing such ordeals. In the three years of his absence Lucy must prove her worth by setting up a school. She succeeds magnificently, inspired by the lessons in discipline and self-discipline that she has learned from her professor.

The relationship between the lovers during Paul's absence is sustained by passionate letters. The novel concludes with a coda which switches dramatically from the past to the present tense: 'And now the three years are past. M. Emanuel's return is fixed.' It was early summer when he left (the roses were in bloom). Now, on the eve of his return, it is autumn and the season of equinoctial storms. Lucy apostrophizes the elements as her demonic foe:

The wind shifts to the west. Peace, peace, Banshee—'keening' at every window! It will rise—it will swell—it shrieks out long: wander as I may through the house this night, I cannot lull the blast. The advancing hours make it strong: by midnight, all sleepless watchers hear and fear a wild south-west storm. (p. 617)

A cataclysmic storm duly rages for seven days, an appropriately de-creating span of time which will, we fear, return Lucy's universe to chaos. The novel concludes with an enigmatic and emotionally exhausted last two paragraphs:

Here pause: pause at once. There is enough said. Trouble no quiet, kind heart; leave sunny imaginations hope. Let it be theirs to conceive the delight of joy born again fresh out of great terror, the rapture of rescue from peril, the wondrous reprieve from dread, the fruition of return. Let them picture union and a happy succeeding life.

Madame Beck prospered all the days of her life; so did Père Silas; Madame Walravens fulfilled her ninetieth year before she died. Farewell. (pp. 617–18)

Does Emanuel drown or does he survive drowning? The reference to Madame Walravens indicates that Lucy is

writing many years after the event, so the outcome must
be known—despite the present tense used to evoke the
storm.

The novel's internal structure of allusion is enigmatic
on the question. The 'banshee' reference looks all the way
back to Chapter 4, which features a terrible storm while
Lucy is in England, in the service of the invalid Miss
Marchmont. That storm is described as being accompanied
by a 'subtle screeching cry'. Looking forward, beyond the
events of Villette's narrative, Lucy records that:

> Three times in the course of my life, events had taught me that
> these strange accents in the storm—this restless, hopeless cry—
> denote a coming state of the atmosphere unpropitious to life.
> Epidemic diseases, I believed, were often heralded by a gasping,
> sobbing, tormented long-lamenting east wind. Hence, I inferred,
> arose the legend of the Banshee. (p. 46)

Miss Marchmont dies that night.

The second of the three occasions alluded to by Lucy in
the above passage is recorded in Chapter 15. The heroine is
now in the less congenial service of Madame Beck. She has
been subject to 'peculiarly agonizing depression' (p. 197)
and feverish delirium. Recovered from her nightmares,
but still weak, she arises from her bed, unable to bear the
'solitude and the stillness' of the dormitory any longer. It
is evening, and the darkening sky is terrible with the
threat of storm:

> from the lattice I saw coming night-clouds trailing low like
> banners drooping. It seemed to me that at this hour there
> was affection and sorrow in Heaven above for all pain suffered
> on earth beneath; the weight of my dreadful dream became
> alleviated. (p. 198)

Lucy unwisely ventures out into the storm in her weakened, semi-invalid state. The end of this chapter marks the
gap between the first and second volumes of the original

three-volume edition brought out by Smith, Elder & Co in January 1853. For the mass of circulating-library readers, rationed by their one-guinea subscriptions to one volume at a time, this gap would entail more than simply reaching for the next volume. There would, probably, be a longish interval during which volume 1 was returned (possibly after a delay while some other member of the family read it) and the second volume borrowed from the library (possibly after yet another delay if one had to visit Mudie's main establishment in Bloomsbury, or if all the second volumes were 'out'). Readers, thus kept in suspense, might reasonably expect that Lucy was about to die. Chapter 15 and volume 1 end with the dramatic statement: 'I seemed to pitch headlong down an abyss. I remember no more.'

Is Lucy dead? Almost dead, it transpires. The opening of the second volume (Chapter 16) picks up on the 'abyss' reference: 'Where my soul went during that swoon I cannot tell.' Lucy has experienced, it seems, an after-death experience:

Whatever [my soul] saw, or wherever she travelled in her trance on that strange night, she kept her own secret; never whispering a word to Memory, and baffling Imagination by an indissoluble silence. She may have gone upward, and come in sight of her eternal home, hoping for leave to rest now, and deeming that her painful union with matter was at last dissolved. While she so deemed, an angel may have warned her away from heaven's threshold, and, guiding her weeping down, have bound her, once more, all shuddering and unwilling, to that poor frame, cold and wasted, of whose companionship she was grown more than weary. (p. 207)

Miss Soul's return (that is to say, Lucy's revival) is further metaphorized in terms of a painful rescue from drowning. This, one assumes, is the second 'banshee' experience in which the victim is pulled back from the very jaws of death. The third banshee-storm-death episode is that connected with Paul Emanuel's return voyage from Guadaloupe and his shipwreck at sea. Does it betoken death (as with Miss Marchmont) or a terrifying brush with death (as with Lucy)?

Charlotte Brontë evidently received some querulous correspondence on the subject of her indeterminate ending. As Mrs Gaskell records, two of the author's female contemporaries wrote demanding 'exact and authentic information respecting the fate of M. Paul Emanuel'. Brontë wrote to her editor at Smith, Elder & Co. saying she had dispatched an answer, 'so worded as to leave the matter pretty much where it was. Since the little puzzle amuses the ladies, it would be a pity to spoil their sport by giving them the key.'

As Margaret Smith and Herbert Rosengarten suggest, in their World's Classics edition of *Villette*, we should also consider in this context Brontë's sharper letter to her publisher, George Smith, on 26 March 1853:

With regard to that momentous point—M. Paul's fate—in case anyone in future should request to be enlightened thereon—they may be told that it was designed that every reader should settle the catastrophe for himself, according to the quality of his disposition, the tender or remorseful impulse of his nature. Drowning and Matrimony are the fearful alternatives. The Merciful . . . will of course choose the former and milder doom—drown him to put him out of pain. The cruel-hearted will on the contrary pitilessly impale him on the second horn of the dilemma—marrying him without ruth or compunction to that—person—that—that—individual—'Lucy Snowe'. (p. 662)

Charlotte Brontë supplies us in this sarcastic letter with the 'key to the puzzle'. That is to say, one could only sustain the 'sunny' reading of the novel's ending if one equated the disaster of Paul's drowning with the 'disaster' of his marrying the woman he loves and who loves him. It is 'moral' for Lucy to prevaricate if Paul Emanuel has indeed died at sea, so as not to discomfit her less emotionally sturdy readers. Hiding her misery is a brave and admirable thing to do. Had Paul Emanuel returned, it would have been reprehensible to have disguised or withheld the fact. Such behaviour could only be construed as a claim for undeserved pity and sympathy.

There is, in short, no problem with the conclusion of *Villette*, if one gives it a moment's thought. Paul Emanuel drowns—end of story (literally). Mrs Gaskell confirms the point by reference to privileged family testimony:

Mr Brontë was anxious that her new tale should end well, as he disliked novels which left a melancholy impression upon the mind; and he requested her to make her hero and heroine (like the heroes and heroines in fairy-tales) 'marry, and live happily ever after'. But the idea of M. Paul Emanuel's death at sea was stamped on her imagination, till it assumed the distinct force of reality; and she could no more alter her fictitious ending than if they had been facts which she was relating. All she could do in compliance with her father's wish was so to veil the fate in oracular words, as to leave it to the character and discernment of her readers to interpret her meaning. (pp. 661–2)

The interpretation is simple enough, and few sensible readers of the novel can have given credence to the spurious 'sunny' ending.[2] More interesting—particularly in the context of 1853—is the device of the double ending, the reader being left free to choose between a 'real' or a 'fairy-tale' version. *Villette* came out in January 1853. In October of the same year Thackeray began to serialize *The Newcomes*. This massive saga-novel was to continue as a monthly serial for the following twenty-three months, until August 1855. The main strand of Thackeray's narrative deals with the careers of the cousins Ethel and Clive Newcome, their true love for each other, and their respective unhappy marriages to less-congenial partners.

The Newcomes ends with one of greatest effusions of

pathos in Victorian fiction, the death of Colonel Newcome,
and Clive and Ethel aching for each other but forever separated. There follows a coda in which Thackeray, apparently *in propria persona*, declares that: 'Two years ago,
walking with my children in some pleasant fields, near to
Berne, in Switzerland, I strayed from them into a little
wood: and, coming out of it presently, told them how the
story had been revealed to me somehow, which for three-
and-twenty months the reader has been pleased to follow'
(p. 1007).

Thackeray then embarks on an extended fantasia about
what his characters are doing in 'Fable-land'. His belief is,
he says, 'that in Fable-land somewhere Ethel and Clive are
living most comfortably together'. That is, as man and
wife. 'You', Thackeray tells his reader:

may settle your fable-land in your own fashion. Anything you like
happens in fable-land. Wicked folks die à propos ... annoying
folks are got out of the way; the poor are rewarded—the upstarts
are set down in fable-land ... the poet of fable-land ... makes the
hero and heroine happy at last, and happy ever after. Ah, happy,
harmless fable-land, where these things are! Friendly reader! may
you and the author meet there on some future day! He hopes so;
as he yet keeps a lingering hold of your hand, and bids you
farewell with a kind heart. (p. 1009)

It seems an uncannily close echo of the Revd Brontë's
demand that his daughter's novel should deny its own
character, and conclude with a 'fairy-tale' ending. And
there is, as it happens, a graphic record of just such
pressure being brought to bear on Thackeray. While lecturing in Coventry during the course of the serial run of
The Newcomes, Thackeray was entertained by the Brays
and Hennells (George Eliot's friends). Miss Hennell, as
the ladies' spokeswoman, said:

'Mr Thackeray, we want you to let Clive marry Ethel. Do let them
be happy.' He was surprised at their interest in his characters

[and replied] 'The characters once created *lead me*, and I follow where they direct.'[3]

None the less, in his fable-land coda, as had Charlotte Brontë a couple of years earlier, Thackeray threw a sop to his soft-hearted readers and Coventry's imperious need for 'sunny' endings.

In April 1854, just over a year after *Villette's* publication and a good year before the end of *The Newcomes'* run, Dickens began to serialize his new novel *Hard Times* in *Household Words*, where it ran weekly until August. *Hard Times* finishes with a visionary coda in which the narrator pictures a series of happy endings, including that of Louisa, released from Bounderby and

again a wife—a mother—lovingly watchful of her children, ever careful that they should have a childhood of the mind no less than a childhood of the body, as knowing it to be even a more beautiful thing, and a possession, any hoarded scrap of which, is a blessing and happiness to the wisest. (p. 397)

'Did Louisa see this?' the narrator asks: 'Such a thing was never to be.'

These three novels, by the three leading novelists of 1853–5, all employ the same striking terminal device of the double ending. One of those double endings is harshly 'realistic', and aimed at tough readers (with whom the novelist is clearly in closer sympathy). For softer-minded readers, of 'sunny' disposition, an alternative 'fairy-tale' ending is supplied (or in Dickens's case, hinted) in which Paul Emanuel returns to the embraces of his little Protestant Lucy, Clive and Ethel are united to the clashing peals of wedding bells, and Louisa recovers from her near seduction by Harthouse to become a respectably fulfilled materfamilias. 'You pays your money and you takes your pick', the novels seem to say.

One can suggest a reason for this epidemic of double

endings in 1853–5. Clearly Charlotte Brontë, Charles
Dickens and Thackeray were responding to the pressure of
a new reading public, one that wanted happy endings and
could make its wants felt. That reading public (with its
representative spokespersons like the Revd Brontë and
Miss Hennell) had been massively organized and
empowered by the new phenomenon of the circulating
library—notably Mudie's. Charles Mudie's 'Leviathan'
had started modestly enough in Southampton Row in the
1840s. In 1852, however, the firm moved into massive new
premises at the corner of New Oxford Street and Museum
Street. As Guinevere Griest records: 'During the ten years
between 1853 and 1862, Mudie added almost 960,000 volumes to his library, nearly half of which were fiction'.[4]
Mudie was suddenly the biggest bulk purchaser of new
novels in the kingdom. And the proprietor of the Leviathan demanded happy endings, on behalf of his customers.
As Griest again records, 'over and over again works were
censured because they were "disagreeable" or "unpleasant", qualities which Mr Mudie's readers did not care to
find in their novels' (p. 136).

The peremptory demands of the library reader for sunshine and their resentment of anything 'disagreeable'
were beginning to be focused on the novelist in 1853–5, by
direct pressure from the publisher, himself under direct
pressure from the bulk-buying libraries. What the endings
of these three high-profile novels of 1853–5 indicate is that
on their part the novelists had registered the demands of
this newly mobilized force of library readers, and
were devising subtle strategies of resistance. This complex tug-of-war between novelist and the tyrannic circulating library was to continue until 1894 and the collapse
of the three-decker novel under the assault of novelists
like George Moore and Thomas Hardy, enraged by
the constraints that Mrs Grundy (alias Mr Mudie, the

'nursemaid' of literature) were imposing on their art and their claims to the privileges of realism.

The Oxford World's Classics *Villette* is edited by Margaret Smith and Herbert Rosengarten. The Oxford World's Classics *The Newcomes* is edited by Andrew Sanders. The Oxford World's Classics *Hard Times* is edited by Paul Schlicke.

What is Hetty waiting for?

In their forthrightly entitled article, 'Victorian Women and Menstruation', Elaine and English Showalter note that:

Few taboos evoke as forceful and as universal a response as that surrounding menstruation. Even the redoubtable Marquis de Sade, who took a prurient delight in moldy feces and decapitated dogs, appears to have regarded menstruation with faint distaste . . . Small wonder that even Victorians as open-minded as Florence Nightingale and John Stuart Mill maintain an almost complete silence on the subject. (p. 83)[1]

'Unlike sexual activities', the authors continue, 'menstruation has no literary reflection, true or false.' In the quarter of a century since the Showalters wrote their article critics have become very ingenious at uncovering the repressed consciousness of nineteenth-century fiction—most aggressively in Eve Kosofsky Sedgwick's polemic, 'Jane Austen and the Masturbating Girl'.[2] None the less, the menstruating woman has not been located and the Showalters' claim about 'no literary reflection' would seem to hold up. There is, however, one exception. Not surprisingly, it is to be found in the toughest-minded of the mid-Victorian novelists, George Eliot.

In what follows, I shall attempt to read the critical middle chapters of *Adam Bede* as a contemporary Victorian woman of the world might have read them—looking shrewdly between the lines for hints, clues, and coded references. Chapter 27, 'A Crisis', begins with specific time-markers (George Eliot is unusually precise about days, weeks, and months in this section of the narrative, a feature which might well alert our notional woman reader).[3] It is, as the crisis looms, 'beyond the middle of August'—the 18th, as we later learn. It is coming up to harvest time in Loamshire, and the local farmers are anxious that the high August winds will damage the crop of wheat, which is ripe in the ear but not as yet gathered in: 'If only the corn were not ripe enough to be blown out of the husk and scattered as untimely seed'.

Untimely seed is being spilled elsewhere. As we apprehend from hints earlier, Arthur and Hetty are meeting in the Chase for clandestine sexual assignations. Walking through these woods at sunset on 18 August, Adam comes across Arthur and Hetty kissing. In his innocence, the young carpenter supposes that the intimacy which he has accidentally witnessed has gone no further than kissing and cuddling. Adam confronts Arthur who—with secret relief—quickly discerns that Adam has not realized how far his misconduct with Hetty has gone. Furtively, the squire notes that 'Adam could still be deceived'. Deceived, that is, not as to the fact that he has stolen Hetty's heart, but that he has stolen her virginity as well. The two young men come to blows, fighting 'with the instinctive fierceness of panthers in the deepening twilight'. Adam, the stronger man, eventually knocks Arthur out.

Chapter 28 of *Adam Bede* opens with a chastened Donnithorne informing his victorious opponent that 'I'm going away on Saturday, and there will be an end of it'. Adam—who is not entirely a fool—inquires as to whether the affair is only a matter of 'trifling and flirting, as you call it' and, on being dishonestly reassured on the matter, he demands that a letter be written, disabusing Hetty of any expectation that Arthur can ever marry her. In Chapter 29 Arthur concludes that Adam '*must* be satisfied, for more reasons than one'. Arthur dimly sees as his salvation

Adam going on to marry Hetty, and never—till his dying day—finding that she has been seduced.

As George Eliot insinuates, Arthur also sees the awful prospect (among other awful prospects) that Hetty may be pregnant:

A sudden dread here fell like a shadow across his imagination—the dread lest she should do something violent in her grief; and close upon that dread came another, which deepened the shadow. But he shook them off with the force of youth and hope. What was the ground for painting the future in that dark way? It was just as likely to be the reverse ... There was a sort of implicit confidence in him that he was really such a good fellow at bottom, Providence would not treat him harshly.

The first dread is that Hetty may kill herself. The second dread, as any wide-awake Victorian adult reader would apprehend, is that she may be with child. Trusting to his luck, as have multitudes of reckless young men before him, Arthur resolves to keep Adam in ignorance. Somewhere too, at the very back of his mind, will be the unformed idea that surely—if she does find herself in trouble—Hetty will know some old woman somewhere who will help her get rid of the unwanted thing.

Chapter 30 describes the delivery of Arthur's letter via Adam. Hetty, before reading it, is also quick to perceive that Adam does not realize how far things have gone between her and Arthur. Chapter 31, 'In Hetty's Bed Chamber', shows Hetty reading the letter that will ruin her life. It contains the awful sentence:

I know you can never be happy except by marrying a man in your own station; and if I were to marry you now, I should only be adding to any wrong I have done, besides offending against my duty in other relations of life.

Clearly enough, Arthur is advising Hetty to marry Adam, and better do it quickly to be on the safe side. The letter finishes with the instruction, 'Do not write unless there is something I can really do for you'. He leaves an address—we infer he is still worried about the possibility of pregnancy.

As the narrator puts it, Hetty's 'short poisonous delights' (by which we may assume that the meetings in the Chase were fumbled and dubiously joyful) have 'spoiled her life forever'. Chapter 33 opens with the harvesting of the barley and the gathering of the season's apples and nuts. It is the annual harvest festival celebrated by country folk on 29 September every year: 'Michaelmas was come, with its fragrant basketfuls of purple damsons, and its paler purple daisies'. Assuming a last sexual encounter on 18 August, Hetty will still be unsure whether her own fruitfulness is to be added to that of the season. If her period is a week or two late, that could well be the effect of the shock of Arthur's letter.

Mrs Poyser notes a 'surprising improvement in Hetty'. The girl is, for a change, quiet and submissive. She is also setting her cap at Adam, which is slightly odd. Hetty is described smiling at her young suitor, 'but there was something different in her eyes, in the expression of her face, in all her movements Adam thought—something harder, older, less child-like'. In Chapter 34 we are told it is now 2 November: and on this Sunday, on the way back from church, Adam proposes to Hetty. He notices as he does so that she exhibits of late 'a more luxuriant womanliness'. This we may gloss as a fuller physical shape—particularly around the bust and waist. Hetty accepts Adam's proposal. Why, since she still loves Arthur, she should do so is not made immediately clear. But, at this stage, we may suspect a half-formed idea that if the wedding comes off quickly, she may still be able to pass off the child she fears she is carrying as Adam's—this, surely, is what a cunning dairymaid like Arabella Donn would have done in Hetty's place. (As will emerge later, I do not think this construction is entirely fair to Hetty.)

Assuming that Hetty was impregnated on her last encounter with Arthur, 18 August, and that date was midway between her periods, she will be, by 2 November, two months pregnant. Disastrously for her, Adam in his prudence postpones the wedding until March next, by which time he will have been able to build the extension to his mother's house, where they will live as man and wife. Over the subsequent months Hetty's forlorn hopes (that she is not after all pregnant, that she may be able to disguise the child as Adam's) slip away. By the time she runs away from Hall Farm to find Arthur at Windsor in February, Hetty must be six to seven months pregnant.

Why has no one, particularly the lynx-eyed Mrs Poyser, noticed Hetty's advanced condition? One reason is that, like Mrs Saddletree at a similar juncture in *The Heart of Midlothian*,[4] Mrs Poyser is made to be indisposed: 'confined to her room all through January' by a bad cold. But it beggars credulity that Mrs Poyser would not at some point over half-a-year have noticed the change in Hetty's shape, more so as they would have to share the same bathing facilities and the dairymaid would be obliged to strip off her outer clothing in the heat of her daily work. When Hetty faints in the Green Man public house the publican's wife, on unlacing the young woman, immediately perceives what is up (Ah, it's plain enough what sort of business it is!'). Why then is it not plain to Mrs Poyser? One may plausibly guess that Hetty's guardians *have* noted her condition. But they assume, logically enough, that Adam is the child's father. At this period of history in rural communities it was the rule rather than the exception that the bride would be with child at the altar. The Poysers might be surprised that the upright Adam would indulge in such immoral behaviour, but in a plighted couple premarital intercourse would not necessarily have been a matter of outrage or even much comment—so long as everything were made well in the church.

Hetty, of course, knows differently. In a passage in Chapter 35 recollecting her state of mind over the wretched months of her secret trial, there occurs the following: 'After the first on-coming of her great dread, some weeks after her betrothal to Adam, she had waited and waited, in the blind vague hope that something would happen to set her free from her terror.' Under its circumspect expression, this is one of the more remarkable passages in Victorian fiction. While the unworldly male and juvenile readers might construe the sense here as Hetty waiting for a letter or some miracle, no mature woman reader could miss the import of what is being said. The 'something' in early November that Hetty is desperately waiting for that will 'set her free from her terror' is her period.

What we may reconstruct is the following. After her last love-making with Arthur in mid-August, and the subsequent non-appearance of her period, Hetty was vaguely apprehensive (like him), but nothing more. As a demure young lady, brought up in a well-regulated religious household like the Poysers', Miss Sorrel would have had only the vaguest idea of where babies came from or— more precisely—the physiological signs and changes characteristic of early pregnancy. On her betrothal to Adam, it was appropriate (indeed a sacred duty) for Mrs Poyser to impart to her young ward 'the facts of life' (such maternal tuition was common well into the twentieth century, before schools got into the 'sex education' business). Now she knew what the missing period meant, Hetty experienced her 'great dread', and desperately prayed all through November and December that her period might belatedly come (Mrs Poyser would have told her that, for a girl her age, only recently past puberty, the occasional lapse of a month or so would not be unusual). When, as the year drew to its end, the 'something' did not happen, the full horror of her situation would have been tragically clear to Hetty: in her maidenly ignorance she had accepted Adam's proposal while carrying another man's child. Having told Hetty the facts of life, Mrs Poyser—noticing Hetty's interesting condition around January or February—would naturally assume that the young hussy could not wait to put her new knowledge into practice. Typical.

To return to the Showalters' claim with which this chapter began. This, surely, is a clear 'literary reflection' of the great unmentionable, menstruation. It is clearly something rather unusual, but doubtless there are other similar coded references in Victorian fiction that the radar of contemporary women readers might pick up.

The Oxford World's Classics *Adam Bede* is edited by Valentine Cunningham.

===

The missing fortnight

===

On its publication in three-volume form in August 1860 (after its triumphant nine-month serialization in *All the Year Round*) *The Woman in White* enjoyed a huge success, sparking off what today we would call a sales mania and a franchise boom. As Wilkie Collins's biographer Kenneth Robinson records:

> While the novel was still selling in its thousands, manufacturers were producing *The Woman in White* perfume, *The Woman in White* cloaks and bonnets, and the music shops displayed *The Woman in White* waltzes and quadrilles ... Dickens was not alone in his enthusiasm. Thackeray sat up all night reading it. Edward FitzGerald read it three times, and named a herring-lugger he owned *Marian Halcombe*, 'after the brave girl in the story'. The Prince Consort admired it greatly and sent a copy to Baron Stockmar.[1]

Nuel Davis, in his life of Collins, goes so far as to claim that '*The Woman in White* was probably the most popular novel written in England during the nineteenth century'.[2] This is demonstrably untrue (*Robert Elsmere* and *Trilby* outsold Collins's novel by many times), but it is quite likely that it was the best-seller of the decade.

Among the chorus of applause there was one discordant voice. *The Woman in White* received a devastating review in *The Times* (then, as now, the country's newspaper of record) on 30 October 1860. In the review E. S. Dallas proved—by close scrutiny of dates in the crucial Blackwater Park episodes—that the events described in the novel *could never have happened*. *The Woman in*

White was, Dallas demonstrated, 'impossible'. As Dallas pointed out the whole of Collins's intricate denouement hinges on a single date—when was it that Laura took her fateful trip to London in late July 1850? If it can be proved that the date of Laura's journey from Blackwater to Waterloo station post-dated her recorded 'death' (in fact, the death of her look-alike half-sister, Anne Catherick) at 5 Forest Road, St John's Wood, then the criminals' conspiracy falls to the ground. With this crucial fact in mind, Dallas dismantled the plot machinery of *The Woman in White* with the ruthless precision of a prosecuting counsel exploding a shaky alibi:

The question of a date is the pivot upon which the novel turns. The whole of the third volume is devoted to the ascertaining of this date. Everything depends upon it. But it is lost in the most marvellous obscurity—it is lost even to Mr Wilkie Collins, who is a whole fortnight out of his reckoning. If we dare trespass upon details after the author's solemn injunction [in his preface to the three-volume edition, that reviewers not give away the plot] we could easily show that Lady Glyde could not have left Blackwater Park before the 9th or 10th of August. Anybody who reads the story and who counts the days from the conclusion of Miss Halcombe's diary, can verify the calculation for himself. He will find that the London physician did not pay his visit till the 31st of July, that Dawson [the doctor who attends on Marian] was not dismissed till the 3rd of August, and that the servants were not dismissed till the following day. The significance of these dates will be clear to all who have read the story. They render the last volume a mockery, a delusion, and a snare; and all the incidents in it are not merely improbable—they are absolutely impossible.[3]

The details of Dallas's criticism are less important than its general thrust. What he was doing, and doing brilliantly, was subjecting a work of fiction to the criterion of falsifiability, in terms of its internal logic and structure. This test was something distinctly new in literary criticism, and a corollary of the fetishistic standards of documentary accuracy which Collins had imported into English fiction as his hallmark. As he says in his 'Preamble', Collins wanted his novel to be read as so many pieces of evidence, 'as the story of an offence against the laws is told in Court by more than one witness'. The reader, that is, should be as alert to clues and discrepancies in evidence as is a jury sitting in judgement. As Henry James astutely observed, Collins was playing a deep game with genre and literary discourse. Collins's novels, James declared, were 'not so much works of art as works of science. To read *The Woman in White* requires very much the same intellectual effort as to read Motley or Froude.'[4]

What James implied by comparing Collins to the leading historians of the age was that one could bring the same truth-tests to *The Woman in White* that a sceptical expert might bring to *The Rise of the Dutch Republic* (1855) or the *History of England from the Death of Cardinal Wolsey to the Defeat of the Spanish Armada* (12 vols., 1856–70). By reading *The Woman in White* as if it were history or science (rather than just a made-up story) Dallas can 'disprove' it.

Collins took Dallas's criticisms immensely seriously. He wrote to his publisher the next day, instructing that no more copies of *The Woman in White* must be put out, until he should have an opportunity to revise the text: 'The critic in "The Times" is (between ourselves) right about the mistake in time . . . we will set it right at the first opportunity', he confessed.[5] The mistake was duly set right in the 'New' 1861 one-volume edition by antedating the crucial Blackwater Park episode a whole sixteen days, and by clipping a couple of days off the crucial death-of-Anne/arrival-of-Laura episode (i.e. making it 25/26 July, rather than 28/29 July). In the revised edition, Collins made other small corrections (changing the wedding date of Percival Glyde and Laura, for instance, so that it did not hit a Sunday in the 1849 calendar—a document which the novelist evidently went back to consult in the course of revision).

Although he took extraordinary pains to reconcile fine points of narrative chronology, Collins left one troubling mote to trouble the reader's eye. In the revised 1861 text, a day or two after 20 June, when Marian falls into her fever, Count Fosco discovers Anne Catherick's whereabouts and treats her heart condition. Having won her confidence, the fat villain passes on to Anne a forged message from Laura, telling her to go to London with her old friend and companion, Mrs Clements. Laura, Anne is reassured, will meet her there. Three days later, Anne having been strengthened sufficiently by Fosco's medicines to undertake the journey, the two women leave for London, where they take lodgings. 'A little more than a fortnight' later (as Mrs Clements later testifies, p. 473) Anne is abducted. By Mrs Clements's reckoning, this must be around 7 July— two to three weeks before Anne's death. But, by Fosco's account in his final written confession to Hartright, it was on 24 July that Anne Catherick was abducted and brought to the house in St John's Wood as 'Lady Laura Glyde' (p. 623). The unfortunate woman died of heart failure there the next day, 25 July, and it was not until the day after that, 26 July, that the true Laura was lured to London. On 27 July she was returned to the London lunatic asylum as 'Anne Catherick', the true Anne Catherick now being prepared for her funeral at Limmeridge on 2 August, as 'Laura'.[6]

Who do we believe? Mrs Clements, by whose account Anne was in the sinister custody of the Foscos and the Rubelles for two weeks? Or Count Fosco, by whose account Anne was in their custody for two days? It does not require much inspection to see that Fosco's confession, for all its superficial candour, is shot through with self-serving falsehoods. Mrs Clements, by contrast, is stolidly honest. In terms of character the reader/jury will find her by far the more credible witness. And if Anne was held for two weeks in St John's Wood, what was she subjected to during that time? A clue is supplied in the famous anecdote of the novel's inspiration, given by J. G. Millais (the painter's son), ten years after Collins's death:

One night in the '50s [John Everett] Millais was returning home to 83, Gower Street from one of the many parties held under Mrs Collins's hospitable roof in Hanover Terrace, and, in accordance with the usual practice of the two brothers, Wilkie and Charles [Collins], they accompanied him on his homeward walk through the dimly-lit, and those days semi-rural, roads and lanes of North London ... It was a beautiful moonlight night in the summer time and as the three friends walked along chatting gaily together, they were suddenly arrested by a piercing scream coming from the garden of a villa close at hand. It was evidently the cry of a woman in distress; and while pausing to consider what they should do, the iron gate leading to the garden was dashed open, and from it came the figure of a young and very beautiful woman dressed in flowing white robes that shone in the moonlight. She seemed to float rather than run in their direction, and, on coming up to the three men, she paused for a moment in an attitude of supplication and terror. Then, suddenly seeming to recollect herself, she suddenly moved on and vanished in the shadows cast upon the road. 'What a lovely woman!' was all Millais could say. 'I must see who she is, and what is the matter,' said Wilkie Collins, as, without a word he dashed off after her. His two companions waited in vain for his return, and next day, when they met again, he seemed indisposed to talk of his adventure. They gathered from him, however, that he had come up with the lovely fugitive and had heard from her own lips the history of her life and the cause of her sudden flight. She was a young lady of good birth and position, who had accidentally fallen into the hands of a man living in a villa in Regent's Park. There for many months he kept her prisoner under threats and mesmeric influence of so alarming a character that she dared not attempt to escape, until, in sheer desperation, she fled from the brute, who, with a poker in his hand, threatened to dash her brains out. Her subsequent history, interesting as it is, is not for these pages.[7]

Fosco, we remember, is a mesmerist: the Rubelles are thugs. What we can plausibly suppose is that, like the other luckless Woman in White, Anne was incarcerated for quite some time in a villa in the Regent's Park district, where she was subjected to barbarous mistreatment, which may well have included sexual abuse. It was this mistreatment which provoked her death from heart failure on 25 July. Fosco, out of guilt, suppresses the fact that he was responsible for Anne's death by torture, claiming instead that she died of 'natural causes', having been in his care only a few hours.

There is, of course, a simpler explanation—namely that Collins simply made another chronological miscalculation. But this seems unlikely. He revised the time-scheme of *The Woman in White* so conscientiously for the 1861 text, and he was so expert in such dovetailing, that it is much more attractive to assume that he left the anomaly for his more detectively inclined readers to turn up. This reading élite should have the privilege of knowing just how subtle and evil the Napoleon of Crime, Count Fosco, really was.

The Oxford World's Classics *The Woman in White* is edited by John Sutherland.

W. M. Thackeray · *Pendennis*
Mrs Gaskell · *A Dark Night's Work*
Anthony Trollope · *Rachel Ray*

———

Two-timing novelists

———

Early nineteenth-century novelists had an engagingly
cavalier attitude to finer points of chronology. One of
Dickens's footnotes in Chapter 2 of the 1847 reissue of *The
Pickwick Papers* is typical of the freedoms they allowed
themselves in such matters. Mr Jingle, in response to
Pickwick's observation that 'My friend Mr Snodgrass has
a strong poetic turn', replies: 'So have I . . . Epic poem—
ten thousand lines—revolution of July—composed it on
the spot.' When asked, he assures the amazed Pickwick
that he was, indeed, there at the event and saw the blood
flowing in the Parisian gutters. Dickens adds the footnote
to this exchange: 'A remarkable instance of the prophetic
force of Mr Jingle's imagination; this dialogue occurring
in the year 1827, and the Revolution in 1830.'[1]

Scott is equally good-natured about his chronological
solecisms in *Rob Roy*. When Andrew Fairservice urges the
hero, Frank Osbaldistone, to accompany him to 'St
Enoch's Kirk, where he said "a soul searching divine was
to haud forth"', the novelist added the bland footnote (evidently as the result of a friend's observation): 'This I
believe to be an anachronism, as St Enoch's Church was
not built at the date of the story [1715].'[2] No more than
Dickens, apparently, did Scott think of changing his
anomalous text.

Scrupulosity about narrative chronology tightened up
during the Victorian period, reaching a fetishistic pitch

with the intricate sensation novels of Wilkie Collins. The older school of novelists were not, however, sure that they altogether liked the new orderliness about such things. Trollope voiced a typically bluff complaint in his comments on Collins in *An Autobiography:*

Of Wilkie Collins it is impossible for a true critic not to speak with admiration, because he has excelled all his contemporaries in a certain most difficult branch of his art; but as it is a branch which I have not myself at all cultivated, it is not unnatural that his work should be very much lost upon me individually. When I sit down to write a novel I do not at all know, and I do not very much care, how it is to end. Wilkie Collins seems so to construct his that he not only, before writing, plans everything on, down to the minutest detail, from the beginning to the end; but then plots it all back again, to see that there is no piece of necessary dove-tailing which does not dove-tail with absolute accuracy. The construction is most minute and most wonderful. But I can never lose the taste of the construction. The author seems always to be warning me to remember that something happened at exactly half-past two o'clock on Tuesday morning . . . (pp. 256–7)

Trollope's underlying gripe would seem to be that by clock and calendar-watching Collins had deprived novelists and readers of valuable traditional liberties. In support of Trollope's preference for the old easygoing ways, we may examine chronological cruxes in three Victorian novels of the 1850s and 1860s, Thackeray's *Pendennis*, Mrs Gaskell's *A Dark Night's Work*, and Trollope's own *Rachel Ray*. Closely examined, they suggest that what looks like slovenliness about chronology in Victorian fiction can plausibly be seen as an artistic device which these three novelists, at least, used to powerful effect.

Pendennis was Thackeray's second major novel and it was, even by Victorian standards, an immensely long work (twenty-four thirty-two-page monthly numbers, compared to the twenty that made up *Vanity Fair)*. It took some twenty-six months in the publishing (November 1848–December 1850), interrupted as it was by the novelist's life-threatening illness which incapacitated him between September 1849 and January 1850. *Pendennis* is also long in the tracts of time its narrative covers. The central story extends over some forty years as the hero, Arthur Pendennis ('Pen'), grows from boyhood to mature manhood. In passing, Pen's story offers a panorama of the changing Regency, Georgian, Williamite, and Victorian ages.

Pendennis is one of the first and greatest mid-Victorian *Bildungsromanen*. The central character, as Thackeray candidly admitted, is based closely on himself. As part of this identification, Thackeray gave Arthur Pendennis the same birth-date as himself—1811. This is indicated by a number of unequivocal historical markers early in the text. Pen is 16 just before the Duke of York dies in 1827. We are told that Pen (still 16) and his mother recite to each other from Keble's *The Christian Year* (1827), 'a book which appeared about that time' (p. 31). Pen's early years at Grey Friars school and his parents' Devonshire house, Fairoaks, fit exactly with Thackeray's sojourns at Charterhouse school and his parents' Devonshire house, Larkbeare. Both young men go up to university ('Oxbridge', Cambridge) in 1829. Both retire from the university, in rusticated disgrace, in 1830. Thackeray clinches this historical setting by any number of references to fashions, slang, and student mores of the late 1820s and 1830s, as well as by a string of allusions to the imminent and historically overarching Reform Bill.

Switch from these early pages to the last numbers of the novel, where we are specifically told on a number of occasions that Pen is now 26. This is supported by any number of historical allusions fixing the front-of-stage date as the mid-to-late 1830s.[3] *Pendennis* is given its essentially nostalgic feel by historical and cultural events dredged up from the past, between ten and twenty years before the period of writing. And yet, there are a perplexing string of references which locate the action in the late 1840s, indeed, at the precise moment Thackeray was writing. In the highpoint scene of Derby Day in Number 19 of the serial narrative we glimpse among the crowd at the racecourse the prime minister, Lord John Russell, who took up office in 1846, and Richard Cobden MP. Cobden did not enter Parliament until 1847. And, by cross-reference to Richard Doyle's well-known Derby Day panorama in *Punch*, 26 May 1849 (a work which inspired Frith's famous *Derby Day* painting), we can see that Thackeray is clearly describing the Derby of the year in which he wrote, which actually took place a couple of months before the number was published.

Thackeray, as has been said, is insistent in this final phase of his narrative that Pen is just 26 years old (p. 797), which gives a historical setting of 1837. But, at the same time, Pen is given speeches like the following (one of his more provokingly 'cynical' effusions to Warrington), in Number 20:

'The truth, friend!' Arthur said imperturbably; 'where is the truth? Show it me. That is the question between us. I see it on both sides. I see it in the Conservative side of the House, and amongst the Radicals, and even on the ministerial benches. I see it in this man who worships by Act of Parliament, and is rewarded with a silk apron and five thousand a year; in that man, who, driven fatally by the remorseless logic of his creed, gives up everything, friends, fame, dearest ties, closest vanities, the respect of an army of Churchmen, the recognized position of a leader, and passes over, truth-impelled, to the enemy, in whose ranks he is ready to serve henceforth as a nameless private soldier:—I see the truth in that man, as I do in his brother, whose logic drives him to quite a different conclusion, and who, after having passed a life in vain endeavours to reconcile an irreconcilable book, flings it at last down in despair, and declares, with tearful eyes, and hands up to heaven, his revolt and recantation. If the truth is with all these, why should I take side with any one of them?' (pp. 801–2)

No well-informed Victorian reading this in 1850 could fail to pick up the topical references. In his remark on the 'ministerial benches' Pen alludes to the great Conservative U-turn over the Corn Laws in 1846 (in which the aforementioned Cobden and Russell were leading players). His subsequent references are transparently to John Henry Newman (1801–90) and his brother Francis William Newman (1805–97). John went over to the Catholic Church in 1845. As Gordon Ray's biography records, Thackeray attended his course of lectures on Anglican difficulties at the Oratory, King William Street, in summer 1850 (this number was published in September). Francis, professor of Latin at University College London, 1846–69, published his reasons for being unable to accept traditional Christian arguments in the autobiographical *Phases of Faith* (1850). According to Gordon Ray, Thackeray was much moved by the book. Clearly Pen's comments to Warrington only make sense if we date them as being uttered in mid-1850, at the same period that this monthly number was being written. And we have to assume that Thackeray was making his hero the vehicle for what he (Thackeray) was thinking on the great current question of Papal Aggression.

These examples of 'two-timing' in *Pendennis* are systematic features of the novel's highly artful structure. Thackeray has devised a technique that was to be later explored and codified into a modernist style by the Cubists. Not to be fanciful, the author of *Pendennis* anticipates Picasso's multi-perspective effect whereby, for example, more than one plane of a woman's face could be combined in a single image. Pen and his mentor

Warrington in the above scene are at the same time young
men of the 1830s and bewhiskered, tobacco-reeking, 'muscular' hearties of the early 1850s, verging on middle-age.
They inhabit the present and the past simultaneously,
offering two planes of their lives to the reader.

Mrs Gaskell first published her novella *A Dark Night's
Work* as a stopgap serial in Dickens's journal, *All the Year
Round*. (Charles Reade needed more time to prepare for
his massively documented sensation novel, *Hard Cash*.)[4]
Mrs Gaskell's tale first appeared as instalments between
24 January and 21 March 1863 in the journal and was
reissued as a one volume book later in the year. It would
seem, however, that the work had an earlier origin. As the
World's Classics editor, Suzanne Lewis, notes, 'although
published in 1863, *A Dark Night's Work* was, according to
a letter from Elizabeth Gaskell to George Smith, begun in
about 1858'.[5] Lewis goes on to connect this double date
(composition beginning in 1858, publication occurring in
1863) with an important dating reference in the story's
first sentence: 'In the county town of a certain shire there
lived (about forty years ago) one Mr Wilkins, a conveyancing attorney of considerable standing' (p. 1). The
editor notes that by simple subtraction we may assume
'that the early events of the tale take place sometime
between 1815 and 1820' (p. 304).

The earliest events told in the tale are Mr Wilkins's
courtship of his wife which, thanks to a reference to the
state visit of the allied sovereigns (p. 3), we can locate as
taking place in the months directly following June 1814,
when the Emperor of Russia and the King of Prussia were
entertained in London. Mr Wilkins is subsequently
widowed very young and left with his daughter, Ellinor, as
his only consolation (a younger daughter dies a baby, soon
after her mother). At 14, as we are told, Ellinor makes a

friend of Ralph Corbet, who is studying with a clergyman-
tutor nearby. And, four years or so later, the two young
people are deeply in love. Meanwhile, Mr Wilkins has conceived a huge dislike for his obnoxiously efficient chief
clerk, Mr Dunster, and his conveyancing business is going
to the dogs.

Already some of the time-markers in *A Dark Night's
Work* are beginning to go astray. As Suzanne Lewis notes,
Ellinor, at some point shortly before 1829, is described visiting Salisbury Cathedral, where she earnestly discusses
'Ruskin's works' with the resident clergyman, Mr Livingstone (p. 47). Nothing of Ruskin's would have been available until decades later, and certainly not *The Seven
Lamps of Architecture* (1849) and its extended discussions
of the beauty of Salisbury Cathedral, which is what Mr
Livingstone and Miss Wilkins are evidently supposed to
be discussing.

Events crowd on quickly, driven by Mrs Gaskell's penchant for melodrama. In one of his drunken rages, Mr
Wilkins strikes out and kills Dunster. In their 'dark
night's work', Ellinor, the loyal servant Dixon, and Mr
Wilkins bury the clerk's body, allowing it to be thought
that he has stolen money from the firm and decamped to
America. Under the strain of complicity, Ellinor falls ill;
the engagement with Ralph Corbet is broken off; Mr
Wilkins declines into chronic drunkenness and dies soon
after, shattered by remorse and guilt. Ellinor is left virtually penniless, and goes to live a retired and self-
punishingly religious life at East Chester. The narrative
specifically dates the heroine's illness (and thus all the
circumambient events) as 1829 (p. 116).

Ellinor remains at East Chester 'sixteen or seventeen
years', before the long feared calamity occurs. Surveyors,
prospecting for a new railway line between Hamley and
Ashcombe, discover Dunster's body and an incriminating

knife belonging to Dixon. Ellinor is at the time of the
exhumation in Italy, and is unable to get back before the
loyally mute Dixon is sentenced to death. The telegraph,
we are informed, is not available to the heroine (as
Suzanne Lewis notes, although introduced in the 1830s it
did not come into general commercial service until the
late 1850s: p. 312). Ellinor eventually does hurry back,
by steamship and railway train, the bustle of which is
graphically described.

The central chronological problem in *A Dark Night's
Work* is explained by Suzanne Lewis, in a note to the '1829'
reference to Ellinor's illness on page 116:

This date does not fit the chronology of the story so far. When
Ellinor is ill she is approximately nineteen; if the date of her
illness is 1829, then the story begins before 1810, earlier than the
date suggested by the 'forty years ago' of the opening paragraph,
and the reference to the visit of the allied sovereigns in 1814.
Moreover, a few days before she falls ill, Ellinor and Mr Livingstone discuss Ruskin's works, but even the earliest of Ruskin's
works were not published until the mid 1830s. (p. 310)[6]

That Ellinor was, in fact, 19 at the time of the dark night's
work is confirmed at the beginning of Chapter 12 where we
are told 'her youth had gone in a single night, fifteen years
ago' and the she is now 'only four-and-thirty' (p. 115).
There would seem, therefore, to be a decade or more's
slippage in the main events of the narrative, according to
where in the text one is reading.

And then there is the strange business of characters'
ages. After the murder, and the disposal of Dunster's body,
while Ellinor is still recovering from her illness her
accomplice, the lugubrious Dixon, is made to say to her:

'Ay! . . . We didn't think much of it at the time, did we, Miss Nelly?
But it'll be the death on us, I'm thinking. It has aged me above a
bit. All my fifty years afore were but as a forenoon of child's play
to that night.' (p. 69)

By which we suppose that he was born in 1829 minus fifty years, that is, in 1779. But later on we are told that he solemnly takes Ellinor to the grave of his first love, 'Molly, the pretty scullery-maid'. The tablet over her grave reads: 'Sacred to the Memory of Mary Greaves, Born 1797. Died 1818. "We part to meet again"' (p. 125). 'I put this stone up over her with my first savings', Dixon tells Ellinor. Now clearly Dixon was not supposed to have been twenty years older than Molly, nor did he have to wait until he was 39 before he had sufficient savings to pay for a simple gravestone. Gaskell has created two Dixons, an old Dixon and a middle-aged Dixon—both of whom uneasily cohabit the narrative.

There is a similar dualism in the character of Miss Monro, Ellinor's governess, and another important secondary character in the tale. After Mr Wilkins's death and the news that there is no longer enough money in the household to employ her, Miss Monro rouses herself pluckily. She declares, 'I am but forty, I have a good fifteen years of work in me left yet' (p. 102). But, when we encountered her on her first arrival at Hamley, some ten years before, Miss Monro is described as 'a plain, intelligent, quiet woman of forty' (p. 11). Either she is gallantly lying when she tells Ellinor that she has fifteen years more of work in her or, more likely, we have another chronological anomaly: a character who does not age with the passing of time.

These anomalies in *A Dark Night's Work* seem to be genuinely irreconcilable. Nor, as with *Pendennis*, can one weave them into some artistic effect, aimed at by the author. They seem rather to belong to a broadbrush historical scheme of the 'before and after' kind in which the only thing that matters is whether something roughly succeeds or roughly precedes a threshold event. It would seem that Mrs Gaskell began *A Dark Night's Work* with a vivid *donnée*—the preparatory excavations for the railways churning up the beautiful English landscape, and discovering a murdered body. This *donnée* had social significance as well as directly personal implications for Ellinor. As Humphry House argues in *The Dickens World* (1941), the coming of the railways in the early years of the 1840s marked for the Victorians the passing of the old, 'innocent' England and the arrival of 'modernity', with all its woes. As a narrative (covering as it does some thirty years) *A Dark Night's Work* is divided into two halves, the world before the railways—a world of horses and sleepy country towns; and the world after the coming of the railways—marked in Gaskell's novel by joyless European tourism, frenetic rush, and the London where Ellinor has her fateful interview with Ralph Corbet.[7] The description of Ellinor's journey to Judge Corbet's house in Hyde Park Gardens to intercede for Dixon gives a vivid impression of the hectic pace of London life in the 1840s:

It was about the same time that she had reached Hellingford on the previous night, that she arrived at the Great Western station on this evening—past eight o'clock. On the way she had remembered and arranged many things: one important question she had omitted to ask Mr Johnson; but that was easily remedied. She had not inquired where she could find Judge Corbet; if she had, Mr Johnson could probably have given her his professional address. As it was, she asked for a Post-Office Directory at the hotel, and looked out for his private dwelling—128, Hyde Park Gardens. (pp. 154–5)

Ellinor sends a hotel messenger to the judge's house, but he is not at home, so she orders a cab for seven the next morning. All this hyperactive toing-and-froing belongs to the high-technology world of the 1840s and 1850s. In the 1820s and 1830s (when the first half of *A Dark Night's Work* is set) Ellinor would have had to lumber up to London by stage-coach and might have taken days tracking down Corbet by personal inquiry and trial and error. The Great Western Railway link referred to in the above passage was (as Suzanne Lewis notes) only completed in 1841. The Post Office Directory was, in the early 1840s, a recent innovation, which came in with Rowland Hill's reforms in the late 1830s. The fast and efficient metropolitan communication system (couriers and cabs arriving promptly at appointed hours) are all features of modern London, a London that has only recently come into being, we feel. In short, what Mrs Gaskell is aiming at in *A Dark Night's Work*, and what she succeeds in, is a novel divided historically into 'then' and 'now', with the arrival of the railway marking the point of division. It is a powerful effect, and one that lingers in the reader's mind.

Rachel Ray has one of the simplest of Trollope's plots. A young girl in an evangelically strict household receives a proposal of marriage from a young man. He is eligible in every way, except that he earns his money from brewing beer and has the reputation (ill-deserved) of being a 'wolf'. Torn between the moral anxieties of her widowed mother and widowed sister, Rachel neither accepts nor rejects Luke Rowan. She seems to have lost him by her vacillation, but finally he proves to be true.

Trollope chose to set *Rachel Ray* in Devon. The provincial setting has plausibly been ascribed to his admiration for George Eliot's recently published (and highly successful) *Scenes of Clerical Life* (1858). But Devon suggested itself for two other reasons. First, because it was historically a stronghold of evangelicalism (something that Trollope refers to in the novel on a number of occasions). Secondly, because Devon was a county Trollope knew intimately. Since childhood, he had spent holidays in Exeter with relatives. And in August 1851, on being

transferred back to England from Ireland by the Post
Office, he had been assigned to a roving mission to the
West Country. 'I began in Devonshire', he records in his
Autobiography, 'and visited, I think I may say, every nook
in that county' (p. 88). Trollope loved Devon, and came to
consider it the most beautiful region in England.

Rachel Ray vividly recalls Trollope's first impressions
of Devon when he returned in the baking heat of
summer 1851. He describes it with an uncharacteristic-
ally sensuous turn of phrase:

in those southern parts of Devonshire the summer sun in July is
very hot. There is no other part of England like it. The lanes are
low and narrow, and not a breath of air stirs through them. The
ground rises in hills on all sides, so that every spot is a sheltered
nook. The rich red earth drinks in the heat and holds it, and no
breezes come up from the southern torpid sea. Of all counties in
England Devonshire is the fairest to the eye; but, having known it
in its summer glory, I must confess that those southern regions
are not fitted for much noonday summer walking. (pp. 16–17)

Peter Edwards, the editor of the World's Classics *Rachel
Ray*, points out that for much of the manuscript Trollope
wrote 'Kingsbridge' for 'Baslehurst' (where the Rays are
supposed to live). The significance of the original name is
that Kingsbridge is an actual town in South Hams, Devonshire. Trollope's diary records that Kingsbridge was virtually the first place that he visited when he came to the
county, staying there on 9 August 1851. Coming as he had
from cool, damp Ireland, he evidently remembered the
heat of that summer week all his life.

One of the most distinctive features of Trollope—'the
lesser Thackeray'—is that unlike his master, or Dickens,
or George Eliot, he did not normally antedate the action
of his fiction. His best-known novel for posterity is probably *The Way We Live Now* (serially published in 1874–5,
set in 1873) and the title could describe most of the

Trollopian *oeuvre*. When he died in 1882, obituarists noted that if later generations wanted a 'photogravure' image of the Victorian age, they might consult Trollope's novels.

Rachel Ray would seem to deviate from the Trollopian norm in this respect. It is clear that in creating the novel's little world Trollope drew on his recollections of South Devon in August 1851. A number of cues in the action mark the action—or portions of it—as taking place well before 1863, the date of publication. So too does the generally sleepy atmosphere of Baslehurst. But at other points in the narrative Trollope specifically alludes to current events and even, at one point, seems to indicate a time-setting of August 1863 (which would be in line with his 'the way we live now' practice).

To summarize some of these chronological contradictions: in Chapter 4, we encounter the following, by way of introduction to the 'low' clergyman, Samuel Prong:

As we shall have occasion to know Mr Prong it may be as well to explain here that he was not simply a curate to old Dr Harford, the rector of Baslehurst. He had a separate district of his own, which had been divided from the old parish, not exactly in accordance with the rector's good pleasure. Dr Harford had held the living for more than forty years; he had held it for nearly forty years before the division had been made, and he had thought that the parish should remain a parish entire,—more especially as the presentation to the new benefice was not conceded to him. Therefore Dr Harford did not love Mr Prong. (p. 51)

Edwards adds a note:

the division of parishes such as Dr Harford's was carried out by the Ecclesiastical Commission, which was instituted in 1835 and was guided by a series of church-reform acts passed in the late 1830s and early 1840s. (pp. 407–8)

The 'Ecclesiastical Estates Commissioners' (set up, as Edwards notes, in 1835) had sweeping powers to equalize and rearrange dioceses, parishes, and clergymen's income. The re-parishioning referred to here must have taken place in the early 1840s at the latest, since the point is clearly made that Dr Harford has held the living for nearly forty years before the division and for just over forty years altogether. We must therefore assume the date of the narrative here also to be in the early to mid-1840s.

This date is confirmed by another reference, at the end of the same chapter, in the scene where Luke Rowan shows Rachel the beauty of the clouds at sunset. The narrator notes, sympathetically enough, that Luke 'was not altogether devoid of that Byronic weakness which was so much more prevalent among young men twenty years since than it is now' (pp. 54–5). The 'twenty years since' reference would also give a setting of the 1840s, which actually 'feels' right for this idyllic chapter.

There are, however, many other references in *Rachel Ray's* text which point to a present, 'way we live now' setting for the novel. There is, for example, an allusion to the early 1860s 'crinoline mania', in Chapter 7, in the description of the massed young ladies at the Tappitts' ball (p. 84).[8] In Chapter 9, as Dorothea contemplates the possibility of divorce, she clearly has the terms of the 1857 Matrimonial Causes Act, in mind (p. 123). There are passing references in the text to such modernistic things as night mail trains. And Mrs Ray's excursion by railway to Exeter in Chapter 21 clearly suggests a late 1850s, early-1860s date. Railways were relatively late to come to Devon (when he was posted there in 1851 Trollope was obliged to go about the county mainly by horse). The GWR did not offer a network service to a little town like 'Baslehurst' (i.e. Kingsbridge) until the early 1850s. In Chapter 21 ('Mrs Ray Goes to Exeter and Meets a Friend') Mrs Ray is described making a day trip to the nearby large town. Rachel commiserates with her mother on the older lady's return, observing she must be tired: 'Yes, I am tired, my dear; very' replies Mrs Ray; 'I thought the train never would have got to the Baslehurst station. It stopped at all the little stations, and really I think I could have walked as fast.' As the narrator tartly notes: 'A dozen years had not as yet gone by since the velocity of these trains had been so terrible to Mrs Ray that she had hardly dared to get into one of them!' (pp. 280–1). The dozen years would seem to refer the reader back to the early 1850s, when trains first arrived in the region. Finally, one may note that in the business of the election which dominates the second half of the narrative Mr Hart, the Jewish candidate, is clearly presenting himself after 1857–8, when it finally became possible for Jews to sit in Parliament (pp. 224, 412).

This two-timing in *Rachel Ray* does not give any impression of error, or narrative confusion. It creates a subtle and pleasing pictorial effect. Trollope paints an essentially contemporary Baslehurst—a thriving little country town of the 1860s, with its modern railways, breweries, and elections. But he throws over this depiction of rural modernity a kind of nostalgic halo, or veneer. Among all the contemporaneity we catch a momentary glimpse of old Devon, as it was fondly enshrined in Trollope's memory. For the reader of *Rachel Ray* it creates a peculiarly idyllic effect, like a sepia tint on a photograph.

In the three instances which have been examined here, structural anachronism, or the double time-setting, is not something one would necessarily want cleared up in any rationalistic spirit of standardized chronological reference. The case can be made, without excessive ingenuity, that these novelists' two-timing practices conduce to effects of historical complexity (in Thackeray's case), a highlighting of the major emotional divide in Victorian social history (in Gaskell's case), and a sensuously rich and cross-embroidered narrative texture (in Trollope's case). As Trollope insists in his *Autobiography*, too much scrupulosity in such matters may not always be the best thing artistically.

The Oxford World's Classics *Pendennis* is edited by John Sutherland; the Oxford World's Classics *A Dark Night's Work and Other Stories* is edited by Suzanne Lewis; the Oxford World's Classics *Rachel Ray* is edited by Peter Edwards; the Oxford World's Classics edition of Trollope's *An Autobiography* is also edited by Peter Edwards.

Anthony Trollope · *Phineas Finn*

———

The phantom pregnancy of Mary Flood Jones

———

Trollope has enjoyed three major revivals in the last fifty years. The first occurred during the years of Britain's siege culture in World War Two. Following a successful radio adaptation of the Barchester Novels in the early days of hostilities, reading Trollope became a cult among the literate middle classes as they whiled away the weary months of war. Dons in uniform like R. W. Chapman and John Sparrow, when they weren't cracking codes at Bletchley Park, exchanged erudite *aperçus* about textual minutiae in Trollope's novels. In a series of articles in the *TLS* they vied with each other to find misprints which had escaped the duller eyes of the novelist himself and his Victorian proof-readers.[1]

The second Trollopian wave came crashing in with the paperback classic reprints series which were pioneered by the Penguin English Library (now Penguin Classics) in the late 1960s. This series was followed by the revived Oxford University Press World's Classics, and the Everyman lines. There are, at the time of writing, up to four budget priced versions of most of Trollope's principal works of fiction in every high-street bookshop in the country.

The third and highest crest of the Trollopian wave came with the successful televisations of the Palliser novels in 1974. These six 'Parliamentary' novels, as Trollope called them (he studiously avoided the term 'political novels') were adapted for the small screen by Simon Raven. Raven was qualified for work on such a mammoth scale by virtue of his own ten-volume-strong 'Alms for Oblivion' saga (published between 1964 and 1975). He was used to the gigantic dimensions of the sequence novel. On the other hand, some viewers might well have thought Simon Raven disqualified by his raffish, and extremely un-Trollopian frankness about matters sexual in his 'Alms for Oblivion' narratives, in which fornication, adultery, and perversion were happenings as routine as breakfast.

In the event Raven did a magnificent job on 'The Pallisers' (as the BBC called the mini-series).[2] But as one might have expected (or feared) he imported into Trollope a vein of explicitness which was occasionally disturbing. This was notably the case with *Phineas Finn, the Irish Member*, the second novel in the sequence. The love plot of *Phineas Finn* is easily summarized. The young Irish hero (the son of a local doctor) wins the heart of a pretty Irish maiden, Mary Flood Jones, in his native Killaloe. He stands successfully for Parliament and leaves Killaloe for the fleshpots of London. Before he goes, he snips a lock of hair from Mary's head, and steals a kiss. She duly regards herself as engaged. In London, Phineas MP falls in love with Lady Laura Standish, and proposes to her: she sensibly rejects the penniless young man (although in her heart she is drawn to him) in favour of a Croesus-rich Scottish landowner, Robert Kennedy. Phineas then turns his attention to a beautiful and spirited heiress, Violet Effingham. She in her turn rejects Phineas, finding a certain moral insubstantiality in a suitor who can direct his affections so briskly from one target to another. Finally, after three years and as a rising politician in dire need of wealth to support his ministerial career, Phineas allows himself to be proposed to by a brilliant society hostess, the immensely wealthy, widowed, and mysterious Madame Max Goesler. He tactfully declines, and returns to the

faithful Mary. Almost penniless, they resolve to marry—
on £150 a year, if necessary. Phineas is rescued from this
awful fate by an appointment (at £1,000 p.a.) as a Poor Law
Commissioner. His political friends have looked after him.
The novel ends with a coy exchange between Phineas and
Mary, indicative of his lover's impatience to enjoy his
marital privileges:

'Oh Phineas; surely a thousand a-year will be very nice.'

'It will be certain,' said Phineas, 'and then we can be married
tomorrow.'

'But I have been making up my mind to wait ever so long,' said
Mary.

'Then your mind must be unmade', said Phineas. (ii. 356)

Phineas's reasons for giving up his London parliamentary
career—which looks potentially glorious—are insufficiently explained by his good-natured difference of opinion with his Liberal leaders on a piece of Irish legislation.
Nor is it entirely clear why he should reject Madame
Goesler (whom he is, after trials and widowerhood, eventually to marry, in *Phineas Redux*).[3] Simon Raven solved
this enigma by a daring stroke—he made Mary Flood
Jones pregnant. Raven's Phineas, having weighed everything up, decided to do the right thing and make Mary an
honest woman.

Although there is no textual warrant, there is a motiv-
ational logic in Raven's narrative improvement. It
explains why Phineas—no fool, and ambitious to a fault—
should have committed political suicide, as he did. Nor is
it, as some commentators on the TV series complained,
an 'Un-Trollopian' invention. Raven was no stranger
to Trollope's fiction in 1974. He had earlier in 1966 adapted
Trollope's great satire, *The Way We Live Now*, for
television, and in the same year he had edited, for
Anthony Blond's 'Doughty Library', Trollope's late novella, *An Eye for an Eye* (1879). In that story Fred Neville, a

young English officer in the hussars, meets an innocent
Irish beauty in Co. Clare. Kate O'Hara is cut from the
same pattern as Mary Flood Jones. Fred (who is by no
means a swine, but lacking in moral fibre) seduces and
impregnates the luckless girl. Trollope does not (by the
strict standards of Victorian fiction) mince his words:

Alas, alas; there came a day in which the pricelessness of the girl
he loved sank to nothing, vanished away, and was as a thing
utterly lost, even in his eyes. The poor unfortunate one—to whom
beauty had been given, and grace, and softness—and beyond all
these and finer than these, innocence as unsullied as the whiteness of the plumage on the breast of a dove; but to whom, alas,
had not been given a protector strong enough to protect her softness, or guardian wise enough to guard her innocence! To her he
was godlike, noble, excellent, all but holy. He was the man whom
Fortune, more than kind, had sent to her to be the joy of her
existence, the fountain of her life, the strong staff for her weakness. Not to believe in him would the foulest treason! To lose him
would be to die! To deny him would be to deny her God! She gave
him all—and her pricelessness in his eyes was gone for ever.
(pp. 108–9)

This echoes similar passages in *Phineas Finn*. In Chapter
16, for example, the hero returns to Killaloe for five months
during the long recess of Parliament. He is now cool
towards Mary, although he does not altogether discard
her. Her mother warns her that Phineas intends to be false.

Mary made no answer; but she went up into her room and swore
before a figure of the Virgin that she would be true to Phineas for
ever and ever, in spite of her mother, in spite of all the world—in
spite, should it be necessary', even of himself. (i. 146)

In *An Eye for an Eye* Fred deserts a now-pregnant Kate,
and returns to his grand life as future Earl of Scroope in
England where he is expected to marry a young lady of his
own class. He returns briefly to Ireland to put his affairs

in order, and Kate's enraged mother pushes him over the cliffs to his death.

There is clear parallelism between the two plots. In both, a free-and easy young man wins a humble Irish girl's heart, and deserts her in order to make his way (and marry someone else) in England. He does not tell the women he pays court to in England about his forlorn Irish sweetheart. In one novel the deserted maiden loses a lock of hair, in the other her maidenhood. Raven was clearly justified in eliding details of the two plots, in the interest of stiffening his adaptation, and making it plausible to 1970s viewers.

The main objection to Raven's taking such a liberty is that it sets a up a train of subsequent contradictions to what Trollope manifestly intended. Mary Flood Jones (who is the most *disponible* of Trollopian heroines) dies in the un-narrated interval (two years, as we are told) between *Phineas Finn* and *Phineas Redux*. It is clear that Mary's death occurs very shortly before the action of the sequel (and thus at least a year after their marriage). As Laurence Fitzgibbon tells the party manager, Mr Ratler, 'the poor thing [Mary] died of her first baby before it was born' (p. 6). 'First baby' suggests that there was no little stranger on its way at the end of *Phineas Finn*. Trollope, one may guess, would have been mightily indignant about the slur cast on the honour of one of his more fragrant and virtuous young ladies.

There are, however, episodes elsewhere in the Palliser series which suggest that Trollope wants us to be aware that at every point more may be going on sexually than he is free to tell us about. There is, for instance, a revealing moment late in the action of the first of the Palliser novels, *Can You Forgive Her?* (1865). By this stage in the narrative the Byronic hero, George Vavasor, has gone utterly to the bad. He early on proposed to his cousin, the long-suffering

Alice, with the sole aim of getting her fortune. Since then his business speculations have gone wrong, he has been disinherited, and when his attempt to establish himself in Parliament fails, he assaults his faithful sister Kate. He compounds his falsehood by blackmailing Alice (who had given him her troth) and tries to murder his rival for her love, John Grey. At the depth of his misfortune, as he contemplates emigration or suicide, George receives a visitor. She reveals herself to be a discarded mistress, called Jane:

She was a woman of about thirty years of age, dressed poorly, in old garments, but still with decency, and with some attempt at feminine prettiness. There were flowers in the bonnet on her head, though the bonnet had that unmistakable look of age which is quite as distressing to bonnets as it is to women, and the flowers themselves were battered and faded. She had long black ringlets on each cheek, hanging down much below her face, and brought forward so as to hide in some degree the hollowness of her jaws. Her eyes had a peculiar brightness, but now they left on those who looked at her cursorily no special impression as to their colour. They had been blue,—that dark violet blue, which is so rare, but is sometimes so lovely. (p. 321)

It emerges in the following conversation that for three years Jane was a kept woman, George's mistress. He installed her in a house. Then, having tired of her, he put her into a 'business' (a small shop, apparently), at a cost of £100. As he brutally puts it, 'That was all I could do for you;—and more than most men would have done, when all things are considered' (p. 323). The shop has failed, she is starving. If he cannot give her something to support herself, only one course is open to her—the streets. He dismisses her without a penny, at one point threatening to call the police if she does not go quietly. As we guess, she will be a whore before the week is out.

What is astonishing about this episode is that nowhere

earlier in the text is any sexual delinquency on George's part hinted at, even in the most distant or coded way. He is, albeit ruthless, a model of social propriety. He does not drink, gamble, or in any way waste his substance. His manners are perfect (even here he claims that he has acted better than other men would have done, 'when all things are considered'). And yet, we are to gather, all the time that we have had his acquaintance in the novel there was that secret compartment of his life about which we were not informed. The door swings open briefly—not to reveal anything very important, but merely to let us know that there are such doors and such secret chambers in Trollope's world.

What we may deduce from this scene in *Can You Forgive Her* is that, in the un-narrated hinterland of all of the Palliser novels, many of Trollope's gentleman characters have sexual lives which, just as they keep hidden from the world, the fiction keeps hidden from the reader. With this in mind, is it likely that a highly sexed, impulsive, handsome young buck like Phineas would keep himself entirely pure for five years in a foreign city? Raven's invention of a pregnant Mary Flood Jones is clearly recalcitrant in going so flatly against the grain of Trollope's narrative. On the other hand, Raven's blatant foregrounding of sex in *Phineas Finn* reminds us that Trollope's young heroes are neither neuters nor angels in their 'private', un-narrated lives.

The Oxford World's Classics *Phineas Finn* is edited by Jacques Berthoud. The Oxford World's Classics *An Eye for an Eye* is edited by John Sutherland. The Oxford World's Classics *Can You Forgive Her?* is edited by Andrew Swarbrick, with an introduction by Kate Flint.

===

Is Will Ladislaw legitimate?

===

It helps to picture the *dramatis personae* of *Middlemarch*
less as a community of English townspeople of the early
nineteenth century than as a Papuan tribe—each connected to the other by complex ties of blood and marriage.
Unknotting these ties requires the skills of the anthro-
pologist rather than those of the literary critic. Let us
start with Casaubon. Early in the narrative, the middle-
aged vicar of Lowick is most vexed when Mr Brooke (making unwarranted deductions from their age difference)
refers to young Will Ladislaw as 'your nephew'. Will, as
Casaubon testily points out, is his 'second cousin', not his
nephew. We learn from questions which Dorothea asks on
her first visit to Lowick, that Casaubon's mother, whose
Christian and maiden names we never know, had an elder
sister, Julia. This aunt Julia—as we much later learn—ran
away to marry a Polish patriot called Ladislaw and was
disinherited by her family. Julia and her husband had one
child, as best we can make out. Ladislaw Jr. (we never
learn his first name) inherited from his father a musical
gift which the son turned to use in the theatre—to little
profit, apparently. In this capacity he met an actress,
Sarah Dunkirk. Sarah, like Casaubon's aunt Julia, had
run away from her family's household to go on the stage.
At some point before or after running away, she
discovered that her father, Archie Dunkirk, who at one
point in the text is alleged to be Jewish (although a practising nonconformist Christian of the severest kind),
was engaged in criminal activities. He is reported to have

had a respectable pawnbroking business in Highbury, and another establishment which fenced stolen goods in the West End. Sarah broke off all relations with her mother and father on making this discovery. They have another child, a boy, and effectively disowned their disobedient daughter.

Sarah was subsequently married to, or set up house with, Ladislaw Jr. The couple had one child (Will) before the father prematurely succumbed to an unidentified wasting disease. Before dying, he introduced himself to Edward Casaubon, who generously undertook to take care of the penniless widow and child. Will is too young to remember anything distinctly about his father. On her part Mrs Ladislaw died in 1825, some ten years after her husband, of what is vaguely described as a 'fall'.

At some point after Sarah Dunkirk's breaking off all relations with her parents, her brother died. Shortly after this her father also died. In the distress of her double bereavement, Mrs Dunkirk (now an old lady, and— although she does not know it—a grandmother) turned to a young evangelical clerk of her husband's, called Nicholas Bulstrode. Eventually, she married the young man. The disparity in age precluded children. As she approached death, a distraught Mrs Bulstrode made desperate attempts to locate her daughter Sarah with the hope of reconciliation. But, although he had discovered their whereabouts, Bulstrode—assisted in his act of deception by another former employee of Dunkirk's, John Raffles—suppressed all information about Sarah and her little boy. Raffles in fact makes contact with Sarah twice, although he only informs Bulstrode about the first encounter (this is important since, for complicated reasons, he only discovers Ladislaw's name on the second occasion). When Mrs Bulstrode died, Bulstrode, by his act of deception, inherited his wife's entire fortune and used it

to set up a bank in Middlemarch. It will help at this point
to refer to a family tree (see Fig. 1). As Farebrother puts it
with uncharacteristic coarseness later in the narrative
(presumably echoing Middlemarch gossip): 'our mercurial
Ladislaw has a queer genealogy! A high spirited young
lady and a musical Polish patriot made a likely enough
stock for him to spring from, but I should never have suspected a grafting of the Jew pawnbroker' (p. 588).[1]

This means, of course, that Bulstrode is Casaubon's distant cousin by marriage—although both are oblivious of
the relationship. In Middlemarch, the still-young, newly
widowed, and now rich Nicholas Bulstrode married Harriet Vincy. She is a sister of Walter Vincy, manufacturer,
husband to Lucy Vincy and father of the novel's *jeunes
premières* Fred and Rosamond. Mrs Vincy's sister was the
second wife of the rich skinflint, Peter Featherstone.
Featherstone's first wife was a sister of Caleb Garth, father
of Mary Garth and other children who feature on the edge
of the novel's plot. Peter Featherstone has no child by
either of these two wives, both of whom predecease him by
some years. But, unknown to his hopeful heirs (among
whom the most hopeful is his nephew Fred Vincy), Peter
Featherstone had a third, common-law wife, called Rigg.
By this Miss Rigg, Featherstone has an illegitimate son,
Joshua, born in 1798. Discarded by Featherstone, Miss
Rigg subsequently married John Raffles, the aforementioned employee of Dunkirk and conspirator with
Bulstrode to defraud Will Ladislaw of his inheritance. It
will help here to refer to another tree (see Fig. 2).

Thus John Raffles, fence, blackmailer, gambler, the most
despicable character in the novel, is related to Casaubon
and (by subsequent marriages in the novel) to Lydgate,
Dorothea Brooke, Will Ladislaw, and Sir James Chettam.
The line of connection goes as follows: Raffles's wife is the
mother of Peter Featherstone's child and heir; Peter

Figure 1

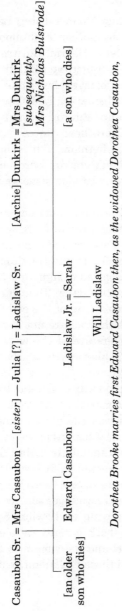

Casaubon Sr. = Mrs Casaubon — [sister] — Julia [?] = Ladislaw Sr.   [Archie] Dunkirk = Mrs Dunkirk [subsequently Mrs Nicholas Bulstrode]

[an older son who dies]   Edward Casaubon   Ladislaw Jr. = Sarah   [a son who dies]

Will Ladislaw

Dorothea Brooke marries first Edward Casaubon then, as the widowed Dorothea Casaubon, Will Ladislaw by whom she has children

Figure 2

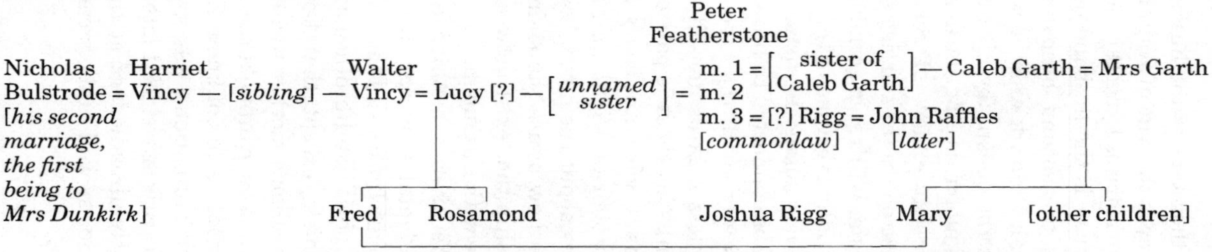

Peter Featherstone   m. 1 = [sister of [Caleb Garth]]   sister of [[Caleb Garth]] — Caleb Garth = Mrs Garth

Nicholas Bulstrode = Harriet Vincy [his second marriage, the first being to Mrs Dunkirk] — [sibling] — Walter Vincy = Lucy [?]

m. 2 = [unnamed sister]   m. 3 = [?] Rigg = John Raffles [commonlaw] [later]

Fred   Rosamond   Joshua Rigg   Mary   [other children]

Fred Vincy subsequently marries Mary Garth, Rosamond Vincy marries Tertius Lydgate

Featherstone is the husband of Lucy Vincy's sister; Lucy
Vincy is the wife of Walter Vincy, the mother of Rosamond
(who marries Lydgate) and the sister of Harriet Bulstrode;
Harriet is the husband of Nicholas Bulstrode; Bulstrode
was the second husband of the former Mrs Dunkirk;
Sarah Dunkirk was the wife of Ladislaw Jr.; Ladislaw Jr.
was the cousin (by his aunt Julia) of Edward Casaubon;
Casaubon is the husband of Dorothea; Dorothea is
the sister-in-law of Sir James Chetham. Put simply,
Bulstrode is (by marriage) Casaubon's cousin, Dorothea's
cousin, Will's step-grandfather, and related in some way to
virtually everyone in the novel.

Every main character in *Middlemarch's* massive plot
can be connected by lines of consanguinity or marriage in
this way—with the exception of Farebrother (who none
the less regards himself as an 'uncle' to the Garth children). Clearly, it is part of Eliot's grand design, and per-
tains to what Rosemary Ashton aptly calls, 'the central
metaphor of *Middlemarch*, the web'.[2] One of the odd features about the novel, however, is that we are not always
sure how aware the main characters are of the webs of
kinship that exist between them. This is particularly the
case with Casaubon.

We know something of Casaubon's background from
incidental remarks. Before their marriage, he tells his
fiancée Dorothea that his mother was one of two daughters, just like Dorothea and Celia. Of his father we know
nothing, except that Lowick is the family home and
Casaubon's mother was a young woman there—whether
she had been brought there as a bride, or had lived there as
a child, we do not know. Edward was a younger son, and—
after ordination—was given the living at Lowick. Subsequently his elder brother died (both parents were evidently already dead at this point) and he came into the
manor as well as the vicarage. All these Casaubon deaths

must have occurred much earlier, in the narrative's distant prehistory. It was evidently as the head of the family that Ladislaw Jr. approached Edward for help, and this was when Will was still too young to know anything about his circumstances other than that he was very hungry.

In this context one may note a remark which the Revd Cadwallader makes early in the narrative to Sir James Chettam. Sir James, still smarting at the absurd idea that Dorothea, whom he loves, should choose to marry such a dry stick as Casaubon, asks what kind of man he is. 'He is very good to his poor relations', Cadwallader says, using the plural form of the word.

he . . . pensions several of the women, and is educating a young fellow [i.e. Will] at a good deal of expense. Casaubon acts up to his sense of justice. His mother's sister made a bad match—a Pole, I think—lost herself—at any rate was disowned by her family. If it had not been for that, Casaubon would not have had so much money by half. *I believe he went himself to find out his cousins*, and see what he could do for them. (pp. 56–7; my italics)

We never discover who these unnamed 'relations', 'women', 'cousins' are. They make no appearance at Casaubon's funeral, nor is any bequest to them mentioned in the subsequent lengthy discussion of the will. Dorothea inherits everything, as we understand (Will, who might have expected 'half', is spitefully excluded). What is interesting, however, is Cadwallader's recollection that Casaubon has made active investigations about his relatives, presumably on coming into his inheritance. He would surely have extended his inquiries to his aunt Julia and her offspring and might even have found out something about the murky world of the Dunkirks.

In conversation with Dorothea shortly after Casaubon's first heart-attack, Will casually tells her that his 'grandmother [was] disinherited because she made what they called a *mésalliance*, though there was nothing to be said

against her husband, except that he was a Polish refugee
who gave lessons for his bread.' Dorothea goes on to ask
what he knew about his parents and grandparents, and
Will replies:

only that my grandfather was a patriot—a bright fellow—could
speak many languages—musical—got his bread by teaching all
sorts of things. They [i.e. grandfather and grandmother] both
died rather early. And I never knew much of my father, beyond
what my mother told me; but he inherited the musical talents. I
remember his slow walk and his long thin hands; and one day
remains with me when he was lying ill, and I was very hungry, and
had only a little bit of bread. (p. 300)

Shortly after, Will recalls, 'my father ... made himself
known to Mr Casaubon and that was my last hungry day'.
And shortly after that, his father died.

An initial mystery is why Julia's alliance with a cultivated Pole should have resulted in such a total alienation
from her family. A second mystery is Casaubon's extraordinary disinclination to discuss anything to do with
Will's origins. He returns all Dorothea's inquiries with
'cold vagueness' and refuses outright to answer any of his
wife's questions about 'the mysterious "Aunt Julia"'
(p. 305). Thirdly, one may wonder why Casaubon, an extraordinarily rectitudinous man, does not make over part of
the family portion to Will, if he is the legitimate grandson
of the older daughter (Julia) who would—had she not
made her *mésalliance*—have inherited half or more of her
parents' wealth, wealth which has all funnelled into the
sole possession of Casaubon.

These questions, particularly the last, should be borne
in mind when scrutinizing Raffles's account of how, all
those years ago, he discovered Will and his mother and
kept the news secret from Mrs Dunkirk, at Bulstrode's
behest. 'Lord, you made a pretty thing out of me,' Raffles
tells Bulstrode, on their reunion at Stone Court: 'and I

got but little. I've often thought since, I might have done
better by telling the old woman that I'd found her daughter
and her grandchild: it would have suited my feelings
better' (p. 431). He goes on, after revealing that Bulstrode
gave him enough to emigrate comfortably to America,

I did have another look after Sarah again, though I didn't tell
you; I'd a tender conscience about that pretty young woman. I
didn't find her, but I found out her husband's name, and I made a
note of it. But hang it, I lost my pocket book. However, if I heard
it, I should know it again . . . It began with L; it was almost all l's,
I fancy. (p. 433)

The name, of course, is Ladislaw. This accounts why it is
Bulstrode does not put two and two together when his
young step-grandson turns up in Middlemarch. But under
what name, then, did Raffles first discover the mother and
child? One has to assume he discovered them as 'Sarah
and Will Dunkirk', It beggars credulity that if he were
charged to find proof of their identity, with £100,000 at
stake, he would not have made some attempt to ascertain
names and identities. Without some name to work with,
how could he (or his lawyers) have found them in the first
place?

This may be taken in conjunction with Ladislaw's
extreme sensitivity on the subject of his mother. Consider,
for example, Raffles's overture to Will, once he has
tumbled to who he is. 'Excuse me, Mr Ladislaw', he asks:

'was your mother's name Sarah Dunkirk?'
  Will, starting to his feet, moved backward a step, frowning, and
saying with some fierceness, 'Yes, sir, it was. And what is that to
you?' . . . 'No offence, my good sir, no offence! I only remember
your mother—knew her when she was a girl. But it is your father
that you feature, sir. I had the pleasure of seeing your father too.
Parents alive, Mr Ladislaw?'
  'No!' thundered Will, in the same attitude as before. (pp. 497–8)

One notes that Raffles does not say—as would be normal—
'was your mother's maiden name Sarah Dunkirk?' One
notes too the extraordinary anger which Raffles's inquiry
provokes. The same angry response is evident in Will's
interview with the repentant Bulstrode, very shortly after:

'I am told that your mother's name was Sarah Dunkirk, and that
she ran away from her friends to go on the stage. Also, that your
father was at one time much emaciated by illness. May I ask if
you can confirm these statements?'

'Yes, they are all true,' said Will ... 'Do you know any
particulars of your mother's family?' [Bulstrode] continued.

'No; she never liked to speak of them. She was a very generous,
honourable woman,' said Will, almost angrily.

'I do not wish to allege anything against her . . . ' (pp. 507–8)

One notes again the use of the name 'Sarah Dunkirk'
rather than, 'your mother's name was Sarah Dunkirk
before marriage'. Also prominent is Ladislaw's touchiness
at any aspersion against his mother's 'honour'.

There seems at least a prima-facie case for wondering
whether or not Will was born out of wedlock. This would
explain why it is he and his mother are first found by Raffles under some other name than Ladislaw (presumably
'Sarah Dunkirk and son'). Irregular unions were common
enough in the nineteenth-century theatre world. It is
worth recalling too that Will Ladislaw is known to be an
idealized portrait of George Eliot's consort, G. H. Lewes.
And, as Rosemary Ashton's recent biography has
revealed, Lewes was illegitimate.[3] As Ashton notes, Lewes
may not himself have known the fact. She adds: 'It is not
surprising . . . that we know nothing about G. H. Lewes's
earliest years. They must have been precarious socially,
and probably financially as well . . . Whatever Lewes was
told about his own father . . . he nowhere mentions [him] in
his surviving writings' (p. 11). There is, of course, a difference. It seems that at some point Ladislaw Jr. did marry

Sarah Dunkirk—possibly as he felt death was coming, and he needed to hand over responsibility to Casaubon, he made an honest woman of Sarah and a legitimate child out of Will. All this is highly speculative. But any ideas we form about this aspect of the novel are driven to guesswork. One could, of course, speculate that Sarah when she left her parents took on a stage-name, and it was under this that Raffles first found her. There is also the baffling detail that at one point in the narrative Raffles seems to refer to Sarah's family name as 'Duncan' (see p. 498).

One is on firmer ground with hypotheses about what must have been going through Casaubon's mind, and agonizing him, as he watched Dorothea and Will forming a close relationship. He may well have known (from his interviews with Ladislaw Jr. and Will's mother, who has been alive until quite recently) about the discreditable 'Jew pawnbroker' business, if only vaguely. Should he tell the young man? Casaubon may also, as I have speculated, have known that Will was born out of wedlock (which would explain why he had not made part of the family fortune over to him, as a legitimate heir). At the very least, it seems strongly probable that Casaubon is possessed of some guilty knowledge and that the anxiety of it hastens his premature death.

The Oxford World's Classics *Middlemarch* is edited by David Carroll with an introduction by Felicia Bonaparte.

Is Melmotte Jewish?

In his monumental survey of anti-Semitism in the works of
Thackeray, *Israel at Vanity Fair* (1992), S. S. Prawer refers
in passing to Melmotte, the financier villain of Trollope's
The Way We Live Now, as a 'Jewish crook' (p. 418). This is
a common assumption among critics and readers of
Trollope and can be found in print in any number of
places. It is, very probably, a misapprehension—although
it is not easy to come to a final resolution on the matter.[1]

The novelist apparently connives at our uncertainty
about Melmotte's origins by not being as straightforward
as he normally is on such matters. There is, for instance,
no ambiguity about the race or religion of Samuel
Cohenlupe, 'Member of Parliament for Staines, a
gentleman of the Jewish persuasion' (i. 84), the amiable
Ezekiel Brehgert, or the less amiable Mr Goldsheiner. Of
Madame Melmotte, it is clearly explained not just that she
is a Jewess, but that she is a particular variety of non-
English Jewess—doubly alien: 'She was fat and fair,—
unlike in colour to our traditional Jewesses; but she had
the Jewish nose and the Jewish contraction of the eyes'
(i. 31). Georgiana Longestaffe's accepting the proposal of
Brehgert provokes an anathema worthy of a medieval
Pope from her despairing, patrician, incurably xenophobic
mother: 'It's worse than your wife's sister. I'm sure there's
something in the Bible against it . . . An accursed race;—
think of that, Georgiana;—expelled from Paradise' (ii.
263). 'Mamma, that's nonsense,' the hard-headed young
lady responds, with the common sense of a commodity

which has been twelve years' unbought on the marriage market and at the end of its shelf-life.

Although he is not generally mealy-mouthed about such things, Trollope deliberately, it seems, casts a pall of racial and national ambiguity around Melmotte. At our first introduction in Chapter 4 ('Madame Melmotte's Ball'), we are given an extensive but radically unclear description:

The giver of the ball was Augustus Melmotte, Esq., the father of the girl whom Sir Felix Carbury desired to marry, and the husband of the lady who was said to have been a Bohemian Jewess. [In the manuscript of the novel 'Italian Jewess' is crossed out, and 'Bohemian Jewess' added.] It was thus that the gentleman chose to have himself designated, though within the last two years he had arrived in London from Paris, and had at first been known as M. Melmotte. But he had declared of himself that he had been born in England, and that he was an Englishman. He admitted that his wife was a foreigner,—an admission that was necessary as she spoke very little English. Melmotte himself spoke his 'native' language fluently, but with an accent which betrayed at least a long expatriation. Miss Melmotte,—who a very short time since had been known as Mademoiselle Marie,— spoke English well, but as a foreigner. In regard to her it was acknowledged that she had been born out of England,—some said in New York; but Madame Melmotte, who must have known, had declared that the great event had taken place in Paris. (i. 30)

Melmotte's speech, which should betray his origins, gives similarly mixed signals. When drunk, for instance, he speaks ungrammatically, and with what sound like Cockneyisms. Demanding to be introduced to the Emperor of China (for whom he has gone to the expense of organizing a lavish dinner) he declares: 'He don't dine there [i.e. in my house] unless I'm made acquainted with him before he comes. I mean what I say. I ain't going to entertain even an Emperor unless I'm good enough to be presented to him' (ii. 39). At other times, especially when addressing his

wayward daughter Marie, Melmotte's native tongue—like
his surname—seems clearly French. 'Pig! ... wicked
ungrateful pig!' (ii. 257), he shouts at his terrified and
beaten daughter in the extremity of his rage. The objurga-
tion does not sound like an English papa laying down the
law to his errant offspring. But nowhere does Melmotte
make errors in his speech, which is characteristically, in
conversation with Englishmen, fluent and idiomatic.
Nor is his speech, like that of Fisker, blemished with
vulgar Yankeeisms—although, as we shall see, there are
good grounds for thinking the Great Financier spent his
formative years in New York.

Some clue to Melmotte's mysterious origins is given in
an incidental reverie of Marie's, early in the narrative:

She could just remember the dirty street in the German portion
of New York in which she had been born and had lived for the
first four years of her life, and could remember too the poor,
hardly-treated woman who had been her mother. She could
remember being at sea, and her sickness,—but could not quite
remember whether that woman had been with her. Then she had
run about the streets of Hamburg, and had sometimes been very
hungry, sometimes in rags,—and she had a dim memory of some
trouble into which her father had fallen, and that he was away
from her for a time. She had up to the present splendid moment
her own convictions about that absence, but she had never mentioned them to a human being. Then her father had married her
present mother in Frankfurt. That she could remember distinctly,
as also the rooms in which she was then taken to live, and the fact
that she was told that from henceforth she was to be a Jewess. But
there had soon come another change. They went from Frankfort
to Paris, and there they were all Christians. (i. 106)

Although she was born in New York's 'German' quarter
with English as the language of her country and city,
the 19-year-old Marie has a poor grasp of English. She
evidently spent some time at Hamburg, where her mother

had died and Melmotte went to prison for fraud (see
ii. 298). On his release, the widowed trickster evidently
won himself a rich wife among the élite Jewish merchant
class in Frankfort. Would Melmotte (or whatever he was
then called)—a gentile—have been allowed to carry off a
Jewish heiress and her dowry? And then there is the odd
phrase in Marie's reverie, 'they were *all* Christians', with
its implication that Melmotte converts, as well.

When he stands for Parliament as the member for
Westminster, Melmotte attracts from his opponents and
their newspaper allies the ironic title of 'the Great Financier'. This sobriquet is invented by the editor of the *Evening Pulpit*, Mr Alf. At this point in his career, despite
his protestations (for electoral purposes) of invincible
attachment to the Protestant faith (accompanied by some
judicious charitable donations), 'it was suspected by many,
and was now being whispered to the world at large, that
Melmotte had been born a Jew' (ii. 52). To any moderately
well-informed reader of 1875 it would have been crystal
clear what Mr Alf's 'Great Financier' slur, and the pervasive rumours of his Jewish origins, alluded to. The
Member of Parliament for the City of London at this time
was Lionel Nathan de Rothschild. Rothschild was elected
in 1847, but was not allowed to sit in the House because as
a Jew he could not conscientiously take the oath. He was
repeatedly re-elected as the most eminent financier in the
City and finally took his seat in 1858. Rothschild was
associated, like Melmotte (although more honourably),
with lucrative French railway speculations. A dashing
man, he was immortalized elsewhere in fiction as Sidonia,
in Disraeli's *Coningsby*. (Trollope, incidentally, loathed
Disraeli and all his works, both political and literary.) In
1872, Rothschild acquired the Tring Park estate, in Hertfordshire (as, in the novel, Melmotte schemes to acquire
the Pickering estate), setting himself up as a landed

English nobleman. Trollope himself hunted with members of the Rothschild family in 1872, but seems to have fallen out with them, shortly before writing *The Way We Live Now*.

All this seems to point in a clear direction. But, in its last pages, the novel plays a last trick on us. After her father's death, Marie finds herself again an eligible heiress, with what little is left from the wreckage of Melmotte's ruin. She is claimed in marriage by the amiably amoral Hamilton K. Fisker. But even with Melmotte out of the way, there remain difficulties in establishing who Marie really is:

At first things did not arrange themselves pleasantly between Madame Melmotte and Marie. The reader will perhaps remember that they were in no way connected by blood. Madame Melmotte was not Marie's mother, nor, in the eye of the law, could Marie claim Melmotte as her father. She was alone in the world, absolutely without a relation, not knowing even what had been her mother's name,—not even knowing what was her father's true name, as in the various biographies of the great man which were, as a matter of course, published within a fortnight of his death, various accounts were given as to his birth, parentage, and early history. The general opinion seemed to be that his father had been a noted coiner in New York,—an Irishman of the name of Melmody,—and, in one memoir, the probability of the descent was argued from Melmotte's skill in forgery. (ii. 449)

It is a plausible pedigree, and confirms details in Marie's faint childhood recollections, quoted above. But it remains tantalizingly vague, even at this last stage of the novel's complicated denouement.

So—is Melmotte English (as his command of the language and accent suggests), French (as his name, and occasional linguistic inflections suggest), American-Irish, or American-Jewish (i.e. sprung from the 'German' quarter of New York)? The clearest clue to what Trollope intended is to be found in his preliminary notes for the novel, which are held at the Bodleian Library, at Oxford. Putting together preliminary notes for his *dramatis personae*, Trollope jotted down the following thumbnail sketches:

~~Marianna Treegrene~~ Marie Melmotte, the heiress, daughter of
~~Samuel Emanuel~~ Augustus ~~S. Treegrene~~ Melmotte
the ~~great American~~ French swindler
Madame Melmotte—fat Jewess.

It seems clear from these alterations that Melmotte began in Trollope's mind as two, and possibly three, separate conceptions. The first conception was Samuel Emanuel Treegrene, a Jewish swindler of German origins, who has anglicized his name from Grünbaum ('green tree'). The other conception was Augustus S. Melmotte, 'the great American Swindler', who has enriched himself by marriage to a rich Jewess in Frankfort, and by fraud in Paris, and who has Gallicized his name and Anglicized his pedigree the better to delude his victims and cover his criminal tracks. It would have been easy and logical for Trollope to have cleared up this confusion, by making Melmotte a thoroughly Jewish rogue (like Cohenlupe and Goldsheiner), or a thoroughly American rogue, like Hamilton K. Fisker. Instead, he dropped the tell-tale American initial ('Augustus *S*. Melmotte), and made his villain both, fusing the two conceptions and retaining a degree of irreconcileability, which he prudently shrouded by vagueness. Finally, he added to the mixture a dash of Irishness (drawing clearly on memories of the great Irish swindler John Sadleir, who committed suicide by cyanide— as does Melmotte—in 1856, and who was popularly presumed to be still alive in 1875, and living in New York). Melmotte, in short, is a national-racial compendium. As such, he can stand for a whole range of 'dishonesties' which the enraged Trollope perceived to be destroying the fabric of England, Europe, and America in the early 1870s (for the historical identity of the swindlers whom Trollope had in mind, see the Introduction to the World's Classics edition of *The Way We Live Now*).

As a satire against a whole gallery of foreign and domestic rascals and rascalities, Melmotte was aptly named. Trollope must surely have had in mind Charles Maturin's Gothic novel, *Melmoth the Wanderer* (1820). The hero, an Irishman, who is a version of the wandering Jew, cannot die for 120 years, and goes through many changes of identity in his long, largely villainous, career. Maturin's novel ends with a magnificent suicide by Melmoth, who casts himself off a crag at his ancestral estate in Wicklow (echoed in Melmotte's suicide in Trollope's novel). The theme of Maturin's novel was picked up by another 'cursed' Irish wanderer, Oscar Wilde, during his post-prison exile in Europe, where he took on the name 'Sebastian Melmoth'. The Christian-name alludes to the long-suffering saint, pierced by tormenting arrows but unable to die. 'Melmoth' echoes both Maturin (who was a distant relative of Wilde's) and Trollope's tormented villain.

Is Melmotte, to return to the question with which this chapter began 'a Jewish crook'? Yes, he is. But he is also a gentile, an Irish, an American, a German, and an English crook.

The Oxford World's Classics *The Way We Live Now* is edited by John Sutherland.

Anthony Trollope · *The Prime Minister*

===

Where is Tenway Junction?

===

The suicide of Ferdinand Lopez is regarded as one of the finest things in Trollope's late fiction. An adventurer of dubious foreign extraction (even he, we are told on the first page, does not know who, or of what nationality, or of what ethnicity were his grandparents), Lopez has successfully invaded the upper echelons of English society. By preying on the susceptibilities of Lady Palliser with his un-English smoothness of manner, he has almost gained election to Parliament. He has won a monied English bride. He has, for a while, been prosperous in the City of London. Finally, Lopez's house of cards falls. He is disgraced politically (bringing down Plantagenet Palliser's administration with him), wholly alienated from his wife (whom he has abused dreadfully), and ruined financially.

The last twelve hours of Lopez's life show him still going mechanically through the forms and rituals of a gentleman's existence. He takes dinner in his club in St James. He then undertakes a long peregrination on foot through nocturnal London. It is March, and a sleety, blustery night. He has an umbrella over his silk top hat. His route through the different quarters of the city is described by Trollope in meticulous topographic detail:

he went round by Trafalgar Square, and along the Strand, and up some dirty streets by the small theatres, and so on to Holborn and by Bloomsbury Square up to Tottenham Court Road, then through some unused street into Portland Place, along the Marylebone Road, and back to Manchester Square by Baker Street. (ii. 188)

One can trace his circuitous route on any *London, A-to-Z*, and it seems that Lopez, as he stands on the brink of eternity, wishes to sees as many facets of fashionable, low-life, and bohemian London as is possible on a single night. On his way, he is 'spoken to frequently by unfortunates of both sexes' (the only reference that I know in decent Victorian fiction to male prostitutes, or 'rent boys', of the kind who were to bring Oscar Wilde to ruin in 1895). Once home in his Manchester Square mansion, Lopez comes face to face with the utter impossibility of his position. Early the next morning he leaves his house for the last time. It is still raining hard. He looks for a cab, but—as is invariably the case in London when it rains—none is to be found. In Baker Street he takes an omnibus (horse-drawn at this date) which carries him as far as 'the underground railway [i.e. what is now the Baker Street station], and by that he went to Gower Street [i.e. what is now the Euston Square station, on the Circle Line]' (ii. 190). As is his usual practice, Trollope has set the action of his novel very close to the present. The underground line (served by steam engines, and not a very attractive mode of transport) had been open since 1863. Lopez then crosses the Euston Road and walks 200 yards or so through the rain to the Euston Station. This great terminus, open since 1847, served in the 1870s as the gateway to the West and North. Again, Trollope gives us real names for these very real London places.

Lopez breakfasts on a mutton chop at the station café. Charmer to the end, he cannot forebear from flirting with the waitress. He then goes into the ticket-hall, and buys 'a first-class return ticket, not for Birmingham, but for the Tenway Junction'. The return ticket suggests that he has not yet decided irrevocably to kill himself—but there seems no other reason for him to go to Tenway Junction. Had he wished merely to disappear from the eyes of men under an alias, or abroad, he would surely have packed a bag and raised some cash. Trollope then embarks on a long description of Lopez's destination which opens, paradoxically, with the statement that any such description is, of course, wholly superfluous:

It is quite unnecessary to describe the Tenway Junction, as everybody knows it. From this spot, some six or seven miles distant from London, lines diverge east, west, and north, north-east, and north-west, round the metropolis in every direction, and with direct communication with every other line in and out of London. It is a marvellous place, quite unintelligible to the uninitiated, and yet daily used by thousands who only know that when they get there, they are to do what some one tells them. The space occupied by the convergent rails seem to be sufficient for a large farm. And these rails always run into another with sloping points, and cross passages, and mysterious meandering sidings, till it seems to the thoughtful stranger to be impossible that the best trained engine should know its own line. Here and there and around there is ever a wilderness of wagons, some loaded, some empty, some smoking with close-packed oxen, and others furlongs in length black with coals, which look as though they had been stranded there by chance, and were never destined to get again into the right path of traffic. Not a minute passes without a train going here or there, some rushing by without noticing Tenway in the least, crashing through like flashes of substantial lightning, and others stopping, disgorging and taking up passengers by the hundreds. Men and women,—especially the men, for the women knowing their ignorance are generally willing to trust to the pundits of the place,—look doubtful, uneasy, and bewildered. But they all do get properly placed and unplaced, so that the spectator at last acknowledges that over all this apparent chaos there is presiding a great genius of order. (ii. 191–2)

Lopez, having contemplated the marvellous geometry of the Junction, walks down the bevelled end of a platform, into the path of the morning express from Inverness to London, which is coming round the curve into the station 'at a thousand miles an hour'. He is 'knocked into bloody atoms'. He who, we are told in the first chapter came from nowhere returns to oblivion.

The description of Tenway Junction and Lopez's suicide reveals an unexpectedly Dickensian aspect to Trollope's genius, recalling as it does Carker's symbolically charged death in *Dombey and Son*. There are added felicities: traditionally, suicides were buried in unhallowed ground at crossroads, and what more impressive crossroads has the world ever seen than this? There are, however, some baffling elements in the scene. As has been noted, Trollope opens with the declaration that it is unnecessary to describe something which he then proceeds to describe at great length. Baffling again is the assertion that 'It is quite unnecessary to describe the Tenway Junction, *as everybody knows it.*' Not every reader does. Elsewhere, to my chagrin, I have identified Tenway as Clapham Junction, which is clearly wrong, since Tenway is specifically indicated as being to the north of London and Clapham lies due south.[1] It must, presumably, be the Grand Junction at Willesden, in Middlesex: the point at which the (then privatized) Great Western, North London, London and North West, and Midland lines converged as they entered and left the Greater London network. (This identification is correctly made by the World's Classics editor, Jennifer Uglow.)

Most baffling, why does Trollope not give 'Tenway' its proper name? The pseudonym is not very brilliant (as Henry James pointed out, unlike his master, Thackeray, Trollope was not gifted in the 'science of names'). And pseudonymy jars with the accuracy of the earlier description of Lopez's night and morning peregrinations through London—all that cartographically exact business about Trafalgar Square, the Strand, and Baker Street. It may be, of course, that Trollope did not want to inspire copy-cat suicides. The Victorian was not as litigious an age as ours, but it may also be that Trollope did not want to libel the Willesden station-master by suggesting that his precautions against injury to passengers were insufficient.[2]

Plausible as these motives may be, it is more likely that Trollope fictionalized Willesden Junction for artistic reasons. Tenway Junction is not merely a busy railway station, any more than the great concourse which Thackeray describes in 'Before the Curtain' (in *Vanity Fair*) is merely a London street fair. Both are allegories of Victorian society. When he wrote *The Prime Minister* Trollope was well aware that his own death was not far off. He had given up the hunting he loved, and his health was failing. Like Lopez, he was standing on the edge of his own mortality. What Trollope desired at the climax of his narrative was a scene which should transcend the mere accidents of London topography. He wanted—like the hero of one of Browning's great monologues—to outreach himself, to exceed, for once, the Trollopian.

The Oxford World's Classics *The Prime Minister* is edited by Jennifer Uglow, with an introduction by John McCormick.

Was he Popenjoy?

Question-marks are everywhere in *Is he Popenjoy?*. They figure on the cover, at the head of chapters, and throughout the text. Questions are profusely interpolated into the authorial commentary and characters interrogate themselves and others constantly. There are, as I count them, some 1,175 question-marks speckling the narrative of *Is he Popenjoy?*. For what the statistic is worth, *Barchester Towers*, written twenty years earlier and much the same length, has only 626.

The big question, of course, is the titular one. In the novel as it opens, Mary Lovelace, the daughter of an amiably combative Dean (only a generation away from 'trade'), marries the younger son of an aristocratic family, Lord George Germain: Although he is not the heir, Lord George has very great expectations. His elder brother (by some ten years), the Marquis of Brotherton, lives in Italy, is in poor health, has dissolute habits, and is unmarried. Even if he does not himself inherit, Lord George may reasonably expect his son to do so. Heirs-apparent to the Marquisate are graced with the title 'Lord Popenjoy'. The Dean lives in eager expectation of having a Popenjoy as his grandchild.

George and Mary marry in June. An announcement is sent to the Marquis in Italy. He has 'never been a good correspondent' (i. 18), but the Marquis does on this occasion honour his brother with a communication of some three of four lines, indicating that (after his ten-year absence abroad) he may soon return to England, and that he will require George to vacate the grand family house. This is a blow; George is not rich, and he, his mother and sisters have grown used to occupying Manor Cross.

Then, 'about the middle of October', comes a bombshell in the form of a longer letter from Brotherton:

My Dear George,

I am to be married to the Marchesa Luigi. Her name is Catarina Luigi, and she is a widow. As to her age, you can ask her yourself when you see her, if you dare. I haven't dared. I suppose her to be ten years younger than myself I did not expect that it would be so, but she says now that she would like to live in England. Of course I've always meant to go back myself some day. I don't suppose we shall be there before May, but we must have the house got ready. (i. 51)

In addition to the distress of having to move into much less grand new accommodation, the letter also raises the possibility that the Marquis, with a ten-year-younger (i.e. in her thirties) wife, may well produce a Popenjoy.

Around November; at a dinner party in London, Mary hears more about the Marchesa, her new sister-in-law, from her neighbour at table, the middle-aged spinster, Miss Houghton:

'So the Marquis is coming,' [Miss Houghton] said. 'I knew the Marquis years ago . . . So he has married?'

'Yes; an Italian.'

'I did not think he would ever marry. It makes a difference to you—does it not?'

'I don't think of such things.'

'You will not like him, for he is the very opposite to Lord George . . . Have you heard about this Italian lady?'

'Only that she is an Italian lady.'

'He is about my age. If I remember rightly, there is hardly a month or two between us. She is three or four years older.'

'You knew her then?'

'I knew of her. I have been curious enough to inquire, which is, I dare say, more than anybody has done at Manor Cross.'

'And is she so old?'

'And a widow. They have been married, you know, over twelve months; nearly two years, I believe.'

'Surely not; we heard of it only since our own marriage.'

'Exactly; but the Marquis was always fond of a little mystery. It was the news of your marriage that made him hint at the possibility of such a thing; and he did not tell the fact till he had made up his mind to come home. I do not know that he has told all now.'

'What else is there?'

'He has a baby—a boy.' (i. 123–4)

Thus, through the malicious obliquities of social gossip, is the awful truth discovered. The Marquis (who told them in October that he was *going to be* married) has, it now emerges, actually been married for two years and has had an heir for twelve months. The lady is not, as he said in his letter, ten years younger than he, but a little older (i.e. well into her forties). At least there should be no more than the one child.

Lord George is appalled by the news—less for the confusion of his ambitions than at the bad manners of it all. The Marquis has not even told his mother, the dowager Marchioness, that she has a grandson. On his part the Dean is wildly suspicious. The mystery is compounded by reports in the newspapers, shortly before the Marquis's return with his new family. In one paper it is reported that the Marchesa Luigi, now the Marchioness of Brotherton, had been born in Orsini. In another paper it is reported 'that she had been divorced from her late husband' (i. 172). The Marquis's English agent is instructed, by telegram from Florence, to issue a public denial that the Marchioness is a divorced woman.

The Brothertons arrive at the end of April, a little sooner than planned. As they progress from the railway station to Manor Cross, 'the world of Brotherton saw them, and the world of Brotherton observed that the lady was very old and very ugly' (i. 199). The family are not permitted even to be introduced to the new Marchioness, nor view the baby. Dark suspicions gather: 'it was very odd that the marriage should have been concealed, and almost more than odd that an heir to the title should have been born without any announcement of such a birth' (i. 217). When pressed by a reluctant George on the matter, however, the Marquis airily observes that 'It's lucky that I have the certificated proof of the date of my marriage, isn't it?' (i. 218)—without actually producing this vital proof. When, belatedly, the young 'Popenjoy' is allowed to be seen by his English relatives, the child seems to Lord George 'to be nearly two years old. The child was carried in by the woman, but Lord George thought that he was big enough to have walked' (i. 228). If he is two years old, he must be either illegitimate or barely legitimate, assuming the marriage itself to have taken place two years earlier. But then, in his October letter, six months since, the Marquis clearly stated that he intended to get married, not that he had been already for some time a married man and a father. It is all very baffling.

The Dean, of course, has convinced himself that this 'Italian brat' who stands in the way of his daughter's ennoblement is illegitimate and that there has been criminal skulduggery. Lord George is prevailed on to write a letter, demanding from the Marquis some 'absolute evidence of the date of your marriage, of its legality, and of the birth of your son' (i. 251). The matter is put in the hands of a lawyer, the aptly named Mr Battle. Battle discovers that 'The Marchioness's late husband—for she doubtless is his lordship's wife—was a lunatic.' The plot thickens with the possibility of an earlier annulment. Battle continues, 'we do not quite know when he [the lunatic husband] died, but we believe it was about a month

or two before the date at which his lordship wrote home to
say that he was about to be married.' Then, asserts the
Dean exultantly, the child cannot be legitimate! Not
necessarily so, points out the more prudent lawyer: 'There
may have been a divorce.' There is 'no such thing in Roman
Catholic countries,' retorts the Dean, 'certainly not in
Italy.' The lawyer is not sure, and adds 'I should not wonder if we found that there had been two marriages' (i. 278).
The three men (Lord George, the Dean, Mr Battle) resolve
to send a confidential clerk to Italy, to learn all the
circumstances of what is evidently a very murky case.

The information which the lawyer's emissary brings
back from Italy is perplexing. The Marquis, as suspected,
had gone through two marriage ceremonies, 'one before
the death, and one after the death, of her first reputed
husband'. There was no divorce. But, 'Mr Battle was
inclined, from all that he had learned, to believe that the
Marchioness had never really been married at all to the
man whose name she had first borne, and that the second
marriage had been celebrated merely to save appearances'
(ii. 35). Enquiries have been made 'at very great expense'.
But no final determination can be made: 'the Luigi family
[i.e. the family of the insane first partner] say that there
was no marriage. Her family say that there was, but cannot
prove it' (ii. 36).

Lord George is sufficiently convinced to give up the
fight, although the Dean remains obdurate. The problem
is finally solved by 'Popenjoy' dying. Contemplating his
son's death (which he discovers affects him more than he
expected), the Marquis remains bitter and venomous to
the end. He confides to Mr De Baron, 'I'll go on living as
long as I can keep body and soul together', adding:

'Poor little boy! . . . Upon my soul, I don't know whether he was
legitimate or not, according to English fashions.' Mr De Baron
stared. 'They had something to stand upon, but—damn it—they

went about it in such a dirty way! It don't matter now, you know, but you needn't repeat all this '

'Not a word,' said Mr De Baron, wondering why such a communication should have been made to him.

'And there was plenty of ground for a good fight. I hardly know whether she had been married or not. I never could quite find out.' Again Mr De Baron stared. 'It's all over now.'

'But if you were to have another son?'

'Oh! we're married now! There were two ceremonies.' (ii. 202)

This is the closest we ever come to a clear determination on the great question. Even the Marquis himself does not know whether his son was legitimate or not; or whether his wife is a bigamist. Nor did he ever know. Nor, apparently, will he ever know. Had the matter gone to trial, litigation would certainly have dragged on inconclusively for years. The question-mark attached to the title of the novel is as firmly attached at the end as it was at the beginning. Only the tense has changed. 'Was he Popenjoy?'—who can say?

Why did Trollope not close this gap, as he easily could have done? It is not his habit to leave such loose ends in his fiction. If ever a novelist liked tidy denouements, it was Anthony Trollope. The explanation is to be found, I suggest, in the dates of the novel's composition—12 October 1874 to 3 May 1875. The novel's title, as the Introduction to the World's Classics edition stresses, is highly topical. It alludes, as readers of the 1870s would immediately have picked up, to the absorbing question of the day: 'Is he Tichborne?' In 1854 Roger, the young heir to the Tichborne baronetcy and estates, had been drowned (as it was thought) at sea. Sir Roger's mother, a weak-minded lady, clung to the belief that her son was still alive. Her advertisements for information about her son were answered in 1865 by an apparent impostor, Arthur Orton, alias Thomas Castro—a loutish butcher from Wagga Wagga. With extraordinary effrontery, Castro came to

England to claim 'his' title and fortune. The family (except for the besotted mother) saw through Castro at once. He was brought to court first to eject him from his usurped title, then on charges of perjury. The case lasted from May 1871 to March 1874. In the way that some crimes do, 'Is he Tichborne?' caught the imagination of the British public. Orton won extraordinary sympathy among the English lower classes. There were public demonstrations and near-riots on his behalf in January 1874. Nevertheless—six months before Trollope began writing *Is he Popenjoy?*—the 'claimant' (as he was universally called) was found guilty, and sentenced to fourteen years' penal servitude.

Had the matter ended at this point, with Orton (Tichborne?) disposed of, Trollope might well have given the reader a clear answer to the 'Is he Popenjoy?' question in his ongoing novel. But the affair did not end in March 1874. In January 1875, with the opening of the new session of Parliament, the claimant's supporters introduced a slew of questions, notices, and petitions seeking a pardon for 'that unhappy nobleman now languishing in prison'.[1] They demanded a Royal Commission (a request that was contemptuously voted down by the House) and accused the judges who had passed sentence of being unfair to their man ('Sir Roger', as they obstinately maintained). Outside Parliament controversy also raged. On 29 March several thousand persons marched in procession with banners and music to Hyde Park for the purpose of making a demonstration in favour of the claimant.

All this put Trollope in something of a quandary. On his part, he had no doubts that the claimant was an impostor and his supporters fools and rogues.[2] But on 1 March he left England by boat for Australia. It was on board that he was obliged to write the last chapters of *Is he Popenjoy?*, finishing on 1 May, the day before landing at Melbourne. All this time he was effectively incommunicado, unable to get recent London papers. What might have happened in the meanwhile? Perhaps all the furore between January and March might have resulted in the verdict being overthrown? Perhaps Orton might have been shown by some legal *coup de théâtre* to be Sir Roger after all? Trollope, as his ship forged through the far Pacific, simply did not know how the 'Is he Tichborne?' question would be answered. Accordingly, the Popenjoy question is left similarly undecided.

The Oxford World's Classics *Is He Popenjoy?* is edited by John Sutherland.

====

R. H. Hutton's spoiling hand

====

The original text of *The Portrait of a Lady* has what is arguably the most delicately understated ending in all Victorian fiction. Isabel has at last come to a true appreciation of her husband, Osmond, and sees a straight path in front of her. In full consciousness of his moral worthlessness, and the worthiness of her loyal suitor, Caspar Goodwood, she has made a decision. The reader is not directly informed what that decision is. Osmond is meanwhile in Italy, and Isabel has been staying in London with her friend, Henrietta:

Two days afterwards Caspar Goodwood knocked at the door of the house in Wimpole Street in which Henrietta Stackpole occupied furnished lodgings. He had hardly removed his hand from the knocker when the door was opened and Miss Stackpole herself stood before him. She had on her hat and jacket; she was on the point of going out. 'Oh, good morning,' he said, 'I was in hopes I should find Mrs Osmond.'

Henrietta kept him waiting a moment for her reply; but there was a good deal of expression about Miss Stackpole even when she was silent. 'Pray what led you to suppose she was here?'

'I went down to Gardencourt this morning, and the servant told me she had come to London. He believed she was to come to you.'

Again Miss Stackpole held him—with an intention of perfect kindness—in suspense. 'She came here yesterday, and spent the night. But this morning she started for Rome.'

Caspar Goodwood was not looking at her; his eyes were fastened on the doorstep. 'Oh, she started—?' he stammered. And without finishing his phrase or looking up he stiffly averted himself. But he couldn't otherwise move.

Henrietta had come out, closing the door behind her, and now she put out her hand and grasped his arm. 'Look here, Mr Goodwood,' she said; 'just you wait!'

On which he looked up at her . . .

As originally published, the novel ends with Caspar's perplexed gaze into Henrietta's face—and very effective the ending is. Most readers assume that Isabel has of course gone back to Osmond. This is a willed, moral, unselfish, hugely courageous, 'ladylike' action. In her article 'Two Problems in *The Portrait of a Lady*', Dorothea Krook is contemptuous of any other construction which might be wished on to the end of James's novel by weak-minded readers:

Why does Isabel go back to Osmond? This problem has, I believe, been somewhat artificially created for modern critics by a failure in critical perspective which arises from the disposition to ignore or minimize the context, historical and dramatic, in which Isabel Archer's final decision is made. I have heard it seriously argued that Isabel 'could after all have done something else'—walked out into freedom (like Nora in *A Doll's House*, presumably), or gone in for charitable works (like Dorothea Brooke in *Middlemarch*), or even perhaps taken a degree and become a pioneer in women's education, or whatever. The short answer to these bracing proposals is that Isabel Archer could have done none of these things. Her circumstances, historical, psychological, and dramatic—in particular the dramatic—absolutely prescribe any 'end' to her life other than marriage, and any duties, responsibilities or even serious interests other than those belonging to or arising out of that estate.[1]

Interestingly, Krook does not even consider; among the absurd alternatives open to Isabel, the absurdest of all: adultery or 'open sexual union' with Caspar. Yet this is one of the possible interpretations of Henrietta's 'Just you wait!'—that is, 'don't worry, she'll come back and then you two can get together at last'.

This may seem a far-fetched gloss to the last paragraphs of the 1881 *The Portrait of a Lady*. But this is precisely how the ending was misread in one of the most important reviews the novel received on its first appearance, that in the *Spectator* (unsigned, November 1881), by Richard Holt Hutton. 'Never before', Hutton thunderously declared in the peroration to his long piece, 'has Mr James closed a novel by setting up quite so cynical a sign-post into the abyss, as he sets up at the close of this book':

He ends his *Portrait of a Lady*, if we do not wholly misinterpret the rather covert, not to say almost cowardly, hints of his last page, by calmly indicating that this ideal lady of his, whose belief in purity has done so much to alienate her from her husband, in that it had made him smart under her contempt for his estimates of the world, saw a 'straight path' to a liaison with her rejected lover. And worse still, it is apparently intended that this is the course sanctioned both by her high-minded friend, Miss Stack-pole, and by the dying cousin whose misfortune had been to endow her with wealth that proved fatal to her happiness.

Hutton delivered himself of much more in the same appalled vein, concluding with: 'We can hardly speak too highly of the skill and genius shown in many parts of *The Portrait of a Lady*. We can hardly speak too depreciatingly of the painting of that portrait itself, or of the moral collapse into which the original of the portrait is made to fall.'[2]

For most modern readers, the idea that Isabel is intending an eventual extra-marital liaison ('moral collapse') is grotesque. Hutton clearly does 'misinterpret' the last page in the most disastrous way. Yet, just as clearly, James worried about this misinterpretation. If an intelligent reader and former of public opinion like Hutton could go wrong, so might multitudes of others, When he revised the novel, together with all his major fiction, in 1908, he added the following postscript to the 1881 ending:

. . . 'just you wait!'

On which he looked up at her—but only to guess, from her face, with a revulsion, that she simply meant he was young. She stood shining at him with that cheap comfort, and it added, on the spot, thirty years to his life. She walked him away with her, however, as if she had given him now the key to patience.[3]

No one reading this version of the text could fall into Hutton's error. James here obliterates the remotest possibility that Isabel will ever throw in her lot with Goodwood. All that Henrietta means by her final instruction ('just you wait!') is that Caspar must be patient, and someone else will come into his life. He has many years ahead of him. It is hard not to feel that a fine Jamesian effect has been lost in order to achieve the corrective, unequivocal stress that the author felt was necessary.

Oddly enough, if Hutton were mounting the endings of major Victorian novels on his wall as trophies, *The Portrait of a Lady* would be joined by *Middlemarch*. The final two paragraphs of George Eliot's 'Study of Provincial Life' are as famous as anything she wrote. Never did the author achieve a more resounding tone of moral authority as—Godlike—she pronounced on the human condition in the middle years of the nineteenth century. None the less, Eliot clearly had authorial doubts about her concluding remarks. As David Carroll reveals in his World's Classics edition, not only did she have second thoughts while composing (see p. 707), she also made her most significant textual alterations in revised editions of *Middlemarch* to these last two paragraphs. Notably, she made a major excision in post-1874 versions of the novel (marked here by square brackets and italics):

Certainly those determining acts of [Dorothea's] life were not ideally beautiful. They were the mixed result of a young and noble impulse struggling amidst the conditions of an imperfect social state, in which great feelings will often take the aspect of error, and great faith the aspect of illusion [*They were the mixed result of young and noble impulse struggling under prosaic conditions. Among the many remarks passed on her mistakes, it was never said in the neighbourhood of Middlemarch that such mistakes could not have happened if the society into which she was born had not smiled on propositions of marriage from a sickly man to a girl less than half his own age—on modes of education which make a woman's knowledge another name for motley ignorance—on rules of conduct which are in flat contradiction with its own loudly-asserted beliefs. While this is the social air in which mortals begin to breathe, there will be collisions such as those in Dorothea's life, where in which great feelings will often take the aspect of error, and great faith the aspect of illusion.*] For there is no creature whose inward being is so strong that it is not greatly determined by what lies outside it. A new Theresa will hardly have the opportunity of reforming a conventual life, any more than a new Antigone will spend her heroic piety in daring all for the sake of a brother's burial: the medium in which their ardent deeds took shape is for ever gone. But we insignificant people with our daily words and acts are preparing the lives of many Dorotheas, some of which may present a far sadder sacrifice than that of the Dorothea whose story we know.

Her finely-touched spirit had still its fine issues, though they were not widely visible. Her full nature, like that river of which Cyrus broke the strength, spent itself in channels which had no great name on the earth. But the effect of her being on those around her was incalculably diffusive: for the growing good of the world is partly dependent on unhistoric acts; and that things are not so ill with you and me as they might have been, is half owing to the number who lived faithfully a hidden life, and rest in unvisited tombs. (pp. 682, 707–8)

As the editor of the Penguin Classics *Middlemarch*, Rosemary Ashton, records, Eliot made this substantial change 'after recognizing that those critics [notably Richard Holt Hutton] were right who pointed out that Middlemarch society did not smile on Mr Casaubon's proposal'. Hutton

was thinking about such things as Mrs Cadwallader's
sarcasms in Chapter 6 about the ill-assorted marriage.

Hutton had reviewed the serial parts *of Middlemarch* as
they came out, in the *Spectator*, of which he was literary
editor. He also reviewed the whole novel when it was published entire in December 1872.[4] He claimed to admire
Eliot's achievement intensely. But he had doubts about
the last paragraphs. Robert Tener and Malcolm Woodfield
sum up Hutton's mixed feelings, and the seriousness with
which Eliot took them:

As Rosemary Ashton has shown, George Eliot's tone of irony
towards her heroine disappears as the novel progresses until, in
the Finale, Dorothea's disappointed life is blamed on 'the society
which smiled on propositions of marriage from a sickly man to a
girl less than half his own age.' Hutton was the first to point out
the change of perspective (since, far from 'smiling' on the marriage, Dorothea's friends utterly disapproved of it). Following his
objection, George Eliot paid Hutton the ultimate compliment,
one which she afforded no other critic before or after, of cutting
the passage from the 1874 book version, the version on which all
subsequent editions have been based.[5]

As with *The Portrait of a Lady*'s Huttonian postscript,
one may question whether the Huttonian excision from
Middlemarch was artistically correct. It is true that Sir
James Chettam and Mrs Cadwallader are scathing about
an old stick like Casaubon (in his early forties) marrying a
19-year-old girl. Even Mr Brooke, in his ineffectual way,
tries to dissuade his ward. But the fact is that Dorothea is
two years short of the age of consent. Had Mr Brooke and
her other guardians felt that strongly about the match,
they could have forbidden it for twenty-four months with
absolute authority and a clear conscience (Casaubon and
Dorothea are the least likely people in all Victorian fiction
to elope to Gretna Green). They (specifically Mr Brooke)
consented to the match, even if 'smiling on it' may be

slightly too strong a term. And why did they consent? Because Casaubon was a rich man. If he were a poor parson with just his living (that is, if his elder brother had not died, leaving him the wealthy heir of Lowick) there is no doubt but that Mr Brooke would have put his foot down very firmly. Eliot's essential point remains valid and could easily have been covered by toning down 'smiled on' to 'acquiesced in'.

There is another reason for regretting the excision. It is not just the one comment about sickly men marrying girls less than half their age which is removed. Eliot also took out the remark about 'modes of education which make a woman's knowledge another name for motley ignorance'. By removing this aggressive note of feminist protest, Eliot effectively depoliticized her ending. It represents a loss, since one of the sharpest themes in *Middlemarch* is that women's education must be improved if English society is to get the best from its women. Not to make this point explicitly and with force is to muffle a conclusion which the novelist has worked hard for.

Finally, there is the rather mysterious remark which Eliot modified about great feelings 'colliding' with society's 'loudly-asserted beliefs' about 'rules of conduct', thus presenting to crasser minds the aspect of error. I would guess that what Eliot is thinking about here is her own unsanctified union with G. H. Lewes. Technically, she and Lewes were living in sin. This is what small-minded contemporaries said about them and, as Gordon Haight records in his biography, 'Mr and Mrs Lewes' (as they liked to be known) encountered persistent social ostracism for their having sacrificed conventional decencies to their 'great feelings'.[6]

In general, Hutton's approach to narrative is one which will be congenial to many readers. He was a close and often bloody-minded scrutinizer of the text, forever looking for nooks and crannies into which to introduce a pedantic or a downright perverse interpretation. But I would suspect that George Eliot was not driven to make her massive (for such it is) change to the conclusion of *Middlemarch* merely because Hutton had perceived a slight contradiction between what was said in the penultimate paragraph and what had been said by some second-rank characters in Chapter 6. What alarmed her was the fact that someone as authoritative as the literary editor of the *Spectator* was looking so closely at the last sentences of her novel. So as not to confuse the moral peroration with secondary distractions, she purged her conclusion not just of its small narrative anomaly (which did not in fact require anything more than a change of phrase) but of its sexual politics and a significant measure of its personal import.

Both Eliot and James made the claim, common enough with great novelists, that the opinions of the critics meant nothing to them. But it is unarguable that in the above instances the reviewer's opinions were not just registered, they were deferred to. Of the millions of twentieth-century readers who have read *Middlemarch* in its post-1874 version and *The Portrait of a Lady* in its post-1908 version, probably less than one in ten thousand could say who Richard Holt Hutton was. And yet, for all time, his messy fingerprints will be all over the conclusions to these novels.

The Oxford World's Classics *The Portrait of a Lady* is edited by Nicola Bradbury.

R. L. Stevenson · *Dr Jekyll and Mr Hyde*

═══

What does Edward Hyde look like?

═══

Say 'Jekyll and Hyde', and the person you are speaking to will see in the mind's eye Spencer Tracy's amiably pudgy features dissolving into the monstrous physiognomy of Edward Hyde. The transformation is one of the high-points of early Hollywood special effects and close-up camera artistry. The World's Classics volume pays tribute to the 1941 film by carrying on its cover a still photograph of Tracy in his Hyde make-up.[1] Thanks to the film, when they think of Jekyll and Hyde modern readers see a face very vividly and in great detail. One of the puzzles in Stevenson's source text, however, is that where Hyde's face ought to be in the narrative there is a blank—rather like the facial features technologically fuzzed out in television documentaries and newscasts 'to protect the innocent'. What precisely was Stevenson's motive for doing this?

The numerous descriptions of Edward Hyde in the narrative agree on a number of points: (1) he is physically small; (2) he is a 'gentleman'; (3) he is young; (4) he is, in some unspecified way, 'deformed'. Jekyll, by contrast, is 'a large, well-made, smooth-faced man of fifty', possessed of a 'large handsome face' (pp. 22–3). The first eyewitness description which we are given of Hyde arises out of the 3 a.m. outrage when he tramples a little girl in the London street (only children and the very aged are at risk from Edward Hyde, who is not, it seems, inclined to tackle fully grown, physically active adults). According to Mr Enfield, the assailant is 'a little man'. That he is also a 'gentleman' is testified to by his having a bank account at

Coutts and his evening dress. Enfield gives no description of the monster's face, but recalls that it was his manner, his 'black sneering coolness', which infuriated the onlookers. Describing the nasty episode to Utterson, Enfield strikes what is to be a recurrent note in response to the question 'What sort of man is he to see?' He is not easy to describe, Enfield recalls:

There is something wrong with his appearance; something displeasing, something downright detestable. I never saw a man I so disliked, and yet I scarce know why. He must be deformed somewhere; he gives a strong feeling of deformity, although I couldn't specify the point. He's an extraordinary looking man, and yet I really can name nothing out of the way. No, sir; I can make no hand of it; I can't describe him. And it's not want of memory; for I declare I can see him at this moment. (p. 12)

Playing the part of 'Mr Seek', Utterson himself comes across Mr Hyde in the streets after one of his horrible nocturnal adventures. The encounter produces the following Identikit picture: 'He was small and very plainly dressed, and the look of him ... went somehow strongly against the watcher's inclination ... Mr Hyde was pale and dwarfish, he gave an impression of deformity without any nameable malformation' (pp. 17–19). Later, arising out of the Carew murder case, the anonymous maidservant who witnessed the crime describes 'a very small gentleman'. This is the best she can do, although she manages a fuller description of Sir Danvers Carew, MP, 'an aged and beautiful gentleman with white hair'. What colour, then, was Hyde's hair? Evidently her eyes are sharp enough to pick up such detail, but something prevents her 'seeing' the assailant. Her identification is exclusively moral: the murderer was 'particularly small and particularly wicked looking' (pp. 25–7). The chapter ends with another highly charged passage which expatiates on Hyde's inscrutability, his powerful nonentity:

He had numbered few familiars . . . his family could nowhere be traced; he had never been photographed; and the few who could describe him differed widely, as common observers will. Only on one point, were they agreed; and that was the haunting sense of unexpressed deformity with which the fugitive impressed his beholders. (p. 29)

It is worth pausing here because, over the last fifty years, Mr Hyde has been very widely 'photographed'—that is to say, he has been depicted in innumerable films and television adaptations. These versions of Mr Hyde invariably agree on what he looks like: simian, excessively hairy, thick-lipped, beetle-browed, swarthy, middle-aged, and physically massive (see the World's Classics cover). One of the 'artist's impressions' loved by newspapers would be very easy to draw up. None the less, in Stevenson's source narrative Hyde continues through the middle and later stages shrouded in physical and physiognomic vagueness. There is, for instance, the strange episode in which Jekyll's servant sees Edward Hyde in his master's laboratory and assumes that—like the Elephant Man—he wears 'a mask upon his face' (p. 45). His subsequent description is as unhelpful as those of all the other witnesses have been ('When that masked thing like a monkey jumped from among the chemicals and whipped into the cabinet, it went down my spine like ice'). When, in the climax of the melo-drama, Dr Lanyon confronts Edward Hyde face to face, any clear description of the monster is once again withheld:

Here, at last, I had a chance of clearly seeing him. I [Lanyon is writing] had never set eyes on him before, so much was certain. He was small, as I have said; I was struck besides with the shocking expression of his face, with his remarkable combination of great muscular activity and great apparent debility of constitution, and—last but not least—with the odd, subjective disturbance caused by his neighbourhood. (p. 56)

On his part, looking at the twitching dying visage of Hyde, Utterson declares, 'the cords of his face still moved with a semblance of life, but life was quite gone' (p. 49). All this tells us is that Hyde is possessed of a face. What that face's lineaments or features are we can only guess.

The sum of the physiognomic description which we are given is very unsatisfactory. The only concrete detail we have is that Hyde's face is 'pale', which does not much help the mind's eye picture him. Henry Jekyll's own final testament adds one small detail, which has been eagerly seized on by film-makers. It occurs during an unwilled metamorphosis when, to his horror, Dr Jekyll discovers he has changed personality during a 'comfortable morning doze':

I was still so engaged when, in one of my more wakeful moments, my eye fell upon my hand. Now the hand of Henry Jekyll (as you have often remarked) was professional in shape and size: it was large, firm, white and comely. But the hand which I now saw, clearly enough, in the yellow light of a mid-London morning, lying half shut on the bed clothes, was lean, corded, knuckly, of a dusky pallor and thickly shaded with a swart growth of hair. It was the hand of Edward Hyde. (pp. 66–7)

Taking this cue, special-effects departments have gone straight for the box marked 'Werewolf'. In the famous Lon Chaney movie, the hero is seen by the technique of stop-frame photography transmuting in front of the camera's eye from respectable middle-class man to disgusting hairy monster. So, too, does Spencer Tracy transmute in the film, *Jekyll and Hyde*. In fact, there is no warrant for assuming a hairy, monstrous Hyde. This is the only reference to hairiness which we are given. There are many more countervailing references in the text to his being 'pale' and 'childlike'; It may well be that a distraught Jekyll is not seeing himself clearly at this point—he may be hallucinating. It is more likely that Hyde now looks different from what he initially did. Jekyll goes on to say in his 'Statement of the Case':

That part of me which I had the power of projecting, had lately been much exercised and nourished; it had seemed to me of late as though the body of Edward Hyde had grown in stature, as though (when I wore that form) I were conscious of a more generous tide of blood . . . (p. 67)

Following the logic of this statement, Mr Hyde should be conceived as changing from young, hairless, juvenile monster in his early manifestations to the hirsute, middle-aged, bulkier monster of his last appearance. No such distinction is traditionally made in film versions. To summarize: there are, it seems, some very good photographs of Mr Hyde—but they are not Stevenson's. In his album there is a perfect blank, apart from the tantalizing snapshot of one enigmatic hand.

The Oxford World's Classics *Dr Jekyll and Mr Hyde* is edited by Emma Letley.

===

Who is Alexander's father?

===

The main element in Robert Louis Stevenson's mind as he embarked on *The Master of Ballantrae* was the idea of an old Scottish family hedging its bets at the time of the 1745 Revolution by dispatching one son to serve with the Pretender while another son remained at home, a loyal servant of King George. Stevenson had an actual historical case in mind.[1] It is, in the story, quite arbitrary which brother will join the rebels. The question is decided by the flip of coin, as are other crucial decisions in the Durie brothers' careers. But what began as an eminently sensible hedging of bets returns as a curse which haunts and eventually destroys the House of Durrisdeer and Ballantrae.

An early, discarded title for the new novel was 'Brothers'. Another was 'The Familiar Incubus'. The incubus in *The Master of Ballantrae* is self-evidently James—the elder brother (or 'Master') who is 'killed' first at Culloden, then in the duel with his brother, and finally in the frozen Adirondacks. On each occasion he rises from the grave to haunt his brother Henry ('Jacob', as he tauntingly calls him, for having stolen the birthright of Esau). The Master, James, finally dies only after he has succeeded in frightening his luckless victim into dying first. It is a surreal conception. And one can perhaps track its meaning by looking more closely into the meaning of 'incubus'. Its primary sense is, as the *OED* tells us: 'A feigned evil spirit or demon, supposed to descend upon persons in their sleep, and especially to seek carnal intercourse with women.' Sexual predatoriness is the salient characteristic of the incubus. One of the most masterly elements in the telling of this most obliquely narrated of tales is the way in which RLS manœuvres the reader into calculations and reckonings which 'prove' adultery, illegitimacy and incest. These things are never actually made clear, but the reader, almost unwillingly, cannot but be conscious of them.

The narrative of *The Master of Ballantrae* opens with the protestation by Ephraim Mackellar that he will give the world 'The full truth of this odd matter'. A couple of pages later, it is made clear that where the 'full truth' is concerned, Mr Mackellar can sometimes be less than forthcoming. Of the early scapegrace history of James (the elder, and from childhood the more wayward of the brothers) he writes:

> One very black mark he had to his name; but the matter was hushed up at the time, and so defaced by legends before I came into those parts that I scruple to set it down. If it was true, it was a horrid fact in one so young; and if false, it was a horrid calumny. (p. 11)

What this 'black mark' is, we never learn. It must be something more than merely spawning bastards and spurning their mothers (Ephraim is later forthcoming enough on that score). Something of the order of rape or murder seems to be alluded to.

The Durie brothers are brought up in the same household with Alison Graeme, 'a near kinswoman, an orphan, and the heir to a considerable fortune'. She and James fall in love, and—we may assume—possibly their love has been consummated. The Master is not one to rein his appetites back in such matters. After the flip of the coin, which decides that James shall join the rebels, the following exchange occurs between the Master and his young mistress:

'If you loved me as well as I love you, you would have stayed', cried she.

'"I could not love you, dear, so well, loved I not honour more",' sang the Master.

'O!' she cried, 'you have no heart—I hope you may be killed!' and she ran from the room, and in tears, to her own chamber. (p. 13)

James goes off to fight with the Pretender, and is reported to have been killed at Culloden. In her grief, Alison upbraids Henry: 'There is none but me to know one thing—that you were a traitor to him in your heart' (p. 16). The significance of this remark is obscure, like much of the sexual underplot of this story.

Although he inherits the estate, Henry is much maligned. Survivors of the Jacobite faction in the neighbourhood call him 'Judas'. As Ephraim recalls: 'One trollop, who had had a child to the Master [i.e. James], and by all accounts very badly used, yet made herself a kind of champion of his memory. She flung a stone one day at Mr Henry' (p.18). The trollop, Jessie Broun, witnesses to the sexual ruthlessness of James, and his none the less irresistible attraction to the women he preys on.

'Miss Alison's money was highly needful for the estates' (p. 16), Ephraim, the steward, notes. Marriage will ensure the survival of the house. In what may be gratitude for the shelter she has received over the years, Alison finally accepts Henry's proposal with the bleak statement: 'I bring you no love, Henry; but God knows, all the pity in the world' (p. 20). They marry, as Ephraim precisely records, on 1 June 1748. By the end of December, as he again precisely records, Alison's baby is 'due in about six weeks' (p. 22). The conjunction of dates is a clear instruction to the reader to do some reckoning. If the marriage took place on 1 June and the baby is due in mid-February (giving an interval of some eight months) one assumes that the child was conceived just before the wedding or on the wedding-night itself.

The first child is a daughter, Katherine, and the birth is harrowingly difficult. Unusually for the period, Henry chose to be present at the delivery, 'as white (they tell me) as a sheet and the sweat dropping from his brow; and the handkerchief he had in his hand was crushed into a little ball no bigger than a musket bullet' (p. 32). Afterwards, we learn, he has difficulty in showing any tenderness towards his little daughter Katherine. Nor is the relationship between man and wife harmonious. As Ephraim tells us:

Mrs Henry had a manner of condescension with him [Henry], such as (in a wife) would have pricked my vanity into an ulcer; he took it like a favour. She held him at the staff's end; forgot and then remembered and unbent to him, as we do to children; burthened him with cold kindness; reproved him with a change of colour and a bitten lip, like one shamed by his disgrace; ordered him with a look of the eye, when she was off her guard; when she was on the watch, pleaded with him for the most natural attentions, as though they were unheard-of favours. (pp. 31–2)

On 7 April 1749 what little serenity the Durie household enjoys is shattered by the arrival of Francis Burke, with the appalling news that James is not, after all, dead but alive in France. 'The seductive Miss Alison', as Burke provocatively calls her, faints when she hears the news (p. 34). There follows the long leeching of money from the estate to the wastrel across the water. News of James's survival also brings about a palpable change in Mrs Henry, what Ephraim calls 'a certain deprecation towards her husband' (p. 74). He, on his part, is tormented by what he conceives to be her 'truant fancies'—that is, a continuing love for James. What is most significant is that there are no more children after Katherine. Ephraim several times alludes to 'estrangement' and, the reader presumes, sexual relations between husband and wife have been suspended. So it goes on for seven years, during which period the estate is bled of £8,000.

On 7 November 1756 James returns. His family still fondly imagine that he is a political exile, in danger of his life should he be discovered. 'Mister Bally', as he is called, taunts and insults Henry from their first encounter. He reminds Ephraim of a cat playing with its prey. Alison, who is visibly affected by the reappearance of her old lover, at first tries to avoid him. Initially, he too seems inclined to keep her at a distance. But, after a furious quarrel with Henry about his refusal to dismiss Ephraim (for refusing, on his part, to drive away the pertinacious trollop Jessie Broun), James's attitude to Alison changes. She, it appears, becomes instrumental in his grand scheme of revenge against his brother. Up to that hour, Ephraim records:

the Master had played a very close game with Mrs Henry; avoiding pointedly to be alone with her, which I took at the time for an effect of decency, but now think to be a most insidious act ... Now all that was to be changed; but whether really in revenge, or because he was wearying of Durrisdeer, and looked about for some diversion, who but the devil shall decide. (pp. 94–5)

There now begins what Ephraim calls 'the siege of Mrs Henry'. James woos her with romantic tales, ballads, and kindness towards little Katherine (whom her father seems unfairly to neglect). 'Presently there came walks in the long shrubbery, talks in the Belvedere, and I know not what tender familiarity' (p. 96). Ephraim may choose not to know, but the reader can easily guess. Alison's infatuation with James is only momentarily cooled by the revelation that he is not—after all—a Jacobite refugee, but a government spy who can move without let or hindrance

between France and England. All the 'Mr Bally' business
was a sham.

Ephraim is convinced that Alison is 'playing very near
the fire' (p. 103) in her intimacy with James. Dark suspicions have formed in his mind, and in those of Mr Henry—
so dark, in fact, that neither man can dare to articulate
them:

> There were times, too, when we talked, and a strange manner of
> talk it was; there was never a person named, nor an individual
> circumstance referred to; yet we had the same matter in our
> minds, and we were each aware of it. It is a strange art that can
> thus he practised: to talk for hours of a thing, and never name
> nor yet so much as hint at it. And I remember I wondered if it
> was by some such natural skill that the Master made love to
> Mrs Henry all day long (as he manifestly did), yet never startled
> her into reserve. (p. 103)

It is, at this point, 26 February 1757, as we learn from
Ephraim's pedantic notation of such matters. The events
of the following night—'the fatal 27th'—occupy a whole
chapter. The evening's tragedy begins with a game of
cards, and too much liquor taken by James, who delivers
himself of a 'stream of insult' against his luckless brother,
'Jacob' (as he tauntingly persists in calling him). There
ensues the crowning insult:

> 'For instance, with all those solid qualities which I delight to
> recognise in you, I never knew a woman who did not prefer me—
> nor, I think', he continued, with the most silken deliberation, 'I
> think—who did not continue to prefer me'. (p. 107)

Henry strikes James, and the inevitable duel takes place
in the long shrubbery. Before they cross swords, James
again alludes to 'your wife—who is in love with me, as you
very well know' (p. 109). In the subsequent fight James
is 'killed', and the woes of the House of Durrisdeer and
Ballantrae begin in earnest.

Not until much later is a crucial date introduced, almost in passing, by Ephraim:

And now there came upon the scene a new character, and one that played his part, too, in the story; I mean the present lord, Alexander, whose birth (17th July, 1757) filled the cup of my poor master's happiness. (p. 139)

Let us review dates at this point. The Duries' first child, Katherine, was born as soon as possible after the marriage on 1 June 1748. Thereafter, for almost nine years, there were no children and—we may suspect—no sexual relations between the 'estranged' husband and wife. On 7 November 1756 James returns to the scene. He is a former lover of Alison (and may have been a lover in the carnal sense). With at least one bastard child, and the mother cruelly cast off, he is no respecter of female persons. He enjoys secret intimacies with his brother's wife in the long shrubbery and elsewhere. On 17 July, some nine months after his arrival and his 'siege' of Alison, Alexander is born. Henry, meanwhile, is so mad with sexual jealousy that he is willing to commit one of the most heinous of primal sins—fratricide.

The dates all point in one direction. So does Ephraim's coyness. It is singular that—during all the period leading up to the 'fateful 27th'—no mention is made of Alison's pregnancy. By March she will be five months pregnant. Her condition must be known—at least to Henry and Ephraim. Why do they not mention it? Because it is one of those things that they dare not even 'hint at'.

The Oxford World's Classics *The Master of Ballantrae* is edited by Emma Letley.

Oscar Wilde · *The Picture of Dorian Gray*

═══

Why does this novel disturb us?

═══

Early critical reaction to *The Picture of Dorian Gray* 'was almost unanimously hysterical', Isobel Murray's introduction to the World's Classics edition tells us.[1] Why? The story would seem to be excessively moralistic—a parable, no less (what shall it profit a man if he keep his good looks and lose his soul?). The homosexual hints are deeply buried beneath Dorian's conventional heterosexual villainies (the seduction of Sibyl Vane, the debauching of society wives, the ruining of young girls, the inhaling of opium). There were enough sops to the straight, late-Victorian world to have kept even Mr Pecksniff happy, one would have thought.

A key to the disturbing quality of *The Picture of Dorian Gray* can be found in the first paragraph of the novel:

The studio was filled with the rich odour of roses, and when the light summer wind stirred amidst the trees of the garden there came through the open door the heavy scent of the lilac, or the more delicate perfume of the pink-flowering thorn. (p. 1)

This is the setting to Dorian's fateful meeting with his evil angel, Lord Henry Wotton, at the studio of his friend, the artist Basil Hallward, for whom he is sitting. The first point to note is the initial emphasis on scent. The chapter continues in the same olfactory vein, with references to Lord Henry's 'innumerable cigarettes', and the 'honey-sweet and honey-coloured blossoms of a laburnum'. These opening sentences fairly reek. The overload of smell references is compounded when we discover that the garden in which the scene is set is actually in central London, which 'roars dimly' in the background, generating its own characteristic repertoire of summer pongs.

Smells are something that the Anglo-Saxon novel is notably deficient in and uneasy about. The whole of Hemingway's fiction does not contain a single smell, as Norman Mailer once reckoned (Mailer likes a good stench in his own narratives). For most novelists in English—particularly in the nineteenth century—smells are indelicate. England has left it to its 'dirty' continental neighbours, particularly the French, to cultivate the arts of the nose in its perfume and wine industry (in which the French bibber is as attentive to aroma as taste). The two greatest novels devoted to the power of smell—Joris-Karl Huysmans' *A Rebours* and Patrick Süsskind's *Perfume*—could never have been written in England, and in translation have never been popular among English readers. Isobel Murray confirms that contemporary English critics condemned *The Picture of Dorian Gray* nose-first. 'Typical of the general outrage', she tells us, 'was an unsigned review in the *Daily Chronicle*, which condemned the novel on all counts, and chiefly as "a poisonous book, the atmosphere of which is heavy with the mephitic odours of moral and spiritual putrefaction"' (p. vii).

The Anglo-Saxon terror of smell is one likely reason why Wilde's novel triggered visceral alarm. Another is the 'unnaturalness' of the horticultural references in the first paragraph and elsewhere. In southern Britain, lilac blossoms and is odoriferous in rainy April, thorn in May ('May' is the common countryside name for it), and roses bloom in blazing mid-June (when, as we are repeatedly told by Wilde, this first chapter is set). It is not inconceivable that the flowers, blooms, and blossoms which Wilde describes (lilac, rose, laburnum, thorn) might just coincide on the branch in mid-June—but not in the full

odoriferousness about which the first chapter is so elo-
quent and which so gratifies Lord Henry.

It is wrong—queer, one might say—that the smell of
blown roses and lilac coincide and that their coincidence
should be repeatedly mentioned throughout the opening
scene of the novel. Sequence has been replaced by a puzzling sychronicity. It is subliminally worrying. Roses, we
instinctively feel, should follow thorn and thorn should
follow lilacs, they should not all merge in this sensory riot,
this nasal orgasm. So too, age should follow youth. But one
of the endeavours of homosexual love, with its cult of the
marvellous boy, is to abolish sequence. This desire to abolish the generational sequences of youth, maturity, and age
is allegorized in *The Picture of Dorian Gray*—the hero is,
at one and the same time, a beautiful boy (the same object
that Hallward worships in the first scene), a mature man
of the world (cultivated, a member of clubs, a brilliant
conversationalist at dinner tables), and a withered old
man (a senility recorded in the portrait secreted in his
attic). *The Picture of Dorian Gray* fantasizes a world
where middle-aged hedonists can be forever boys, equated
in a timeless plane composed half out of lust, half out of
the wish-fulfilling visions of the fairy story. Dorian Gray
is, to play with the word, two kinds of fairy—the Faustian
hero who sells his soul for youth, and the middle-aged,
mutton-dressed-as-lamb gay, who *would* sell his soul to
look young again.

This denial of sequence also operates in the larger
frame of the story's chronology. It is clear that the first
scene and the narrative up to the death of Sibyl take place
in the 1890s. There are unmistakeable cultural references
locating the action in this period. For instance: the cult
of Wagner and Schumann; the young dandies' taste
for 'vermouth and orange bitters' (p. 73); the 'Yellow
Book' that Dorian meaningfully glances at (p. 125); the

fashion for marrying American heiresses; the 'seventeen photographs' of Dorian in different poses which Lord Henry has acquired; the repeated references to the writings of Walter Pater with which the young men first became acquainted at Oxford. The annotations to the World's Classic edition clearly indicate the time of the narrative's early action as coinciding with the period of Wilde's writing the novel, 1888–90. Looking back through literary history, we recognize it as the brief and soon-to-be curtailed golden age of aestheticism, a florescence that Wilde's own disgrace would extinguish five years later.

There are, additionally, precise chronological markers, putting the action in the late 1880s-to-1890 period. In Chapter 9 Hallward desperately tries to persuade Dorian to alter his increasingly dissipated ways. And he asks for the portrait back as he means to exhibit it, giving as his reason, 'Georges Petit is going to collect all my best pictures for a special exhibition in the Rue de Sèze, which will open the first week in October' (p. 112). Petit's gallery (which is clearly well established at this point in the narrative) was set up in 1882, in the Rue de Sèze. This must, logically, be happening at some later point in the 1880s. A little later in the novel, in Chapter 10, Dorian comes across a work of literature which will change his life:

It was a novel without a plot, and with only one character, being, indeed, simply a psychological study of a certain young Parisian, who spent his life trying to realize in the nineteenth century all the passions and modes of thought that belonged to every century except his own, and to sum up, as it were, in himself the various moods through which the world-spirit had ever passed, loving for their mere artificiality those renunciations that men have unwisely called virtue, as much as those natural rebellions that wise men still call sin. The style in which it was written was that curiously jewelled style, vivid and obscure at once, full of *argot*

and of archaisms, of technical expressions and of elaborate
paraphrases, that characterizes the work of some of the finest
artists of the French school of *Symbolistes*. (p. 125)

This novel is, unmistakably, Huysmans' *A Rebours*, which
was first published in 1884.

Not to labour the point, the early chapters of *The
Picture of Dorian Gray* are clearly signalled to take place
in 1889–90 or, at most, a couple of years earlier. To place
the action much earlier than that would be a gross
misreading of the novel. How, then, do we make sense of
the encounter 'eighteen years later' (as we are told)
between Dorian and Sibyl's vindictive sailor-brother,
Tom? Dorian escapes the knife meant for his breast only
by showing his still-young face. He cannot be the 40-year-
old man Tom is looking for, possessing as he does the
unblemished features of someone half that age. Dorian's
quick-thinking ruse is plausible, and makes an effective
coup de théâtre. But, if we calculate, the last chapters of
the novel must—given the passage of eighteen years—take
place in 1903–5 at the earliest. After, that is to say, the
death of Queen Victoria, the disgrace and death of Oscar
Wilde, and the anathematization of the aestheticism of
which Dorian is the flower. It is also a decade-and-a-half
after the publication of *The Picture of Dorian Gray* in 1891.

Clearly the last chapters of Wilde's novel are not
visionary glimpses of the future. The season has changed
(it is murky midwinter, opposed to the high midsummer of
the first chapter) but the date has not. It is still, we
apprehend, 1889–90. Sequence has again been abolished.
It is—as with the out-of-order flowers in the first
paragraph—very disturbing. And this disturbance, I suggest, working seismically beneath the surface of what is,
in most respects, a hyper-moralistic narrative, provokes
those shudders which early critics and readers felt, and

their invincible suspicion that there was something very queer indeed about *The Picture of Dorian Gray.* Reviewers were right to suspect that the novel's author was going to come to a very sticky end.

The Oxford World's Classics *Dorian Gray* is edited by Isobel Murray.

Thomas Hardy · *Tess of the d'Urbervilles*

═══

Is Alec a rapist?

═══

There has been an interesting slippage in critical discussion of the climax of 'Phase the First' ('The Maiden') of Hardy's *Tess of the d'Urbervilles: A Pure Woman* over the last century. Victorian critics, to a man and woman, assume that the luckless maiden is at least partly the author of her own misfortune. As Mowbray Morris put it in the *Quarterly Review* (April 1892):

For the first half of his story the reader may indeed conceive it to have been Mr Hardy's design to show how a woman essentially honest and pure at heart will, through the adverse shocks of fate, eventually rise to higher things. But if this were his original purpose he must have forgotten it before his tale was told, or perhaps the 'true sequence of things' was too strong for him. For what are the higher things to which this poor creature eventually rises? She rises through seduction to adultery, murder and the gallows.[1]

Writing a month earlier in *Blackwood's Magazine*, Mrs Oliphant is fierce against Tess for not having withstood temptation better:

We have not a word to say against the force and passion of this story. It is far finer in our opinion than anything Mr Hardy has ever done before. The character of Tess up to her last downfall ... is consistent enough, and we do not object to the defiant blazon of a Pure Woman, notwithstanding the early stain. But a Pure Woman is not betrayed into fine living and fine clothes as the mistress of her seducer by any stress of poverty or misery; and Tess was a skilled labourer, for whom it is very rare that nothing can be found to do. Here the elaborate and indignant plea for Vice, that is really Virtue, breaks down altogether.[2]

Morris and Oliphant take it for granted that Tess was 'seduced'—that is, led astray, not violated or forced into sexual intercourse against her will. Compare this Victorian view with the downrightness of Tony Tanner, writing in 1968:

Hardy's vision is tragic and penetrates far deeper than specific social anomalies. One is more inclined to think of Sophocles than, say, Zola, when reading Hardy . . . Tess is the living demonstration of these tragic ironies. That is why she who is raped lives to be hanged.[3]

She who was seduced in 1892 is she who is raped in the permissive 1960s. Even those modern commentators unwilling to go the whole way hedge their bets. Thus, the first edition of the *Oxford Companion to English Literature* (1932) declares 'Tess is seduced'. Margaret Drabble's fifth edition of *OCEL* (1984), while retaining the substance of the *Tess* entry, states 'Tess is cunningly seduced'. The 1993 literary encyclopaedia *The 1890s* backs both horses by opening its *Tess* entry with the statement: 'This simple story of seduction-cum-rape', and goes on to describe what happens in the Chase as 'virtual rape'.[4] Ian Gregor, in his influential study of Hardy's major novels, goes all the way by declaring that 'it is both a seduction *and* a rape' (try that in court).[5] The World's Classics editors, Juliet Grindle and Simon Gatrell, use the ambiguous term 'betrayed' (as does OUP's blurb-writer) and the non-felonious 'violated' ('violation' will not land you with a ten-year prison term, 'rape' will). Writing in the 1990s, with the complexities of 'date rape' hovering in the air, James Gibson refers edgily to Tess's 'sexual molestation by Alec' and his 'sexual harassment of his victim'. In his outline of the crucial episode in the 'Text Summary' section of the

'Everyman' edition, Gibson reverts to a more Tannerian reading of events:

Chapter 11
Alec rides with Tess into the Chase—works on her by appearing to be worried about her safety and emphasising the presents he has sent to her family—he deliberately loses the way—after pretending to go in search of the way he returns and rapes her.[6]

So what does happen in the Chase on that September night—seduction, cunning seduction, betrayal, sexual molestation, sexual harassment, violation, 'virtual rape', or rape? The first point to note is that Hardy himself was somewhat unsure about the 'naughty chapters' (as Mrs Oliphant called them). In the serialization of the story in the *Graphic* newspaper (July–December 1891) he was prevailed on by nervous editors to drop the Chaseborough dance and subsequent seduction/rape sequence altogether, putting in its place an entirely new sub-plot. In the *Graphic* version of *Tess*, the heroine is tricked into a fake marriage, and is thus deflowered with her full (if deluded) consent. This venerable device had been used earlier by Charles Reade in *Put Yourself in his Place* (1870), by Thackeray in *Philip* (1862), and, aboriginally, by Scott in *St Ronan's Well* (1823). The attraction of the bogus-marriage gimmick was that it enabled the hoodwinked heroine to commit the act of fornication innocently, thus preserving her 'purity'. In the three-volume edition, which came out in November 1891, Hardy repudiated artifice and insisted on reprinting the original rape/seduction text, with the prefatory proclamation: 'If an offence come out of the truth, better is it that the offence come than that the truth be concealed.'

Even in the frank versions of 'The Maiden', however, much is left inscrutable, if not entirely concealed. The rape/seduction episode begins with a description of the Trantridge peasantry's loose morals and hard drinking, which are given free rein in their Saturday night festivities at the nearby 'decayed market-town', Chaseborough. Tess, we are told, likes to go to these Saturday night affairs, although she does not participate in the revelry. On the misty September Saturday night in question, Tess makes her way from Chaseborough to a barn in a nearby 'townlet' where her fellow Trantridge cottagers are at a 'private jig'. She wants their company on the way home, since there has been both a fair and a market day at Chaseborough, and there may be drunken men in the country lanes. When she arrives at the dance, Tess discovers a surreal scene. The barn floor is deep in 'scroff'—'that is to say the powdery residuum from the storage of peat and other products, the stirring of which by [the dancers'] turbulent feet created [a] nebulosity that involved the scene . . . [a] floating, fusty *débris* of peat and hay' (p. 66). The dusty haze thrown up by the dancers' muffled stamping merges with the mist, and later the fog, which enshrouds the whole of the seduction/rape episode in a corresponding moral 'nebulosity'.

The dustily indistinct picture of the dance has been connected with the pictorial influence of French Impressionism on Hardy and is one of his fine visual set-pieces. At a more physical level, the scene alludes to a common belief in country communities—that flying dust, as it gets trapped in their underwear, has a sexually exciting effect on women dancers. It is part of the folklore of barn-dances in America that unscrupulous young men—intending to induce wantonness in their partners—scatter pepper on the boards before the evening gets under-way. Certainly the 'scroff' seems to have had an aphrodisiac effect at Chaseborough. Hardy hints at sexual orgy by a string of meaningful classical references:

They coughed as they danced, and laughed as they coughed. Of the rushing couples there could barely be discerned more than the high lights—the indistinctness shaping them to satyrs clasping nymphs—a multiplicity of Pans whirling a multiplicity of Syrinxes; Lotis attempting to elude Priapus, and always failing. (pp. 66–7)

Each of these three allusions signals 'rape'. Tess is invited to join in by a dusty, sweating swain. But she refuses. She becomes aware of the glowing tip of Alec's cigar in the gloom behind her. He offers to take her home, but although she is very tired she declines, not quite trusting him—perhaps forewarned by the phallic heat of his Havana on her neck. But later, when Car Darch (one of Alec's cast mistresses) threatens violence, Tess allows herself (a maiden in distress) to be rescued by Alec, now on horseback. This is the prelude to Chapter 11. Chaseborough is only three miles from Trantridge, and the journey on Alec's stallion should take twenty minutes or so. But he deliberately loses his way turning his horse into the foggy wilderness of the Chase—'the oldest wood in England'. Tess, who has been up since five every day that week, is exhausted. As she falls asleep in the saddle, Alec puts his arm around her waist. 'This immediately put her on the defensive,' we are told, 'and with one of those sudden impulses of reprisal to which she was liable she gave him a little push from her' (p. 74). Alec almost tumbles off the horse. It is a significant detail. The push looks forward to Tess's eventually stabbing Alec to death, which—we apprehend—is another reflexive 'impulse of reprisal'. Here it stresses that even when her body is dormant, Tess's purity is vigilant and well capable of defending itself. This is important, since she will be sleeping when the seduction/rape occurs.

The point is also stressed that Alec has not directed his horse's head into the Chase with any overtly mischievous intention, but merely 'to prolong companionship with her' (p. 76). Tess repulses his love-making as they ride, without ever distinctly denying that she loves him. He is much encouraged by her lack of 'frigidity'. He contrives further to weaken her resolve with the information that he has bought her father a new horse, to replace the luckless Prince, who died as a result of her falling asleep on the road. Once again, it seems that Tess is failing into dangerous slumber. Alec, who by now is completely lost in the fog and trees, wraps her in his coat, makes a 'sort of couch or nest' for her in the newly dropped leaves, and goes off on foot to look for some landmark. He eventually locates the road, and returns to find Tess fast asleep. He bends down to her, 'till her breath warmed his face, and in a moment his cheek was in contact with hers. She was sleeping soundly, and upon her eyelashes there lingered tears' (p. 77).

This is the last image Hardy leaves us with. It could be Prince Charming about to wake Sleeping Beauty, or it could be ravishing Tarquin. The narrative averts its gaze from whatever happens next and moralizes loftily for three paragraphs. The clearest clue as to what is meanwhile going on between Tess and Alec is given in the second of these paragraphs:

Why it was that upon this beautiful feminine tissue, sensitive as gossamer, and practically blank as snow as yet, there should have been traced such a coarse pattern as it was doomed to receive; why so often the coarse appropriates the finer thus, the wrong man the woman, the wrong woman the man, many thousand years of analytical philosophy have failed to explain to our sense of order. One may, indeed, admit the possibility of a retribution lurking in the present catastrophe. Doubtless some of Tess d'Urberville's mailed ancestors rollicking home from a fray had dealt the same measure even more ruthlessly towards peasant girls of their time. But though to visit the sins of the fathers upon the children may be a morality good enough for divinities, it is scorned by average human nature; and it therefore does not mend the matter. (p. 77)

As Thackeray says in *Vanity Fair*, the novelist knows everything. Hardy must know what is going on here, even if he chooses not to tell us. Clearly intercourse is taking place while the narrator turns away and prates about olden times. But what kind of intercourse? All the narrative divulges to the reader is that Alec is not as 'ruthless' as those ancient ravishers, Tess's ancestors, taking their seigneurial rights. It is clear that Alec has not set out with the explicit purpose of assaulting Tess; when he leaves her in her leafy couch, it is genuinely to find the road home, not to lull her into defencelessness. Not that she would normally be defenceless. The point is made earlier in the chapter that even when asleep, Tess is able to fend off unwanted sexual advances. Why does she not protect her imperilled virtue with one of those timely 'impulses of reprisal'?

More significantly, when—a maiden no more—Tess upbraids Alec, she does not accuse him of rape, but of having duped her: 'I didn't understand your meaning till it was too late' (p. 83), she says. Nor, when upbraiding her mother for not warning her against men, does Tess claim that she has been raped. As the narrative glosses her thoughts:

She had never wholly cared for [Alec], she did not at all care for him now. She had dreaded him, winced before him, succumbed to adroit advantages he took of her helplessness; then, temporarily blinded by his ardent manners, had been stirred to confused surrender awhile: had suddenly despised and disliked him, and had run away. (p. 87)

Alec, we understand, has been 'adroit'—some cunning caresses with his hands are implied. His 'ardent manners' (an odd conjunction—ardour is rarely well mannered) had 'stirred' Tess—erection is hinted at. The verb 'stirred' is significant, suggesting as it does physical reciprocation on Tess's part. Did she consent? 'Confused surrender' suggests that she did, but that she was blinded at the time by his stimulating foreplay and the power of her own aroused feelings.

By Victorian legal lights it was clearly seduction; there was nothing forcible in Alec's actions, although, as he himself avows ('I did wrong—I admit it'), they were the actions of a cad. He 'took advantage' of her. This is immoral, but not criminal. Even by the strict 1990s definition of rape on North American campuses, his behaviour would probably not be criminal. It is not recorded that Tess clearly told Alec to stop, once he had started to make love to her.' Stirred' as she was, she may well have encouraged him to continue making love by body movements of her own. That is, neither seduction nor rape may be the proper term; Tess was a willing, if misguided, participant in her own undoing.

Why then do modern critics and readers assume that Alec is a rapist? For the same reason that they are unwilling to see Tess as a murderess. Here again, Hardy manipulates our response in his heroine's favour less by what he describes than by what he omits to describe. To summarize: hearing unusual 'sounds', Mrs Brooks, the landlady at the Herons, the inn where Alec and Tess have taken an apartment, looks through the keyhole. She sees Tess in distress at the breakfast table, and hears a long complaint ('a dirge rather than a soliloquy') from her lips. Tess is berating herself for her weakness in surrendering again to Alec's 'cruel persuasions'. She sees herself as an irredeemably fallen adulteress. Mrs Brooks hears 'more and sharper words from the man', then 'a sudden rustle'. Tess soon after hurries away from the inn, dressed in black. Alec's body is discovered on the bed, stabbed through the heart (pp. 367–70).

Tess's subsequent explanation to Angel is not entirely satisfactory.

'But how do you mean—you have killed him?'

'I mean that I have,' she murmured in a reverie.

'What—bodily? Is he dead?'

'Yes. He heard me crying about you, and he bitterly taunted me; and called you by a foul name; and then I did it; my heart could not bear it: he had nagged me about you before—and then I dressed myself, and came away to find you.' (p. 372).

Hardy does not give us any details of the subsequent trial, leaping straight from Tess, arrested on the sacrificial slab at Stonehenge, to her execution at Wintoncester Gaol. But it would be interesting to know what came out in court. By Mrs Brooks's testimony (as we have it), it would seem that Alec—justifiably vexed by Tess's long diatribe against himself—said something 'sharp' ('bitterly taunted' seems an overstatement). It is hard to think up a 'foul name' applicable to a man ('no-balls eunuch'?) which would justify what followed. Tess then picked up the carving knife from the breakfast table, walked all the way across the length of the living room to the bed on which Alec was still lying, and stabbed him through the heart, One precisely aimed stroke has killed him. It is hard to imagine how this could be done—given Alec's superior strength and agility—unless Tess waited until he relapsed into sleep, as people do before breakfast. An awake Alec would hardly watch Tess stalking towards him with an upraised knife without raising a hand to defend himself or shifting his torso away from the path of the murder weapon.

It is conceivable that a legal defence could be made for Tess along the lines that lawyers successfully defended Lorena Bobbit—the aggrieved Virginian who cut off her husband's penis with a carving knife while he slept.

Possibly a 1990s jury might acquit Tess, on the grounds that she, like Lorena, had suffered years of abuse from her partner (although Alec is not recorded as ever striking or beating Tess). But the jury would not, one imagine, acquit her as readily and absolutely as do the literary critics, This, for instance, is how James Gibson summarizes the climactic chapter:

Chapter 56
The landlady of the lodging-house is curious—hears Tess moaning in her room and sharp words—she sees Tess leaving the house and then a red spot on the ceiling—Alec is dead.[7]

'Alec is murdered' would seem to be truer to the facts. Hardy's rhetoric allows the critic to overlook the simple wrongness of Tess's act, and mask it in a neutral phraseology more appropriate to suicide or death by natural causes than homicide. The holes in Hardy's account allow us to jump to conclusions ('Alec is a rapist who gets what is coming to him') and sanction such exonerating imagery as Tony Tanner's: 'Tess is gradually crucified on the oppugnant ironies of circumstance and existence itself'. On objective legal grounds, one might retort, Tess deserves crucifixion rather more than do the two thieves and their famous companion. It would be much harder to sustain the 'Tess as Christ figure' line if readers had before them a clear image of her plunging the carving knife into Alec's sleeping body, choosing her spot carefully so as to kill him with one blow—all because he had applied some unspecified 'foul name' to her husband. Nor would it be easy, I imagine, to sustain the 'Tess is a victim of rape' line (which leads directly into the 'justifiable homicide' line) if one had a clear image of her making reciprocal love to Alec in the Chase. Hardy's novel is like a court case in which all the material evidence is left out, and the jury (readers) rushed to judgement on the basis of the defendant's beauty and pathetic suffering alone.

All this is not to suggest that Tess is a murderous slut who gets what is coming to her. But one should perhaps give more credence to Mrs Oliphant's Victorian common-sensical view. Alec is not a rapist and, although her innocence makes her vulnerable, Tess must take some small responsibility for what happens in the Chase. Tess does have a saleable skill, and she did not have to surrender a second time to Alec purely for economic reasons. Nor, having surrendered, did she have to compound adultery with wilful murder. Had Hardy, in the manner of some Victorian John Grisham, supplied us with two closely described trials in the body of the novel (the first of Alec for rape, the second of Tess for murder), our verdict would surely be harder on Tess, and lighter on Alec.

The Oxford World's Classics *Tess of the d'Urbervilles* is edited by Juliet Grindle and Simon Gatrell, with notes by Nancy Barrineau.

Arthur Conan Doyle · *Sherlock Holmes*

Mysteries of the Speckled Band

'The Adventure of the Speckled Band' is one of Sherlock Holmes's best-known early cases.[1] The affair is recalled by Watson, much later in life. The lady who initially implored the great detective's assistance has, we guess, recently died (prematurely, it would seem), allowing Watson to divulge her story to the world. As Watson recalls, in April 1883 Miss Helen Stoner, a handsome but clearly distressed young woman with prematurely white strands in her hair, called at 221B Baker Street, early in the morning. Her tale was intriguing. Raised in India, she had returned to England some ten years earlier with her mother, her twin sister Julia, and her stepfather. The girls' mother has died eight years since, 'in a railway accident near Crewe' (p. 175). Helen's stepfather; who evidently married his wife for her money (some £1,100 a year, shrunk by current agricultural distress to £750), is an unredeemable brute, the degenerate offspring of a 'dissolute and wasteful' family on whose decayed estate, Stoke Moran in Surrey, they now live in reduced circumstances. A doctor by profession, Roylott is suspected of having murdered a servant in India and—as Holmes astutely deduces—routinely brutalizes his stepdaughters (the detective's sharp eyes note bruises on Miss Stoner's wrist and arm). The Misses Stoner, on marriage, will take to their husbands a portion of their mother's inheritance. Julia, however, has died very recently in suspicious circumstances after indicating an intention to marry.

Helen describes the enigmatic events surrounding her

sister's death in some detail. On the evening she died, the young ladies, as had happened before, heard a 'low whistle', for which they had no explanation. There was also heard a clanging sound, which was similarly mysterious to them. The girls have separate bedrooms and, after retiring, Helen was roused by a hideous shriek. She rushed out to encounter Julia emerging from her room, 'swaying like a drunkard'. The unfortunate woman convulsed and died seconds later, in agony. There were no marks apparent on her body, nor any evident cause of death. Julia's final words are baffling in the extreme:

as I bent over her she suddenly shrieked out in a voice which I shall never forget, 'Oh, my God! Helen! It was the band! The speckled band!' There was something else which she would fain have said, and she stabbed with her finger into the air in the direction of the Doctor's [i.e. her stepfather's room], but a fresh convulsion seized her and choked her words. (p. 178)

The doctor, it emerges, has lately been intimate with a band of gipsies on his 'plantation'. These are the only human beings with whom he has any civilized intercourse. Possibly, conjectures Miss Stoner, the mysterious speckled band may refer 'to the spotted handkerchiefs which so many of them [i.e. gipsies] wear over their heads' (p. 180). But since no one has been seen entering or leaving the room, what we would seem to have here is a version of the 'locked room mystery'—that master-class problem for all great sleuths.

These, Holmes opines, 'are very deep waters'. Helen goes on to say that she too is about to be married, to 'Percy Armitage—the second son of Mr Armitage, of Crane Water, near Reading' (p. 180). Her stepfather has offered no objection to the match, but she has anxieties. More so, since she has been moved by his instruction into the very bedroom that her unlucky sister formerly occupied, and has the previous night heard the same ominous whistle that they heard on the night of Julia's death. After Miss Stoner has left, Holmes and Watson receive an unpleasant call from Dr Grimesby Roylott, of Stoke Moran. He confirms his stepdaughter's unflattering account. An old man possessed of almost superhuman strength (he bends a poker double to add emphasis to his threats), his face is 'marked with every evil passion'. He utters some inarticulate but very horrible imprecations against Holmes, should he interfere.

Holmes later admits that at this initial stage he had formed 'an entirely erroneous conclusion, which shows, my dear Watson, how dangerous it always is to reason from insufficient data'. The presence of the gypsies, and 'the use of the word "band"' had thrown the sleuth on an 'entirely wrong scent' (p. 196). We never discover what Holmes's erroneous 'conclusion' was—presumably that Roylott summoned gipsy assassins to his daughter's chamber for light-footed murder.

After the visits of Miss Stoner and Dr Roylott, Holmes and Watson take the train down to Stoke Moran. They discover in the dead girl's bedroom a dummy bell-pull. The bed is bolted to the floor, so that it must always be directly underneath the tasselled cloth band, which is odd. Holmes's sharp eyes also detect an air-vent which has been recently constructed. Its passage does not connect, as would be logical, to an outside wall, but to the doctor's adjoining bedroom. This vent allows the rank odour of Roylott's cigar and even gleams of light to penetrate into Helen's chamber. It is not said outright, but we deduce that the vent could also serve as a spy-hole for anyone with voyeuristic intentions. Dr Roylott, of course, is no gentleman and a young lady's privacy would not be sacred to him.

In every way Stoke Moran gives Holmes and Watson the impression of being an 'evil household'. The outlying

Arthur Conan Doyle

estate is similarly infested with signs of evil. 'There was little difficulty in entering the grounds,' Watson recalls:

for unrepaired breaches gaped in the old park wall. Making our way among the trees, we reached the lawn, crossed it, and were about to enter through the window, when out from a clump of laurel bushes there darted what seemed to be a hideous and distorted child, who threw itself upon the grass with writhing limbs, and then ran swiftly across the lawn into the darkness.

'My God!' I whispered; 'did you see it?'

Holmes was for the moment as startled as I. His hand closed like a vice upon my wrist in his agitation. Then he broke into a low laugh, and put his lips to my ear.

'It is a nice household,' he murmured. 'That is the baboon.' (p. 193)

Baboons, of course, are not native to Surrey. This beast is a relic from an menagerie of Indian animals which the doctor tried unsuccessfully to set up on his return from the subcontinent. But, for astute readers of detective stories, the introduction of the baboon will recall that archetype of the locked-room mystery genre, Edgar Allan Poe's 'The Murders in the Rue Morgue' (1841), where the murderer is finally revealed to be an orang-utan. Might the baboon have somehow been responsible for Julia's death?

The denouement is quickly told. In a metal safe (with a sonorously clanging door) in his bedroom Doctor Roylott keeps a trained swamp adder—the 'deadliest snake in India'. This beast has been trained to respond to whistled signals. It is capable of slithering through the connecting vent and down the fabric bell-rope. (It defies plausibility, incidentally, that it could slither back up— some variant of the Indian rope trick was apparently in Doyle's mind.)[2] This serpent is the 'speckled band' of which the inarticulate and dying Julia spoke. Surprised by Holmes and Watson as it slithers towards its second victim, the infuriated snake insinuates its way up the bell-pull and back into Roylott's bedroom and stings him to death. Holmes has, quite advertently as he later confesses, engineered the doctor's death. 'I cannot say that it is likely to weigh very heavily on my conscience' (p. 197), he complacently informs Watson.

There remain, even after the thrilling denouement, profound mysteries to this case. The deceased Miss Stoner was, like her twin sister Helen, brought up in India where she spent what we can calculate to be her first fifteen years or so of life. This experience would certainly have educated her as to the existence of snakes. Why, then, after having been agonizingly stung and clearly having seen what stung her, does she waste her last words talking about 'speckled bands' as if she had never seen such a thing as a swamp adder, or its serpentine cousins? Even if an old India hand might have had a momentary confusion on waking from sleep, it would quickly have been dispelled by the sinuous movements of the 'band', and its bite. That bite, incidentally, is anything but painless. The Doctor emits a 'dreadful shriek' on being bitten which is audible in the nearby village. One might also carpingly note that, although a swamp adder might be trained to return to its nest on command, it could scarcely be trained to bite on command.

When one looks more closely at it, the whole question of what it is Julia sees is vexed. According to Helen, when she ran out, alarmed by Julia's 'wild scream', into the passage connecting their bedrooms: 'By the light of the corridor lamp I saw my sister appear at the opening, her face blanched with terror, her hands groping for help, her whole figure swaying to and fro like that of a drunkard' (p. 178). As Helen puts her arms around the dying woman, 'she suddenly shrieked out in a voice which I shall never forget, "O, my God! Helen! It was the band! The speckled band!"' At this point, she falls speechless, although as

Helen notes, 'there was something else she would fain have said, and she stabbed with her finger into the air in the direction of the Doctor's room' (p. 178).

While writing the scene Conan Doyle evidently realized that, in order for the victim to have seen the 'speckled band', there must be some source of light in Julia's room. If there were too much light she would naturally see the reptile slithering up and down the bell-pull, and make too correct an identification. Thus, in reply to Holmes's question, 'Was your sister dressed?', Helen is made to reply, 'No she was in her nightdress. In her right hand was found the charred stump of a match, and in her left a matchbox' (p. 179). The feeble light afforded by a Victorian Lucifer would explain how a snake might look like a ribbon. But how, one may ask, when she emerged into the corridor did Julia's hands 'grope for help', or her finger point towards the doctor's room?[3]

Why, as a further mystery, did Julia not complain at the doctor's knocking a hole into the adjoining wall between their bedrooms, violating her privacy and adding nothing to the freshness of her boudoir? Why do the girls not leave Stoke Moran? There is no reason for Julia to have remained there: she was of age, and her prospective in-laws would certainly have given her a haven (as, of course, would the Armitages of Reading for Helen, were she to ask them). There is, one deduces, a strong suggestion of sexual bondage. The girls, for some reason, cannot leave. We never learn how Helen came by the bruises on her wrists that Holmes discerns at their first interview in Baker Street. All that she says, by way of blushing explanation, is that 'He is a hard man ... and perhaps he hardly knows his own strength' (p. 181). This, notoriously, is what battered wives tell the police and magistrates in defence of their brutal husbands. 'Miss Roylott', says Holmes, 'You are screening your stepfather' (p. 181). Why, in saying this, does Holmes, who has the best brain in England, miscall Miss Stoner 'Miss Roylott'—is he hinting at a closer relationship than that of stepfather and stepdaughter? Has the unspeakable Dr Roylott somehow mixed his identity with that of the young woman? Helen Stoner, we note, does not correct Holmes when he calls her 'Miss Roylott'—is he not subtly probing for evidence of incest, and has he not found it?[4]

This whole episode recalls a vivid exchange between Holmes and Watson in another exciting early case, 'The Adventure of the Copper Beeches'. As they travel into rural Hampshire Watson enthuses about the beauty of the scene. 'Good heavens!', he exclaims, 'Who would associate crime with these dear old homesteads?' Holmes replies bleakly that such idyllic landscape fills him with more 'horror' that 'the lowest and vilest alleys in London':

the reason is very obvious. The pressure of public opinion can do in the town what the law cannot accomplish. There is no lane so vile that the scream of a tortured child, or the thud of a drunkard's blow, does not beget sympathy and indignation among the neighbours, and then the whole machinery of justice is ever so close that a word of complaint can set it going, and there is but a step between the crime and the dock. But look at these lonely houses, each in its own fields, filled for the most part with poor ignorant folk who know little of the law. Think of the deeds of hellish cruelty, the hidden wickedness which may go on, year in, year out, in such places, and none the wiser. (p. 280)

Reading 'The Adventure of the Speckled Band' at a deeper level than the sleuth's slick cracking of the case, there remains a surplus of unresolved questions. Why did Helen, after being released from Stoke Moran, die so prematurely? Was it some ineradicable legacy of shame? Why does Holmes feel justified in killing Dr Roylott as justifiably as one might squash a dung beetle? He is not normally given to such acts of vigilantism. What 'hidden wickedness' may we surmise was going on at Stoke Moran under the doctor's corrupt regime? Much more, we apprehend, than the amiably dull-witted Watson suspects.

The Oxford World's Classics *The Adventures of Sherlock Holmes* is edited by Richard Lancelyn Green.

Thomas Hardy · *Jude the Obscure*

═══

What does Arabella Donn throw?

═══

Most readers will, if they have learned nothing else from
Jude the Obscure, know how a pig of the nineteenth century was killed, dressed, and its carcass disposed of. 'The
pig-sticking and so forth', as D. H. Lawrence dismissively
calls it in his *Study of Thomas Hardy*, is uncomfortably
prominent. Hardy's proclaimed intention in *Jude* was to
tell his story 'without a mincing of words'. Where things
porcine are concerned, his words are notably unminced.
There are, however, some aspects of this strand in the
novel which may elude the modern reader, and are perhaps
designed by Hardy to be elusive. Take, for example, the
irruption of Arabella into Jude's life, with the 'missile':

In his deep concentration on these transactions of the future
[Jude is dreaming of becoming a bishop], Jude's walk had slack-
ened, and he was now standing quite still, looking at the ground
as though the future were thrown thereon by a magic lantern.
On a sudden something smacked him sharply in the ear, and he
became aware that a soft cold substance had been flung at him,
and had fallen at his feet.

A glance told him what it was—a piece of flesh, the characteristic part of a barrow-pig, which the countrymen used for
greasing their boots, as it was useless for any other purpose.
(p. 35)

What strikes one here is the odd tentativeness which
masks an obvious knowledgeability about country matters.
The parodic cupid's dart is described with the maximum
of periphrasis compatible with not actually disguising
what the organ is, 'a piece of flesh, the characteristic

part of a barrow-pig'. Twice more in the scene it is referred
to. Arabella saucily observes: 'If I had thrown any thing at
all, it shouldn't have been *that*' (p. 35). Later on it occurs
to the otherwise gullible Jude that 'it had been no vestal
who chose *that* missile for opening her attack on him'
(p. 39). In neither case is 'that' specified any more than it
was on its first appearance.

Hardy's delicacy of description serves a number of
purposes. First, and most simply, he could not be as frank
on matters of sexual detail as he might have liked. Mrs
Grundy—in the form of his editors and publishers—would
not let him. More artistically, the lack of specification
aptly mimics the coyness of the 'maidens' and conveys the
prim disgust of Jude, who shrinks from naming the object
('*that*'), even in the private recesses of his own mind. The
maidens' motive for avoiding the word is aggressive sexual
mock-modesty, his is genuine sexual timidity. And, at the
rhetorical level, yet another function is performed. Hardy
must have been aware that relatively few of his public
(townees all) would have known what part of pork offal
was used for boot-dubbin in the West Country.

The reader is thus teased into supplying his or her own
suggestion for what '*that*' might be. Not everyone gets it
right. Kate Millett, for example, in her otherwise acute
discussion of *Jude* in *Sexual Politics*, writes that the
lovers 'first meet when Arabella pitches the scrotum of a
butchered barrow-pig at Jude's head'.[1] This is a misapprehension which leads to a misreading of the episode.
A barrow-pig is a castrated boar reared for pork, not
breeding, and *sui generis*, has no scrotum. That part of
the beast's sexual equipment is cut away while it is still a
piglet, so that it will grow a fat, porcine eunuch. What
Arabella throws at Jude is a pizzle or penis. But nor is
it quite sufficient merely to describe it as a 'penis', as
Patricia Ingham does, in her account of how Hardy was

forced to bowdlerize this scene for its various form of publication (p. 435). The stress is on the observation 'it was useless for any other purpose'. It is a dysfunctional penis. The 'message' is not one of sexual invitation, but one of taunting. Arabella's missile is not a symbol of animal potency but of animal impotency. The message is mischievously provocative ('Is yours as useless as this, young man?') This aggressive sexual taunting is a note which will reverberate through the lovers' subsequent relationship until Arabella finally disposes of her thoroughly emasculated mate at Christminster.

The Oxford World's Classics *Jude the Obscure* is edited by Patricia Ingham.

R. L. Stevenson · *Weir of Hermiston*

What is Duncan Jopp's crime?

The Oedipal struggle between Archie Hermiston and his awesome, hanging-judge father reaches a crisis in Chapter 3—'In the Matter of the Hanging of Duncan Jopp.' The chapter opens:

It chanced in the year 1813 that Archie strayed one day into the Judiciary Court. The macer made room for the son of the presiding judge. In the dock, the centre of men's eyes, there stood a whey-coloured, misbegotten caitiff, Duncan Jopp, on trial for his life. His story, as it was raked out before him in that public scene, was one of disgrace and vice and cowardice, the very nakedness of crime; and the creature heard and it seemed at times as though he understood—as if at times he forgot the horror of the place he stood in, and remembered the shame of what had brought him there. He kept his head bowed and his hands clutched upon the rail; his hair dropped in his eyes and at times he flung it back; and now he glanced about the audience in a sudden fellness of terror, and now looked in the face of his judge and gulped. There was pinned about his throat a piece of dingy flannel; and that it was perhaps that turned the scale in Archie's mind between disgust and pity. The creature stood in a vanishing point; yet a little while, and he was still a man, and had eyes and apprehension; yet a little longer, and with a last sordid piece of pageantry, he would cease to be. And here, in the meantime, with a trait of human nature that caught at the beholder's breath, he was tending a sore throat. (p. 103)

There is a striking anticipation here of a passage in George Orwell's 'A Hanging':

It was about forty yards to the gallows. I watched the bare brown back of the prisoner marching in front of me. He walked clumsily with his bound arms, but quite steadily, with that bobbing gait of the Indian who never straightens his knees. At each step his muscles slid neatly into place, and the lock of hair on his scalp danced up and down, his feet printed themselves on the wet gravel. And once, in spite of the men who gripped him by each shoulder, he stepped slightly aside to avoid a puddle on the path.

It is curious, but till that moment I had never realized what it means to destroy a healthy, conscious man. When I saw the prisoner step aside to avoid the puddle I saw the mystery, the unspeakable wrongness, of cutting a life short when it is in full tide.[1]

As an increasingly appalled Archie watches, Jopp and his slatternly mistress, Janet, are ruthlessly mocked by the judge in his braid-Scots dialect—'Godsake! ye make a bonny couple.' Janet is spared, but Duncan is summarily sentenced to execution. In the course of passing sentence, Weir delivers himself of a particularly brutal *obiter dictum:* 'I have been the means, under God, of hanging a great number, but never just such a disjaskit [untidy] rascal as yourself'. As the narrative observes: 'The words were strong in themselves; the light and heat and detonation of their delivery, and the savage pleasure of the speaker in his task, made them tingle in the ears' (p. 104).

Duncan Jopp leaves the dock, a pathetic spectacle in the eyes of court: 'Had there been the least redeeming greatness in the crime, any obscurity, any dubiety, perhaps he might have understood'. For Archie the trial—more particularly the cosmic insignificance of Jopp as a defendant—has soiled his father irredeemably: 'It is one thing to spear a tiger, another to crush a toad; there are aesthetics even of the slaughter-house; and the loathsomeness of Duncan Jopp enveloped and infected the image of his judge' (pp. 104–5). But neither here nor elsewhere does Stevenson indicate what Jopp's 'crime' is, other than in the contemptuous vagueness of 'His story . . . was one of disgrace and vice and cowardice, the very nakedness of crime'.

The short interval between sentencing and execution passes as a 'violent dream' for Archie. He is present at the public hanging of Jopp (in Edinburgh's Grass Market, presumably):

He saw the fleering rabble, the flinching wretch produced. He looked on for a while at a certain parody of devotion, which seemed to strip the wretch of his last claim to manhood. Then followed the brutal instant of extinction, and the paltry dangling of the remains like a broken jumping-jack. He had been prepared for something terrible, not for this tragic meanness. He stood a moment silent, and then—'I denounce this God-defying murder', he shouted; and his father, if he must have disclaimed the sentiment, might have owned the stentorian voice with which it was uttered. (pp. 105–6)

It is Archie's first overt act of rebellion against his father, and as such a threshold event in his life. He compounds his rebellion at the place of execution by proposing that evening at the 'Spec' debating society the 'Jacobinical' motion: 'Whether capital punishment be consistent with God's will or man's policy?' All this inevitably gets back to Hermiston who, with his habitual, unmanning, insolence banishes Archie to the family estate at Hermiston. The scene is thus set for the events which will lead (had Stevenson lived long enough to write it) to Archie's being brought up before his own father on a charge of murder and—presumably—being sentenced to the same fate as the luckless Jopp.

Stevenson devotes a great deal of space in Chapter 3 to the description of Duncan Jopp. But he nowhere tells us what his offence is. As is well known (and as RLS pointed out in letters to friends), Weir of Hermiston is based closely on the 'Scottish Jeffreys', Robert MacQueen, Lord Braxfield (1722–99). As Emma Letley explains, in her notes to the World's Classics edition:

Braxfield became an advocate in 1744 and, in 1766, was appointed a Lord of Session; in 1788 he became Justice-Clerk, in effect head of the Criminal Court in Scotland. He was known for being particularly harsh with political offenders, and was noted for his brutality and insulting treatment of such plaintiffs as appeared before him. (p. 215)

A 'coarse and illiterate man' (as Henry Cockburn called him) and spectacularly drunken to boot, who loved to use broad dialect on the bench, Braxfield made himself hated (and earned his 'Jeffreys' sobriquet) in the brutal repression of the Duns rioters over which he presided in 1793–4. His conduct was, Cockburn declared, 'a disgrace to the age'. But *Weir of Hermiston* is set in a later age—1813. Whatever else, Jopp is not guilty of any offence against civil order; his, we may be sure, is no 'political' crime. But what kind of crime is it? It is some two decades before the Peel reforms and Jopp could, in 1813, be hanged for the theft of a loaf of bread to feed his starving offspring. But his crime seems more sordid than this. 'Grant he was vile', Archie tells his father, 'why should you hunt him with a vileness equal to his own?' Some squalid sexual crime seems to be indicated. The point is necessary to assist the readers in arranging their sympathies towards father and son. If Jopp, for instance, had killed a man, or a woman, or a child, in cold blood we might well feel—even with the enlightened sympathies of the twentieth century—that the hanging was no 'God-defying murder', but justice. If, on the other hand, Jopp was a petty thief, or some wretched sexual delinquent, hanging would indeed strike the modern reader as judicial murder. By not instructing on this matter Stevenson, for his own artistic purposes, leaves us, like Jopp, twisting in the wind.

The Oxford World's Classics *Weir of Hermiston* is edited by Emma Letley.

H. G. Wells · *The Invisible Man*

Why is Griffin cold?

H. G. Wells was keen that his 'scientific romances' should be just that—scientific. He devotes a whole section of *The Invisible Man* (Chapter 19, 'Certain First Principles') to authentication of the central concept in the novel. It is, for the lay-reader at least, an extraordinarily plausible performance. 'Have you already forgotten your physics?', Griffin asks his old class-mate, Kemp, before launching into a lecture on optics:

Just think of all the things that are transparent and seem not to be so. Paper, for instance, is made up of transparent fibres, and it is white and opaque only for the same reason that a powder of glass is white and opaque. Oil white paper, fill up the interstices between the particles with oil so that there is no longer refraction or reflection except at the surfaces, and it becomes as transparent as glass. And not only paper, but cotton fibre, linen fibre, woody fibre, and *bone*, Kemp, *flesh*, Kemp, *hair*, Kemp, *nails* and *nerves*, Kemp, in fact the whole fabric of a man except the red of his blood and black pigment of hair, are all made up of transparent, colourless tissue. So little suffices to make us visible one to the other. For the most part the fibres of a living creature are no more opaque than water. (p. 92)

'Of course, of course', responds Kemp, suddenly remembering his undergraduate physics, 'I was thinking only last night of the sea larvae and all jelly-fish!'

Wells managed to finesse the business about the black pigment in hair by making Griffin albino. But one feature of his invisibility hypothesis continued to bother the author, and evidently remained insolubly inauthentic.

As he later explained in a letter to Arnold Bennett:

Any alteration of the refractive index of the eye lenses would make vision impossible. Without such alteration the eyes would be visible as glassy globules. And for vision it is also necessary that there should be visual purple behind the retina and an opaque cornea and iris. On these lines you would get a very effective short story but nothing more.[1]

There are other irrationalities flawing the central conception of *The Invisible Man* which Wells seems not to have commented on. The most memorable episode in the novel is Griffin's recollection to Kemp of how, newly invisible in London, he discovered himself not omnipotent (as he fondly expected) but more wretched than the most destitute of street beggars, wholly impotent, a modern version of Lear's poor forked animal:

'But you begin to realise now', said the Invisible Man, 'the full disadvantage of my condition. I had no shelter, no covering. To get clothing was to forego all my advantage, to make of myself a strange and terrible thing. I was fasting; for to eat, to fill myself with unassimilated matter, would be to become grotesquely visible again. (p. 116)

This sticks indelibly in the mind. Like Midas, Griffin's dream of vast power turns to a terrible curse. It is January. What more distressing than to be naked and starving in the cold streets?

And yet, if we think about it, Griffin could have been as comfortably covered and as well fed as any of his visible fellow-Londoners. As he tells Kemp, describing his first experiments, he discovered early on that any fibre, vegetable, or woody matter can be rendered invisible— particularly if it has not been died or stained.[2] Griffin proves this in his earliest experimental trials:

I needed two little dynamos, and these I worked with a cheap gas engine. My first experiment was with a bit of white wool fabric.

It was the strangest thing in the world to see it in the flicker of
the flashes soft and white, and then to watch it fade like a wreath
of smoke and vanish. (p. 96)

Griffin moves on to his neighbour's white cat, and the
white pillow on which the animal's drugged body is
lying—both of which are rendered invisible by his little
gas-powered machine.

It is clear that, with a little forethought, Griffin could
quite easily make himself an invisible white suit of clothing. He could also render food invisible before eating it, so
that its undigested mass did not show up in his otherwise
transparent entrails. He could, if he were patient enough,
construct himself an invisible house out of invisible wood.
If due to the invasions of suspicious neighbours, he had
no time to do this in London he might certainly do it
during his many weeks at Iping (where, as he tells Kemp,
most of his efforts seem to be vainly directed towards
finding a chemical formula which will enable him to be
visible or invisible at will).

The naked, starving, unhoused Griffin would, logically,
seem to be that way not because of any fatal flaw in his
science. He could, as has been said, walk around in an
invisible three-piece suit, with an invisible top hat on his
invisible head, an invisible umbrella to keep himself dry,
and an invisible three-course meal in his belly. That he
does not avail himself of these amenities may, conceivably,
be ascribed to a mental derangement provoked by the
excruciating pain of the long dematerialization process.

I had not expected the suffering. A night of racking anguish,
sickness and fainting. I set my teeth, though my skin was presently afire; all my body afire; but I lay there like grim death.
I understood now how it was the cat had howled until I chloro-
formed it. Lucky it was I lived alone and untended in my room.
There were times when I sobbed and groaned and talked.

But I stuck to it. I became insensible and woke languid in the darkness. (p. 101)

But, closely examined, Griffin's derangement seems to originate in the condition of his life well before his agonizing passage into invisibility. His aggrieved sense of alienation evidently began early, probably with the bullying and jeers he attracted as a child, on account of his physical abnormality. It is his physical repulsiveness that strikes those who remember him as an adult. Kemp recalls Griffin at University College as 'a younger student, almost an albino, six feet high, and broad, with a pink and white face and red eyes—who won the medal for chemistry'. This evidently was six or seven years since. In his last years as a student, and in his first employment as a lecturer in an unfashionable provincial university, Griffin (who, one guesses, has neither men nor women friends) has deteriorated into a condition of clear paranoia:

I kept it [i.e. his discovery] to myself. I had to do my work under frightful disadvantages. Oliver, my professor, was a scientific bounder, a journalist by instinct, a thief of ideas,—he was always prying! And you know the knavish system of the scientific world. I simply would not publish, and let him share my credit. I went on working. I got nearer and nearer making my formula into an experiment, a reality. I told no living soul, because I meant to flash my work upon the world with crushing effect,—to become famous at a blow ... To do such a thing would be to transcend magic. And I beheld, unclouded by doubt, a magnificent vision of all that invisibility might mean to a man,—the mystery, the power, the freedom. Drawbacks I saw none. You have only to think! And I, a shabby, poverty-struck, hemmed-in demonstrator, teaching fools in a provincial college, might suddenly become—this. (pp. 93–4)

Griffin, in his maniac delusions of divine superiority, despises humanity. When, therefore, he goes among the London crowds naked and starving it is because, like the self-divested Lear on the heath, he is deliberately refusing to wear the uniform of his herd-like fellow man. He has chosen to strip himself. Nakedness is the sign of his difference, and his godlike superiority over the lesser, visible beings, he despises. He no more needs trousers than Jove or Satan. It is beneath his notice to concern himself with such minutiae.

The Oxford World's Classics *The Invisible Man* is edited by David Lake with an introduction by John Sutherland. (For copyright reasons, this volume is only available in the United States.)

Why does the Count come to England?

Our obsession with vampires supports a commercial empire which mass-produces books, films, cartoons, television dramas, comics, and novelties (such as plastic vampire teeth and Bela Lugosi capes). Like the great Transylvanian monster himself, it would seem that the vampire industry cannot die. Just when you think it is finally exhausted, along come a couple of big-budget, millions-at-the-box-office-earning movies like Francis Ford Coppola's *Bram Stoker's Dracula* (1993) and the Anne Rice-originated, Neil Jordan-directed, Tom Cruise-starring *Interview with the Vampire* (1995).

The essential book on the vampire *cultus* is Paul Barber's *Vampires, Burials and Death*.[1] Barber's survey is massively debunking and wholly convincing, drawing as it does on the resources of folklore scholarship, anthropology, mythography, and forensic pathology (particularly the evidence of post-mortem medical investigators and autopsies). Barber shows how superstitions about vampires—which are found in cultures as remote from Transylvania as China—originate not in the epic misdeeds of Vlad the Impaler, but in the behaviour of the human corpse after death. The dead body is not inert, but a veritable hothouse of chemical and physiological activities. It moves, makes noises, and excretes fluids. This post-mortem activity, Barber suggests, is rationalized by primitive peoples into the vampire (or 'undead') myth.

Dracula, as A. N. Wilson pointed out in his World's Classics introduction, is a mishmash of elements picked

up from the author's experience in the popular theatre
(exactly at that moment when it was about to transmute
into the cinema industry) and from Gothic predecessors
such as John Polidori's *The Vampyre* (1819), J. M. Rymer's
Varney the Vampire (1847), and Sheridan Le Fanu's
superior novella, *Carmilla* (1872). On to this Stoker pasted
some new-fangled psychiatric theory, derived from the
French alienist Charcot, one of Freud's main precursors
(see p. 191, where Van Helsing indicates he is a disciple).
Overlaying the whole work is the kind of paranoid anxiety
induced by the 'invasion fantasies' which (following Colonel
George Chesney's *The Battle of Dorking* in 1871) were a
popular fictional genre at the end of the century.[2] Like
Wells's Martians (which also sent shivers down English
spines in 1897), Stoker's monstrous vampire is a deadly and
alien invader, bent on destroying England's green and
pleasant land (both the Martians and Dracula support
themselves on a diet of English blood, interestingly enough).

As its title proclaims, Francis Ford Coppola's sumptuously produced *Bram Stoker's Dracula* prides itself on
being more authentic than its predecessors. Coppola
strips away the superstructural mythologies which originate in F. W. Murnau's 1922 film, *Nosferatu*; principally the
convention (which is not found in Stoker) that Dracula is
destroyed by sunlight. Coppola observes Stoker's less
florid conception, which is that Dracula can only exercise his superhuman powers fully at night. During the
day he is obliged to take a mundane, human form, and
his wings are correspondingly clipped. But he is quite
capable of moving around by daylight with the freedom
of any other gentleman. Traditionally, film-makers have
loved the Murnau final twist of Dracula surprised by
sunlight and turning first to gorgonzola and then to bones
and sawdust. It makes wonderful cinema. When the first
(of six) Hammer versions of *Dracula* came out in 1958,

the last sequence, in which Christopher Lee deliquesced in a shaft of morning sunshine, was thought so horrible that the British censor demanded it be cut.

None the less, Coppola's *Dracula* deviates from Stoker's original text in two important ways. First, by inventing a wildly romantic reason for Dracula's coming to England (he sees in Mina the reincarnation of the wife whom he loved and lost while still human: it is this undying love that brings him to England). Secondly, Coppola throws the film back into a 'Gothic' nineteenth-century England, lush as a Leighton oil-painting, but essentially as ahistorical as Ruritania.

The key to reading *Dracula* and recovering Stoker's artistic intention is, I would suggest, close attention to the large number of spikily contemporary references in the text to recent gadgetry, communications technology, and scientific innovation. It is significant, for example, that Jonathan Harker records his journal in shorthand (p. 1). Later, he refers in passing to his 'Kodak', with which he has photographed the English estate in which Dracula is interested (p. 23). Mina, we are told, is learning to 'stenograph', so that when she marries Jonathan she can be his 'typewriter girl' (p. 53). There are numerous references to the New Woman vogue, something that peaked in 1894 (Mina, although an advanced member of her sex, draws the line at aligning herself with New Women, what with their outrageous 'open sexual unions'; see, for example, p. 89). Lucy Westenra's life is prolonged, but not saved, by a blood transfusion (this is one of many references to up-to-the-minute medical advances—see, for example, the reference to brain surgery, p. 276). Lucy's phonograph cylinders are used by Dr Seward to make memoranda (p. 142). Van Helsing even develops an early version of radar employing Mina's powers as a mesmeric medium to locate the fleeing monster.

On his part, Dracula hates modernity—or, at least, he is nervous of it. He cannot read shorthand and throws Harker's encrypted writings on the fire in disgust. He chooses to come to England by sail, not steamboat. He studiously avoids the railway for the transport of his earth-filled boxes, choosing instead gipsy carts. What this means is that in the struggle between Van Helsing and Dracula, we have a contest between the 'pagan world of old' and 'modernity' (p. 134). A demon from the Dark Ages pitted against men of the 1890s armed with Winchester rifles, telegrams, phonographs, modern medicine and science. Stoker's Transylvania is certainly Gothic and ahistorical. But his England is as up-to-date as that week's edition of *Tit-bits*.

Why, it may be asked, does Dracula want to come to England? It would seem he has something more than tourism in mind. When we first encounter him, through Harker; he is practising his English to make it flawless, and is studying

books ... of the most varied kind—history, geography, politics, political economy, botany, geology, law—all relating to England and English life and customs and manners. There were even such books of reference as the London Directory, the 'Red' and 'Blue' books, Whitaker's Almanack, the Army and Navy Lists, and—it somehow gladdened my heart to see it—the Law List. (p. 19)

One apprehends from this that Dracula does not want to visit England—he wants to invade it, conquer it, make it his own infernal kingdom. It is notable that his activities in England are very different from those in Transylvania where, apparently, his depredations on the local populace are random, infrequent and rather circumspect (the only local victim we learn of is one baby). In Transylvania Dracula is apparently careful about propagating his kind, keeping his retinue of undead companions to a handful. But in England his promiscuity triggers off a potential infectious epidemic. Lucy becomes one of the undead, and as the 'Bloofer Lady' promptly embarks on infecting any number of children who in their turn will infect others. In a year or so, we can calculate, England will be a pest-hole.

There are huge risks in Dracula moving from his castle fastness in Transylvania. The business of the fifty boxes makes him very vulnerable. The journey itself involves what would seem to be unacceptable risks—his ship is almost wrecked off Whitby (and death by drowning is, together with a stake through the heart, one of the sure ways in which Dracula can be exterminated). Why do it, and if he must do it, why not choose Germany, which at least would shorten the distance back to his lair and would not entail passing over the dangerous element of water?

The reason for Dracula's coming to England is divulged late in the narrative by Van Helsing. 'Do you not see', he asks Harker, 'how, of late, this monster has been creeping into knowledge experimentally?' (p. 302). Dracula, in other words, is learning how to think scientifically. The point is elaborated by the perspicacious professor a little later:

With the child-brain that was to him he have long since conceive the idea of coming to a great city. What does he do? He find out the place of all the world most of promise for him. Then he deliberately set himself down to prepare for the task. He find in patience just how is his strength, and what are his powers. He study new tongues. He learn new social life; new environment of old ways, the politic, the law, the finance, the science, the habit of a new land and a new people who have come to be since he was. His glimpse that he have had whet his appetite only and enkeen his desire. Nay, it help him to grow as to his brain; for it all prove to him how right he was at the first in his surmises. He have done all this alone; all alone! from a ruin tomb in a forgotten land. What more may he not do when the greater world of thought is open to him? (pp. 320–1)

Dracula, we apprehend, has chosen England because it

is the most modern country in the world—the most modern that is, in its social organization, its industry, its education, its science. Put in its most banal form, he has come to England to learn how to use the Kodak, how to write shorthand, and how to operate the recording phonograph in order that he may make himself a thoroughly modern vampire for the imminent twentieth century.

The Oxford World's Classics *Dracula* is edited by Maud Ellmann.

Rudyard Kipling · *Kim*

═══

How old is Kim?

═══

Alan Sandison notes in his introduction to the World's Classics edition of *Kim* that 'As a physical being, Kim remains a rather shadowy figure' (p. xvii). One of the shadowier aspects of Kipling's young hero is his precise age during the first half of the narrative—the period of his Indian liberty before he is (reluctantly) made a 'Sahib'. The opening encounter finds Kim—indistinguishable from Hindu lads of his age—playing 'King of the Castle' astride the great gun Zam-Zammah (a symbol of the mastery of the Punjab, as Sandison points out). 'King of the Castle' is, of course, child's play. The brief description which Kipling gives of the game suggests the players are very childish indeed:

'Off! Off! Let me up!' cried Abdullah, climbing up Zam-Zammah's wheel.

'Thy father was a pastry-cook, Thy mother stole the *ghi*,' sang Kim. 'All Mussalmans fell off Zam-Zammah long ago!'

'Let *me* up!' shrilled little Chota Lal in his gilt-embroidered cap. His father was worth perhaps half a million sterling, but India is the only democratic land in the world.

'The Hindus fell off Zam-Zammah too. The Mussalmans pushed them off. Thy father was a pastry cook—' (p. 4)

At this point, Kim has his first astonishing sight of the Lama, whose *chela*, or guide, he is to become.

In passing we are given the bare details of Kim's parentage. His father was a young colour-sergeant in the Mavericks, an Irish regiment. Kimball O'Hara married a nursemaid in a Colonel's family (given the shortage of

eligible young European women in India, Sergeant
O'Hara must have been a dashing fellow). After marriage,
he resigned the service and took a post on the Sind, Punjab, and Delhi railway. A child arrived soon after and soon
after that Annie O'Hara died of cholera in Ferozepore.
The husband, left with a 'keen three-year-old baby', went
to the bad, took to opium, and died. From his very
imperfect English (he thinks, for example, that his father
served in an 'Eyerishti' regiment, p. 86), Kim must have
been left a young orphan. He has been brought up by a
lady of easy virtue in the bazaar.

The keynote in early descriptions of Kim, 'the little
friend of the world', is the incantatory use of the term
'little'. Take, for example, the early instance of his street-
wise resourcefulness in kicking away the bull (a sacred
beast to Hindus) from the stall of the vegetable seller, thus
ensuring a charitable donation of food for the Lama:

The huge, mouse-coloured Brahminee bull of the ward was
shouldering his way through the many-coloured crowd, a stolen
plantain hanging out of his mouth. He headed straight for the
shop, well knowing his privileges as a sacred beast, lowered his
head, and puffed heavily along the line of baskets ere making his
choice. Up flew Kim's hard little heel and caught him on his
moist blue nose. He snorted indignantly, and walked away across
the tram rails, his hump quivering with rage. (p. 14)

'Hard little heel' suggests a hard little fellow. When he
falls in with the Mavericks, the chaplain (seizing on the
charm around his neck which contains his birth certificate) tells Kim: 'Little boys who steal are beaten. You
know that?' (p. 84). A couple of pages on, in the same vein,
the narrative observes that 'small boys who prowl about
camps are generally turned out after a whipping. But
[Kim] received no stripes' (p. 86). On the next page he is 'a
phenomenal little liar' (p. 87) and a 'little imp' (p. 96) and a
'little limb of Satan' (p. 97).

Answering from their general impressions, most readers would see Kim as somewhere between 9 and 12. There is some confirmation of this when we are told that 'Kim had many dealings with Mahbub *in his little life,*—especially between his tenth and his thirteenth year' (p. 18; that is, between the ages of 9 and 12). When Kim falls into the hands of his father's regiment, it is clear that he is too 'little' to be recruited as a drummer-boy—young soldiers who are 14 and up. One (later discarded) plan is to send the little waif 'to the Military Orphanage at Sanawar where the regiment would keep you till you were old enough to enlist' (pp. 104–5). Kim could, of course, enlist on his fourteenth birthday, as have other drummer-boys in the regiment. As the son of a not very illustrious colour-sergeant, this would seem quite appropriate.

It is fair to say that most readers see the Kim of Kipling's early chapters as a 12-year-old urchin, rather young and small for his years. It is partly because he is so 'little' that the Mavericks adopt him as a mascot, to be treated with unusual care. Hollywood, which has to be definite about such things, made Kim the same very juvenile age as Sabu the Elephant boy, or 'Boy' in the Tarzan films, in the 1950 film (starring Errol Flynn as Mahbub, and the child-star Dean Stockwell as Kim).

Perplexingly, a different calculus of Kim's age emerges in the Maverick scenes—one which would make him significantly older. On the face of it, one can see why this happens. It is specifically stated in the first chapter that Sergeant Kimball O'Hara was demobilized from his regiment, which duly 'went home without him' (p. 1). Kim cannot have been born long after—at most a couple of years and conceivably less. What this means is that the Mavericks have been posted home from India to Ireland, and then posted out again. Moving a thousand men and all their *matériel* twice across the globe is no small thing,

even for the rulers of the British Empire, and two such
tours of duty in peacetime could not possibly have taken
place without an interval of many years, and possibly decades. Father Victor; who was evidently a young Catholic
chaplain on the earlier Indian posting, recalls 'I saw
Kimball married myself to Annie Shott' (p. 86). The impression the reader gets is that it happened a long time ago.

By this second chronological scheme, Kim is something
over 14—on the brink of adolescence. It is, of course, hard
to square this with his playing 'King of the Castle' and
flashing his 'hard little heel' at the Brahminical bull. But,
by reference to specific date-markers in the book, we can
calculate that Kim spends something under three years at
St Xavier's, where he makes remarkable progress:

It is written in the books of St Xavier in Partibus that a report of
Kim's progress was forwarded at the end of each term to Colonel
Creighton and to Father Victor, from whose hands duly came the
money for his schooling. It is further recorded in the same books
that he showed a great aptitude for mathematical studies as well
as map-making, and carried away a prize (*The Life of Lord
Lawrence*, tree-calf, two vols., nine rupees, eight annas) for proficiency therein; and the same term played in St Xavier's eleven
against the Allyghur Mohammedan College, his age being
fourteen years and ten months ... Kim seems to have passed an
examination in elementary surveying 'with great credit', his age
being fifteen years and eight months. From this date the record
is silent. His name does not appear in the year's batch of those
who entered for the subordinate Survey of India, but against it
stands the words, 'removed on appointment.'

Several times in those three years, cast up at the Temple of the
Tirthankers in Benares the lama, a little thinner and a shade
yellower, if that were possible, but gentle and untainted as ever.
(pp. 164–5)

It is earlier indicated that graduation from the school will
happen when Kim is 17 (pp. 118, 176), which indicates that
he enters at 14, or something over.

The cricket-playing Kim seems significantly older than the King-of the-Castle-playing Kim of eight months earlier ('little Kim', as we may call him). Possibly, as young boys do, Kim had his growing spurt at this period, and started on the dramatic physical changes and enlargements involved in puberty.[1] What seems more likely is that Kipling has two Kims in his mind. One, 'little Kim', corresponds to the 'Indian' Rudyard, who left India at the age of 6, and who idealized his early experience of the subcontinent in Kim's early escapades in the bazaar. Kipling saw this early segment of his life as immensely important. He begins his autobiography, *Something of Myself*, with the statement: 'Give me the first six years of a child's life, and you can have the rest.'[2] That formative phase of his life would seem to be memorialized in the early chapters of *Kim*, and Kim is correspondingly infantile.

The other Kim corresponds to the pubescent Kipling who was enrolled at the age of 13 in the United Services College at Westward Ho!, in Devon (an institution with clear similarities to St Xavier's—both institutions train English boys for the colonial service). One Kim is a diminutive urchin, the other a coltish schoolboy. A third, and more stable Kim, the adolescent on the verge of manhood, dominates the second half of the novel. How old is Kim? It depends on the angle.

The Oxford World's Classics *Kim* is edited by Alan Sandison.

Can Jane Eyre be Happy?

Daniel Defoe · *Robinson Crusoe*

—

Why the 'Single Print of a Foot'?

—

J. Donald Crowley is amusingly exasperated about Defoe's
many narrative delinquencies in *Robinson Crusoe*. 'Perhaps the most glaring lapse', Crowley says in his edition of
the novel,

> occurs when Defoe, having announced that Crusoe had pulled
> off all his clothes to swim out to the shipwreck, has him stuff his
> pockets with biscuit some twenty lines later. Likewise, for the
> purpose of creating a realistic effect, he arranges for Crusoe to
> give up tallying his daily journal because his ink supply is
> dangerously low; but there is ink aplenty, when, almost twenty-
> seven years later, Crusoe wants to draw up a contract. . . Having
> tried to suggest that Crusoe suffers hardship because he lacks
> salt, he later grants Crusoe the salt in order to illustrate his
> patient efforts to teach Friday to eat salted meat. Crusoe pens a
> kid identified as a young male only to have it turn into a female
> when he hits upon the notion of breeding more of the animals.
> (p. xiii)

Such inconsistencies convince Crowley that 'Defoe wrote
too hastily to control his materials completely'. His was a
careless genius.

   Haste and carelessness could well account for some
baffling features in the famous 'discovery of the footprint'
scene. It occurs fifteen years into Robinson's occupation
of his now thoroughly colonized and (as he fondly thinks)
desert island. At this belated point the hero is made to
describe his outdoor garb. He has long since worn out
the European clothes which survived the wreck. Now his
coverings are home-made:

Clark & Pine S[c]

1. Frontispiece from the first edition, 1719

I had a short Jacket of Goat-Skin, the Skirts coming down to about the middle of my Thighs; and a Pair of open-knee'd Breeches of the same, the Breeches were made of the Skin of an old *He-goat*, whose Hair hung down such a Length on either Side, that like *Pantaloons* it reach'd to the middle of my Legs; Stockings and Shoes I had none, but had made me a Pair of somethings, I scarce know what to call them, like Buskins to flap over my Legs, and lace on either Side like Spatter-dashes; but of a most barbarous Shape, as indeed were all the rest of my Cloaths. (p. 149)

This sartorial inventory has been gratefully seized on by the novel's many illustrators, from 1719 onwards (see fig. 1). The salient feature is that Robinson goes barefoot. And it is to rivet this detail ('Shoes I had none') in our mind that at this point Defoe describes Crusoe's wardrobe. In the preceding narrative, if it crosses the reader's mind, we assume that Crusoe has some protection for the soles of his feet (the island is a rough place). Oddly, Robinson seems not to have taken a supply of footwear from the ship's store nor any cobbling materials with which to make laced moccasins from goatskin. Shortly after being marooned he found 'two shoes' washed up on the strand, but they 'were not fellows', and were of no use to him. Much later, during his 'last year on the Island', Robinson scavenges a couple of pairs of shoes from the bodies of drowned sailors in the wreck of the Spanish boat. But, when he sees the naked footprint on the sand, Crusoe is barefoot.

The footprint is epochal, 'a new Scene of my Life', as Crusoe calls it. He has several habitations on the island (his 'estate', as he likes to think it) and the discovery comes as he walks from one of his inland residences to the place on the shore where he has beached his 'boat' (in fact, a primitive canoe):

It happen'd one Day about Noon going towards my Boat, I was exceedingly surpriz'd with the Print of a Man's naked Foot on the Shore, which was very plain to be seen in the Sand: I stood like one Thunder-struck, or as if I had seen an Apparition; I listen'd, I look'd round me, I could hear nothing, nor see any Thing. I went up to a rising Ground to look farther, I went up the Shore and down the Shore, but it was all one, I could see no other Impression but that one, I went to it again to see if there were any more, and observe if it might not be my Fancy; but there was no Room for that, for there was exactly the very Print of a Foot, Toes, Heel, and every Part of a Foot; how it came thither, I knew not, nor could in the least imagine. (pp. 153–4)

2. Lynton Lamb, cover design for Oxford University Press, 1957

Two big questions hang over this episode. The first, most urgent for Robinson, is 'Who made this footprint?' The second, most perplexing for the reader, is 'why is there only one footprint?' In the above passage, and later, Crusoe is emphatic on the point. We are not much helped by illustrations of the scene, such as that above by Lynton Lamb to an early World's Classics edition, which shows the footprint, on a flat expanse of beach, with nothing else for yards around. (It's a lovely picture; but Lamb has erroneously given Crusoe a pair of Scholl sandals.[1])

Was the single footprint made by some monstrous hopping cannibal? Perhaps Long John Silver passed by, from *Treasure Island*, with just the one foot and a peg leg? Has someone played a prank on Robinson Crusoe by raking over the sand as one does in a long-jump pit, leaving just the one ominous mark? More seriously, one might surmise that the ground is stony with only a few patches of sand between to receive an occasional footprint. This is the interpretation of G. H. Thomas in the next version of this scene (note the shoes, again). The objection to the thesis of this illustration is that Crusoe would scarcely choose such a rocky inlet as a convenient place to beach his boat.

Robinson has no time for investigation of the footprint. He retreats in hurried panic to his 'Castle', not emerging for three days. Is it the mark of the Devil, he wonders, as he cowers inside his dark cave? That would explain the supernatural singularity of the footprint, since the devil can fly. In his fever vision, years before, Robinson saw the Evil One 'descend from a great black Cloud, in a bright Flame of Fire, and light upon the Ground' (p. 87)— presumably leaving an enigmatic footprint in the process, if anyone dared look. But if the mark in the sand is the devil's work it would seem lacking in infernal cunning or even clear purpose: 'the Devil might have found an

3. Illustration by George Housman Thomas, from an edition of 1865

abundance of other Ways to have terrify'd me than this of
the single Print of a Foot', Robinson concludes.[2] Similar
arguments weigh against the footprint's being a sign from
the Almighty. It is more plausible, Robinson finally concludes, 'that it must be some of the Savages of the main
Land over-against me, who had wander'd out to Sea in
their *Canoes*'. Will they now come back in force, to
'devour' him?

Fear banishes 'all my religious Hope' for a while. But
gradually Crusoe's faith in Providence returns, as does his
trust in rational explanation. 'I began to perswade my self
it was all a Delusion; that it was nothing else but . . .the
Print of my own foot' (p. 158). He emerges from his hole
and, stopping only to milk the distended teats of his goats,
he returns to examine the print more carefully. In three
days and nights one might expect it to have been covered
over by the wind, but it is still there, clear as ever. Crusoe's
rational explanation proves to be wrong: 'When I came to
measure the Mark with my own Foot, I found my Foot not
so large by a great deal.' Panic once more.

We are never specifically told who left the print, nor why
it was just the one. But the experience changes Robinson
Crusoe's way of life. No longer supposing himself alone,
he adopts a more defensive ('prudent') way of life. He is
right to be prudent. Some two years later, on the other side
of the island, he sees a boat out at sea. That far coast, he
now realizes, is frequently visited—unlike his own: 'I was
presently convinc'd, that the seeing the Print of a Man's
Foot, was not such a strange Thing in the Island as I imag-
in'd.' Providence, he is grateful to realize, has cast him
'upon the Side of the Island, where the Savages never
came' (p. 164). Never? Who left the print then—friendly
Providence, as a warning that there were savages about?

Gradually Crusoe comes, by prudent anthropological
observation, to know more about the Savages—a process

that culminates ten years after the footprint episode with the acquisition of his most valuable piece of property, Man Friday. The savages are, as Robinson observes, opportunist raiders of the sea—black pirates with a taste for human flesh. When they find some luckless wrecked mariner, or defenceless fellow native in his craft, the savages bring their prey to shore to cook and eat them. Then they leave. In their grisly visits they never penetrate beyond the sandy beach to the interior of the island (perhaps, as in Golding's *Lord of the Flies*, there are legends of a terrible giant, dressed in animal skins, with a magical tube which spurts thunder). It is likely that the footprint must have been left by some scouting savage making a rare foray to the far side of the island. He noticed Crusoe's boat, concluded on close inspection that it was flotsam, and went off again. Luckily the hero's residences, livestock, and plantations were some way distant and could not be seen from this section of the shore.

But why the single footprint? Before attempting an answer one needs to make the point that although careless in accidental details (such as the trousers and the biscuits), Defoe usually handles substantial twists of plot very neatly. A good example is the corn which Crusoe first thinks is providential manna but which later proves to have a rational origin. Defoe sets this episode up by mentioning, on page 50, that Robinson brought back some barley seed from his wrecked ship, 'but to my great Disappointment, I found afterwards that the Rats had eaten or spoil'd it all'. He threw it away in disgust. Then, twenty-eight pages later, the seed sprouts. Robinson at first believes the growing barley to be a miracle. Then he puts two and two together and realizes it is the result of his thoughtlessly shaking out the bags of spoiled chicken-feed some months earlier. It is an accomplished piece of narrative.

A few pages before the episode of the footprint Defoe has Crusoe describe, in great detail, the tides which wash the island and their intricate ebbs and flows. Many readers will skip over this technical and unexciting digression. Ostensibly, Crusoe's meditation on the 'Sets of the Tides' has to do with navigation problems. But the ulterior motive, we may assume, is to imprint in the reader's mind the fact that the island does have tides and that they are forever lapping at its shoreline.

What we may suppose happened is the following. Crusoe has beached his boat, not on the dead-flat expanse which Lamb portrays, but on a steeply inclined beach. The unknown savage came head-on into the beach and pulled his boat on to the sand. He investigated Crusoe's canoe, all the while walking below the high-tide line. Having satisfied himself that Crusoe's vessel had no one in it, he returned to his own craft. Coming or going, one of his feet (as he was knocked by a wave, perhaps, or jumped away from some driftwood) strayed above the high-water mark. This lateral footprint (i.e. not pointing to, or away from, the ocean) was left after the tide had washed all the others away together with the drag marks of the savage's boat.

Robinson Crusoe's discovery of the footprint is, with Oliver Twist's asking for more, one of the best-known episodes in British fiction—familiar even to those who would scarcely recognize the name of Daniel Defoe. It is also one of the English novel's most illustrated scenes—particularly in the myriad boys' editions of *Robinson Crusoe*. Most illustrations I have seen make one of three errors (as does Lamb above): they put the footprint too far from the waves; they picture Robinson as wearing shoes; they show the beach as too flat. These errors, I think, reflect widespread perplexity at the scene and a fatalistic inclination not to worry too much about its illogical details. But there are, as I have tried to argue, ways of making sense of the single footprint. And at least one illustrator has interpreted the scene as I have. Despite its rather melodramatic *mise en scène*, the most persuasive pictorial interpretation I have seen is this by George Cruikshank (although he too gives Robinson shoes).

The Oxford World's Classics *Robinson Crusoe* is edited by J. Donald Crowley.

Illustration by George Cruikshank,
from an edition of 1890

John Cleland · *Fanny Hill*

Where does Fanny Hill keep her contraceptives?

I first read *Fanny Hill* (or, more properly, *Memoirs of a Woman of Pleasure*) in the 1950s, when it was still a banned book. A friend loaned me a much-thumbed copy, vilely printed in Tangiers, and evidently smuggled in by a merchant sailor. Any bookseller handling Cleland's 'erotic masterpiece' in 1955 would have faced prosecution. British schoolboys caught with the book might expect instant expulsion. Adults found in possession would probably receive a formal police warning[1] and summary confiscation of the offending object (which, one guesses, would be eagerly pored over at the station). *Fanny Hill* was a much less exciting text after it—along with *Lady Chatterley's Lover*—was 'acquitted' and became a legal high street commodity.[2] It was elevated to classic status by Penguin in 1985 and by OUP as a World's Classic in the same year. Doubtless some of the more adventurous A-level boards will soon be prescribing *Fanny Hill* as a set text and the BBC will chip in with a 'Book at Bedtime' version.

Fanny Hill was, one suspects, a subversive presence in English literature during its long career as an 'underground' text—particularly in the moralistic Victorian era. It seems likely that Dickens read it, and at a number of points one can plausibly detect its mark in his fiction. Mr Dick, the amiable, kite-flying idiot in *David Copperfield*, conceivably owes his name—and possibly more—to the idiot in *Fanny Hill:* 'The boys, and servants in the

neighbourhood, had given him the nickname of *Good-
natured Dick*, from the soft simpleton's doing everything
he was bid to do at the first word, and from his naturally
having no turn to mischief' (p. 160).

In a spirit of lascivious mischief Fanny and Louisa
undress Good-natured Dick. His *membrum virile* amazes
them: 'prepar'd as we were to see something extraordinary, it still, out of measure surpassed our expectation, and
astonish'd even me, who had not been us'd to trade in
trifles' (p. 162). Modest Fanny merely looks but the wanton
Louisa must sample the aptly named Dick's 'maypole'. And
so, we learn, do other women, inflamed by Louisa's 'report
of his parts'. As a sexual toy, Dick has the advantage that
since he remembers nothing he can be trusted to be discreet. He is no more likely to blab than a king-sized,
battery-operated vibrator. Obviously Miss Trotwood
would not, like Louisa, misconduct herself with her
Dick—whose 'King Charles's head' keeps poking in
everywhere (Fanny's true love is called Charles, we recall;
he too is a great one for poking). But a spinster living
alone with an adult man would surely give rise to bawdy
speculation among the locals. It was Victorian folklore
that all idiots had massive penises (something that features in depictions of the age's favourite mascot, Mr
Punch, and his phallic truncheon). Every schoolboy would
have a sniggering awareness of the *double entendre* in Mr
Dick's name.

Joss Lutz Marsh, in a perceptive article,[3] notes another
interesting echo from *Fanny Hill* in Dickens's *Dombey and
Son*. When Florence Dombey loses her way in London she
is abducted by a horrible crone who calls herself 'Good
Mrs Brown'. 'A very ugly old woman, with red rims round
her eyes', Mrs Brown deals in rags and bones in a small
way. She incarcerates Florence in a filthy back room in a
shabby house in a dirty London lane. Mrs Brown then

strips off all Florence's clothes and gives her rags to cover
herself with. For a few moments we picture the little girl
either in her underclothes or stark naked. Suddenly Mrs
Brown catches sight of Florence's head of luxuriant hair
under her bonnet and is gripped by the lust to clip the
tresses off and sell them. She obviously has further plans
to make money out of the child's body which are happily
forestalled when Florence escapes to be rescued by Walter.

Mrs Brown's predatoriness should be read metaphoric-
ally, Marsh suggests. With a little adjustment we can see
'Good Mrs Brown' as a procuress of underage girls for
immoral purposes, one of the suppliers of the 'tribute of
Babylon'. When she has stripped and shorn Florence, Mrs
Brown will sell what is left to some expensive London
brothel specializing in juvenile virgins. As Marsh is
apparently the first to notice, there is an echo here from
Cleland's novel. When 15-year-old Fanny Hill comes to
London the first of the procuresses she falls in with is Mrs
Brown. A 'squob-fat, red-fac'd' woman of 'at least fifty',
possessed of Messalina's appetites, Cleland's Mrs Brown
is not an attractive personage, if not quite as revolting as
her Dickensian namesake. Cleland's bawd tries to sell
Fanny's maidenhead to the odious Mr Crofts but when
that fails (Fanny having heroically kept her legs crossed)
Mrs Brown treats the young virgin not at all badly. She is
put in the charge of a kind-hearted trull, 'Mrs' Phoebe
Ayres, 'whose business it was to prepare and break such
young Fillies as I was to the mounting-block' (p. 9). Phoebe
is Fanny's 'tuteress'. By cunning (and gentle) lesbian
caresses the older woman stimulates Fanny's latent sen-
suality and by voyeuristic spectacles she instructs the
child in the mechanics of sex and its repertoire of 'pleasures'. Phoebe also inducts her pupil into 'all the mysteries
of Venus'. They probably include, as we deduce from
Fanny's later career, planned parenthood.

Having benefited from Phoebe's tuition, Fanny is now
ready for the next phase of her career. She elopes with her
19-year-old 'Adonis', Charles, to a convenient public house
in Chelsea, where she finally surrenders her maidenhead.
The young lovers enjoy each other many times and with
excesses of mutual 'pleasure'. Physically Charles is both a
man of wax and a man of means. The only son of a prosperous revenue officer, he is also the favourite of a wealthy
grandmother. Charles rescues Fanny from Mr Brown's
clutches and promptly sets her up as his mistress in
apartments with another bawd—Mrs Jones. Fanny, looking back on events, expresses a strong dislike for this new
protector. Mrs Jones is a 'private procuress . . . about forty
six years old, tall, meager, red-hair'd, with one of those
trivial ordinary faces you meet with everywhere . . . a
harpy' (pp. 51–2). On the side she engages 'in private pawnbroking and other profitable secrets' (abortion, as we
apprehend).

Fanny resides under Mrs Jones's uncongenial roof for
eleven months, at which point she is, as she tells us, 'about
three months gone with child'. One deduces that she is
pregnant by policy not accident. Over the months Charles
has been 'educating' her—expunging her rusticity, making her a lady 'worthier of his heart'. His love, she protests, is of 'unshaken constancy', and he 'sacrificed to me
women of greater importance than I dare hint' (p. 53). It is
clear that Fanny fondly expects to marry Charles—despite
the class difference and the fact that he found her in a
London brothel. It is to this end that she has allowed herself to become pregnant—to force his hand.

What follows in Fanny's account is highly suspect. She
herself confesses that she will 'gallop post over the particulars' (p. 54). According to her skimped version of
events, Charles (who has just learned that Fanny is with
child) is kidnapped by his father and put on a boat leaving

that hour for the South Seas where a rich uncle has just died. He is not allowed to dispatch any messages (or money) back to shore. Although it is said that he later sends letters, they all 'miscarry'. Implausible, one might think.

Fanny learns from a maid that Charles has left the country and that any attempt to communicate with him is hopeless. She is alone again in the world, penniless and pregnant. Her ruse, if ruse the pregnancy was, has backfired. What actually happened seems clear enough, if we discount (as probability suggests we should) Fanny's version of events. Charles confessed to his father that he had made a woman of the town pregnant. Her bawd would swear the child was his. It would be very embarrassing for the revenue officer—and expensive. Aged 20, Charles could not marry without paternal consent even if he wanted to, and he probably does not intend to ruin his prospects by setting up house with a reformed whore. He is sent abroad for a couple of years until the whole thing blows over. The traditional solution for young men of good families who got into this kind of pickle was to send them away— preferably as far and for as long as possible.

According to Fanny she swoons when she hears the news of her lover's disappearance and, after 'several successive fits, all the while wild and senseless, I miscarried of the dear pledge of my *Charles*'s love' (p. 56). What seems more likely is that Mrs Jones aborted the child. Fanny now has only one resource—to sell herself, preferably as a 'virgin' newly up from the country. She owes Jones a huge sum for rent (over £23), and unless she can go on the game she will find herself in prison—as her landlady unkindly reminds her. Carrying Charles's 'pledge' to term is out of the question unless she wants to enter motherhood in Bridewell.

Under Mrs Jones's guidance, Fanny for the first time

takes paying clients. Some welcome stability enters her
professional life when she becomes the mistress of Mr
H—. But, after seven months, in sheer boredom, she surrenders to her protector's massively endowed footman,
Will. When she is discovered *in flagrante*, Mr H— turns
her into the streets with 50 guineas (he is not a hard-
hearted man, we apprehend). Thus Fanny, still only 16,
comes under the care of the third and most amiable of her
bawds, Mrs Cole. Mrs Cole is not only good-natured, but
conscientiously instructs her whores in 'prudential economy'. She is a skilled madame. 'Nobody', Fanny says, had
'more experience of the wicked part of the town than she
had [or] was fitter to advise and guard one against the
worst dangers of our profession' (p. 88). One main danger is
disease; the other, we guess, is pregnancy.

Enriched by three years' service with Mrs Cole, Fanny
('not yet 19') finds herself possessed of a fortune and,
thanks to her patroness, knows how to look after her nest-
egg. She is now an independent woman and has been making desultory enquiries about the whereabouts of the
errant Charles. On a triumphant trip to show herself off in
her native Lancashire village she is finally reunited with
her lover by accident. He has been shipwrecked coming
back from the South Seas. More to the point, he is now a
poor man. The tables are turned but Fanny's heart is true.
She accepts him as her husband and they go on to have
'those fine children you have seen by this happiest of
matches'.

Over the five years of our acquaintance with her, Fanny
avoids pregnancy when it would be professionally
inconvenient. She becomes pregnant when (as she wrong-
ly thinks) it will coerce Charles into marriage. She has
legitimate children after marriage. How does she control
her reproductive functions so efficiently? *Fanny Hill* is
unusual among works of popular pornography in that it

does not assume that the sexual act has no consequences—
venereal disease and pregnancy are always darkening the
edge of the heroine's 'pleasures'. The house of accommodation under the supervision of a knowledgeable bawd
offers invaluable prophylaxes for someone in Fanny's position. It is clear that Mrs Cole screens clients to eliminate
the grosser disease carriers.[4] It is only slightly less clear
that the Cole establishment is furnished with an efficient
contraceptive apparatus for the working girls. The nature
of the apparatus is obliquely described in the scene where
Fanny has to fabricate a broken hymen for the benefit of
Mr Norbert.

In each of the head bed-posts, just above where the bed-steads are
inserted into them, there was a small drawer so artfully adapted
to the mouldings of the timber-work, that it might have escap'd
even the most curious search, which drawers were easily open'd
or shut, by the touch of a spring, and were fitted each with a
shallow glass tumbler, full of a prepar'd fluid blood; in which lay
soak'd, for ready use, a spunge that requir'd no more than gently
reaching the hand to it, taking it out, and properly squeezing
between the thighs. (p. 135)

The defloration of virgin would be a relatively rare
event in Mrs Cole's house. Rich fools like Mr Norbert are
not come by every day. But the sponge and the tumbler
would have a more quotidian usage, justifying the expensive alterations to the bedroom furniture. As Peter Fryer
records in his history of birth control, there were in the
eighteenth century five approved forms of contraception:
coitus interruptus, anal intercourse, primitive condoms,
exotic prophylactic potions (spermicides or abortifa-
cients), and vaginal sponges—usually dipped first in a
tumbler of some such spermicide as brandy or vinegar.[5]
There is no coitus interruptus in *Fanny Hill*—the 'bal-
samic fluid' is invariably 'inspers'd' in the woman's 'seat of
love'. Fanny, her fellow whores, and her bawds have a holy

horror of sodomy. There is no mention of condoms—which
in this period are associated less with the class of whore-
mongers who patronize Fanny than with virtuoso liber-
tines like Casanova (whose 'English overcoat' was made of
sheep's gut). Vaginal sponges, however, would seem to be
quite at home in the world of *Fanny Hill*, conveniently
available on every bedpost.

The Oxford World's Classics *Memoirs of a Woman of Pleasure*
(Fanny Hill) is edited by Peter Sabor.

Henry Fielding · *Tom Jones*

—

Who is Tom Jones's father?

—

According to the scholar John Mullan, even readers who
know Fielding's novel well will struggle with the above
question, without recourse to the book. One can see why
Tom's paternity should be something of a poser. The crucial information is held back until the very last pages and
then passed over quickly. Maternity is something else.
That young Jones is Bridget Allworthy's offspring will be
picked up early by astute readers. It is implicit in Miss
Allworthy's instant partiality for the foundling—a partiality which continues even after she has a legitimate
child of her own (whom she evidently hates as his father's
son)—and her refusal to join in the persecution of Jenny
Jones. Fielding sows a number of such hints in the early
chapters. But the author tantalizingly withholds the identity of Tom's father—even from the characters themselves
at crucial junctures. It was, as Jenny tells Mr Allworthy,
always Bridget's intention 'to communicate it to you'. But
when she sends her deathbed confession via Dowling, it is
frustrating (particularly for Blifil, who intercepts the
message) that Bridget does not, even on the brink of
eternity, name Tom's father. 'She took me by the hand,'
Dowling recalls, 'and as she delivered me the letter, said, "I
scarce know what I have written. Tell my brother Mr
Jones is his nephew.—He is my son.—Bless him," says she,
and then fell backward, as if dying away. I presently called
in the people, and she never spoke more to me, and died
within a few minutes afterwards' (p. 840). Her son, and who
else's?

Finally, at the denouement of the novel, Mrs Waters (formerly Jenny Jones) enlightens Allworthy Tom's father, we at last learn, was 'a young fellow' called Summer. We never learn his Christian name, nor is his surname mentioned before this point. Allworthy remembers the young fellow well: 'he was the son of a clergyman of great learning and virtue, for whom I had the highest friendship.' Apparently Summer was orphaned and there was no immediate family. Allworthy 'bred the young man up, and maintained him at university'. He came to reside at Mr Allworthy's house on graduation—beating the trail later followed by Square and Thwackum. Allworthy treated Master Summer like a son.

Young Summer 'was untimely snatched away' by smallpox leaving Miss Allworthy pregnant. For reasons which are not entirely clear, Bridget then confided her plight to Jenny Jones and to Jenny's mother—but not to her own brother. Jenny had recently been dismissed from service with the Little Baddington schoolmaster, Partridge (later one of Tom's putative fathers), on grounds of sexual looseness—not, one would have thought, a strong recommendation for her to be taken into the moralistic Miss Allworthy's service. But the lady had her reasons.

It is a stroke of fortune for the conspirators that Mr Allworthy is away on a three-month sojourn in London. When Bridget's time comes the unreliable Deborah Wilkins is sent off on a wild-goose chase to Dorset to investigate the character of a prospective servant (Bridget has dismissed her personal maid three months earlier—clearly the girl knew too much about the affair with Summer). As Jenny recalls, 'It was . . . contrived, that my mother and myself only should attend at that time'. The plan was that Jenny should 'own' Bridget's child—in return for a handsome sum of money 'The child was born', Jenny tells Allworthy, 'in the presence only of myself and my mother, and was by my mother conveyed to her own house, where it was privately kept by her till the evening of your return, when I, by the command of Miss Bridget, conveyed it into the bed where you found it' (p. 833). Thus begins the novel.

There is little encouragement for us to go back and reread the early chapters in the light of Jenny's last-page revelation. Bridget is a shadowy presence in the narrative after the death of Captain Blifil. Any residual curiosity we have about her is deliberately damped down. There are only a few offhand references to Miss Allworthy in the last seventeen years of her life. She dies, as she has largely lived, off-stage.

If, however, we do make the effort to go back and insert Jenny's information about Summer into the early chapters an interestingly enigmatic subplot can be reconstructed. At the time of Tom's birth Bridget Allworthy is 'past the age of thirty' (p. 32)—a euphemism for nearly 40, as we learn at the time of her courtship by Captain Blifil. She is a woman 'whom you commend rather for good qualities than beauty' (p. 32). Since her good qualities are headed by religious hypocrisy, duplicity, and sexual incontinence, her beauty must be small indeed. She is not quick-witted (as Jenny is). Why would Summer, almost twenty years her junior, and university educated, be attracted to Bridget? He was, as Jenny recalls with suspicious warmth: 'the handsomest person I ever saw, he was so genteel, and had so much wit and good breeding.'

The Allworthy fortune, of course, may add a golden lustre to Bridget's otherwise meagre attractions. Some five years earlier Allworthy's three children and his wife were wiped out in a previous smallpox epidemic, as we assume. Bridget, much younger than her brother, is now his inheritrix. Who, then, seduced whom? What deduction should we draw from Bridget's sordid liaison, a few months after giving birth to Tom, with Captain Blifil? Rather than announce his suit to Mr Allworthy (whom he fears would not approve the match) Blifil methodically sets out to seduce Bridget Allworthy into a clandestine marriage. To this end, he assaults her virtue on three occasions. Twice she responds, *'nolo episcopari'* ('I do not want the bishopric'—with the stress on the last syllable). On the third occasion, it emerges she does want the bishopric. A month later they are secretly married. Eight months after the marriage, Blifil is born (p. 69). Did young Summer, like Blifil, impregnate the spinster with a view to guarantee-ing Allworthy's acquiescence to an otherwise unpropi-tious match?

Summer leaves no residue in the early part of the narrative—although he must have died shortly before the story opens and as an adoptive 'son' to Allworthy must have been a heavy loss. The secret birth of Tom Jones is just plausible, given the absence of Allworthy, Wilkins, and the personal maid. But there are a number of contingent puzzles. Why did Bridget choose to confide in Jenny? Why, when Jenny was examined before Allworthy as magistrate, was evidence not taken as to her pregnancy? While a gentle-lady with private apartments like Bridget might keep her interesting condition secret, a servant like Jenny could surely not, any more than Molly Seagrim can, twenty years later. If Jenny were pregnant, that would be known; if she were not pregnant that would be known too. The foundling Tom would need a wet-nurse—why was Jenny not offered the position? If she were, it would be very suspicious if she said she was unable to suckle because she had no milk.

These puzzles should be taken in conjunction with the piece of news that, a few months later, inflames Anne Partridge to physical violence on her luckless spouse, precipitating his ruin and exile from Little Baddington. One of Anne's gossips tells her, in response to a casual inquiry after Jenny Jones: 'You have not heard, it seems that she hath been brought to bed of two bastards; but as they are not born here . . . we [i.e. the parish] shall not be obliged to keep them.' The two bastards must none the less have been begotten in the parish, Mistress Partridge calculates, 'for the wench hath not been nine months gone away' (p. 77). What provoked the series of events that led to her going away, many months earlier, was a dinner-table *contretemps* in the Partridge household:

the husband and wife being at dinner, the master said to his maid, '*Da mihi aliquid potum*', upon which the poor girl smiled, perhaps at the badness of the Latin, and, when her mistress cast her eyes on her, blushed, possibly with a consciousness of having laughed at her master. Mrs Partridge, upon this, immediately fell into a fury, and discharged the trencher on which she was eating, at the head of poor Jenny, crying out, 'you impudent whore, do you play tricks with my husband before my face?' (p. 73)

Where, or from whom, has Jenny learned better Latin than the schoolmaster who taught her the language? What seems possible is that Summer, having got Bridget pregnant, fell in with the precociously clever Jenny Jones and put her in the family way as well. Jenny, having raised herself above Partridge's level of scholarship, willingly succumbed to the 'handsomest person I ever saw', with his university Latin, his 'wit', and 'gentility'. Tom Jones, it would seem, has inherited his cheerfully polygamous instincts. As Tom can be in love with Sophia Western and simultaneously lust after Mrs Waters (i.e. Jenny Jones), so could Summer with Bridget and Jenny. Like father, like son.

It was, one may hypothesize, their common plight that created the unlikely bond between Miss Allworthy and Miss Jones. The fact that Jenny was pregnant herself would make it easier for her to take charge of Miss Bridget's baby; both children could be looked after by old Mrs

Jones until they were disposed of in their different ways. Hence the gossip about the girl having *two* bastards—a piece of garbled information that must have leaked out via Jenny's mother. There were two bastards in the Jones household for a while—but only one of them was truly Jenny's.

Obviously, in these unhappy circumstances, Miss Allworthy could not marry the promiscuous Mr Summer (a foreshadowing of Sophia's problems with the similarly promiscuous Tom Jones). This impossibility would also explain her vehement reaction to Mr Allworthy's suggestion that she might consider marrying Summer—a vehemence that still mystifies the good old gentleman, two decades later:

I confess [he tells Jenny] I recollect some passages relating to that Summer, which formerly gave me a conceit that my sister had some liking to him. I mentioned it to her: for I had such a regard to the young man, as well on his own account as on his father's, that I should willingly have consented to a match between them; but she expressed the highest disdain of my unkind suspicion, as she called it, so that I never more spoke on the subject. (p. 833)

Why would Bridget not consent to such a suitable arrangement, with a comely, clever, supremely eligible young man; not consent, moreover, when she was carrying his child? Because she did not want to be linked in scurrilous gossip with Jenny Jones who was also carrying Summer's child—thus making herself a figure of ridicule in her community.

The Oxford World's Classics *Tom Jones* is edited by John Bender and Simon Stern.

Laurence Sterne · *Tristram Shandy*

—

Slop Slip

—

'Has anyone noticed that Sterne seems to have over-reached himself and slipped in Volume Two, Chapter 8 of *Tristram Shandy*?' Barbara Hardy asks, in *Notes and Queries*.[1] Her query, and the explanatory note she offers, lead into a beguiling Shandean brain-twister. The 'slip' (which is chronological) is the more remarkable in that Sterne is a writer obsessively concerned with time in his novel. But is it, in fact, a slip?

The passage in question is found on page 83 of the World's Classics edition. At last the hero, Tristram, is about to be born. It has been a long wait for would-be readers of his life and opinions. A commotion has been heard upstairs, where a very pregnant Mrs Shandy is confined with women attendants. Downstairs, Uncle Toby and Mr Shandy anxiously wait on natal events. On hearing the tell-tale noises and bustle above their heads, Uncle Toby has summoned the servant Obadiah by ringing the bell. It is not clear exactly when he performed this act—there have been so many Shandean digressions. But, at some point previously, Obadiah has been sent off post-haste to fetch the man midwife, Dr Slop.

Chapter 8 begins: 'It is about an hour and a half's tolerable good reading since my uncle *Toby* rung the bell, when *Obadiah* was order'd to saddle a horse, and go for Dr. Slop, the man-midwife.' Just a few lines higher up the page, at the end of chapter 7, 'a devil of a rap at the door' has been heard, which has caused Mr Shandy to snap his pipe in two—an event of great significance in the little world of Shandy Hall. The pipe-shattering rap, of course, betokens the arrival of the man midwife (much beslopped, as it will appear, from having fallen in the stable-yard, just outside the house). How did Slop get to Shandy Hall so quickly? It is an eight-mile ride, a sixteen-mile round trip.

Sterne side-steps what the reader really wants to know at this point (has Tristram been born?) for a characteristically subtle disquisition—apropos of Slop's miraculously prompt journey—on real and imaginary duration, which ultimately becomes a cogitation on the nature of fictionality. The issue can be simplified as follows: (1) The 'real' time which has intervened between the ringing of the bell and the knock on the door betokening the arrival of Slop is very short—'no more than two minutes, thirteen seconds, and three fifths', as Sterne 'hypercritically' calculates;[2] (2) in between describing the ringing of the bell and the arrival of Slop, Sterne has digressed to give us a mass of antecedent information: 'I have brought my uncle *Toby* from *Namur*, quite across all *Flanders*, into *England* ... I have had him ill upon my hands near four years; and have since travelled him and Corporal *Trim*, in a chariot and four, a journey of near two hundred miles down into *Yorkshire*' (p. 84). In these digressions, Sterne has chronicled large tracts of imaginary historical time— four years, at least; (3) reading about Uncle Toby's history, in the interval between ring and knock, will occupy the average reader, as Sterne estimates, an hour and a half. The clock time (two minutes, odd) is too short, the narrative time (four years plus) is too long, the reading time (an hour and a half) is just right for the sixteen-mile gallop at ten miles an hour.

The paradox is familiar from films which centre on a long flashback or dream. For example, at the beginning of *The Wizard of Oz* Dorothy is knocked out during a tornado which strikes her family farm in Kansas. She is unconscious, as we reckon, for a few hours at most. During this real time (shown in black and white) Dorothy has a vivid and lengthy Technicolor dream. She and her dream companions make a long journey to the land of Oz which takes several weeks, as we reckon. The film itself lasts an hour and a half in the watching. So when Dorothy, the Tin Man, the Cowardly Lion, and the Scarecrow skip up the yellow-brick road, how long does it take? In Dorothy's unconscious mind, it can occupy only a microsecond or two. In implied narrative time, the journey will take several days. On screen, the yellow-brick road sequence is abbreviated into ten or so minutes. Which is the 'right' answer?

Having posed a similar problem in *Tristram Shandy*, Sterne rudely knocks it down by informing the reader that 'Obadiah had not got above threescore yards from the stable-yard before he met with Dr Slop'. In other words, Obadiah was not, after all, obliged to travel the eight miles to fetch the man midwife. Slop was already on his way and almost arrived at Shandy Hall (all that remained was for him to fall in the stable-yard mire). It's a typical piece of Sterneian one-upmanship. He sets up an elaborate intellectual puzzle, draws the reader into it, and then lets him/her down, like Slop, with a terrific bump.

It's nicely done. But, as Barbara Hardy points out, Sterne spoils the effect of his little ambush on the reader by what looks like a clumsy slip. This slip stands out prominently from the opening sentence of volume II, chapter 8: 'It is about an hour and a half's tolerable good reading since my uncle *Toby* rung the bell.' In fact, as Hardy notes, it is at the beginning of volume II, chapter 6 (only a couple of pages earlier) that the bell was rung. There (II.6) we are given a vignette of Uncle Toby 'taking as I told you, his pipe from his mouth, and striking the ashes out of it as he began his sentence;—I think, replied he,—it would not be amiss, brother, if we rung the bell.' As Hardy points out, 'all that comes between the ringing and the rapping is a two-chapter conversation' between Uncle Toby and Mr Shandy. For even the most primitive reader, this couple of pages would not require more than ten minutes. Where, then, did Sterne get his 'hour and a half' from? It is, Hardy observes, 'a strange lapse since it involves forgetting what happened only two chapters ago'. It is, for a writer as attentive to details of time as Sterne, more than strange— grotesque, even. Hardy surmises that even Sterne, like Homer, can nod, and that an uncharacteristic error has been made.

To return to Hardy's opening query ('has anyone noticed'); another critic, H. K. Russell, thirteen years earlier, noticed the same 'slip'.[3] But Russell picks up that when Sterne writes 'taking *as I told you*, his pipe from his mouth . . . as he began his sentence', the phrase 'I told you' refers to something a long way back in the text, as far back as volume I, chapter 21, in fact (page 51 of the World's Classics edition). There it was that the narrator first told us about the sudden commotion among the ladies upstairs, and (prefiguring the opening of II.6) we find the following passage: 'I think, replied my Uncle *Toby*, taking his pipe from his mouth, and striking the head of it two or three times upon the nail of his left thumb, as he began his sentence,—I think, says he:—but to enter . . .' (Sterne embarks on the long series of digressions that will take us to Namur, Uncle Toby's wound, the journey to Yorkshire, etc.). Clearly, the 'I think' was to be followed (as it finally is in II.6) by 'it would not be amiss, brother, if we rung the bell'. Getting from the interrupted sentence in I.21 to its completion in II.6 and II.8 will certainly take most readers an entertaining hour and a half.

So, what happened? Did Sterne momentarily forget that

in 1.21 Uncle Toby failed to complete his sentence? It is plausible. But there is, I think, another explanation which exonerates Sterne from the charge of having made a slip so injurious to his text (and not correcting it in proof—which seems a strange oversight). To demonstrate that there may not, after all, be a slip, consider the following pairs of sentences:

1. 'I think it is time for a drink,' he said, and poured himself a whisky.
2. He poured himself a whisky; 'I think it is time for a drink,' he said.

1. 'This bottle is empty,' he said, raising it up to the light.
2. He raised the bottle up to the light. 'This bottle is empty,' he said.

Sequentially, the act and the description of the act in the above sentences are reversible. In formulation (1), the utterance is predictive or proleptic (he will imminently pour himself a drink, check the contents of the bottle). In formulation (2), the utterance is explanatory of what has just happened (he has poured himself a drink, he has checked the contents of the bottle).

Consider, in the same light, the following pair of statements, as they apply to *Tristram Shandy*:

1. Uncle Toby rang for Obadiah, and began knocking the ashes out of his pipe. 'I think it would not be amiss, brother, if we rang the bell,' he said.
2. Uncle Toby began knocking the ashes out of his pipe. 'I think it would not be amiss, brother, if we rang the bell,' he said, and rang it.

To my eye and ear, the first of these is if anything more natural than the second. It is natural for masters summoning servants to act peremptorily, then pronounce on their act ('he kicked the footman down stairs: "You are dismissed", he muttered'). Nor is it easy to picture Toby scraping the ashes out of his pipe *then* pulling the bell-cord. The natural order would be to pull the bell-cord and occupy the fidgety moments until the arrival of Obadiah by nervously tapping one's pipe. The strongest support for the hypothesis that Uncle Toby rings, then fiddles with his pipe, then speaks, is that Sterne does not specifically say when the bell was rung. Had he written, for example, as opening to 11.6, the following there would be no grounds for argument:

—What can they be doing, brother? said my father.—I think, replied my uncle Toby,—taking as I told you, his pipe from his mouth, and striking the ashes out of it as he began his sentence;—I think, replied he,—it would not be amiss, brother, if we rung the bell. *He duly rang the bell.*

But Sterne did not add the italicized comment, or anything equivalent. Nowhere, in fact, is the statement 'he rang the bell' to be found. It floats un-narrated, wherever we choose to place it. It is as logical to place it in I.21 as in II.6. In these dubious circumstances, and with the author's chronic punctiliousness in mind, it seems reasonable to assume that there is no error here, or at most an ambiguity within which 'hypercriticks' can muddle themselves.

The Oxford World's Classics *The Life and Opinions of Tristram Shandy* is edited by Ian Campbell Ross.

Jane Austen · *Mansfield Park*

═══

Pug: dog or bitch?

═══

If there was ever an inconsequential quibble in Austen
scholarship, the changing sex of Lady Bertram's lap-dog
would seem to be it. Tony Tanner, who has done more than
any living critic to instruct us how to read the six novels,
sees it as a litmus test, dividing what is useful to discuss
from what is irredeemably petty.[1] Quixotic as it may
appear, there is something worthwhile to be dredged up
from this, admittedly picayune, detail in *Mansfield Park*'s
background. It does not substantially alter our reading of
the novel, but it does offer a sharper outline of one of its
principal characters.

The core of the puzzle is an incidental reference in volume I, chapter 8, as the Mansfield Park party depart in
their carriages to visit Sotherton. Whether or not Fanny is
to be one of the party is the main preceding issue. Mrs
Norris is adamant she shall not go; Mr Rushworth gallantly wants her included; it is left to Edmund to find a
solution. In the minutes before departure, there is some
fierce skirmishing between Julia and Maria as to who
shall be on the barouche-box seat, alongside Henry Crawford. The younger sister wins. Lady Bertram, who is too
'fatigued' to make the trip, sees the company off: 'Happy
Julia! Unhappy Maria! The former was on the barouche-
box in a moment, the latter took her seat within, in gloom
and mortification; and the carriage drove off amid the
good wishes of the two remaining ladies, and the barking
of pug in his mistress's arms' (p. 72). It's a vivid tableau.
Our eyes are firmly on the carriage and the sexual warfare

seething within it (in her quiet way, Fanny is just as much a combatant as her cousins). But the little dog's bark may momentarily catch our attention. And, we may note from the use of 'his', it is a dog not a bitch.

Pug does not reappear until the third volume. Sir Thomas and Lady Bertram have by now resolved that Fanny must marry Henry. They are using every carrot and stick at their disposal to induce the unexpectedly stubborn young woman to conform to their wishes. 'You must be aware,' Lady Bertram tells her niece, 'that it is every young woman's duty to accept such a very unexceptionable offer as this.' The narrative continues by throwing the spotlight back on the mistress of Mansfield Park:

This was almost the only rule of conduct, the only piece of advice, which Fanny had ever received from her aunt in the course of eight years and a half.—It silenced her. She felt how unprofitable contention would be. If her aunt's feelings were against her, nothing could be hoped from attacking her understanding. Lady Bertram was quite talkative.

'I will tell you what, Fanny,' said she.—'I am sure he fell in love with you at the ball, I am sure the mischief was done that evening. You did look remarkably well. Every body said so. Sir Thomas said so. And you know you had Chapman to help you dress. I am very glad I sent Chapman to you. I shall tell Sir Thomas that I am sure it was done that evening.'—And still pursuing the same cheerful thoughts, she soon afterwards added,—'And I will tell you what, Fanny—which is more than I did for Maria—the next time pug has a litter you shall have a puppy.' (p. 302)

The episode perfectly catches Lady Bertram's moral obtuseness and her selfishness. But, out of the corner of our eye, we may note that 'pug' would now seem to be a bitch—the proud mother of puppies.

Pugs are 'toy dogs' (miniaturized bulldogs—the plucky mastiff peculiarly associated with John Bull) and, although they are short-coated, their sex may not be immediately apparent without indecently close inspection. Narrators are only human and may make the same mistakes as all of us do about such things. A devious reader might further argue that highly strung thoroughbred dogs like pugs are carefully mated, with their owners in watchful attendance as the deed takes place. Typically, the sire's owner takes an agreed share (as much as half) of the subsequent litter. So when Lady Bertram says 'the next time pug has a litter' she could conceivably mean that the next time 'he' sires one, Fanny shall have one of pug's offspring.

Pug makes two other fleeting appearances in *Mansfield Park*. In the first chapter, when it is agreed that Fanny will come to the Park House, not the Rectory, Lady Bertram observes: 'I hope she will not tease my poor pug . . . I have but just got Julia to leave it alone' (p. 8). Pug is here the neuter 'it'. There is a follow-up reference a few pages later in Chapter 2, when we are told that Lady Bertram is 'a woman . . . of little use and no beauty, thinking more of her pug than her children'. Pugs are ugly beasts like their full-sized ancestor. Unlike bulldogs, however, they are entirely useless—there being no miniature bulls for them to bait. We are to assume that the un-beautiful and useless Lady Bertram, like other dog-lovers, has come to resemble her pet. The dates implied by these early references are perplexing. Fanny, we are told, is 'just ten years old' when she comes to Mansfield Park, where—we may be sure—she will never tease Lady Bertram's pet. Assuming that pug was housebroken before Lady Bertram took possession of 'it', and that it has been in the family some time (otherwise how could 12-year-old Julia have been in the habit of teasing it?) the animal must be going on 11 or 12 years old when Lady Bertram promises 19-year-old Fanny one of its puppies—if she consents to accept Crawford. I am no dog-breeder, but this seems rather late in the day for thinking

of future litters. It might be, that as with other small
dogs (miniature poodles, King Charles's spaniels) it is chic
to have more than one. The consistent lower-casing ('pug'
not 'Pug') suggests a generic rather than an individual
beast. But descriptions such as that of Lady Bertram as 'a
woman . . . of little use and no beauty, thinking more of her
pug than her children' (pp. 16–17)[2] make it clear that she
has just the one pet dog. Otherwise it would be 'thinking
more of her pugs than her children'. One might hypothesize that the old (male) pug died and a younger (female)
pug was acquired in the interval between the Sotherton
and Portsmouth episodes—but this would be very far-
fetched.

One assumes that Jane Austen did make a tiny error
and—as Tanner says—it matters not a jot to any sensible
reader. The *de minimis* rule applies to literary criticism as
it does to law. But once our attention is drawn to the dual-
sexed pug with its unusually long sex life, some other useful points can be made. First, about pugs themselves. As
the *Oxford English Dictionary* notes, the little dogs 'came
into fashionability in 1794'. They are supposed to have
come across with William III, and are among the most
venerable of 'toy dogs'. Their tininess made them peculiarly useful as women's accoutrements, as did their placid
temperament. The placidity went with a tendency to obes-
ity ('Has anyone ever seen a thin pug?', asks one history of
the English dog). By the early decades of the nineteenth
century pugs were commonly 'ornamentally' mutilated
(ears cropped, tail docked) and the species was generally
felt to be almost bred out. It was revived, in the mid-
nineteenth century, by enterprising pug-breeders.

Pugs, then, were cherished fashion accessories because
they were *petite*, docile dogs which could be held in the
arms by women as a kind of canine muff. Essentially
they were 'masculine' beasts—mastiffs—genetically re-

modelled as ornaments for the weaker sex. The pug's miniaturized 'bulldog' lineaments rendered it not just fashionable in the late eighteenth century but—at a period of war with France—patriotic. Like the 'Blenheim spaniel' which Tory Mrs Transome has in *Felix Holt*, the pug made a political statement, in an acceptably feminine way.

The main events of *Mansfield Park* are commonly taken to be set between 1805 and 1811, during the Napoleonic Wars,[3] and the novel opens with the dating phrase: 'About thirty years ago . . .' It would seem that Lady Bertram (who after the birth of her children never can be troubled to go to London during the season) has retained the tastes of her youth, when she was the belle who captivated Sir Thomas Bertram of Mansfield Park. The pug, so fashionable when she was Miss Maria Ward, is a Miss Havisham-like attempt to stop the clock which has rendered her middle-aged and *fade*.

It is also relevant that pugs were the outcome of a strenuous and artificial breeding programme. In this they make another statement about the attitude of Lady Bertram's class to the all-important question: who should marry whom? Lady Bertram's sister, Frances, marries, 'in the common phrase, to disoblige her family . . . fixing on a Lieutenant of Marines'. The Prices' breeding is thereafter undisciplined in the highest degree. When she implores Lady Bertram to take Fanny, Mrs Price 'was preparing for her ninth lying-in'. Since they have been married eleven years (a period of frigid estrangement between the sisters), one wonders when it was that Lieutenant Price ever went to sea. On his part, the lieutenant is in the habit of cursing his unruly pack of children as 'young dogs' (p. 348)—mongrels all.

As elsewhere in *Mansfield Park*, Jane Austen sets up a thought-provoking opposition. Too much attention to breeding results in the odious pug, a useless, ugly, 'inbred' fashion accessory. Too little attention to breeding leads to the jungle of the Price household at Portsmouth—with its stravaiging pack of 'ill-bred' young dogs. None the less, Portsmouth—for all its undisciplined breeding—produced William and Fanny. Mansfield Park has produced Julia and Maria. Austen would seem to endorse the principle known to all dog breeders and eugenicists—that breeds must be regularly reinvigorated from outside the pedigree line. The aristocratic Bertrams, on the verge of inbreeding (as was the pug in 1810), need an admixture of mongrelized Price blood.

The Oxford World's Classics *Mansfield Park* is edited by James Kinsley, with an introduction by Marilyn Butler.

Jane Austen · *Emma*

How vulgar is Mrs Elton?

In 1994 Pat Rogers published an elegant article on a small piece of fashionable (or perhaps not) slang in *Emma*, entitled: ' "Caro Sposo": Mrs Elton, Burneys, Thrales, and Noels'.[1] The Italian endearment ('dear husband') is associated indelibly in the reader's mind with Mrs Elton (née Augusta Hawkins)—heiress of Bristol, whose money is very new and breeding rather dubious. We first hear her favourite phrase when she returns, victrix, with the Revd Elton ('Mr E.') in tow as her newly wed husband.

Among the flood of offensive things which Mrs Elton pours out to Emma (whom she regards as a bested opponent in love) one remark causes unforgivable offence. Mrs Elton is talking of the descriptions her husband has given her of his circle at Highbury. ' "My friend Knightley" had been so often mentioned,' she tells Emma, 'that I was really impatient to see him; and I must do my caro sposo the justice to say that he need not be ashamed of his friend' (p. 250). Fuming after their meeting, Emma thinks savagely that her new neighbour at the vicarage is 'A little upstart, vulgar being, with her Mr. E., and her *caro sposo*, and her resources, and all her airs of pert pretension and underbred finery'.

As Rogers points out, Mrs Elton's slangy speech, particularly her 'easy application of a cant Italianate phrase . . . is a strong pointer towards her affectation and vulgarity'. But *caro sposo*, he further suggests, may be something more than 'a mark of pretension'. Arguably it carries a subtler satirical load. He goes on to survey the

rise and fall of the phrase (in the mouth of the middle- and
upper-class English) as something fashionable. Its heyday
was in the 1770s and 1780s, when it was often used in the
conversation and correspondence of younger members of
noble and literate families, such as the Noels, Burneys,
and Thrales. It was less commonly used in the 1790s, largely because it had become hackneyed. The latest non-ironic
usage Rogers can find is 1808 (used by an elderly member
of the Burney family). By this date, also the putative
period of *Emma, caro sposo* would be very vieux jeu—
rather like someone in the 1990s resurrecting trendy jargon from the swinging sixties ('Cool, man!'). Such cultural
infelicities make the sensitive listener's skin crawl. Rogers's history of the currency of *caro sposo* is learned and
wholly convincing. He concludes that 'Mrs Elton's
attempts at "smart talk" reveal her not just as
uncultivated, but as badly out of date with fashionable
slang . . . people were not saying *caro sposo* any more'.

It's a satisfying demonstration of the value of historical
philology to the general reader. Unfortunately textual
bibliography steps in to complicate things. Rogers relies
on the R. W. Chapman text (on which the 1988 World's
Classics edition is also based). When he prepared *Emma*
(initially for the Clarendon Press in 1923) Chapman made
some silent alterations to the original 1816 text which
materially affect the *caro sposo* business. In the first (1816)
edition the offending words of Mrs Elton read as follows:
'"My friend Knightley" had been so often mentioned, that
I was really impatient to see him; and I must do my cara
sposo the justice to say that he need not be ashamed of his
friend. Knightley is quite the gentleman.' Not *caro sposo*,
that is, but the ungrammatical *cara sposo*.

The next time Mrs Elton uses the jarring term is after
having received some routine courtesy from Emma's
father over dinner. If anything, the notion that her aged

parent might be sexually interested in Mrs Elton infuri-
ates the heroine even more than the gross impertinence
about 'my friend Knightley'. 'I wish you had heard his gallant speeches to me at dinner,' Mrs Elton tells a frozen-
faced Miss Woodhouse. 'Oh! I assure you I begin to think
my cara sposa would be absolutely jealous. I fancy I am
rather a favourite.'

Now it is 'cara sposa' which Chapman again silently
emends to 'caro sposo'. His editorial judgement was evidently that these linguistic lapses were printer's errors
which might be cleaned up without distracting comment.
English printers often make errors with foreign phrases,
particularly when working from handwritten copy-text.

Not all editors and readers (when it is pointed out to
them) agree with Chapman's correction, on the grounds
that what Austen is trying to get across—with sly wit—is
Mrs Elton's blundering ignorance of Italian. Such is the
line taken by the Penguin Classic and the 'Norton Critical
Edition' editors, who religiously retain the misspelled versions of 1816. These lapses from strict grammatical correctness, it is assumed, are intended satire on Austen's
part. She knows, Emma knows, we know, Mrs Elton has
got *caro sposo* wrong. The only person who doesn't know is
Mrs Elton herself.

What, then, are the arguments in favour of Chapman's
emending all the usages to 'caro sposo'? First, Mrs
Elton— incorrigibly tactless as she may be—is a woman of
the world. She has seen more of that world (specifically
Bath, as she incessantly points out) than Emma. She has
almost certainly been to the theatre. Much slang and cant
Italian would be heard in these places. Bristol, where Miss
Hawkins originated, is a large cosmopolitan city (it was
also the centre of the British end of the African slave
trade, from which we may assume the Hawkins money
came—Sir John Hawkins was a well-known slave-trader

and Austen presumably intends us to pick up the allusion).
From her comments on music, the young Augusta
Hawkins evidently had the services of an expensive governess. She is obnoxious, but no fool. It is quite clear in the
above exchange about Mr Woodhouse's gallantries that
she knows she is galling Emma: she *wants* to gall her rival
and does it with malicious and practised expertise. The
phrase 'caro sposo', as Pat Rogers demonstrates, was
extremely well known by the early nineteenth century—so
well known that people of real *ton* took great care not to
use it any more. One would have to be very vulgar and very
ignorant to misquote or mispronounce it in 1810. And, as
even Emma grudgingly admits, Mrs Elton does have a
modicum of 'accomplishment'. She quotes Gay and
Gray from memory (reasonably accurately) and uses
French terms like *carte blanche* and *chaperon* correctly.
Mr Elton is a conceited man; but an educated clergyman
like himself who has been to university would not marry a
complete ignoramus, and if his wife were consistently
misusing Italian to his public embarrassment he would
have a quiet word with her *('caro sposo*, my love, *caro
sposo!')*.

There is also some textual support for the correction.
Immediately after the first 'caro sposo' insult, a furious
Emma inwardly passes the irreversible verdict: 'Insuffer-
able woman ... A little upstart, vulgar being, with her
Mr E., and her *cara sposo*, and her resources, and all her
airs of pert pretension and under-bred finery'. It could be
argued that Emma is spitefully mimicking the gross error,
or that she does not register it as an error. But if she did
mark 'cara' as a mistake, surely Austen would have indicated her heroine's contempt for the solecism a little more
clearly for the duller reader's benefit. It is not, on the face
of it, an Austenish kind of humour. It seems more likely
that the printer was unsure of the spelling from the

author's manuscript and hopefully reproduced what he had printed a few lines up.

There is a third use of the phrase which, I think, lends further support to Chapman's decision to correct and regularize. In volume III, chapter 6, during the planning for the picnic, a relentlessly talkative Mrs Elton—whose proposals are becoming more and more impractical—declares: 'I wish we had a donkey. The thing would be for us all to come on donkies, Jane, Miss Bates, and me—and my caro sposo walking by (p. 331)' (the 1816 text has 'caro sposo'). Now it seems she can get it right. Why then did she butcher the phrase two different ways a few weeks earlier? One could argue that Mr Elton has finally had a word in her ear, or she may have been tactfully instructed by her dear Miss Fairfax, who knows quite a lot about Italy.[2] But if that were the case, Mrs Elton would surely have avoided 'caro sposo' altogether in these latter days, embarrassed at the awful gaffes she had made earlier.

This is a very tiny puzzle. Its value is that it obliges readers to determine for themselves just how vulgar they think Mrs Elton is, and what kind of vulgar. Is she the kind of grossly uneducated woman who would mangle a well-known Italian phrase? Or is she merely someone who would use a once-fashionable phrase correctly, but long after it had ceased to be fashionable, and in provincial company where it would strike her listeners as disgustingly 'slangy'? Is she coarse; or merely egotistic and insensitive to social nuance? Readers will determine the issue for themselves; myself, I tend towards Chapman's view of Mrs Elton—she is vulgar, but not so ignorantly vulgar that she would say 'cara sposo'.

The Oxford World's Classics *Emma* is edited by James Kinsley, with an introduction by Terry Castle.

James Fenimore Cooper · *The Last of the Mohicans*

═══

Whose side is Hawk-eye on?

═══

The first half of *The Last of the Mohicans* is taken up with
the perilous journey through the Indian-infested wilderness which lies between Fort Edward and Fort William
Henry in the war-torn summer of 1757. There is much mystery attaching to this section of Cooper's tale. Why does
Colonel Munro want his daughters to join him at the very
moment that the poorly defended fort under his command
is about to be attacked by an overwhelming force of
French soldiers and their savage Huron allies? Does he
want his daughters to be scalped, or worse? Why does he
release one of his senior aides, Major Duncan Heyward, to
bring his daughters to him instead of a junior officer? It is
the more mysterious since Heyward, as it emerges, does
not know the route and gets hopelessly lost. Why does
Heyward employ as scout the treacherous Magua, whom
he knows to have a burning grudge against Colonel
Munro? If ever a trip through the woods was destined for
disaster, this is it.

Such questions fade with the series of exciting events
which ensue—particularly after Heyward's little band
picks up with the frontiersman Hawk-eye (Natty Bumppo)
and his two Mohican comrades, Chingachgook and Uncas.
Thanks to Hawk-eye's cunning, Heyward's party finally
fights its way through to Fort William Henry at precisely
the same time as the encircling French set up their siege.

It is what happens next, between chapters 15 and 19,
that I want to explore here. It seems that almost as soon as
he arrived with Heyward and the Munro girls, Hawk-eye

was dispatched back to Fort Edward, to implore the commander, General Webb, to send reinforcements. Some 1,500 men have been promised and they are desperately needed. There are 20,000 enemy with superior artillery surrounding Fort William Henry. The defenders' provisions, ammunition, and morale are running low.

A few days later, Heyward, now commanding an entrenched forward position beyond the fort's wall, sees a prisoner being escorted back to William Henry, under flag of truce. It is Hawk-eye:

[Heyward] walked to an angle of the bastion, and beheld the scout advancing, under the custody of a French officer, to the body of the fort. The countenance of Hawk-eye was haggard and care-worn, and his air dejected, as though he felt the deepest degradation at having fallen into the power of his enemies. He was without his favourite weapon, and his arms were even bound behind him with thongs, made of the skin of a deer. (pp. 168–9)

Hawk-eye is uninjured. It seems that he was captured on his return journey and that a letter from Webb to Munro was taken from him. Montcalm now has it. It is of the utmost importance that Munro should know what is in the letter. If reinforcements are on their way, the commander must, at all costs, hold out—to the last man and the last bullet, if necessary. But, equally, he must know *when* Webb's relief column will arrive. We learn in passing from Munro that Hawk-eye was returned unharmed as a gesture of Montcalm's 'accursed politeness'. It seems an odd kind of politeness, to return such an accomplished warrior to the ranks of your enemy. It is even odder since Hawk-eye will have useful verbal information to impart to Munro.

It emerges that Webb's letter, now in Montcalm's possession, instructs Munro to surrender. No reinforcements are on their way. It also emerges that, from some spy, Montcalm knows exactly the state of the opposing army:

'twenty-three hundred gallant men', as he serenely informs the fort's commander. How did he come by this valuable information? With the knowledge from the letter that no battle may now be necessary, the French general is disposed to be generous. Munro bows to the inevitable and capitulates. Montcalm has offered generous terms and may intend to keep them. But he cannot control his Indian irregulars, who run amok and massacre up to 1,500 of the defenceless British soldiers (who have surrendered their ammunition), their wives, and children.

We do not see Hawk-eye (or his Mohican comrades) again until three days after this atrocity. Where he has been we do not know. He reappears on the scene to help Heyward and Munro track Cora and Alice, who have once more been abducted by Magua (who lusts to make Cora his squaw). It is striking that at this point in the narrative Hawk-eye again has his formidable rifle, 'Deer-slayer', by his side and ammunition. It is manifestly the same weapon that he had before.

A first question is: how did Hawk-eye, a disarmed prisoner of war, get his rifle back? He did not have it when he was returned to the fort. It would have been madness for the French to have allowed the best marksman in North America to retain his *longue carabine* with which to take pot-shots at them from the fort's battlements. Deer-slayer would surely have been snatched by some Indian chief as a trophy. How, then, did Hawk-eye repossess it?

This leads on to other questions. How was it that Hawk-eye was taken uninjured by the French? Did he not put up a fight? Why did he not destroy the letter he was carrying before he was captured? We never know the details of how he was taken, nor is it easy to picture the event, knowing the man as we do. Where was he during the massacre?

We can work out possible answers to these questions from Hawk-eye's behaviour at other hazardous moments in the narrative—moments when he has to balance prudence against his frontiersman's code of chivalry. It is never Hawk-eye's practice to risk his life foolishly. In the siege at Glenn's Cave Uncas and Chingachgook—realizing that further resistance is useless—elect to save themselves by allowing the rapid current to carry them downstream to safety (or death by drowning; it's a desperate remedy). Their thinking is eminently practical: a live Mohican warrior is more use to his nation than a live white squaw. As a white officer and a gentleman, Heyward elects to stay with the ladies even though he knows it will be death for him, will not help them, and that he is needed to help defend Fort William Henry. His and the women's scalps (unless they are taken as concubines) will be dangling from some Indian's belt within a few hours. *Noblesse oblige.* White men act one way in these crises, red men another way.

Hawk-eye seems to allow himself to be persuaded by Cora's argument that he can leave the cave with the Mohicans, get to the fort, and bring back help. In acquiescing, however, he says something to his Indian comrades in the Delaware tongue which they listen to 'with deep gravity'. Of course Cora, Heyward, and the scout himself know that there is no hope that even someone as fleet-footed as Hawk-eye can bring back aid in time (assuming that British soldiers could battle their way through hostile Indian country). They are simply giving their friend a pretext for saving his skin which the more gallant Heyward scorns to avail himself of.

Hawk-eye duly jumps into the flood with the two Mohicans. It later turns out, however, that the three men do not—once out of the clutches of the enemy—make their way to safety. They secretly return to observe the capture of Heyward and the white women—intending to intervene if they can be of use, but to do nothing if intervention will be hopeless. As it happens, they are able to save Heyward and the women as, bound to the stake, they await fiendish Indian torture.

Hawk-eye, one deduces, is shrewd and pragmatic about such matters. He does not take unnecessary risks. If he has to lie or deceive in order to save his skin, he will. Better a live dog than a dead lion is his motto. There is another illustrative moment in the second half of the novel which highlights his pragmatism. On the track of Magua and the abducted maidens (if Cora is still such), the white men are pursued in their canoe. The Hurons fire on them. Hawk-eye tells Heyward and Munro to lie down on the floor of the canoe, so as to present a smaller target. With a dare-devil smile, Heyward demurs: 'It would be but an ill example for the highest in rank to dodge, while the warriors were under fire!' This officer's bravado provokes a blistering retort from the scout:

Lord! Lord! that is now a white man's courage ... and like too many of his notions, not to be maintained by reason. Do you think the Sagamore [Chingachgook], or Uncas, or even I ... would deliberate about finding a cover in a skrimmage, when an open body would do no good! (p. 207)

Like a good poker player, Hawk-eye knows when to stand and when to fold. What, then, may we assume happened when he (and his letter) were 'captured'? On his mission to Fort George he evidently perceived that there was to be no relief column from the pusillanimous Webb. Hawk-eye was aware of the massive ten-to-one superiority of the attacking force of French, having passed through their lines a few hours earlier. For the occupants of Fort William Henry fighting 'would do no good'. Why then fight? It would be 'white man's courage' and red man's foolishness. Hawk-eye, no white fool, calculated that the best thing was to collaborate with the French to minimize the bloodshed. He surrendered himself, gave up the letter to Montcalm, and requested that—as a cover—he be taken back as a prisoner. His weapon 'Deer-slayer' was taken on the understanding that it would be returned to him at some later point. He slipped out of the fort during the surrender negotiations, retrieved his beloved rifle, and watched events. He could not prevent the massacre, so he did nothing. He could help Munro and Heywood rescue the Munro women, so he rejoined them, fully armed again.

Cooper inserted a clue to this interpretation—namely, that Hawk-eye is playing his own game during the siege. Heyward's first question to Munro after Hawk-eye has been escorted back is: 'I hope there is no reason to distrust his fidelity?' (p. 150). Heyward—who has recently had the opportunity to observe Hawk-eye in action—has his doubts. Munro, not a perceptive commander as we apprehend, blankly refuses to believe Hawk-eye has betrayed them, 'though his usual good fortune seems, at last, to have failed'. The reader will probably concur with Heyward's scepticism in this matter.

The Oxford World's Classics *The Last of the Mohicans* is edited by John McWilliams.

Charles Dickens · *The Pickwick Papers*

━━━

What does Mr Pickwick retire from?

━━━

This is a short puzzle because it is about something that
seems not to exist, twice—namely, Samuel Pickwick's
occupation in life. At the end of the novel, in which 'everything is concluded to the satisfaction of everybody', Mr
Pickwick announces to his club *confrères* that events have:

> rendered it necessary for me to think soberly and at once upon my
> future plans. I determined on retiring to some quiet, pretty
> neighbourhood in the vicinity of London; I saw a house which
> exactly suited my fancy. I have taken it and furnished it. It is fully
> prepared for my reception, and I intend entering upon it at once,
> trusting that I may yet live to spend many quiet years in peaceful
> retirement. (p. 714)

Retirement from what? At the beginning of the novel it is
clear that Mr Pickwick is a gentleman in late middle-age,
already retired from the hurly-burly of whatever sector of
professional life he was previously engaged in. For two
years he conducts his 'Club'—which is not an occupation
as such, but an amateur society, or hobby. So, it would
seem, Mr Pickwick retires to his haven at Dulwich from
retirement.

This relates to a larger perplexing aspect of the novel,
Mr Pickwick is a man entirely without a *curriculum
vitae*—rather like those aliens who fall to earth in Hollywood science-fiction stories. Readers will search in vain
for clues as to what Samuel Pickwick has done, been, or
experienced in life before 12 May 1827. He has, apparently,
no family; no parents; no siblings; no married relations;

even no personal servant until Sam Weller comes along to look after him. We do not know what occupation Mr Pickwick followed—if indeed he has ever done a day's work—nor how he came by his evidently substantial source of personal wealth (pretty houses in Dulwich village, if not as expensive as they are now were not cheap in 1829).

Is Pickwick's money earned, inherited, won, counterfeited, or stolen? He is clearly not a military man, from his comical ignorance of firearms; he is not a lawyer, as we may guess from his ineptitude in Bardell versus Pickwick. Was he in business? Trade? The 'Exchange'? We do not know from which part of the country or the metropolis he originates. His incompetence with horses suggests he is a townee. He lives in London, but his ignorance of nearby Stroud, Rochester, Chatham, and of suburban Brompton make one wonder under what stone he has spent his fifty or so years of life previous to 12 May 1827. He has no house, but 'rooms' in Goswell Street (apparently a nonexistent address in 1827—although honorary Goswell Streets sprang up all over the English-reading world with the popularity of the *Papers)*. In the case of Bardell versus Pickwick we learn a lot about the plaintiff, his landlady, the custom officer's relict. All we learn about Pickwick is that he has rented rooms on her first floor for three years and that he likes tomato sauce with his chops. He has no political affiliations. He apparently has no friends or acquaintance until the formation of the club—which also gives him his only known occupation, G. C. M. P. C. (General Chairman: Member Pickwick Club). He claims the title 'Esquire', which indicates at least gentry status. He can write and speak correctly which argues education. But we do not know if Mr Pickwick went to university or what other professional or learned societies he may belong to. He has no detectable regional accent and uses

no dialects or specialized jargons in his speech which
would help us place him.

There are other men of mystery in Victorian fiction. We
do not, for example, know Heathcliff's Christian name nor
his parentage. But we do know that he was found in a
gutter in Liverpool. It's not much of a pedigree—but more
than we know about Samuel Pickwick, Esq. According to
Dickens, 'I thought of Mr Pickwick, and wrote the first
number'. Was Mr Pickwick so brilliant an invention that
everything around him was obscured? At only one point in
the text does Dickens relent about the blank context of
nothingness surrounding his hero. In his farewell speech,
Mr Pickwick vouchsafes that 'Nearly the whole of my previous life having been devoted to business and the pursuit
of wealth ...' It's a tantalizing fragment ('Goodbye for
ever: oh, by the way, I used to be in business'). What business? Import-export, retailing, finance?

We shall never know. What we can usefully ask is why
Dickens created Pickwick as a man without a past. As he
recalls in his preface to the first book edition of the novel,
when he began the *Papers* he had no idea of what the
novel would grow into. In the early numbers he was working within various 'machineries'—such as the 'Club'
gimmick—which were eventually outgrown. It seems likely that Dickens initially devised his hero as an antithesis
to Mr Jingle. Mr Jingle is a man with many pasts—too
many. In the first few minutes of his encounter with the
astonished club members it emerges that he has written an
epic poem of 10,000 lines on the July 1830 Revolution
(interesting, since it is 1827 and the Parisian uprising is
three years in the future); he was the owner of a literate
dog called Ponto; and he has conducted a passionate
affaire de coeur with the Spanish beauty, Donna Christina.
The joke is, that for all the wealth of biographical information that keeps spewing out, we know as much about

Mr Jingle's real past as we know about Mr Pickwick's—
precisely nothing. Unlike the 'Club' (and the ominous
'Posthumous Papers') this opposition between Pickwick
(man with no past) and Jingle (man of a hundred pasts) is
a joke that Dickens chose to keep running to the end of his
novel.

The Oxford World's Classics *The Pickwick Papers* is edited by
James Kinsley.

Charles Dickens · *Oliver Twist, Great Expectations*

Why is Fagin hanged and why isn't Pip prosecuted?

The Dickens scholar Michael Slater reports that two of
the questions most often asked him by lay readers are
those above. First, why is Fagin hanged? Everyone is
familiar with Cruikshank's great illustration of the prisoner in his death cell, 'the night before he was stretched'.
Like his illustrator, Dickens rises to the occasion, both in
the accompanying description of the Jew's last night in
Newgate, and in the preceding trial with its nail-biting
suspense as the jury returns with its verdict:

At length there was a cry of silence, and a breathless look from
all towards the door. The jury returned, and passed him [Fagin]
close. He could glean nothing from their faces; they might as well
have been of stone. Perfect stillness ensued—not a rustle—not a
breath—Guilty.

The building rang with a tremendous shout, and another, and
another, and then it echoed deep loud groans that gathered
strength as they swelled out, like angry thunder. It was a peal of
joy from the populace outside, greeting the news that he would
die on Monday.

The noise subsided, and he was asked if he had anything to say
why sentence of death should not be passed upon him. He had
resumed his listening attitude, and looked intently at his ques-
tioner while the demand was made; but it was twice repeated
before he seemed to hear it, and then he only muttered that he
was an old man—an old man—an old man—and so, dropping into
a whisper, was silent again.

The judge assumed the black cap, and the prisoner still stood

Fagin in the condemned cell

with the same air and gesture. A woman in the gallery uttered some exclamation, called forth by this dread solemnity; he looked hastily up as if angry at the interruption, and bent forward yet more attentively. The address was solemn and impressive, the sentence fearful to hear. But he stood, like a marble figure, without the motion of a nerve. His haggard face was still thrust forward, his under-jaw hanging down, and his eyes staring out before him, when the jailer put his hand upon his arm, and beckoned him away. He gazed stupidly about him for an instant, and obeyed. (pp. 428–9)

It is magnificent. But a number of awkward thoughts suggest themselves. On a legal technicality, it is Friday—two weekend days would hardly seem to give the remotest chance of the appeal to which Fagin surely has a right. And how does the crowd outside *know* that Fagin will be hanged on Monday, before the judge has put on his black cap and pronounced sentence? Are they deciding the matter? Is the bigwig judge dancing to the mob's savage tune?

More importantly, what capital offence has Fagin committed? He has, we know, trained boys in pickpocketing and appropriated their daily haul. He has received stolen goods and keeps a secret store of them in his den. He has been an accessory before and after the crime of housebreaking. Fagin has connived with Monks to keep Oliver out of his patrimony. He has verbally provoked Sikes to murder Nancy. None of these is, in the context of the mid 1830s (when the novel must be set, to justify its passionate assault on the 1834 New Poor Law) a hanging crime. As Philip Collins notes, 'from 1832 onwards . . . murder was virtually the only crime for which capital punishment was exacted'.[1] The Bloody Code, by which fences might conceivably be hanged for handling stolen goods, was—since Peel's 1828 reforms—a thing of the past. Fagin richly deserves punishing: but a longish term of imprisonment or a term of transportation (such as his original, Ikey Solomon, received in 1831) would seem a condign sentence. 'What right have they to butcher me?' he plaintively asks his jailer. It is a good question.

Fagin's most heinous offence is complicity in the beating to death of Nancy—a character who has been raised from the status of burglar's moll to sanctified heroine during the course of the novel. Fagin's involvement in this 'worst' of deeds is, however, equivocal.[2] Morris Bolter (i.e. Noah Claypole) has eavesdropped on Nancy's conversation with Rose Maylie and Mr Brownlow, by London Bridge. Nancy informs on Monks, but is careful not to implicate Sikes (whose surname she studiously avoids mentioning) and specifically refuses to give up Fagin. Her reason is 'thieves' honour'. She will betray Monks, because he is gentry, but she will not 'peach' on one of her own. 'I'll not turn upon them who might—any of them—have turned upon me, but didn't, bad as they are.'

Claypole duly tells Fagin what he has heard. The Jew sees danger for himself. He knows too much about prostitutes to trust Nancy's 'honour'. When, just before dawn, Sikes arrives to drop off some swag, Fagin plies him with a series of hypothetical questions about what he would do to someone who 'peached' on him. The robber gives predictably blood-curdling answers as his temper flares at the thought. Fagin climaxes his provocative catechism with the insinuation that 'NANCY' has betrayed him (Fagin cunningly does not say as much, he leads Bill to jump to the conclusion). Bolter, meanwhile, is roused from sleep and is prompted to spill the beans by Fagin:

'Tell me that again—once again, just for him to hear,' said the Jew, pointing to Sikes as she spoke.

'Tell yer what? asked the sleepy Noah, shaking himself pettishly.

'That about—NANCY,' said the Jew, clutching Sikes by the

wrist, as if to prevent his leaving the house before he had heard enough. You followed her?'

'Yes.'

'To London Bridge?'

'Yes.'

'Where she met two people?'

'So she did.'

'A gentleman, and a lady that she had gone to of her own accord before, who asked her to give up all her pals, and Monks first, which she did—and to describe him, which she did—and to tell her what house it was that we meet at, and go to, which she did—and where it could be best watched from, which she did—and what time the people went there, which she did. She did all this. She told it all every word without a threat, without a murmur—she did—did she not?' cried the Jew half mad with fury.

'All right,' replied Noah, scratching his head. 'That's just what it was!' (pp. 380–1)

All this is, as it happens, quite true. Nancy 'did' all that Fagin and Claypole say here. What she did *not* do, and what neither Fagin nor Claypole claim she did, is 'peach' on 'Bill' by surname—which would, of course, lead to his immediate arrest. She specifically refused to do that. Fagin's report is malicious but accurate.[3]

In what follows, it is not clear whether Fagin is trying to restrain Sikes's homicidal rage, stoke it up still further, or direct it into a devilishly cunning act of blood:

'Let me out,' said Sikes. 'Don't speak to me; it's not safe. Let me out, I say.'

'Hear me speak a word,' rejoined the Jew, laying his hand upon the lock. 'You won't be—'

'Well,' replied the other.

'You won't be—too—violent, Bill?' whined the Jew.

The day was breaking, and there was light enough for the men to see each other's faces. They exchanged one brief glance; there was a fire in the eyes of both, which could not be mistaken.

'I mean', said Fagin, showing that he felt all disguise was now useless, 'not too violent for safety. Be crafty, Bill, and not too bold.'

Sikes made no reply; but, pulling open the door, of which the Jew had turned the lock, dashed into the silent streets. (p. 382)

Fagin's parting words could be seen as incitement ('Goading the Wild Beast', as the running head puts it). They could also be interpreted as a coded instruction— don't use your pistol (which Sikes, with an uncharacteristic prudence, avoids doing, apparently heeding Fagin's advice). But in his defence Fagin could argue that he never actually stated that Nancy had informed on Bill, he was simply advising him to make inquiries in his usual direct way—beat her up if you have to, but don't kill her. Nor did *he*, Fagin, commit the subsequent awful deed, and moreover, he specifically cautioned Sikes against 'violence', in the presence of a witness. He might be seen as an accessory before the crime, but hardly an accomplice to it. Nor does he give Sikes refuge after the murder. Above all, everything that he told Sikes was perfectly true.

Why, then, is the populace so enraged against Fagin? Why the 'peal of joy' when they learn that he is to be hanged in forty-eight hours' time, without any hope of reprieve? It seems rather excessive for a receiver of silk handkerchiefs, silver snuff-boxes, and gold watches. (And, to be snobbish, the mob outside Newgate do not seem to belong to the silver snuff-box-owning class; why do they care if 'swells' are relieved of some of their surplus finery?) Had Fagin personally bludgeoned Nancy the lynch-mob jubilation outside the court would have been comprehensible.

We have to assume that London's blood-lust has been fanned by sensational accounts of Sikes's crime in the newspapers, and with Sikes already dead the crowd's rage has discharged itself on his nearest henchman. Dickens does not describe the trial, and we do not know what charges and what evidence were brought against Fagin, but it must, from the outcome, be conspiracy to murder. From one of his more sanguinary ramblings in his cell ('Bolter's throat, Bill; never mind the girl—Bolter's throat as deep as you can cut. Saw his head off!') we deduce that Fagin was shopped by Claypole. This is confirmed in the epilogue, which flashes forward to give us the apprentice crook's future career:

Mr Noah Claypole: receiving a free pardon from the Crown in consequence of being admitted approver against the Jew: and considering his profession [i.e. pickpocket] not altogether as safe a one as he could wish: was for some little time, at a loss for the means of a livelihood, not burthened with too much work. After some consideration, he went into business as an Informer, in which calling he realises a genteel subsistence. (p. 438)

As Kathleen Tillotson suggested in her notes to the World's Classics edition, we may assume that Noah has 'improved on' his evidence—perjured himself, that is. To whip up sufficient wrath in the newspapers, and through them the London populace, Claypole must have laid the main responsibility for the murder squarely on 'the Jew'. In point of fact, as any competent defence counsel could have elicited, Claypole was as much an inciter to the killing as Fagin. It was Claypole's gratuitously sneering report that Nancy had duped Bill by dosing him with laudanum that drove him to an uncontrollable pitch of fury. Claypole is, we assume, a perjurer—and a very culpable perjurer, in that his tainted evidence sends a man to the gallows. He is also a thief (after his first day Fagin congratulates him on making 'six shillings and nine-pence halfpenny'). A good defence counsel could discredit him very easily. At the very least, Noah should spend a little time in clink. Instead, his reward is perfect freedom to pursue his pickpocketing and informing trades for many years to come—presumably under the protection of the police. He suffers the lash of Dickens's sarcasm, but no ill comes to him in the future.

Seen in this light, the rush to execute Fagin—for a murder someone else committed, on the basis of perjured evidence from a petty criminal—is akin to the hysteria that sent Derek Bentley to the gallows in 1952—for allegedly 'inciting' Christopher Craig to kill a policeman (Bentley was in custody at the time of the murder). Londoners did not behave very well on that occasion, either. And many readers, I suspect, feel as I do a kind of savage pleasure (a reverberation of the populace's 'peal of joy') at the thought of Fagin's being hanged. Why, when even by the stern standards of pre-Victorian justice he does not merit the punishment? Because—if I am honest with myself on the subject—Fagin is presented to me in the novel as old, ugly, racially alien, and is monotonously associated with dirt, grease, and physical uncleanliness. I want the world to be rid of him. The reader is, I think, prejudiced by Dickens's rhetoric. He knew what he was doing. In his various revisions of the scene of Fagin in the cell, Dickens judiciously interchanged 'Fagin' and 'Jew', so that the loaded word echoes most effectively in the reader's ear. In as much as we concur with the crowd's 'peal of joy', it is not the trial verdict we are responding to so much as the indelible first impression we received of Fagin on his introduction in Chapter 8:

The walls and ceiling of the room were perfectly black, with age and dirt. There was a deal table before the fire: upon which were a candle, stuck in a ginger-beer bottle: two or three pewter pots: a loaf and butter: and a plate. In a frying-pan which was on the fire, and which was secured to the mantelshelf by a string, some sausages were cooking; and standing over them, with a toasting fork in his hand, was a very old shrivelled Jew, whose villanous-looking and repulsive face was obscured by a quantity of matted

red hair. He was dressed in a greasy flannel gown, with his throat
bare. (pp. 60–3)

A throat which we already itch to put into a noose. Fagin,
we are made to feel, is the unclean denizen of an unclean
lair. It complicates one's response that Dickens is at gratuitous pains to make the point that Fagin is not even a
good Jew—no need to ask if the sausages are pork.

If one worries about equity in *Oliver Twist*, it seems
wrong that Fagin should be so over-punished. It also seems
wrong that 'respectable' offenders with clean linen round
their clean-shaven chins get off scot-free in the novel. Losberne and the Maylies knowingly harbour a criminal and
obstruct police officers investigating the burglary in
which Oliver is wounded and left behind. They foil the
Bow Street Runners from the kindest of middle-class
motives. But their act—which is plainly felonious—has
serious consequences. If the Runners had been able to
question Oliver immediately after the crime and had their
wits about them they might have arrested the whole gang,
including Fagin, Crackit, and Sikes. Nancy's murder
would have been prevented. Many London houses would
have been spared Sikes's nocturnal visits. It is, however, as
unthinkable that Losberne should answer for his actions
in court as that Fagin should come to any other end than
the rope.

Middle-class gentlefolk harbouring criminals also figure in *Great Expectations*. The novel's climax hinges on
Magwitch's melodramatic utterance to Pip in volume III,
chapter 20:

'Caution is necessary.'
  'How do you mean? Caution?'
  'By G——, it's Death!'
  'What's death?'
  'I was sent for life. It's death to come back.' (p. 318)

Magwitch was initially sentenced to fourteen years' transportation for the crime of putting stolen notes into circulation. The sentence, already severe, was subsequently increased to transportation 'for the term of his natural life' for the offence of escaping (the episode which led to his first encounter with Pip in the churchyard, twenty years before). Any attempt to return to England, even after he is a free man in Australia, will result in a very unnatural ending to Magwitch's life (he indicates what it will be to an appalled Pip by 'giving his neck a jerk with his forefinger'). Transportation to Australia began in the 1760s and continued to the mid-1840s. As the editor calculates in the World's Classics edition, the narrative of *Great Expectations* opens in the early years of the nineteenth century (around 1805), and at this point we are in the 1820s—certainly not earlier. As Philip Collins points out, Magwitch's apprehensions are historically ungrounded:

Magwitch ends up under sentence of death, of course, not for killing Compeyson (though they were ready enough to kill each other, and Compeyson certainly died through trying to arrest him), but for returning from Transportation. He dies while awaiting the Recorder's Report and the result of Pip's appeals for mercy. As it happens, he need not have feared hanging, though Dickens conceals or ignores the fact that this offence had notoriously ceased to be *de facto* capital by the time when the action of the novel takes place.[4]

As Robin Gilmour points out, 'The last returned transport to be hanged was in 1810, though the crime remained technically a capital offence until 1835.'[5]

In the world of Dickens's novel the law is not disposed to be lenient to illicitly returned convicts from New South Wales—even when they have reformed themselves into model capitalists. The judge picks Magwitch's case out of the thirty-two death sentences he is delivering that day as

the most 'aggravated' and most deserving of the extreme
penalty. In the circumstances, Magwitch was quite right to
be 'cautious'. But so should those inclined to help him
have been cautious. Assisting criminals in the commission
of their capital crimes is no light thing at any period of
history—and never more so than when the 'Bloody Code'
held sway. Pip is specifically warned on this matter, by
Jaggers:

'Now, Pip,' said he, 'be careful.'

'I will, sir,' I returned. For, I had thought well of what I was
going to say coming along.

'Don't commit yourself,' said Mr Jaggers, 'and don't commit
any one. You understand—any one. Don't tell me anything; I
don't want to know anything; I am not curious.'

Of course I saw that he knew the man was come. (p. 331)

On his part, Jaggers is certainly 'careful' to give himself
deniability. So too, although he is more directly helpful to
Pip, is Wemmick (who uses such circumlocutions as
'gentlemen of a not uncolonial nature' to avoid direct
'knowledge' of who Pip's 'Uncle Provis' actually is). Pip
and Herbert are anything but careful. They shelter Magwitch, they give him concealment, they help him evade
agents of the law, after he has been denounced to the
authorities by Compeyson. It must surely be a serious
offence. And Pip's explanation—if he told 'nothing but
the truth'—would stand up very weakly in court: 'I am not
related to the man; he disgusts me; but I have taken huge
amounts of money from him over the years; I knew perfectly well that he was a wanted criminal; I none the less
helped him escape.' A prosecuting counsel would slash
such a witness to pieces.

When Magwitch is arrested, on the river, it must be
known to the authorities that Pip is aiding and abetting a
known felon in the commission of a most serious offence.
Apart from anything else, by returning to England Mag-

witch has rendered his fortune forfeit to the Crown, and Pip is assisting in a fraud on the Exchequer. Pip's house has been under surveillance, he himself has been tailed. Compeyson would have fingered him, and Herbert as well, as Magwitch's accomplices. The most superficial enquiries by the Bow Street Runners among boatmen, innkeepers, and other witnesses would determine, beyond all reasonable doubt, that Pip was not just accompanying Magwitch—he was arranging the felon's escape down to the last detail and paying for it out of his pocket. And if there were the smallest smidgen of doubt about his involvement, Pip erases it in the self-incriminating petition for mercy which he sends to the Home Secretary, 'setting forth my knowledge of [Magwitch], and how it was that he had come back for my sake'. A wideawake minister would automatically confirm the sentence on the convict and initiate proceedings against the young rogue who assisted the old rogue. Too much of that kind of thing, nowadays. But there is no suggestion before, during, or after Magwitch's trial that any charges will be brought against Pip or Herbert. Incredibly, it seems the police do not even question Mr Pirrip.

Of course, no one will protest this miscarriage any more than we protest the miscarriage of justice which brings Fagin to the gallows—although, as Michael Slater notes, readers occasionally worry about the fickleness of Dickensian law. Why, then, is Fagin hanged and Pip not prosecuted? Because one is a dirty old man and the other is a nice young gent.

The Oxford World's Classics *Oliver Twist* is edited by Kathleen Tillotson with an introduction by Stephen Gill; *Great Expectations* is edited by Margaret Cardwell with an introduction by Kate Flint.

Emily Brontë · *Wuthering Heights*

Who gets what in Heathcliff's will?

Heathcliff's death is among the most unusual in Victorian fiction. A man in rude health, 38 years old, dies of inanition. He does not eat or drink for four days (a short period, incidentally for someone in Heathcliff's physical condition to starve to death). Every time he makes to eat or drink, he is interrupted—as we deduce—by a distracting vision of his lost love Catherine. 'I'm animated with hunger; and, seemingly, I must not eat' (p. 328), he observes. Nelly makes him coffee, breakfast, lunch, dinner. But something always comes between him and sustenance. 'I vainly reminded him of his protracted abstinence from food', the housekeeper says in her stilted fashion: 'if he stirred to touch anything in compliance with my entreaties, if he stretched out his hand to get a piece of bread, his fingers clenched, before they reached it, and remained on the table, forgetful of their aim' (p. 331). It is a version of the Tantalus torture. 'By God! she's relentless', Nelly overhears Heathcliff say. And, eventually, the relentless Cathy ('she') succeeds in killing him.

Wuthering Heights, with its enigmatic opening and ending (Lockwood's dream and 'They's Heathcliff and a woman, yonder, under t'Nab') leaves open the issue of whether ghosts exist or not. Assuming they do exist—at least in Emily Brontë's fictional universe—and that they have motives, why does the spectre of Catherine choose this moment to kill Heathcliff? There would seem to be other, more appropriate, occasions. Is it simply that after all these years she wants to be united with her old comrade and lover—that she is lonely and dissatisfied with the spectral Edgar, as anaemic in death as in life? This is the interpretation supplied by the MGM film, which ends with a vignette of the two young lovers (Cathy and Heathcliff) skipping, as carefree ghosts, over Penistone Crags. But if it were simply post-mortem sexual union that Cathy wanted, surely she would have intervened sooner. She is not a patient woman in life; it is hard to think her so in her afterlife.

The explanation for Cathy's sudden resolution to haunt Heathcliff is to be found, I believe, in the fact that she interrupts not just one activity (his intake of food, drink, and rest) but two. The trigger for Cathy's return is an oddly ruminative comment Heathcliff makes to Nelly, summing up his life's work:

It is a poor conclusion, is it not . . . An absurd termination to my violent exertions? I get levers and mattocks to demolish two houses, and train myself to be capable of working like Hercules, and when everything is ready, and in my power, I find the will to lift a slate off either roof has vanished! My old enemies have not beaten me—now would be the precise time to revenge myself on their representatives—I could do it; and none could hinder me— But where is the use? (p. 323)

This is the only occasion on which Heathcliff indicates his long-term aim—the dispossession of Hareton and Catherine from the Wuthering Heights and Thrushcross Grange inheritance. Over the years he has centralized the two estates in his own hands—by extracting gambling IOUs from Hareton, by eloping with Isabella, by forcing his son to marry Cathy, by making his son, on his deathbed, leave everything to his father. Heathcliff can now stop Hareton and Catherine from coming into their parents' property by drawing up a will which specifically disinherits them. This is what he means by 'now would be the precise time to revenge myself on their representatives'.

Already Heathcliff is, as he tells Cathy, 'half conscious' of some power robbing him of the will to carry through this consummating act of revenge. There is, as he tells Nelly, 'a strange change approaching—I'm in its shadow at present'. The shadowy change will, over the next few days, 'materialize' as the wraith of Cathy. Heathcliff becomes a man possessed under her 'relentless' spell. But still the intention to change his will lurks at the back of his mind. On the evening before his death, in a state bordering on distraction, he tells Nelly, 'When day breaks, I'll send for Green [the solicitor] . . . I wish to make some legal inquiries of him while I can bestow a thought on those matters, and while I can act calmly. I have not written my will yet.' Heathcliff then becomes even more distracted, telling Nelly, 'It's not my fault, that I cannot eat or rest . . . I'll do both, as soon as I possibly can. But you might as well bid a man struggling in the water, rest within arm's length of the shore! I must reach it first, and then I'll rest. Well, never mind Mr Green' (pp. 332–3).

Heathcliff dies intestate, the property descends—as it should—to the young lovers, and the two great houses revert to their dynastic owners. But what if Heathcliff had not been conveniently haunted to death at this juncture? He would have written his vengeful will dispossessing Hareton and Catherine. Why then does Cathy return from beyond the grave at this specific moment? To forestall Heathcliff making his will, I would suggest. Cathy has three characters in the novel: she is Edgar's wife, Heathcliff's lover, and Catherine's mother. It is as the last of these that she returns. Her primary aim is not to starve Heathcliff to death in order that they may be reunited for a spot of posthumous adultery. It is to starve Heathcliff to death lest he do what he is just now threatening to do—

make a will which will evict Cathy's descendants for ever from their ancestral lands. If one were doing a screenplay, it should not (MGM-style) show young Cathy and young Heathcliff idyllically united. It should show an adult, maternal Cathy gloating over a raging and thoroughly tricked Heathcliff. In the last analysis, she reverts to type: she is the mistress, he the outsider at Wuthering Heights. He may have a share of her grave, but not the Earnshaws' family house.

The Oxford World's Classics *Wuthering Heights* is edited by Ian Jack, with an introduction by Patsy Stoneman.

Charlotte Brontë · *Jane Eyre*

Can Jane Eyre be happy?

Margaret Smith's introduction to the World's Classics *Jane Eyre* summarizes the formative influence of Charlotte Brontë's reading in the Bible, Bunyan, Shakespeare, Scott, and Wordsworth. Smith expertly identifies the Byronic and Miltonic elements which fuse into the mighty conception of Edward Fairfax Rochester. There is, however, a principal source for *Jane Eyre* which Smith does not mention—a 'fairy story' which, one assumes, was read by or to the Brontë children in their nursery years.

The story of Bluebeard ('Barbe Bleue') was given its authoritative literary form in Charles Perrault's *Histoire du temps passé* (1697). Perrault's fables were much reprinted and adapted by the Victorians into children's picture books, burlesque, and pantomime. By the 1840s the story of the bad man who locked his superfluous wives in his attic would have been among the best-known of fables. In the twentieth century the Bluebeard story, with its savagely misogynistic overtones, has fallen into disfavour.[1] It survives as the source (sometimes unrecognized) for such adult productions as Maeterlinck's play, *Ariane et Barbe Bleue* (1901), Béla Bartok's *Duke Bluebeard's Castle* (1911), John Fowles's *The Collector* (1963), and Margaret Atwood's *Lady Oracle* (1976).[2] Among its other distinctions, *Jane Eyre* can claim to be the first adult, non-burlesque treatment of the Bluebeard theme in English Literature.

Perrault's 'Bluebeard' is the story of a rich, middle-aged gentleman, named for his swarthy chin and saturnine manner, who marries a young woman. They take up residence in his country castle. Mr Bluebeard leaves on a trip, giving his wife the keys to the house with a strict instruction not to go to 'the small room at the end of the long passage on the lower floor'. The wife's curiosity is piqued and she disobeys his instruction. In the little room she finds the butchered corpses of Bluebeard's previous wives. In her shock, she drops the key into a pool of blood. On his return Bluebeard sees the stain on the key and deduces what has happened. She must die too, he declares. She is saved in the nick of time by her brothers, who ride to her rescue. They kill Bluebeard and enrich his young widow with her former husband's possessions.

The echoes of 'Bluebeard' in *Jane Eyre* are obvious. Rochester is a swarthy, middle-aged, rich country gentleman, with a wife locked up in a secret chamber in his house. He wants another wife—like Bluebeard, he is a man of voracious sexual appetite. Bertha is 'saved', after a fashion, by her brother. Ingenuity can find numerous other parallels.[3] But what is most striking is Brontë's inversion of the conclusion of the fable. In *Jane Eyre* we are encouraged, in the last chapters, to feel sympathy for Bluebeard—a husband more sinned against than sinning. The locked-up wife is transformed into the villain of the piece. It is as if one were to rewrite Little Red Riding Hood so as to generate sympathy for the wolf, or Jack and the Beanstalk to generate sympathy for the giant who grinds Englishmen's bones to make his bread.

Not only is sympathy demanded. We are to assume that—after some moral re-education—Jane will be blissfully happy with a Bluebeard who has wholly mended his ways. It is the more daring since (putting to one side the intent to commit bigamy), Edward Rochester is responsible for Bertha Rochester's death. Although he claims that 'indirect assassination' is not in his nature, this is

exactly how he disposes of his superfluous first wife. Why
did he not place her in one of the 'non-restraint' institutions which were transforming treatment of the insane in
England in the late 1830s? The York Retreat (where Grace
Poole and her son previously worked, we gather) and John
Conolly's Hanwell Asylum in Middlesex were achieving
remarkable results by *not* immuring patients in 'goblin
cells' but allowing them a normal social existence within
humanely supervised environments.[4] Bertha Mason, we
learn, has lucid spells which sometimes last for weeks. In
squalid, solitary confinement, with only Grace Poole as
her wardress, what wonder that she relapses? Why, one
may ask, does Rochester not put his wife into professional
care? Lest in one of her lucid spells she divulges whose
wife she is. What 'care' does he provide for her? An alcoholic crone, a diet of porridge, and a garret.[5] And then
there is the business of Bertha's actual death, as related
by the innkeeper at the Rochester Arms: 'I witnessed, and
several more witnessed Mr Rochester ascend through the
skylight on to the roof: we heard him call "Bertha!" We
saw him approach her; and then, ma'am, she yelled, and
gave a spring, and the next minute she lay smashed on the
pavement' (p. 428).

It is clear from the form of words ('I witnessed and several more witnessed') that the innkeeper (formerly the
Thornfield butler) is parroting verbatim his testimony at
the coroner's inquest. As a pensioner of the Rochesters, he
doubtless said what was required. There is no clear evidence that Edward went up to the burning roof to save
Bertha—it could well be that he said something, inaudible
to those below, that drove her to jump. His 'Bertha!' may
have been uttered in a threatening tone. At the very least
Mr Rochester, if no wife-murderer, might be thought
indictable for manslaughter by virtue of persistent neglect. There have been previous warnings that Bertha is a

threat to herself, and to others, under the gin-sodden care
of Mrs Poole. Who is responsible for the fire at
Thornfield—the madwoman, the drunk woman, or the
husband who, despite these warnings, did not dismiss the
drunk woman and put the madwoman under proper supervision? Is Edward Rochester a man to whom we entrust
Jane Eyre with confidence, should she suffer a *crise de
nerfs* later in life?

The main grounds for a reversal of the traditional
antipathy towards Bluebeard the wife-killer are stated by
Rochester himself in his explanations to Jane after their
disastrously interrupted wedding. Edward was spoiled as a
child. It is only late in life that he has gained moral maturity. His father and elder brother intended he should marry
money, and conspired with the Mason family in Jamaica
to unite him with Bertha. He was kept in the dark as to the
madness rampant in the Mason line. Besotted by lust he
married, only to discover that his much older wife was
incorrigibly 'intemperate and unchaste' (less unchaste,
perhaps, than Edward Rochester during his ten-years'
philandering through the ranks of 'English ladies, French
comtesses, Italian signoras, and German Grafinnen',
p. 311). But before the aggrieved husband can use her vile
adulteries as grounds for divorce, Bertha cheats him by
falling victim to the Mason curse. Lunatics cannot be
held responsible in law for their acts. Edward is chained
to Bertha. He brings her to England, where no one knows
he is married. Nor shall they know. Servants who are
necessarily aware of her existence assume she is 'my bastard half-sister; my cast-off mistress' (p. 291). He is free to
range Europe in search of sexual relief from mistresses
not yet cast off. Sexual fulfilment eludes him. Only
another marriage will answer his needs. Bigamy it must
be.

Is Bluebeard-Rochester justified in his attempted act of

bigamy? Are there mitigating circumstances, or just a middle-aged roué's glib excuses? In answering the question it is necessary first to determine the date of the action: more particularly, whether Rochester's foiled union with Jane takes place before or after the English Marriage Act of 1835. It was this act which clearly stated that marriage with a mad spouse could not be dissolved if the spouse were sufficiently sane at the time of the ceremony to understand the nature of the contract involved. Subsequent lunacy was no grounds for divorce even if compounded with other offences (violence, infidelity, desertion, cruelty). If the marriage in *Jane Eyre* is construed as taking place after 1835, then Edward is clearly guilty of a serious felony (intent to commit bigamy). It would be the responsibility of the clergyman, Mr Wood, to report Rochester (and Mr Carter, the physician, who criminally conspired with him) to the police. It is one of the small mysteries in *Jane Eyre* that Rochester seems to suffer no consequences, nor any visits from the authorities, following the 'bigamous' service.

If the marriage ceremony is construed as taking place before the firmer legislation of 1835, then Rochester may have a case for thinking that his earlier marriage is either null, or dissoluble on grounds of Bertha's premarital deceits, her subsequent adulteries, or the fact that the marriage may not have been consummated. He persistently refers to his wife as 'Bertha Mason', not 'Bertha Rochester', which suggests that he does not regard himself as married to the horrible woman. A good lawyer might fudge the issue for his client—not sufficiently to get him off the hook, but sufficiently to suggest that he honestly felt himself justified in making a second marriage.

When, then, is *Jane Eyre* set? The 1944 Orson Welles film explicitly declares that the central events occur in 1839.

But in the novel dates are a minefield. The editor who has
looked into them most clearly, Michael Mason, identifies
two conflicting pieces of dating evidence. When she came
over from France (a few months before Jane's arrival at
Thornfield, p. 101), Adela recalls 'a great ship with a chimney that smoked—how it did smoke!' Steam-driven vessels
were plying up and down the eastern coast of Britain as
early as 1821. Scott travelled down by one ('the Edinburgh') to the coronation in 1821. Like Adela, he found
the vessel exceptionally smoky and he nicknamed it the
'New Reekie'. Cross-channel steam services seem to have
started later in the 1820s.

If steam-driven ships are momentarily glimpsed (or
smelled) in *Jane Eyre*, steam-engined trains are wholly
absent. This is the prelapsarian world of the stage coach.
When Jane waits for her coach at the George Inn at Millcote she has leisure to examine the furniture. On the wall
there are a number of prints: 'including a portrait of
George the Third, and another of the Prince of Wales, and
a representation of the death of Wolfe.' Clearly this is
some point before the mid-1830s, when Millcote (Leeds)
would have been served by the railway. But it would be
interesting to know how faded those prints on the wall
are. George III died in 1820; his son ceased to be Prince of
Wales, and became Prince Regent, in 1811. West's famous
picture of the death of Wolfe as engraved by John Boydell
was most popular from around 1790 to 1810.

The clearest but most perplexing date-marker occurs
late in the narrative when Jane is with St John Rivers at
Morton School. On 5 November (an anti-Papist holiday) St
John brings Jane 'a book for evening solace'. It is 'a poem:
one of those genuine productions so often vouchsafed to
the fortunate public of those days—the golden age of
modern literature. Alas! the readers of our era are less
favoured ... while I was eagerly glancing at the bright

pages of Marmion (for Marmion it was), St John stooped to
examine my drawing' (pp. 370–1).

Scott's long narrative poem *Marmion* was published in
late February 1808 as a luxurious quarto, costing a guinea
and a half. The month doesn't fit, although the year might
be thought to chime with the earlier 'Prince of Wales' reference. But 1808 makes nonsense of critical elements in
the characters' prehistories. It would give Jane, for
instance, a birth-date of 1777. It would mean that Rochester impregnated Céline with Adela (if he is indeed the
little girl's father) around 1799. We would have to picture
him, an Englishman, gallivanting round France during
the Napoleonic Wars, crossing paths with the Scarlet
Pimpernel and Sidney Carton. Those wars would still be
going on in the background of the main action of *Jane
Eyre*.

Sea-going steamers aside, Charlotte Brontë's novel does
not 'feel' as if it is taking place in the first decade of the
nineteenth century. There are numerous incidental allusions which place it at least a couple of decades later.[6]
What seems most likely is that the 'new publication' of
Marmion is the 'Magnum Opus' edition of 1834. This
cheap edition (which came out with Scott's collected
works) was hugely popular, and cost 6 shillings—more
appropriate to the frugal pocket of St John Rivers than
the *de luxe* version of 1808. It is quite possible that
what Brontë is recalling in this little digression is the
excitement which the purchase of the same, Magnum Opus,
volume excited at Haworth Parsonage when she was 19.

A 'best date' for the main action of *Jane Eyre* would be
the early to mid-1830s—a year or two before the critical
date of 1835, which may be seen as foreshadowing but
not as yet clearly defining the grounds for, divorce or
annulment. This historical setting would not exonerate
Rochester's intended bigamy, but in the legally blurred

context of pre-1835 it would not be as deliberately felonious an act as it would be in the film's 1839.

Rochester is an inscrutable man whom we never know
on the inside. If we want to prognosticate whether, in the
years of their marriage, he will make Jane Eyre happy it is
important to extricate his motives for marrying her in the
first place—more particularly the series of events that
lead to his dropping Blanche Ingram in favour of 'You—
poor and obscure, and small and plain as you are'.

When Mr Rochester brings Blanche Ingram and her
grand entourage to Thornfield Hall, there is every expectation of an imminent happy event. 'I saw he was going to
marry her', says Jane (p. 186) and so, apparently, does
everyone else. Negotiations have been in train for some
time. Lawyers have been consulting. It is common knowledge that the Ingram estate is entailed, which is why they
are smiling on a match with an untitled suitor who happens to be very wealthy. It augurs well that Blanche has
the physical attributes to which Rochester is addicted.
Like her predecessor, Miss Ingram is 'moulded like a Dian';
she has the same 'strapping' beauty and jet-black tresses
that captivated Edward in Jamaica fifteen years before.

The visit of the Ingram party calls for unprecedented
preparations at the hall, as Jane observes:

I had thought all the rooms at Thornfield beautifully clean and
well-arranged: but it appears I was mistaken. Three women were
got to help; and such scrubbing, such brushing, such washing of
paint and beating of carpets, such taking down and putting up of
pictures, such polishing of mirrors and lustres, such lighting of
fires in bed-rooms, such airing of sheets and feather-beds on
hearths, I never beheld, either before or since. (pp. 163–4)

The pre-nuptial junketing at Thornfield is interrupted by
the unannounced arrival of Richard Mason from the West
Indies. Rochester is not present to greet him (he is mounting his gypsy fortune-teller charade), but his reaction on

being told of the Banquo visitation at his feast is dramatic:

'A stranger!—no: who can it be? I expected no one: is he gone?'

'No: he said he had known you long, and that he could take the liberty of installing himself till you returned.'

'The devil he did! Did he give his name?'

'His name is Mason, sir; and he comes from the West Indies: from Spanish Town, in Jamaica, I think.'

Mr Rochester was standing near me: he had taken my hand, as if to lead me to a chair. As I spoke, he gave my wrist a convulsive grip; the smile on his lips froze: apparently a spasm caught his breath.

'Mason!—the West Indies!' he said, in the tone one might fancy a speaking automaton to enounce its single words. (p. 203)

There follows Mason's disastrous interview with his demented sister, uproar in the house, and a new bond of intimacy between Rochester and Jane. Shortly after Mason has gone (back to Jamaica, as Rochester thinks, see p. 223), Jane is called to the Reeds' house fifty miles away at Gateshead. There she remains a month settling old scores. After her return, Mr Rochester is then himself away for some weeks. During this interval 'nothing was said of the master's marriage, and I saw no preparation going on for such an event'. It seems from a later conversation with Jane that Rochester has suddenly decided to put Miss Ingram to the test, and found her wanting in affection. 'I caused a rumour to reach her that my fortune was not a third of what was supposed, and after that I represented myself to see the result: it was coldness both from her and her mother' (p. 254).

Having found Blanche and her mother lacking in warmth towards him, Edward proposes to Jane. It is no fashionable wedding that he offers. Their union will be private, furtive even. There are no relatives (apart from the distant Mrs Fairfax) on his side, and as Jane puts it (with an allusion to the dragonish Lady Ingram), 'There will be no-one to meddle, sir. I have no kindred to interfere.' There is a month of courtship—long enough for the banns to be discreetly called. Three short months after the world supposed Edward Rochester to be affianced to Miss Ingram, Rochester takes Jane Eyre up the aisle. The difference between the two planned weddings could not be greater. After the ceremony with Jane, the newly weds will leave immediately for London. There is to be no wedding breakfast. The ceremony itself takes place in a deserted church. There are 'no groomsmen, no bridesmaids, no relatives' (p. 287) present. The assembled congregation is one person—Mrs Fairfax (what Rochester is to do for witnesses is not clear). The proceedings are then interrupted by the two strangers whom Jane has seen lurking around the graveyard: 'Mr Rochester has a wife now living', it is proclaimed. The strangers are, of course, Rochester's bad-penny brother-in-law and a London solicitor.

This is the second time that Richard Mason has arrived to foil Rochester's imminent marriage. On both occasions his appearance is out of the blue and uncannily timely. At Thornfield Hall, Rochester evidently thinks his brother-in-law dead, gone mad like the rest of the Masons, or safely ignorant of what is going on 3,000 miles away. Why does Richard turn up at this critical moment in Rochester's life, and what does he say to his brother-in-law about the law that joins them, and the impending 'marriage' with the Hon. Miss Ingram? After seeing him off Rochester clearly thinks that Richard is on his way back to Jamaica. He refers twice to this fact (pp. 213, 216). But Richard Mason, it emerges in the Thornfield church, is not safely in the West Indies. Moreover, during the three intervening months he has had sent him a copy of Edward and Bertha Rochester's marriage certificate.

Who informed Mason of details of the forthcoming

nuptials with Jane Eyre? It would have to be some insider
in possession of two privileged pieces of knowledge: (1)
the date, exact time, and place of the clandestine
marriage—something known only to the two principals,
the clergyman, and the three servants at Thornfield
Hall; (2) that Richard Mason was the brother-in-law of
Rochester's still-living wife, Bertha.

As Rochester later discloses, only four people in England are in possession of that second piece of information:
himself, Bertha during her lucid periods, Carter the physician, and Grace Poole (p. 309). There is, however, one
other who may have penetrated the mystery. Rochester
suspects that his distant kinswoman Mrs Fairfax 'may . . .
have suspected something'. Certain of her remarks suggest that this is very likely. Mrs Fairfax, alone of all the
Thornfield household, dismisses out of hand the likelihood that her relative will ever marry Blanche Ingram
('I should scarcely fancy Mr Rochester would entertain an
idea of the sort', p. 160). And Mrs Fairfax is very alarmed
when she subsequently learns that Jane is to marry her
master and very urgent in her dissuasions (pp. 264–5). It is
also relevant that, immediately after the wedding débâcle,
Rochester dismisses Mrs Fairfax from his employment at
Thornfield (p. 427). Nor is she called back after his blinding, when her presence would seem desirable as his only
living relative and former housekeeper.

The most likely construction to put on this series of
events is the following. Rochester had every intention
of marrying Blanche Ingram, until the unexpected arrival
of Richard Mason at Thornfield Hall. Who summoned
him? Mrs Fairfax (although Rochester probably thought
at the time that it was an unlucky coincidence). We do not
know what was said between the two men. But Richard,
timid though he is, would hardly give his blessing to bigamy and the threat of exposure would be implied, if not

uttered. His hopes with Blanche dashed, Rochester still longed for a wife. Another marriage in high life, such as the Rochester–Ingram affair, would attract huge publicity. That option was now too dangerous. Having packed Richard Mason back to the other side of the globe, Rochester put his mind to a partner whom he might marry without anyone knowing. He wanted nothing to get into newspapers which might subsequently find their way to the West Indies. Up to this point, Rochester must have thought of Jane Eyre as a potential future mistress. Now, with Blanche Ingram out of play, she was to be promoted. Carter was somehow squared. Poole was no problem; neither was Bertha. But, unfortunately for Rochester, Jane wrote to her uncle in Madeira, who fortuitously conveyed the news to Richard Mason (who happened to be in Madeira for his health). We can assume that it was Mrs Fairfax, again, who alerted Mason as to the exact time and place of the wedding (something that Jane did not know, when she wrote). He in turn took legal advice and came back to Thornfield with his legally drawn-up 'impediment'. At this point, his marriage hopes in ruins, Rochester discerned who had betrayed him and sent Mrs Fairfax 'away to her friends at a distance' (p. 427). Being the man he is, he also settled an annuity on her, presumably with the understanding that she stay out of his presence for ever (she is not mentioned in Jane's ten-years-after epilogue).

Bluntly, Rochester proposed to Jane as a *faute de mieux*—the *mieux* being Blanche Ingram. The notion sometimes advanced that the Ingram courtship was a charade designed to 'test' Jane is unconvincing. There was no need to test her, and if there were a need something much less elaborate might be devised (at the very least, something that might not land Rochester in a breach-of-promise suit). With many of Rochester's amoral acts (his adoption of Adela, for example) there is a kind of careless grandeur. His courtship of Jane Eyre, by contrast, has something sneaking about it. Would he have proposed to the governess had Mason not arrived to foil his courtship of the society beauty? Probably not.

Like Samson, Rochester is ultimately humbled by tribulation and physical mutilation. 'A sightless block', he discovers Christianity and for the first time in his adult life has 'begun to pray' (p. 446). But again, Jane would seem to be a *faute de mieux*. Supposing Edward Rochester had emerged from the blazing ruins of Thornfield with his limbs and organs intact, would it have been Jane he cried for at midnight? Possibly, possibly not. Blind and crippled, no comtesse, Blanche Ingram, or signorina will have him now. Only Jane will. Doubtless if, instead of killing Bluebeard, the wife's brothers had merely blinded him and cut off a hand (with the threat that if he did not behave himself they would come back and cut off some more), the old rogue might have become a tolerably good husband. But what if, like Edward Rochester, after ten years of marriage, his sight were to return and—barring the minor blemish of a missing hand (common enough, and even rather glamorous in these post-war years)—Bluebeard still cut a handsome figure. Could one be entirely confident that his wife-killing ways would not return?

The Oxford World's Classics *Jane Eyre* is edited by Margaret Smith, with an introduction by Sally Shuttleworth.

W. M. Thackeray · *Vanity Fair*

How many pianos has Amelia Sedley?

Like other well-brought up girls of her era and class (early
nineteenth century, London *nouveau riche)*, Amelia
Sedley has been taught to sing and play the piano. She is
neither as gifted in this department nor as industrious as
her bosom friend at Miss Pinkerton's Academy, Becky
Sharp. Miss Sharp, we are told, 'was already a musician'
when she was taken in as a non-paying boarder, and she
practises 'incessantly' (p. 19). None the less, Amelia can
handle the instrument well enough to make a private
recital the pretext of flirting with George Osborne in the
'back drawing-room'. It is there that the Sedleys' family
piano is situated ('as pianos usually are', the narrator
notes on page 39—pianos, incidentally, are omnipresent in
Vanity Fair). This back-drawing-room piano makes a later
appearance at the auction where Mr Hammerdown disposes of the ruined Mr Sedley's household effects two
years later. It is, we are informed as it comes up for sale, a
'state grand piano' (p. 205). Presumably it is as vulgar a
piece of furniture as the 'great carved-legged, leather
cased grand piano' in the Osbornes' hateful upstairs drawing-room, in their house on the other side of Russell Square.

At the auction, the point is made that there are in fact
two pianos in the Sedleys' household. Amelia has, as her
private possession in her own room, 'a little square piano'.
It is with the changing fortunes of this modest instrument
over the years that I am concerned here. It first makes an
appearance in chapter 2. Amelia has brought Becky back
to stay with her for a week or so at Russell Square, before

328   W. M. Thackeray

Miss Sharp takes up her new position as governess at Queen's Crawley. Becky has clearly never been to the Sedleys' home before. As soon as they arrive, Amelia excitedly shows Rebecca 'over every room of the house, and everything in every one of her drawers; and her books, and her piano, and her dresses, and all her necklaces, brooches, laces, and gimcracks' (p. 21). Guessing from the context, 'her piano' is the little square instrument in her bedroom, not the great monster downstairs.

The little square piano is not heard of again until months later, in chapter 17 ('How Captain Dobbin Bought a Piano'), where it briefly has a starring role. It is the auction following Sedley's bankruptcy and Dobbin, good-hearted as ever, has resolved to buy the little piano and return it to Amelia. But his agent finds that someone else is interested. To the auctioneer's surprise the bids rise to 25 guineas, at which inflated level Dobbin secures the instrument. It emerges that his rival in the bidding has been Becky. She takes her loss with typical good spirits: 'I wish we could have afforded some of the plate', she tells her husband, Rawdon (they are newly wed, and setting up house); 'Five-and-twenty guineas was monstrously dear for that little piano. We chose it at Broadwood's for Amelia, when she came from school. It only cost five-and-thirty then.' As the World's Classics note records: 'John Broadwood, the piano maker, had his business in Great Pulteney Street. In 1782 he patented his hugely successful design for a domestic pianoforte' (p. 914). There is already a small narrative inconsistency, however. Becky's recollection that the instrument was bought 'when Amelia came from school' indicates that it was acquired during that June 1813 holiday she spent at Russell Square, after the girls had left Miss Pinkerton's for good. But, in chapter 2, it is suggested that Amelia already has a piano in her room. Are we to assume that the

Broadwood is a replacement? Or, as seems more probable, is Becky fibbing?

Dobbin, having secured the piano, makes arrangements for it to be sent to the 'little house where the Sedley family had found refuge' (p. 223) after the crash. Tactfully, he does not accompany it with a note drawing attention to his generosity. A desperate Amelia, clutching at straws, assumes that the piano has come from George. Although their parents have called off the engagement he still loves her, she deludes herself. At the end of her note to George accompanying the return of his presents ('made in happier days'), she adds a postscript: 'I shall often play upon the piano—your piano. It was like you to send it.' In their quarters at the barracks, George shows Dobbin this letter, and he reads all of it. Surprisingly, there is no recorded conversation along the lines of: 'Who the deuce sent her that piano? You did, Dobbin? Gad! What a trump you are.'

The next day, Dobbin calls on the Sedleys in their refuge. He finds Mrs Sedley 'greatly agitated by the arrival of the piano, which, as she conjectured *must* have come from George and was a signal of amity on his part'. Captain Dobbin, we are told, 'did not correct this error of the worthy lady'. And he sets in motion the events that will lead to the marriage of George and Amelia in defiance of old Osborne's tyrannic prohibition and his (Dobbin's) own forlorn hope that Amelia might one day be his.

At this point, we may digress to indicate where Thackeray got the idea for this Broadwood square-piano subplot. In volume 2, chapter 8 of *Emma*, the heroine learns from her friend Mrs Cole that Jane Fairfax, who is staying with her aunt, Miss Bates, has had a mysterious gift:

Mrs Cole . . . had been calling on Miss Bates, and as soon as she entered the room had been struck by the sight of a pianoforté—a very elegant looking instrument—not a grand, but a large-sized square pianoforté . . . this pianoforté had arrived from

Broadwood's the day before, to the great astonishment of both aunt and niece—entirely unexpected; that at first, by Miss Bates's account, Jane herself was quite at a loss, quite bewildered to think who could possibly have ordered it—but now, they were both perfectly satisfied that it could be from only one quarter;—of course it must be from Col. Campbell.

No, as we later discover, it was not from the colonel, but from Jane's secret admirer, Frank Churchill. Frank, like Dobbin, does not enlighten the world, noting only with an enigmatic smile to Emma (who entirely misinterprets its meaning), 'It is a handsome present'. Thackeray evidently thought that this was too good a subplot to be used only once in English fiction.

After its return to the Sedley household the little square piano is lost once more in the background of *Vanity Fair*. It is glimpsed again when, shortly after her wedding, Amelia makes a trip to her parents, now in a cottage at Fulham (supported by an annuity from their nabob son, Jos). Things are going badly for Mrs Amelia Osborne. George is already kicking over the traces—spending too much, drinking too much, gambling too much and, as Amelia dare not admit to herself, consorting adulterously with other women. She falls down by the maidenly white bed she slept on as a girl and prays (prayers which, the narrator sternly informs us, we have no right to overhear). Then she goes downstairs and, to cheer up her father, 'she sat down at the piano which Dobbin had bought for her, and sang over all her father's favourite old songs' (p. 321).

For twelve long years the little square piano disappears from view while momentous things happen. Napoleon is defeated, George is killed, Becky is presented to her sovereign then taken in adultery, Amelia loses Georgy to the Osbornes, everyone (including the piano) gets suddenly middle-aged. When a grizzled Major Dobbin, CB, returns in 1827 from India he makes his first call on the Sedleys, now in lodgings at Brompton. At last, he fondly hopes, he may make his proposals to Amelia. He is admitted into the Sedleys' drawing-room: 'whereof he remembered every single article of furniture, from the old brass ornamented piano, once a natty little instrument, Stothard maker, to the screens and the alabaster miniature tombstone, in the midst of which ticked Mr Sedley's gold watch' (p. 740).

At the auction Becky specifically recalls the instrument's being bought at Broadwood's. Robert Stothard was Broadwood's great rival. They did not sell each other's pianos. There is more confusion to come. Dobbin is with Amelia a few days later, as arrangements are being made to move her family to Jos's grand new house (he has returned from India with Dobbin). To the major's pleasure, he sees that she is taking with her the piano:

that little old piano which had now passed into a plaintive jingling old age, but which she loved for reasons of her own. She was a child when first she played on it: and her parents gave it her. It had been given to her again since, as the reader may remember, when her father's house was gone to ruin, and the instrument was recovered out of the wreck.

Dobbin's hopes are raised by Amelia's special attention to 'this old music box'. He is glad she has kept it, he tells her:

'I was afraid you didn't care about it.'

'I value it more than anything I have in the world,' said Amelia.

'*Do* you, Amelia?' cried the major. The fact was, as he had bought it himself, though he never said anything about it, it never entered into his head to suppose that Emmy should think anybody else was the purchaser, and as a matter of course, he fancied that she knew the gift came from him. 'Do you, Amelia?' he said; and the question, the great question of all, was trembling on his lips, when Emmy replied—

'Can I do otherwise?—did not he give it to me?'

'I did not know,' said poor old Dob, and his countenance fell.
(pp. 758–9)

The Indian fevers he has suffered from must have affected
the major's brain. He was shown Amelia's letter to George
in April 1815 mistakenly thanking him (George) for the
gift of the piano. Shortly afterwards he (Dobbin) gallantly
declined to correct Mrs Sedley's misapprehension that
George was the donor. At that point in the narrative
Dobbin clearly did know that Amelia mistakenly thought
that the piano came from George, not him. There are other
little mysteries swirling about the episode. Did Amelia
and George never talk about the piano? Are we to assume
he lied on the subject after their marriage, or deliberately
left her in the dark? If so, it adds a new and uncharacter-
istically sly dimension to his villainy.

Shortly after the above exchange at Brompton, a morti-
fied Amelia suddenly realizes the truth: 'it was William
who was the giver of the piano.' She now hates the thing:
'It was not George's relic. It was valueless now. The next
time that old Sedley asked her to play, she said it was
shockingly out of tune, that she had a headache, that she
couldn't play.' The instrument is never heard of again in
Vanity Fair. Perhaps Amelia keeps it, more likely it is
thrown into some lumber-room and forgotten.

There are three problems in charting the long career of
the little square piano. Did Amelia get it as a little girl, or
did she buy it in company with Becky, as a young woman.
Is it a Broadwood or a Stothard? Does Dobbin know that
Amelia doesn't know who gave it to her? By tying oneself
in knots, one can find ingenious solutions. There was more
than one (perhaps as many as three) little pianos over the
years at Russell Square—in his palmy days, old Sedley was
certainly rich and doting enough to shower his daughter
with expensive luxuries. Dobbin has hoped so obsessively

that Amelia will love him that his memory has warped. Freudian analysis throws up any number of examples of this 'willed amnesia' phenomenon. When she made her remark about 'We chose it at Broadwood's . . . it only cost five-and-thirty', Becky is not remembering an event, but prodding Rawdon to take her, that very minute, to the nearby emporium in Great Pulteney Street to buy her an instrument just like the one she has lost to Dobbin at auction.

Attractive as ingenuity is, it would be misplaced here. As Stephen Blackpool would say, 'it's aw a muddle'—but only if we read *Vanity Fair* the wrong way. What we learn from following the story of the piano is something important about Thackeray's writing habits, something to which we must adjust our own reading habits when we come to his novels. He loved long perspectives and the resonant recurrent detail. No author handles such effects better. But Thackeray could not be troubled, or was too hurried, to turn back the pages of his novel to see what he had written earlier. His memory—wonderfully sure in essentials—played tricks with small details, tricks that the reader happily indulges.

The Oxford World's Classics *Vanity Fair* is edited by John Sutherland.

Charlotte Brontë · *Shirley*

Will she ever come back?

Shirley opens with a robustly drawn 'then and now' framework. 'Of late years,' the unidentified narrator tells us, 'an abundant shower of curates has fallen upon the north of England ... but in eighteen-hundred-eleven-twelve that affluent rain had not descended.' *Shirley*'s 'then' is self-evidently 1811–12. Its 'now' (as Brontë's subsequent reference to the Oxford Movement makes clear) is the period of writing and first publication of the novel, 1848–9. The location of the novel is as precisely staked out—the West Riding of Yorkshire, a setting from which the narrative will not stray by so much as a yard into any neighbouring county.

In her opening paragraphs, the narrator (a Yorkshire-woman, as we deduce) promises a story strenuously purged of sensational event:

Do you anticipate sentiment, and poetry, and reverie? Do you expect passion, and stimulus, and melodrama? Calm your expectations; reduce them to a lowly standard. Something real, cool, and solid, lies before you; something unromantic as Monday morning. (p. 1)

This promise is belied by the novel which follows. *Shirley* is passionate, stimulating, and melodramatic: a page-turner; as a modern publicist would say. Much is compressed into the eighteen months of chronological time which the narrative covers (February 1811 to August 1812). Caroline Helstone almost dies for frustrated love of Robert and discovers her long-lost mother in the shape of Mrs Pryor

There are riots, machine-breakings, and an assassination attempt on Robert. Both he and Caroline are fortunate to reach the marriage altar in one piece. On her part, Miss Keeldar fends off several proposals, before defying her guardian's instructions by falling in love with the unprepossessing Louis Moore. On the memorable 'Summer Night' of chapter 19, Shirley and Caroline heroically fight off a workers' uprising. The narrative concludes with festivities for the victory at Salamanca (events in the Peninsula and in Russia are alluded to throughout the novel) and a spectacular double wedding, neatly settling the destinies of all four principal characters. It is, we may conclude, an eventful year-and-a-half in the West Riding of Yorkshire. If we are curious about such things, events in *Shirley* exactly coincide with those at Mansfield Park, some 200 miles away in Hampshire. In so far as such things can be measured, Brontë's novel contains at least twenty times as much narrative matter as Austen's mild comedy.

When Jane Austen finishes a narrative, it is like a door slamming in the reader's face. At the end of *Emma*, for instance, we are blandly told that the union of the Knightleys will be 'perfectly happy'—with the implication 'that is all ye know, and all ye need to know'.[1] In Brontë's fiction the door at the end of the novel is often left ajar, allowing us to see over the edge of the narrative. The most striking such glimpse in *Shirley* concerns the beyond-the-novel fortunes of the Yorke family. They are introduced at full length in chapter 9, 'Briarmains' (the house where the family has lived for six generations). An idyllic portrait is given of the patriarchal Yorkshire manufacturer (whose name is emblematic of his northern county's rugged virtues), his wife, and of the six children happily gathered round his knee. The apple of his paternal eye is young Jessy. Suddenly, the narrator throws a cloud across the sunny group picture of the Yorkes at home. Mr Hiram

Yorke, she confides to the reader, 'has no idea that little
Jessy will die young, she is so gay and chattering'. The
narrator—now well into her gloomy stride—widens her
clairvoyant view to include the fate of the older daughter,
stolid Rose. Having made her dismal forecast to the reader
she goes on to inform Mr Yorke himself (who presumably
hears her words as a cold gust, as when someone—as they
say—walks over your grave):

Mr Yorke, if a magic mirror were now held before you, and if
therein were shown you your two daughters as they will be
twenty years from this night [in spring 1812], what would you
think? The magic mirror is here: you shall learn their destinies—
and first that of your little life, Jessy.

Do you know this place? No, you never saw it; but you recognise
the nature of these trees, this foliage—the cypress, the willow,
the yew. Stone crosses like these are not unfamiliar to you, nor
are these dim garlands of everlasting flowers. Here is the place;
green sod and grey marble headstone—Jessy sleeps below. She
lived through an April day; much loved was she, much loving. She
often, in her brief life, shed tears, she had frequent sorrows; she
smiled between, gladdening whatever saw her. Her death was
tranquil and happy in Rose's guardian arms, for Rose had been
her stay and defence through many trials: the dying and the
watching English girls were at that hour alone in a foreign country, and the soil of that country gave Jessy a grave.

Now, behold Rose, two years later. The crosses and garlands
looked strange, but the hills and the woods of this landscape look
still stranger. This, indeed, is far from England; remote must
be the shores which wear that wild, luxuriant aspect. This is
some virgin solitude: unknown birds flutter round the skirts of
that forest; no European river this, on whose banks Rose sits
thinking. The little, quiet Yorkshire girl is a lonely emigrant in
some region of the southern hemisphere. Will she ever come
back? (pp. 149–50)

Charlotte Brontë seems to have wandered out of *Shirley*
(whose chronological horizons are 1811–12, and whose

geographical boundaries the West Riding of Yorkshire) into another, wider-ranging narrative set two decades later in Catholic Europe (presumably Belgium) and, as we guess, in Australasia. The Yorkes, we apprehend, have been ruined—how, the reader is not informed. Six generations have ended with penury and exile. Should I store these details in my mind? the reader wonders. Are they going to be needed again later in the novel? They are not. The business about Rose, pining in a far country, is left hanging. Where she is, and whether she ever comes back, is left a mystery.

To add to the mystery, a later aside indicates that the narrator was actually present as one of the 'watching English girls' at Jessy's burial, twenty years later ('and some years ago' from the time of writing) when the little girl's remains were laid to rest 'in a heretic cemetery' overseas. Why was she buried in an alien grave? How did she die? Where were her parents? Charlotte Brontë does not tell us. What we can infer is that Brontë's narrative has trespassed well beyond *Shirley* (whose recorded events conclude in summer 1812) deep into afterlife territory.

Although Charlotte is inscrutable, the editors of the World's Classics edition help out with a brief note— namely, that the Yorkes are 'closely based' on Brontë's friends, the Taylor family. Investigation in the standard Brontë lives turns up the information that the head of the family, Joshua Taylor, was, like Hiram Yorke, a textile mill-owner who fell on hard times. There were six children. The Taylors lived, in the years of their prosperity, at the 'Red House' on which Briarmains is closely modelled. Rose is based on Mary Taylor. The prematurely deceased Jessy is based on Martha Taylor, who died in Brussels in 1842 aged 23, and was buried in a Protestant graveyard in the city (the Taylors were Presbyterians). Given the historical antedating of *Shirley*, Brontë gets into something of a muddle with dates here (it wasn't 'twenty years from this night' in 1812—which would make it 1832—but 1842; but then, if Jessy had died aged close on 40, it would hardly be a premature death).

In short, this vignette of the Yorkes in their parlour is a family photograph of the author's particular friends, slipped in from 'the real world'. Charlotte Brontë, as is her wont (though usually not as disruptively as here), has torn a gaping hole in the fabric of her fiction. Fact floods in, and—once we know there are facts to be had—we want more of them. If the novel won't inform us, who will? Not the *Dictionary of National Biography*. Mary Taylor is not listed. In fact, the best place to begin is the *Times Literary Supplement*, in summer 1996. In the issue for 31 May, Juliet Barker (author of a recent group biography of the Brontës) gives a concise pen portrait of Mary Taylor. An old school friend of Charlotte's at Roe Head school, Mary grew up:

a Radical in politics and a Dissenter in religion [who] defied custom and propriety throughout her long and active life. After the death of her father, when she was still a young unmarried woman, she earned her living as a teacher in an all-boys boarding-school in Germany, before emigrating, in 1845 to New Zealand, where she set up shop with such success that, fourteen years later, she was able to retire to her native West Riding of Yorkshire; an intrepid mountaineer and regular visitor to Switzerland, she led an expedition of four young women on an ascent of Mont Blanc when she was almost sixty.[2]

The answer to Charlotte's question, then, is: yes, 'Rose' did return in 1859. And in some style, it would seem. But the author of *Shirley* did not live to welcome her friend home to the West Riding, having died in 1855.

It is safe to say that, until summer 1996, very few people knew of Mary Taylor. And those who did thought her worth nothing more than a passing reference and a foot-

note in the standard lives of Charlotte Brontë. But 103
years after her death Mary Taylor was to get her Warho-
lian moment of world fame. It all revolved around a novel
which Taylor began writing in the late 1840s, parallel in
many ways to *Shirley*, and eventually published as *Miss
Miles*, in 1890, three years before the author's death.
Taylor had corresponded with Charlotte Brontë about her
unpublished novel-in-progress in the early 1850s. Like
Shirley, Taylor's story was set in the West Riding and
could loosely be described as an 'industrial novel'. But
Miss Miles embodied more aggressive ideas about women
and their right to work. *Shirley*, as Taylor pugnaciously
informed her friend Charlotte, was notably 'cowardly' on
this topic, insinuating merely that *'some'* women may
work, 'if they give up marriage and don't make themselves
too disagreeable to the other sex'.[3] Taylor was an absolut-
ist on such matters—a feminist *avant la lettre*. To her mind
all women had a right to work. It was a view she promul-
gated throughout the 1860s and 1870s, in her writings for
the militant *Victoria Magazine*. *Miss Miles* is similarly
downright on the question.

A furore was caused in early 1996 when an Edinburgh
bookseller, Ian Watson King, announced to the world that
he had found a lost work of Charlotte Brontë's. Moreover,
it was no piece of juvenilia (those had been turning up for
years). It was Charlotte's last, major work of fiction, her
masterpiece. And it *was—Sarah Miles* (alias *Miss Miles*).
'Rights' to the new work (since it was long out of copyright, it was not clear what these meant) were rumoured to
have been sold to the American publisher Random House
for a reported six-figure sum. This commercial interest
was shrewd. The reading public has an insatiable curiosity
about 'newly discovered' works by great writers. The
inclusion of the lyric 'Shall I Fly?' in OUP's Shakespeare
edition generated a huge amount of publicity for the book

in the 1980s. The 'new chapters' *of Huckleberry Finn* were published in the *New Yorker* in the 1990s—and very boring they were. A major work by Charlotte Brontë could be a gold-mine for whoever staked the first claim.

King's thesis depended on a number of interlocking hypotheses. First, that Charlotte Brontë wrote *Miss Miles*. Secondly, that all the correspondence from Mary Taylor to Charlotte (of which a large amount survives in different depositories) was forged by the Victorian bibliophile, T. J. Wise, to disguise Brontë's authorship. Thirdly, that Wise and Taylor conspired in 1890 to pass off *Miss Miles* as Taylor's work to the publisher Remington, who duly produced a three-volume edition which was singularly short-lived. King deduced that somehow Remington got wind of what was going on and 'spiked' the edition. King further claimed that computer analysis supported his claims about *Miss Miles* being a lost work by Charlotte Brontë.

King's claims provoked a storm of angry denial from Brontë scholars, and most authoritatively from Juliet Barker. She pointed out the physical impossibility of Wise's having forged those letters between Charlotte and Mary Taylor specifically discussing *Miss Miles*. The notion that Taylor would have conspired to pass off, or allow to be passed off, her friend Charlotte's novel as her own was preposterous and slanderous. And why go through this charade anyway? If *Miss Miles* was by Charlotte Brontë, there was no reason on earth for not proclaiming the fact to the skies and coining money from it. There were, in point of fact, more copies circulated of *Miss Miles* than King realized. The reason the novel failed was that it was irredeemably second-rate. Dull, tendentious three-volume novels were anyway on the way out in 1890.[4]

If one followed King's line of argument, yes, 'Rose Yorke' did indeed come back from New Zealand; and once back she robbed the grave of the author of *Shirley*. Better that Miss Taylor had stayed out there with the exotic birds rather than return to commit such a dirty deed. Few of those without a direct commercial interest in *Miss Miles* did follow Mr King, it must be conceded. But, whatever else, Mary Taylor had at last, a century after her death, become a significant figure on the Victorian landscape. There will now be a long entry on her in the *New DNB*, due out in 2003. Nor, in future, will anyone be able to read the description of the Yorkes and Charlotte's poignant question about Rose in quite the same way. She has returned—from New Zealand, and from oblivion.

The Oxford World's Classics *Shirley* is edited by Herbert Rosengarten and Margaret Smith.

Nathaniel Hawthorne · *The Scarlet Letter*

——

What are the Prynnes doing in Boston?

——

The Scarlet Letter's many enigmas have been exhaustively explicated. The novel is a literary-critical battleground (with the feminists probably slightly in the ascendant at the moment). But no one, as far as I know, ever asks what series of events brought Hester Prynne to Massachusetts, where so much obloquy is heaped on her. One is not encouraged to be curious on this score. Hawthorne's text is studiously inscrutable about events antecedent to Hester's being branded adulteress. The fullest account of her past life is given in sketchy flashback, as she endures her three hours of public shame in the Boston pillory:

Standing on that miserable eminence, she saw again her native village, in Old England, and her paternal home; a decayed house of gray stone, with a poverty-stricken aspect, but retaining a half-obliterated shield of arms over the portal, in token of antique gentility. She saw her father's face, with its bald brow, and reverend white beard, that flowed over the old-fashioned Elizabethan ruff; her mother's, too, with the look of heedful and anxious love which it always wore in her remembrance, and which, even since her death, had so often laid the impediment of a gentle remonstrance in her daughter's pathway. She saw her own face, glowing with girlish beauty, and illuminating all the interior of the dusky mirror in which she had been wont to gaze at it. There she beheld another countenance, of a man well stricken in years, a pale, thin, scholar-like visage, with eyes dim and bleared by the lamplight that had served them to pore over many ponderous books. Yet those same bleared optics had a strange, penetrating power, when it was their owner's purpose to read the human soul. This figure of the study and the cloister, as Hester Prynne's womanly fancy failed not to recall, was slightly deformed, with the left shoulder a trifle higher than the right. Next rose before her, in memory's picture-gallery, the intricate and narrow thorough-fares, the tall, gray houses, the huge cathedrals, and the public edifices, ancient in date and quaint in architecture, of a Continental city; where a new life had awaited her, still in connection with the misshapen scholar; a new life, but feeding itself on time-worn materials, like a tuft of green moss on a crumbling wall. Lastly, in lieu of these shifting scenes, came back the rude market-place of the Puritan settlement, with all the townspeople assembled and levelling their stern regards at Hester Prynne,—yes, at herself,—who stood on the scaffold of the pillory, an infant on her arm, and the letter A, in scarlet, fantastically embroidered with gold thread, upon her bosom! (p. 58)

It seems that Hester (whose maiden name we never know) was the only child of a genteel but impoverished English family. She married an elderly scholar for money as a self-less act of duty to her parents. Her mother has since died. Her father may be living. Further fleeting details emerge in Chillingworth's conversation with onlookers, as Hester stands at the pillory. She is, Chillingworth learns, 'the wife of a certain learned man, English by birth, who had long dwelt in Amsterdam, whence, some good time agone, he was minded to cross over and cast in his lot with us of the Massachusetts. To this purpose, he sent his wife before him, remaining himself to look after some necessary affairs.' Hester Prynne, a new American, has only been some two years in Boston. Since Pearl is, at the time of her mother's pillorying, three to four months old we can calcu-late that Hester succumbed to the Reverend Dimmesdale ten or so months after arriving in the colony. Or perhaps he succumbed to her. From various hints, it seems that the couple only committed adultery once. 'Once in my life I met the Black Man!', Hester tells Pearl. 'This scarlet letter

is his mark!' On his part, we are told, Arthur Dimmesdale
'had never gone through an experience calculated to lead
him beyond the scope of generally received laws;
although, in a single instance, he had so fearfully trans-
gressed one of the most sacred of them'.

Meanwhile no word was heard of Mistress Prynne's
husband who was considered 'most likely . . . at the bottom
of the sea'. If the lovers really believed this, Hester might
have pleaded with her judges to have the scarlet letter
commuted to 'F', for 'fornication'—a lesser, non-capital
crime. Of course, Roger is not at the bottom of the ocean
but has been captured by Indians in the south. He is
brought back by his captors, on the very day of Hester's
public punishment, to be exchanged for ransom (whether
he will pay it, or the community, is not clear—if Roger
Chillingworth is paying, one would like to know how he
gets access to Roger Prynne's funds in his disguised identity). During their interview in prison (where he visits
Hester in his guise as physician) more details of the
Prynnes' marriage emerge. He married her as a 'book
worm of great libraries—a man already in decay'. He
hoped, like many a bookworm, that his 'intellectual gifts
might veil physical deformity'. They did not. 'Thou
knowest', says Hester, 'that I was frank with thee. I felt
no love nor feigned any.' She married him for his
money—not to enrich herself, but to relieve her parents'
wants.

There remain a number of puzzles. What was Roger
Prynne, an Englishman, doing in Amsterdam? He is, as he
frequently says, an 'alchemist'. He is addicted to libraries,
'ponderous books', and dabbling in potentially criminal
arts. Why does he subsequently leave Amsterdam? Above
all, why does Prynne decide on Massachusetts, a colony
not well supplied with ponderous books or the wherewithal for an ambitious scholar. Nor—as a place where

they like to burn witches and wizards—is it somewhere
that a prudent alchemist would choose to set up his stall.
Roger Chillingworth is not religious—his remarks on his
Puritan neighbours indicate scorn for their fanaticism.
'He knew not that the eye and hand were mine!' he says of
Dimmesdale's sufferings; 'With the superstition common
to his brotherhood, he fancied himself given over to a
fiend.' Clearly Chillingworth does not share that superstition although at one point he recalls that he was religious
in his distant youth. As we know him, Roger has more in
common with the pagan Indians, from whom he has learned many valuable herbal secrets during his period of
captivity.

Nor is it poverty that drives Roger Prynne to emigration. When he dies, 'by his last will and testament . . . he
bequeathed a very considerable amount of property, both
here and in England, to little Pearl, the daughter of Hester Prynne'. Why did he send Hester ahead of him to Massachusetts? Why was she not accompanied by a servant, or
at least a maid? (Had she been, the servant might well have
recognized her master Roger Prynne, confounding his
scheme of revenge.) Apparently, Mistress Prynne was sent
to Massachusetts without funds, or access to funds. If
Roger Prynne has a 'considerable amount of property . . .
here', why is his wife so poor that she has, from the beginning apparently, to earn her living by her needle? Why—in
the seven years that Roger is assumed dead—does she
receive no money from his estate?

To summarize: the reader may reasonably assume that
the Prynnes' marriage was mercenary on her side and
over-optimistic on his. Perhaps his optimism had a scientific origin. Like other alchemists Prynne has been searching for the fabled 'elixir' which will change lead to gold.
The same elixir also serves as the bodily restorative and
aphrodisiac which Epicure Mammon apostrophizes in

Jonson's *The Alchemist* (II. ii). With the elixir's aid he intends:

> To have a list of wives and concubines,
> Equal with Solomon, who had the stone
> Alike with me; and I will make me a back
> With the elixir that shall be as tough
> As Hercules, to encounter fifty a night.

Once he discovered the elixir, Roger doubtless expected to be able to satisfy his beautiful young wife.

Although his substantial property is in England, Prynne pursued his studies in Amsterdam—presumably because of its better libraries and a more tolerant attitude towards alchemy. So much the reader may legitimately suppose. It is with the subsequent events—between the Prynnes' marriage and Hester's punishment—that mysteries multiply. Why did the Prynnes decide to emigrate to Boston? Not because of religious persecution or religious attraction. It is more feasible that things became too hot for Roger Prynne in Europe—his experiments may have attracted official disapproval. Perhaps he was delayed in accompanying Hester by the need to get his laboratory together, or to clear himself with the authorities, or to transfer his property to England.

Or perhaps the reason lay in the marriage bed. From the name she chooses for her child, it is feasible that Hester lost her 'Pearl above Rubies', her virginity, not to her husband, but to Arthur Dimmesdale. It may be that Prynne sent his wife ahead, without servant or adequate money, to an excessively puritanical community as one might send a daughter to a convent. The Prynnes' marriage, this is to say, may not have been consummated. Prynne sends his spouse to Massachusetts for the same reason that Wycherley's Pinchwife keeps his wife in the country, so no one gets to her first. This might also explain Roger

Chillingworth's morbid fear of being revealed as Hester's husband, since his impotent inability to enforce his conjugal rights might emerge as well.

This is deeper into hypothesis than most readers will find it useful to go. But the questions are relevant if we are to balance mitigating circumstance against innate evil (or female rebelliousness) in Hester Prynne's great act. She does not 'belong' in the Boston that judges her so cruelly. She was neither born nor brought up in that peculiar environment. It was not her choice to be in Massachusetts, one assumes. Had she remained in the bosom of her English family, among her own folk, making the kind of marriage normal for a beautiful girl of her class, there would have been no scarlet letter. It points towards a central question in *The Scarlet Letter*. Have the extraordinary conditions of Puritan Boston stripped away external trappings to reveal the 'true' Hester within; or, is she, like the Salem 'witches', the victim of distorting institutionalized paranoia?

The Oxford World's Classics *The Scarlet Letter* is edited by Brian Harding.

What happens to Mrs Woodcourt?

During the libel trial which entertained the nation in July 1996, cricketer Ian Botham was asked under cross-examination if it was true that he had said after a tour of Pakistan, 'it is the kind of place where you would send your mother-in-law for a week's holiday—all expenses paid'. No, the great sporting hero replied, he would never say such a thing. What he had said was that Pakistan was the kind of place you would send your mother-in-law for *two* weeks—all expenses paid. When the laughter died down, Botham was pressed by the cross-examining counsel on whether this was not a racist slur—a kind of verbal Paki-bashing. No, Botham replied, it was a slur against mothers-in-law.

No one likes mothers-in-law, and they are fair game for any basher. It is to Esther Summerson's advantage that she brings no maternal appendage to her marriage. Lady Dedlock would not make an easy in-law. Esther does, however, acquire a mother-in-law at the end of *Bleak House* in the shape of the first Mrs Woodcourt. And her relationship to this lady, if we read the text for its symptomatic silences, shows an unexpected strand of cruelty in the otherwise tender-hearted Dame Durden.

Mrs Woodcourt is a fringe character in *Bleak House* but the centre of an interesting subplot. She is presented through the lens of Esther's retrospective narrative which is written, we can deduce, some five to seven years after the main events of the novel. Written not by Miss Summerson but by Mrs Woodcourt the second, that is. The older Mrs Woodcourt is introduced to the reader in chapter 17. Allan himself we know to be a doctor. He has been in practice in London three or four years but has not prospered. He has resolved to go 'to China, and to India, as a surgeon on board ship'—the resort of second-rate physicians. Esther is already attracted to Allan, although she has not apparently admitted the fact to herself. 'I believe—at least I know—that he was not rich', she says. The lapse into present tense ('I know') indicates subsequent intimacy. She goes on: 'All his widowed mother could spare had been spent in qualifying him for his profession.' He is her only child, we gather, and she has made painful sacrifices to help him make his way in the world.

When Allan comes to Bleak House to make his adieu to Esther he brings Mrs Woodcourt with him. Evidently there has been some conversation between mother and son in which he has intimated his hopes. One of the purposes of the visit is to show Esther off. Esther's first impression of Mrs Woodcourt is mixed: 'She was a pretty old lady, with bright black eyes, but she seemed proud.' Since Allan is only in his mid twenties (seven years older than Esther) Mrs Woodcourt cannot be very ancient. But proud she certainly is. Esther describes Mrs Woodcourt's tedious obsession with the blood of Morgan-ap-Kerrig that flows in her and Allan's veins. More to the point, the mother clearly warns Esther off:

Mrs Woodcourt, after expatiating to us on the fame of her great kinsman, said that, no doubt, wherever her son Allan went, he would remember his pedigree, and would on no account form an alliance below it. She told him that there were many handsome English ladies in India who went out on speculation ... She talked so much about birth, that, for a moment, I half fancied and with pain—but, what an idle fancy to suppose that she could think or care what *mine* was! (p. 256)

Allan, clearly embarrassed, changes the subject. The

meeting has gone very badly. There is one other encounter between Esther and Mrs Woodcourt (they meet only twice in the recorded narrative—itself an oddity, given their eventual close family relationship). It takes place during Allan's long absence abroad. Mrs Woodcourt visits Bleak House at her son's request (he evidently wants news of his intended). During the interview that ensues Esther finds Mrs Woodcourt 'irksome' (a uniquely negative term on her lips). What is it, Esther wonders, that so 'irks' her about Mrs Woodcourt? Not her upright carriage, not the general expression of her face (it was 'very sparkling and pretty for an *old* lady'). 'I don't know what it was. Or at least if I do, now, I thought I did not then. Or at least—but it don't matter' (p. 433). This, I believe, is the only grammatical solecism Esther perpetrates in her long narrative. She is clearly under the stress of conflicting emotions.

What so discomfits Esther, as she clearly knows 'now' (i.e. five years later, at the time of writing), is that Mrs Woodcourt is again warning her off. The mother prates interminably about her son's high birth: 'my son's choice of a wife, for instance, is limited by it; but the matrimonial choice of the Royal family is limited in much the same manner' (p. 434). She is even prepared to malign Allan in the cause of deterring Esther, telling the young lady that he 'is always paying trivial attention to young ladies'. Shrewdly, Mrs Woodcourt then predicts that Esther 'will marry some one, very rich and very worthy, much older— five and twenty years, perhaps—than yourself. And you will be an excellent wife, and much beloved, and very happy.' In other words, Esther will marry her guardian, Mr Jarndyce. She may be a snob and callous about a vulnerable girl's feelings, but Mrs Woodcourt has eyes in her head.

The interview leaves Esther with a suspicion that Mrs Woodcourt is 'very cunning' (p. 436). The ladies are not recorded in the novel as meeting again. When Allan comes back he is unmarried and not much richer. He takes up lodgings in London, where he practises medicine among the poor. Surprisingly, he does not install his mother as housekeeper, as would seem normal. She is, after all, an impecunious widow and a doting parent. One gathers there have been words between mother and son. During his first, emotionally charged, interview with Esther (she has been disfigured by smallpox, he has not made his fortune), Allan asks fondly about Miss Flite. The subject of that other old lady, Mrs Woodcourt, does not come up. Esther does not inquire after her, Allan offers no information.

In fact, the subject of Mrs Woodcourt never comes up again, nor does the widow make any appearance, except as a problem for the omnicompetent Mr Jarndyce to dispose of, in chapter 60. Dickens's working notes for this chapter begin with the entry: 'Mrs Woodcourt and Allan. Prepare the way.' More accurately, Allan's mother is to be got out of the way. 'I come to Mrs Woodcourt,' Jarndyce says, and goes on to ask: 'How do you like her, my dear?' Esther finds the question 'oddly abrupt', and replies mechanically that 'I liked her very much, and thought she was more agreeable than she used to be.' Her guardian concurs: 'I think so too ... Not so much of Morgan-ap—what's his name?' (pp. 849–50). When and where Esther has recently found Mrs Woodcourt more agreeable we do not know; as far as the reader is aware, there have been no meetings since Mrs Woodcourt's highly disagreeable visit to Bleak House in chapter 30, when Morgan ap—what's his name was very much to the fore. But clearly Esther and Mrs Woodcourt have subsequently met, and the older lady has been bested.

Mr Jarndyce then tells Esther that, since the lady has mended her snobbish ways, he intends to 'retain Mrs

Woodcourt here'. There are a number of deductions which
we make from this apparently impulsive act of charity.
Jarndyce, as we now learn, has arranged for Allan to take
up a promising practice as 'medical attendant for the
poor . . . at a certain place in Yorkshire'. At last Dr Woodcourt will have income sufficient to set up a home and it
would be normal for a dutiful son to install his mother in
it. That must not happen. Instead, Mrs Woodcourt is to be
'retained' at Bleak House with Jarndyce's menagerie of
dependants, as a kind of female Skimpole.

Jarndyce duly surrenders his claim on Esther, freeing
her to marry Allan—now a thriving professional man able
to support a family. The courtship and proposal exchanges
are missing from the narrative. It would be interesting to
know what was said of Mrs Woodcourt, Esther's prospective mother-in-law. We then leap forward to Esther's vale-
diction, written seven years later. She tells us about Ada
(much recovered), little Richard (to whom Esther is a second mama), her own two daughters ('my pets'), Charley
(prosperous), Caddy (prosperous—but with a handicapped
baby), and even Peepy (prosperous). As for Esther herself,
life has been very good to her: 'The people even praise Me
as the doctor's wife. The people even like Me as I go about,
and make so much of me that I am quite abashed. I owe it
all to him, my love, my pride! They like me for his sake, as I
do everything in life for his sake' (p. 913). Not *quite* everything: she also, it is clear, does much for the sake of her
guardian. 'With the first money we saved at home,' she
tells us, 'we added to our pretty house by throwing out a
little Growlery expressly for my guardian which we
inaugurated with great splendour the next time he came
down to see us.' As it happens, she continues, 'my darling
[Ada] and my guardian and little Richard . . . are coming
tomorrow'.

Where is 'the doctor's mother' in all this welter of happy

ever after? It is clear that Mrs Woodcourt is not living with Allan, his wife, and her grandchildren in Yorkshire. It is equally clear that she is not coming with the party tomorrow. If Mrs Woodcourt has died in the interval, it would surely have warranted half-a-sentence of filial obituary among the detail of Peepy Jellyby's successful career in the Custom House or Mr Turveydrop's increasingly worrisome blood pressure.

We assume that Mrs Woodcourt has been left behind, to languish in Hertfordshire. She is not wanted in Yorkshire. Given Esther's incessant gush of kindness for all and sundry, it seems wantonly cruel. Whatever her crotchets, Mrs Woodcourt's snobbery originates in love of her son and a desire that he shall do well in the world. At no point in the novel is she shown as wanting anything for herself. She is a widow who has spent her every mite in the prosecution of Allan's career, stinting herself so that Esther can eventually be 'the doctor's wife'. If Esther can build a Growlery for her guardian, why not build an extension for her daughters' grandmother?

Esther's cuckooing Mrs Woodcourt out of her Yorkshire nest can be seen as necessary in terms of domestic *Realpolitik*. As 'mother Skipton . . . mother Hubbard . . . Dame Durden . . . Dame Trot . . . Mistress of the Keys', Esther cannot, in territorial terms, contemplate any power-sharing with a mother-in-law (when her daughters grow up, that will be something else; there will be a subordinate place for them in the domestic hierarchy). There cannot be two mistresses of the keys at either Bleak House. Jarndyce perceived as much, when he made arrangements for Mrs Woodcourt to live with him. It was not out of kindness to the older woman, but to make space for Esther that he took in Esther's mother-in-law (she will, of course, henceforth be a pensioner, and tied to him financially).

There is clearly much of significance between the two

Mrs Woodcourts which is not narrated in the text of *Bleak House*. Interviews and meetings are recorded as having taken place about which we know nothing (it would also be interesting to know what has been said between mother and son on the subject of Miss Summerson). But one thing is clear. If there was a power struggle between mother-in-law and daughter-in-law, Esther has come out on top. Nor is it easy to picture the doting Mrs Woodcourt easily giving up her sovereignty over her wonderful son, the only child who is such a credit to her. If we think about it, Mrs Woodcourt must be wretched as she remains, in solitude, at the southern Bleak House, thinking about the jollifications in Yorkshire. Esther, we surmise, has inherited some of Lady Dedlock's steel. On the whole it augurs well for the marriage. Allan is clearly a spineless kind of fellow—a philanthropic friend to the poor but lacking drive and the ability to rise in his profession. He needs a strong woman, a ruthless woman indeed, behind him. The doctor's wife fits the bill.

The Oxford World's Classics *Bleak House* is edited by Stephen Gill.

≡

The Barchester Towers *that never was*

≡

Readers attentive to the calendar will be arrested by the opening words of chapter 9 of *Barchester Towers*: 'It is now three months since Dr Proudie began his reign.' The time reference is perplexing. Trollope's novel began vividly with old Bishop Grantly dying 'in the latter days of July in the year 185–'. There follows the magnificent episode of the bishop's son, Archdeacon Grantly, torn between filial grief and ecclesiastical ambition, dispatching a telegram to Downing Street in the hope that it will arrive before the government falls. He is too late (if only his father had died earlier, he thinks—then hates himself for thinking such a thing). A new administration, Palmerston's as we infer, comes in and the Archdeacon's hopes of slipping into his father's *caligulae* are dashed forever. The obnoxiously reforming Dr Proudie is elected Bishop of Barchester. The story of his and his domineering wife's administration will be covered over the massive length of the subsequent Barchester Chronicles (1855–67).

With the above 'July' reference in mind we may make some chronological deductions. They are unsettling. On page 9 we were informed that 'just a month after the demise of the late bishop, Dr Proudie kissed the Queen's hand as his successor elect'. Calculation suggests, therefore, that Bishop Proudie's 'reign' began at the end of August, which means that this new phase of the narrative (marked by the opening of chapter 9) begins 'three months' after the August ceremony, at the end of November and the beginning of December (1854, as we may deduce). But, as a number of specific references indicate, the narrative following on from this point is set in August and the early autumn months thereafter. Three or four months have apparently come adrift. See, for instance, the letter from Mr Harding on page 108, which is dated '20th August, 185–'. Miss Thorne's *fête champêtre* takes place in September following, on a fine autumn day. The end of September sees 'Mrs Proudie Victrix', a week or so after the great affair at Ullathorne. The happy ending of the novel—crowned by the union of Arabin and Eleanor and the final downfall of the Proudie–Slope party—occurs 'in the beginning of October'. So if one is literal about it the Proudies will have returned to Barchester at the beginning of chapter 9 in November 1854 *after* the subsequent events of the novel. When they alight at the station the epic war between Archdeacon Grantly and the Slope faction will be over; Slope and Arabin's personal duel for the hand of Eleanor will have been settled; the wardenship contest between Dr Harding and the Revd Quiverful will have been decided. But, of course, Bishop and Mrs Proudie are principal actors in these contests. They must be in Barchester for the novel which we know as *Barchester Towers* to happen; but, chronologically—if we credit that pesky 'three months' reference—they cannot be.

The easiest way for Trollope to have ironed out the contradictions would have been to pre-date the opening sentence of the novel ('In the latter days of July in the year 185–') to 'In the latter days of April in the year 185–', and make a few minor seasonal adjustments. He did not, probably because he did not notice the anomaly. He was often indifferent to minor inconsistencies in his narratives. Nor should the reader intent on enjoying Trollope linger on such blemishes, unless they point to something interesting in the author's thinking about his novel. Here the confusion about months can indeed lead us to discover something of importance about *Barchester Towers*.

It is plausibly surmised that Trollope began writing *Barchester Towers* in January 1855, and that with eighty-five manuscript pages done he stopped writing.[1] Given Trollope's invariable 235–50 words per handwritten page, and the fact that the whole manuscript came in at 1,018 pages (the manuscript is lost, but we know how long it was), it is very likely that the break occurred between chapters 8 and 9, or chapters 7 and 8. After this first stint of composition there followed an immensely long interval, during which Trollope worked at his anatomy of English society, *The New Zealander*, from February 1855 to April 1856. It was not until 12 May 1856, nearly fourteen months after writing the first eighty-five pages, that Trollope resumed writing *Barchester Towers*. Thereafter, he wrote swiftly, finishing the work on 9 November 1856. It was never, in my experience, Trollope's practice to go back and substantially modify earlier sections of his manuscript once it was on paper. One may reasonably assume that chapters 1 to 8 represent the early, January–February 1855, stratum of composition in its original shape, pristine archaeological evidence of his first thinking about the novel.

The strong presumption is that in the nearly fourteen months' interval during which no work was done on *Barchester Towers* (i.e. between February 1855 and May 1856), Trollope's conception of his novel changed radically. In the early days of January 1855, he had seen *Barchester Towers* as less a proliferating Victorian soap opera (which it becomes) than a 'second part' of *The Warden* (*The Warden II*, as a modern film-maker would call it). *The Warden* had come out in early 1855. *Barchester Towers* was to be in every sense a partnering work, that is, of about the same dimensions and concentrating on precisely the same central issues: the incumbency of the wardenship of Hiram's Hospital (contested between Quiverful and Harding), the wooing of Eleanor (now an eligible widow, as previously she had been an eligible maiden). *The Warden* was, of course, a slim one-volume novel (284 pages in the World's Classics edition). *Barchester Towers*, as it eventually emerged, is a majestically sprawling three-volume novel (553 pages in World's Classics).

In his first mention of the embryonic *Barchester Towers* to his publisher, Longman, on 17 February 1855, Trollope says that: 'I intended to write a second part for publication [i.e. *Barchester Towers*] in the event of the first part [i.e. *The Warden*] taking and the tale was framed on this intention. I have written about one third of the second part.'[2] If eighty-five pages represents 'about one third' of the total manuscript at this stage of conception, the length of the putative whole—some 260 manuscript pages—indicates that *Barchester Towers*, 'the second part', was originally intended like *The Warden* to be a one-volume work. Trollope's first conception, then, was for something only one-third the size of the eventual *Barchester Towers*. And it was to this tight, one-volume scale that he framed the early layer of his narrative which we have as chapters 1–8.

It would seem, from several earlier references, that in the initial one-volume *Barchester Towers* it was intended that the Proudies would spend most of their time in London, off-stage. In the eighty-five-page prelude, Proudie would be a political bishop who made occasional forays into Barchester when the season was over (i.e. in August), when Parliament was in recess, and at important festivals of the year when his attendance at the cathedral was unavoidable. Hence Mr Slope's grandiose musings on page 27: 'He, therefore, he, Mr Slope, would in effect be bishop of Barchester . . . [Mr Slope] flattered himself that he could out-manœuvre the lady. She must live much in London,

while he would always be on the spot.' It would seem that
in his first plans for *Barchester Towers*, and while writing
the first eighty-five pages in January 1855, Trollope foresaw a long-distance war lasting three months between the
Proudies in London, and the Grantly faction in Barchester, with Slope as very much a free agent. Trollope set this
up in the early layer of narrative. At the end of chapter 1
Proudie is appointed the new bishop (at the end of August,
as has been noted). The Proudies are introduced in chapter 3 at full length, with heavy stress laid on their attachment to London. Dr Proudie, we are told:

by no means intended to bury himself at Barchester as his predecessor had done. No: London should still be his ground: a comfortable mansion in a provincial city might be well enough for the
dead months of the year. Indeed Dr Proudie had always felt it
necessary to his position to retire from London when other great
and fashionable people did so [i.e. in the hot summer months, and
at Christmas]; but London should still be his fixed residence, and
it was in London that he resolved to exercise that hospitality so
peculiarly recommended to all bishops by St Paul. How otherwise
could he keep himself before the world? how else give to the government, in matters theological, the full benefit of his weight and
talents? (pp. 20–1)

Trollopians will find the above passage perplexing. In the
episodes of the Barsetshire Chronicles that follow—
the multi-volume saga that extends through to the *Last
Chronicle* in 1867—the Proudies are wholly resident in
Barchester: provincial through and through. What happened to the plan of having their main base in London? It
is never mentioned again.

In the four chapters that follow we apprehend that the
Proudies are making only a fleeting visit to Barchester—
some three or four days' duration, as we are told, during
which Slope gives the obnoxiously low-church sermon
in the cathedral which sets 'all Barchester by the ears'.

Leaving Slope to fight their reformist battles, the bishop and his wife return to their natural habitat at the end of chapter 7 ('Dr and Mrs Proudie at once returned to London ... they left Mr Slope behind them'). The next chapter sets up what, in his early conception for the novel, Trollope evidently saw as his main plot-lines. It is entitled 'The ex-Warden rejoices in his probable Return to the Hospital', and at the end of the chapter Slope makes his wooer's visit to Eleanor. Ominously, she is not displeased by his addresses. It leads to some friction between father and daughter. Although he is gratified by the thought of being Warden again, Dr Harding is not overjoyed by the prospect of Mr Slope as son-in-law. All this, of course, is a replay of *The Warden*, where Harding's disputed wardenship and his personal distaste for his daughter's suitor, John Bold, are the novel's main plot elements.

There follows, at the beginning of chapter 9, the 'impossible' dating reference: 'It is now three months since Dr Proudie began his reign.' I surmise that just before this point the fourteen-month hiatus occurred. When Trollope picked up his manuscript again there was a momentary confusion in his mind in which two schemes for the novel conflicted. In the first of those schemes the Proudies were to be absent in London from August to October—while all the manœuvring for the wardenship and Eleanor's hand took place at Barchester, with Slope centre-stage. The Proudies would reappear from the wings in early winter. The second scheme was what we now have as *Barchester Towers*: with the Proudies prominently and permanently installed at the Palace—meddling indefatigably—during those same August-to-October months. The mark of the temporary confusion, like the jolt of a train as it couples itself to new carriages, is that 'three months' anomaly.

The main reason why Trollope did not persist with *Barchester Towers* in February 1855, dropping it for many months, is because Longman blew very cold on the project. *The Warden* (first published in January 1855) had not been an immediate sales success although during the course of 1855 it began to attract attention and to build up what was to become a huge popularity with the British reading public. But all this was in the future in February 1855, when the first edition of *The Warden* was still hanging fire. Had Longman presciently encouraged Trollope in February 1855, posterity would very likely have had a short, one-volume, stripped-down 'Barchester Towers' by the middle of the year: something markedly different from what we now have. But, as I say, they did not encourage him and the project was put into cold storage.

For the fun of it we may hypothesize in detail what this ghostly one-volume 'Barchester Towers' would have been. As I have speculated, it would not have featured the Proudies, except as absent potentates in London—dispatching haughty missives, probably, but not involving themselves directly. The narrative would have centred on a head-to-head struggle about the disposal of the wardenship (Harding or Quiverful?) between the contenders' champions, Archdeacon Grantly and Chaplain Slope.[3] The amiable Mr Harding would once again be caught painfully in the middle. From early references in the first chapter, the *Jupiter* and Tom Towers would have grossly interfered, as they did in *The Warden*. Trollope evidently killed off John Bold (whom he never liked very much, as he confessed) so as to make Eleanor marriageable and a main prize in the ecclesiastical in-fighting. Conceivably Slope would have tried to blackmail her into giving him her hand, with the promise of her father's return to Hiram's Hospital—if he were also Mr Slope's father-in-law. The unwritten (or uncompleted) 'Barchester Towers' would have been altogether more plot-driven and less episodic. The Stanhopes (for whom there is no early foundation),[4] the Thornes (first introduced in chapter 22), and Mr Arabin (first introduced in chapter 14) would probably not have made any appearance in the short 'Barchester Towers'. The widowed Eleanor might well have been married off, but to whom is not clear. Trollope might conceivably have left her in young widowhood.

One admires Trollope's deft changing of the scale and focus of his manuscript novel and there is pleasure to be had in speculating about the 'Barchester Towers' that never was. There is another, larger consideration. As he makes clear in his *Autobiography*, the gradual success of *The Warden*, and the Barchester Chronicles it inaugurated, marked Trollope's belated entry into the ranks of the great British novelists. He was 40 years old in 1855, the author of six novels, and at best a respected middle-rank author. *The Warden* and *Barchester Towers* changed all that. By 1860 he was at the top of the tree—the new Thackeray. In the change from the short 'unwritten' 'Barchester Towers' to the full-sized novel we have, Trollope crossed a significant threshold. He moved away from novels of tight plot, to a kind of fiction *sans frontières* which creates not a story but a world. This new style of fiction-writing—what we think of as the essentially Trollopian style—emerged with the expanded sequel to *The Warden*. Between the 'Barchester Towers' that never was, and the *Barchester Towers* that was finally written, the mature Anthony Trollope came into being.

The Oxford World's Classics *Barchester Towers* is edited by John Sutherland.

George Eliot · *Adam Bede*

━━

Why doesn't the Reverend Irwine speak up for Hetty?

━━

When the Reverend Irwine informs Adam Bede that Hetty has been charged with infanticide, the young man reacts with understandable violence. Adam's first response is an explosive 'It *can't be*!' (p. 408), by which the honest fellow means that, for all he has done, Hetty is still a virgin. Of course, as her intended husband in a couple of weeks (the very day she goes to the gallows, as it turns out), the general scurrilous assumption may well be that he is the father of Hetty's murdered baby and that she ran away and smothered it rather than spend the rest of her life as Mrs Adam Bede.

When Irwine persuades him—by means of the magistrate's letter—that the awful news from Stoniton is probably true, Adam extracts from the parson an assurance that he will inform the Poysers that he, Adam, is innocent of seducing Hetty. Adam's other reactions are equally constructive—if vehement. He apprehends that Captain Donnithorne, his once-idolized 'friend', lied to him when he said that the affair with Hetty had not gone beyond harmless flirting. 'It's *his* doing', Adam mutters:

if there's been any crime, it's at his door, not at hers. *He* taught her to deceive—he deceived me first. Let 'em put *him* on his trial—let him stand in court beside her, and I'll tell 'em how he got hold of her heart, and 'ticed her t'evil, and then lied to me. Is *he* to go free, while they lay all the punishment on her . . . so weak and young? (p. 409)

Irwine does not answer. Tacitly, yes, he intimates: Hetty is to bear all the blame and the heavy legal consequence. Adam continues: 'I'll go to him—I'll bring him back—I'll make him go and look at her in her misery ... I'll fetch him, I'll drag him back myself' (p. 410). Arthur, of course, is serving his country in Ireland (an active-service posting) with the Loamshire Militia. When Adam threatens to 'fetch' Arthur, Irwine at last responds. 'No, Adam, no,' he counsels. He (Adam) must stay here (in the Hayslope area) for *her* (Hetty). 'Besides', Irwine adds, reassuringly: '[Arthur] is no longer in Ireland: he must be on his way home or would be, long before you arrived; for his grandfather, I know, wrote for him to come at least ten days ago. I want you now to go with me to Stoniton.'

This is the first we have heard of the old squire's summons—presumably it concerns the removal of the Poysers from Hall Farm. It is no life-and-death matter. And since the Loamshires were posted to Ireland only a few weeks since, there is no guarantee that Arthur will hurry back. (What would his fellow officers say if—in the face of the enemy—he turned tail because his grandfather was having a spot of bother with one of his tenants?) There is every likelihood that Arthur will take his time in returning to Hayslope.

Suppose, at this point, Irwine had said to Adam something along the lines of:

Yes, Adam, you must indeed fetch Captain Donnithorne back, the sooner the better. Take the best horse from my stable and ride like the wind. Here is fifty guineas for your expenses. Stint nothing. I learn from the commandant of the Loamshires that Arthur's troop is quartered in Dublin. Gallop post-haste to Liverpool. Leave a message there, and at every coaching inn on the road, telling Arthur *to make all speed to Stoniton: It is a matter of life and death!* If you have to, hire a ketch to cross the Irish channel. On my part, I will request the commandant to dispatch a regimental courier, as fast as may be practical, to fetch Captain Donnithorne back. I will also petition the judge at Stoniton to delay the trial until the arrival of this most material witness. With God's help, we can still avert this awful tragedy. What are you waiting for, Adam? Be off!

And supposing Arthur, having been brought back in time, had addressed the court with remorseful demeanour, clad in his regimentals, as follows:

My lord and gentlemen of the jury. Miss Sorrel was the ward of one of my grandfather's tenants. She was a very guileless girl, of previously excellent character, but easily impressed and perhaps too vain of her beauty. I selfishly seduced her and (unknowingly) left her with child. I lied to the honest man of her own class she was engaged to marry. He trusted me, and I callously betrayed him. I was called away to serve my country. It was in Miss Sorrel's vain attempt to follow me and in a desperate condition—for which I hold myself entirely responsible—that this terrible thing happened. I entreat you to be merciful with her, and reserve your just recriminations for me.

Would any jury, faced with such testimony, convict for murder?

Irwine, however, seems determined not to let the above scenario happen. He persuades Adam to do nothing, and on his own part does nothing to hurry Arthur back. Why should Irwine claim that Adam Bede is needed at Stoniton? As it turns out, Hetty will not see her intended husband, nor is Adam permitted to give evidence in court. The carpenter is wholly out of his depth in all this legal business. Why does Irwine want Adam to cool his heels for ten days, doing nothing?

After the interview with Adam in which he learns that Arthur is Hetty's seducer Irwine returns home to discover that the old squire has suddenly died. Arthur is now squire-elect of Hayslope. A messenger has already been sent to await his arrival at Liverpool, with the news of his

grandfather's death. It is Wednesday. The trial is set for
Friday week.

Given the uncertain nature of the post in the early nineteenth century, it would seem more than ever urgent to
dispatch a courier to speed Arthur on his way. But Irwine
does not even send a letter to Liverpool for Arthur to find
on his return from Ireland, so that he might come directly
to Stoniton. One of the things that goes hard with Hetty in
the trial is that she at first refuses to give her identity and
obdurately denies that she ever had a baby, let alone killed
it. Her motives for this disastrous plea are never clearly
explained, but evidently she wants to protect Arthur. If
she denies having a baby, no cross-examining counsel can
ask who the father was.

On the eve of the trial, Irwine tells Adam, that 'Arthur
Donnithorne is not come back ... I have left a letter for
him: he will know all as soon as he arrives.' But, it now
seems clear, Donnithorne will not arrive in time to take
part in the trial. When Adam again protests about the
author of all this misery getting off scot-free, Irwine again
counsels patience and forgiveness: 'he *will* know—he *will*
suffer, long and bitterly ... why do you crave vengeance in
this way?' (p. 422). The parson goes on to deliver an elo-
quent sermon on Christian acceptance. As always, he is
preparing Adam for the worst—Hetty must hang. Had he
been less distraught, Adam might well have replied that it
is not Captain Donnithorne's blood he wants so much as
his truthful testimony.

The morning session of the trial itself is given obliquely
through Bartle Massey's account to Adam. There has
been damaging evidence from the doctors. Martin Poyser
has been called by the prosecution to identify his niece.
But, Massey adds reassuringly, 'Mr Irwine is to be a witness himself by-and-by, on her side'. He adds, 'Mr Irwine'll
leave no stone unturned with the judge'. Fortified by the

prospect of Irwine telling all, Adam attends the afternoon session where he hears further evidence from various witnesses—one of whom testifies conclusively to the birth of the babe, the other to its murder. The prosecution case is, as Adam perceives, wholly damning. Then comes the Revd Irwine's testimony, about which Bartle was earlier so hopeful. But by now Adam is beyond hope: he

heard no more of the evidence, and was unconscious when the case for the prosecution had closed—unconscious that Mr Irwine was in the witness-box, telling of Hetty's unblemished character in her own parish, and of the virtuous habits in which she had been brought up. (p. 435)

The narrator adds: 'This testimony could have no influence on the verdict, but it was given as part of that plea for mercy which her own counsel would have made.'

What, one may ask, happened to the 'leaving no stone unturned with the judge'? Why does not Irwine—once he has the ear of the jury—thunder out the truth: 'Hetty was seduced and abandoned by a man she trusted and whose duty was to protect her virtue, not debauch it.' He knows the facts of the case, why does he not utter them? And why, as the fiancé of Hetty and the possible father of the dead child in the eyes of the world, is Adam not called—if only to clear his name? His nobility of character would surely deflect judicial severity from Hetty to her culpable seducer.

Irwine's feeble character-witness ('she was a very good girl until she murdered her baby') has no effect. The judge dons his black cap and Hetty is sentenced to hang on Monday. Meanwhile, on the same Friday as the trial, Arthur finally makes his way to Liverpool. There he opens the letter informing him of his grandfather's death. There is no accompanying letter from Irwine on the more serious matter at Stoniton. Had there been, it being early Friday morning, Arthur might conceivably, by fast galloping, have intervened.

Instead he wends his happy way by coach to 'dear old Hayslope', fantasizing all the way about how wonderful his tenure as squire will be. He arrives home in the 'late afternoon'. He finds the servants oddly subdued (they have been talking to the Poysers). Arthur bathes and refreshes himself. At last he reads Irwine's letter and its awful announcement, 'Hetty Sorrel is in prison and will be tried on Friday for the crime of child-murder.' Eliot breaks off the report of Irwine's letter at this point, so we do not know what advice, if any, Irwine went on to give ('Come at once'? 'Do nothing till you hear further from me'?). Arthur rushes to the stables, instructing the butler to 'Tell them I'm gone—gone to Stoniton'. He springs into the saddle 'and sets off at a gallop'. Stoniton is twenty miles distant, and he will be there in an hour and a half.

It is, of course, too late now to give evidence. Sentence has been passed. The trial is over by sunset (as we are told) and the March days are short. It is not clear what Arthur does at Stoniton when—around six or seven o'clock presumably—he gallops into town. What he should do is secure an interview with the judge and crave a stay of execution. He does not, apparently. He does not visit Hetty nor contact Adam, who remains unaware that Arthur is back in the country (had the men met at this moment, Adam might well have killed him—as Irwine constantly fears). Of course there must be a meeting between Arthur and Irwine, but we do not know what the two men say to each other. What seems likely from subsequent events is that Irwine instructs Arthur not to announce his presence in Stoniton but to ride at once to London and intercede privately with friends in high places for a reprieve. Meanwhile, in a scene which Eliot does narrate at length, Dinah prepares Hetty for public hanging—

a fate which is forestalled by Arthur's dashing reappearance in Stoniton, at the eleventh hour, riding pell-mell
through the crowd, 'in his hand a hard-won release from
death'.

In the public mind Arthur probably gets credit from this
exploit. Most onlookers will see him as a heroic squire
saving one of his shiftless tenants from deserved punishment. The circle of people who do know Arthur's culp-
ability in the sorry affair are restricted to the Poysers and
their close associates. Arthur's treachery was not bruited
in court and will not make the newspapers. The world at
large will continue to think that Adam was the father of
the murdered infant and obscurely responsible for Hetty's
flight from Hayslope by some pre-marital unkindness.

What should the reader make of Irwine's equivocal
behaviour in all this? At any one of a number of points he
could have been more effective in Hetty's defence, if that
had been his primary concern. He could have let Adam
fetch Arthur and have made strenuous efforts himself in
that direction. He could have sent a letter to Liverpool,
rather than leaving one to be found, eventually, at Hayslope. He could have given frank evidence as to Arthur's
misconduct at the trial—or have had defence counsel put
Adam on the stand to do it. He could have told Arthur,
when he finally arrived at Stoniton, to make a public proclamation of his responsibility for the girl's pregnancy and
request a stay of execution so that his evidence might be
considered by the authorities. He did none of these things.

One assumes that Irwine is trying to maintain an awkward balance. Of course he wants to mitigate Hetty's punishment if he can, but he is also obliged to preserve as
much of Arthur's reputation as he can. It is not just
partiality. These are dangerous times. Britain is at war.
Jacobinical principles are abroad. Methodism is attacking
the very foundations of the Anglican Church. It could be

very dangerous if Arthur were publicly disgraced. The crowd who come to witness the hanging might well become an angry mob and Stoniton gaol their Bastille. Apart from anything else, if the fact that he had lied to one of his most loyal retainers came out—what regiment would ever offer Arthur Donnithorne a commission? Rogering peasant girls might possibly be blinked at. But a squire who would cold-bloodedly betray a loyal retainer like Adam Bede will not make an officer to whom men can trust their lives in battle. The whole English squirearchy and the complex mutual fealties which go with it, would be tainted at a time when it needed to be upheld. A loophole *must* be left for Arthur's redemption.

Irwine, we may assume, methodically limits the damage to Arthur. He does so partly for selfish reasons: his living is in the Donnithornes' manor (it may be in their gift) and it is his duty to protect his protectors. There are also reasons of state. The trustworthy parson and the trustworthy squire are the twin pillars of rural life. Shake them, and Britain may experience what France went through a decade before. There are three prongs to Irwine's strategy in the matter of Hetty's trial. First, he must rein in and neutralize Adam—which he does by confining the violent young man to Stoniton and keeping him out of the witness box. Secondly, he must if possible keep Arthur out of the way. He must also prevent his name coming up in court. And when the young man finally turns up in Stoniton, he is bundled away to London. The 'release from death' (commutation to transportation) carries no public stigma for Arthur, as his self-incriminating evidence in court or in judge's chambers would have done. And the last, sharpest, prong of Irwine's strategy is that Hetty must be sacrificed.

Irwine's strategy works. Adam obediently ends up shaking hands with Arthur, instead of becoming an English

Defarge. Whatever political fire there is in his belly will be extinguished by Dinah and her Methodism. Arthur goes off to win glory in the Peninsula. As Colonel Donnithorne he is, on his return, a rather melancholy old dog—but a true English hero. Conceivably he will still be around to play his part at Waterloo. A respectable cousin will take over as squire if 'the colonel' dies in action. If he survives Arthur will return to take up his squire's duties, purged of all scandal by his feats on the battlefield. The old order is thus preserved by Irwine's manœuvres. He has done his small bit to avert revolution. The loser in all this, of course, is Hetty.

Had the full story of Arthur's seduction, mendacity, and abandonment come out—particularly if it had been reiterated in court by Irwine, Adam, and Arthur himself— she might have won a full pardon, or at least a light cus- todial sentence in England. What actually happens to her is politically necessary (if one shares Irwine's politics) but horribly unjust. As an attractive young woman with the reputation of a hardened trull, she will be subject to sex- ual molestation from her male guards and, all too likely, from other convicts.

As Robert Hughes points out, the lot of the 24,000 women convicts transported to Australia in the early nineteenth century was not enviable:

Convict men might in the end redeem themselves through work and penance, but women almost never. It was as though women convicts had passed the ordinary bounds of class and become a fiction, not far from pornography: crude raucous Eve, sucking rum and mothering bastards in the exterior darkness, inviting contempt from her social superiors, rape rather than help from men.[1]

Thank you, Reverend Irwine, thank you, Captain Donnithorne.

Hetty in fact lives only a few years in Australia, and wretched years we can imagine them to be. It seems a hard fate for a girl whose main fault was a fondness for glass earrings. But, as Irwine would doubtless point out, sorrowfully but firmly, the security of England's institutions is more important than the fate of a light-headed milkmaid.

The Oxford World's Classics *Adam Bede* is edited by Valentine Cunningham.

George Eliot · *The Mill on the Floss*

──

How good an oarswoman is Maggie Tulliver?

──

For all his admiration of its author, Henry James did not like the ending of *The Mill on the Floss* one bit:

The story is told as if it were destined to have, if not a strictly happy termination, at least one within ordinary probabilities. As it stands, the *dénouement* shocks the reader most painfully. Nothing has prepared him for it; the story does not move towards it; it casts no shadow before it. Did such a *dénouement* lie within the author's intentions from the first, or was it a tardy expedient for the solution of Maggie's difficulties? This question the reader asks himself, but of course he asks it in vain. For my part, although, as long as humanity is subject to floods and earthquakes, I have no objection to see them made use of in novels, I would in this particular case have infinitely preferred that Maggie should have been left to her own devices.[1]

On his part, Leslie Stephen (writing in 1909) could 'not help wishing that the third volume could have been suppressed'.[2] F. R. Leavis concurred with James, if less dismissively:

The flooded river has no symbolic or metaphorical value. It is only the dreamed-of perfect accident that gives us the opportunity for the dreamed-of heroic act—the act that shall vindicate us against a harshly misjudging world, bring emotional fulfilment and (in others) changes of heart, and provide a gloriously tragic curtain. Not that the sentimental in it is embarrassingly gross, but the finality is not that of great art, and the significance is what I have suggested—a revealed immaturity.[3]

One could multiply examples and it is difficult to find a critic of weight prepared to commend the last chapter of *The Mill on the Floss*. The principal objections are that the drowning of Tom and Maggie is arbitrary (no foreshadow is cast, as James puts it) and that it is sentimental. It is odd that so few of the critics who dislike the climax of *The Mill on the Floss* adduce another objection—namely, that the scene of the Tullivers' drowning is, by any understanding of the laws of hydrodynamics and the lesser science of river-boating, incredible.[4]

The final chapter of *The Mill on the Floss* (volume III, chapter 5) is entitled 'The Last Conflict'. It opens with Maggie's life in ruins. She is estranged from her stern brother, Tom, who is living again at the Dorlcote Mill. Stephen Guest, just returned from Holland, cannot understand why Maggie will not see him. He has written her a violently passionate and hurtful letter. As a woman to whom public scandal attaches following her unchaperoned escapade in the boat with Stephen, Maggie has been advised by the friendly local minister, Dr Kenn, 'to go away from St Ogg's for a time'. The hoped-for position as governess is now out of the question. 'Gossip and slander' have condemned her. Before taking this step she has found refuge at good-hearted Bob Jakin's humble house, by the riverside.

Outside, the equinoctial storms of mid-September are raging. The rain is incessant. The Floss (which Eliot based on the Trent, although the St Ogg's region is clearly in Warwickshire) is running ominously high. A tidal river, its current is swollen both from the teeming heavens and from the surging ocean. The old men of St Ogg's shake their heads and talk 'of sixty years ago, when the same sort of weather, happening about the equinox, brought the great floods, which swept the bridge away, and reduced the town to great misery'.

It is 'past midnight'. While Bob, his wife, and their child sleep upstairs a sleepless Maggie sits in 'her lonely room'. Later called a 'parlour', this room is on the ground floor with a window looking out to the river. Foreseeing the wretched life that lies ahead of her ('how long it will be before death comes! I am so young, so healthy'), Maggie fights down a brief temptation to suicide. But she tacitly pleads that God will end her misery soon. 'At that moment' she feels 'a startling sensation of sudden cold about her knees.' The Floss has broken its banks. She wakes Bob, who is upstairs.

They must get to the two boats belonging to the house, she shouts (this is an error, of course; the sensible thing to do would be to go quietly to the upper storey of the house, and wait until the deluge subsided). As Maggie gives the alarm there is a 'tremendous crash'. One of the rowing-boats has banged through the parlour window. (Was it not moored? Apparently so—how then has it risen so high in the water?) The boat remains, 'with the prow lodging and protruding through the window'.

It turns out that both boats are conveniently jammed against the window, ready for the house's occupants to embark. Bob, who now has a lantern, gets his wife and baby into one boat. Maggie boards the other—no easy task, one would have thought, given the rocking boat and the awkwardness of clambering through the broken window-frame wearing a full-bodied, ankle-length dress (see the illustration at the end of this chapter). But Maggie contrives to do it. Once in the boat she 'gets possession of an oar' and pushes off. We are given a vivid vignette of her by Bob's fitful lantern flare, 'as she stood in the rain with the oar in her hand and her black hair streaming'. The boat is, we apprehend, a narrow-beam, shallow-draft rowing-boat or skiff, designed for river and estuary work close to the land. Lacking a keel, such craft are inherently unstable (as anyone who has been in one on a river will know). Standing up in such a boat would be risky at any time and suicidal in the eddying turbulence of a flash flood which has been violent enough to raise the water-level many feet in a few minutes. But things are moving fast. Suddenly 'a new tidal current' catches Maggie's little vessel, and she finds herself alone on the broad expanse of the swollen Floss in the pitch black. The stream carries her along although she has her oar with which to scull (or possibly two with which to row—the detail is not clarified), as she drifts at some speed downstream to St Ogg's.

Maggie's first thought is the Mill ('which is the way home?' she cries). She is now in smooth water 'perhaps far on the over-flooded fields' (St Ogg's is in low-lying Fen country). Day is at last breaking. Maggie seizes her oar again, and paddles 'with the energy of awakened hope' (if she paddles, presumably she is sitting down again, but it is not clear that with one oar she could direct the boat where she wants it to go. Possibly she is sculling, like a gondolier, with the oar secured on a stern rowlock). Her every thought is bent towards her brother and his safety.

Soon the 'dark mass' of St Ogg's looms up. The Mill is at the junction of the faster-flowing tributary, the Ripple, and the main channel of the Floss. Maggie is obliged to navigate her little craft through the swirling crosscurrents to get to Tom: '*now*, she must use all her skill and power to manage the boat and get it if possible out of the current ... With new resolution, Maggie seized her oar, and stood up again to paddle.' What 'skill', one may ask? The point was made earlier in the text that it was only a few months earlier that Maggie had—for the first time in her life—learned how to handle an oar.

During a summer outing on the river with Lucy and Stephen, 'she thought she would like to learn how to row' (p. 336). The young man gallantly instructed her in the rudiments of rowing (taking the opportunity to clasp her hand when her foot slips getting out of the boat). Those few minutes of tuition from Stephen on still water represent the sum total of Maggie's experience of handling a boat. Although, as G. S. Haight notes, she has been brought up as something of a tomboy in a water-mill alongside a river, neither boatcraft nor swimming seem to have featured in her childhood.

Now, in the midst of the most turbulent flood stream for sixty years, Maggie can balance herself, encumbered by a wet, full-length dress and petticoats, and vigorously ply a single oar in such a boat as we see in the illustration. Stephen must, we assume, be a teacher of genius and Maggie a similarly gifted pupil. How else could she stand up, on a rocking craft, and 'paddle' (scull, using the rowlock? Or direct her strokes strategically on one side then the other?). Grace Darling herself would be proud of Maggie's boating feats on the Floss. George Eliot, one assumes, has fallen into the landlubber's common error of thinking that rowing is as easy as it looks.

By energetic 'paddling' Maggie successfully directs her boat to the mill. The flood is now at a level with the 'upstairs windows' (the water must have risen some twenty feet in six hours). Fortuitously, Tom is stranded in the house by himself. Leaving, as Maggie did, by a window, he 'steps into the boat' (wiser, one would have thought, to have lowered himself into it). Once on board he takes the 'oars' (there are now two). They push off, and Tom rows 'with untired vigour'. Their plan is to row downstream to Tofton, and Park House, which 'stands high up out of the flood'. Then comes the tremendous climax:

Nothing else was said; a new danger was being carried towards them by the river. Some wooden machinery had just given way on one of the wharves, and huge fragments were being floated along. The sun was rising now, and the wide area of watery desolation was spread out in dreadful clearness around them—in dreadful clearness floated onwards the hurrying, threatening masses. A large company in a boat that was working its way along under the Tofton houses, observed their danger, and shouted, 'Get out of the current!'

But that could not be done at once, and Tom, looking before him, saw death rushing on them. Huge fragments, clinging together in fatal fellowship, made one wide mass across the stream.

'It is coming, Maggie!' Tom said, in a deep hoarse voice, loosing the oars, and clasping her.

The next instant the boat was no longer seen upon the water— and the huge mass was hurrying on in hideous triumph.

But soon the keel of the boat reappeared, a black speck on the golden water.

The boat reappeared—but brother and sister had gone down in an embrace never to be parted: living through again in one supreme moment the days when they had clasped their little hands in love, and roamed the daisied fields together. (p. 521)

It is magnificent, but as Gordon Haight points out, it is not realistic fiction. First, the meteorology is wrong. Flash floods, of the kind which suddenly and without warning inundate a whole town under many feet of swirling water, only occur in mountainous areas or where dams break creating a tidal wave. This is flat fen-country As Haight neatly puts it: 'the water could not have risen above the hedgerows of Dorlcote if the whole twenty-five-inch rainfall of Lincolnshire had dropped there in one night'.[5]

As unconvincing as the flash-flood-in-the-fens is the business about the 'huge fragments' of 'wooden machinery'. The adjective 'wooden' was an afterthought added by George Eliot to the second edition of *The Mill on the Floss*, when it occurred to her that metal machinery does not float. But 'wooden machinery' is an oxymoron that strains the imagination. It certainly strained the artist's imagination (see the details on the 'huge fragment' above). The notion that in 1839, with Britain well into the

'It is coming, Maggie!' Tom said, in a deep hoarse voice, loosing the
oars, and clasping her

Industrial Revolution, in a go-ahead place like St Ogg's (substantially Coventry), dockside factories would be using wooden cog wheels six feet in diameter beggars belief.

Most bewildering, as Haight points out, is the depiction of these large masses of wood 'rushing' at a much faster speed than Tom and Maggie's wooden boat, when both are in the same line of the current. These 'fragments' will, like icebergs, have most of their bulk beneath the water, and—dragging on the bottom—will be moving much slower than the shallow-draft rowing-boat. Unless their vessel is snagged on something the Tullivers are in no danger whatsoever. But in contravention of the laws of hydrodynamics, the 'huge mass hurries on' to its 'hideous triumph' and crushes Tom and Maggie's boat. If the illustrator is to be credited, brother and sister stand up to embrace for the last time. At this point, one supposes, it hardly matters if they capsize.

George Eliot was addicted to tremendous scenes of women in little boats. But although the pictorial, poetic, and dramatic aspects of women drifting attracted Eliot, the practical business of navigating boats was clearly unknown territory. Nor, although she undertook laborious research for her novels, did she make any investigation into boating matters. An hour with the oars would have prevented much of the implausibility in 'The Last Conflict'. George Eliot compares poorly in this respect (though in few others) with Wilkie Collins, who loved to mess about in boats and is very accurate about boating details.

The Oxford World's Classics *The Mill on the Floss* is edited by Gordon S. Haight with an introduction by Dinah Birch.

—

How good a swimmer is Magwitch?

—

Great Expectations has the most vivid of all Dickensian openings, designed to burst explosively on the first page of *All the Year Round*, where it was initially serialized. Pip mournfully regards the graves of his parents and five little brothers, 'who gave up trying to get a living exceedingly early in that universal struggle'.[1] The narrative halts for a paragraph to depict the dreary marsh landscape on a late winter afternoon. It is all too much for the 7-year-old orphan, who begins to cry:

'Hold your noise!' cried a terrible voice, as a man started up from among the graves at the side of the church porch. 'Keep still, you little devil, or I'll cut your throat!'

A fearful man, all in coarse grey, with a great iron on his leg. A man with no hat, and with broken shoes, and with an old rag tied round his head. A man who had been soaked in water, and smothered in mud, and lamed by stones, and cut by flints, and stung by nettles, and torn by briars; who limped, and shivered, and glared and growled; and whose teeth chattered in his head as he seized me by the chin.

'O! Don't cut my throat, sir,' I pleaded in terror. 'Pray don't do it, sir.' (p. 4)

It is not until much later in the novel (II.3), and sixteen years later in Pip's life, that we learn the details of how Abel Magwitch, Pip's 'fearful man', escaped from the hulks and came to be hiding behind the gravestone (of Pip's father, as illustrators have felicitously assumed). He tells Pip and Herbert about his criminal intrigues with the

villainous Compeyson, their conspiracy to put stolen
banknotes into circulation, the grossly discrepant sentences he and his accomplice received, Compeyson's
infuriating taunt after the trial. The two men are consigned to the 'hulks' to await transportation:

I had said to Compeyson that I'd smash that face of his, and I
swore Lord smash mine! to do it. We was in the same prison-ship,
but I couldn't get at him for long, though I tried. At last I come
behind him and hit him on the cheek to turn him round and get a
smashing one at him, when I was seen and seized. The black-hole
of that ship warn't a strong one, to a judge of black-holes that
could swim and dive. I escaped to the shore and I was a hiding
among the graves there, envying them as was in 'em and all over,
when I first see my boy! (pp. 347–8)

The prison ships, or 'hulks', lie—as Mrs Joe tells Pip
(with the unkind prediction that he will one day know
them from the inside)—across the marshes. Decommis-
sioned naval vessels, crudely converted, they lay in the
Medway estuary (although Dickens seems in *Great
Expectations* to put them at the mouth of the Thames). The
hulks held prisoners before passage could be found for
them to Australia. It might be a long wait—transportation
was an expensive business. For security's sake the hulks
were moored some way from shore in deep water—floating
Alcatrazes. They fell into disuse as transportation fell out
of favour, and the last of the hulks was taken out of service in 1858, a couple of years before *Great Expectations*.

By Dickens's own private reckoning, Magwitch is
around 45 years old when he leaps on Pip in the graveyard.
For a middle-aged man and a heavy smoker, he is in truly
excellent physical shape. Diving into the current-ridden
Thames estuary in winter and swimming several hundred
yards to the shore fully clothed is no mean athletic feat.
Doing it weighed down with a 'great iron' suggests superhuman powers. Nor, it would seem, is Magwitch unique.

On his way to the graveyard with the required 'wittles' and file, Pip meets Compeyson, who has also gone overboard from the hulk; 'He was dressed in coarse grey, too, and had a great iron on his leg.' Like Magwitch, Compeyson must be a remarkable swimmer.

When Dickens repeatedly talks of a 'great iron', he intends us to visualize a large, heavy, metal fetter, which serves the same hobbling purpose as the ball and chain beloved by cartoonists. Even Mark Spitz in his heyday would not be able to swim the distance from the hulk to the shore thus burdened down. Magwitch would never break surface from his dive. This nonsense came about, I imagine, because for Victorians of Dickens's generation 'swimming' (as opposed to 'bathing') was an unusual practice. Magwitch's swim to shore was generally unremarked on because Dickens's readers shared his vagueness about what human limits are in the water. At best Victorians could float, dog-paddle, or thrash about a bit. A tonic 'dip' at the seaside or in the Serpentine would be the extent of their knowledge. Most of the readers of *All the Year Round* were, one guesses, non-swimmers.

As it happened, this widespread ignorance was being corrected, especially among the younger generation of Victorians. In the 1850s Muscular Christianity (with its strong vein of latent homosexuality) was popularizing manly sports like boxing and swimming, which required young men to display their naked bodies to each other. The novelist Charles Kingsley was the main propagandist for the muscular cult, and *The Water Babies* (1863) was, among other things, a long advertisement for the manifold joys of water sport.

In the period between the 1850s and Captain Matthew Webb's swimming the English Channel in August 1875 (the period of what has been called the 'Victorian sports mania'), swimming became a popular national exercise in which, for many decades, Britain led the world. In the early 1870s there were two important developments. In 1873 the 'trudgen' or 'crawl' stroke was developed, allowing much higher speeds in the water (if you had asked Dickens what 'stroke' Magwitch used in his magnificent swim, he would, I suspect, have been puzzled how to answer). Also in the 1870s, the newly founded Amateur Swimming Association began establishing a set of 'world records'. They make comical reading. In 1878, for instance, the record for the free-style 100 yards stood at 76 and three-quarter seconds.

A younger novelist like Wilkie Collins would not have made the error that Dickens makes in *Great Expectations*. Nor, as a keen amateur yachtsman, would Collins make the primitive errors about boating that George Eliot makes at the end of *The Mill on the Floss* (see the previous chapter). For older novelists, like Dickens and Eliot, water was something you drown in (like Quilp, Headstone, Riderhood, the Tullivers) or get shipwrecked on.[2] There are many reasons, most of them inarticulate, why Gwendolen, in *Daniel Deronda*, lets Grandcourt drown after she perceives, with surprise, that he can't swim. But even if Gwendolen had wanted to save her husband, it is not certain that she could have done so. It is suggested in the narrative that she could have thrown him a rope (this assumes there was one to hand, and that Gwendolen had the physical strength to fling it far enough and accurately enough). What is clear is that Gwendolen could not do what a young woman of today might do: tear off her clothes, dive in, reach him with a few powerful strokes, turn him on his back, incapacitate him if necessary with a firm blow to the jaw, and bring him back to the yacht with powerful frog-kicks.

For these writers of an earlier generation, the water was not the playground or gymnasium it later became. It is what Conrad called it, 'the destructive element'. Wilkie Collins's *Armadale* is the first novel in English, I think, to be almost entirely based on yachting as a sport; it was written in the first flush of Collins's acquiring his own pleasure-yacht. Similarly R. M. Ballantyne's *The Coral Island* is the first popular novel aggressively to promote swimming as an activity for boys—something 'manly', but also immensely pleasurable (it was to be many decades before girls, or women, would be encouraged to swim rather than 'bathe').

Ballantyne everywhere celebrates the joys of the plunge. Swimming in *The Coral Island* is not merely functional as it was in the novel's prototype, *Robinson Crusoe*. Robinson is, as he tells us, a 'good swimmer' (for practical reasons, sailors saw it as a necessary skill, like knotting).[3] He swims from the wreck to the shore of his desert island. Later he swims back to and around the stranded vessel. But once he is established on his island, with his little economy in good order, Robinson hunts for pleasure but never swims for pleasure. The idea would doubtless have struck him as grotesque.

It is different with Ballantyne's castaways. Ralph, as he modestly tells us, is 'really a good swimmer and diver too'. But he cannot 'equal Jack, who was superior to any Englishman I ever saw'. Peterkin, on the other hand, 'could only swim a little, and could not dive at all'. Peterkin is thus cut off from the wonderful underwater world open to the two other boys as, naked (although illustrations in later editions invariably show them decently covered), they dive down to the reef:

As I have before stated, the water within the reef was as calm as a pond; and, as there was no wind, it was quite clear from the surface to the bottom, so that we could see down easily even at a depth of twenty or thirty yards. When Jack and I dived into shallower water, we expected to have found sand and stones, instead of which we found ourselves in what appeared really to be an enchanted garden. The whole of the bottom of the lagoon, as we called the calm water within the reef, was covered with coral of every shape, size, and hue. Some portions were formed like large mushrooms, others appeared like the brain of a man, having stalks or necks attached to them; but the most common kind was a species of branching coral, and some portions were of a lovely pale pink colour, others were pure white. Among this there grew large quantities of seaweed of the richest hues imaginable, and of the most graceful forms; while innumerable fishes—blue, red, yellow, green, and striped—sported in and out amongst the flower-beds of the submarine garden, and did not appear to be at all afraid of our approaching them.

On darting to the surface for breath, after our first dive, Jack and I rose close to each other.

'Did you ever in your life, Ralph, see anything so lovely?' said Jack, as he flung the spray from his hair.

'Never,' I replied. 'It appears to me like fairy realms. I can scarcely believe we are not dreaming.' (pp. 35–6)

Maybe they were. Unless they were wearing goggles, or were in diving-suits, none of this submarine detail would be clearly visible. What Ralph and Jack would 'see' underwater is not a 'fairy realm' in all its magic detail but a polychromatic blur with a few vague shapes. And the salt content of the water would irritate their eyes horribly. This unnatural underwater clarity is a main feature of the subsequent 'Diamond Cave' scenes, which are central to the plot.

Ballantyne was in most respects a fetishist about accuracy. As J. S. Bratton points out, in the interest of getting the details of his novels just right 'he visited lighthouses, rode on fire engines, and tried out diving suits on the bottom of the Thames'. He must, presumably, at some point have opened his eyes underwater. What then went wrong in *The Coral Island*? If not an error on the same scale as Ballantyne's famous unhusked coconuts,[4] the translucent

Pacific water is clearly a high-order inaccuracy. The point, surely, is that whereas in *Great Expectations* Dickens was writing for readers of his own generation (he was in his late forties) entirely indifferent to 'swimming as sport', Ballantyne was writing for much younger readers enthusiastic about swimming but still not very knowledgeable—readers, that is, who would assume that swimming in the lucid Pacific might be entirely different from what they had experienced in the chilly and opaque waters of Margate.

Within fifty years swimming would be a universally familiar recreation. One still, however, encounters what one might call the 'Magwitch Great Iron' paradox in popular narrative—that is, stories which trade on audience ignorance about 'extreme' physical activities. Although most men and women in the Western world will have swum, relatively few have scaled mountains. In the film *Cliffhanger*, Sylvester Stallone is shown catching with one hand the wrist of a falling companion as she hurtles down. This is, I would guess, physically impossible (even with biceps as well developed as Stallone's). Either the grasp would slip, or the climbers' shoulders would be wrenched from their sockets,

Ice tobogganing is another thrilling sport which only an élite of sportsmen practise, although most of us have seen it on TV. In the James Bond thriller *On Her Majesty's Secret Service* a villain dies horribly when he pitches on to a toboggan run and slides to the bottom—by which time he is hamburger. It was later pointed out to Ian Fleming that a human body on a toboggan run would not slither more than three yards before stopping.

As with mountaineering and tobogganing, few members of a film audience have first-hand experience of sky-diving. In a spectacular stunt in *Eraser*, Arnold Schwarzenegger overtakes as he drops from a plane the parachute which was thrown out many seconds earlier. Is this not against the laws of physics? Objects, however heavy, fall at the same rate. Although he can alter his aerodynamic configuration to go faster (by adopting a forward dive position and lessening air resistance), Arnold could never streamline himself into a narrower mass than the parachute—and he would have to spend precious seconds adjusting for the lateral distance created by the time interval between the pack's being dropped and his jumping from the plane. Schwarzenegger would make a sizeable crater in the ground many seconds after the parachute bounced to rest on its surface, some half-a-mile away. Victorian authors, like Dickens, are as free to make use of these pockets of audience ignorance as modern film-makers. But they may well look as odd to later generations as our breath-taking stunts will, a hundred years hence.

The Oxford World's Classics *Great Expectations* is edited by Margaret Cardwell with an introduction by Kate Flint. *The Coral Island* is edited by J. S. Bratton.

═══

What, precisely, does Miss Gwilt's purple flask contain?

═══

Wilkie Collins wrote *Armadale* under an unusual set of pressures. As the follow-up to his all-conquering *The Woman in White*, he had been offered a huge sum by the publisher George Smith for the new novel—£5,000. 'Nobody but Dickens has made as much', he jubilantly told his mother. Smith wanted *Armadale* for serialization in *his* all-conquering *Cornhill Magazine*. Collins would have to be on his mettle to keep company with such works as Trollope's *Framley Parsonage* and George Eliot's *Romola*.

Unfortunately, Collins—whose health was chronically poor and not helped by his addiction to narcotics—suffered a health collapse as he prepared to embark on his new novel. Originally scheduled to start serialization in January 1863, *Armadale* was postponed for almost two years, the first instalment not appearing in *Cornhill* until November 1864. And even when he was in a position to start composition (around June 1864), Collins was not as well prepared as he would have liked to be for such a challenge.

For novelists like Collins and his friend Charles Reade—rising stars of the 1860s—preparation was a crucial phase of work. They wrote what were often called 'matter-of-fact romances'. That is to say, their fiction was underpinned by a more solid foundation of authenticity than a 'domestic' novelist like Trollope or an out-and-out 'sensationalist' like Elizabeth Braddon. Reade, for instance, created mountainous archives in preparation for his work, with newspaper clippings and other research materials. His fiction is constipated with the factual ingredients he stuffed into it. Collins, although not as fetishistic as Reade, took professional pride in the factual accuracy of his fiction. In his 'Appendix' to *Armadale*, for instance, he tells us that: 'Wherever the story touches questions connected with Law, Medicine, or Chemistry, it has been submitted, before publication, to the experience of professional men.' He was careful about such things.

As Collins came up to the last instalments of *Armadale*, he was working against the calendar. The novel was serialized between November 1864 and June 1866, and for the latter sections Collins was evidently running only a month or two ahead of *Cornhill*'s printers (who, as George Smith told the author, were enjoying *Armadale* immensely). It would seem that, in autumn 1865, Collins had not worked out in his mind how to wrap up his fiendishly complex plot—with the murderous, bigamous, *femme fatale* Lydia Gwilt at its centre. Something spectacular was needed.[1]

On 30 November 1865 there appeared in *The Times* a report which must have seemed to Collins a gift from the gods:

POISONOUS GAS—At the Liverpool Coroner's Court yesterday an inquiry was held touching the deaths of three men who were suffocated within a few days of each other while acting as shipkeepers on board the ship *Armadale* lying in the Huskisson Dock. Dr Trench, medical officer of health, and Mrs Ayrton gave evidence to the effect that death had been caused by inhalation of carbonic acid gas, which, in consequence of the prevailing high winds, had been forced back into the deckhouse where the men slept, and where they had kindled fires. The jury returned a verdict: 'That death resulted from suffocation caused by defective ventilation.'

The coincidence of the ship being called *Armadale* was

amazing—more than amazing, it was ominous. For someone like Wilkie Collins, with his belief in 'fate' (a main
theme in *Armadale*), it must have seemed like a clear sign
from his tutelary spirit: 'this is how to end your novel'.
Moreover, the story was in *The Times*—the nation's
'newspaper of record'. What better provenance for a
'matter of fact' romancer looking for a neat way to tie up
the threads of his novel in progress?

Collins duly wove *The Times'* report into the climactic
section of *Armadale*, entitled 'The Purple Flask'. The
denouement is complex in the extreme. Allan Armadale
has inconveniently returned from a watery grave, foiling
Lydia's bigamous plans *vis-à-vis* Ozias. She conspires with
the villainous Dr Le Doux (alias Downward), now the
proprietor of a sanatorium for nerve-racked women in
Hampstead. Between them they intend to do away with
Allan. To this end the guileless young man is lured to the
Sanatorium, and tricked into spending the night there.

Meanwhile Le Doux (careful always to give himself
deniability should the case come to the notice of the
police) hints to Lydia how she may perform the awful deed.
While showing some prospective clients round his establishment, the doctor makes sure that Miss Gwilt is thoroughly familiarized with the workings of the ingenious
'fumigation' device which he has devised for his patients.
Ostensibly he is showing this Victorian air-conditioning
system off to his visitors; in reality he is instructing Lydia
as to how it may be misused:

Epidemic disease, in spite of all my precautions, may enter this
Sanatorium, and may render the purifying of the sick-room
necessary. Or the patient's case may be complicated by other than
nervous malady—say, for instance, asthmatic difficulty of breathing. In one case, fumigation is necessary: in the other, additional
oxygen in the air will give relief. The epidemic nervous patient
says, 'I won't be smoked under my own nose!' The asthmatic

nervous patient gasps with terror at the idea of a chemical
explosion in his room. I noiselessly fumigate one of them; I noiselessly oxygenize the other, by means of a simple Apparatus fixed
outside in the corner here. It is protected by this wooden casing;
it is locked with my own key; and it communicates by means of a
tube with the interior of the room. Look at it! (pp. 773–4)

Miss Gwilt, together with the assembled visitors, duly
'looks at it'. The fumigation and oxygenation apparatus
comprises a large stone jar with a glass funnel and a pipe
leading into the room. There is no pumping apparatus, the
gas, vapour, or fumes merely siphon or drift into the
adjoining room—according to whether they are heavier or
lighter than air. The occupant, as Le Doux points out, will
be unaware of what is going on.

A little later Le Doux describes to Lydia the chemical
reactions which will produce what we assume to be deadly
carbonic gas. An unnamed fluid in a flask (evidently sulphuric acid) is poured on to a 'common mineral substance'
(evidently limestone) in six small measured doses, producing a quantity of gaseous bubbles. 'Collect the gas in
those bubbles', Le Doux tells Lydia, 'and convey it into a
closed chamber—and let Samson himself be in that chamber, [the gas] will kill him in half an hour.' Not only that,
the cause of death will appear to any medical examiner or
coroner to be wholly natural—'apoplexy or congestion of
the lungs'. The perfect murder, in other words.

This, then, is how the deed will be done. Le Doux early
in the evening places quantities of limestone (as we
assume) in the stone jar connected to Room Number Four.
Alongside the jar he places a small 'purple flask', containing acid (as we again assume) with six levels marked on the
outside. It is arranged that Lydia shall have a key to the
room's fumigation apparatus. Allan arrives at the Sanatorium and is assigned to number four. But, unexpectedly,
he is accompanied by Ozias who—anticipating some

villainy—switches bedrooms with his friend. At a quarter past one in the morning, Lydia begins her deadly work, unaware of the room-change. After she has poured four doses from her lethal purple flask into the stone jar, at the prescribed five-minute intervals, she discovers to her horror that she has almost asphyxiated the man she loves—it is Ozias, not Allan, in Room Number Four. She drags Ozias out unconscious (but still living), pours in the sixth and final dose from her purple flask, kisses the recumbent Ozias, then enters the chamber of death herself:

'Good-by!' she said softly.

The door of the room opened—and closed on her. There was an interval of silence.

Then, a sound came dull and sudden, like the sound of a fall.

Then, there was silence again. (p. 807)

It is tremendously effective, but it is, I suspect, scientific nonsense. And, as he wrote this last scene, Collins must have become increasingly nervous about its authenticity. It seems clear that he was misled by a scientific error in *The Times'* report. It is evident that the men on the *Armadale* were suffocated by the massive build-up of carbon monoxide from a heating fire in their bunk-room on board the vessel, forced back by wind pressure on the outside vents. (This is still a hazard with such things as charcoal-fired indoor barbecues.) 'Carbonic acid gas' seems to have got into the report by mistake. Dissolving small amounts of limestone with tiny measures of acid (which is what Collins has in mind with Miss Gwilt's purple flask and the stone jar) would produce negligible amounts of carbon dioxide. In very confined chambers (something the size of a goldfish bowl), this could have a narcotic or even a fatal effect—but not diffused in an area as large as a bedroom. A scientist tells me that it would be like trying to poison someone with the emissions from a fizzing Coca Cola can.

Lydia would need gallons of acid and rock-sized chunks of limestone, many hours of chemical reaction time, and a sophisticated powered pumping mechanism to move the resultant gas into a room. With the toxic apparatus at her disposal, she might conceivably kill a mouse in a glass jar.

In a letter Collins admitted to having encountered problems in 'reconciling certain facts with the incidents in the last chapter'. He handled the problem in a way which must have been deeply unsatisfactory to his artistic conscience. In the text of *Armadale* he never specifies what is in the 'purple flask', nor on what substance it is to react in the stone jar. He knew that if he did so ('there is sulphuric acid in the flask, limestone in the jar') he would invite the kind of deadly 'disproof' of his veracity that *The Times* had brought to bear on *The Woman in White*. That episode was deeply embarrassing to him.[2] Ironically, it was the same paper which had got him into the pickle he was now in. With more time, he could doubtless have got it right— although it is not easy to see how you could poison someone with Le Doux's primitive fumigation apparatus. In the circumstances the only resource open to Collins was a smoke-screen of lurid Gothic horror—the kind of Radcliffian rhetoric which, as a 'matter of fact' novelist, he despised. 'What is inside Lydia's purple flask?' Something too terrible to describe, words fail me—don't ask, just shudder.

The Oxford World's Classics *Armadale* is edited by Catherine Peters.

George Eliot · *Felix Holt, the Radical*

====

Lemon or ladle?

====

Readers of my generation often bemoan the passing of the 'old' World's Classics. They can still be found (although they are becoming increasingly expensive) in second-hand bookshops. Pocket-book sized, with hard covers (stamped prominently with the Oxford University crest and motto) they were beautiful things. Launched in 1906, they marked OUP's entry into the world of general trade publishing.[1] The World's Classics came into their own in the 1920s and ran to 500 titles by the end of the decade.

If the old World's Classics had any introductions at all (most didn't) they were short belletristic effusions by writers such as Virginia Woolf or G. K. Chesterton. Latterly, in the 1960s, the series attempted to rejuvenate itself with bumper-value 'double volumes' and pictorial dust jackets by Lynton Lamb which are, in my opinion, the best modern illustrations of the Victorian novel we have.[2] They were books of an earlier, less transatlantic, less anxious literary culture. And, with a span of sixty years, they lasted longer than most reprint series of their kind.

Nostalgia aside, there is much to be said in favour of the new (i.e. post-1980), soft-cover World's Classics. They are cheaper. The texts are better. The typography is sharper. Most valuably, unlike their predecessors, the new World's Classics have an *apparatus criticus*—introductions, chronologies, textual notes, explanatory notes, select bibliographies, and often appendices of relevant material.

Even in what is usually the most technical section of the apparatus, inquisitive readers can usually find

thought-provoking material. In the 'Note on the Text' to
Felix Holt, for instance, the editor, Fred C. Thomson,
records: 'One oversight by George Eliot, which persists in
the manuscript and all editions, has been emended by the
editor: in chapter 25 (p. 208), Christian is said to have
dropped a "punch-ladle", whereas in chapter 7 (p. 85) it
was "a lemon".'[3]

Apparently minor, this emendation leads to what I think
is an illuminating puzzle. The scene in question is striking
and well worth Thomson's running repair—if that repair
is really needed. The background is simple enough—
although it gets fiendishly complicated later on. When
Philip Debarry, heir-apparent to his father's baronetcy,
returns to Treby Manor from Oxford he brings with him a
'factotum', Maurice Christian. The omnicompetent Christian is a figure of mystery. He is 50, grey-haired, and
distinguished-looking.

Christian serves as Mr Debarry's 'man'—what in modern parlance we would call a 'personal assistant'. He is
very much what the Victorians thought of as an 'upper
servant'—that is, one who has frequent intercourse with
the gentlefolk of the household and partakes of many of
their privileges and perquisites. Christian's fellow servants are awed by the rumour that he was once a gentleman himself and fought a duel. He lords it over them. He is
also haughty to the point of insolence with his betters,
abasing himself only to Philip Debarry (who treats Christian with more deference than he would an equal, we are
told). Christian speaks French, takes opium for an
unspecified bodily weakness, and has a 'past' that no one
knows about.

We are introduced to the mysterious Mr Christian at
length in volume I, chapter 7. As the genteel company
upstairs relaxes after dinner, the scene shifts to below-
stairs, to the even more convivial steward's room:

where Mr Scales, house-steward and head-butler, a man most solicitous about his boots, wristbands, the roll of his whiskers, and other attributes of a gentleman, distributed cigars, cognac, and whisky, to various colleagues and guests who were discussing, with that freedom of conjecture which is one of our inalienable privileges as Britons, the probable amount of Harold Transome's fortune ... (p. 83)

Present are Scales, Mr Crowder ('an old respectable tenant'), the head-gardener Brent, and the supercilious Christian. A small altercation breaks out among the company when Christian corrects Crowder's French. As it happens, things French (for reasons we will discover later) make Christian uneasy. Scales, an impulsive and foolish man, is in danger of losing his temper. He resents Christian's 'airs', feeling diminished by his presence. Christian moves to lower the temperature: 'Don't be waspish, man', he tells Scales. 'I'll ring the bell for lemons, and make some punch. That's the thing for putting people up to the unknown tongues.' He gets up and slaps Scales's shoulder, with false *bonhomie*, as he walks over to the bell-pull.

Already there are features of this scene which would make any Victorian householder shudder. The sedulous aping of their betters (to the absurd point of ringing for their own servants!) could be thought amusing. Less amusing is the fact that these servants are drinking heavily in their place of work. This is worrying. Moreover, they are not drinking the servant's traditional porter or ale, but 'punch'. The point has already been made, in the description of Treby in chapter 3, that punch is a tipple for the gentry. 'In no country town of the same small size as Treby', we are informed, 'was there a larger proportion of families who had handsome sets of china without handles, hereditary punch-bowls, and large silver ladles with a Queen Anne's guinea in the centre.' Here, it would seem, even the servant's hall has its hereditary punch bowl and large silver ladle.

It would also be noted by a Victorian that lemons were not easily come by in Britain. Those that Christian calls for must have come from the Treby conservatory, warmed laboriously with 'a nether apparatus of hot-water pipes' (p. 43). They would be a luxury, to be used sparingly by the master of the house himself. They would be a fantastic luxury for the servants—lemons, forsooth! Whatever next? Caviare? *En passant*, the Victorian would feel (as in 1866, with the second great 'Bill' on the horizon, George Eliot felt) that 'reform' was getting out of hand; the aristocracy, the ruling classes, have lost their grip. Important social distinctions are blurring.

Punch, as the nineteenth century knew it, was a concoction of wine or spirits, hot water or milk, sugar, and lemons. It was mixed in a bowl, and served piping hot. Best drunk fresh, punch required a series of ritual operations: getting the utensils (heat-resistant bowl, ladle, and special cup-shaped punch glasses), preparing the hot water, fetching the basic alcoholic ingredients, and mixing them carefully. Eliot does not describe the making of the punch in Scales's room and we have to picture it happening in the background while the conversation about how rich or poor the Transomes are continues in its desultory way.

One thing leads to another, and Crowder—apropos of the law-suits which have so impoverished the family at Transome Court—recalls:

'There was the last suit of all made the most noise, as I understand . . . but it wasn't tried hereabout. They said there was a deal O' false swearing. Some young man pretended to be the true heir—let me see—I can't just remember the names—he'd got two. *He* swore he was one man, and *they* swore he was another. However, Lawyer Jermyn won it—they say he'd win a game against the

Old One himself—and the young fellow turned out to be a scamp. Stop a bit—his name was Scaddon—Henry Scaddon.'

Mr Christian here let a lemon slip from his hand into the punch-bowl with a plash which sent some of the nectar in to the company's faces.

'Hallo! what a bungler I am!' he said. (p. 85)

The little accident is vivid (we can almost feel the hot liquor scalding our cheeks). The vividness is an effective device for 'fixing' the episode, like a snapshot, in the reader's memory. It is, of course, Eliot's intention that we should recall it a hundred matter-packed pages later, in chapter 21, when Jermyn drops his bombshell on Christian: 'A—your name—a—is Henry Scaddon.' It's fair to say that very few first readers of *Felix Holt* will have already guessed that Maurice Christian is Henry Scaddon (nor, at this point in the narrative, will they guess the further twist to come). It is equally fair to say that most readers will vividly recollect the episode of the splashing punch, as if it were the page before. 'That's why he was so clumsy,' we think, as the detail slides pleasingly into place.

There are, however, some things not quite right with the punch-making scene, closely examined. For one thing, the timing isn't right. We are in continuous real time—that is to say there are no breaks in the narrative—and only a page-worth (mid-84 to mid-85 in the World's Classics edition) passes, all of it dialogue, between Christian getting up to ring the bell and subsequently dropping the lemon in the punch. If one speaks the dialogue at the speed it would have been spoken, the time elapsed is a bare four minutes. This is insufficient time for the lemons to have arrived. The servant's servant would come in, having been summoned by the bell; he would be told to go and fetch the fruit. It would be some way away—perhaps still in the conservatory, perhaps in a cold store. Certainly such precious objects would not be left around in the kitchen for anyone to help themselves to and keys would have to be used.

It would be several minutes (probably more than four) before the servant could make the return trip with the fruit. Meanwhile, the punch-making apparatus has to be assembled, the bottles uncorked, measured, poured out and so on. Water needs to be heated (although possibly there is a kettle steaming on the hob). Clearly Christian is presiding over all this complicated procedure himself (he is described, a couple of pages on, 'ladling out the punch'). Nor, if one is petty-minded enough to think about it, would a lemon (or half a lemon, if Christian is so far forward as to be squeezing the juice out) make a considerable enough 'plash' to spatter the faces of the assembled company—unless they had their noses virtually in the bowl. It's a fine scene, but nigglingly off centre in a few important details.

The reader remembers the episode, and so does George Eliot. She refers directly to it again at the end of the second volume (p. 208). Christian has just had his interview with Rufus Lyon, who mistakenly thinks he has discovered an appalling secret about Esther's parentage. What is going on is by no means clear to Christian, and he is increasingly anxious. He is also keen to provide for his retirement with some judicious blackmail. Eliot writes:

He held various ends of threads, but there was danger in pulling at them too impatiently. He had not forgotten the surprise which had made him drop the punch-ladle [the World's Classics edition has 'lemon'], when Mr Crowder, talking in the steward's room had said that a scamp named Henry Scaddon had been concerned in a lawsuit about the Transome estate. (p. 208)

'Punch-ladle' is clearly a mistake, but why did Eliot make it? Because, I surmise, her artist's mind was trying, retroactively, to get the lemon-in-the-punch business right.

There was a timing readjustment. In Eliot's subconscious rewriting of the scene the splash was pushed further along the mixing process, from the stage when lemons are appropriate to the later point at which Christian is stirring and ladling out the drink.

This left the rather more serious avoirdupois problem. Something heavier than half-a-lemon (which would make little more than a feeble plop) was needed to drop into the steaming liquid so that it might splash several feet on to the expectant faces. Why not one of those massive silver ladles, described so graphically in chapter 3? If this is what happened, Eliot's subconscious mind (what elsewhere she called the 'not self' that took over in her most inspired passages of writing) solved the problems rather neatly. Unfortunately, it neglected to inform its conscious colleague, and the revision, made so effectively in the mind, was not made on the page.

Clearly, no entirely satisfactory solution can be found now without gross interference in the text of *Felix Holt*. But, as a record of George Eliot's unrealized intention, I would rather like the anomalous punch-ladle to remain as a mark of her artistic, unsleeping, conscience.

The Oxford World's Classics *Felix Holt, the Radical* is edited by Fred C. Thomson.

Anthony Trollope · *Ralph the Heir*

═══

Why 'Captain' Newton?

═══

The names in *Ralph the Heir* are very confusing—no less
than four 'Ralph Newtons' figure in the plot, for instance.
But the romantic story at the novel's centre is straightforward enough. Ralph Newton ('the heir') is parentless
and has been looked after by the lawyer Sir Thomas
Underwood in the office of guardian. Underwood—a
superannuated widower—has two daughters. Patience,
the elder, is her father's housekeeper and is 'certainly not
pretty'. The younger, Clarissa, is 'a beauty' and the family
pet. Underwood also has another ward living in his Fulham villa, Mary Bonner, a surpassingly beautiful young
orphan from the West Indies. Ralph opens proceedings by
lightly proposing marriage to Clarissa ('Dear, dear
Clary,—you know I love you') during a summer's day loun-
ging by the Thames, dressed fetchingly in his straw hat
and Jersey shirt. She tacitly accepts his offer. Clarissa,
meanwhile, is loved faithfully by Ralph's younger brother,
Gregory, a dutiful clergyman. Gregory glumly knows that
his suit has no hope against that of his dashing brother.
Ralph (who disdains work) subsequently attempts to stave
off his increasingly pressing creditors by borrowing from
his breeches-maker, Neefit, and is persuaded by the
socially aspirant tradesman to propose to his jolly young
daughter, Polly. Polly Neefit—although an eminently
sensible girl (more so than her besotted father)—is flattered sufficiently by Ralph's addresses to turn down the
son of a bootmaker, Onty Moggs. Onty knows that he cannot compete with a West End swell, even if that swell is a

'butterfly' and he, Onty, an honest working man. Without clearly cancelling either of these earlier proposals, Ralph goes on to propose marriage to yet a third young woman, Mary Bonner, who is beloved by another Ralph Newton (an illegitimate cousin). Bastard Ralph, who is no heir, feels that he cannot stand in the way of legitimate Ralph. Finally, at the end of an eventfully romantic year, Ralph proposes to a fourth young lady, Gus Eardham, for whom in truth he does not much care. Thus, the great question posed by the novel is 'who will Ralph the heir marry?'

It is, to be honest, not a very exciting question. Looking back on *Ralph the Heir* in his autobiography, Trollope marked it down as one of his failures, noting bleakly that 'a novelist after fifty should not write love stories' (he was 54 when he wrote *Ralph the Heir*). The great weakness in the love plot of the novel, as Trollope perceived, was that Ralph the Heir is so chronically and incurably 'weak'. Moral weakness is demonstrated by his reckless proposals of marriage to every attractive woman who crosses his path and—more significantly—his disinclination to work, or do anything useful. He is a drone, and there is no lower order of life in the Trollopian universe than idlers.

Although *Ralph the Heir* was not one of Trollope's great successes, everyone liked the vulgar breeches-maker, Neefit (it was Neefit's character that was exploited in the dramatic adaptation of the novel).[1] Trollope catches the tradesman's breezy cockney dialect with great skill. There is, however, an oddity in the breeches-maker's patronizing mode of address to Ralph—the young man whom he fondly thinks he has 'bought' as Polly's husband. On being told, for instance, that Ralph is having difficulty with a bill owing to Moggs, the bootmaker, Neefit

told Ralph to come to him when Moggs's 'bit of stiff' came round. Moggs's 'bit of stiff' did come round, and 'the Captain' did as he had been desired to do. Neefit wrote out the cheque without saying a word about his daughter. 'Do you just run across to Argyle Street, Captain,' said the breeches-maker, 'and get the stuff in notes'. For Mr Neefit's bankers held an establishment in Argyle Street. 'There ain't no need, you know, to let on, Captain, is there?' said the breeches-maker. (p. 225)

Why does Neefit repeatedly apostrophize Ralph as 'Captain'? If readers register it as something odd, they probably assume it is a Victorian cockneyism along the lines of 'Squire' ('Right you are, Squire'), 'moosh' ('Watch it, moosh'), 'mate' ('don't you worry your head about it, mate') or cock ('Wotcher, cock'). But, unlike these others, 'Captain' has not survived in popular usage.

This explanation is plausible but wrong. 'Captain' is not a cockneyism. Its origin can be found in cancellations in the manuscript of *Ralph the Heir*. Up until chapter 8, the manuscript reveals, Ralph was a captain in the Coldstream Guards. Trollope subsequently changed the early part of his novel extensively so as to write out this detail, rendering Ralph nothing more than an unemployed heir-expectant. Neefit's 'Captain' survives as an enigmatic hangover from this earlier conception of the novel. Either it crept in as a lapse of memory, or Trollope allowed it to stand as a private joke.

The protrusion of 'Captain Newton' into the revised text is an interesting but not very significant detail—like those earlier designs that X-ray photography sometimes finds under the surface of old master paintings. But why, one may go on to ask, did Trollope make the change? It was not his habit to alter what was written and there are other examples of his going to some lengths not to rewrite, even where it might be advisable.[2]

There are, I think, two answers to the puzzle 'why did Trollope demobilize Captain Newton?' The first of these is that at some point, well into his novel, the novelist remembered, or someone pointed out to him, an awkward article in Queen's Regulations. Junior officers in the British army require their commanding officer's permission to marry or they are obliged to resign their commission. A well-disposed colonel in the Household Brigade might permit Captain Newton to marry Miss Underwood, Miss Bonner, or Miss Eardham (although only one at a time). He would never permit one of his junior officers to marry the daughter of the regiment's supplier of breeches. Captain Newton would not merely be required to resign his commission, he would be hooted out of the service, never to lift his head again in the company of officers and gentlemen.

There was another objection to Ralph's being a serving officer in a crack regiment. *Ralph the Heir* was written in spring and summer 1869—the same period that the novel's action is set. This was the time of Prussian expansionism, culminating in the overrunning of France in 1870. It was also a period of general alarm in Britain about the readiness and competence of the country's armed forces—particularly its soldiers. It was this mood of alarm which set the scene for Colonel Chesney's phenomenally successful invasion fantasy, *The Battle of Dorking* (1871), in which the Prussians are shown doing to London what they have just done to Paris. *Ralph the Heir* completed its serial run and the three-volume edition was published in June 1871, when British war panic was at its height. Trollope did not want one of his 'domestic' novels to get embroiled in all this (what did he, Anthony Trollope, know about the army?), so he demobilized Captain Ralph Newton. It was a prudent move, but it fatally weakened the 'hero' of the novel by making him, like Othello, a man without 'occupation'.

The Oxford World's Classics *Ralph the Heir* is edited by John Sutherland.

Thomas Hardy · *A Pair of Blue Eyes*

What is Elfride's rope made of?

One of the zanier stories in the American press in 1993 told of an inmate in a high-security prison who had escaped using a rope made out of the dental floss which his custodians had thoughtfully provided over the years. It is the kind of article that sticks in the mind (was it *used* floss? one wonders). There is a similar episode, similarly memorable, in Thomas Hardy's early novel *A Pair of Blue Eyes*. The blue-eyed heroine, Elfride Swancourt, is the daughter of the rector of Endelstow (i.e. St Juliot), whose deserted parish is on the 'sea-swept' Wessex (Devonshire and Cornwall) coast. The nearest town is Castle Boterel (i.e. Boscastle).

Elfride is beloved by two very different men—close friends before they became rivals for her hand. Stephen Smith is a gifted young architect. Born into the Wessex peasantry, he has risen above his origins but remains socially insecure, particularly in his addresses to a genteel rector's daughter with distant connections to nobility. Henry Knight is a man of letters, older, richer, and endowed with the *savoir faire* which Stephen lacks. But Knight is sexually insecure and less physically attractive.

The episode in question occupies chapters 21 and 22. It is an overcast summer's afternoon and Elfride (sadly torn between her suitors, although she is at the moment pledged to Stephen) resolves to walk over the cliffs to catch an early glimpse of the steamer *Puffin* which is bringing her fiancé back to Castle Boterel. She carries with her a heavy old telescope with which to spy the vessel as it rounds the coast-line from Bristol. It is a whimsical 'act of supererogation', as Hardy calls it. But placing Elfride on a headland, watching for the ship carrying her lover, creates a resonance with Tristram and Isolde which forecasts the novel's eventual tragic conclusion.

On her way to the cliffs Elfride meets Henry Knight—a coincidence which provokes a 'rebellious' thrill of pleasure. She is something of a flirt at heart. Knight offers to accompany her; she does not tell him exactly why she is going to the coast, merely that she intends to look for a ship. Perversely, not only do Elfride and Knight see the *Puffin* as it puffs into view, but Stephen standing on the deck, sees *them* outlined against the skyline. It is a sight which can only inflame his jealousy.

It threatens rain and Knight suggests that they hurry back. To shorten the way, he proposes they follow a steep path which will take them to the crest of a towering cliff from where they can walk over the downs to Endelstow. The sheer cliff face is composed of a 'vast stratification of blackish-grey slate, unvaried in its whole height by a single change of shade' (p. 202). With some effort, they reach the summit which looms 650 feet over the ocean below. The path on which they now stand is banked. Beyond the bank on the seaward side is a yard or two of level ground. Beyond the strip of level ground there is a 'short steep preparatory slope' (a one-in-three incline, as we later learn), slaty and with only the sparsest vegetation. Beyond the slippery slope is 'the verge of the precipice'.

Knight, an inveterate pedant, does not make love to Elfride, Instead, he gives her a lecture on the wind's aerodynamic peculiarities in the spot where they are standing. Carried away by his exposition, he leans forward and his hat is sucked off by the updraft. Feeling foolish, he goes over the bank and the level ledge on to the steep slope to

Elfride's attempt to help Knight

retrieve his headgear. Elfride loses sight of him. A couple of minutes pass and it begins to rain.

Finally Elfride goes over the bank herself to see what has happened. Below her, crouching on the slope on his hands and knees, is Knight. His hat is again on his head (a nice touch), but he now has other things to worry about. The rain has made the surface of the shale slimy and he cannot find the purchase on it to clamber back up. There are beads of perspiration on his brow. He is very frightened. Elfride is an intrepid 'new woman' (although she is dressed in high Victorian style, in a long walking-dress). She ventures on to the 'treacherous incline' herself, to give Knight the necessary hand up. We are told she 'propped herself with the closed telescope', although this is hard to picture. Knight, still crouching, takes her hand, but in trying to haul himself up only succeeds in pulling Elfride down. They slip together, until his foot comes to rest on 'a bracket of quartz rock, standing out like a tooth from the verge of the precipice'. They are almost on the brink. As a reminder of what will happen if they slip further, the telescope rolls down and vanishes over the edge 'into a nether sky'.

Knight and Elfride are now lying prone against the incline side by side. 'Hold tightly to me,' he tells her, and she flings her arms around his neck 'with such a firm grasp that whilst he remained it was impossible for her to fall'. Knight is in no condition to appreciate this exciting physical closeness. Their plight is increasingly desperate. No one comes along this path from one week to the next. Knight realizes that, unless they can ascend the slope 'with the precision of machines', they are doomed.

He makes a 'stirrup' out of one of his hands (presumably steadying himself with the other) and instructs Elfride to lever herself up then step on to his shoulder. With 'trembling limbs' she does as he tells her. Knight will have a good view of those trembling limbs because, as she raises herself on to his shoulder, he will be looking directly up her skirt. Elfride lifts herself up as instructed, and with a 'spring' from Knight's shoulder reaches the safety of the narrow strip of level ground above them. But the force of her spring, added to Knight's weight, breaks the tooth of quartz on which he is balanced. It moves. Knight grabs two tufts of sea-pink. The quartz tooth now completely dislodges and tumbles into the void. One of the tufts in his hands comes away by the roots, and 'inch by inch' Knight begins to 'follow the quartz'. He manages to arrest his fall by grabbing 'the last outlying knot of starved herbage ere the rock appeared in all its bareness'.

Knight is now holding on for dear life by his hands on the very edge of the precipice. How long will it take her to run to Endelstow and back, he shouts up. Three-quarters of an hour, Elfride answers. 'That won't do; my hands will not hold out ten minutes', he forlornly estimates. At this point, Hardy closes the chapter. *A Pair of Blue Eyes* was first serialized in *Tinsley's Magazine* (a monthly), and the instalment finished here—a literal cliffhanger. How, *Tinsley's* readers must have wondered over the next four weeks, will Knight get out of this? ('With one bound he was free!'?) Not one in a thousand can have come up with the solution Hardy had in mind.

Chapter 23 spends its earlier pages describing Knight's state of mind as he hangs, Prometheus-like, on the rock. In one of the most effective of Hardy's digressions on evolution, Knight ('a good geologist') contemplates the fossil of a trilobite embedded in the rock in front of his eyes: 'Time closed up like a fan before him', Hardy observes. Knight's metaphysical speculations on his cosmic insignificance are interrupted by gusts of rain which bite into his flesh like 'cold needles'. All the while his hands are weakening. Three minutes have passed (it seems like ten to Knight).

Where is Elfride? Has she fainted? Run away? What can a mere *woman* do, anyway?

Suddenly Elfride reappears to ask 'how much longer can you wait?' Four minutes he replies. And with good hope of being saved? 'Seven or eight,' he hazards. Desperate as he is, Knight notices two oddities: Elfride looks strangely slimmer than she did and the sinuous contours of her body, where the wet clothing sticks to them, are remarkably—not to say voluptuously—visible. And in her arms she has 'a bundle of white linen'.

This linen, we apprehend, is Elfride's petticoat. The three minutes' absence were spent stripping and putting her outer clothes back on. Elfride now sets to work making 'a perfect rope . . . six or seven yards long'. She does so by tearing the linen (of the petticoat, presumably) into long strips, knotting the ends together, twisting them into braid, and binding the twine in place with thinner strings of linen. It takes some time to describe this process; actually performing it would take even longer.

When she has finished Elfride tests the knots one by one, by standing on the 'linen rope' and yanking it. Some repairs are needed. She then ties one end of the rope around her waist and leans forward on the outward edge of the gently sloping bank of the path, holding hard with her hands and feet—like the 'anchor' in a tug-of-war team. On a prearranged signal (three twitches) to indicate she is ready, Knight uses the rope to crawl up the incline (never putting more than half his weight on the rope, as Hardy carefully notes).

When he reaches safety, they impulsively embrace. It is not the usual decorous Victorian encounter. Elfride has 'absolutely nothing between her and the weather but her diaphanous exterior robe or "costume"' (p. 216). Her flimsy outer covering is wet and clings to her like a 'glove'—or a modern body-stocking. While Knight was waiting for

death on the cliff face, we are now informed, 'she had taken
off her whole clothing, and replaced only her outer bodice
and skirt. Every thread of the remainder lay upon the
ground in the form of a woollen and cotton rope.'

After their embrace, Elfride runs off 'through the pelt-
ing rain like a hare; or more like a pheasant when, scampering away with a lowered tail, it has a mind to fly, but does
not'. Her wet dress, without a petticoat to keep it away
from her thighs, impedes her. In her modest confusion, she
leaves everything behind her. Ever the gentleman, Knight
'gathers up her knotted and twisted plumage of linen, lace
and embroidery work' to take back for her (the Rector may
have some awkward questions about how he came by this
'plumage', one imagines).

A number of puzzles hover over this episode. Essentially
Hardy recycles a Victorian version of the Rapunzel fable
('Rapunzel, Rapunzel, let down your hair'), but unlike
Grimm's story, one expects a degree of *vraisemblance* in a
novel of 1873. Is it feasible that Elfride could make a
seven-yard linen rope, as described, in as many minutes?
Probably not. Given an area of two square yards, and
strips of nine inches, could a 'walking' petticoat—closely
twisted and tightly knotted—supply such a length of
rope? Probably not. Could such a rope bear half (or
more) of Knight's weight—say six to nine stone? Probably not.

In the interest of a terrific action scene one would not
linger on such picayune calculations about measurement
and breaking-strain. But one may legitimately ponder just
what garments the rope is made of. The description seems
oddly contradictory. Hardy's initial and repeated
emphasis that it is a 'linen rope' implies the petticoat.
That garment alone could supply the lengths Elfride
needs. But Hardy explicitly states a little later on that
Elfride has shed everything except her 'diaphanous exter-

ior robe'. Every 'thread' of her other clothing has gone
into what is later called 'a woollen and cotton rope'.

Linen (derived from flax) is a stout material suitable
for sheets, shirts, and petticoats. It is too coarse for
underclothes which come into direct contact with the
skin—at least for a fine lady like Elfride. The 'wool' which
Hardy refers to presumably comes from Elfride's vest. The
cotton comes from her long drawers, or knickers (Elfride
would not waste her fine silk underclothes on a solitary
walk along the cliffs). Finally, still later, the rope is
described as a 'knotted and twisted plumage of linen, lace,
and embroidery work'. Elfride's corsetry (the lace and
embroidered brassiére, what the Victorians would call an
'under bodice') is now also woven into the rope,
apparently.

We experience the thrills of the mountain rescue
entirely through Knight's perceptions. As he perceives it,
the life-line which dangles down to him is a 'linen rope'.
Then, when he sees it on the ledge, it has become a 'woollen and cotton rope'. When he eventually picks it up and
can examine it at leisure, it is 'linen, lace, and embroidery
work'. How does one account for these changes?

There is, I think, a plausible explanation. Modest young
woman that she is, Elfride used the petticoat—least intimate of her underthings—for the end which Knight would
grab hold of, and indeed for the main part of the rope he
would climb. The notion of him hurtling down to his death
holding her drawers was not to be thought of. The end of
the rope which she tied around her waist was made up of
her more intimate undies, her vest, long knickers, and
under bodice. No man's hand should touch those. When he
gets to the top, and sees the rope's entire length, Knight
perceives that more than linen went into its making.

Victorian modesty—even *in extremis*—is the key to this
ingenious scene. Just how ingenious Hardy has been in

controverting Victorian mores can be demonstrated by a small mind experiment. Suppose one were to get all the great novelists of the age—Dickens, Eliot, Thackeray, the Brontës, Trollope—into a room and set them the following problem: 'I want you each to devise a scenario in which a well-bred young lady allows a polite young man who is neither her fiancé nor her physician (1) to embrace her tightly and feel the outline of her breasts; (2) to look up her skirt at leisure; (3) to hold and examine in the closest detail all her underwear—articles which you will minutely describe. Neither of these young people is to suffer the slightest damage to their moral reputation in the eyes of the world, or the reader.' It would, one guesses, be a tough competition and the wise money would be on young Thomas Hardy.

The Oxford World's Classics *A Pair of Blue Eyes* is edited by Alan Manford.

George Eliot · *Daniel Deronda*

———

Is Daniel Deronda circumcised?

———

The question is posed, and an elegant answer proposed, by
Kenneth Newton in an article in *Essays in Criticism*.[1]
Newton's starting-point is an apparently devastating
objection to the *vraisemblance* of *Daniel Deronda* noted by
Steven Marcus, who in turn was alerted to the anomaly by
one of his sharp-eyed graduate students, Lennard Davis:

Mr Davis has discovered a detail—or a missing detail—in *Daniel
Deronda* that throws the whole central plot of the novel out of
kilter. Deronda's identity is a mystery to himself and has always
been. It is only when he is a grown man, having been to Eton and
Cambridge, that he discovers he is a Jew. What this has to mean—
given the conventions of medical practice at the time—is that he
has never looked down. In order for the plot of *Daniel Deronda* to
work, Deronda's circumcised penis must be invisible, or nonexistent.[2]

As the author of *The Other Victorians*—a study of the
period's pornography—Marcus knows more about the
lineaments of the Victorian penis than most people. Is
Daniel Deronda, then, a narrative built on sand?

Any response to this conundrum must begin from the
position that Eliot would certainly care about such a
detail. She was scrupulous to the verge of fanaticism
about authenticity in her fiction. And circumcision is not
just a minor feature of Judaism but as central to its ritual
as is baptism to Anglicanism. Eliot took expert advice on
the finer points of Judaic practice and Jewish culture for
Daniel Deronda (as elsewhere she took advice on the legal

intricacies in her plots). Gordon Haight outlines her
extensive reading and notes that 'her lively concern with
the idea of Jewish nationalism sprang directly from her
friendship with Emmanuel Deutsch. Born in Silesia,
Deutsch was educated by his uncle, a rabbi, and then at the
University of Berlin before coming to London in 1855 to
work as a cataloguer of books at the British Museum.'[3] In
the period preceding the writing of *Daniel Deronda*,
Deutsch visited weekly to give Eliot lessons in Hebrew.

It is most unlikely that the rite of infant circumcision
(*bris*), symbolizing Abraham's covenant with Jehovah,
would not have been touched on in Deutsch's explanations
of Jewish religious practices. And there were other, closer,
sources of information accessible to Eliot. In her 1996 life
of Eliot, Rosemary Ashton quotes a hitherto unregarded
letter of G. H. Lewes's about *Daniel Deronda*. Writing on
Christmas Eve, 1876, to the palaeontologist Richard
Owen, Lewes alludes to the unpopularity of *Deronda's*
Jewish plot among Gentile readers:

The English public seem to have been amazingly dead to the
attempt to enlighten it about the Jewish race; but the Jews
themselves—from Germany, France, and America, as well as
England—have been deeply moved, and have touchingly
expressed their gratitude. Learned Rabbis, who can alone
appreciate its learning, are most enthusiastic. Is it not psycho-
logically a fact of singular interest that she was never in her life
in a Jewish family, at least never in one where Judaism was still a
living faith and Jewish customs kept up? Yet the Jews all fancy
she must have been brought up among them; and in America it is
positively asserted that *I* am of Jewish origin![4]

Lewes's origins are not entirely clear and the hypothesis
that he was at least partly Jewish still surfaces from time
to time.[5] What one does know is that he had a training in
medicine. And, in the very unlikely event that Eliot was in
some doubt as to what was physically entailed in circum-

cision, Lewes—of all people—would be uniquely qualified to enlighten her.

In *Daniel Deronda*, as the Princess—the hero's mother—records, the baby Daniel was given up at 2 years old, to be raised as an aristocratic gentile, wholly ignorant of his racial origins. By this age every Jewish male child routinely would have gone through the *bris*. Why wasn't Daniel circumcised, and why didn't he—as Marcus puts it—'look down' and draw the obvious conclusion?

Newton's approach to what looks like a damaging *lacuna* in *Deronda's* plotwork is scholarly and methodical. He starts with the proposition that: 'Circumcision may be present in the novel even if not specified: literary criticism would be extremely restricted if it had to confine itself to what was directly referred to in a text.' This weakens Marcus's damaging syllogism that Eliot does not explicitly use the 'C' word, therefore Daniel must be uncircumcised, therefore the novel falls apart. Newton chooses for the thrust of his refutation Marcus's phrase, 'the conventions of medical practice at the time'. The 'time' of Daniel's infancy is the late 1830s (the main action takes place in the mid-1860s). Infant circumcision, for general sexual hygienic motives, became a widespread medical practice in Britain towards the end of the nineteenth century.[6] But—Marcus assumes—in the early decades of the century only Jewish (and some Muhammadan) babies would have their foreskins snipped.

Is this true? Not entirely. Newton turns up evidence that, particularly among surgeons in London, circumcision was a routine intervention. Evidence can be found in handbooks as early as the 1820s. Robert Hooper's *Lexicon Medicum* (1839), for example, has a succinct entry which clearly defines medical thinking and practice on the topic during Daniel's babyhood: '*Circumcision*: The removal of the prepuce from the glans penis. This is a religious rite among the Jews and Mahomedans. It is also practised by surgeons in some cases of phymosis.' Phymosis is tightness of the foreskin, or preputial orifice. Circumcision was also recommended as a surgical procedure where the prepuce was excessively long. There is some evidence that circumcision may also have been practised as a preventive against masturbation, although it is hard to think of Sir Hugo being severe on that subject.

Newton builds on the medical evidence that gentile children were circumcised—particularly upper-class children delivered by qualified physicians rather than midwives or female relatives. As the putative illegitimate son of Sir Hugo Mallinger, Daniel would have had the best-available medical attention. A boy in his position could quite conceivably have been non-ritually circumcised, were he born with a congenital deformity. If he were circumcised, it would explain why Daniel gives so much credence to Mordecai's intuitive conviction that his new friend is 'one of us'. There is, in short, a physical, not a purely mystical, explanation for the instant sense of 'belongingness' that Daniel experiences with Mordecai and his family.

Newton's argument is intellectually attractive and his scholarship is extremely persuasive. Like him, I believe that an author as attentive to detail as Eliot would have been at pains to accommodate the circumcision issue in her novel—reticent although the Victorian writer had to be on sexual matters.[7] But, on balance, I do not believe that Daniel was—until his full adoption of his Judaic destiny—circumcised. Curative circumcision in the early nineteenth century was, as far as one can deduce, as rare as congenital deformities of the male sexual organs. It would, one guesses, be fairly rare, even among the upper classes. A circumcised child would certainly wonder about why he was different—assuming (1) he was moderately curious; and (2) he knew what other boys of his age looked like naked.

The point is made early on that Daniel is an intellectually precocious child. It is from reading Sismondi at the age of 13 that he deduces the 'fact' of his illegitimacy. We are told that at the same period he had 'read Shakespeare'. It is hard to believe that he would not have asked his tutor (as he asked him 'how was it that the popes and cardinals always had so many nephews?') what was the meaning of Othello's final words:

> And say besides, that in Aleppo once,
> Where a malignant and turban'd Turk
> Beat a Venetian and traduc'd the state,
> I took by th' throat the circumcised dog,
> And smote him—thus.

Mr Fraser (who seems unusually candid on sexual matters) would doubtless have replied that circumcision was a ritual operation performed on the *membrum virile*, universal among Jews and some Muhammadans—a racially identifying mark.

After he discovers the fact (as he thinks) of his birth, Daniel is sent to Eton. In the school's communal sleeping and bathing facilities he would surely—given his dark, Semitic appearance and tell-tale penis—have been taunted as a Jew, if only in sport. If, that is, he were circumcised. From books, and from the commonplace anti-Semitic jibes of the English public school, he would have had implanted a seed of suspicion in his mind. Yet Eliot nowhere alludes to this, leaving us to suppose that Mordecai's suggestion is a thunderbolt, that never until late in life has it crossed Daniel's mind that he is Jewish.

Does George Eliot, then, leave room and clues for the reader, curious about the matter, to assume that Daniel is uncircumcised? I think she does. Quite early in the novel, after he has introduced Mirah to the Meyricks, Daniel is surprised to hear her confess that she is not a 'good Jewess':

'In what way are you not a good Jewess?' said Deronda.

'I am ignorant, and we never observed the laws, but lived among Christians just as they did. But I have heard my father laugh at the strictness of the Jews about their food and all their customs, and their not liking Christians . . .' (p. 313)

The implication here is that a dissident, or non-conformist, Jewish parent (even one who fathered the ultra-devout Mordecai) might neglect circumcision ('their food and *all their customs*'). There are much broader hints that Daniel's mother might have been similarly inclined to flout Judaic strictness, as it is embodied in her ultra-orthodox and 'iron-willed' father:

He never comprehended me, or if he did, he only thought of fettering me into obedience. I was to be what he called 'the Jewish woman' under pain of his curse. I was to feel everything I did not feel, and believe everything I did not believe. I was to feel awe for the bit of parchment in the *mezuza* over the door; to dread lest a bit of butter should touch a bit of meat; to think it beautiful that men should bind the *tephillin* on them, and women not,—to adore the wisdom of such laws, however silly they might seem to me. I was to love the long prayers in the ugly synagogue, and the howling, and the gabbling, and the dreadful fasts, and the tiresome feasts, and my father's endless discoursing about Our People, which was a thunder without meaning in my ears. (p. 540)

'I saved you from it', she tells Daniel. On the face of it, the 'saving' refers to her giving Daniel to Sir Hugo, to be brought up out of the faith. But it could as well refer to her keeping him intact from the possessive rituals of Judaism as a baby. Her father died three weeks after her arranged marriage to her cousin Ephraim—'the only one left of my father's family that he knew'. Her mother had been long dead. There were no parental constraints on her as a married woman and mother; nor any extended family to impose on her. Ephraim is a poor creature, and wholly subject to his wife: 'he made it the labour of his life to devote himself to me: wound up his money-changing and banking, and lived to wait upon me—*went against his conscience for me*' (p. 543, my italics).

Ephraim would not stand in her way, should she choose not to submit 'her' child to ritual and 'barbarous' mutilation by tribal elders whom she hates. Her father gone, no family to interfere, a weakling husband who suppresses his 'conscience' in deference to her will—why should she have her baby circumcised?

This hypothesis is easier to sustain if one reconstructs the episode. The *bris*, or ritual circumcision, takes place eight days after birth. The child is taken from the mother, and the operation, performed by the mohel, is a predominantly male affair (it is the father's duty to arrange it). The mother is not necessarily present. No anaesthesia is used. For a woman like the Princess, such a ceremony might well seem a vivid assertion of Judaism's patriarchal tyranny—its ruthless appropriation of 'her' child, and its relegation of a mere woman like herself to the inferior status of a procreative vessel. Would she *allow* Ephraim to take the child away to the *bris*, completely under her thumb as the poor fellow was? She would not, one imagines.[8]

This female rebellion on a point of religious ritual would strike a sympathetic chord with Eliot. The critical—and most agonizing—moment in her early progress to intellectual independence was her refusal to attend church with her father. It provoked, as Gordon Haight records, an explosion in the Evans household: 'Mr Evans, after a fruitless outburst of parental authority, lapsed into stony silence, refusing to discuss the question of religion with his disobedient child. How was he to hold a plate on Sunday mornings at Trinity [church], the father of an avowed free-thinker?'[9] The rift was patched but never mended. The rebellion was, as all biographers agree, necessary that the woman of letters might emerge. Had Eliot borne a baby, she would not, I think, have allowed it to be baptized in the church of her father, however much pressure were put on her.

Kenneth Newton is right, I think, to assume that circumcision is a significant thread in *Daniel Deronda*'s rich narrative tapestry. But it seems more likely that Eliot considered the problem, and accommodated it in the subplot of the Princess's rebellion—her wilful *non serviam* on points of ritual. This seems both plausible, and in keeping with Eliot's understanding of female psychology and its modes of resistance to patriarchal oppression. And if one assumes that Daniel is not circumcised it gives what seems like a sly undercurrent of meaning to Sir Hugo's injunction to Daniel in chapter 16, 'for God's sake, *keep an English cut*, and don't become indifferent to English tobacco'. 'Cut' here means 'style' (as in, 'I like the cut of his jib'). But one would like to think there is an allusion to that unkinder cut that Sir Hugo alone (at this point in the narrative) knows Daniel has never had inflicted on his private parts.

The Oxford World's Classics *Daniel Deronda* is edited by Graham Handley.

Anna Sewell · *Black Beauty*

Is Black Beauty gelded?

If one takes the autobiography of a horse 'translated from the original equine' at face value, it is clear that Black Beauty must be gelded at some point around chapter 5 but, as the World's Classics editor puts it, 'delicacy prevents Anna Sewell from making any reference at all to the painful surgery' (p. xxiv). Clearly, in the series of tasks that Black Beauty is called on to perform during his working life (running in harness with the sprightly mare Ginger, for instance), his masters would not want him distracted by wayward sexual urges. But even the most oblique allusion to how these urges were normally dealt with in the Victorian horse-trade was problematic. When, infamously, Anna Sewell sold the copyright of *Black Beauty* for £20, it was to a publisher, Jarrold's, specializing in books for children—who have traditionally made up a loyal element in the novel's readership. The *pas devant* rule would certainly extend to the castrating shears, however familiar the instrument might be in the stable. Had Miss Sewell included a reference to Black Beauty's removed bodily parts, it too would have been removed. Victorians were as expert at gelding texts ('bowdlerizing') as livestock. It remains a delicate subject, at least in popular entertainment. How many film-goers, for example, could say offhand whether Trigger, Champion, or Silver are stallions, mares, or geldings?

This 'delicacy' evidently offended Tolstoy, who in his autobiography translated from the equine, 'The Romance of a Horse', makes gelding the central and harrowing episode ('On the following day I became what I am now, and left off neighing for ever'). Generations of readers have happily ignored Sewell's delicacy and enjoyed her story none the less. And the Tolstoyan objection only has force if we assume that *Black Beauty* is primarily about horses. There is a good case for thinking that it is not. Victorian society ran on two mighty sources of power— horses were one and servants were the other. In a quite subtle way Sewell runs the two categories together. Black Beauty is a talking, thinking, social horse—like Swift's Houyhnhnms. The difference is that Swift's beasts are masters: Sewell's are servants. That he is born to service (although, if he is well behaved, he may regard himself as destined to be an 'upper servant') is the first lesson that Black Beauty's mother instils into him:

One day, when there was a good deal of kicking, my mother whinnied to me to come to her, and then she said:

'I wish you to pay attention to what I am going to say to you. The colts who live here are very good colts, but they are carthorse colts, and of course, they have not learned manners. You have been well bred and well born; your father has a great name in these parts, and your grandfather won the cup two years at the Newmarket races; your grandmother had the sweetest temper of any horse I ever knew, and I think you have never seen me kick or bite. I hope you will grow up gentle and good, and never learn bad ways; do your work with a good will, lift your feet up well when you trot, and never bite or kick even in play.' (pp. 3–4)

In his subsequent life, Black Beauty has many masters and mistresses—farmers, fine ladies, 'cockneys', hackney-cab drivers. Some are good, some careless, some sadistic. But masters and mistresses there always are. It is Black Beauty's duty, like that of all horses, to work for humans— to serve. That is his 'station'. The moral of the book is as applicable to human as to equine servants: 'We horses do not mind hard work if we are treated reasonably' (p. 155).

As well as in nurseries, it is likely that *Black Beauty* was distributed lavishly below stairs—as were tracts and 'improving' moral tales designed to reconcile Victorian servants to their lot.

As a treatise on what Carlyle called 'servantship', *Black Beauty* makes a plea on two fronts as to what 'reasonable' treatment by masters should be. It can be summed up as: don't treat your horses like beasts, don't treat your servants like slaves. Anna Sewell makes the slavery point by direct allusion to *Uncle Tom's Cabin* (and its polemic against the breaking up of negro families) in chapter 5:

When John went into the stable, he told James that master and mistress had chosen a good sensible English name for me, that meant something, not like Marengo, or Pegasus, or Abdallah. They both laughed, and James said, 'If it was not for bringing back the past, I should have named him Rob Roy, for I never saw two horses more alike.'

'That's no wonder,' said John, 'didn't you know that farmer Grey's old Duchess was the mother of them both?'

I had never heard that before, and so poor Rob Roy who was killed at that hunt was my brother! I did not wonder that my mother was so troubled. It seems that horses have no relations; at least, they never know each other after they are sold. (pp. 17–18)

Not even an advocate as friendly as Anna Sewell would propose that horses' family units should be respected. But the insidious effects of 'service' on the human family members employed in middle-class houses clearly worried her, as it worried other *bien pensant* mistresses.

Another main source of worry was sexuality. Two-legged servants could not, like their four-legged colleagues, be mated to order, operated on to remove troublesome urges, or shot in the head if they proved hopelessly recalcitrant. As elsewhere, Victorian doctrine divided into the physical forcers and the moral forcers. A master or mistress who believed in physical force would enforce virtue, by insisting on a good 'character' (i.e. references), by constant inspection of the servants' most intimate affairs, by minimizing free time, by severe rules about visitors. There is an interesting piece of business in Trollope's *Barchester Towers* when Mrs Proudie (a physical forcer if there ever was one) is complaining to Archdeacon Grantly about the physical dilapidation of the Palace, and notes that the locks on the servants' bedrooms are defective from the outside. It is clear that the Bishop's wife is in the habit of locking her servants in their rooms at night. If English law allowed her to, doubtless she would geld and spay her menials, as freely as she does her other livestock.

Moral forcers would try to control their servants' sexuality by instilling a high level of self-control. This could be done by good example, by frequent family prayers, by precept. A 'good' servant could be trusted to restrain himself or herself from straying sexually. It is clear that in her first lesson to Black Beauty (which, as he says, 'I have never forgotten') his mother is enjoining self-restraint and 'manners' ('I hope you will grow up gentle and good, and never learn bad ways'). As it happens (although Harriet Beecher Stowe, like her sister-novelist, is too delicate to mention it), slaves in America before 1865 could, like other cattle, be gelded if their masters so determined. In *Black Beauty*, at least in its aspect as a treatise on servantship, Sewell argues that such extreme and inhumane measures are not necessary. Well trained by his mother, and with a good master, Black Beauty will be able to control himself without recourse to the dreaded shears. Is Black Beauty gelded? Yes (in so far as he is a four-legged servant) and no (in so far as he represents the two-legged class of servant). Self-control will answer.

The Oxford World's Classics *Black Beauty* is edited by Peter Hollindale.

What does Mrs Charmond say to Grace?

The Woodlanders is a novel resting sedately on a huge chronological flaw. In a narrative oddly lacking in clear historical markers, there is a stark contradiction between the only two which the attentive reader will find. Perplexingly, Hardy seems to go to some pains to etch the clash of dates on our consciousness. The first is signposted relatively early in the narrative. When Giles meets the strange gentleman at the midsummer festivity who has terrified the local girls ('We saw Satan pursuing us'), he feels justified in asking some close questions of the interloper:

'You come from far, seemingly?'

'I come now from the South of Europe.'

'Oh indeed, sir. You are an Italian or Spanish or French gentleman, perhaps?'

'I am not either.'

Giles did not fill the pause which ensued and the gentleman, who seemed of an emotional nature, unable to resist friendship, at length answered the question: 'I am an Italianized American, a South Carolinian by birth,' he said. 'I left my native country on the failure of the Southern cause, and have never returned to it since.' (p. 151)

The strange gentleman is, we learn, one of Felice Charmond's more importunate lovers (and eventually her assassin). His reference to the 'Southern cause' unmistakably indicates the American Civil War, 1861–5. And if he has since 'Italianized' himself (a process which would take some years), the present date is presumably around the mid-1870s, or later. His reason for leaving his homeland is a superfluous piece of information (we are not usually so open about our personal histories to complete strangers). One must assume that Hardy intends us to take careful note, as we do.

The American's *curriculum vitae* is, however, wholly irreconcilable with Fred Beaustock's excited information to Mellbury later in the novel that Grace may get her release from Fitzpiers by a 'new' divorce law. Under this just-passed ordinance, the former law-clerk tells Mellbury:

A new court was established last year, and under the new statute, twenty and twenty-one Vic., Cap. eighty-five, unmarrying is as easy as marrying. No more Acts of Parliament necessary, no longer one law for the rich and another for the poor. (p. 267)

It used to be held by Hardy scholars that what Beaustock is here referring to is a modification to British divorce law introduced in 1878. But, as Michael Millgate pointed out in 1971, the legal dating jargon (twenty and twenty-one years after Victoria's accession in 1837) makes the reference to 1857 unequivocal.[1] Beaustock is a habitual drunkard, and as the World's Classics editor, Dale Kramer, notes: 'perhaps Hardy intends to suggest that Beaustock is so befuddled that the passing of the recent 1878 Act has jogged his memory of what had been current legal news during his sober years.' But if this were the case, Hardy would surely have made Beaustock's error crystal-clear to the reader. Again, by inserting more information than would realistically be given in casual conversation ('twenty and twenty-one Vic., Cap. eighty-five' hardly rolls off the tongue) Hardy seems set on grinding a specific date into our minds—the year after this legislation, 1858.

What is as odd as the glaring, two-decade (1858/1878), discrepancy between these two bearing points is the almost total lack of other historical markers. Hardy has deliberately, as it seems, purged his text of any other clues as to period. We are not sure whether Grace comes to Hinstock by train or horse-drawn coach: nor whether Mrs Charmond travels on the Continent by train or coach. There seems to be no steam-powered, or mechanized equipment in the Mellbury sawmill—as there would be in 1878. But we cannot be sure of the point. There is no clear reference to clothing fashions which would help us date the action (steel-hooped crinolines, for instance, or bustles; the 'chignon' which Mrs Charmond has made out of Marty's hair might, conceivably, be linked to the fashion of the 1870s, but this is not conclusive). Fitzpiers's late-night reading is all in 'metaphysical' and 'Idealist' sources which are more appropriate to a Bulwer-Lyttonish 'student' of the 1830s and 1840s than to a late Victorian physician up-to-date with the latest advances in medical science. But again we cannot be sure. Many books and titles are mentioned in passing, but none are later than the mid-1850s (if only Fitzpiers had quoted some late Browning, or early Swinburne, like Sue Bridehead; his favourite poet, however, is the pre-Victorian Shelley). The only cultural marker I note is in the exchange between Grace and Fitzpiers, when they first meet at Hintock House:

'And now, doctor,' she said, 'before you go I want to put a question to you. Sit round there in front of me on that low chair, and bring the candles, or one, to the little table. Do you smoke? Yes? That's right—I am learning. Take one of these; and here's a light.' She threw a match-box across. (p. 186)

This seems a clear reference to the 'new' practice of cigarette smoking (a tobacco pleasure in which middleclass women could indulge for the first time) brought back by British troops from their Russian foe in the Crimean War, after 1855.

David Lodge, who has examined the evidence thoroughly
for his Macmillan edition, advises that we should not try
to hunt down clinching chronological evidence in *The
Woodlanders*—although he personally leans to 'an earlier
rather than a later dating'. The fact that for a hundred
years critics were happy to mislocate the narrative by
twenty-odd years (twenty of the most transformative years
in nineteenth-century history) is not evidence of the
critics' impercipience so much as the novel's inscrutability. As Lodge puts it:

Nobody before Millgate, it would appear, has noticed the contradiction between the divorce law reference and the Civil War reference: they occur at widely separated points in the narrative and
the reader is not naturally inclined to check one against the
other. This reinforces my own feeling that *The Woodlanders* has a
distinctly mythopoeic, dreamlike quality about it. History seems
suspended—something that goes on in the world outside the
woods.[2]

This is probably as satisfactory a solution to the chronological puzzle in *The Woodlanders* as we shall get. Hintock
is like Brigadoon, a village out of historical time. There
remains, however, a smaller puzzle on which one has less
editorial guidance. It has to do with Fitzpiers's mysterious
omnipotence over women, and his predatory sexual habits.

Grace's suspicions about her husband develop soon
after marriage and harden into the kind of evidence that
would satisfy any modern divorce court as to Fitzpiers's
incorrigible misconduct (if not the court set up by 'Vic. 20,
21', which required, on the male side, adultery compounded by gross violence, incest, sodomy or desertion
without reasonable cause for over two years). Grace sees
Suke Damson furtively leaving Fitzpiers's rooms 'between
four and five' and soon discovers that his explanation that
she had maddening toothache is a lie. There is only one
explanation for a hoyden like Suke spending the night

with a handsome young man like Edred. Night after night Fitzpiers goes out, sometimes not returning till morning, on spurious calls that Grace knows are pretexts for visiting Hintock House. One morning, returning asleep on his horse, he miscalls his wife 'Felice'—Mrs Charmond's Christian name.

Grace's suspicions explode into accusation when, by accident, she comes across Mrs Charmond walking in the woods at twilight. The older woman is astonished at Grace's unexpected 'toughness'. Grace begins with the warning: 'You may go on loving him if you like—I don't mind at all. You'll find it, let me tell you, a bitterer business for yourself than for me in the end. He'll get tired of you soon, as tired as can be—you don't know him so well as I!—and then you may wish you had never seen him!' (p. 236). Warming to her theme, Grace pours scorn on her patrician rival:

Before I came I had been despising you for wanton cruelty; now I only pity your weakness for its misplaced affection. When Edred has gone out of the house in hope of seeing you, at seasonable hours and unseasonable; when I have found him riding miles and miles across the country at midnight, and risking his life, and getting covered with mud, to get a glimpse of you, I have called him a foolish man—the plaything of a finished coquette. I thought that what was getting to be a tragedy to me was a comedy to you. But now I see that tragedy lies on your side of the situation no less than on mine, and more. (p. 237)

Every reader will apprehend that Grace *knows*. She may have spent a year with fine folks in town, but she is a country girl by upbringing and is quite familiar with the facts of life. Fitzpiers has been unfaithful to her—both with the low-born Suke, and with the high-born Felice Charmond. Grace's only consolation is that he will treat them as callously in love as he has treated his wife. Their triumph will be short-lived.

A discomfited Mrs Charmond rushes off, loses herself in the wood, and falls exhausted by the way. It is now night, and cold. She is again met by Grace, who is still walking by herself. Out of mere humanity, Grace comforts her rival. And to warm themselves, the women cling close together under Mrs Charmond's furs until she feels strong enough to get to her feet. In this nocturnal intimacy, Mrs Charmond finds herself obliged 'to make a confession'. She '*cannot*' give up Fitzpiers, she tells Grace, 'until he chooses to give me up!' Surely, says Grace, as the partner in the superior station, 'the cut must come from you'. There then occurs the following mysterious exchange:

'Tchut! Must I tell verbatim, you simple child? O, I suppose I must! It will eat my heart if I do not let out all, after meeting you like this and finding how guileless you are.'

She thereupon whispered a few words in the girl's ear, and burst into a violent fit of sobbing.

Grace started roughly away from the shelter of the furs, and sprang to her feet.

'O my great God!' she exclaimed, thunderstruck at a revelation transcending her utmost suspicion. 'He's had you! Can it be—can it be!' (p. 240)

When she next speaks to Mrs Charmond, it is with a voice 'grown ten years older'. At last rested sufficiently to be able to move, they part with the following words:

'I have told you something in a moment of irresistible desire to unburden my soul which all but a fool would have kept silent as the grave,' [Mrs Charmond] said. 'I cannot help it now. Is it to be a secret, or do you mean war?'

'A secret, certainly,' said Grace mournfully. 'How can you expect war from such a helpless, wretched being as me!'

'And I'll do my best not to see him. I am his slave; but I'll try.' (p. 241)

In her earlier strictures on Mrs Charmond's 'coquetting', it is manifest that Grace knew that the affair had gone further than flirting. Whatever it was Felice whispered must have been shocking beyond belief. Grace's lapse into country coarseness, 'He's had you', is amazing in a Victorian novel, recalling as it does the yokel ballad 'Oi had 'er; Oi had 'er; Oi upped and Oi had 'er; Oi had 'er on Saturday noight'.[3] The hyperbole suggests something far exceeding mere adulterous congress, that Fitzpiers has 'had' something more than sexual relations conventionally offer ('Can it be—can it be!').

Mrs Charmond, one reminds oneself, is no *ingénue*. She is a woman of the theatre and a woman of the world who has had a string of lovers. She has travelled widely (disposing her favours wherever she goes, as gossip claims), and has cold-bloodedly married an older man whom she did not love for money. He died soon after. This courtesan-cum-Black Widow is ill-cast as a sexual victim.

Initially Grace accused Mrs Charmond of making a conquest of Edred (he was 'the plaything of a finished coquette'), as she had conquered other men. Now, it seems, she has told Grace something that convinces her that Edred has made a conquest of Felice—a conquest which has reduced this sophisticated *femme fatale* to the degraded condition of a sexual slave. There is only so far one can go along this route, depending as it does on an inaudible whisper, but it seems that what is hinted at here is some 'French practice', some refinement of *Ars Amatoria* picked up on the Continent. When Felice talks of 'war' she may be implying that perhaps, after all, were she to face the horrible publicity, Grace may indeed have grounds for divorce under Vic. 20, 21.

The Oxford World's Classics *The Woodlanders* is edited by Dale Kramer.

Thomas Hardy · *Tess of the d'Urbervilles*

━━━

Who will Angel marry next?

━━━

The bitter ending to *Tess of the d'Urbervilles* is well known and much quoted. Angel Clare and his pubescent sister-in-law, Liza-Lu (Elizabeth Louise Durbeyfield), are standing vigil outside Wintoncester Gaol:

Upon the cornice of the tower a tall staff was fixed. Their eyes were rivetted on it. A few minutes after the hour had struck something moved slowly up the staff, and extended itself upon the breeze. It was a black flag.

'Justice' was done, and the President of the Immortals (in Aeschylean phrase) had ended his sport with Tess. And the d'Urberville knights and dames slept on in their tombs unknowing. The two speechless gazers bent themselves down to the earth, as if in prayer, and remained thus a long time, absolutely motionless: the flag continued to wave silently. As soon as they had strength they arose, joined hands again, and went on. (p. 384)

Went on to what? The image, as critics have noted, evokes the end of *Paradise Lost*: 'They hand in hand with wandering steps and slow | Through Eden took their solitary way.' Adam and Eve are, of course, man and wife, carnally united. Is this what will happen here? Will Angel 'go on' to marry Liza-Lu? Tess, as we learn early in the novel, has six siblings. They are: Liza-Lu (four years younger than Tess), then in descending order Abraham, Hope, Modesty, and two unidentified younger children. At the beginning of the story Liza-Lu was described as twelve-and-a-half, and Abraham is apparently around nine.

Throughout the subsequent narrative the younger offspring of the Durbeyfields remain shadowy characters, Tess, apparently, has no intimate relationship with any of them, and the only recorded conversation between her and a sibling is the exchange about 'blighted stars' with Abraham in which he feeds his older sister ingenuous questions about the human condition. None the less, after her father's death Tess feels obliged to support her family, and her sense of a bread-winner's duty is one of the means by which Alec blackmails her.

The fact that Angel only has Liza-Lu with him at Wintoncester Gaol could imply that the other Durbeyfield children are still too young for such a grisly ordeal. It could further imply that he has taken on the protector's role for the surviving Durbeyfields—he will henceforth be their good Angel. Most likely, of course, is that he and Liza-Lu will form some kind of marital, or sexual, liaison. Hardy endorses this likelihood by offering, in this last chapter, our first clear visual image of Tess's sister: 'a tall budding creature—half girl, half woman—a spiritualized image of Tess, but with the same beautiful eyes—Clare's sister-in-law, Liza-Lu.' The suddenly nubile Liza-Lu, as we can work out from the four-year age gap, must be just under 16 at this point—too young to marry for a month or so, but eligible if Angel is patient.

If Angel does take up with Liza-Lu it might strike the reader as in keeping with the cheerfully callous morality of the English ballad, an ethos which hangs over much of *Tess of the d'Urbervilles*—a case, that is, of 'so I kissed her little sister, awful sorry Clementine'. It would be less hard on Angel to suppose that the union with Liza-Lu was a fulfilment of Tess's fervent wishes: 'Why didn't you stay and love me when I—was sixteen', she complained to Angel, 'living with my little sisters and brothers, and you danced on the green? O, why didn't you, why didn't you?' Liza is now verging on 16—and, we assume, a virgin (the word Tess cannot bring out). Angel is now in a position to rectify his mistake—not with Tess herself but with 'the spiritualized image of Tess'.

So what will happen? Hardy is careful in the last chapter to notate not just that Liza-Lu is the image of Tess, but that the girl is Angel's 'sister-in-law'. No Victorian would have missed the cue: with the hoisting of the black flag Liza-Lu becomes Angel's 'Deceased Wife's Sister'—a phrase heavy with legal baggage. Ever since the Act of 1835, marriage with a deceased wife's sister had been determined by the law of England to be within the degrees of incest. Incest, by this statute, was conceived to extend not just to *consanguinei* (those related by blood), but to certain *affines* (those related by marriage). The dead wife's sister was one (but not the dead husband's brother).

As the eleventh edition of the *Encyclopaedia Britannica* puts it: 'For many years [after 1835] an active and ceaseless agitation was prosecuted on behalf of the legalization in England of marriage with a deceased wife's sister.' Bills to reform the anomaly were brought into the House of Commons from 1850 onwards. There were some twenty-six abortive initiatives between 1850 and 1896. In most cases the bill passed in the Commons but was rejected in the Lords. Finally the 'deceased wife's sister' law was belatedly reformed in 1906, although marriage between such *affines* as adoptive parents and children, and adoptive siblings, remained within the prohibited degrees.

If Angel wishes to marry Liza-Lu, he has a number of options. *Tess* finishes around the early 1880s: he can wait a quarter of a century until, in the fullness of time, the English law changes (Liza-Lu will still be of childbearing age—just). Alternatively the couple can emigrate to one of the many self-governing British colonies, which had already revoked the 'deceased wife's sister' legislation (Australia, New Zealand, South Africa, Canada). Given the stigma attached to being relatives of a hanged murderer, this would be a sensible course of action on other grounds. As a third option, Angel and Liza-Lu can stay in England and enter into an 'open sexual union'—the kind of relationship celebrated in such 'New Woman' novels as Grant Allen's *The Woman Who Did* (1895). They can, in other words, flout Mrs Grundy. This last option is highly unlikely, given Angel's moral fastidiousness and (we may guess) his sexual timidity. It could also be dangerous: Angel could conceivably be prosecuted for incest, the more so if the union begins before Liza-Lu's sixteenth birthday.

The key to the future of the relationship lies probably in the term 'spiritualized'. Angel will love, but not violate, Liza-Lu, as the disincarnate relic of Tess. Liza-Lu will remain an ethereal and virginal version of her sister: the Pure Woman's purer essence. The relationship between Angel and Liza-Lu will be 'blank'—white and sexless. Angel will nobly undertake not to impose his animal appetites on the woman he worships, fulfilling himself with a 'higher' spiritual and intellectual union. One of the favourite conundrums of medieval theologians was whether angels had sexual organs and if so whether they used them. This one has, and doesn't.

The Oxford World's Classics *Tess of the d'Urbervilles* is edited by Juliet Grindle and Simon Gatrell.

Charlotte Perkins Gilman · *The Yellow Wall-Paper*

What cure for the Madwoman in the Attic?

One of the achievements of feminist literary criticism over the last few decades has been the establishment of a canon enriched with 'rediscovered' works. If you had asked typical American readers of *Scribner's* or the *Century Magazine* in 1897, 'what novelist of the day will "last" and still be read in 1997?' they might well have backed Silas Weir Mitchell, whose historical romance of Quaker pacifism in the Revolutionary War, *Hugh Wynne*, was the best-selling novel of 1897. Few of them, I suspect, would have backed Kate Chopin or Charlotte Perkins Gilman for immortality. But it is one of literary history's ironies that, if Mitchell has any name-recognition in the 1990s, it is as not as a novelist but in his other professional capacity as a physician specializing in women's nervous disorders. Specifically, it is his demonized appearance as the advocate of the 'rest cure' in Chopin's *The Awakening* and—most dramatically—in Gilman's *The Yellow Wall-Paper* that has ensured Mitchell a place in modern consciousness.[1]

With the new literary map drawn by Sandra Gilbert and Susan Gubar's *The Madwoman in the Attic* (1979), two texts have been elevated to supreme status in the feminist canon: *Jane Eyre* (particularly as rewritten from the madwoman in the attic's point of view, in Jean Rhys's *Wide Sargasso Sea*) and *The Yellow Wall-Paper*. Gilman's story features another madwoman locked in 'the nursery at the top of the house'. *The Yellow Wall-Paper*—which has been out of print for most of the twentieth century (and virtu-

ally unavailable in the UK)—is now one of the most studied texts in literature departments across the English-
speaking world.

Gilman's story takes the form of a monologue by a
doctor's wife who has been confined to convalescent
inactivity 'for her own good' by her ostensibly well-
meaning husband. He has taken a short locum position for
three months in an unnamed resort town—it seems that he
is not a particularly successful physician. The house he
has rented for the short period of his stay is grander than
what they are used to, as the woman's opening comments
make clear:

It is very seldom that mere ordinary people like John and myself
secure ancestral halls for the summer.

A colonial mansion, a hereditary estate, I would say a haunted
house, and reach the height of romantic felicity—but that would
be asking too much of fate!

Still I will proudly declare that there is something queer
about it.

Else, why should it be let so cheaply? And why have stood so
long untenanted? (p. 3)

The woman, whose name we never learn, has recently
had a baby and has suffered a breakdown ('a temporary
nervous depression—a slight hysterical tendency'). As the
stylistic flourishes indicate, she has 'literary' pretensions
of which her husband disapproves—'He says that with my
imaginative power and habit of story-making, a nervous
weakness like mine is sure to lead to all manner of excited
fancies, and that I ought to use my will and good sense to
check the tendency. So I try.' John has brought his sister
Jennie (also called 'Jane' at one point[2]) to assist him as
housekeeper during his wife's indisposition. A servant
called Mary looks after the baby.

John is a firm believer in Weir Mitchell's 'rest cure'

therapy, and his wife is accordingly kept in a state of virtual sensory deprivation. She is denied reading materials, forbidden visitors, and may not even see her baby, because 'it makes me so nervous'. It is clear that, to forestall other sources of 'nervousness', she and John are not sleeping together. She is confined to what seems like a nursery at the top of the house, but which may have served a more sinister purpose. It is:

a big, airy room, the whole floor nearly, with windows that look all ways, and air and sunshine galore. It was nursery first and then playroom and gymnasium, I should judge; for the windows are barred for little children, and there are rings and things in the walls. (p. 5)

Over the subsequent weeks, the woman's *idée fixe* about the room's yellow wallpaper develops into full-blown dementia. The story, given entirely in her own words, chronicles her descent into madness, with the implication that her condition is 'iatrogenic'—caused, not relieved, by the medical treatment to which she is subjected, medical treatment which is merely a mask for patriarchal oppression. The cruelties of that oppression are hinted at by the apparatus of Bedlam ('rings and things in the walls').

I taught *The Yellow Wall-Paper* for ten years, on and off, to what would seem the least congenial pupils imaginable: a freshman class composed almost entirely of males, all of them intending eventually to major in science, and many of them from non-English-speaking backgrounds. They were, however, extraordinarily intelligent—all selected for entry into the California Institute of Technology by virtue of superior ability in mathematics. Their reactions to *The Yellow Wall-Paper* were refreshingly heterodox. One of the objections which they regularly brought to Gilman's story was that John was no villain. He was applying the latest scientific theory to his wife's case. This was the right thing to do—the scientific thing. If you can't trust the latest scientific thinking, what can you trust? Why was Gilman so down on the man? Another objection, typically brought by Asian-Americans, was that the woman was a bad mother, thinking always and only of herself. This censure was even more rigorously applied to Edna Pontellier, whose suicide at the end of Chopin's *The Awakening* was seen as the worst kind of maternal dereliction. All she cared about was her own selfish 'liberation'—what about her two children?

Most perplexing, however, was these students' literalistic reaction to a puzzling feature of *The Yellow Wall-Paper* which more sophisticated students of literature overlook: namely, the change in the status of the document which we are (1) reading, and (2) listening to. *The Yellow Wall-Paper* is a fragmentary narrative, mainly composed of one-sentence, barely grammatical paragraphs, without any apparent internal architecture other than that of the fugue from neurosis to psychosis. There is, however, a significant middle point in the story when the woman declares: 'Well, the Fourth of July is over!' The 'fourth' is, of course, 'Independence Day' in the United States. And independence is marked in the story by a tacit change in the narrative mode of address. Before Independence Day, it is clear that the woman is writing. There are, in fact, four references to this activity, concluding with:

There comes John's sister. Such a dear girl as she is, and so careful of me! I must not let her find me writing.

She is a perfect and enthusiastic housekeeper, and hopes for no better profession. I verily believe she thinks it is the writing which made me sick!

But I can write when she is out, and see her a long way off from these windows. (p. 8)

We have to assume that, up to Independence Day, what

we have is a written record—a text. After the Fourth, there are no more references to writing. We now understand that what we are listening to is a stream of consciousness which some omniscient author is recording for us—something more akin to a live broadcast. The narrative is now interior monologue, reporting present sensations and events as they happen:

> I quite enjoy the room, now it is bare again.
> How those children did tear about here!
> This bedstead is fairly gnawed!
> But I must get to work.
> I have locked the door and thrown the key down into the front path. (p. 17)

The reader is no longer reading the story as words on the page (as in the first half of the text) but is 'hearing' it *through* the words on the page. Students of literature make the required epistemological gear-change effortlessly—so effortlessly that they are unaware of it. Literalistic readers (as I have called them) worry about the altered status of the 'data'. There is a difference in creditworthiness between what is written and what is merely thought and transcribed by an intuitive third party. The woman, that is, loses authority with the surrender of her authorial role—eyewitness testimony becomes hearsay. Where there was previously a relationship of two (woman and reader), there are now three persons involved (woman, reader, and an unidentified narrator who has stepped in to take charge). Once this is pointed out, it becomes a troubling detail.

The problem could, I think, be solved if we had one piece of information which Gilman denies us. The passage immediately before Independence Day alludes to Jenny's hostility to the woman's writing ('I verily believe she thinks it is the writing which made me sick'). Did Jenny

take the woman's writing materials away from her, tipping
her over the edge into madness (as might happen in *A Tale
of Two Cities* with Dr Manette, if you took away his cobbler's last)? Or has the woman simply deteriorated to the
point that she can no longer write, even though she still
has her pen and paper by her? This would be the implication of some earlier references to her writing, in which she
records how increasingly difficult the task has become:

I did write for a while in spite of them; but it *does* exhaust me a
good deal . . . I haven't felt like writing before, since that first day
. . . I think sometimes that if I were only well enough to write a
little it would relieve the press of ideas and rest me.
    But I find I get pretty tired when I try. (pp. 1–7)

This uncertainty relates to an enigma at the heart of
The Yellow Wall-Paper. Is the woman 'everywoman'—more
specifically every wife and every mother in the prison of
the bourgeois home, Ibsen's infernal 'Doll's House'. Or is
she a superior kind of woman—a novelist, deprived of the
means of self-expression, and thus of her sanity? A superficial reading of *The Yellow Wall-Paper* might suggest
that, in reaction to Mitchell's 'rest cure', Gilman is advocating a 'writing cure' (a variant on Freud's talking cure),
particularly necessary to an unusually gifted woman like
herself. Not every woman in the prison of the domestic
home is a frustrated writer. Jenny and Mary, for instance,
clearly aren't—what is their status in the story? Quislings
collaborating with the enemy, or a lower order of
womanhood?

The enigma at the heart of *The Yellow Wall-Paper*
(crudely: is the woman mentally ill or has she been driven
mad by solitary confinement?) relates to Gilman's own
experience, which she describes in a 1913 essay, 'Why I
wrote *The Yellow Wall-Paper*'. It seems that after the birth
of her first child, Gilman suffered severe post-natal

depression. Her husband (an artist, not a doctor) referred her to the great Dr Silas Weir Mitchell. He prescribed his famous rest cure. She was sent home, 'with the solemn advice to "live as domestic a life as . . . possible [and] never to touch pen, brush, or pencil again" as long as I lived'. She followed the advice for three months, 'and came so near the borderline of utter mental ruin that I could see over. Her glimpse into this heart of darkness is given literary expression in *The Yellow Wall-Paper*. Gilman divorced her husband (on the grounds that marriage was driving her insane) in 1892—the same year that her story was published. The 'divorce cure' wasn't entirely successful, although it worked better than Mitchell's rest cure. Gilman suffered frequent relapses into depression over the next four decades but was not incapacitated by them. She wrote a large number of aggressively feminist tracts (e.g. *Man-Made World*, 1911) and novels (e.g. *Herland*, 1915).

Even in their heyday, R. D. Laing and Thomas Szasz allowed that some schizophrenics are genuinely mentally ill—not everyone is *driven* mad by external circumstances. But assuming that the woman in the story has been driven mad, how could she be brought back to sanity? Clearly Mitchell's rest cure is a non-starter—a form of torture to rank with the snake pit, pre-frontal lobotomy, and the 'liquid cosh' (the megadose-of-tranquillizer regime, beloved by some prison governors). At times the story suggests that giving the woman more 'rights' within the commonwealth of the family might work: she could tend her baby, have visits from 'Cousin Henry and Julia', take over from the odious Jenny (a lineal descendant of Jane Murdstone) the superintendence of the household. But taken as a whole, *The Yellow Wall-Paper* does not make much of a case for domestic power-sharing. The woman won't be cured by a better pre-nuptial contract. Allowing her a zone of freedom within which to express herself artistically—Dr Manette's last, leather, and hammer—might also help; but it, too, would only be a palliative, not a cure—a re-papering of the prison walls that have to be torn down or leapt over. Gilman's bleak assertion would seem to be that of the Scottish peasant: if you want to get there, don't start from here (marriage, that is); or—to adapt Mr Punch's advice to young men about to marry—'Don't!' In answer to the question in the title, if you need a cure, the condition is already incurable.

The Oxford World's Classics *The Yellow Wall-Paper and Other Stories* is edited by Robert Shulman.

Jack London · *The Sea-Wolf*

====

Who is George Leach?

====

The Sea-Wolf opens brilliantly—the fog-bound ferry-boat
Martinez hooting its way across the San Francisco Bay at
night, in an atmosphere shrouded in gloomy foreboding.
On board the middle-aged littérateur, Humphrey van
Weyden, is mightily pleased with himself—more particularly he is pleased with his literary reputation and power.
He idly observes, as an entomologist might look at an
unusual genus of ant, one of his fellow passengers—a man
with no legs who walks on artificial limbs. During Humphrey's complacent reverie the *Martinez* collides with
another vessel, is holed, and rapidly sinks. So 'civilized' is
Humphrey that at first he simply watches the spectacle as
a disinterested observer. This commotion surely cannot
affect *him*—the 'Dean of American Letters the Second'?
Why are these women squealing like 'pigs'? He is too
refined even to struggle for his life—at least initially. He
reacts rather more energetically when he feels the sting of
the cold bay water on his limbs. At the point of drowning,
that mystical moment when the whole of one's life is supposed to flash in front of the eyes, Humphrey is plucked
from his doom by a god-like Wolf Larsen. As Humphrey is
drifting towards final oblivion and certain death, the
Ghost sweeps silently past (it is sail-driven—unlike the
noisy steam-powered vessels which collided in the Bay).
Humphrey glimpses a man on the boat's bridge,

who seemed to be doing little else than smoke a cigar. I saw the
smoke issuing from his lips as he slowly turned his head and
glanced out over the water in my direction. It was a careless,

unpremeditated glance . . . His face wore an absent expression, as of deep thought, and I became afraid that if his eyes did light upon me he would nevertheless not see me. (p. 9)

Wolf Larsen nevertheless does 'see' Humphrey and brings the *Ghost* about to rescue the nearly drowned man.

It emerges that Wolf Larsen has remarkable powers of vision—second sight, it seems. After he has contemptuously refused Humphrey's offer of $1,000 to transfer him to a passing pilot vessel, Larsen presses the appalled 'Dean of American Letters the Second' (or 'Hump', as he crudely rechristens him) into service as the *Ghost's* cabin-boy on its long voyage to the northern seal-hunting grounds. Cabin-boy is all Hump is good for. Captain Larsen then summons the fellow who previously held the menial post. He is now to be 'promoted' (much against his will—serving as a seaman under Larsen is no picnic). It is clear that the two men have never met before. 'What's your name, boy?', Wolf demands:

'George Leach, sir,' came the sullen answer, and the boy's bearing showed clearly that he divined the reason for which he had been summoned.

'Not an Irish name,' the captain snapped sharply. 'O'Toole or McCarthy would suit your mug a damn sight better. Unless, very likely, there's an Irishman in your mother's woodpile.'

I saw the young fellow's hands clench at the insult, and blood crawl scarlet up his neck.

'But let that go,' Wolf Larsen continued. 'You may have very good reasons for forgetting your name, and I'll like you none the worse for it as long as you toe the mark.' (p. 24)

Larsen has deduced that 'Leach' is on the run from the authorities. So much any astute skipper with a knowledge of the riff-raff on the San Francisco waterfront might have done. But what is very strange—superhuman, it would seem—is that Larsen has divined the seaman's true name. He has 'seen through' Leach's disguise. Later in the voyage Leach realizes that Larsen is going to kill him in reprisal for the failed mutiny he and Johnson have led (Larsen eventually carries out his vengeance in a peculiarly sadistic way, calmly watching the two men struggle in a small boat in a heavy sea, tantalizing them all the while with the possibility that he may heave the *Ghost* to and save them).

Before making his vain attempt to escape, Leach comes to speak to Hump, who has now risen to the rank of mate ('Mr Van Weyden') on the *Ghost:*

'I want to ask a favor, Mr Van Weyden,' he said. 'If it's yer luck to ever make 'Frisco once more, will you hunt up Matt McCarthy? He's my old man. He lives on the Hill, back of the Mayfair bakery, runnin' a cobbler's shop that everybody knows, and you'll have no trouble. Tell him I lived to be sorry for the trouble I brought him and the things I done, and—and just tell him "God bless him", for me.' (p. 139)

London does not draw our attention to it, but there is something very puzzling in this confidential exchange. How did Larsen know earlier that 'Leach' was, in fact, called 'McCarthy?' If it was a shot in the dark, it was uncannily accurate: there are many common Irish names, most of which would come more readily to the tongue.

The mystery is compounded by the fact that London was more careful than most authors about such details, and had his friends look through his manuscript for possible factual errors or anomalies. More than with many authors, one can be sure that he was aware of the 'McCarthy' coincidence.[1]

It seems likely that London intended to leave this teasing detail as a mote to trouble the reader's eye. Leach is a minor character and the fact that Larsen effortlessly penetrated his incognito has no central plot significance. Its effect in the text is to suggest that Larsen has god-like powers of divination that flash out at unexpected moments. It consolidates his image as Nietzschean *über-mensch* and his tyrannical power over the mere mortals under his command.[2]

The Sea-Wolf has been filmed several times. In the most famous adaptation, that by Warner Bros in 1940, the pregnant 'George Leach' detail is exploited to create what is effectively a new story for the taste of a later age. The film was directed by Michael Curtiz, and had a screenplay by Robert Rossen, who had evidently studied London's text with some care.

Warner's cast was star-studded and their apparatus state-of-the-art for 1940. The studio had recently invested in a huge new tank (for scenes at sea) and a fog machine. Both were used in the gloomily atmospheric opening on the ferry. Van Weyden, now 'a novelist', was played in the film by Alexander Knox, an actor fresh from the London West End stage who projected a desiccated, patrician image of his character. On the ferry he is approached by an escaped convict, 'Ruth Webster' (spunkily played by Ida Lupino), who is trying to hide from two detectives. Van Weyden refuses to aid the girl, but just at this point the ferry is rammed by the *Ghost* and sinks.

Wolf Larsen (played by Edward G. Robinson) rescues the couple, but refuses to let them go ashore. Humphrey is made assistant to the cook, Mugridge (played by the Irish character actor Barry Fitzgerald). Ruth is kept for the captain's own nefarious purposes: to warm his bunk on cold nights, as we apprehend. In port Larsen has earlier shanghaied a mysterious young sailor—in fact another escaped convict—George Leach (played by the film's principal box-office star, John Garfield). Ruth and Leach fall in love. The middle parts of Curtiz's *The Sea-Wolf* more or less follow London's, but with the role of Humphrey (lover and bookworm) split between the glamorous Garfield and the rather stuffy Knox. As redesigned for the silver screen,

Leach shares the 'lead' with Larsen, with Humphrey Van Weyden trailing some way behind.

The story's climax is strikingly changed. In the novel, Leach is murdered by Larsen. Van Weyden and the high-born Maud Brewster (very unlike the 'moll' Ruth Webster) escape to 'Endeavor Island', where they spend an idyllic, Crusoe-like couple of years discussing poetry and Darwin and virtuously not making love. Larsen, blind and abandoned by his crew, is eventually washed up on the island and slowly dies of creeping paralysis—watched by a forgiving Humphrey. At the end of the novel Humphrey and Maud sail off to Japan in the rejigged *Ghost*. They will marry and doubtless set up a fine literary salon in San Francisco.

In the film all this is altered to revolve around the heroic character of George Leach, now the central character. Leach is not murdered, but is clapped in irons on the sinking *Ghost* by the blind and vengeful Wolf Larsen. Humphrey engages in a battle of wills and wits with Larsen, and contrives to allow Ruth and Leach to escape to a nearby island. What they will do there, how they will square their accounts with the 'Frisco authorities, we do not know—everything is left in Hollywood's blissfully 'happy ever after'. Humphrey, who has been shot, goes down to Davey Jones's Locker, with Larsen and the *Ghost*. The film ends with a vignette of Leach and Ruth, happily united in their little love boat.

Hollywood traditionally takes liberties with classic texts and the history of film adaptation is one of wholesale travesty. But in this instance, London seems to have anticipated the needs of a youth-centred, more proletarian, more sentimental public for whom his superannuated and Brahminical Humphrey Van Weyden would be insufficiently heroic. In the character of Leach/McCarthy, and the unsolved mystery attached to his character (who is he?

where does he come from?), he deliberately left a niche for other fictioneers to work in. There's a story here, he seems to say with his Leach mystery, fill it in as you will.

The Oxford World's Classics *The Sea-Wolf* is edited by John Sutherland.

═══

Wanted: deaf-and-dumb dog feeder

═══

Edmund Wilson scored some easy points against *The Hound of the Baskervilles* in his amusing essay 'Mr Holmes, they were the footprints of a gigantic hound!' It is not hard to poke holes in this most Gothic of the great detective's cases. What is more interesting, perhaps, is to see Arthur Conan Doyle himself doing running patchwork on some of those holes, as they became apparent to him while writing and serializing his story in the *Strand Magazine*.

The 'gigantic hound' of the title is built up in the reader's imagination by the horrible legends attaching to it and by the fact that to see it is manifestly to risk death by heart attack (as happens with Sir Charles Baskerville). Holmes and Watson's first physical encounter with the beast does not disappoint:

I sprang to my feet, my inert hand grasping my pistol, my mind paralysed by the dreadful shape which had sprung out upon us from the shadows of the fog. A hound it was, an enormous coal-black hound, but not such a hound as mortal eyes have ever seen. Fire burst from its open mouth, its eyes glowed with a smouldering glare, its muzzle and hackles and dewlap were outlined in flickering flame. Never in the delirious dream of a disordered brain could anything more savage, more appalling, more hellish, be conceived than that dark form and savage face which broke upon us out of the wall of fog. (p. 151)

It is rather an anti-climax to learn, as we do in the last chapter, that this monster is in fact a cross between a bloodhound and a mastiff, and that it was purchased from

Ross and Mangles, the dog-dealers in Fulham Road. Of course, the firm's animals do not come bathed in fiery incandescence. 'The man who called himself Stapleton' (alias Vandeleur, alias Baskerville) daubed it with the phosphorescent paste that had recently become all the rage on Victorian watch-faces.

Painting watches would seem to be an easier option (although, as was soon to become evident with the epidemic of 'fossy jaw', working with phosphorescent substances had dangers that even Holmes did not guess at). The 'demon dog' may not be as big as 300 years of rumour suggested, but it is undoubtedly a fierce canine. Stapleton stokes its savagery by keeping it 'half-starved'. In these circumstances it would be a brave man who dared put the animal's fearsome make-up on, before it ventured out on its night's hunting on Dartmoor. It is good-natured of the dog not to lick the paint off. Since it is suggested that its eyeballs are daubed as well, it is surprising that the animal can concentrate on tracking its prey. As a further quibble, one might wonder how the hound—unlike all the unfortunate ponies that keep getting sucked down to their deaths—avoids the quicksands of Grimpen Mire.

A more serious query is, what exactly does Stapleton intend to achieve by setting his hound on Sir Henry? Clearly Sir Charles Baskerville, with his weak heart and superstitious fears, is an easy prey. But Sir Henry has been brought up on the prairies of North America. He will have faced wolves and bears. He carries a firearm. He is not likely to be frightened to death. Rather weakly, Holmes supposes that Stapleton's motive is to 'paralyze Sir Henry's resistance'. If he is out to murder Sir Henry, all the business with the hound (and stealing one of his shoes in London, for the dog to pick up his scent) would seem somewhat unnecessary. Why not just shoot him and pitch him into the bog?

The most worrying of the loose ends which straggle from the denouement ('A Retrospection') is the explanation of who looked after the hound while Stapleton, in his bearded disguise, trailed the new baronet in London (meanwhile his treacherous wife was locked up in her hotel room—it was a busy week or so). The problem of the hungry dog evidently occurred to Doyle only as he was wrapping the story up. He improvised a solution. In his debriefing session with Holmes, Watson asks, 'What became of the hound when its master was in London?' Holmes replies:

I have given some attention to this matter and it is undoubtedly of importance. There can be no question that Stapleton had a confidant, though it is unlikely that he ever placed himself in his power by sharing all his plans with him. There was an old man-servant at Merripit House, whose name was Anthony. His connection with the Stapletons can be traced for several years ... This man has disappeared and has escaped from the country. It is suggestive that Anthony is not a common name in England, while Antonio is so in all Spanish or Spanish-American countries. The man, like Mrs Stapleton herself, spoke good English, but with a curious lisping accent. I have myself seen this old man cross the Grimpen Mire by the path which Stapleton had marked out. It is very probable, therefore, that in the absence of his master it was he who cared for the hound, though he may never have known the purpose for which the beast was used. (p. 164)

Holmes may have seen him, but this is the first that the reader learns of 'Antonio'. It seems clear that Doyle has invented the South American factotum to cover a little local difficulty which suddenly became apparent to him in the last instalment of the serial. But the insertion of a newly devised character into this late stage of the narrative weakens much of what has gone before. Awkward questions crop up. Is it likely that Antonio would not wonder why his master was keeping a gigantic, half-starved hound in the middle of a marsh, together with a supply of luminous paste, traces of which would still be visible on the animal? Might he not put two and two together upon learning that Sir Charles Baskerville had died—reputedly after seeing a spectral hound? If he knew the 'Stapletons' back in Costa Rica, would he not also know that his master was then called by his birth name? If Anthony is 'not a common name in England', neither is 'Baskerville' a common name in Costa Rica. If he did not know 'the purpose for which the beast was used', why has Antonio fled the country? Was he involved with the dastardly series of robberies by which Stapleton supported himself while he pursued his schemes against the successive heirs to the Baskerville title? Did he side with the remorseful Beryl, or the remorseless Stapleton?

Obviously Doyle was torn between making Antonio a version of the deaf-mute servant, beloved by the villains of Gothic fiction, and making him a co-conspirator—as guilty as his master. Or possibly he might be like Beryl, an unwilling accomplice. It is a small thread which will forever now dangle from the otherwise neat design of Doyle's story.

The Oxford World's Classics *The Hound of the Baskervilles* is edited by W. W. Robson.

Whose daughter is Nancy?

The Good Soldier is, Eugene Goodheart claims, 'one of the most puzzling works of modern fiction'.[1] It is notoriously hard to make sense of Ford's characters, their backgrounds, and their actions. There is critical dissension on such issues as whether the title (in so far as it refers to Captain Edward Ashburnham's 'goodness') is ironic or not. The narrative is speckled with what look like factual contradictions (about such crucial data as when and where the Dowells first met the Ashburnhams).[2] Close inspection reveals that the chronology is awry at almost every point. 'Is this', Martin Stannard asks, 'Fordian irony or simply carelessness about details?'[3] Should we lay the inconsistencies at the door of an artfully unreliable narrator (John Dowell), or at the door of a slipshod writer (Ford Madox Ford)? Some critics, Vincent Cheng for instance (who has assembled a convincing chronology of *The Good Soldier*), believe that Ford is writing in 'the French mode of *vraisemblance*', and that it is legitimate to ask 'what actually happens?'[4] with a reasonable expectation of getting 'right' answers. Other commentators, such as Frank Kermode, see *The Good Soldier* as the *locus classicus* of modernist indeterminacy. 'We are in a world of which it needs to be said not that plural readings are possible (for this is true of all narrative) but that the *illusion of the single right reading is possible no longer*'.[5]

I want to look at a puzzle recently highlighted by Ian Hamilton, reviewing the latest biography of Ford Madox Ford, by Max Saunders, in the *London Review of Books*.[6] A number of reviewers felt that the fifty-three pages of close exegesis which Saunders lavished on *The Good Soldier* might be too much of a good thing. Hamilton did not. He was particularly grateful for 'a single right reading' that Saunders brought to a traditionally difficult text:

Saunders has found a real-life model for John Dowell and argues persuasively (with biographical support) that Ashburnham's suicide was forced on him by the knowledge that Nancy was actually his daughter. Has this theory been proposed before? Not that I know of. All in all, Saunders's *Good Soldier* chapter had the effect of altering my reading of a book I thought I knew—a book I thought was marred by Ashburnham's implausible exit. So I for one am grateful.

The Good Soldier is a text well trodden by critical explication and a couple of weeks later Edward Mendelson wrote to the *LRB* (18 July) pointing out that Dewy Ganzel had contributed a 'persuasive' article to the *Journal of Modern Literature* (July 1984), arguing that Nancy was Edward's natural daughter. The insight was not quite as new as Hamilton thought.[7]

Questions of priority aside, what is the case for thinking that Edward's relationship with Nancy Rufford is not merely treacherous and adulterous, but incestuous? *Prima facie* it is odd that Edward reacts as remorsefully as he does to this last of his affairs. He is inhibited, as he tells Dowell, by a 'tabu' round Nancy. There are very few taboos in modern life; sleeping with one's daughter is certainly one of them. In other of his philanderings Ashburnham is wholly uninhibited. As far as we can make out he is a sexual addict, incapable of keeping his hands off any woman who takes his fancy. Prudence counts for nothing when his carnal pleasures are involved. He compromises his position in English society by assaulting a servant ('the Kilsyte girl') in a third-class railway carriage. In

India, he seduces brother-officers' wives ('Mrs Major
Basil', 'little Maisie Maidan'), exposing himself to blackmail and possible court-martial. He is prepared to bank-
rupt his estate and publicly humiliate his wife by buying
the favours of a courtesan (La Dolciquita) for an outrageous £60,000. For nine years he callously cuckolds his
best friend, the gullible Dowell (Florence meanwhile
denies Dowell his conjugal rights on the grounds of
'heart'). Florence, as Dowell belatedly discovers, poisons
herself when she believes Ashburnham has thrown her
over in favour of the much younger Nancy.

Why then should a late-life fling with Nancy precipitate
Edward's own suicide, Nancy's madness, and a nervous
breakdown in Leonora? The Ashburnhams, at least, must
be habituated to his incorrigible infidelity by now and it
would seem that the worst (Florence's death, financial
ruin, a court-case, blackmail) has already happened. It is
true that Nancy is Leonora's ward but on past record this
would prove no bar to Edward's making her his mistress.

In explaining the traumatic effects of the Ashburnham–
Nancy affair, Ganzel points to some odd inconsistencies in
the accounts we are given of Nancy's background. First
we are told that Nancy was 'Leonora's only friend's only
child', and that 'she had lived with the Ashburnhams ever
since she had been of the age of thirteen, when her mother
was said to have committed suicide owing to the brutalities of her father'. Later we are told that Nancy was sent
to boarding-school and 'her mother disappeared from her
life at that time. A fortnight later Leonora came to the
convent and told her that her mother was dead.' Finally,
nine years later, we learn that 'Nancy Rufford had a letter
from her mother. It came whilst Leonora was talking to
Edward, or Leonora would have intercepted it as she had
intercepted others. It was an amazing and horrible letter.'
What amazing horrors the letter contains we are not

specifically told—except that she may not be Colonel Rufford's daughter (he has retired from the army, and is now a tea-planter in Ceylon).

There are further mysteries about Mrs Rufford: it is implied at one point that she has descended to the condition of a common street-walker in Glasgow. Then it emerges that she is living reasonably prosperously, with a man whose telephone number Ashburnham knows well. There are, as Ganzel points out, loose ends here, and the explanation he comes to is 'that Nancy is Edward Ashburnham's natural daughter'. Edward knew, Leonora knew, and after receiving the 'horrible' letter from her mother, Nancy knew. The only person who doesn't know is the narrator, Dowell (and the bulk of his readers, one might add). Just as he couldn't see what was going on under his nose with Florence and Ashburnham, Dowell is blind to the relationship between Edward and Nancy.

If, against Kermode's instruction, one believes in 'single right readings', this would seem to be extraordinarily satisfactory. Certainly Max Saunders found it so: 'I had known the novel for nine years', he writes (echoing the nine years the Dowells knew the Ashburnhams), 'before the thought occurred to me, but then immediately details began to fall into place.'[8] Saunders's 'thought' is framed slightly more cautiously than Ganzel puts it: 'the girl with whom Ashburnham has become infatuated might be his own illegitimate daughter'. 'Might' leaves open the possibility that Ashburnham and Leonora cannot be sure—it's a wise philanderer that knows his own daughter. But none the less the 'touch of incest' insight is, for Saunders, the key to *The Good Soldier*, discovered only after years wrestling with the text.

Attractive as it is, the 'Nancy is Edward's daughter' interpretation is flawed. There is, one may note, no physical resemblance. Edward is fair-haired ('golden-haired' as he grows older), with striking porcelain-blue eyes. Nancy has 'the heaviest head of black hair that I have ever come across'. Given recessive genes, hair colour is by no means a clinching factor. Dates are. When the four principals meet at Nauheim in summer 1904, Edward is 33. This gives a birth-date of 1870 or 1871. When Florence kills herself it is 1913, and Nancy is something between 21 and 22, which gives a birth date of 1891 or 1892. When Nancy was conceived (1890 or 1891), Edward was between 20 and 21. It was at the age of 22 that he married Leonora, at which time he was, Dowell tells us, 'almost as pure in mind as Leonora herself. It is odd how a boy can have his virgin intelligence untouched in this world.' Edward's career in extra-marital 'libertinism' begins with the Kilsyte case, in 1895.[9]

Dates are notoriously slippery in *The Good Soldier*. But those I have listed here are among the most reliable we can determine in the novel. They are the pegs on which the narrative hangs. If they are not reliable, nothing is—even the names of the characters and the places they visit. It is hard, almost inconceivable, to picture 'virginal' Edward in his early twenties fathering Nancy, by the wife of a Scottish officer in a Highland regiment. Such acts belong to his later life. Probably like the mad (if she is mad) governess in James's *The Turn of the Screw*, Nancy's paternity will become one of modernism's chewed bones. But the balance of evidence is against its being Edward Ashburnham.

The Oxford World's Classics *The Good Soldier* is edited by Thomas Moser.

Clarissa's invisible taxi

It is not an easy novel to read, but Virginia Woolf's *Mrs Dalloway* is the easiest of novels to summarize. 'A day in the life of a middle-aged upper-class London woman planning her party', is how the *Oxford Companion to Twentieth Century Literature* encapsulates it. The long prelude to the novel is Clarissa Dalloway's morning walk through the West End on a brilliant June morning (the 13th) in 1923 to select the flowers for the entertainment she and her politician husband are giving that evening. One of the pleasures of *Mrs Dalloway* is that you can follow quite exactly the route taken by Clarissa on her morning walk.[1] OUP has helpfully provided a map for pedestrian-minded readers. They should also set their watches. Woolf originally called her novel 'The Hours', and Clarissa Dalloway's early morning peregrination through the London streets is precisely measured by the chimes of two clocks, Big Ben and the slightly belated St Margaret's (the parish church of the House of Commons). It is with Mrs Dalloway's morning excursion that I am concerned—specifically, the puzzle of how she makes her return journey.

The novel opens, 'Mrs Dalloway said she would buy the flowers herself'—the servants are busy preparing the house for the grand evening party. She and her Conservative MP husband, Richard, live in Westminster (within a stone's throw of the House of Commons and Westminster Abbey). As she crosses busy Victoria Street, Big Ben tolls 'the hour, irrevocable' (p. 4). It is not indicated what hour

A Map of Mrs Dalloway's London

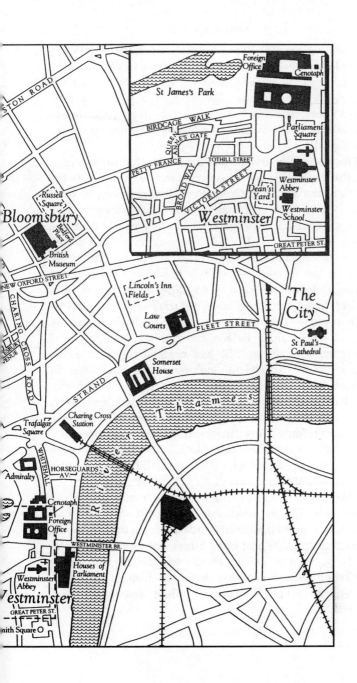

is sounding but we assume it is ten o'clock.[2] Mrs Dalloway is, we learn much later, carrying a parasol (p. 25), although it is not clear that she yet needs it. It is 'early' but London is already bustling. Mrs Dalloway, who is 'in her fifty-second year' and has a weak heart, is in no condition to bustle with it. We assume that her walking pace is a moderate stroll.

The next landmark the text gives us is that she is 'entering the Park'. This is evidently St James's Park, just to the south of the Mall and Green Park. It is not clear by what route she got here—presumably the short distance along Storey's Gate to Birdcage Walk. In St James's Park she meets her old friend Hugh Whitbread, on his way to the House of Commons. Reveries about the past (mainly concerning her former lover Peter Walsh, and the country house, Bourton, where they had their affair thirty years earlier) bring her to the 'middle of the Park'. The shortest path would lead her to the exit gate on the Mall, just to the east of Buckingham Palace. But the next topographical reference we have is: 'She had reached the Park gates. She stood for a moment, looking at the omnibuses in Piccadilly' (p. 7). From this we deduce that she has absent-mindedly passed through *both* St James's Park, and Green Park. She has, presumably, passed in front of the palace and up Queen's Walk, to the hurly-burly of Piccadilly (where the Green Park tube station and Ritz Hotel now are). At her presumed pace, Clarissa will be some twenty-five minutes into her walk.

Clarissa turns right along Piccadilly, remaining on the south side. She is making for Bond Street (Old Bond Street, as it now is) some 200 yards down, on the other side. She actually walks past Bond Street (without crossing the road), to browse awhile at the window of Hatchard's Bookshop, where she toys with the idea of buying a present for Hugh Whitbread's ailing and menopausal wife, Evelyn (whom she does not much like). Nothing suits, so 'Clarissa ... turned and walked back towards Bond Street'. She is now in the fashionable shopping area of London: 'Bond Street fascinated her; Bond Street early in the morning in the season; its flags flying; its shops; no splash; no glitter; one roll of tweed in the shop where her father had bought his suits for fifty years; a few pearls; salmon on an iceblock' (p. 9). She stops at the fishmongers (to look, not to buy) and the glove shop 'where, before the War, you could buy almost perfect gloves'. Mrs Dalloway proceeds up Bond Street to Mulberry's the florists, 'where they kept flowers for her when she gave a party'. As far as we can make out, this fictional shop is located at the junction with Brook Street—well into New Bond Street (p. 15). Another reverie about her daughter Elizabeth (who is modern and difficult) and about Elizabeth's former governess, the unpleasant Miss Kilman, preoccupy Clarissa in the seconds before pushing through the shop's swingdoors. Once inside she is attended on by Miss Pym ('whose hands were always bright red, as if they had been stood in cold water with the flowers'—the spiteful comment explains why she fictionalizes Mulberry's but not Hatchard's). Clarissa spends some time with Miss Pym, sampling the shop's extensive stock of blooms, relishing the colours and scents. She is uplifted. The sensations are 'a wave which she let flow over her and surmount that hatred, that monster, surmount it all; and it lifted her up and up when—oh! a pistol shot in the street outside.'

Her mood is shattered. It is not, however, a pistol shot. Miss Pym goes to the window and reports that it is merely a car backfiring (Londoners are still jumpy from the Zeppelin raids, we assume). The time elapsed up to this point in the narrative would be some thirty-five minutes easy walking (I timed it myself, on foot, in June 1996) with some ten minutes to a quarter-of-an-hour's conference in Mulberry's with Miss Pym. It is, therefore, around 10.45 to 10.50 a.m.

Up to this point the narrative has been solely attached to Clarissa's consciousness. Now, with the 'violent explosion', it becomes detached. We in fact see little more of Clarissa until she is back at her house in Westminster. Instead, we follow the repercussions of the backfiring motor car. It is no ordinary automobile, but a limousine containing 'a face of the very greatest importance'. Whose face? 'Rumours were at once in circulation from the middle of Bond Street to Oxford Street.' Was it the Prince of Wales, the Queen, the Prime Minister? No one is sure. Septimus Smith, a shell-shocked World War One veteran, overhears people discussing the matter. He too is evidently passing Mulberry's shop, on his way north to Regent's Park with his wife, who has brought him out for his daily exercise. Septimus has heard the report of the car backfiring and it terrifies him (in fact, it sows the seed of the suicide he will commit, later that day). Rezia Smith wonders, with other passers-by, whether the Queen herself is in the car.

After this introduction to the Smiths we follow the mysterious car, which proceeds, 'with inscrutable reserve', south to Piccadilly. Meanwhile, Mrs Dalloway (thinking like others, 'It is probably the Queen') emerges from Mulberry's 'with her flowers'. The car 'glides across Piccadilly', turns left, and then left again down St James's Street, through London's clubland. Gentlemen looking out of the great window at White's 'perceived instinctively that greatness was passing, and the pale light of the immortal presence fell upon them as it had fallen upon Clarissa Dalloway' (p. 16). It passes the sentries at St James's Palace, who salute, then turns right along the Mall to Buckingham Palace (the flag is flying, so it may indeed be the Queen in the car), where a crowd of hopeful onlookers is gathered.

Suppositions about the occupants of the mysterious car ripple among them, as they did among the pedestrians in Bond Street (readers never learn who actually was in the car, although Woolf's working materials indicate it was the Prime Minister, who makes an appearance later at Mrs Dalloway's party). Suddenly, in addition to the great person's limousine, there is another distraction. Above the gawpers clustered outside the Palace an aeroplane is skywriting a message. It is evidently an advertisement, but no one can quite make out the words. A Mrs Bletchley hazards it is 'Kreemo'; Mr Bowley thinks he sees 'toffee'. As Londoners silently gaze into the sky, 'bells struck eleven times' (p. 18).

Meanwhile, in the time taken by the limousine to get from Bond Street to Buckingham Palace, Septimus and Rezia have reached the fountains at the southern end of Broad Walk in Regent's Park. Given the fact that it is about a mile-and-a-half (it takes me twenty brisk minutes to walk it), they may have taken a bus or a tube from Oxford Circus to Regent's Park Station (which Woolf mentions on page 22) although for one stop it would hardly seem worth it. They too see the skywriting: 'It was toffee; they were advertising toffee, a nursemaid told Rezia. Together they began to spell t . . . o . . . f . . . "K . . . R . . ." said the nursemaid.' Septimus, enclosed in his private psychosis, thinks 'So . . . they are signalling to me'. Evidently this too is happening at eleven o'clock—although Regent's Park is (unlike Buckingham Palace) beyond earshot of Big Ben and St Margaret's. The narrative remains for a few pages with people in the park.

Suddenly, on page 25, the narrative reverts to Clarissa. She is now, we discover, home. 'What are they looking at?' she asks the maid who opens the door to her house in

Westminster. Presumably 'they' are pedestrians, and what they are looking at is the Kreemo toffee message in the sky. This would suggest a third simultaneity: Mrs Bletchley's remarks outside the Palace; Rezia's conversation with the nursemaid in Regent's Park; Clarissa's return home to her house in Westminster—all occur with the chimes at eleven o'clock. This is confirmed, a few pages (but only a couple of minutes) later, when—hearing that she has a visitor (her old lover, Peter Walsh, as it turns out)—Clarissa finds it 'outrageous to be interrupted at eleven o'clock on the morning of the day she was giving a party' (p. 34).

The question is—how did Clarissa get back from upper Bond Street so quickly? Although we are given a minute topographic description of her walk to Mulberry's, we have no idea how she returned. It is accomplished, we may calculate, in the time it takes a chauffeured limousine to make its sedate way from upper Bond Street through the Mall to Buckingham Palace—ten minutes, fifteen at most if the traffic is heavy. A good middle-distance runner could hare down Bond Street and across the parks to Westminster in that time. Doubtless many commuters with trains to catch at Victoria do it every working day. But if Mrs Dalloway did it walking (carrying a large bunch of flowers, a handbag, and a parasol), she should cancel the next appointment with her heart specialist.

The solution, once one thinks of it, is blindingly obvious. She took a taxi. But why are we not told this fact? None of the student guides I have seen (*Coles Notes*, for instance) mentions this invisible taxi. Clarissa's morning expedition is assumed to be, going and coming, entirely on foot. But unless those feet are very swift indeed, a taxi there must be. The taxi hypothesis would also explain why, until she alights from the vehicle outside her front door, Mrs Dalloway has been blissfully ignorant of the skywriting that all pedestrian London is looking at.

But even if one inserts the unmentioned taxi, there are still loose ends. The last we saw of Clarissa in the West End was at Bruton Street, watching the queenly limousine. Was it there she got her taxi? Or did she walk down to Piccadilly? What route did her vehicle take (did she, for instance, pass in front of Buckingham Palace, a few feet from Mrs Bletchley and Mr Bowley?) What sights did she see on the way? It is not entirely inconceivable that there was no cab: she walked up to Oxford Circus (possibly along-side Septimus and Rezia) and got the underground to Westminster—although carrying flowers it would not have been an inviting prospect. The taxi seems more likely.

The reason why Woolf does not mention the taxi is to be found, I think, in her and Mrs Dalloway's class habits when in town. For 'upper-middle-class ladies' in 1923 to take a mile's walk to a florist's to save a servant's legs was unusual to the point of eccentricity ('What a lark! What a plunge!' Clarissa thinks as she sets out on her stroll). The wife of Richard Dalloway, MP, would routinely hail a taxi when shopping in Bond Street, or have some shop assist-ant do it for her. The act is so natural that there is no need to mention it: any more than one need mention that there are pigeons in Trafalgar Square—or that there are under-paid, unidentified servants who keep things shipshape in the Dalloway household. (When she was writing her fam-ous polemic about a room of one's own and £500 a year, the Woolfs had two live-in female servants, Lotte and Nellie, who earned £76 per annum between them. They did not, one suspects, have rooms of their own.)

In his essay on Tolstoy, the Marxist critic Georg Lukacs argues that in reading *Anna Karenina* or *War and Peace*, we should always insert into the narrative 'the invisible serf'. That is, we should visualize (as the novels often do not) the vast servile infrastructure which made the prin-cipals' drama possible. Similarly, in *Mrs Dalloway* we should recall the 'invisible taxi'—the fleets of carriages (they used to be called 'horseless'), the armies of servants (now sadly thinned by post-war democracy and insubordination), the attentive shop assistants (only visible when, like the luckless Miss Pym with her cherry-red hands, they are ludicrous or clumsy)—all of which exist to make Clarissa Dalloway's life bearable.

The Oxford World's Classics *Mrs Dalloway* is edited by David Bradshaw.

Who Betrays Elizabeth Bennet?

Daniel Defoe · *Moll Flanders*

Why is Moll's younger brother older than she is?

As Ian Watt notes in *The Rise of the Novel*, the attentive reader will find an 'inordinate number of cracks' in the plot of *Moll Flanders*. Some, in fact, are less cracks than gaping fissures. There are, Watt goes on to observe, two possible lines on the inconsistencies in Moll's account of her life. We can read her narrative 'ironically'. In this mode of reading 'errors' are assumed to have been cun-ningly planted by Defoe to be picked up by the wideawake reader.[1] Defoe *designed* such glaring anomalies as Moll's remembering to the farthing the value of gold watches she stole twenty years ago, but forgetting the names (and even, apparently, the number) of her children. These are to be taken 'ironically' as signs of her incorrigible callousness. Similarly ironic are such jarring pieties as her reflection, after stealing a little girl's gold necklace, that by her theft she had 'given the parents a just reproof for their neg-ligence, in leaving the poor lamb to come home by itself, and it would teach them to take more care next time' (p. 194). Like the sadistic Victorian flogger telling his victim that 'this hurts me more than it hurts you', Moll is—if we follow this line of explanation—a double-dyed hypocrite.

Ian Watt eschews this super-subtlety. He prefers a read-ing of *Moll Flanders* which sees Daniel Defoe as a hurried writer, catering for readers who were not trained—as modern 'sleuthing' readers are trained—in the intricacies of detective fiction. The novel had not fully risen, nor had the skills of the novel's consumers. 'We take novels much more seriously today,' Watt claims. Defoe, in his day, was a hasty writer for unserious readers; an artist who worked 'piecemeal, very rapidly, and without any subsequent revision'.[2] Watt calculates that Defoe put out 'over three thousand pages of print in the year that saw *Moll Flanders'* and, we may assume, blotted very few of those pages.

There are, to the modern eye, some astonishing anomalies in the novel. Moll, for example, signs off on the last page in 1683, with the information that she is 'almost seventy Years of Age'. This means that during the 1640s—while Moll is swanning around Virginia—there is a civil war going on in Britain. The conflict was particularly savage in Colchester, where the heroine has deposited two of her (nameless) children. That momentous upheaval is never mentioned, any more than is the execution of King Charles (worth a parenthesis, one would have thought) or the Restoration. The 'Great Fire of London' ravages the capital without Moll, apparently, noticing. She does, however, tell us in some detail about a household fire in which she is bruised by a mattress thrown out of a top window by a desperate occupant.

One can, of course, rationalise these oversights in terms of Moll's class origins. The great waves of history wash over the working classes without their noticing. When Winston Smith (in *Nineteen Eighty-Four*) tries to extract from the old man in the pub what life before the Revolution was like, he is absolutely frustrated by the old prole's inability to *know* what he remembers or remember what he knows:

A sense of helplessness took hold of Winston. The old man's memory was nothing but a rubbish heap of details ... They remembered a million useless things, a quarrel with a workmate, a hunt for a lost bicycle pump, the expression on a long-dead sister's face, the swirls of dust on a windy morning seventy years ago; but

all the relevant facts were outside the range of their vision. They
were like the ant, which can see small objects but not large ones.[3]

So too with Moll. She remembers the mattress, but forgets all the great historical events of what Dryden called
the 'Annus Mirabilis', 1666. The Great Fire of London, the
Dutch invasion of the Thames, the Wren rebuilding of the
capital all pass unobserved. Dryden is the laureate's history. Moll's is 'prole' history. Bicycle pumps and mat-
tresses. Like the 'ironic' approach, it's another flattering
way of reading Defoe's fiction—flattering both to him and
to us. But Watt's analysis is more convincing, in my view,
than subtle readings which cast Moll as an 'unreliable
narrator' and her omissions as 'symptomatically' self-
revealing. Even Kurt Waldheim's amnesia did not extend
to forgetting there was a war going on in 1939–1945.[4]

Ian Watt concludes that *Moll Flanders* is not a 'work of
irony' but it is an 'ironic object' (p.135). By which he
means we can read it more sophisticatedly than Defoe
wrote it but should be careful about reading our sophistication *into* the novel. None the less, one of the striking
things about Defoe is how, in some important aspects, his
narratives hold together well. Moll's age, for instance, is
accurately recorded throughout all the complex vicissi-
tudes of her life and emblazoned on the 1721 title-page (see
overleaf).

If, as Watt suspects, Defoe wrote at reckless speed he
must surely have had a 'Memorandum' to hand to remind
him of Moll's current age as he wrote. The narrative offers
a chronologically coherent account of Moll's childhood
until, at 'between seventeen and eighteen' (p. 18), she
leaves the household where she has been seduced by one
brother to marry the other. 'Betty' (as she is then called)
is married five years, before Robin dies (p. 58). She
promptly disposes of her two children to the care of their

THE
FORTUNES
AND
MISFORTUNES
Of the FAMOUS

Moll Flanders, &c.

Who was Born in NEWGATE, and during a
Life of continu'd Variety for Threescore Years,
besides her Childhood, was Twelve Year a
Whore, five times a *Wife* (whereof once to her
own Brother) Twelve Year a *Thief*, Eight Year a
Transported *Felon* in *Virginia*, at last grew *Rich*,
liv'd *Honest*, and died a *Penitent*.

Written from her own MEMORANDUMS.

LONDON: Printed for, and Sold by W.
CHETWOOD, at *Cato's-Head,* in *Russel-
street, Covent-Garden*; and T. EDLING, at
the *Prince's-Arms*, over-against *Exerter-Change*
in the *Strand*. MDDCXXI.

grandparents and, as a 23-year-old widow, marries (after a few months' courtship) her gentleman draper. Their marriage lasts 'about two years and a quarter' (p. 62) before they part company (rendering Moll's subsequent 'marriages' bigamous—something that she conveniently forgets in her 'penitent' phase of life).

At this point, Betty becomes 'Mrs Mary Flanders'—a handsome 25- or 26-year-old young woman of (apparent) means and respectability. After 'half-a-year's' interval (p. 66) in this character, Mary marries her American sea-captain. He takes her back as his new bride to his home in old Virginia, where they have three children; at which point, to her horror, she discovers that her husband is her half-brother.

After eight years in America, Mary returns to Britain (p.104), leaving her 'brother-husband' free to claim that she has died. He may thus marry again, if he wishes (she will, if she can). Moll is, she says, 'far from old' (p. 106) and must be, we calculate, around 34 when she migrates back to England. Although the years abroad have been hard on her, she is still a viable, if hardly nubile, commodity in the sex market. She now takes up residence in Bath, picking up (after a couple of seasons) with a wealthy man whose wife is insane. This arrangement lasts 'near two years', at which point, Mary must be 36 or 37.

As her sexual charms wane she declines from 'friend' to 'whore'. 'Thief' is still to come, with menopause. Over the next 'six years' she bears three children (that we know about) to her 'protector' (p. 120). As she now assesses her life, Moll ruefully notes:

I had the World to begin again; but you are to consider, that I was not now the same Woman as when I liv'd at *Redriff* [i.e. Rother-hithe], for first of all I was near 20 Years older, and did not look the better for my Age, nor for my Rambles to *Virginia* and back again; and tho' I omitted nothing that might set me out to

Advantage, except Painting, for that I never stoop'd to ... yet there would always be some difference seen between Five and Twenty, and Two and Forty (p. 127)

By Moll's own several accounts, we can confirm that she was indeed around 26 when she married her Virginian captain. He, we know, was born in the colony. As her 'mother-in-law' ('mother') tells Moll, when she (the older woman) arrived in Virginia, 'she very luckily fell into a good Family, where behaving herself well, and her Mistress dying, her Master married her, by whom she had my Husband and his Sister' (p. 88). We are told that this lady's son, Moll's husband, 'was above thirty' at the time of their arrival in Virginia—when Moll is, as calculated, 26–7. He is, therefore, some five years older than she (as a 'captain', he could scarcely be in his early twenties).

There is a major problem here, created by Defoe's punctiliousness about his heroine's dates and chronology. If they were born to the same mother Moll must have entered the world in England at least five years before her mother can: (1) have emigrated to Virginia; (2) have worked as a servant until her mistress died; (3) have married her master; (4) have borne a son. That son (subsequently Moll's 'husband') must be significantly *younger*, not significantly older than his English sister.

It could be one of the many 'cracks' in Defoe's narrative. But the anomaly usefully directs us back to Moll's brief, superficially clear, but actually very perplexing account of her origins. Her mother, as she says, was convicted of 'borrowing three pieces of fine *Holland*'. Of this crime, Moll says, 'the Circumstances are too long to repeat, and I have heard them related so many Ways, that I can scarce be certain which is the right Account' (p. 8). In the weeks while awaiting trial at Newgate, Moll's mother took the precaution of getting herself pregnant (by the gaoler, we assume). Hence the private joke in her later assumed name, 'Flanders'—three pieces of Holland procreated her.

Moll's mother 'pleaded her belly' to escape, got herself a seven-month reprieve (she must have just made it), and subsequently had her sentence commuted to transportation. At six months, young Moll was consigned to the 'bad Hands' of 'some Relation of my Mothers' (p. 8). Her first conscious recollection is as a 3-year-old child among a nomadic company of *Gypsies*, to whom she was sold—evidently to be used as a child beggar or whore. Luckily, she somehow got away from this gypsy band, and found herself in Colchester—where her next fifteen years were to be spent.

There are a number of oddities in this account. Clearly Moll knows her true name—although we never do. It is by this name that she identifies her mother, a quarter of a century later in Virginia. How *does* she know her name? The gypsies would surely have renamed her, to protect themselves. She can hardly have been baptized. Who was it who told her the circumstances of her mother's arrest and trial, 'so many Ways' that she cannot be sure 'which is the right Account'?

If her unnamed maternal relatives told her, a 2-year-old girl at the time, the account would surely have fallen on uncomprehending ears. Who were these relatives of her mother, anyway? How did the gypsies come by her? And why—if the gypsies bought or abducted her—did they simply let her go? As a 3-year-old child, Moll can, by her own account, have known nothing of her origins—certainly not enough to fill in, as she does, missing parts of her mother's recollections many years later. It is difficult, on the narrative evidence, to see how she could even have known her own name.

'Gypsy abduction' is a favourite childish fantasy. In order to make sense of the gross disparity of age between the heroine and her Virginian husband (more so given Defoe's accuracy elsewhere about this aspect of his plot), one is driven to assume that Moll is lying. She was more than 3 when she arrived in Colchester, and there is some prehistory which we do not know about. Moll, we deduce, is some years older than she claims and is clumsily masking what she knows of her birth and that disreputable 'Relation of my Mothers'. Whores' penitential confessions are, by their nature, suspect documents. By opening with a precise, but so easily exploded (and arguably romantic), account of her origins, Moll brands herself as untrustworthy, but not for that reason entirely unsympathetic. Who, with Moll's past, would not tell a few fibs about her childhood?

The Oxford World's Classics *Moll Flanders* is edited by G. A. Starr.

Who has Susan been talking to?

According to Coleridge, the three best-constructed plots in world literature are *Oedipus Rex, The Alchemist*, and *Tom Jones*.[1] In Fielding's novel the chapters in the inn at Upton show the plot-wright's art at its most virtuosic. Few now read his plays, but the novelist's long apprenticeship on the stage must have prepared him in handling the intricate plot machinery of Books 9 and 10—a section of the narrative which, as Tony Richardson's 1963 film showed, adapts wonderfully to the conventions of high-speed theatrical farce.

To summarize: the Upton sequence begins with Tom taking a leisurely farewell from the Man of Hill at dawn, before starting on his way. The two gentlemen enjoy a philosophic view of the early morning landscape from a neighbouring eminence, Mazard Hill. (Partridge, who is not philosophical, has elected to stay in bed.) The idyll is disturbed when Tom spies a lady being murdered (or worse than murdered) in a thicket. The would-be murderer turns out to be none other than the hero's old foe, Northerton (who escapes to do more bad things). The voluptuous victim is—although Tom does not know it—Mrs Waters, alias our old friend Jenny Jones.

Rather oddly, Mrs Waters does not now or later tumble to Tom's identity (there are so many Tom Joneses in the world, presumably), although tumbling is much on her mind. Manfully, the young man resists her delicate invitation to take his rescuer's reward, and conducts the lady to a convenient inn at 'the famous town of Upton'

(p. 430). The sleepy Partridge is directed to follow in his own time.

A near-naked woman, accompanied by a dishevelled young buck, are not the custom the landlord and his wife think appropriate to their genteel establishment. A brawl ('the Battle of Upton') ensues, elaborately described in Fielding's mock-heroic style. Tom is saved from mortal injury at the hands of the broom-wielding landlady by the nick-of-time arrival of Partridge, who is promptly belaboured by the inn's 'robust and manlike' maid-of-all-work, Susan. Enter a sergeant of musketeers, who recognizes Tom's companion as 'Mrs Waters'—his commander's 'wife'. As an officer's lady she is, of course, now made welcome at the inn and peace breaks out.

While the debris of the fracas is being cleared up, a mysterious lady and her attendant have arrived in a coach and four. Tom is bent over the distraught (and still interestingly undressed) Mrs Waters, and Partridge is washing blood from his nose at the courtyard pump. Neither takes any notice of these newcomers. The alert reader suspects that they may be Sophia and Honour. But they are, as later emerges, Mrs Fitzpatrick—a lady in flight from her violent husband—and her attendant. It is their intention only to rest an hour or two, and travel on post-haste, overnight.

It is now teatime, and a number of strands of the plot run concurrently. In her private apartments, Mrs Waters takes some refreshment with Tom who finally surrenders to her charms (incestuously?). This is an afternoon engagement, to be followed up by further nocturnal action(s). Meanwhile, downstairs in the kitchen, a relaxed Partridge, the ladies' coachman, the sergeant, and (between their duties) the landlord and landlady chat and drink the evening away.

The sergeant tactfully describes Mrs Waters's fondness

for errant young officers like Northerton (with whom she was eloping, before he decided to kill her for her diamond ring and ninety guineas). Partridge, who like Cassio has very poor brains for drinking, boasts about his 'friend' Mr Jones and what great expectations 'the heir of Squire Allworthy' has. As the drink flows, quarrels break out, a thoroughly drunk sergeant and coachman come to blows—but so overcome are they with the landlady's dubious 'perry', that they can do each other no harm.

The coachman is now far too drunk to take Mrs Fitzpatrick away from the inn and she reluctantly decides to stay the night. By midnight, only Susan is up—'she being obliged to wash the kitchen, before she retired to the arms of the fond, expecting ostler'. Enter, furiously, an Irish gentleman looking for his escaped wife. Susan assumes Mrs Waters must be the runaway, and directs Mr Fitzpatrick (as it turns out to be) to the lady's bedroom. It may, of course, be that Susan's motives are mischievous—she knows full well that something untoward is going on in Mrs Waters's room.

Misdirected by Susan, the irate husband bursts in to be confronted by a naked Jones. On seeing the woman's clothes around the bed, and a form therein, Fitzpatrick naturally assumes that he is being cuckolded in front of his very eyes. A furious fight ensues. The uproar brings in another Irishman who is sleeping in an adjoining bedroom (the narrator has been too busy to tell us about *his* arrival at the inn).

'Mr Maclachlan' is, it turns out, known to Fitzpatrick and—candles now being brought—he points out to his friend that the lady in the bed is not Mrs Fitzpatrick caught *in flagrante delicto* but some other lady. Quick-wittedly, Mrs Waters further protests that Mr Jones, in an adjoining room, was himself drawn in by the noise of Fitzpatrick's irruption. To proclaim her innocence before

the world, she begins to shout out hysterically 'Help!
Rape! Murder! Rape!'

The landlady finally arrives and all is more or less set
straight. Fitzpatrick, not thinking to search other rooms
in the inn, retires to share Mr Maclachlan's bed ('errant
scrubs', the landlady disgustedly comments; she has been
cheated out of a fee). Partridge now comes down to the
kitchen. He too has been wakened by the noise and terrified, as he says, by a 'screech owl' outside his window. He
persuades Fitzpatrick's two manservant's to keep him
company, and takes to drinking again.

Susan now admits two women travellers into the inn.
They turn out to be Sophia and her maid, Mrs Honour.
Partridge, however, does not recognize them, muffled up as
they are at this time of night. Moreover, it has been many
years since he resided in their village. Sophia retires to a
bedroom to rest; Honour comes down to the kitchen and—
despite the hour—peremptorily demands cooked food.
Susan and Partridge are vexed and the schoolmaster-
barber lets slip, talking to the landlady, that his sleeping
friend is 'Jones . . . Squire Allworthy's son'. Mrs Honour
'pricks up her ears', returns to tell Sophia what seems like
good news, then returns to the kitchen.

A thoroughly confused Partridge, under the imperious
maid's interrogation as to where Jones is, informs her
'plainly that Jones was in bed with a wench, and made use
of an expression too indelicate to be here inserted'. Exit
Mrs Honour again, to pass on this awful intelligence to
Sophia. Distraught, Sophia summons Susan to her bedroom. She and Mrs Honour cross-examine the maid, and
by a mixture of bullying and bribery (Susan's price is an
exorbitant two guineas) persuade the wench to test the
truth of what Partridge has said by going to Jones's bedroom. It is empty, Susan reports. Mr Jones must be with
Mrs Waters. On being told, Sophia 'turns pale':

Mrs Honour begged her to be comforted, and not to think any more of so worthless a fellow. 'Why there,' says Susan, 'I hope, madam, your ladyship won't be offended, but pray, madam, is not your ladyship's name Madam Sophia Western?' 'How is it possible you should know me?' answered Sophia. 'Why, that man that the gentlewoman [Mrs Honour] spoke of, who is in the kitchen, told about you last night.' (p. 471)

Susan goes on to say that Partridge further said that Sophia was 'dying for love of the young squire, and that he was going to the wars to get rid of you'.

Sophia now sees that Tom Jones has played her false. He is not her true love. She gives Susan a third guinea and instructs the serving-woman to place the muff Jones gave her in the unfaithful young man's room, with her name attached on a piece of paper. This will lead to further complications after she has left (which she and Mrs Honour do forthwith), shortly before Squire Western arrives.

The Upton chapters are done in masterly fashion, and there is a touch of justified bravado in Fielding's challenge to the 'reptile critics' to find fault with his design, if they can. The narrator succeeds, against all the odds, in keeping Partridge and Mrs Waters (Tom's two putative parents), apart while keeping Tom and Partridge together. The schoolmaster-barber might plausibly fail to recognise Sophia and Honour. He would certainly remember the fascinating Jenny Jones.

There is, however, a puzzle embedded in this virtuosic stretch of narrative. How does Susan know Sophia's name, and how has she come by the remarkably untrue allegation that Mr Jones was running away to the wars to be rid of Sophia? If we look back at what Partridge actually said in the kitchen (Susan, incidentally, is not recorded as being present at the time), it is very different. After he has boasted that he is Mr Jones's friend, *not* his servant, and that Mr Jones is the 'heir of Squire Allworthy' (a magnate known, even at this distance, to the inn's hosts), Partridge is asked by the landlord: 'how comes it . . . that such a great gentleman walks about the country afoot?' It is a shrewd question. 'I don't know', Partridge lamely retorts, then gets into his stride:

'. . . great gentlemen have humours sometimes. He hath now a dozen horses and servants at Gloucester; and nothing would serve him, but last night, it being very hot weather, he must cool himself with a walk to yon high hill, whither I likewise walked with him to bear him company.' (p. 446)

Hereafter, the discussion disintegrates into drunken quarrelling and even more drunken fisticuffs.

How, one may ask, did Susan get hold of her (nearly accurate) version of things? There are a number of possibilities. In his cups, Partridge may have drivelled out a whole string of indiscretions, at a time when Susan was moving in and out of the kitchen about her business. This might have taken place during some un-narrated portion of the story, while the reader's attention was directed elsewhere. It is, however, very hard to find an occasion when Partridge's public indiscretions could have occurred. All the chinks are filled. And no one but Susan seems to be privy to them.

Alternatively, one might think that Susan—who is mischievous (*vide* the business with Mr Fitzpatrick)—is making it all up. But there is a garbled version of the truth here, and she knows Sophia's identity (she is, in fact, the only person in the inn to penetrate the disguise). There is a strong kernel of truth in what she knows, or thinks she knows. She must have had it from someone in the know.

What seems most likely is the following. After their epic battle at the beginning of the Upton episode, Partridge and Susan make up, as we are told. He forgives his scratches, she forgives the black eye he has given her: 'between these two, therefore, a league was struck, and those hands became now the mediators of peace.' Flirtation, we deduce, may have followed amity—with the promise of even closer intimacies, when Susan should have time for them.

Susan, we infer, must be a paragon of chambermaids. She is manifestly on duty at crack of dawn on the two days covered by the Upton business (see pp. 473, 480). Thus it is, for instance, that she can participate in the morning 'Battle of Upton'. As is made clear, the day's business at the inn in this summer-time of year begins two hours before dawn, at five o'clock. This estimable servant is still, as we are told, working at midnight. First up, she is last to go to bed. Nor can she expect sleep even when she does get to bed. The ostler will doubtless want to keep her from slumber for a little while, at least.

What seems plausible is the following. Susan cemented her 'league' with Partridge by retiring with him, or visiting his bedroom, shortly after he retired—an arrangement made earlier in the day, after the 'battle'. Before leaving Partridge's embrace for that of the ostler (in the straw, with his horses) she indulged in some pillow talk. Partridge, indiscreet as ever, told her things he should not have done. On her part, she cunningly milked him for anything she could learn about who his master was, and any details of his amours. It was while she was on her way from one bed to another (the business about 'being obliged to wash the kitchen' was a lie) that Susan chanced to be up at midnight when Fitzpatrick arrived.

There is some warrant for this line of speculation. In her inquest after the Fitzpatrick imbroglio we are told that 'the landlady, remembering that Susan had been the only person out of bed when the door was burst open', goes on to ask some searching questions. She clearly is suspicious

about the maid being up at midnight. Susan, we are told,
'related the whole story which the reader knows already,
varying the truth only in some circumstances, and totally
concealing the money she had received'. Among those
'varied circumstances', we may suppose, is the true
account of what she happened to be doing out of bed (or
between beds) at that ungodly hour.

The Oxford World's Classics *Tom Jones* is edited by John Bender
and Simon Stern, with an introduction by John Bender.

≡

Who betrays Elizabeth Bennet?

≡

Elizabeth Bennet's final put-down of Lady Catherine de Bourgh in Volume III, Chapter 14 *of Pride and Prejudice* ranks with Lady Bracknell and the handbag as one of the most memorable scenes in literature. As Jane Austen tells it, it is a conflict of battleaxe versus rapier with the old battleaxe comprehensively vanquished. Lady Catherine flies the field with her magnificently hollow rebuke: 'I take no leave of you, Miss Bennet. I send no compliments to your mother. You deserve no such attention. I am most seriously displeased' (p. 318).

What has so seriously displeased Lady Catherine is the report that Elizabeth is about to become engaged to Darcy—a marital prize she has reserved for her own daughter Anne. The couple are 'tacitly' engaged—she loftily tells Miss Bennet. But, as she is obliged to add:' The engagement between them is of a peculiar kind' (p. 315). The de Bourghs have not troubled, that is, to secure the young man's compliance in the matter.

Elizabeth holds her ground, parrying all the older woman's attempts to coerce her into an 'undertaking'—a surrender, that is, of any claim to Darcy. By sheer dialectical skill, Elizabeth neither admits any intention of marrying the gentleman nor offers any guarantee that she will not. Her sub-zero *politesse* drives de Bourgh to paroxysms of fury and what even she, imperceptive as she is, dimly perceives to be foolishness: 'Obstinate, headstrong girl! I am ashamed of you! Is this your gratitude to me for my attentions to you last spring? Is nothing due

to me on that score?' (p. 316). After her antagonist bustles
away in a rage, Elizabeth wonders:

> from what the report of their engagement could originate,
> Elizabeth was at a loss to imagine; till she recollected that
> *his* [Darcy's] being the intimate friend of Bingley, and *her*
> [Elizabeth's] being the sister of Jane, was enough, at a time when
> the expectation of one wedding, made every body eager for
> another, to supply the idea. (p. 319)

It's a weak supposition—unworthy of the sharp-witted
Miss Bennet. And it is exploded immediately by her father.
He has received a perplexing letter from Mr Collins: 'He
begins with congratulations on the approaching nuptials
of my eldest daughter [Jane and Bingley], of which it
seems he has been told, by some of the good-natured, gos-
siping Lucases' (p. 321). Jane Austen laid this train of gossip at the end of Volume III, Chapter 13, when Mrs Bennet
goes to her sister, the lawyer's wife, and 'was privileged
to whisper it to Mrs Philips, and *she* ventured, without
any permission, to do the same by all her neighbours in
Meryton' (p. 311). Among whom, we deduce, are the Philips
family's close neighbours at Lucas Lodge. As we follow the
line of clues, Lady Lucas has written to her daughter
Charlotte, now Mrs Collins, and she has passed the news
of Jane and Bingley's engagement on to her husband and
his patroness over dinner at Rosings.

All this is transparent enough, and fits in with the gos-
sipy world of Longbourn and Meryton (separated, as we
are told, by only a mile's 'short walk', p. 14). But Mr
Collins's letter contains something else. He goes on to
felicitate Mr Bennet on the impending marriage of his
daughter Elizabeth to 'one of the illustrious personages in
the land' (p. 321). Who can this 'illustrious personage' be,
Mr Bennet wonders? It must be Darcy. But, to a common-
sensical man like him, it *cannot* be 'Mr Darcy, who never

looks at any woman but to see a blemish, and who probably never looked at *you* in his life! It is admirable' (p. 322). And preposterous. The effect of this double-fronted attack is — of course—to put any possible union between Mr Pride and Miss Prejudice entirely out of the question. Wheels are being spoked (particularly if, as we suspect, similar rumours are being cast to embarrass Darcy).

There is a puzzle underlying this interesting tangle, pointed out to me by Kathleen Glancy:

How could there be a report in Meryton about *anyone*, much less one of Mrs Bennet's daughters, getting married, which has *not* reached the ears of Mrs Bennet herself? It can't have done or her attitude to Darcy would have undergone its dramatic meta-morphosis far sooner than it does. Her sister Mrs Philips can't have heard it either, for she would have passed it onto Mrs Bennet at once. It is all the more amazing because it is known to Sir William and Lady Lucas.

Does such a report exist? Is Mr Collins, for heaven knows what reason, *lying* when he informs Lady Catherine in conversation and Mr Bennet by letter about Elizabeth's impending marriage to one of the most illustrious persons in the land? Or, even more horrible, has Jane Austen blundered. Can the puzzle be made sense of, Miss Glancy asks?

It is indeed puzzling. The Philips' house, Lucas Lodge, and Longbourn are all at a convenient walking distance from each other, and gossip flashes between them as fast as ladies can move between the establishments on their daily round of 'calls'. Why then are Mr and Mrs Bennet in the dark, and Mr Collins and Lady Catherine—the two most obtuse and imperceptive characters in the novel— all-knowing on this confidential matter? Mrs Bennet, of course, is obtuse and imperceptive on all subjects save one—her daughters' marriage prospects. If there were so much as a whisper about the possibility of a match for Elizabeth with Darcy, she would have been on fire with the intelligence.

There is, I think, a plausible explanation to Miss Glancy's puzzle. The most interesting character in the novel, who Jane Austen clearly does not have room to develop fully, is Charlotte Collins (née Lucas). Formerly Elizabeth Bennet's particular friend, Charlotte delivers her opinions with impressive authority. Early in Chapter 6, on the subject of the relation of the sexes, Charlotte utters what I think is the longest speech (the irrepressible Miss Bates excepted) of any woman in all the six novels. Laden with Johnsonian epigram ('if a woman conceals her affection with the same skill from the object of it, she may lose the opportunity of fixing him; and it will then be but poor consolation to believe the world equally in the dark', p. 17) it eloquently expresses Charlotte's pragmatic philosophy of sex:

'There is so much of gratitude or vanity in almost every attachment, that it is not safe to leave any to itself. We can all *begin* freely—a slight preference is natural enough; but there are very few of us who have heart enough to be really in love without encouragement. In nine cases out of ten, a woman had better shew *more* affection than she feels.' (p. 17)

Charlotte evidently believes that women are so socially disadvantaged that they must strike, like bandits, when opportunity offers—and if necessary dissimulate to get their prize. This is theory. It is put in practice when Charlotte takes Mr Collins on the rebound, only hours after Elizabeth has rejected his proposal of marriage. No woman with a scintilla of 'pride' would do such a thing. A 27-year-old woman driven by cold reason might—if the calculation were to her advantage. Such a woman would weather out the scorn of being thought second-best. Words will never hurt her. Charlotte's acceptance of Mr

Collins leads to a painful rupture between the former friends. Elizabeth is surprised by the intelligence into a wounding tactlessness:

'Engaged to Mr. Collins! my dear Charlotte,—impossible!'

The steady countenance which Miss Lucas had commanded in telling her story, gave way to a momentary confusion here on receiving so direct a reproach; though, as it was no more than she expected, she soon regained her composure, and calmly replied,'

Why should you be surprised, my dear Eliza?—Do you think it incredible that Mr. Collins should be able to procure any woman's good opinion, because he was not so happy as to succeed with you?' (p. 113)

Charlotte was quick to perceive subliminal attraction between Elizabeth and Darcy: 'I daresay you will find him very agreeable' (p. 81) she tells her friend, as early as Chapter 18. Over the years Charlotte has had to put up with many slights from the Bennets. In Chapter 5 Mrs Bennet, recalling the glories of the ball, complacently tells her:

'*You* began the evening well, Charlotte,' said Mrs. Bennet with civil self-command to Miss Lucas. '*You* were Mr. Bingley's first choice.'

'Yes;—but he seemed to like his second better.'

'Oh!—you mean Jane, I suppose—because he danced with her twice. To be sure that *did* seem as if he admired her—indeed I rather believe he *did*. . .'(pp. 14–15)

Women as clever as Miss Lucas do not forget these things.

Charlotte is off-stage for the second half of the novel— disposed of in the great marriage auction. But simply because she is not seen, we should not imagine that she is getting less clever or less sharp. Having to dine every evening with the Revd Mr William Collins and the Rt. Hon. Lady Catherine de Bourgh would turn a saint's milk of human kindness to vinegar. What we may assume is that an embittered Charlotte is determined to settle accounts with Elizabeth. She will poison Elizabeth's prospects, with

a pre-emptive strike that she knows will provoke an outburst of the young woman's incorrigible 'prejudice'. It is a
stroke of well-conceived malice. It fails—but only just. [1]

Postscript

Friends on whom I have tried this essay have responded sceptic-
ally—as does my correspondent Kathleen Glancy (see pp. 739–40).
The reason is that, supporting character though she is, most
readers form a benign image of Charlotte Lucas. Apart from
her one petulant outburst at Elizabeth's 'incredulity' when
she accepts her (Elizabeth's) discarded suitor, there is little on
the surface of the text to suggest malignity in the Miss Lucas
we see or the Mrs Collins of whom we see so little.

I cannot claim to be the first to have thrown a spotlight on
Charlotte. In 1997 Kim Damstra hypothesized a subplot in which
Charlotte is detected as 'scheming' behind the scenes throughout
most of the narrative, much more ambitiously and constructively
than my 'betrayer'. Dr Damstra's argument is subtle and sets out
to show in detail Charlotte as a mastermind behind much that
turns out well in *Pride and Prejudice*, not least her own success
in life.

I stand by my conception of a betraying Mrs Collins, although I
feel rather shakier about it than I once did. Readers can judge for
themselves by reading Dr Damstra's piece, which is published
as an article, 'The Case Against Charlotte Lucas' in *Women's
Writing* (Vol. 7, No. 2, 2000). Dr Damstra kindly sent me an early
draft of his article (well before I wrote this chapter). It is an
embarrassment to me that I did not acknowledge it in the earlier
impressions of *Who Betrays Elizabeth Bennet?* and I apologize
for the omission. Dr Damstra is, as far as I know, the first critic
to have written on the plausible, behind-the-scenes activities
of Charlotte Lucas and I look forward to reading other
puzzle-pieces from his pen.

The Oxford World's Classics *Pride and Prejudice* is edited by
James Kinsley and Frank W. Bradbrook, with an introduction by
Isobel Armstrong.

What do we know about Frances Price (the first)?

In a short note in the Jane Austen Society *Report* for 1982 Deirdre Le Faye points out a problem in the sketched background to *Mansfield Park*. It relates to the three Ward sisters, each of whom plays a significant, if supporting, role in the novel's plot.[1] The problem is laid out in Jane Austen's typically crisp *mise en scène* in the first two pages of the narrative. 'About thirty years ago,' the novel opens, 'Miss Maria Ward of Huntingdon, with only seven thousand pounds, had the good luck to captivate Sir Thomas Bertram, of Mansfield Park, in the county of Northampton' (p. 1).

Given its date of publication, 1814, the 'thirty years ago' reference would set Maria's happy catch in the 'season' of 1784 or thereabouts. Huntingdon and Northampton are neighbouring counties and the same social set attends the same events. We get a momentary glimpse of the family behind the bride, but no more than a glimpse: 'All Huntingdon exclaimed on the greatness of the match, and her uncle, the lawyer himself, allowed her to be at least three thousand pounds short of any equitable claim to it.'

The lawyer uncle and the dowry (albeit three thousand short) indicate professional respectability and a middle rather than upper station in life (the younger sons of the nobility go into the church or the army, not the law; noble wives bring with them property, not money). We know absolutely nothing of the Ward parents. But Maria,

we are told, 'had two sisters to be benefited by her elevation
... Miss Ward and Miss Frances'. The honorific 'Miss
Ward' (without the Christian name, which we never know)
indicates that she is the oldest of the trio. 'Half-a-dozen'
years later (1790-ish) Miss Ward, having now been somewhat long in the shop window, is obliged to lower her
sights and accept 'the Rev. Mr Norris, a friend of her
brother-in-law with scarcely any private fortune'. Why
Miss Ward, unlike her younger sister, has little or no
dowry we are not told.

Sir Thomas's patronage gives Mr Norris a living in the
environs of Mansfield Park in Northamptonshire and
with it a comfortable income of 'a very little less than a
thousand a year'. The Norrises have no children (and are
careful not to adopt one, in the shape of young Fanny),
and we may suppose that Mrs Norris takes wise precautions against any expensive little strangers. The 'less than
a thousand pounds' does not admit of such extravagances.
The less constrained Lady Bertram has four children: two
boys and two girls. It is, as Deirdre Le Faye plausibly surmises, at some point shortly after Mrs Norris's wedding
that the third sister, Frances Ward, makes her disastrous
choice of partner. She 'married, in the common phrase,
to disoblige her family, and by fixing on a Lieutenant of
Marines, without education, fortune, or connections, did
it very thoroughly'. He was evidently wholly unknown to
the Ward family. Sir Thomas can do nothing in this
unfortunate case. Lieutenant Price's line of profession
'was such as no interest could reach'. And, to seal the
rupture, there is a sharp exchange of letters in which
Frances makes 'disrespectful reflections on the pride of
Sir Thomas'.

Over the next eleven years, in their series of married
quarters in Portsmouth, Mrs Price goes on an orgy of
childbearing, with nine lying-ins. A contrite letter gets

a helpful response from Mansfield Park—leading to the launching of the two oldest Price children, William and Fanny, into more respectable courses of life than their parents. Frances's husband has not risen in his branch of the service. He is still only a lieutenant—indeed is no further forward ten years later, in 1808-11, the date at which the novel proper begins.[2]

The questions which Deirdre Le Faye asks are the following:

1. How did Miss Frances Ward—of Huntingdon—fall into the way of a lieutenant of marines in faraway Portsmouth? Unlike Northampton, this is not neighbouring territory.

2. Did Frances Ward elope with Lieutenant Price, prefiguring Maria Bertram's conduct? That she did is hinted by the tart comment: 'to save herself from useless remonstrance, Mrs Price never wrote to her family on the subject, till actually married' (p. 1).

3. 'Why cannot Sir Thomas's 'interest' help Lieutenant Price?

Le Faye surmises, plausibly, that Frances cannot have been working as a governess in Portsmouth—that being the only line of away-from-home work which someone of Miss Ward's class might take up. As we see her in later life, Mrs Price is incompetent to have filled such a role. She might, conceivably, have been visiting relatives in the south-west. But, as Le Faye sees it, elopement is the most likely scenario. It is a case of 'family history repeating itself'.

Le Faye's speculations are as convincing as any speculation can be. We assume, if only from the evidence of the sexual activity, that there was a kind of Mellors-the-gamekeeper masculinity about Lieutenant Price which made him irresistibly attractive to the lawyer's genteel niece. Those manly attractions had probably worn rather thin by the time of her ninth pregnancy—but by then Frances's lot was fixed.

There are some other deductions to be drawn from the parental Price plot, once it is brought to the reader's attention. The marines were responsible for discipline in the shipyards and ports. The navy—manned as it was in large part by press-ganged crews, with discipline enforced by the cat—was in a constant state of seething discontent and mutiny. Major garrisons of marines were kept in the principal ports such as Chatham and Portsmouth.

An oddity of the marines was that commissions were not by purchase after 1755 (they remained so in the regular army until the 1870s). This explains why it is that Sir Thomas cannot instantly help Lieutenant Price. As a branch of the services, the marines had earned great credit for their part in putting down the 1796 mutinies at the Nore and Spithead. It is more than likely that Lieutenant Price played a part in this operation. As a mark of favour, they were renamed the 'Royal Marines' in 1802, although Jane Austen does not use that title.

It is clear from Fanny's experiences when she is given her punishment posting to Portsmouth that Lieutenant Price is not a pleasant paterfamilias. He drinks in his mess, is coarsely sarcastic at home, neglects his worn-down wife, and evidently rules his wayward children harshly. But, as Fanny notes in her father's conversations with Henry Crawford, on duty he is not unprepossessing in public. He would seem to be a good marine.

We have, I think, to leave the courtship of Frances Ward and Lieutenant Price in the dark in which Austen chose to keep it. But an authorial motive can be discerned in Austen's having made her heroine's father a marine. The marines were famous throughout their long history, but particularly after 1796 (and particularly at Portsmouth), as the embodiment of martial discipline of a ruthless kind.

It is as just such an act of discipline that mutinous Fanny is sent back to Portsmouth, to bring her to her senses with—metaphorically—a touch of the lash (it is not inconceivable that she might get the odd physical cuff from her drunken lieutenant father).

Meanwhile—ironically—discipline at Mansfield Park falls to pieces with the elopements. I think Jane Austen chose a lieutenant of marines not because she had, stored away in the back of her mind, some 'pre-plot' in which she saw the courtship of Miss Ward and her unsuitable suitor in any detail. She chose him because he fitted into the thematic pattern of her novel: *Mansfield Park: or Discipline.*[3]

The Oxford World's Classics *Mansfield Park* is edited by James Kinsley with an introduction by Marilyn Butler.

Apple-blossom in June—again

In *Is Heathcliff a Murderer?* I defended what is thought to be Jane Austen's most egregious 'error' in her fiction, arguing that it was no error at all if one read it aright. The company go for a picnic to the grounds of Donwell Abbey.[1] It is 'the middle of June', 'almost Midsummer', as we are precisely informed (the actual day can be calculated as the 22nd of the month). Strawberries are in prospect:- 'the best fruit in England—every body's favourite'. They are in plentiful supply, we understand. It has been a good crop—and on time. During a quiet moment on the expedition, standing on a hill, Emma gazes at the Surrey landscape spread out before her. It is 'a sweet view—sweet to the eye and the mind. English verdure, English culture, English comfort, seen under a sun bright, without being oppressive.'

Emma is content, not to say downright pleased with herself. She has successfully removed Harriet from the 'degrading' connection with her former suitor, Robert Martin of Abbey-Mill Farm. She is at this moment looking down on the farm. Her protege (who is also looking down at the farm) is now destined for much better things than Mr Martin:

There had been a time ... when Emma would have been sorry to see Harriet in a spot so favourable for the Abbey-Mill Farm; but now she feared it not. It might be safely viewed with all its appendages of prosperity and beauty, its rich pastures, spreading flocks, orchard in blossom, and light column of smoke ascending. (p. 326)

As the notes to the Oxford World's Classics edition comment: 'the anomaly of an orchard blossoming in the strawberry season' was noticed by some of the novel's first readers, notably Jane's brother Edward who archly requested: 'Jane, I wish you would tell me where you get those apple-trees of yours that come into bloom in July'. None the less, the novelist did not correct 'the mistake' because, the family surmised, 'it was not thought of sufficient consequence'.

It is, of course, late June, not July. None the less, the anomaly is singular—Miss Austen, as R. W. Chapman notes, seldom makes such mistakes. But it is not, I suggested, 'a mistake'. Not, that is, if one takes into consideration that there are three 'anomalies' in the offending sentence: (1) the late blossom; (2) a fire burning at Abbey-Mill Farm on a scorching day in late June; (3) that "spreading flocks" would more plausibly refer to the lambing season, in early spring, when flocks enlarge dramatically'.

We should, I suggested, read the passage not as a snapshot of what is before Emma as she stands on the hill, but as a montage—a sequence of the turning seasons. I directed the reader to a passage which performs the same kind of trick in a poem by one of Austen's favourite poets, William Cowper, in which the poet, looking on a winter landscape, simultaneously sees features of spring and summer. What Austen implies by the 'spreading flocks, orchard in blossom, and light column of smoke ascending' sentence, I suggest, is: 'now Harriet, so effectively separated from Mr Robert Martin, the occupant of Abbey-Mill Farm, is immune to its varying attractions over the course of the year—whether in spring, early summer, midsummer; or autumn.'

I received a number of polite objections to this admittedly ingenious line of argument—on the score of all three anomalies'. As to the sheep, Claire Lamont commented: 'I query whether the reference to "spreading flocks" is seasonal. Sheep spread out in the field when they are content, and huddle together when they are frightened. Shepherds take pleasure in seeing their flocks well spread out and it is just the sort of reference the passage needs to imply prosperity and calm.' It's a nice point, although not entirely clinchingly so, I think.

Dr Lamont also has some misgivings about the June kitchen fire:

I don't know what happened to summer fires in Surrey; if the passage were set further north I would not hesitate to believe that a fire would be burning all the year round, and that the summeriness of the scene is indicated by 'light column' as a description of its smoke. I am haunted by references to domestic fires which are never let out until the goodwife dies—but they are probably all Scottish references.

Deirdre Le Faye (as the editor of the most recent edition of Austen's letters) also took exception to the 'anomaly' of summer smoke—claiming that it was a perfectly normal feature of the rural landscape:

There would have to be a fire all the year round in the kitchen for cooking and hot water. Kitchens *were* notoriously hot and awful; that's why cooks had a free beer issue as well as wages, and are always portrayed as red-faced and sweaty. Abbey-Mill Farm would have been big enough, and the Martins rich and socially rising enough (they are quite literate, and Mrs Martin's daughters go to the respectable boarding school in Highbury), to have a separate dining room.

The question is, I think, open. I have looked, for example, at John Constable's numerous studies of home-county farms and mills in summer, over the period 1810–20, and see no smoke whatever from chimneys.[2] This is not, of course, conclusive evidence. But, at midday, in midsummer, on a scorching hot day, there was, I suspect, little likelihood of a kitchen fire at Abbey-Mill Farm.

There is, however, one other piece of evidence, pointed out to me by Brian Nicholas. As Professor Nicholas observes:

> In spite of the weather, a fire had been kept going 'all the morning' at the Abbey, in preparation for Mr Woodhouse's arrival, and its 'slight remains' were still hot enough for Frank Churchill to sit as far away from them as possible when he arrived in the late afternoon. Emma is on Mr Knightley's ground [Abbey-Mill Farm is clearly close to Donwell Abbey], able to look both down to the farm and up to the Abbey. Perhaps the two are conflated in her idyllic vision (or maybe there was another damp-fearing hypochondriac living at the farm).

Professor Nicholas's acute observation is, I think, slightly favourable to my reading (although the 'conflated vision' hypothesis is beguiling). Clearly, fires are exceptional.

Another assault on my suggested reading came from an unexpected source—namely an article in the scientific journal *Nature*. It was brought to my attention by Professor Judah, of the Department of Physiology at University College London. The article in question is by Euan Nisbet, a member of the Geology Department, Royal Holloway College, London. In his article Dr Nisbet correlates weather references in the text of *Emma* with data from an early nineteenth-century survey of the British weather; *The Climate of London* (1833), by Luke Howard. Howard's book is 'one of the founding texts of British meteorology'. On her part, Jane Austen, as Dr Nisbet notes, was 'an acute observer of the weather'— an amateur meteorologist, one might go so far as to say. *Emma* was written over 1814–15, and can plausibly be seen as accurately reflecting the weather conditions of that period, specifically those of summer 1814. As Dr Nisbet notes:

The crisis in the book occurs just before midsummer's day. Austen makes the fascinating observation of an 'orchard in blossom', her famous 'error'. What are apple trees doing in flower in mid June? But is this error—or clue? The weather was unusual in 1814. The annual mean temperature was one of the coldest in Howard's record, and in May and June the means were colder than 1816, 'the year without a summer' after the eruption of the Tambora volcano in what is now Indonesia. In the cool spring of 1996, mild in comparison to 1814, apple trees flowered as late as early June. . . Is it presumptuous to attempt to match the weather to the novel? Possibly—an author has the light of imagination. But Austen is accurate. If she says the orchard was in bloom, then it surely was in bloom.[3]

This is very elegant research and, on the face of it, convincing. There are, however, some niggling objections to the hypothesis that Jane Austen is mirroring 1814's anomalous weather patterns in *Emma*. If it had been an unusually cold spring, one would expect some clue in the text such as 'orchards *still, even at this late time of year*, blossoming'. If Jane Austen were an acute meteorologist, she would surely offer some other incidental comment on the huge abnormality of the seasons. One also has to take into account that, internally, there are no references to a wintry spring elsewhere in Jane Austen's narrative, which covers a period of many months (in 1814, as Dr Nisbet would have us believe). There is snow at the Westons' Christmas party, which throws poor Mr Woodhouse into panic—but snow in December is not unexpected. In fact, as spring draws on the weather around Highbury seems generally clement. When Mr Weston reports that young Churchill is coming (it must be around March) he says:

'Frank comes to-morrow—I had a letter this morning—we see him to-morrow by dinner time to a certainty—he is at Oxford to-day, and he comes for a whole fortnight; I knew it would be so. If he had come at Christmas he could not have stayed three days; I was always glad he did not come at Christmas; now we are going to have just the right weather for him, fine, dry, settled weather. We shall enjoy him completely . .' (p. 168)

A couple of paragraphs later, we are informed:

Emma's spirits were mounted quite up to happiness. Every thing wore a different air; James [the coachman] and his horses seemed not half so sluggish as before. When she looked at the hedges, she thought the elder at least must soon be coming out; and when she turned round to Harriet, she saw something like a look of spring, a tender smile even there. (p. 169)

Elder is the most forward of the common English trees. Normally elder would come into leaf in late February or March, and into blossom in late April or May. There is nothing here to suggest retardation of this normal sequence of events. Indeed, if 'come out' means 'blossom', spring would seem to be early this year. And, of course, there are the strawberries. If the year were so behind as for blossom to be on the apple trees, the picnickers would have no strawberries to picnic on. Unless, that is, Frank Churchill did one of his mysterious trips to France.

Beguiling as the 'freezing 1814' thesis is, it is—on inspection—less than overwhelmingly persuasive. The balance of evidence seems to me still to warrant reading the 'orchards in blossom' sentence as a montage of the turning year rather than a snapshot. But, clearly, not everyone will be convinced.

The Oxford World's Classics *Emma* is edited by James Kinsley, with an introduction by Terry Castle.

Walter Scott · *Rob Roy*

How old is Frank?

Middle-aged readers will take heart from the fact that Walter Scott did not publish his first novel until the age of 43, with *Waverley* (1814). Once started, the Wizard of the North made up for lost time, writing eighteen novels in ten years. Churning out three- and four-deckers at his factory rate of production (and he did much else than write novels) meant that Scott was occasionally obliged to be rough and ready in the finer points of construction. His fiction is speckled with piddling errors for his pedantic editor ('Dr Dryasdust', as Scott called the genus) to clear up. On his part, Scott did not fret about his slips, seeing them as a small tax to be paid for his speed of composition.

Rob Roy (1817) has a lot of narrative errors: the hero crosses over an historically yet-to-be-built bridge to reach the inn at Aberfoil where so many exciting events occur; he attends an historically yet-to-be-built church in Glasgow; and reads yet-to-be-published books. One possible explanation is that the narrator's memory may not be all it once was. Old men forget, and they embellish what they dimly remember. This explanation would be more convincing, however, if we knew exactly what was going on in Frank's life as he tells his story, and how old he actually is. In fact, we have only the sketchiest portrait of the narrator in old age (if it is old age). We apprehend that he is telling the adventures of his early youth by letter to his friend Will Tresham, and that all ends happily with his marriage to Die Vernon. But since then, we gather, great sadness has supervened:

How I sped in my wooing, Will Tresham, I need not tell you. You
know, too, how long and happily I lived with Diana. You know
how I lamented her. But you do not—cannot know, how much she
deserved her husband's sorrow. (p. 452)

This is tantalizing. Has Diana died? Has she run away?
Fallen into madness? Why, after a long and happy marriage, should Frank feel such 'sorrow' for his departed
wife—if she is indeed departed and was his wife. Are there
children? The novel breaks off before offering any explanation, with the terse editorial statement: 'Here the original manuscript ends somewhat abruptly. I have reason to
think that what followed related to private affairs' (p. 452).

It is all very baffling. Nor is it easy to work out exactly
how ancient a man is talking to us, because the evidence
points in a number of irreconcilable directions. In his
opening comments Frank implies that he is very far gone
in years. He is, he avers, in 'the decline of my life'; the
narrative is offered to those 'who love to hear an old man's
stories of a past age' (p. 65). The 'past age' is we may assume
1714–15, at which point Frank is 'some twenty years old'—
born in 1694 or 1695, we can calculate.

But how old is the 'old man' now talking to us? Here
again one encounters perplexing anachronism. On one
side, a string of references date the narrator's 'now' as the
1770s, which would put Frank in his mid-eighties. On page
72, for example, he refers to Postlethwayte's *Universal
Dictionary of Trade and Commerce* (1766) with a comment
that indicates he knows the date of its publication. On
page 89, Frank quotes from Adam Smith's *Wealth of
Nations* (1776). Most precisely, on page 96 he observes,
apropos of irresponsible politicians: 'We have seen
recently the breath of a demagogue blow these sparks into
a temporary flame, which I sincerely hope is now extinguished in its own ashes.' A footnote explains: 'This seems

to have been written about the time of Wilkes and Liberty'
(p. 461). Modern readers probably need to have it explained
that the allusion is to the period 1762–8, when John Wilkes
was most aggressive in his political provocations. The
remark about 'now extinguished' must refer to Wilkes's
expulsion from the House of Commons in 1769. All this
points one way: Frank is narrating probably around
1770–5.

How, then, do we account for another footnoted passage,
in Chapter 32 (p. 370), referring to the surprise attack by
Rob Roy's caterans on the English horsemen under Captain Thornton? Scott observes: 'It was not indeed expected
at that time, that Highlanders would attack cavalry in an
open plain, though late events have shown that they may
do so with success.' A footnote clarifies the allusion: 'The
affairs of Prestonpans and Falkirk are probably alluded
to, which marks the time of writing the Memoirs as subsequent to 1745' (p. 464). But it cannot be *long* after. The
phrase 'late events' suggests that the 1745 battles (chronicled by Scott in *Waverley*) are recent, not more than a
year or so since, one would guess. Certainly one would
never say 'late events have shown' about something that
happened thirty years ago.

Is Frank a quavering 80-year-old, writing in the 1770s? Or
is he in his full-throated early fifties, writing around 1748?
If we are to respond intelligently to the novel, we must
'hear' the narrator's voice, its timbre, tone, and strength.
Age is a factor. Perhaps there are two layers of composition, one belonging to the 1740s, the other to the 1770s.
But why, then, talk about 'the time of writing the Memoirs'
as one time? Why, as in the other cases mentioned, high-
light this awkward anomaly with a footnote which only
serves to plunge the reader into gratuitous quandaries?

It would be plausible to argue, as an older school of
commentators liked to, that *Rob Roy* is a hopelessly

ramshackle piece of fiction with some wonderful moments and memorable characters. Or one might argue, as some modern critics have, that the flawed surface of *Rob Roy* is artful in the highest degree. Scott, that is, carefully inserted the errors into his novel as some Victorian geologists believed God put the fossils into the rocks.[1]

The explanation, in my view, lies between these extremes. Scott, as has been noted, wrote *Rob Roy* hurriedly. There was nothing exceptional about that; he wrote everything *currente calamo*. But *Rob Roy* faced other difficulties than the routine tight schedule. In March, a couple of months before signing the contract for his new novel, Scott had been taken ill with stomach cramps at a dinner party. He rose from the table with a scream of agony which electrified his guests, and for a few days seemed to be at death's door.

Over the next few months, as he embarked on *Rob Roy*, he remained ill and 'weak as water'. R. P. Gillies, who saw him in Edinburgh that summer, describes a living corpse, 'worn almost to a skeleton'. Scott told Gillies: 'the physicians tell me that mere pain cannot kill; but I am very sure that no man would, for another three months, encounter the same pain and live.'[2] The cramps (which turned out to be gallstones) continued into the autumn. Against the recurrent agony, Scott took dangerously large amounts of opium. But despite the devastating pain, and the dulling narcotics, he raced ahead with his novel in hand. The first volume of *Rob Roy* was finished in August, and the whole thing wrapped up by December. It was, as Scott told his friend and printer James Ballantyne with characteristic understatement, 'a tough job'.

What I suspect happened was that Scott, attacked as he was by pain and dulled by painkillers, slipped without noticing btween his own age (47 in 1817) and Frank's putative four-score and more. Listening to *Rob Roy* we should school ourselves to hear an aged narrator but, every so often, allow the rich mellow tones of middle-aged Walter Scott (with their Lowland burr) to break through. How old is Frank? It's hard to say.

The Oxford World's Classics *Rob Roy* is edited by Ian Duncan.

Clachan of Aberfoyle[3]

Mary Shelley · *Frankenstein*

━━

Why is the monster yellow?

━━

Simon Levene writes wittily in response to *Is Heathcliff a Murderer?*, correcting an error and pointing out an unobserved other puzzle in *Frankenstein*:

without seeming ragingly pedantic, may I mention p. 27, where you refer to a 'metallic bolt' attaching [the monster's] head to its body? In fact, it is not a bolt but the ends of the electrodes through which the electricity flows into the monster. More to the point, why should Victor Frankenstein ever *construct* a body? Why wouldn't *one* body have done quite as well?

Mr Levene's 'one body' question sticks in the mind. After wrestling with it, I would offer two possible lines of explanation. The first is to be found in the epigraph from Milton's *Paradise Lost* (x. 743–5) on the novel's title-page:

> Did I request thee, Maker, from my clay
> To mould Me man? Did I solicit thee
> From darkness to promote me?—

As commentators have often noted, Mary Shelley's novel conforms closely to Milton's epic as source text. We are not shown how God creates Adam from his constituent clay. But it is quite clear how he creates that lesser order of creation, Eve. He takes a body-part—Adam's rib—and out of that *membrum* makes woman. This notion of making the whole new person out of the part(s) of another person is clearly alluded to in Mary Shelley's description of the scientist-hero's midnight raids: 'I collected bones from charnel houses; and disturbed, with profane fingers, the tremendous secrets of the human frame ... The

dissecting room and the slaughter-house furnished many
of my materials' (pp. 36–7). Victor seems to be doing two
things here: investigating the anatomy of the 'human
frame' and assembling the wherewithal—the 'Adam's
ribs'—with which to compose such a frame.

The other objection to Victor's using an intact body for
his monster is theological. There are any number of
accounts of hanged criminals being taken down too soon,
and crossing back from death to life. Much fiction has
built itself around the conceit.[1] As Marilyn Butler notes
in her Oxford World's Classics edition of the 1818 text:

a number of well-known attempts had been made to induce life,
whether by animating single-cell creatures, such as body para-
sites, or by reviving dead bodies, including executed criminals.
Some of the best-known were associated with Luigi
Galvani. (p. 255)

The problem (for Mary Shelley) was that such back-
from-the-dead survivors—prisoners taken down prematurely from the gallows, for example—come back not
as newborn babes, but as their former selves. So too, if
Galvani had succeeded in reviving a dead body it would
have returned as its former self. Shelley wanted 'creation',
not 'resurrection'. It was necessary to dissolve the pre-
existing personalities (and by implication the multiple
'souls') of the bodies from whom the miscellaneous parts
were gathered.

Significantly, this is an area in which the archetypal film
version, that by James Whale in 1931, goes directly against
Mary Shelley's portrayal. The deformed servant, Fritz, is
shown breaking into the anatomy laboratory to steal a
brain, and—having accidentally dropped the brain of a
genius—takes instead that of a psychopathic criminal
(without telling his master). We are to assume that traces
of the criminal's previous criminality infect the monster,

although Whale does not follow up this line in the melo-dramatic middle and late sections of the film narrative.

It would be interesting to know how Mary Shelley imagined that a brain could be transplanted, without trailing clouds of the previous owner's character. She sidesteps the problem by artfully hazing over the descrip-tion of how the monster is actually made. And she goes on to imply (without ever clearly asserting) that the monster is less a kind of physiological jigsaw man—assembled from bits and pieces gathered from hither and yon—than a culture *grown* from a soup, or distillate, extracted from all the *membra disjecta* Victor has assembled from his mid-night raids. Wisely, perhaps, Mary Shelley does not go into detail about what goes on in Victor's 'filthy workshop' as, to their detriment, all film versions of *Frankenstein* have done.

Shelley does, however, go into some detail about the physical appearance of the newborn (newly assembled) monster:

It was already one in the morning; the rain pattered dismally against the panes, and my candle was nearly burnt out, when, by the glimmer of the half-extinguished light, I saw the *dull yellow eye* of the creature open; it breathed hard, and a convulsive motion agitated its limbs.

How can I describe my emotions at this catastrophe, or how delineate the wretch whom with such infinite pains and care I had endeavoured to form? His limbs were in proportion, and I had selected his features as beautiful. Beautiful!—Great God! His *yellow skin* scarcely covered the work of muscles and arteries beneath; his hair was of a lustrous black, and flowing; his teeth of a pearly whiteness; but these luxuriances only formed a more horrid contrast with his water eyes, that seemed almost of the same colour as the *dun white sockets* in which they were set, his shrivelled complexion, and straight black lips. (pp. 38–9; my emphasis)

Jonathan Grossman raises an interesting query about this. 'Last semester' (i.e. winter 1997), he writes:

I heard Professor Anne Mellor (whose work I very much like) give an interesting talk about Frankenstein's monster as an 'Oriental' menace. The problem with the argument was that it rested wholly on the thinnest of evidence: the creature's infamous yellow eyes and yellow skin. It seems to me a long way from these yellow eyes and yellow skin to the 'Yellow Peril'. How does one build an Asian body out of the corpses of Europeans?

I tend to agree with Professor Grossman—thought-provoking as Professor Mellor's thesis is. But, as Grossman says, the yellow eyes are perplexing. He pursues the problem, arguing that we should not assume 'that the irises themselves are a cat-like yellow'. As he confesses, Victor has raided slaughterhouses in his midnight expeditions. But it is extremely unlikely (unless he ventured as far afield as Korea, which would give substance to the Yellow Peril hypothesis) that he found cats' heads in the local shambles or butcher-shop. We assume, therefore, that it is the 'whites' of the monster's eyes which are yellow—or 'dun white'.

Grossman concludes that 'the poor creature is born with jaundice.' He called up a doctor friend, who confirmed that 'the whites of the eyes as well as the skin do turn yellow and that it is one of the main signs of jaundice. Diagnosis: a liver condition? Bad liver transplant?'

There is a persuasive biographical explanation for the yellow monster being jaundiced. As commentators (particularly feminist commentators) have noted, the creation scene in *Frankenstein*, and the concomitant disgust of Victor for his creation, can be read as an allegory of post-natal shock and depression. In February 1815 Mary Wollstonecraft, aged 17, gave premature birth to a daughter—Clara—who died a few days later; of what, we do not know.

Frankenstein

515

In January 1816 she gave birth to a son, William. Mary and Percy Shelley did not marry until December 1816. While she was completing *Frankenstein* in May 1817 Mary was pregnant with her third child. She knew about natal depression and was familiar with the physical appearance of newborn children.

Jaundice is a very common and (to the mother's eye) alarming condition in newborn babies. One (or both) of Mary's children may well, one assumes, have been born with it, possibly fatally in Clara's case. Interestingly, no later references seem to be made to the monster's having a yellow skin or eyes. He is 'ugly' and 'loathsome', but not—as far as we know—'yellow'.

The Oxford World's Classics *Frankenstein* is edited by Marilyn Butler.

Charles Dickens · *Oliver Twist*

═══

Does Dickens lynch Fagin?

═══

The above title might be rephrased: 'Does Dickens *lynch* Fagin? or is "the Jew" executed fairly, after due process of law?' In *Can Jane Eyre Be Happy?* I pointed to what struck me as a number of oddities in the trial which climaxes *Oliver Twist*. Specifically:

(1) We are never distinctly told what offence (let alone what capital crime) Fagin has committed.

(2) Dickens gives no direct description of the court proceedings, focusing instead (with great literary effect) on Fagin's distracted reactions.

(3) By the best judgement we can make, Fagin is convicted on 'conspiracy' to murder Nancy, or 'complicity' in that murder (which is in fact committed, without Fagin's knowledge, by Bill Sikes). Fagin himself had nothing to do with the deed, told no lies to Bill Sikes who *did*, most brutally, commit the murder, and is—apparently—sent to the gallows on the perjurious evidence of Noah Claypole.

(4) As a petty criminal, bent on saving his own skin, Claypole's testimony would seem self-evidently tainted. 'A good defence counsel', I wrote, 'could discredit him very easily'.

(5) The trial takes place on Friday. As soon as the verdict is announced, before sentence is passed, the crowd outside the courtroom utter 'a peal of joy . . . greeting the news that he would die on Monday'. This is disquieting: 'Two weekend days would hardly seem to give the remotest chance of the appeal to which Fagin surely has a right. And how does the crowd outside *know* that Fagin will be hanged on Monday, before the judge has put on his black cap and pronounced sentence? Are they deciding the matter? Is the bigwig judge dancing to the mob's savage tune?'[1]

The whole process was, I suggested, a legal lynching; Fagin ('the Jew') is railroaded to the gallows because the mob—infuriated by accounts of the inquest in the press—has been denied revenge on Sikes and want a scapegoat to satiate its appetite for blood: 'Jewish blood?—so much the better!'. Injustice was done. Fagin should certainly have been transported, or imprisoned: he is a criminal.[2] But hanging seems vindictive and racially motivated.

A number of readers wrote to point out that there is, in fact, a clear premonition of the charge Fagin will be brought up on and its inevitable outcome. Donald Hawes directed my attention to Kags's forecast in Chapter 50: 'if they get the inquest over, and Bolter [i.e. Claypole] turns King's evidence: as of course he will, for what he's said already: they can prove Fagin an accessory before the fact, and get the trial on Friday, and he'll swing in six days from this, by G—!' (p. 405). Professor Hawes adds: 'George Saintsbury (in his chapter on Dickens in the *Cambridge History of English Literature* quotes G. S. Venables: Dickens hanged Fagin for being the villain of a novel.'

Missing Kags's prediction is a culpable oversight but does not, I think, invalidate the main points about the unfairness of the legal process which Dickens describes. A letter from Andrew Lewis, Senior Lecturer in Laws at University College London, did, however, hole my arguments below the waterline. His letter is so interesting (and informative) tha I will quote it at length. 'Dear Professor Sutherland,' Mr Lewis began:

I hope you will forgive the following mixture of comment, query and sheer impudence from a colleague. I have just been reading, as holiday pleasure, your latest Puzzles in Literary Fiction and cannot forbear to add to the perils of the terrible meshes of the law!

In your chapter on Fagin you seem to me to fall into error

regarding the management of criminal trials in the mid-nineteenth century. You are surely right that it is for the murder of Nancy that we are to suppose that Fagin is tried, though for inciting rather than conspiracy, and so as a principal. You are wrong to think that he could not be an accomplice, legally-speaking. The penalty for this was death by hanging and was, as now with life imprisonment, fixed by law, giving the judge no option but to pass sentence of death. It is for this reason that the crowd outside can anticipate the sentence on hearing of the verdict.

The judge had no option to sentence to death for murder and no control over the timing of the execution unless he ordered a respite. There were no appeals from criminal convictions before 1907—though a judge could refer a case to higher authority if he were troubled by a result. Fagin therefore has no prospect of such a hearing. He could seek a royal pardon, but again these requests were normally channelled through the judge. The judge shares our prejudices against Fagin and has no cause to postpone giving sentence and no reason to order a respite of execution. Execution will therefore proceed as normal at the conclusion of the current court sittings: we are to suppose therefore that Fagin's is the last trial in the current session which will end on Friday or Saturday—courts sat on Saturdays in the nineteenth century. Execution of sentences will commence on the next weekday, the date of which will have been known well in advance, not least to those in the crowd intending to view the scene. There are two other incidental problems with your account. You suppose that Fagin could argue 'in his defence' that he never expressly mentioned Nancy's informing on Bill. As noted above, even if demonstrated this seems irrelevant on a charge that he incited Bill to kill her. But in any case prisoners were barred from giving evidence in their own behalf before 1898. They were allowed to make unsworn statements from the dock but it can be assumed that these carried little weight. Moreover before 1836 those accused of felony were not allowed counsel except to argue legal points. There is plenty of evidence that this provision was frequently ignored in practice, even in the Old Bailey, but barristers had to be paid and we cannot discount the possibility that Dickens intends us to understand that the wicked old Jew is being deprived, quite lawfully, of even such protection as a 'good defence counsel'.

This comprehensively contradicts the case I was making. More importantly, however, it vindicates Dickens's accuracy. The novel is, I think, much stronger for Mr Lewis's expert commentary. There was, however, a related puzzle which seemed to complicate Lewis's explanation. Dickens's *A Tale of Two Cities* has in its early chapters a vividly described criminal trial, again at the Old Bailey. It is a 'Treason Case', prosecuted by the Attorney-General, for which the penalty at this period (the late eighteenth century) is 'quartering'. As one of the vulturous spectators tells Jerry Cruncher:

'he'll be drawn on a hurdle to be half hanged, and then he'll be taken down and sliced before his own face, and then his inside will be taken out and burnt while he looks on, and then his head will be chopped off, and he'll be cut into quarters. That's the sentence.'

'If he's found Guilty, you mean to say?' Jerry added, by way of proviso.

'Oh! they'll find him guilty,' said the other. 'Don't you be afraid of that.' (p. 70)

But Charles Darnay is not found guilty of being a French spy. He is saved by his resourceful defence team, Messrs Carton and Stryver. By cross-examination of the (suborned) witness, Stryver gets him to admit he could not tell the difference between Darnay and Stryver's learned friend, Mr Carton. Therefore the identification of Darnay as the man who committed the alleged act of espionage is invalid. 'The upshot . . . was, to smash this witness like a crockery vessel, and shiver his part of the case to useless lumber' (p. 86). Darnay is duly acquitted. Now it is quite clear that in this case at the Old Bailey, the same court where Fagin will be tried in fifty or so years time, the prisoner most certainly *does* have a defence counsel. And that counsel can demonstrably cross-examine witnesses aggressively and to great effect. If Darnay can be saved from quartering by his resourceful defence counsel, why can't Fagin be saved from hanging?

I put this apparent anomaly to Andrew Lewis. Again, however, I had underestimated the meshes of the law. 'Dear Professor Sutherland,' he replied:

I am currently down in Cornwall so do not have a *Tale of Two Cities* with me. However from what you say about the charge against Carton it is probably Treason. For this (more serious) category of crime counsel seemed always to have been allowed (as they were in cases of misdemeanour). No one seems to have a satisfactory explanation for this apparent anomaly.

What one deduces from this is that, where the law was concerned, Dickens was more historically accurate than a modern reader may appreciate. And where the law itself was not consistent, or even 'an ass' (as in the anomaly about prisoners not being able to testify in their own defence), Dickens faithfully followed its idiocies.

The Oxford World's Classics *Oliver Twist* is edited by Kathleen Tillotson with an introduction by Stephen Gill. The Oxford World's Classics *A Tale of Two Cities* is edited by Andrew Sanders.

Charles Dickens · *A Christmas Carol*

———

How do the Cratchits cook Scrooge's turkey?

———

At Christmas 1997 I set ten puzzles from Dickens's *Christmas Carol* for the readers of *The Sunday Telegraph*, offering a small prize (a 'shiny half-crown') for the best answers. The puzzles were:

1. In what sense is it a 'carol'? (even with the *sotto voce* addition 'in prose').
2. We are told that Scrooge is 'an excellent man of business'; what business?
3. How can Scrooge run his 'firm' (as it is called in the fifth stave) with just one, 15s. a week, clerk?
4. When Scrooge goes to his 'empty house' on Christmas Eve, there is 'a small fire in the grate; spoon and basin ready; and the little saucepan (Scrooge had a cold in his head) upon the hob'. Who has lit his fire and prepared his supper? The house is clearly deserted when the ghost of Marley appears—otherwise Scrooge's first act would be to ring for his servant.
5. What happens to the destitute woman and child collapsed opposite Scrooge's house in the small hours of the morning. The 1951 Alistair Sim-starring film gets round the problem by having her expire during the night. Which means that we should visualize a regenerate Scrooge blithely ordering his turkey from the 'clever boy' across two corpses. Dickens says nothing more of her. Has she, like Jo in *Bleak House*, been 'moved on'? Or was she, like the 'wandering spirits', visionary?
6. At the end of 'Stave One' and his interview with Marley's ghost, we are told that Scrooge 'went straight to bed, without undressing, and fell asleep upon the instant'. But when he

awakes in 'Stave Two' he is 'clad but slightly in his slippers, dressing-gown, and nightcap'. When did he undress?

7.   It is 'past two' (on Christmas morning, presumably) when Scrooge falls asleep. He wakes up on the stroke of twelve, for his encounter with the Spirit of Christmas Past. Is it Boxing Day, or has the interview with Jacob Marley (which took place between midnight and two) never happened?

8.   The Spirit of Christmas Past takes Scrooge back to critical moments in his former life. Why cannot he 'do a Marley' and tell his younger self to mend his ways. If he did so would he, Scrooge as we know him, be erased?

9.   The Spirit of Christmas Present allows Ebenezer to eavesdrop on the Christmas parties—those of the Cratchits, and of his nephew Fred and his wife. But, after his regeneration, these parties will be very different (Scrooge will physically attend Fred's, and Bob's will be dominated by the mysterious turkey). The vision of 'Christmas Present' is, in the event, not that. Nor is it Christmas Past, nor Christmas future. Is it then, Christmas Might-Have-Been? Where in time is it?

10.   In 'Christmas yet to Come' we foresee two deaths the following Christmas: Tiny Tim's (who is dead and about to be buried) and Scrooge's (who dies and is laid out on Christmas Eve). The postscript tells us specifically, that 'Tiny Tim did NOT die'—presumably thanks to Scrooge's providing expensive medical treatment. Will Scrooge die next Christmas, at the 'appointed' date?

I received a number of ingenious solutions to these puzzles. Many more than I had half-crowns. It was generally agreed that Scrooge must be a moneylender. The principal evidence is the exchange between husband and wife in 'Stave Four', when they anxiously enquire between themselves to whom their debt will be transferred, and the husband says: 'I don't know. But before that time we shall be ready with the money and even though we were not it would be bad fortune indeed to find so merciless a creditor in his successor' (p. 78). The 'time puzzles' were explained in terms of Scrooge's observation 'The Spirits have done it all in one night. They can do anything they like'—so, therefore, can Dickens the narrator do anything he likes with chronology. As for the midnight change of dress, it was suggested that, as old men with grumbling prostates do, Scrooge got up during the night. The preparation of Scrooge's gruel was probably the work of the slatternly laundress who is described gloating over the old miser's death in the last stave. She evidently comes in for a few hours each day and leaves before her employer returns from work. Tiny Tim will not die, it was agreed. Nor would Scrooge die next Christmas, on the basis of the remark in the last paragraph: 'it was *always* said of him, that he knew how to keep Christmas well' (my emphasis). That 'always' prophesies that Scrooge will be around for many years to come.

The most delightful and comprehensive set of answers came from Class 7E (aged 10 to 11) of St Christopher's School, Isa Town, in the State of Bahrain. Their English teacher, Mrs G. M. G. Stevenson, set the puzzles as a class assignment on her pupils' return from the Christmas Holiday. I would have disbursed a sack of half-crowns, if I'd had them, for Class 7E. I was particularly taken by a 'puzzle for you', from Anna Jordan, Jessica Salah, and Lily Constantine (see overleaf; the relevant pages in the Oxford World's Classics edition are 85–7).

Children often read adult novels in very rational ways. There is, I think, a thought-provoking puzzle here. Scrooge awakes at the beginning of Stave Five in his own bed. The sun is pouring into his bedroom and the church bells ('Clash, clang, hammer; ding, dong, bell. Bell, dong, ding; hammer, clang, clash!') are calling the London faithful to prayer. It is, presumably, eleven o'clock in the morning. Scrooge calls out from his window to the 'remarkable boy', and sends him off for the huge prize turkey ('it's twice the size of Tiny Tim').

Now we have a question for you!

On page 82-84 New Windmill Edition Scrooge sends the prize turkey to Bob Cratchit's house. However the turkey was unplucked & uncooked, so how on earth did they manage to cook it in time for Christmas lunch?

By our estimation, to prepare a turkey it takes at least 1 hour to pluck, 1 hour to clean and stuff and in the case of a very large turkey ,8 hours to cook - a total of 10 hours. In any case, would they have a big enough oven to cook it in?

SIGNED,

Anna Jordan
Jessica Salah
Lily Constantine
and
the sleuths of 7E
ST.CHRISTOPHER'S SCHOOL
BAHRAIN

We may wonder that a butcher's will be open at this hour on Christmas Day—and that the turkey should still be unsold. But open the shop is, and unsold the bird is. Scrooge sends the turkey off, by cab, to Camden Town. The poulterer's man is not, apparently, instructed to say that the bird comes from an anonymous donor. And he must know who is paying for it, or at least where the purchaser lives. But it is quite clear from Bob's demeanour the next day that he does not know that the turkey came from Scrooge. Another mystery. Did the Cratchits not think to ask about their mysterious benefactor? Do vast turkeys arrive at their door every holiday?

The turkey will not arrive much before noon. Scrooge does not go to the Cratchits for dinner—but to his nephew Fred's. Fred and his wife have their Christmas dinner at a 'civilized' hour, 'in the afternoon'. Unless they have a taste for raw poultry the Cratchits, as the sleuths of Class 7E point out, have many hours' preparation ahead of them. It is hard to think that they will be able to sit down at table until the small hours of the morning.

But, if we read carefully, this seems to be Scrooge's plan. As we are told:

> But he was early at the office next morning. Oh, he was early there. If he could only be there first, and catch Bob Cratchit coming late! That was the thing he had set his heart upon.
>
> And he did it: yes, he did! The clock struck nine. No Bob. A quarter past. No Bob. He was full eighteen minutes and a half behind his time. (p. 89)

Scrooge remembers that, in return for getting Christmas Day off, Bob undertook to be at work 'all the earlier next morning' (Boxing Day). And here he is fully eighteen-and-a-half minutes late. How did Scrooge know that Bob, as presumably he never is (otherwise he would be out of a job), would be late on this day of all days? Because Scrooge knew that the Cratchits would be up till all hours of the morning cooking that monstrous turkey. Scrooge, that is to say, may have undergone a dramatic change of heart. He may even have become the most un-Scrooge-like philanthropist. But he has not become a fool, nor has he lost all his malice—even though it now takes the form of malicious gamesomeness. Bob Cratchit's life in the office will not necessarily be a bed of roses henceforth.

The Oxford World's Classics volume of Dickens's *Christmas Books* is edited by Ruth Glancy.

W. M. Thackeray · *Vanity Fair*

━━

How many siblings has Dobbin?

━━

In a late 'Roundabout Paper' Thackeray makes a charming *mea culpa* on the subject of his propensity to small narrative error:

I pray gentle readers to deal kindly with their humble servant's manifold shortcomings, blunders, and slips of memory. As sure as I read a page of my own composition, I find a fault or two, half-a-dozen. Jones is called Brown. Brown, who is dead, is brought to life. Aghast, and months after the number was printed, I saw that I had called Philip Firmin, Clive Newcome. Now Clive Newcome is the hero of another story by the reader's most obedient writer. The two men are as different in my mind's eye, as—as Lord Palmerston and Mr Disraeli let us say. But there is that blunder at page 990, line 76, volume 84 of the *Cornhill Magazine*, and it is past mending; and I wish in my life I had made no worse blunders or errors than that which is hereby acknowledged.[1]

It is uncivil of the reader to dwell upon these little slips. George Saintsbury, noting Thackeray's tendency to misquote from memory, is even in two minds as to whether the conscientious editor should correct such errors. Saintsbury, in his authoritative 'Oxford' edition of the collected works, decided not to for the good reason that, as he says, Thackeray's misquotations are usually improvements—improvements, that is, on such sources as Horace, Shakespeare, or the Bible (Saintsbury had a high opinion of his author).

Thackeray's slips of name or detail cannot be said to be improvements of this kind, but they often witness to the suppleness of his narrative and his serialist's quick wits.

It is to catch in motion this agility in Thackeray that I want to follow the inconsistent line indicated in the above title. Put another way, what happens to Dobbin's siblings, and why?

Of the five principal characters in *Vanity Fair*, we know a lot about the family backgrounds of the Sedleys, the Osbornes, and the Crawleys. We know tantalizingly little about Becky's (unrespectable) and Dobbin's (respectable) families. It is with the Dobbins that I shall be concerned here. One can assemble a patchy family history, but it needs putting together from clues, hints, and circumstantial evidence. And there remain, after all the evidence is assembled, some teasing holes.

William Dobbin is introduced in Chapter 5 of *Vanity Fair* in a showcase chapter, 'Dobbin of Ours' ('Ours' being military slang for his regiment).[2] We know, from manuscript evidence, that the idea of Dobbin, as George Osborne's *fidus Achates* came late during Thackeray's five-year-long meditation of his 'novel without a hero'. In a flashback to William's and George's schooldays at 'Dr Swishtail's Academy' we learn about the respective backgrounds of these two 'not heroes'—one the embodiment of snobbishness, the other of good-hearted clumsiness. It is the early years of the nineteenth century (1801–2, as we can deduce). Osborne, the younger boy by a year or two, is a merchant's son. Dobbin is horribly bullied by his schoolfellows at Dr Swishtail's when it is discovered (after young Osborne 'sneaks' on him) that his father is a grocer. His 'nobler' schoolfellows tease the tradesman's son—whom they nickname 'Figs'—mercilessly. Not only is Mr Dobbin a grocer, he is—we deduce—a penurious grocer:

it was bruited abroad that [Dobbin] was admitted into Dr. Swishtall's academy upon what are called 'mutual principles'— that is to say, the expenses of his board and schooling were defrayed by his father in goods, not money; and he stood there—

almost at the bottom of the school—in his scraggy corduroys and jacket, through the seams of which his great big bones were bursting—as the representative of so many pounds of teas, candles, sugar, mottled-soap, plums (of which a very mild proportion was supplied for the puddings of the establishment), and other commodities. A dreadful day it was for young Dobbin when one of the youngsters of the school [Osborne], having run into the town upon a poaching excursion for hardbake and polonies, espied the cart of Dobbin & Rudge, Grocers and Oilmen, Thames Street, London, at the doctor's door, discharging a cargo of the wares in which the firm dealt. (p. 48)

A crisis comes in Dobbin's schoolboy life when he is writing a letter to his mother, 'who was fond of him, although she was a grocer's wife, and lived in a back parlour in Thames Street'. Cuff, the school 'cock', insults 'old mother Figs', provoking the great fight in which, to everyone's surprise, 'Figs' licks his opponent and his fortunes rise.

We jump forward to 1813. It seems that William Dobbin Sr.'s fortunes have risen even more precipitately than those of his son. George is now a lieutenant, and the slightly older Dobbin a captain, in a regiment of the line ('Ours'). George visits the house of his sweetheart, Amelia Sedley, and the subject of his inseparable comrade (and slavish admirer) Dobbin comes up. As usual, the company jeers. Dobbin has a lisp, big feet, and awkward manners. They recall an event, seven years ago, when he 'broke the punch-bowl at the child's party'. 'What a gawky it was!', Mrs Sedley recalls, 'good naturedly':

'and his sisters are not much more graceful. Lady Dobbin was at Highbury last night with three of them. Such figures, my dears.'

'The Alderman's very rich, isn't he?' Osborne said archly. 'Don't you think one of the daughters would be a good spec for me, ma'am?'

'You foolish creature! Who would take *you*, I should like to know, with your yellow face? [He is just back from service in

the malarial West Indies.] And what can Alderman Dobbin leave
among fourteen?' (p. 57; see also note, p. 892)

The 'fourteen children' reference was published in the *first*
serial version of *Vanity Fair*. Subsequent editions remove
it.[3] Mrs Sedley's 'three daughters' reference (with the
implication that there are many more than 'three of them')
was let stand, although it does not fit with what follows
later in the narrative.

We may note in passing that the 'fourteen children' reference identifies the Dobbins as a lower-class kind of
people. Genteel middle-class families like the Osbornes
(who have three children) and the Sedleys (who have two)
practised decent restraint—possibly even some primitive
form of birth control. It was only the socially undisciplined
lower classes who bred like rabbits.

None the less, it would seem that the Dobbins have in a
very short time risen meteorically in the world since those
black days when 'Figs' was the butt of schoolboy humour
at Swishtail's. Even with fourteen children to look after,
'Sir William Dobbin' still has enough to buy his son a
commission in 'Ours'. Army commissions were expensive
commodities in the early nineteenth century—it could
have cost the Alderman up to £5,000 to make his son a
captain.

From the coincidence of names we assume that William
is the oldest son and, in the nature of things, favoured.
English primogeniture will assure him the lion's share of
his father's fortune eventually—and clearly Dobbin *père*
will cut up extremely well. But one recalls that the grocer,
partner of the mysterious Rudge, could not even afford Dr
Swishtail's modest school fees. A parenthetic history of
Dobbin Sr.'s rise is given on page 59:

Dobbin, the despised grocer, was Alderman Dobbin—Alderman
Dobbin was Colonel of the City Light Horse, then burning with

military ardour to resist the French Invasion. Colonel Dobbin's corps, in which old Mr. Osborne himself was but an indifferent corporal, had been reviewed by the Sovereign and the Duke of York; and the colonel and alderman had been knighted.

He is a 'Colonel', not on the basis of any military prowess, but because he is paying for all the men's uniforms, steeds, and equipment.

Where has the Dobbin money come from? And how has 'Sir William' enriched himself so quickly? Not, surely, from rice, dried figs, and sugar. Fortunes were made in provisions—but not rapid fortunes. The key, I suspect, is that Dobbin and Rudge, as we are informed, dealt in 'oil'; and their premises in Thames Street were conveniently close to where the freighters carrying it would unload. In his description of the London background to George and Amelia's wedding, the narrator mentions the revolutionary changes in street-lighting which were taking place in the early years of the century (see p. 262). The first, and temporary, breakthrough was whale-oil street-lamps. In 1807 the 'New Patriotic Imperial and National Light and Heat Company' demonstrated the glories of coal-gas lighting in Pall Mall. This inspired a huge boom (although gas, as a source of lighting, was not introduced into homes for many years). We may assume that Dobbin & Rudge got in on the street-lighting boom early—initially as suppliers of whale oil.

Whatever the source of their sudden wealth, the Dobbin family is now middle class—if rather uneasily so. Thackeray duly subjects them to a little behind-the-scenes *embourgeoisement* himself. From subsequent passing references we deduce that Dobbin now has two (not three or more) unmarried sisters. On page 218 (Chapter 18) we learn their names: Miss Ann (the elder, apparently) and Miss Jane. There are, apparently, no married Dobbin sisters or brothers.

What happened to the other eleven children? Has some awful plague swept through Thames Street? One assumes that they have gone the same way as Dobbin's lisp and his big feet. Thackeray, as he penned the early chapters, saw a rather more dignified narrative future for William. As part of this 'dignifying' process, the rabbit-sized brood of Dobbins was thinned down to a genteel three offspring.

The Misses Dobbin are spiteful about the long-suffering Amelia (currently being neglected by George), and Dobbin jumps down their throats: 'You're the wit of the family,' he bitterly tells Ann (who has archly suggested that he should offer for Miss Sedley), 'and the others like to hear it.' That phrase, 'the others', suggests that some of those fourteen Dobbins have survived Thackeray's slaughter of the innocents. Who are they? Apart from Jane (whose name Thackeray seems to forget—he never mentions it again) we never know.

In Chapter 35 Sir William Dobbin makes his only direct appearance in the action when, at his son's request, he calls on Mr Osborne to try and soften the brutish merchant's attitude towards the just-widowed Amelia, his daughter-in-law. There are no physical details given—but we assume, from the act itself, that he is a considerate man. During his long years in India, Major Dobbin (the promotion must have been another expensive purchase) keeps in touch by letter with his 'two' sisters—both still unmarried. Ann—the 'clever' one—is his principal correspondent.

At Dobbin's instruction the Misses Dobbin (now forty-something genteel old-maids) call on Amelia in their splendid 'family carriage' and take young Georgy off to their 'fine garden-house at Denmark Hill, where they lived, and where there were such fine grapes in the hothouses and peaches on the walls'. Later this establishment is called 'Sir William's suburban estate' (p. 762). It is evidently very grand—much grander than the Osborne town-house in Russell Square. Denmark Hill, south of the Thames, was very much in the country at this point. It was a favourite residential area for tradesmen who had struck it very rich. Ruskin's family (John Ruskin Sr. had made *his* money in sherry) resided there, and the author gives a vivid description of the bucolic beauties of the place in the early chapters of his autobiography, *Praeterita*. It is pleasant to think of Sir William Dobbin raising his hat to Mr and Mrs John Ruskin when their carriages crossed paths at Camberwell Green.

The grown-up Dobbin does not, apparently, write to his mother. We assume that Lady Dobbin—who was fond of her boy at Dr Swishtail's when nobody else was—is a poor penwoman. Possibly she worked in the Dobbin & Rudge establishment as a servant, or perhaps she was Rudge's daughter. A later reference to the plural 'parents' (whom he does not immediately visit on his return from India, in his haste to get to Amelia, see p. 748) indicates that Mrs Dobbin is still alive in the early 1820s. The Misses Dobbin remain as spiteful in middle age as they were in youth. Ann (p. 550) maliciously informs Amelia that Dobbin is going to marry the irresistible Glorvina. Ann also maliciously writes to Dobbin to tell him that Amelia is about to marry the Revd Mr Binney. This bombshell it is which brings Dobbin back post-haste from India to England.

Apart from one interesting reference (which I shall come to later), the Dobbin family fades into the background over the next ten years of Thackeray's panoramic narrative. When he returns to England, as has been noted, Dobbin on his first visit to Amelia, 'did not like to own [to Amelia] that he had not as yet been to his parents' and his dear sister Anne'. 'Ann' has become 'Anne' (Thackeray's gremlin strikes again)—but what has become of Jane? Surely she is too far gone in age to have found a husband? And only a few months earlier, the 'Misses Dobbin' were visiting Amelia. Has Jane Dobbin suddenly died? Was it this that William gave as his excuse to Colonel O'Dowd for rushing back to England?

In his will Osborne leaves Dobbin, in recognition of his many years of support of Amelia and her son, 'such a sum as may be sufficient to purchase his commission as a lieutenant-colonel'. Dobbin, however, is obliged to wait until a vacant colonelcy comes up. He is still a major during the Pumpernickel episode, a few months later. Finally, on page 862, he gets the promotion after he has given up his allegiance to Amelia and returned to active service: 'I'll go into harness again,' he thinks, 'and do my duty in that state of life in which it has pleased Heaven to place me ... When I am old and broke, I will go on half-pay and my old sisters shall scold me' (p. 863). One notes that Colonel Dobbin has *sisters* (not just Ann) again.

Why, one wonders in passing, cannot Sir William buy Major William his promotion to lieutenant-colonel? Too much is happening, however, for the reader to dwell on such tangential questions. There is the tremendous reconciliation between Dobbin and Amelia ('God bless you, honest William!—Farewell, dear Amelia—Grow green again, tender little parasite, round the rugged old oak to which you cling!', p. 871). Amelia is now rich with her Osborne bequest.

Dobbin duly retires and has his half-pay pension. He is—as we deduce—the oldest son and principal heir of a very rich London merchant. Between them, Colonel and Mrs Amelia Dobbin should be very 'warm' indeed. But Colonel and Mrs Dobbin do not live like excessively wealthy people. 'When Colonel Dobbin quitted the service,' we are told:

which he did immediately after his marriage, he rented a pretty
little country place in Hampshire, not far from Queen's Crawley
. . . Lady Jane and Mrs. Dobbin became great friends—there was a
perpetual crossing of pony-chaises between the Hall and the
Evergreens, the colonel's place (rented of his friend Major Ponto,
who was abroad with his family). (p. 872)

The Dobbins seem well off; but not excessively so. They
rent, but do not buy a house. If he were Croesus-rich, Dobbin would surely go into politics. Instead of which, he bur-
ies himself in the country, in a house which is not his own,
writing a history of the Punjab.

What, one may idly wonder, has happened to all Sir William's wealth? A possible, if hypothetical, explanation
may be found in the narrative's most tantalizing reference
to the Dobbin family. It occurs in Chapter 46, ('Struggles
and Trials'), during the period of Dobbin's long Indian
exile—around 1825 in historical time. Amelia is still living
in poverty at Fulham, but has not yet surrendered Georgy
to his grandfather. The Dobbin ladies, at William's
instruction, are being kind to the impoverished widow.
They particularly want little George to visit them at Denmark Hill. Amelia suspects (correctly) that the Misses
Dobbin have been conspiring with Miss Osborne and
George's grandfather:

Of late, the Miss Dobbins more than once repeated their
entreaties to Amelia, to allow George to visit them . . . Surely,
Amelia could not refuse such advantageous chances for the boy.
Nor could she: but she acceded to their overtures with a very
heavy and suspicious heart, was always uneasy during the child's
absence from her, and welcomed him back as if he was rescued
out of some danger. He brought back money and toys, at which
the widow looked with alarm and jealousy: she asked him always
if he had seen any gentlemen—'Only old Sir William, who drove
him about in the four-wheeled chaise, and Mr. Dobbin, who
arrived on the beautiful bay horse in the afternoon—in the green

coat and pink neckcloth, with the gold-headed whip, who promised to show him the Tower of London, and take him out with the
Surrey Hounds.' (p. 583)

Mr Osborne ('an old gentleman, with thick eyebrows,
and a broad hat, and large chain and seals') is also lurking
around, Amelia discovers—scheming to abduct Amelia's
boy. But it is the Dobbins who attract the reader's attention. Sir William, of course, is the former alderman, Dobbin's father. He is still *nouveau riche* enough to be
delighted with his four-wheeled chaise. But who—one
wonders—is this dashing 'Mr Dobbin' with the colourful
clothes, the bay horse, and the gold-headed whip?

It is, one has to assume, one of Sir William's offspring
and—by the look of things—a prodigal son. William Dobbin (as Thackeray's illustrations make clear) is no model
of fashion:

A fine Summer Evening

This newly introduced 'Mr Dobbin' is, we assume a scapegrace younger brother: one who dresses like a 'swell', adorns himself with expensive jewellery, and rides to hounds in neighbouring Surrey. He presumably works in his father's firm ('Dobbin and Son'). Why did Thackeray insert a passing reference to this dandy brother so late in the narrative? He could, of course, be a ghostly survivor from the horde of fourteen which has been so ruthlessly culled. But 'Mr Dobbin' is so sharply etched here that one feels Thackeray must have had a role—or a potential role—for him to play. This is late in the narrative; Thackeray had lived with his 'people' for more than a year. Why add at this stage to his dramatis personae?

One knows that Thackeray was in some doubt as to how to wind up his story; whether, for example, to conclude in eighteen or expand to twenty numbers. In fact, he and his publishers decided on twenty instalments, and Thackeray devised the Pumpernickel interlude to create the necessary extension. One is very glad he did so; it is a delightful excursion. What Thackeray also held in reserve, I suspect, was a never-written (but there if needed) subplot in which Sir William Dobbin's business was to be ruined (as, in the event, Jos Sedley is ruined in the last pages, as was his father before him).

In this unwritten turn of plot, The 'dandy Mr Dobbin', scapegrace that he was, would take over the family firm, on the death or retirement of Sir William and ruin it. Amelia would take Colonel Dobbin not as a rich, but as a poor man—thus atoning for her 'selfishness' over the years, and repaying his kindness when *she* was penniless.

If he intended to follow this line, Thackeray in the event decided differently. The dandy Mr Dobbin never reappears after his one dashing entrance. Georgy never gets his visit to the Tower of London, nor his gallop with the Surrey hounds. It tingles, rather like a phantom narrative limb.

One would like to have seen more of the dashing Dobbin younger brother, cutting a swathe through the family fortune so virtuously acquired by his father.

The Oxford World's Classics *Vanity Fair* is edited by John Sutherland.

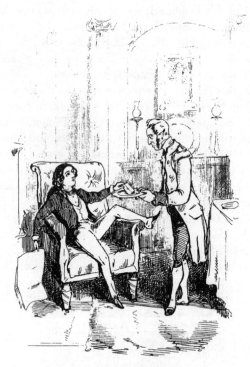

Georgy a Gentleman

==

Heathcliff's toothbrush

==

Judged purely by his actions Heathcliff is a villain: a wife-beater; a child-abuser, a white-collar thief, and—as I would maintain—a murderer. The murder, moreover, is a peculiarly sordid and cold-blooded crime. None the less readers, even those who accept that he probably killed his foster-brother Hindley, persist in seeing Heathcliff as a heroic and tragic figure. There is no obvious clash when glamorous matinée idols like Laurence Olivier and Timothy Dalton, or paragons of showbiz Christianity like Cliff Richard, play him on film, television, or stage.

An explanation for this 'sympathy for the devil' paradox is to be found in a muttered ejaculation of Heathcliff's, overheard by Nelly in the intensity of his grief and sexual frustration after Cathy's death: 'I have no pity! I have no pity! The [more the] worms writhe, the more I yearn to crush out their entrails! It is a *moral teething*, and I grind with greater energy, in proportion to the increase of pain' (p. 152; my italics). The key to our sympathy for Heathcliff, I have suggested, is to be found in that arresting phrase, 'moral teething', and what it implies—particularly to parents:

When a baby savagely bites its teething ring, it is because it (the baby) is experiencing excruciating pain from the teeth tearing their way through its gums. So Heathcliff may be seen to inflict pain on others (hurling knives at his wife, taunting Edgar, striking young Catherine, lashing his horse) only because he feels greater pain himself.[1]

Middle-class Victorian parents popularized the so-called

'teething ring' as a home remedy for the baby suffering the pangs of first dentition. The term is first recorded as a dictionary item in 1872 (Mark Twain, interestingly, is the first writer cited as using it). It is clear, however, that as objects of everyday nursery use teething rings had been around for many years before the 1870s. The rings—fashioned out of ivory, bone, or other semi-precious materials—were popular christening gifts throughout the nineteenth century. Since dentition can start as early as the fourth month of life they were, like silver spoons, matinee coats, or 'christening cups', articles of immediate practical use to the mother. In the early twentieth century vulcanized rubber was favoured, and latterly hard plastic.

For the Victorians, coral teething-rings had a particular vogue: hence Browning's little rhyme (a jeweller is speaking, trying to push his wares on an unwilling customer):

> 'Which lies within your power of purse?
> This ruby that would tip aright
> Solomon's sceptre? Oh, your nurse
> Wants simply coral, the delight
> Of teething baby, the stuff to bite!'

The teething ring, as standardized by Victorian mass production, combines a number of sensible design features. It is larger than a baby's mouth, so as not to be swallowed; it is circular, so little users should not poke themselves in the eye. It is hard, so that it should not be broken, dented, or abraded and become a harbour for germs. Ideally it is shiny (but not coated), so it can be rinsed in boiling water between use.

In *Wuthering Heights* this sudden snapshot of Heathcliff as a baby munching angrily on his little teething ring takes us back to his first appearance, a waif abused by his fostersiblings (including the young Nelly—who hates him as a usurper of *her* adoptive privileges). It evokes a reflexive pang of parental solicitude in the reader. This brute was once a helpless infant, we apprehend. The effect is to soften our feelings: the kind of 'goo-goo! diddums!' response which even the starchiest adults indulge in when presented with a babe in arms.

There are, in fact, two images embedded in Heathcliff's outburst—the merciless stamping and the baby's ferocious chomping of its toothless gums. One may digress for a moment on the worms, whose entrails Heathcliff imagines grinding into the dust. In the first place, it might be objected that earthworms don't have entrails as such ('intestines', 'bowels', 'internal organs') but a kind of digestive fluid. The digestive processes of *lumbricus terrestris* are strikingly simple. As M. S. Laverack puts it in *The Physiology of Earthworms* (New York, 1963): 'the alimentary canal is virtually a straight tube with little specialism in its structure, save for the muscular triturating gizzard.' C. A. Edwards and J. R. Lofty are even terser in *The Biology of Earthworms* (London, 1972): 'The alimentary canal or gut of earthworms is basically a tube extending from the mouth to the anus.' Nutrition-rich dirt goes in one end, pure dirt comes out the other.

I have never stamped on worms, although I have accidentally trodden on them. It wasn't entrails that came out, so much as squish and dirt. This objection to 'entrails' is pedantic, but I guarantee that if Ms Brontë submitted her novel to an American publisher in the 1990s, some bright-eyed young editor, hot out of Radcliffe or Yale, would insist on a change to bring Heathcliff into line with zoological fact.

On one level, Heathcliff's 'writhing' allusion is clearly to the proverbial truth that, given sufficient provocation, 'even a worm will turn'. One may also catch a faint Shakespearian echo of Lear's despairing cry: 'as flies to wanton boys are we to the gods, they kill us for their

sport.' Stamping on worms is, similarly, not an adult form
of rage. Nor is it 'babyish'—their aim isn't good enough,
and one wouldn't want to do it without shoes. Lear's 'wantonly schoolboyish' fits the action rather well.

There are other literary antecedents which may well
have been consciously or unconsciously in Brontë's mind.
The notes to the Oxford World's Classics edition of *Wuthering Heights* draw attention to a premonitory passage in
Scott's *The Black Dwarf*, a gothic effusion, more popular
with the nineteenth century than with us (p. 354). I suspect that Heathcliff's graphic and unpleasant worm-
stomping image may also owe something to another
famous hero-villain of nineteenth-century fiction. In 1832
Bulwer-Lytton wrote a novel about a glamorous 'scholar'
murderer, Eugene Aram. Sensationally, the novelist
implied in his text and declared outright in his preface
that Aram was justified in his homicide, because he was
intellectually superior to his victim and could make good
scholarly use of the money he stole. The novel caused a
terrific furore.[2] Eugene Aram was duly reissued, with a
new apologetic foreword and a 'morally' revised text, in
1840.

Aram was a historical character (1704–59). One of the
paradoxical features in his personality was that—
although a proven murderer and misanthropic in a fash-
ionably Byronic way—he was, in his everyday life, so
'benevolent' that he would even avoid stepping on worms.
As the narrator puts it in the novel:

A resistless energy, an unbroken perseverance, a profound, and
scheming, and subtle thought, a genius fertile in resources, a
tongue clothed with eloquence—all, had his ambition so chosen,
might have given him the same empire over the physical, that he
had now attained over the intellectual world. It could not be said
that Aram wanted benevolence, but it was dashed, and mixed
with a certain scorn: the benevolence was the offspring of his

nature: the scorn seemed the result of his pursuits. He would feed the birds from his window; he would *tread aside to avoid the worm on his path.*[3]

Bulwer-Lytton's preface confirms that this business about worms was a matter of historical record. 'That a man . . . so benevolent that *he would turn aside from the worm in his path* should have been guilty of the foulest of human crimes, viz.—murder . . . presents an anomaly in human conduct so rare and surprising, that it would be difficult to find any subject more adapted for metaphysical speculation and analysis.'[4]

The *Eugene Aram* controversy continued throughout the early 1840s—and was picked up, I suspect, even in remote Haworth, to be echoed in Emily Brontë's enigmatic murderer. Heathcliff, however, is—while similarly 'Byronic'—a more complex and callous conception than Aram. Unlike Bulwer-Lytton's murderer, he harbours no benevolent feelings towards earthworms. None the less, the oddly tentative '*yearn* to crush out their entrails' suggests that he may not actually do it. He merely *wants* to, when he sees them writhing. 'Is Heathcliff a worm-murderer?' Perhaps not.

The Aram and *Black Dwarf* allusions are speculative. But I felt I was on rock-firm ground with the 'moral teething' analysis. It was cut from under my feet (and arguably Emily Brontë's as well) by a letter from Dr Graham Turner. After some courtesies about how much he had enjoyed *Is Heathcliff a Murderer?*, Dr Turner launched the following torpedo:

I am afraid I must differ regarding the contents of the second paragraph on page 57. I should explain that before I retired I was a part-time consultant in paediatric dentistry at the Leeds Dental School. I fear you are repeating what is now widely regarded as an old wives' tale! The primary dentition in general will erupt from the age of four months to perhaps 30 months in late erupting mouths. Very often the initial eruption is accompanied by fever, malaise and what appear to be sore gums. Many mothers are familiar with the grizzling unhappy child, who may have a temperature of 38 or 39 degrees. An aspirin brings relief and, hey presto, the mother believes that the drug has relieved the pain. I believe this is nothing to do with the teeth.

Dr Turner, who has spent a lifetime learning about such things, declares that proverbial 'teething pains' are an 'old wives' tale', despite young mothers' beliefs to the contrary. The industry which turned out those thousands of Victorian teething rings was as redundant as the charlatans who sell 'Pixie's charms' to gullible magazine readers. Instead of 'the more the worms writhe ... entrails ... it is a moral teething', Heathcliff should have ejaculated something along the lines of:

The more the earthworms writhe, the more I yearn to squeeze out with my foot the complex liquid enzymes which serve to break down the nutritious proteins which they absorb through their body sacs. It is a feverish infection of the gums which frequently accompanies first dentition and which is frequently mistaken for 'teething pains', which of course it is not, although typically it coincides with the eruption of the infant's milk teeth.

One might go on from Dr Turner's 'Old Wives' fallacy to note as significant the fact that Emily Brontë was a spinster and that Haworth Parsonage was that rarity among Victorian households, a populous home without babies: neither Elizabeth, Anne, nor Emily bore a child; Branwell never married and Charlotte died in pregnancy before giving birth. What did the Misses Brontë—compared to, say, Mrs Gaskell—know, at first hand, about little strangers?[5]

But the 'old wives' tale' about teething is, I think, obstinately adhered to as folk-wisdom by a majority of young mothers, even those of the present day. My own wife, for instance, is convinced that our child underwent agonizing 'teething pains', and got relief from biting down on his teething ring (she contorts her face into a mime of his furious 'chomping' while telling me this). The guides to baby care to be found in today's high street bookshops confidently assert that babies undergo pain when cutting their teeth. They get relief from vigorous—even violent—chewing during this phase, the mother is instructed. Many baby-care manuals continue to recommend teething rings—scrupulously cleaned and chilled—but not frozen (just like James Bond's martinis).

These are not matters on which literary criticism can adjudicate. But Dr Turner's letter demonstrates what I have always believed—namely, that dentists read novels differently from academics. So do clergymen, deep-sea divers, and ballet-dancers. That is to say, we each of us as readers bring our life experiences to novels and find aspects of that life experience reflected in them. It is extremely valuable, and sometimes a salutary lesson, to see novels as others, with different backgrounds, see them.

Alerted by Dr Turner, one may think more about the subject. I cannot recall dental care featuring prominently in English fiction until Graham Greene, who is obsessed with teeth to an almost pathological degree. The Victorians, I think, were generally philosophical about dental decay—although the middle and upper classes (particularly the upper) were not entirely negligent of oral hygiene. As the German historian Treitschke scathingly noted, 'the English think Soap is Civilization'.[6] Doubtless the Victorians had the same illusion about toothpaste (or 'powder') and they were probably more careful than their continental neighbours. There is, for example, a telling moment in *Anna Karenina*, where Levin looks in the mirror and subjects himself to an honest physical inventory: Yes! There were grey hairs on his temples. He opened his mouth: his double teeth were beginning to decay.

He bared his muscular arms. Yes, he was very strong'
(p. 348).

Levin is an aristocrat, and, at 32, still a young man.
None the less, he clearly regards tooth decay in the same
fatalistic spirit that Vronsky (another; and more dashing
young man) regards his baldness. These are less marks
of premature decay than of physical maturity. For the
Russians, what mattered was not the man's outer physiological casing, but his 'soul'. We see things in a less philo-
sophically Russian way. No Hollywood director, contemplating a big-budget production of *Anna Karenina*, would
cast a bald actor for Vronsky, or a black-toothed actor
with halitosis for Levin.

Dr Turner's letter, in its wider context, makes one curious about Heathcliff's teeth. They are, manifestly, in
extraordinarily good shape for someone of his age (39,
going on 40), in his age (the early nineteenth century),
and—most importantly—his class of society (a 'slovenly
squire' is how Lockwood first describes him). Heathcliff is
routinely described during the course of the narrative as
grinding, clenching, and gnashing his teeth. That he has a
perfect set (as well as an ungrizzled and still-thick head of
hair) in middle age is revealed in Nelly's recollection to
Lockwood of finding his emaciated corpse at the window,
where he has starved to death waiting for his spectral love,
Cathy:

'I hasped the window; I combed his black long hair from his fore-
head; I tried to close his eyes—to extinguish, if possible, that
frightful, life-like gaze of exultation, before any one else beheld
it. They would not shut—they seemed to sneer at my attempts,
and his parted lips and sharp, white teeth sneered too!' (p. 335)

How one may wonder, has Heathcliff managed to keep
his 'sharp, white teeth' in such good condition? As a young
man at Wuthering Heights, reduced to the condition of a

serf by the malevolent Hindley, bodily cleanliness was the least of young Heathcliff's concerns. As Nelly recalls:

Nobody but I even did him the kindness to call him a dirty boy, and bid him wash himself, once a week; and children of his age seldom have a natural pleasure in soap and water. Therefore, not to mention his clothes, which had seen three months' service in mire and dust, and his thick uncombed hair, the surface of his face and hands was dismally beclouded. (p. 52)

It is hard to imagine his teeth gleaming, with Tom Cruise-like brilliance, through these dingy clouds. It is, in fact, a point of honour with young Heathcliff to be uncleanly. When Cathy seems to look down on him, he blurts out, 'I shall be as dirty as I please, and I like to be dirty and I will be dirty' (p. 53). All the signs are that Heathcliff's teeth will go the same way as Joseph's. From his 'mumbling', his dyspepsia, and his invariable diet of porridge, we gather that the old servant, 'hale and sinewy' though he may be, is as toothless as a hen.

After his mysterious three years' absence, Heathcliff returns 'transformed', as Nelly wonderingly observes. He is well dressed, neatly barbered, and 'athletic'. Above all, Heathcliff is 'clean'. We may plausibly infer that he has also acquired habits of dental hygiene in the great world. What would they be? There were, at the turn of the nineteenth century, three favoured modes of teeth-cleaning, described by J. Menzies Campbell in *Dentistry Then and Now* (Glasgow, 1963). The commonest utensils were toothpicks—a means of oral hygiene raised to a high level in ancient Rome, and in many ways still the most efficient technique. Shakespeare makes several references to toothpicks and, as Menzies Campbell notes, characteristically does so in such a way as to suggest that they were 'a symbol of gentility and not in general use in England'.

As Jaques's 'sans teeth' suggests in *As You Like It*, ordinary working-class folk who were lucky enough to survive to old age did not expect to bring their teeth with them. In the 1790s, when Heathcliff was on his travels, toothpicks would still have been associated with a gentleman's toiletry—like personal razors. As Menzies Campbell notes, 'In a 1791 newspaper advertisement, Sharp of 131 Fleet Street, London, was offering for sale an extensive choice of elegant tooth-pick cases'. The second approved method was a kind of primitive 'brushing', using the index finger covered with cloth. Sponges, with dentifrice lotions or powders to whiten the teeth, were a further refinement. It was Lord Chesterfield's habit, in the 1750s, to clean his teeth daily with a sponge dipped in tepid water with a few drops of arquebasade (an aromatic liquor). Brushes of the kind we are familiar with were available in the late eighteenth century, but again only to the upper classes. As Menzies Campbell points out:

In the late eighteenth century exquisite silver tooth-brush sets were manufactured and sold by certain leading silversmiths, located in both London and the Provinces. These consisted of: (a) a tooth-brush with bristles inserted in a wooden or ivory base; (b) a tooth-powder box with two compartments and closely adjusted lids, and (c) a tongue scraper resembling a very thin spatula. They fitted into straight grained red goatskin (usually) covered cases of an exterior design similar to one holding razors.[7]

The point is made that, on his return, Heathcliff has learned the gentlemanly use of the razor during his absence. On first seeing his face, Nelly notes that his cheeks are '*half* covered with black whiskers'. Other male denizens of Wuthering Heights, we gather from Lockwood's appalled description, have shaggy beards. Hareton's whiskers, for example, 'encroach bearishly over his cheeks'. We may assume that Heathcliff has brought back in his portmanteau with his razors a set of toothbrushes. The whiteness of his teeth—which Nelly observes on his corpse—is evidently helped by the fact that, unlike Joseph and Hareton (who are described sitting by the fire of an evening, pulling on their clay pipes 'like automatons', p. 312), he does not smoke.

It would be quite in character for Heathcliff's care of his teeth to be kept decently off-stage. Unlike continentals and Americans, who promiscuously picked their teeth in public (something that infuriated Dickens on his first visit to the USA almost as much as their public spitting), the British have always regarded cleaning teeth as a private act. As private, that is, as bathing; if not quite as private as defecation.

Heathcliff, for all his savagery, maintains a certain decorum, even *in extremis*. Like other 'slovenly squires', he almost certainly sleeps in his shirt of a night. But when Lockwood cries out during his nightmare in Cathy's room, and Heathcliff bursts in, he is described as standing 'near the entrance, in his shirt *and trousers*; with a candle dripping over his fingers, and his face as white as the wall behind him' (p. 24, my emphasis). Heathcliff is quite indifferent to the searing pain of the boiling wax seeping over his fingers, is at his wits' end with shock, but has none the less taken time to put on his unmentionables before rushing out of his bedroom. This may be Yorkshire, but he is no barelegged savage.

The Oxford World's Classics *Wuthering Heights* is edited by Ian Jack, with an introduction by Patsy Stoneman. The Oxford World's Classics *Anna Karenina* is translated by Louise and Aylmer Maude, with an introduction and notes by Gareth Jones.

Charles Dickens · *Dombey and Son*

Does Carker have false teeth?

Dentists, as I observed in the previous chapter, read novels differently. Under their specialist gaze, nineteenth-century fiction, particularly, reveals itself as even coyer about teeth—particularly artificial dentures—than about sex. The point is made by John Woodforde in his delightful chronicle, *The Strange Story of False Teeth:*

Embarrassment dates from the nineteenth century. By about 1840 laboured attempts at a natural appearance had brought false teeth into the category of the modern male toupeé: however blatantly artificial and loose, they had to be passed off as the work of nature ... The trials of wearers were made the more embarrassing by post-Regency puritanism which decreed it a vanity, like dyeing one's sidewhiskers, to resort to artificial teeth at all ... The extreme reticence enforced by propriety inhibited the Victorian novelists, despite their liking for lengthy descriptions of the person. Just as one might read all the works of Dickens or Thackeray without learning of the existence of prostitutes, so one might read a whole library of Victorian novels without learning that anyone's teeth were artificial. An occasional reference to fierceness was as much as convention would allow.[1]

Woodforde's peer into the mouth of nineteenth-century fiction is extraordinarily stimulating. The remark about 'an occasional reference to fierceness' means, I take it, that anyone who makes a 'show' of their gnashers should be suspected of falsity. It usefully directs us back to Thackeray's famous portrait of the Marquis of Steyne in *Vanity Fair* and the 'suppressed woodcut' which accompanies it:

The candles lighted up Lord Steyne's shining bald head, which was fringed with red hair. He had thick bushy eyebrows, with little twinkling bloodshot eyes, surrounded by a thousand wrinkles. His jaw was underhung, and when he laughed, two white buck-teeth protruded themselves and glistened savagely in the midst of the grin. (pp. 473–4)[2]

This is the early 1820s. It is not preposterous to suppose that Steyne has ornamented himself with what were called 'Waterloo teeth'. As Woodforde notes, there was at this period a healthy market

for human teeth plundered from the corpses of [the] battlefield by characters known as resurrectionists. These could sometimes deceive the eye provided they were kept steady on the gums and slightly covered by the lips. Even when a corpse was badly decomposed, its front teeth remained saleable ... Many people unknowingly wore teeth extracted from young men on the field of Waterloo ... Gruesome and downright unhygienic as the use of such objects now seems, it may be surmised that in the twenty-first century it will be thought equally unpleasant that the best wigs and toupees of the 1960s were made of human hair.[3]

It would surely cross the mind of an alert reader of 1847 that those prominent, half-covered 'buck [i.e. front] teeth' of the balding (his 'red' hair must be the result of dye), physically decayed, morally degenerate Steyne were not *his* teeth. They might even—to pursue the thought to a macabre conclusion—be George Osborne's, yanked from his stiffening jaws at Waterloo by some corpse-robbing resurrectionist.

Astute as Woodforde's comments are, he is wrong to imply that Thackeray and Dickens, to take the two eminent names he mentions, *never* mention false teeth in their fiction. They do. In Thackeray's *Pendennis*, for instance, old Major Pendennis (known irreverently as Wigsby' behind his back) has teeth as false as his magnificent head of hair. 'Chatter your old hivories at me, do you ... ?' his rebellious servant, Morgan, has the gall to ask him in their great showdown with each other (p. 878). The Major has a 'Wellington nose' and slavishly models his haughty manner on that of the Iron Duke. It is not far-fetched to imagine that he too has Waterloo teeth, to complete his Wellingtonian toilette.

In *The Virginians* (a sequel to *Esmond*) Thackeray actually builds a whole comic sub-plot around a false-teeth joke. The young American, Harry Esmond Warrington, comes to England and, in his innocence, is entrapped by the wiles of the not-so-young Lady Maria. Harry's aunt, Baroness Bernstein (formerly Beatrix Castlewood, the belle of *Esmond*, now a terrifying dowager), schemes to free her young relative from his unwise infatuation. The old lady is too cunning to attempt a frontal attack. As they play picquet one evening (Maria having retired, indisposed), the Baroness sets to work on the young man.

'That absurd Maria!' says Madam Bernstein, drinking from a great glass of negus, 'she takes liberties with herself. She never had a good constitution. She is forty-one years old. All her upper teeth are false, and she can't eat with them. Thank Heaven, I have still got every tooth in my head. How clumsily you deal, child!'

Deal clumsily, indeed! Had a dentist been extracting Harry's own grinders at that moment, would he have been expected to mind his cards, and deal them neatly . . . Maria is forty-one years old, Maria has false—oh, horrible, horrible! Has she a false eye? Has she a wooden leg? I envy not that boy's dreams that night.[4]

In fact, Maria's teeth are her own, the narrator ('who knows everything') later informs us. But the damage is done. Harry can never love a woman with 'false—oh, horrible'.

Dickens also introduces false teeth into his fiction, notably *Dombey and Son*. Our first introduction to Mrs Skewton, via Major Bagstock, highlights the many artificial aids to the lady's superannuated beauties. 'How long have you been here, bad man?', she archly quizzes Bagstock from her wheelchair, when they meet (his friend Mr Dombey and her daughter Edith in attendance) in the street at Leamington:

'One day,' replied the Major.

'And can you be a day, or even a minute,' returned the lady, slightly settling her false curls and false eyebrows with her fan, and showing her false teeth, set off by her false complexion, 'in the Garden of what's-its-name—'

'Eden, I suppose, Mama,' interrupted the younger lady, scornfully (p. 241)

There are at least three subsequent references to Mrs Skewton's false teeth—all barbed with Dickensian satire at her preposterous attempts at 'juvenility', even after the stroke which totally paralyses her. She dies, false teeth in frozen jaw. 'Cleopatra' Skewton's flashing dentures are, like Yorick's 'chapfallen grin' in *Hamlet*, a *memento mori*.

More enigmatic are Carker's teeth, to whose gleaming and suspicious perfection we are directed, time and again, in *Dombey and Son*. They are prominent in the first description we are given of the 'general manager' in Chapter 13:

Mr Carker was a gentleman thirty-eight or forty years old, of a florid complexion, and with two unbroken rows of glistening teeth, whose regularity and whiteness were quite distressing. It was impossible to escape the observation of them, for he showed them whenever he spoke; and bore so wide a smile upon his countenance (a smile, however, very rarely, indeed, extending beyond his mouth), that there was something in it like the snarl of a cat. (p. 144)

As Woodforde notes, 'in even lighthearted Victorian photographs people smile with closed lips'. Carker's promiscuously displaying every perfect tooth in his head (something which is commented on repeatedly in the novel) would be as shocking as flaunting a wantonly unzipped fly. Dickens evidently gave instructions to his illustrator, Phiz, to draw attention to the general manager's toothsome smile and a set of snappers that would do the Cheshire Cat proud:

Mr Carker introduces Himself to Florence and the
Skettles Family

Carker's 'glistening' teeth, in the mouth of a 40-year-old man, and their astonishing 'regularity and whiteness', are surely too good to be true. They must be porcelain, we suspect. One of the problems with ivory, animal, or human bone false teeth was that they discoloured and became unpleasantly smelly, generating awful bad breath. Porcelain-based or 'mineral-paste' false teeth did not yellow or rot, and preserved the wearer from this added embarrassment of halitosis. Porcelain snappers had a vogue in Britain in the early to mid-nineteenth century. But, as Woodforde records, 'so-called mineral or porcelain teeth . . . had a very artificial appearance in the mouth and made a grating sound when brought together. They were over-white, opaque and brittle.' John Gray, in *Preservation of the Teeth* (1838), was dismissive: 'The things called mineral, or Jews' teeth, are now plentifully manufactured of porcelain; but they always look like what they are, and can never be mistaken for teeth.'[5]

Are Carker's magnificent white teeth his own? Most middle-aged Victorian readers (Dickens was 36 years old at the time of writing *Dombey and Son*) would have been very suspicious. We never know for certain. It would be revealing to examine the bodily remains of Carker that only the dogs seem interested in on the railway line. And it may be significant how often the word 'false' enters the final explosive quarrel between him and Edith. In the two pages recording their last, melodramatic exchange, 'false' comes up six times, and direct allusion is made to Carker's 'shining' teeth. Subliminally, the echo thrown back from this exchange is 'denture'. Myself, I think all that glistens in Carker's mouth is not tooth—human tooth, that is.

As the century progressed, dentistry professionalized itself, legislation against quacks was introduced, and standards of dental hygiene improved—led by America with its (to Dickens) obnoxious toothpicks. Toothbrushes

became common articles of bathroom furniture. Initially
there would be only one toothbrush for the whole Victorian family, as there were common hair- and boot-brushes
for everyone to use. With the suction plate, and more reliable spring mechanisms and better equipped workshops,
false teeth and bridges for the masses became an afford-
able 'cheap luxury'; so much so that in the early twentieth
century, among the self-improving working classes, it was
common as a dowry for a young bride to have all her teeth
pulled so that she might go to the altar with a perfect (if
artificial) dazzling smile.

The first 'unembarrassed' reference to false teeth in
Victorian fiction is, I believe, in *King Solomon's Mines*
(1885). Captain Good, Alan Quatermain, and his friends,
are confronted by a savage African tribe:

'What does the beggar say?' asked Good.

'He says we are going to be scragged,' I answered grimly.

'Oh, Lord!' groaned Good; and, as was his way when perplexed,
he put his hand to his false teeth, dragging the top set down and
allowing them to fly back to his jaw with a snap. It was a most
fortunate move, for the next second the dignified crowd of Kukuanas gave a simultaneous yell of horror, and bolted back some
yards.

'What's up?' said I.

'It's his teeth,' whispered Sir Henry excitedly. 'He moved them.
Take them out, Good, take them out!'

He obeyed, slipping the set into the sleeve of his flannel shirt.

In another second curiosity had overcome fear; and the
men advanced slowly. Apparently they had now forgotten their
amiable intention of doing for us. (pp. 112-13)

False teeth are not a matter of private shame here, but of
imperial pride—'white man's magic'—one of the 'wonders
of civilization' with which to dazzle the backward peoples
of the earth. Perhaps if Carker had slipped his dentures
out from time to time as a party trick we might like him

more. Or possibly, like the Kukuanas, we might merely find him even more terrifying than he already is.

The Oxford World's Classics *Dombey and Son* is edited by Alan Horsman. The Oxford World's Classics *King Solomon's Mines* is edited by Dennis Butts. The Oxford World's Classics *Pendennis* is edited by John Sutherland.

Charlotte Brontë · *Villette*

═══

Lucy Snowe, cement-mixer

═══

One of the most emotionally charged scenes in *Villette* is
that in Chapter 26 ('A Burial'). Lucy Snowe discovers
that Madame Beck has invaded her bureau and has read
her 'triply-enclosed packet of five letters' from Dr John.
Not quite love letters, they are none the less dear to Lucy
And she is apprehensive that her ruthless enemy will
again steal her letters and show them to M. Emmanuel.
Rather than destroy them (to do so would be to destroy
part of herself), Lucy determines to secrete the letters
where the prying eyes of Madame Beck can never find
them.

The act is highly ritualistic. First she makes a 'little
roll' of her precious letters, wraps them in 'oiled silk', and
binds them with twine. In one of the town's pawnshops she
discovers what she next needs, 'a thick glass jar or bottle'.
She inserts her little roll, then gets 'the old Jew broker
to stopper, seal, and make it air-tight'. He looks at her
suspiciously while doing so, as well he might.

All this takes place during 'a fine frosty afternoon'. At
seven-thirty the same night, Madame Beck being occupied
with the boarders, Lucy shawls herself (it is bitterly cold)
and goes through the garden into the *'allée defendue'*. This
was earlier described in Chapter 12. It is a lane at the back
of the house, 'forbidden to be entered by the pupils'
(p. 132). At the end of the walk is a relic from the long-
distant days when the pensionnat was a convent—an
ancient, largely dead, pear-tree, nicknamed (for its age)
Methuselah. At its root, as we are told in Chapter 12

you saw, in scraping away the mossy earth between the half-bared roots, a glimpse of slab, smooth, hard, and black. The legend went, unconfirmed and unaccredited, but still propagated, that this was the portal of a vault, emprisoning deep beneath that ground, on whose surface grass grew and flowers bloomed, the bones of a girl whom a monkish conclave of the drear middle ages had here buried alive, for some sin against her vow. (pp. 130–1)

It would seem that curious passers-by are in the habit of inspecting the slab—may even dare to lift it one day. None the less it is here, alongside the putative remains of this rebel, her predecessor, that Lucy will bury her precious cargo:

Methuselah, though so very old, was of sound timber still; only there was a hole, or rather a deep hollow, near his root. I knew there was such a hollow, hidden partly by ivy and creepers . . . I cleared away the ivy, and found the hole; it was large enough to receive the jar, and I thrust it deep in. In a tool-shed at the bottom of the garden, lay the relics of building-materials, left by masons lately employed to repair a part of the premises. I fetched thence a slate and some mortar, put the slate on the hollow, secured it with cement, covered the whole with black mould, and, finally, replaced the ivy. This done, I rested, leaning against the tree; lingering, like any other mourner, beside a newly-sodded grave. (p. 369)

This is an important scene in the novel—a climax of renunciation and self-denial—symbolized by the act of 'burying', in a sealed cylinder; the emotional part of herself. But a number of questions protrude. The earlier references to 'scraping' away at the base of Methuselah, with all its grisly associations, suggest that it is something which the horrified girls (braving Madame Beck's punishments) do—to give themselves the delicious *frisson* of contemplating the murdered nun's grave. This is not, one would have thought, a sensible place to hide one's intimate letters. Sooner or later, someone will go beyond 'scraping' and dig.

And what has happened, between Chapters 12 and 26, to the 'vault' and the smooth, hard, black slab? In the later chapter it is just a hole in the ground. And then, coming down to practical matters, there is the business with the 'mortar'. One thing any bricklayer would have told Miss Snowe is, 'don't mix cement during a frost'—it won't hold. If cement freezes while still 'setting', it will simply crumble.

But what, exactly, is the mortar for? To create a cover over the 'slate', over the bottle with its edges against the dirt sides of the hole? The cement simply would not hold—there is no adhesive surface for it to bond against. You would just lift the slate out. And has Charlotte Brontë realized that you have to mix mortar—the substance is a precisely measured mixture of sand, water, and cement? I suspect that here she is confusing it with ready-to-use putty.

It creates an odd and distracting image—distracting because it works against the solemnity with which Brontë clearly wants to invest this episode. We have to imagine this gentlewoman mixing cement (since the temperature is below freezing, a fruitless task), getting the water from we know not where (the garden pump?). There are the other distractions of the disappeared slab. Where it either was, or was not, Lucy Snowe has laid another slab, or slate. This, even if her cement holds (which it will not), will be easily lifted, since it adjoins loose earth. Lucy should really have done what any other young Victorian maiden would have done in the circumstances: thrown the letters in the fire.

The Oxford World's Classics *Villiette* is edited by Herbert Rosengarten.

═══

Is Betsey Trotwood a spinster?

═══

In *Can Jane Eyre Be Happy?* I referred in passing to Miss Trotwood, in *David Copperfield*, as a 'spinster'. Donald Hawes writes to correct the error: 'Of course she uses her maiden name and lives as a single woman (as we're told in Chapter 1). But she was a married woman, in fact, who separated from her husband.' Professor Hawes adds:

what I find slightly puzzling is her telling David that she believes that her husband 'married another woman' (Chapter 47). No explanation is given of the legality or illegality of this marriage as far as I know. I also find it strange that John Forster in his *Life of Dickens* refers to her as 'Mrs Trotwood'.

The second wife is indeed puzzling, as is the mis-titling of Miss ('Mrs') Trotwood by someone as close to Dickens in the planning of his fiction as Forster. Once pointed out, it is tempting to follow up the 'Mrs Trotwood' puzzle for what it reveals about Dickens's use of peripheral detail, and his habit of keeping latent plots 'in reserve' (as I will argue).

Dickens, writing serially to the month as he did, clearly left much to his powers of extemporization. His working notes indicate that, even in the privacy of his own study, he did not hazard long-term projections about the future directions of his story (hence our frustrations with the tantalizingly incomplete *Edwin Drood*). But in order to extemporize effectively he had at every stage to keep a range of possibilities open—any of which might lead up to alternative plot-lines, if required. If never used, these untaken narrative options (roads not taken) might well remain as small motes to trouble the pedantic reader's eye.

David Copperfield opens with a teasing uncertainty as to what will follow: 'Whether I shall turn out to be the hero of my own life, or whether that station will be held by anybody else, these pages must show.' The details of Miss Betsey Trotwood's early life seem, however, certain enough:

An aunt of my father's, and consequently a great-aunt of mine, of whom I shall have more to relate by-and-by, was the principal magnate of our family. [She] . . . had been married to a husband younger than herself, who was very handsome, except in the sense of the homely adage, 'handsome is, that handsome does'— for he was strongly suspected of having beaten Miss Betsey, and even of having once, on a disputed question of supplies, made some hasty but determined arrangements to throw her out of a two pair of stairs' window. These evidences of an incompatibility of temper induced Miss Betsey to pay him off, and effect a separation by mutual consent. He went to India with his capital, and there, according to a wild legend in our family, he was once seen riding on an elephant, in company with a Baboon; but I think it must have been a Baboo—or a Begum. Anyhow, from India tidings of his death reached home, within ten years. How they affected my aunt, nobody knew; for immediately after the separation, she took her maiden name again, bought a cottage in a hamlet on the sea-coast a long way off, established herself there as a single woman with one servant, and was understood to live secluded ever afterwards, in an inflexible retirement. (pp. 2–3)

The time reference 'within ten years' is significant. And it is clear, from subsequent events, that all this happened— including her widowing—before the marriage of Mr and Mrs Copperfield, and the birth of David.

We never know what Miss Trotwood's married name was, nor her errant husband's Christian name. He was

born in Hornsey, as we discover much later (although the
manuscript shows that this was not Dickens's first intention). 'Born in Hornsey' is the sum total of his given
biography—apart from the elephant, the Begum, and the
mysterious other wife. On David's birth, Miss Betsey cut
off all communication with the Copperfields, on grounds
of their having perversely brought a boy, not a girl (a little
Betsey), into the world.

When, aged 10, David runs away to Dover and is adopted
by Miss Trotwood (who promptly changes his name to
'Trotwood Copperfield'), he learns something about Mr
Dick, his aunt's inseparable companion. The amiable
lunatic had been sent away 'to some private asylum-place'
by an unsympathetic brother. He was, however, ill treated
at the asylum, 'So I [Miss Betsey] stepped in . . . and made
him [the brother] an offer . . . after a good deal of squab-
bling . . . I got him' (p. 199).[1] As with David, she promptly
changed her ward's name: Richard Babley (her 'babbling
baby') became 'Mr Dick'. Miss Trotwood has an odd passion for changing names, we note (before 1837 there was no
obligation to enter them with the Registrar of Births,
Marriages, and Deaths). Mr Dick is not, however, a penniless waif like David. He has, we later learn, an income of
£100 a year. On her part, Miss Trotwood, as we later learn,
has £5,000 in the consols, which at their standard yield of
3 per cent would give her an annual income of £150. We
may assume, if he too has his funds in the consols, that Mr
Dick has some £3,000 invested.

Unless Miss Trotwood settled this sum on him (which
is doubtful, given her own slender resources) she must
have had some claim other than innate benevolence to
ownership, and—as one guesses, power of attorney. Mr
Dick is a valuable commodity—adventurers would marry
'heiresses' with that kind of dowry. It is unlikely that
Mr Dick—a man of property—would be *given away* for

adoption to an eccentric old woman who felt sorry for him in his asylum, and who had no near connection with him. What was she doing inspecting the inmates of asylums anyway? Was she perhaps locked up in one herself for a while, after the catastrophe of her marriage?

It emerges, about a third of the way through the narrative, that Miss Trotwood's husband is not, after all, dead. It is not clear from his notes (where he refers to him as 'My Aunt's persecutor') that Dickens foresaw this resurrection from the beginning, or whether—as seems more likely—it was a mid-narrative brainwave. In his notes Dickens debates with himself whether to introduce the persecutor early or hold him back until a more effective moment in the narrative. He decides, on reflection, to hold him back. What else he held back about the man we can only guess.

The first enigmatic clue the reader gets about the 'persecutor' is from Mr Dick, in conversation with David, in Chapter 17 ('Somebody Turns Up'): 'Soon after' the time that King Charles turned up (i.e. after the fever and psychosis induced by his brother's and the asylum's ill treatment) 'the man first came', he tells David. 'The man' hung about the house by night. When she saw him, Miss Trotwood was painfully affected: she shivered, held on to the palings, wept, and 'gave him money'. Miss Betsey was evidently surprised, as well as distressed, by this apparition. Mr Dick, as he tells David, has since seen the man again.

David dismisses Mr Dick's account as another King Charles's head. But later, in Chapter 23, when Miss Trotwood comes up to London to pay for David's articles, they pass a 'lowering, ill-dressed man' in the street who evidently recognizes Betsey. She certainly recognizes him. 'I don't know what I am to do,' she tells David, 'in a terrified whisper, and pressing my arm' (p. 340). David sees nothing but an importunate 'sturdy beggar' to be sent on his way. But the old lady gathering herself, tells him she must go off with the ill-dressed man in a coach. She and David will meet later in St Paul's churchyard. When they meet, a confused David notes that her purse is empty of the guineas it formerly contained. What David sees in London corroborates Mr Dick's story about the mysterious 'man' who preys on Miss Trotwood. But he does not learn the man's identity until years later. Alarmed by a light at midnight in his guardian's cottage in Highgate, he goes across the short distance between their dwellings. In the garden, he sees and hears 'the man' drinking and demanding money. 'What have I to do, to free myself for ever of your visits, but to abandon you to your deserts?' Miss Trotwood says. Why doesn't she, he asks, tauntingly: 'You ask me why!', she replies, 'What a heart you must have' (p. 669). It would be interesting to know, exactly, what lies behind that 'why!'

After the man has gone on his way, Betsey confesses all to David: 'Trot . . . it's my husband.' She tells the whole sad story. He wasted her fortune and 'nearly' broke her heart.

I left him. . . I left him generously. He had been so cruel to me, that I might have effected a separation on easy terms for myself; but I did not. He soon made ducks and drakes of what I gave him, sank lower and lower, married another woman, I believe, became an adventurer, a gambler, and a cheat. (p. 670)

From this 'grumpy, frumpy, story' we understand there was no divorce, but a deed of separation. After she had cut herself off from the Copperfields (her only living relatives, apparently) and set herself up as a spinster in Dover—the husband reappeared on the scene. There is a novel's-worth of incident in these few months of Miss Trotwood's life. If, however, the man had indeed 'married again' he would, one assumes, be a bigamist, and in no position to apply any blackmailing pressure at all on his abused former wife. He would be in mortal fear of criminal prosecution. Why then, is Miss Trotwood so frightened of him? She is, in other departments of her life, a plucky woman well able to fight her corner. She declines to be browbeaten by the much more dangerous Uriah Heep (whom she physically assaults) or the 'murdering' Murdstones (whom she fearlessly tongue-lashes). What hold does her former husband have over her?

The 'persecutor' makes his final appearance in the novel as a corpse. He has died in hospital in Canterbury and is about to be borne away by a hearse (paid for by Miss Trotwood) to be buried at Hornsey, where—as Betsey tells David—he was born. On his deathbed, it emerges, he sent for Miss Trotwood, and asked her forgiveness. 'Six-and-thirty years ago, this day my dear', she tells David, 'I was married' (p. 763).

We learn nothing more about the man from Hornsey. But what we do know provokes some teasing speculations. What happened to his second 'wife'? Why was she not in attendance at the hospital, did he not have apologies to make to her? *Was* there a second wife? Did Miss Trotwood really believe he was dead, when—as Mr Dick recalls—he 'first' reappeared in Dover to persecute her? Additionally, there is the odd business of 'Miss' Trotwood's name. Obviously, for informal purposes, people can call themselves what they want. There are no regulations regarding nicknames. If Miss Trotwood wants to call Mr Babley 'Mr Dick', and David Copperfield 'Trotwood' Copperfield, so be it. It is of no more significance than Mr Dombey renaming his servant 'Richards' on the grounds that 'Toodle' is beneath his household dignity. But changing one's name for legal purposes and transactions is not so easy. At the very least, one would need to keep one's solicitor informed. Names have to be kept straight on legal documents. Since Agnes carefully calls David 'Trotwood Copperfield', it would seem that Betsey took the precaution of informing Mr Wickfield about this matter.

It also seems clear that Miss Trotwood and her husband were not divorced but separated. Legally, she would still be known, at least on certain important legal documents, by his surname, whatever it was. Her legal advisers, Spenlow and Jorkins, evidently know her only as 'Miss Trotwood'. Her 'married name' is never brought up. But it would need to be known about and recorded in order to make her papers entirely legal. The married name ('Mrs X, also known as "Miss Trotwood"') would surely also have to be entered somewhere on her deeds of trust (which Wickfield has, and which Heep embezzles), if only in parenthesis.

Also, if Miss Trotwood is not divorced, her property would not be her own but her husband's—unless some form of legal agreement were entered into with him, under his legal name, at the time of separation. This may well be the reason for Miss Trotwood's uncharacteristic nervousness—a fear that the persecutor will enforce his conjugal rights and seize the £5,000 portion remaining to her from her fortune (we learn, later, that she has prudently secreted £2,000, presumably for just such an eventuality). Forster's slip about 'Mrs Trotwood' arose, I would suggest, from a logical but erroneous train of thought. He recalled, subliminally, that Miss Betsey was still 'married', and that she must for the legal purposes which figure so centrally in the plot have used a married name and that name must therefore have been 'Trotwood'.

Another incidental puzzle is: did 'the persecutor' ever go to India? Did he in fact ride an elephant and consort with a baboo or a begum? (He clearly didn't die in India—as family legend also has it.) 'Emigration' and the spiritual regeneration that it permits is a major theme in

David Copperfield. But unlike Em'ly and Micawber, the persecutor seems an unlikely candidate. His Indian career is, most likely, a flight of Trotwoodian fancy—like the foreign investments in which (to protect Wickfield) she claims to have lost all her money. Miss Trotwood is quite capable of exotic lies in an honest cause.

This hypothesis is supported by one's difficulty in fitting the Indian business into a logical time frame. Miss Trotwood announces her thirty-sixth wedding anniversary at a period (Dora's death) when David is around 26. Presumably, then, the marriage took place 10 years before his birth. Yet, it is said that after the marriage (which must have lasted some years, if the persecutor contrived to squander the greater part of Miss Trotwood's considerable fortune) he went to India (a journey which would have taken many months), where he died 'within ten years' (the news, of course, would have taken many months to return). All this took place before David's birth, and even his parents' wedding. By no manipulation of time schemes can one make this order of events work. We must assume, I think, that the 'persecutor' never went to India. On the other hand, from her shock at his reappearance, we may well assume that Miss Trotwood *thought* him dead.

There is no easy answer to the puzzles which swarm around Miss Trotwood's past, and any attempt at explanation needs to take into account Dickens's working methods. If Dickens, opening his narrative, was uncertain as to who 'the hero' of 'these pages' would be, he may just as well not have determined—at that early stage—who the villain was to be. As a kind of 'defence in depth', Dickens may well have laid the ground for a potential sub-plot, to fall back on if need be.

One can speculate about that unwritten (because unneeded) subplot. There is, in Chapter 33 of *David Copperfield*, a strangely digressive paragraph describing some proceedings in court in Doctors' Commons (where divorce business was done at this period) undertaken by Spenlow and the newly articled David:

Mr. Spenlow and I went into Court, where we had a divorce-suit coming on, under an ingenious little statute (repealed now, I believe, but in virtue of which I have seen several marriages annulled), of which the merits were these. The husband, whose name was Thomas Benjamin, had taken out his marriage licence as Thomas only, suppressing the Benjamin, in case he should not find himself as comfortable as he expected. *Not* finding himself as comfortable as he expected, or being a little fatigued with his wife, poor fellow, he now came forward by a friend, after being married a year or two, and declared that his name was Thomas Benjamin, and therefore he was not married at all. Which the Court confirmed, to his great satisfaction. (pp. 465–6)[2]

This little excursus has no relevance to the plot that one can see. Mr Benjamin never reappears. It seems entirely by the way. Unless, of course, Dickens were keeping it in reserve as what I have called a 'fall-back' plot-line. In this unwritten narrative we might find that, like Thomas Benjamin, the persecutor 'entraps' eligible women. He 'married' the ancient heiress, Miss Trotwood, using a false, or imperfect name. The subsequent 'separation'—which involved a huge pay-off on her part—was not a divorce. It could not be a divorce, because the couple were never legally married. In one sense he was still her 'husband' (he had presumably enjoyed conjugal physical rights). But, in another sense, she was still a spinster ('unmarried woman . . . old maid'). Miss Trotwood was never obliged to change her name back to its maiden form. Since the marriage was invalid, this had always been her legal name, anyway.

As a gullible victim of this kind of confidence trick, Miss Trotwood would be terrified of the humiliating publicity of being exposed, and susceptible to blackmail. Legally, the persecutor—like Mr Benjamin—would be

untouchable. Not a bigamist, that is, but a serial confidence trickster. His 'second wife' presumably fell victim
to the same ruse as Miss Trotwood. She was another dupe.
In the imagination one can see an unwritten narrative in
which all this would come out. But, in the event, Dickens
did not need to fall back on this reserve plot, if that's what
it was. Uriah Heep and Mr Murdstone (another serial
predator on marriageable ladies) served the novel's needs
for villainy quite adequately. Is, then, Miss Trotwood a
spinster?—strictly no; but one *can* make a case that she
was never anything else.

Postscript: Are Bella and Laura married women?

John Carey and David Grylls have raised in conversation
with me other puzzles of a similar nature to the Benjamin–
Miss Betsey–man from Hornsey kind. As Professor Carey
points out, Bella Wilfer marries the 'Secretary' in *Our
Mutual Friend* believing him to be John Rokesmith. She
becomes, in good faith, Mrs John Rokesmith. They have a
child who is, presumably, baptized and registered in the
name Rokesmith. But, of course, John Rokesmith is—
legally—John Harmon (alias Julius Handford). All this
comes out in the denouement. The penultimate chapter of
the novel ('Persons and Things in General') opens: 'Mr.
and Mrs. John Harmon's first delightful occupation was
to set all matters right that had strayed in any way wrong'
(p. 803). Was one of these 'matters' to go through a new
wedding under their proper names? Was there no legal
reprisal for John Harmon's passing himself off as 'John
Rokesmith'? Was their child effectively bastardized for the
period that he was a 'Rokesmith'?

The problem in *The Woman in White* is, as Dr Grylls
points out, even more perplexing. Walter Hartright and

Marian Halcombe rescue Lady Glyde (née Laura Fairlie)
from the asylum where she is known as the patient 'Anne
Catherick'. The three of them go into hiding in a 'poor
neighbourhood' in the 'Far East' of London (pp. 420, 440). It
is 1851, the year of the census. The two women, Hartright
tells us, are 'described as my sisters'. Although he does not
say so outright (he is, in fact, very vague on the subject)
they must all be sheltering under the same assumed name.
They know themselves to be in 'serious peril' if Fosco and
Glyde track them down. Presumably Walter makes a false
return on the census return (as Wilkie Collins did in 1861,
to protect his mistress Catherine Graves).

Marian and Walter set themselves to discover the
'Secret'. It will, they believe, lead to the unmasking of the
villains and the restitution of Laura. On their part Fosco
and Glyde know that Anne has escaped but they do not, at
this stage, know that Walter is involved. Nor, of course, do
they know where the artist and his two 'sisters' are living.
If they did, more vile skulduggery would ensue.

The 'Secret' leads Walter to Mrs Catherick at Welmingham. He evidently introduces himself to her *in propria
persona* (she calls him 'Mr Hartright'). Walter discovers
that the 'Secret' lies buried in the registers of Old
Welmingham church. But before he can get at them Glyde
arranges to have him taken up by the magistrates for
assault. It is, of course, a set-up. But, we deduce, Walter
gives a false address (and possibly a false name) to the
authorities. To do otherwise would be to give Fosco and
Glyde directions to the whereabouts of his 'sisters', and
would surely lead to the incarceration of Laura once more.

Sir Percival Glyde is incinerated in the fire in the
church, attempting to destroy the evidence of his
illegitimacy (the 'Secret'). Walter, who led the attempt to
save his rival's life, is called as a witness at the inquest.
Surprisingly (given the fact that Glyde was his closest

friend and his fellow conspirator), Fosco is not in attendance at Welmingham. We assume that again Walter gives a false name and address.

Four months later the trio spend a 'fortnight [at] the seaside'. They have 'earned a little holiday' (p. 571), Walter says. When in town, they are now living at Fulham. During their seaside holiday ('the third day from our arrival') Walter confesses to Marian his desire to marry Laura. 'I am so happy' (p. 576), Laura responds. There follows the enigmatic parenthesis: 'Ten days later, we were happier still. We were married . . . In a fortnight more we three were back in London' (p. 576).

Do they then marry at the seaside? There is no time for the banns to be called, so it must be a civil marriage. They could hardly marry at Fulham where, presumably, Laura is known as Walter's 'sister'. What name does Laura Fairlie–Glyde–Catherick marry under? And does she declare herself a 'spinster', or a widow (Lady [Laura] Glyde)? However mitigated there must be a degree of wilful misrepresentation. Laura is, legally, 'dead'. Corpses cannot marry. And is it, legally, a marriage? Is it in any sense a marriage? The wedding takes place in 1851. It is not until a couple of years later, after Laura has been brought back to life and legality, that she and Walter have their first child, little Walter. When they return to Fulham, do Walter and his 'wife' continue a chaste existence as brother and sister?[3]

The Oxford World's Classics *David Copperfield* is edited by Nina Burgis, with an introduction by Andrew Sanders. The Oxford World's Classics *Our Mutual Friend* is edited by Michael Cotsell. The Oxford World's Classics *The Woman in White* is edited by John Sutherland.

Elizabeth Gaskell · *Ruth*

=====

How does Ruth end up in Wales?

=====

Frances Twinn, a graduate student working on the fiction
of Elizabeth Gaskell, points to a troubling inconsistency
at the heart of *Ruth*. The narrative opens with a depiction
of the poor-but-genteel heroine apprenticed to a harsh
milliner, Mrs Mason, in 'an assize town in one of the eastern counties'. It is 'many years ago' (p. 3). We should
picture, it seems, a sleepy county town like Ipswich or
Norwich in the 1830s. The heroine, Ruth Hilton, is an
orphan. Her mother had been the daughter of a Norfolk
curate—a 'delicate, fine lady' (p. 36); her father had been a
farmer—a good-hearted but tragically unlucky man. The
delicate Mrs Hilton died early of physical exhaustion,
unable to cope with the physical demands of being a
farmer's wife. He followed soon after of a broken heart and
bankruptcy. Ruth, alone in the world, falls into the unfeel-
ing custody of a 'hard-headed' guardian, who disposes of
the waif to Mrs Mason so as to be rid of her, at the small
expense of her indenture fee.

At the shire-hall new-year celebrations, 15-year-old
Ruth Hilton catches the eye of a 23-year-old sprig of the
gentry. In return for the girl's deftly mending the torn
dress of his partner (the haughty Miss Duncombe), Henry
Bellingham gives Ruth a camellia. The gentleman's trifling gift goes to the humble dressmaker's heart. Over the
following six months Bellingham pursues Ruth. She is a
beautiful girl—although chronically shy and deferential.
It is not clear whether he intends to seduce her or to enjoy
some risky flirtation: he is no villain, merely feckless. She

is no trollop, merely innocent of the ways of the world. As Mrs Gaskell emphasizes time and again, she has no *mother* to guide her.

On a nostalgic visit to her former home, Ruth is seen in the company of Bellingham by Mrs Mason and dismissed on the spot ('I'll have no slurs on the character of my apprentices . . . I shall write and tell your guardian tomorrow', pp. 54–5). Her guardian, of course, will now disown her—glad to be rid of the expense. Ruth is now that most unfortunate of Victorian women, a 'castaway'. Bellingham at first seems perplexed as to what to do: 'It is very unfortunate; for, you see, I did not like to name it to you before, but, I believe—I have business, in fact, which obliges me to go to town to-morrow—to London, I mean; and I don't know when I shall be able to return' (p. 56).

The news that he too is about to abandon her plunges Ruth into paralytic despair. But, on the spur of the moment, Bellingham sees a solution: 'Ruth, would you go with me to London . . . you must come with me, love, and trust to me.' It is the serpent's invitation. 'Young, and innocent, and motherless'—Ruth succumbs. Bellingham goes off to get the carriage that will carry the young milliner to her eternal shame.

Chapter 4 of Gaskell's novel (which has been rattling along) ends: 'Ruth was little accustomed to oppose the wishes of any one—obedient and docile by nature, and unsuspicious and innocent of any harmful consequences. She entered the carriage, and drove towards London' (p. 61).[1] As Mrs Twinn puts it:

So the reader is left expecting the couple to arrive in London as they turn over the page. Therefore it is with some astonishment that the reader finds himself transported to 'a little mountain village in North Wales.' Why did Gaskell change her mind? Are there any clues that she has intended to do this all along?

It's a good question. Without explanation or any further mention of London, we find ourselves at the beginning of Chapter 5 in the Welsh village Mrs Twinn mentions. It is unnamed, but some 17 miles from 'Pen trê Voelas'—somewhere in the north of the principality, near Snowdonia we may guess. It is early July—only two months can have passed since Chapter 4 (as Mrs Twinn calculates). It turns out that the inn in which Henry and Ruth are now staying is familiar to him from his varsity days. He knows 'its dirt of old', as Gaskell ominously puts it. He and his fellow undergraduates used to bring 'reading parties' there.

From the disreputable nature of Mrs Jenny Morgan, the landlady, it is clear that the inn does not uphold strict rules of morality among its patrons. 'Young men will be young men,' Mrs Morgan thinks indulgently when she apprehends that Ruth is 'not his wife . . . His wife would have brought her maid, and given herself twice as many airs about the sitting rooms'. Ruth, presumably, is wearing gloves, so the ring, or its absence, are invisible to the innkeeper's sharp eyes. Clearly 'Mrs Bellingham'—as she will have been introduced—has *some* luggage (at least a change of clothes and toilet articles) with her, if no maid. From Mrs Morgan's indulgent reflections, we may assume that when the young students last came, three years ago, they brought some loose company ('Cyprians') with them in addition to their books. Ruth is just such another *belle amie*.

It is said that the couple intend only 'a week's enjoyment of that Alpine scenery', although it seems from other comments that he may be looking for a house to set her up in. Even in private conversation Ruth still timidly addresses Bellingham as 'sir', but it is clear they have slept together and are currently sharing a bed. Although she does not yet know it, Ruth is already pregnant with baby

Leonard. Bellingham, ominously, is beginning to be bored with the little dressmaker. It has been the best part of a week and the evenings drag without livelier company. But before their relationship can work itself to the inevitable conclusion, Bellingham falls into a fever and is repossessed by his vengeful mother, who self-righteously casts out the little minx who has clearly entrapped her son.

So begins Ruth's long travail as a Victorian lone parent and the main business of the novel. But the question remains, why does it begin in North Wales, not London? It may, of course, be a bad join in the narrative. But there is a possible explanation, more flattering to Gaskell's art and her tender sensibility. The first question that strikes the reader is: did Henry Bellingham *really* have to go to London? Probably not. His uncertain and stumbling choice of words ('I *believe*—I have business') and his claim to have just this moment remembered that he has business in the capital suggest a spur-of-the-moment brainwave. It strikes him that, since Ruth is fortuitously homeless and friendless, now is the time to make his move.

Secondly, what is the route that the couple have taken in Bellingham's carriage? If they are going from the general direction of an 'eastern assize town' to northern Wales, they would almost certainly have to go cross-country through London. So it would not be illogical for the carriage to drive, on its first leg, in that direction, as we are told at the end of Chapter 4. What subsequently happens in London? First, Bellingham would put up in some convenient (but discreet) hostelry and do what seducers do when innocent young things fall into their clutches. Then, on the next day, he would buy some clothes and other necessaries for his new mistress (who has left without luggage—not that her milliner's-apprentice outfits would be appropriate for her new station in life as 'Mrs Bellingham').

Elizabeth Gaskell

It would be difficult for Bellingham to stay in town—his mother might find out. She might tell Ruth's guardian. The girl is 15—three years over the age of consent for sexual intercourse but six years below the age of consent for marriage in England. It would look bad if Ruth laid a bastard to his charge in the 'assize town' where he lived, and claimed that he had promised marriage. Even if this disaster were averted, Mrs Mason might find out what has happened to one of her charges (she is *in loco parentis*) and make all sorts of trouble. Where would be a convenient place to install the young lady where she might be available, but not publicly visible? As a 23-year-old, Henry has little experience in such worldly matters as setting up a mistress. But, he remembers, there was that place in Wales where, as a student, he and his friends had that jolly time, and where the landlady was so accommodating. Just the ticket! The journey is around 200 miles, and they will arrive in a couple of days in his hired carriage. He will find some remote (and cheaply rented) house for Ruth well out of the world's eye. He can visit her at his discretion. The name 'Bellingham' will mean nothing in rural Wales.

Why did Gaskell not describe the London episode: the defloration of Ruth? Because it was painful and (as with the murder in *Mary Barton)* she did not like painful scenes and would go to some lengths to avoid them. Secondly, it would have been difficult to present Ruth to the reader in such a way as not to make her seem in some part guilty of her own downfall—unless, that is, she also presented Bellingham as a Lovelace-like rapist (something else she did not want to do). Ruth did not have to get in the carriage and go to London. She could have taken her chances with her guardian, explained her innocence to Mrs Mason, even have gone to the local clergyman. Even in the London inn—or house of assignation—where her pearl without price was lost, Ruth did not *have to* give in (assuming that Henry did not force her). A firm 'no' would have sufficed to preserve her virtue. A decent veil is drawn, so that we do not think too ill of the poor motherless child. The ever-motherly Mrs Gaskell will not cast the first stone.[2]

The Oxford World's Classics *Ruth* is edited by Alan Shelston.

What is Henry Esmond's 'great scheme'?

I have read *The History of Henry Esmond* many times and have examined the manuscript and written on changes Thackeray made to it. I have transcribed the notebook which the author compiled for the novel, and have even edited the novel itself (not, unfortunately, for Oxford World's Classics).[1] But I cannot make sense of the Restoration plot which makes up the main business of *Henry Esmond's* third volume. Nor have I read any account which does make sense of it. Commentators and editors (including myself and the Oxford World's Classics editor) tactfully ignore the problem as something insoluble and best passed over.

The Restoration plot was evidently suggested by that in Scott's *Woodstock*, and in many details follows its original closely. In *Henry Esmond* the hero intends to win Beatrix's (indelibly Jacobite) heart by changing the succession of royal families in England. He will bring the Pretender back from France, arrange a clandestine meeting with Queen Anne, and thus win her support for him as heir. She has, of course, no child of her own to put on the throne. The 'great scheme' is set up and played out in Chapters 8 and 9 of Volume III of *Henry Esmond*.

In Chapter 8, Esmond travels to France. It is May 1714. He goes incognito as 'Monsieur Simon', giving it out to the *monde* in London that he (Mr Esmond) 'was sick, and gone to Hampshire for country air' (p. 398). He leaves his

faithful manservant, John Lockwood, at Castlewood (in
Hampshire). 'The circumstance on which Mr Esmond's
scheme was founded' is the fact that young Viscount Castlewood, currently resident in France and a fervent Jacobite, 'was born in the same year as the Prince of Wales;
had not a little of the Prince's air, height, and figure;
and . . . took no small pride in his resemblance to a person
so illustrious' (p. 399).

In France 'M. Simon' persuades the Prince and the Viscount to join in the 'scheme'. Esmond prepares the ground
by sending back to the London house of the Castlewoods
in Kensington Square a portrait of the Viscount, done by
Rigaud. In fact, it is a portrait of the Prince. It is 'hung up
in the place of honour in her ladyship's drawing-room'.
This is a dangerous game the Castlewoods are playing. On
23 June 1714 Parliament posts a reward of £5,000 for anyone discovering the Pretender in England. The authorities
were nervous of his reappearing on the scene during the
last, tense days of Anne's reign.

Esmond's intention with the Rigaud portrait, clearly
enough, is to delude the world as to the facial appearance
of the Viscount, Frank. As a further precaution, 'All the
old domestics at the little house of Kensington Square
were changed.' It was given out that Frank would be
returning to England 'about the 17th or 18th day of June,
proposing to take horse from Paris immediately, and
bringing but a single servant with him'. He has been away
for five years. The essence of the 'scheme' is given in a
coded message sent on 10 June 1714 which 'told those that
had the key, that

*the King will take the Viscount Castlewood's passports and travel
to England under that lord's name. His Majesty will be at the Lady
Castlewood's house in Kensington Square, where his friends may
visit him; they are to ask for the Lord Castlewood.* (p. 406)

So far, the outline of the 'scheme' is crystal clear. The Prince will come to England impersonating the Viscount Castlewood, who will accompany him as his personal servant. The complications arise in Chapter 9 ('The Original of the Portrait comes to England'). The chapter opens:

'Twas announced in the family that my Lord Castlewood would arrive, having a confidential French gentleman in his suite, who acted as a secretary to his lordship, and who being a Papist, and a foreigner of good family, though now in rather a menial place, would have his meals served in his chamber, and not with the domestics of the house. (p. 408)

This also seems clear enough. The Viscount—in the person of 'Monsieur Baptiste', is to be kept out of the way. It will be assumed by the brighter servants that—Frank Castlewood having converted to Catholicism during his five years in France—M. Baptiste is actually his chaplain.

The unclarity begins with Esmond's riding down with John Lockwood to Rochester, to await 'the king in that very town where his father had last set his foot on the English shore' (p. 409). A room has been reserved in an inn 'for my Lord Castlewood and his servant.' But when the two men appear, Lord Castlewood is Lord Castlewood and the *Prince* is playing the part of M. Baptiste (very badly— he does not take orders well and 'runs after barmaids'). What happened to the business about his taking the Viscount's passports? The Prince has evidently travelled to England under M. Baptiste's name. Confusing.

Confusion intensifies. The three men gallop to London, reaching Kensington at nightfall. Lockwood has been left behind at Rochester to take care of the tired horses. He will follow the next day. The principals arrive at the Castlewood residence—Lord Castlewood *in propria persona*, the Prince still as M. Baptiste, and 'constantly neglecting his part with an inconceivable levity' (p. 413). Both visitors have, of course, been seen by all the servants of the house gathered to welcome their homecoming master. It may cross their minds that he does not resemble the portrait hanging upstairs. But let that pass.

There then follows the most perplexing passage. Next day, John Lockwood reappears:

Esmond's man, honest John Lockwood, had served his master and the family all his life, and the colonel [i.e. Esmond] knew that he could answer for John's fidelity as for his own. John returned with the horses from Rochester betimes the next morning, and the colonel gave him to understand that on going to Kensington, where he was free of the servants' hall, and indeed courting Mrs. Beatrix's maid, he was to ask no questions, and betray no surprise, but to vouch stoutly that the young gentleman he should see in a red coat there was my Lord Viscount Castlewood, and that his attendant in grey was Monsieur Baptiste the Frenchman. He was to tell his friends in the kitchen such stories as he remembered of my lord viscount's youth at Castlewood . . .

Jack's ideas of painting had not been much cultivated during his residence in Flanders with his master; and before my young lord's return, he had been easily got to believe that the picture brought over from Paris, and now hanging in Lady Castlewood's drawing-room, was a perfect likeness of her son, the young lord. And the domestics having all seen the picture many times, and catching but a momentary imperfect glimpse of the two strangers on the night of their arrival, never had a reason to doubt the fidelity of the portrait; and next day, when they saw the original of the piece habited exactly as he was represented in the painting, with the same periwig, ribbon, and uniform of the Guard, quite naturally addressed the gentleman as my Lord Castlewood, my lady viscountess's son.

The secretary of the night previous was now the viscount; the viscount wore the secretary's grey frock . . . (pp. 46–17)

Why switch identities now? If it were necessary, why was not the change done at Rochester, or behind some convenient hedge outside London? And, most confusingly, why did they not stick to the original plan of having the Prince travel as the Viscount? In the above passage, it seems from the opening sentences that John Lockwood is in on the 'scheme'. But then all the business about his being ignorant of art and 'easily got to believe that the picture brought over from France . . . was a perfect likeness of . . . the young lord' indicates that he is *not* in on the 'scheme', but a dupe like the other domestics. But then, later in the chapter (after the Prince has fondled his sweetheart) it is made clear that Lockwood—who fought six campaigns in Flanders with the real Viscount—is quite well aware who 'M. Baptiste' is. And, of course, he was at Rochester when the Viscount and Baptiste disembarked. He must be 'in'.

Throughout July the Prince, in the person of Viscount Castlewood, keeps to his rooms on the pretext of an old war wound breaking out. He has an interview with the terminally ailing Queen in Kensington Palace Gardens (as Viscount Castlewood, paying his respects to the sovereign), and all looks hopeful. But when Frank and Henry confront him with their suspicions that he intends to dishonour Frank's sister Beatrix (who is loyally willing to be dishonoured by her monarch), the Prince flounces out of the safe house in Kensington Square. He has the co-conspirator Bishop Atterbury install him in the house of a curate in nearby Kensington Mall. Here he is known as 'Mr Bates' (p. 448). The reader gathers that, in this character, he is in the habit of going abroad. Presumably a sharp-eyed servant in the Castlewood household might have seen this mysterious personage on the night of his arrival as Monsieur Baptiste, on the next day as the Viscount Castlewood, and now promenading the streets of Kensington as Mr Bates.

A reward of £5,000 awaits any British citizen who identifies the Prince. Short of wearing a crown, the Prince could hardly make it easier for some Kensington resident to get rich quick. 'Mr Bates' is meanwhile accompanied by a Castlewood servant ('Martin') who, from a number of comments in the narrative, evidently still thinks the Prince ('Mr Bates') is the Viscount. Stupid Martin, presumably, is not talking to his old friends at the servants' hall a few hundred yards away in Kensington Square. And those servants might wonder where the 'Viscount' has mysteriously disappeared to, and why he has left M. Baptiste behind. Some scheme.

On the last day of July, the conspirators decide that it is 'now or never'. They summon 'Mr George' (yet another pseudonym for the Prince) to attend on the dying Queen in her bedchamber and be proclaimed by her the next monarch, King James III of England. But 'Mr George' (alias 'Mr Bates') is not to be found at the curate's house. Other bedchambers are on his mind. He has gone into Hampshire (as Viscount Castlewood!) to seduce Beatrix. Her brother and mother have sent her to the Castlewood seat in the country; to be away from the attentions of the Prince. She has foiled them with a secret note to her royal lover.

Frank and Henry gallop down to Castlewood. They save Beatrix's honour in the nick of time. Or perhaps they don't (the narrative is slightly vague on the matter). But when they return to London with the Prince, it is too late: King George has been proclaimed: 'all the vain hopes of the weak and foolish young pretender were blown away' (p. 461). The Prince is smuggled back to the safety of France: whether as the Viscount Castlewood, M. Baptiste, Mr Bates, or Mr George, the narrative does not say.

What was Thackeray thinking of in this dog's dinner of an episode? My guess is that the original 'simple' scheme ('The Pretender impersonates the Viscount') was clouded in his mind when he came to write it down by the sudden realization of a fatal flaw. As conceived by Thackeray, the Prince has very imperfect English. This, in fact, is one of the many disqualifications for kingship which emerge during his clandestine six weeks in England. He might take the Viscount's passports, but any inspector— particularly on the English side of the Channel—would quickly realize that this was no English nobleman, but a French impostor. Hence, the plot was changed so that the Prince was smuggled in as M. Baptiste.

On the other hand, a French servant could hardly be smuggled into Kensington Palace for a private interview with the Queen of England. Only a lofty (and loyal) English nobleman would serve that purpose. Hence the change of identities, the day after arrival. That change of identities also validated the business of the Rigaud portrait which Thackeray had gone to some trouble in setting up. The John Lockwood threads were left dangling, but readers pay very little attention to servants. The original 'simple scheme' was overlaid with a fussier scheme. And the fit was somewhat less than perfect.

Why did Thackeray not sort out this mess? Because as he came to the end of the novel, he was in a great hurry. He was leaving for America, and had to prepare for a hectic lecture tour over there.[2] He patched over the bad joins between the two schemes and hoped for the best. Hoped, that is, that readers would not notice. Nor, in general, do they. There are much better things to concentrate on in this wonderful novel than a few hanging threads.

The Oxford World's Classics *The History of Henry Esmond* is edited by Donald Hawes.

Charles Dickens · *Bleak House*

——

What kills Lady Dedlock?

——

A recent disagreement between two Dickensian critics highlights a central puzzle in *Bleak House*. In a 1983 article, entitled 'The Fever of *Bleak House*', Fred Schwarzbach noted that 'disease plays a central part' in the novel's plot, 'as both subject and metaphor'.[1] Few readers will disagree. Many characters in *Bleak House* die, of many ailments, ranging from opium poisoning, through cerebral stroke, to that most controversial of causes of death, 'spontaneous combustion'. But 'What is not clear; and has puzzled modern critics', Schwarzbach notes, 'is why Dickens has Jo contract smallpox. Should he not have written instead about cholera, the most feared of all fevers in mid-Victorian England, which recently had ravaged the nation in the epidemic of 1848–9?'

Two suggested explanations are offered, both pertinent to the novel's design. Smallpox (unlike typhus) is contagious and serves a 'symbolic' function by linking all the otherwise divergent lines of character and action. 'Connection' is a major theme in the novel, and nothing connects like the pox. Secondly, on the level of plot device, the disease serves the practical purpose of 'disfiguring Esther so that no one will notice her resemblance to her mother.'

In a subsequent article, '"Deadly Stains"; Lady Dedlock's Death', Schwarzbach elaborates this insight, arguing that—although Dickens does not clearly indicate the fact—it *must* be smallpox that kills Lady Dedlock.[2] The moment of contagion occurs in Chapter 16 when, disguised in her servant's clothes, she pays a night-time visit to her lover, Captain Hawdon, resting in his pauper's 'berryin' place'. Dickens accompanies the contagious episode with a charnel-house description of the miasmic infection swirling around the graveyard, and its deadly deposits of 'witch ointment' and 'Tom's [i.e. Tom-all-alone's] slime' (p. 243). In this gothic effusion, Schwarzbach detects a 'key detail' which 'evidently has escaped the notice of modern critics' in the sentence: 'The servant [i.e. Lady Dedlock in her maid's gown] shrinks into a corner—into a corner of that hideous archway, *with its deadly stains contaminating her dress*; and . . . so remains for some moments.' The stains are 'deadly' because they contain the virus (literally 'poison'). Dickens selected the scene for illustration in the serial version of the novel:

Consecrated Ground

Smallpox, as Schwarzbach notes, has 'a variable incuba-tion period', and it is the fever phase of this disease which, we are to assume, eventually kills Lady Dedlock. In her last hours, we are told by eyewitnesses that she is 'hoarse', 'pale', and 'unable to eat'; symptoms compatible with those of the smallpox fever (a sceptic might note, however, that they are symptomatic of much milder ailments than smallpox). Schwarzbach informs us that Victorians believed smallpox could lie dormant until 'a period when the physical system was fatigued or under stress—that is why Jo becomes seriously ill only after Bucket forces him to "move on" ceaselessly.'

Lady Dedlock is certainly under stress in the last two days of her life. Her world collapses with a letter accusing her of killing Tulkinghorn, and a visit from the obnoxious Guppy indicating that her secret past is secret no more. She will shortly be unmasked before the world as a 'harlot' (which she is) and charged as a murderess (which she is not). 'There is no escape but in death' (p. 790), she resolves.

But she does not, in fact, kill herself—or at least not directly. It is morning. Dashing off a letter to her husband (which will induce a paralytic stroke when he reads it), she confesses guilt for everything but the murder, and promises 'I will encumber you no more'. By which we understand, she will disappear without trace. She veils and dresses for the outside weather; it is winter, and bit-terly cold. She 'leaves all her jewels and her money' (although she evidently keeps her watch), and slips out into the early morning London streets.

It is not at all apparent at this stage what Lady Dedlock's intentions are—but it is clear enough that she has a plan of some kind. As we reconstruct it, her first intention is to go down to Saint Albans to have a last unseen sight of Esther. She does not intend to speak to her daughter, merely to gaze at her from afar. Why she does not take money sufficient for the train or coach is mysterious. Presumably she thinks that travel on public transport would make her too conspicuous. But, as subsequent events make clear, a well-dressed gentlewoman, walking the winter roads of outer London, is a sight that sticks in observers' minds. The lady is, we deduce, not thinking straight.

For whatever reason, Lady Dedlock resolves to *walk* the twenty-odd miles into Hertfordshire and to Bleak House. When she arrives, many hours later, she discovers that Esther is in fact in London. She evidently gives up hope of having a last sight of her daughter. Lady Dedlock persuades the brickmaker's wife, Jenny, to change clothes with her, and travel on in a northwards direction. This, she hopes, will throw any pursuers off the scent. Jenny's brutish husband is bribed into complicity with the last of Lady Dedlock's valuables, her watch—something that, presumably, she had hoped to give to Esther.

Now dressed less conspicuously in Jenny's clothes, Lady Dedlock retraces her steps, walking back to London. Why, one wonders? Meanwhile, Esther and Bucket are in close pursuit. Conceivably, their paths actually cross on the London–Saint Albans road: they galloping post-haste north, she limping painfully south on the road that is now the A1. Before leaving London, Bucket has cast a shrewd eye over Lady Dedlock's private apartments. He notes, among other things, that she has taken no money or valuables with her ('rum', he thinks). His first deductions are clear. A woman who does not need money is one who is going on her last journey in life, for which there is no charge—the river, that is. Bucket's first stop is by Limehouse, to check if Lady Dedlock has thrown herself in the Thames, off one of the metropolitan bridges favoured by desperate females.

Esther observes Bucket make his discreet enquiries of

the river warden, whose job it is to scoop the day's harvest of corpses out of the water: 'A man yet dank and muddy, in long swollen sodden boots and a hat like them, was called out of a boat, and whispered with Mr Bucket, who went away with him down some slippery steps—as if to look at something secret that he had to show' (pp. 803–4). But the woman's corpse which the warden shows Bucket is, evidently, not that of a gentlewoman, or this particular gentlewoman ('thank God').

Bucket and Esther continue their pursuit of Lady Dedlock, by fast private coach, to the edge of Saint Albans, arriving between five and six in the morning. Lady Dedlock had passed the same way between eight and nine the previous evening. When they arrive at the brickmakers' cottage, Bucket and Esther discover that neither Lady Dedlock nor Jenny is there. The astute Bucket (but not the sweetly unsuspicious Esther) penetrates the 'change of clothes' ruse at once. But for inscrutable reasons of his own, the detective keeps Esther in the dark. (As his notes show, Dickens was in two minds whether to keep the reader in the dark as well, and decided against it.)

Bucket and Esther retrace their steps to London. It is now snowing hard. They arrive back in the capital around four. In Holborn, they pick up Lady Dedlock's trail again at the Snagsby household (Esther still thinks that they are, for reasons she cannot fathom, following Jenny). Woodcourt now joins them. Guster has a letter from Lady Dedlock, which she has been asked to deliver by hand. The girl has also been told to delay any pursuit as best she can. Bucket quickly gets possession of Lady Dedlock's letter, and shakes the truth out of a feebly obstinate Guster.

In her letter Lady Dedlock declares that she has only two objects left in life: 'to elude pursuit, and to be lost.' 'I have no purpose but to die,' she says bleakly. 'Cold, wet, and fatigue, are sufficient causes for my being found dead;

but I shall die of others, though I suffer from these. It was right that all that had sustained me should give way at once and that I should die of terror and my conscience' (p. 841, my emphasis).

Guster; under pressure from the remorseless Bucket, reveals that Lady Dedlock has asked directions to 'the poor burying ground . . . where the man was buried that took the sleeping stuff' (p. 843; i.e. where Hawdon, having committed suicide with an overdose of opium, is buried).[3] One element in Lady Dedlock's plan is now clear; she wishes to be buried as a destitute vagrant alongside her lover. This is why she has taken no money, and disguised herself as a working-class woman. (Although Dickens is too delicate to mention the fact, we have to suppose that she has exchanged her fine silk underclothes with Jenny as well, and discarded her wedding ring and those 'sparkling rings' which so impressed Jo, when she made her earlier visit to the 'berryin' place', p. 243). Her body will be found and, without any identifying marks, deposited without ceremony in a pauper's grave alongside Hawdon's, or so she hopes.[4]

Woodcourt, Bucket, and Esther now hurry to the 'berrying place'. There, beneath the 'horrible arch', lies a body. At last Bucket tells Esther the truth ('They changed clothes at the cottage'), but the distracted girl cannot take the information in.

I saw before me, lying on the step, the mother of the dead child [i.e. Jenny]. She lay there, with one arm creeping round a bar of the iron gate, and seeming to embrace it. She lay there, who had so lately spoken to my mother. She lay there, a distressed, unsheltered, senseless creature. She who had brought my mother's letter, who could give me the only clue to where my mother was; she, who was to guide us to rescue and save her whom we had sought so far; who had come to this condition by some means connected with my mother that I could not follow, and might be passing beyond our reach and help at that moment; she lay there, and they stopped me! I saw, but did not comprehend, the solemn and compassionate look in Mr Woodcourt's face. I saw, but did not comprehend, his touching the other on the breast to keep him back. I saw him stand uncovered in the bitter air, with a reverence for something. But my understanding for all this was gone.

I even heard it said between them:

'Shall she go?'

'She had better go. Her hands should be the first to touch her. They have a higher right than ours.'

I passed on to the gate, and stooped down. I lifted the heavy head, put the long dank hair aside, and turned the face. And it was my mother, cold and dead. (p. 847)

Esther falls ill at this point, and we learn nothing of the inquest, nor what verdict is passed on the death of Lady Dedlock.

Schwarzbach's 'smallpox' thesis is beguiling. Lady Dedlock is, as in coroners' terminology, 'a well nourished woman' with no history of invalidism. *Something*, we assume must have killed her. Those 'filthy stains' are a plausible 'cause of death'. Susan Shatto, in an answering article entitled 'Lady Dedlock and the Plot of *Bleak House*',[5] begs to disagree and gives powerful reasons for her disagreement. While accepting that smallpox infects Jo, Charley, and Esther, she is entirely unconvinced that Lady Dedlock contracts the disease. Nor does she believe that smallpox kills Jo. He finally succumbs to pulmonary tuberculosis, she maintains.

The time-scheme, as Shatto points out, contradicts Schwarzbach's 'fever' hypothesis. There are *two years* intervening between the 'filthy stains' contamination in Chapter 16, and Lady Dedlock's death in Chapter 59. It stretches credulity to imagine that the disease would have remained latent for two years in its host: 'Dickens would surely [have] known the average period of incubation [was] usually ten to twelve days, and at the maximum seventeen days.' It is true that Victorians (as Carlyle's famous description of the infected shirt in *Past and Present* indicates) believed that clothing could harbour disease and spread it to the upper classes. But Lady Dedlock's servant would have been much more at risk than the mistress who, only once, borrowed her clothes—assuming, as is extremely unlikely—she did not wash (and decontaminate) those clothes after Lady Dedlock returned them. There is no intervening source of contagion that we know about.

It is a persuasive refutation. The smallpox hypothesis is attractive, but unsustainable—unless one assumes wilful medical ignorance on Dickens's part, and among his readers. Less persuasive, perhaps, is Shatto's theory of what *does* kill Lady Dedlock: 'most readers would consider a forty-two mile journey on foot through a snowstorm sufficient for a cosseted lady suffering great emotional stress to grow pale, exhausted, hoarse, miserable, and ultimately, to die.' If for 'cosseted' one were to read 'well fed', 'most readers' might not wholeheartedly agree. Lady Dedlock is in her mid-forties, or just under 50 (Dickens is delicate about the precise age). We are given no hint that she is an invalid. In fact, the evidence suggests that she is anything but a weakling. She has borne a child in secret and defied conventional morality by none the less making her way in the world with nothing but her looks and will to assist her. This, we deduce, is a tough woman. She is capable of making trips at night in disguise to graveyards in slum areas of London. She evidently knows how to look after herself on the streets. On her last journey to Saint Albans and back she has had rest, shelter (and some liquid refreshment) at both the brickmakers' cottage and in Holborn.

Lady Dedlock obviously *intends* to die by her lover's

grave. This is the script she has written for her last act.
But death does not come on time simply because it is
dramatically 'right' that it should do so—except in fairy
stories and melodrama. There is also the strange business of Bucket and Woodcourt's reactions when they see
the body on the steps. How—from a distance of many
yards—do they *know* it is a corpse? Why do they take
their hats off? Woodcourt is a medical man. Noble as the
gesture is, holding back until Esther has had time to
examine the body of her mother ('she has a higher
right') would seem to contravene his Hippocratic oath.
Unless, that is, he knew that any medical attention is
now entirely useless.

If it were merely exhaustion that had felled Lady Dedlock, the doctor's duty (with the detective at his heels)
would be to rush forward, elbowing Esther out of the way
if necessary, shouting—'make way, make way, I'm a medical man'. He would feel her pulse, chafe her wrists, apply
restoratives and smelling salts, burn feathers under her
nose. If there were any flicker of life, he would punch her
chest, try artificial respiration, wrap her in warm
coverings.

And although exhausted (if it were only exhaustion that
had rendered her insensible) there would be every expectation that some life might remain in a healthy, 40-year-old
woman after a day-and-a-half's exposure and that the
prompt attention of a medical man might revive it. Well-
fed, warmly clothed, middle-aged people have survived the
London streets longer than that—and do so around us
every day.

On her part, Esther assumes the body slumped on the
steps is 'senseless', not dead. But Bucket evidently knows
better. It is too late. There are a string of clues as to how
he knows that the body lying in front of them is lifeless,
beyond resuscitation. The fact that she stripped herself of

money and jewels initially persuaded him that the woman intended to do away with herself, and had a plan for doing so—quickly and efficiently (when did Lady Dedlock ever dither?). Hence Bucket's first stop at the river. Having met a dead end there, Bucket deduced (from the evidence of Esther's handkerchief in Lady Dedlock's jewel case) that the mother will have gone to take a last glimpse of her child in Saint Albans (as she thinks). There are further clues for Bucket in Lady Dedlock's statement that 'I shall die'—but not of cold, wet, and fatigue. She has asked directions to where 'the man was buried that took the sleeping stuff' (as Guster gratuitously adds). Dickens, evidently, does not want us to forget that Hawdon took his own life by overdosing on opium (easily acquired by anyone at this period). Someone like Lady Dedlock, given to midnight insomniac walks in London and in Lincolnshire, would certainly have had a supply of opium or laudanum in her medicine cabinet. How does Bucket know, from many yards distant, that Lady Dedlock is dead as a doornail? Because he has (correctly) worked out that she has killed herself. How? With the desperate woman's best friend, opium.

The balance of probability is, we deduce, not that Lady Dedlock died of delayed smallpox, nor cold and exhaustion, but that like Hawdon, she poisoned herself. The prospect of being revived, unmasked as the mother of an illegitimate child, publicly tried, and haled off to prison for murder would be too awful. Nor would Lady Dedlock *risk* that happening.

Why then, do Bucket and Woodcourt not say something? Bucket—in the business of Jenny's clothes—has shown an ability to keep facts to himself. There was a particular reason for taciturnity where suicide was concerned. Nineteenth-century regulations as to the interment of those guilty of 'felo de se' were savagely punitive. Up to

1823 the suicide was required to be buried at a crossroads, in unconsecrated ground, with a stake through the heart (the barbarous ceremony was, for obvious reasons, rarely carried out). Until 1880 the suicide was required to be buried without rites of Christian sepulture. For this reason magistrates, investigating police, and doctors signing death certificates were generously vague, misleading, or simply silent as to cause of death. As, indeed, Woodcourt is when he is called to Hawdon's body. He does *not want to know* if Hawdon took an overdose:

'He has died,' says the surgeon, 'of an over-dose of opium, there is no doubt. The room is strongly flavoured with it. There is enough here now;' taking an old teapot from Mr Krook, 'to kill a dozen people.'

'Do you think he did it on purpose?' asks Krook.

'Took the over-dose?'

'Yes!' Krook almost smacks his lips with the unction of a horrible interest.

'I can't say. I should think it unlikely, as he has been in the habit of taking so much. But nobody can tell.' (pp. 153–4)

Guster is less circumspect.

The suspicion of suicide explains a little exchange between Jo and 'the servant', Lady Dedlock, in which she is particularly inquisitive on the question of whether Hawdon has been buried in consecrated ground:

'The servant [Lady Dedlock] shrinks into a corner—into a corner of that hideous archway, with its deadly stains contaminating her dress; and putting out her two hands, and passionately telling him to keep away from her, for he is loathsome to her, so remains for some moments. Jo stands staring, and is still staring when she recovers herself.

'Is this place of abomination, consecrated ground?'

'I don't know nothink of consequential ground,' says Jo, still staring.

'Is it blessed?'

'WHICH?' says Jo, in the last degree amazed.

'Is it blessed?'

'I'm blest if I know,' says Jo. (p. 248)

Hawdon, evidently, *does* lie in consecrated ground and had some form of Christian burial, even though he took his own life. Ironically, Lady Dedlock is buried in the Mausoleum in Lincolnshire: separated in death from her lover. But, it is clear, the verdict on her at the Coroner's Inquest cannot have been suicide. Nor would Bucket, or Woodcourt, say anything to put such a thought in the investigating magistrate's mind.

The death of Lady Dedlock is no minor episode in *Bleak House*. Dickens gives it pride of place as a 'number ending', with a vivid 'curtain line' and one of the novel's forty illustrations. It is a narrative highpoint. The reader is bound to be curious as to how she dies, and we have—I think—four options. The smallpox hypothesis is attractive, but medically unsound in ways that Dickens would certainly have been aware of. Exhaustion is more likely, but the timing of the death is unsettlingly convenient— more convenient than such deaths are in real life.

This leads to what one might call the 'melodrama' option. In melodrama, heroines can and do die of such non-pathological conditions as 'broken heart' or 'grief' at precisely the right theatrical moment. In life, 'stress' and 'despair' do kill—but usually in undramatic, protracted, messy, and untimely ways. The melodramatic option is plausible but not flattering to Dickens's 'art', nor does it fit in a novel which is elsewhere so successfully realistic.

The fourth option is that Lady Dedlock, like Hawdon (whose death she in other ways imitates, as I have suggested), did away with herself by the opium which she would surely have to hand in her medicine box. (The drug was not even minimally controlled in Britain until the Pharmacy Act of 1868; before then it was more easily available—and cheaper—than beer.) As with Hawdon, the benevolent authorities gloss over the fact of her suicide— Sir Leicester will not know; Esther will not know; the world will not know. The place in Lincolnshire can have its grand funeral. Of the options, I prefer the fourth, although it is unenforceable by clinching evidence.

The Oxford World's Classics *Bleak House* is edited by Stephen Gill.

What are Mr Hale's 'doubts'?

The Victorians had a soft spot for novels about the 'agony' of religious uncertainty. The most popular, by far, was *Robert Elsmere* (1888) by Mrs Humphry Ward. Mrs Ward's hero is a young Anglican minister, tormented by spiritual anxiety—'doubts'. Specifically, Robert cannot accept Christ's divinity, the biblical miracles, or the 'damnatory psalms'. Yet, the Revd Mr Elsmere 'believes'.

Elsmere is a product of Oxford in the 1850s. The university had been, since Newman's first 'Tract for the Times' in 1833, the epicentre of religious doubt and what Gladstone (reviewing *Robert Elsmere*) called 'the battle of belief'. After much spiritual battling, Elsmere moves towards a Unitarian position on matters of theology. He resigns his country living, and starts a 'settlement' for the poor ('The New Brotherhood') in the East End of London. At the end of the novel he dies of consumption. His monument, the New Brotherhood, lives on.

With its Gladstonian endorsement, *Robert Elsmere* sold by the thousand in Britain and the million in America where, at the height of its popularity, it was given away free with 4-cent bars of soap, on the principle evidently that cleanliness is next to godliness. Since there was at this period no international copyright, Mrs Ward got nothing from the sale of either book or bar.

The Victorian reading public had an insatiable appetite for this kind of fiction. From the 1840s onward there was a regular annual supply of 'novels of faith and doubt', a survey of which is offered in Margaret Maison's delightfully entitled *Search your Soul, Eustace!* (1961). The twentieth-century reader does not have much time for Eustace's soul-searching. If there is one category of Victorian fiction which has died the death, it is novels of faith and doubt. Even the greatest of them, *Robert Elsmere* (to my personal regret), has been unable to hold its place in the Oxford World's Classics catalogue. *Sic transit.*

Elizabeth Gaskell's *North and South*, although normally categorized an 'industrial novel', pivots on an act of religious conscience by the heroine's father. The Revd Mr Hale has been for a quarter of a century a clergyman in Hampshire. A morally weak, but scrupulous man, Hale out of the blue informs his appalled daughter that he must resign his living forthwith. Moreover, he charges the girl to pass the news on to his invalid wife. He has 'doubts', Mr Hale explains to Margaret, reiterating the resonant word three times. 'Doubts, papa! Doubts as to religion?' (p. 34) his shocked daughter asks. (With a rare flash of humour, Gaskell observes that Margaret wonders if her father 'were about to turn Mahometan'.) 'No! not doubts as to religion; not the slightest injury to that,' Mr Hale firmly replies.

He will, he tells Margaret, just this once answer any questions as to his changed views on religion: 'but after tonight let us never speak of it again.' None the less, during this single question-and-answer session, Mr Hale is sadly unspecific as to what his 'painful, miserable doubts' actually are. The whole point about doubts is that they can go in any number of directions. If not Islam, Mr Hale could be moving anywhere on a whole spectrum of doctrinal positions from high Catholicism to low Methodism.

Mr Hale does not answer his daughter's barrage of anxious enquiries directly. Reaching up to his bookshelf he reads out a long—and not very illuminating—peroration from 'a Mr Oldfield', a country minister in Derbyshire, 'a hundred and sixty years ago, or more' (p. 34). The Revd Hale's recitation is not easy to follow and even harder to apply to his own case. Oldfield is not a household name, nor was he in 1854 (rarely, incidentally, have Oxford World's Classics notes been so necessary). Oldfield was, with 2,000 others as we discover, ejected from his living in 1662 (on the return of the monarch) on grounds of his refusal to 'conform'.

The only thing to the point which Mr Hale says to Margaret is that the bishop has recently offered him a new living, and the offer crystallized his spiritual uneasiness, and brought it to the pitch of rebellion—or at least resignation. 'I should have had to make a fresh declaration of conformity to the Liturgy' (p. 36), he tells his daughter. This means, apparently, that he would be obliged to make a new affirmation to the Thirty-Nine Articles, as he earlier did at college, at ordination, and on taking over his present living. Even refusing the preferment and staying at Helstone is now beyond him. He must resign.

But why? What precisely is it in the declaration of conformity which causes Mr Hale such agony at this moment? Which of the articles are difficult for him?— presumably those great bones of theological contention, the Apostolic Succession or the Trinity, although one cannot know.[1] He has been at Helstone, as far as we can make out, for going on thirty years. Why resign now? The Oldfield comparison is not apt since he, and the two thousand others, were 'ejected'—driven out. If he just keeps his head down, no one is going to *eject* the vicar of Helstone if he drifts towards a broad, or low-church position. As long as he does nothing wilfully provocative, he has considerable freedom to redefine his personal position on matters of faith and conscience. The only person who can eject Mr Hale is the vicar of Helstone. He is, as we gather; a conscientious and caring parish priest much loved by his 'people'.

Mr Hale is an Oxford man (a significant detail), and has evidently kept in touch with his alma mater. His old tutor at 'Plymouth College' (Exeter College, we apprehend, from the geographical clue), Mr Bell, has connections in the north of England and has arranged for him to be a private tutor in 'Milton-Northern' (Manchester we apprehend) in 'Darkshire' (Lancashire, self-evidently).

A less pliant young lady than Margaret Hale might bridle at all this. For obscure reasons, she was obliged to leave home at the age of 9 and was billeted on relatives in London. The Shaws were kind enough—but they were not her beloved parents. In the interim, the Revd Mr Hale and his wife lavished their attention on her feckless brother Frederick—who after participating in a naval mutiny has been forced to join the Spanish army. A Spanish bride is in prospect. Now, at last, Margaret has returned to rural Helstone, a Hampshire village which she loves. She is a nubile 18 and, as she fondly thinks, is being prepared for a suitable marriage. Now she discovers—after only three months at home—that her father is intent on packing her off to the satanic mills of Darkshire. None the less, she does her duty—taking charge of the household from the incompetent hands of her invalid and neurotic mother whom the Revd Mr Hale, for all his 'conscience', has left entirely in the dark as to his intentions.

On the face of it, Mr Hale's 'agony' seems a mirror image of Robert Elsmere's, as does his drift towards Unitarianism—Christianity based on a 'human' conception of Christ, and ritual stripped to its minimal and most 'rational' form. With its intellectual core at Oxford, 'doubt' pulled mid-century Anglicans in two opposite directions. Rome and Newman was one; Manchester and the arch-Unitarian, James Martineau, was the other. Mrs

Gaskell's husband, William, was of course a Manchester Unitarian, as was she. Mr Hale too, we assume, will gravitate towards Martineau and Unitarianism, although it is not made entirely clear in the novel that he does so. His son Frederick (another 'rebel') gravitates towards Catholicism.[2]

Tempting as the comparison with Robert Elsmere is, Angus Easson specifically warns us in his notes to the Oxford World's Classics edition not to jump to it. The novels, he reminds us, are divided by almost thirty years— decades which were momentous for the Victorian Church. Elizabeth Gaskell did not intend a 'novel of religious doubt' of the kind popular later in the nineteenth century, but more of a 'crisis of conscience' novel. Mr Hale's dilemma is not, specifically, theological but temporal. He cannot accept that the Church of England has any right to *compel* men's beliefs. His position is akin to that of the rebellious dissenters of the seventeenth century. It is coercion, not doubt, which principally agonizes him.

Easson has tracked down the sources and the actual book from which Mr Hale lengthily quotes to Margaret. John Oldfield (1627?–82) was an obscure Derbyshire rector, ejected in 1662 under the Uniformity Act. Mr Hale quotes him as cited in a later text, *The Apology of Theophilus Lindsey* (1774). Lindsey—a dissenter even more obscure than Oldfield—was one of the founders of what later became Manchester Unitarianism. Angus Easson, as far as I am aware, is the only reader to have cracked this nut. Until he wrote an article on it in the *Review of English Studies*,[3] the Oldfield-Lindsey business was a secret between him and Elizabeth Gaskell. Few readers of the 1850s, and fewer in the 1990s, will pick up the intricate allusion to remote texts of forgotten religious controversies. Elizabeth Gaskell, it seems, was playing a very deep game. But what game, and why?

It is the more tantalizing since, after he leaves Helstone, Mr Hale seems to have no religion whatsoever. Over the next three years, during which he is a central personage in the novel, we never know what church in Milton he attends; what religious company he consorts with; whether or not he takes Communion. In one sense, this disinclination to specify could be temperamental—a Gaskellian trait. She is characteristically vague on a number of crucial narrative occasions. There is part of her, apparently, which thinks it bad form to be too direct about such personal matters as religion and health. When, for instance, Mrs Hale falls ill, Margaret alone is told by Mr Donaldson what fatal ailment she has: 'He spoke two short sentences in a low voice, watching her all the time.' Margaret blanches, and exclaims: 'Oh, my God, my God! but this is terrible. How shall I bear it? Such a deadly disease! no hope!' (p. 127). Mrs Hale is a long time dying, and we are given close descriptions of her 'spasms'. But what, specifically, the 'deadly disease' is we know no more than what Mr Hale's 'miserable and painful doubts' are.

One can, however, profitably pursue the puzzling religious doubts. Elizabeth Gaskell is insistent about the contemporaneousness of her 1854 narrative. It is, on the face of it, odd that in the late 1840s–early 1850s Mr Hale (MA Oxon.) should evoke obscure martyrs of 180 years ago. There were nearer martyrs than John Oldfield to evoke. Richard Hale (55 at the time of his death) must, we calculate, have been a student at Oxford in the 1820s at the same time as Newman and Keble. He would certainly, as a bright young undergraduate with a religious vocation, have come into contact with 'Oxford's agony'. He would have been immersed in the debate on Tractarian 'doubts' and the spiritual counter-movements which were tearing the university apart, and with it the Church of England.

Moreover (as the first readers of *North and South* would

have appreciated), there were some notorious novels on the subject of religious doubt written alongside Elizabeth Gaskell's. In 1849, five years before *North and South*, J. A. Froude published *The Nemesis of Faith*, 'the most notorious religious novel of the century', as it has been called. Its literally incendiary impact can be indicated by a brief summary:

The story is told in confessional autobiographical form. Markham Sutherland, a young Oxford undergraduate, prepares for ordination in the Anglican Church, but is agonized by doubts which are expressed in a series of letters to a friend, Arthur, in the early 1840s. He cannot believe in the savage God of the Old Testament. At his family's urging and after six months' inward struggle, he takes orders, but resolves only to give ethical, not religious instruction. He is denounced by his co-religionists and obliged to give up his living. At this point of the narrative, Markham's epistolary record becomes the 'Confessions of a Sceptic', comprising straight theological disquisition ... The novel was publicly burned (for its manifest blasphemy) at Oxford by William Sewell.[4]

Sewell was a fellow of Exeter College, who had written his own novel strenuously opposing 'doubt', *Hawkstone, A Tale of and for England* (1845), tilting principally at Newman (fellow at Oriel). Newman—shortly after going over to Rome—weighed in with *his* novel about 'doubt', *Loss and Gain, the Story of a Convert* (1848).

If one accepts the Plymouth College–Exeter College link, one could argue that Mr Bell—the Revd Hale's mentor and intimate friend—must have taken dinner several nights a week with the choleric Revd Sewell, and have heard his colleague's thunderous denunciations of 'atheist' Froude and 'apostate' Newman. It is, of course, probable that the Mancunian Bell is a covert Unitarian—uncomfortable in his faith, but unwilling to discommode himself by any act of rebellion that would mean no more sinecure, no more high table, no more good college wine. Best say nothing and put up with Sewell's nightly rant.

The Nemesis of Faith was not, in Angus Easson's term 'popular'—indeed, it was sufficiently unpopular in some quarters to be incinerated; a rare distinction it shares with Hardy's *Jude the Obscure*. But Froude's novel was certainly well known, and it is inconceivable that the inmates of Helstone's vicarage would not have heard of it, even if they had not read it. Helstone (which has a railway service) must be very cut off, and Mr Hale must be very out of it in 1850, if he has not heard of the current book-burnings in the Anglican Church. And any well-informed Victorian reading about Mr Hale's doubts in 1854 would, one may be sure, recall the Oxford furore provoked by Newman, Froude, and Sewell. There was, surely, no need for Mr Hale to go back 180 years to find precedents for his 'doubts' and his act of conscience. Markham Sutherland gives up his living, on what look like remarkably similar grounds. Why, then, is Elizabeth Gaskell not as forthright on the subject of Mr Hale's doubts as Froude is? The question relates to another area of referential fogginess in *North and South*: that concerning 'Milton-Northern' and 'Darkshire'. These locations are, self-evidently, Manchester and Lancashire. Why not, then, use the proper names? *North and South* was Elizabeth Gaskell's third novel. Her first, *Mary Barton*, is boldly subtitled 'A Manchester Story' and introduces any number of actual urban locations. Why this topographical masquerade in *North and South*?

In order to makes sense of the veiled names, it is necessary to consider the journal for which Gaskell's novel was first written. Unlike *Mary Barton* (which was published first in two volumes), *North and South* was serialized in *Household Words*, a 2*d*. weekly journal 'conducted' by Charles Dickens. It followed hard on Dickens's own serial

for the paper, *Hard Times*. Both novels are 'social problem' novels (sometimes called 'Condition of England'
novels) set in the industrial north, around Manchester.
And both were directly inspired by the bitter Preston
Strike of 1854, in which textile-mill workers demanded a
raise in their hourly rate of pay and the masters locked
them out for months, precipitating great hardship and the
eventual collapse of the workers' action. *Hard Times's*
'Coketown' is an amalgam of Manchester and Preston.
Although no strike features directly in the narrative,
union agitators from London are shown working up the
mill-hands to an act of desperation.

In *North and South* Gaskell pivots her story on a strike
(see, for example, the chapter 'What is a Strike?'). The
conflict between 'Masters and Men' makes up the central
events of the narrative. And, in a larger sense, Gaskell's
novel is a meditation on civil disobedience—in the form of
industrial action, military mutiny, and religious dissent.
But, no more than Dickens in *Hard Times*, does she directly mention the great Preston strike—something that
must have been in the forefront of the mind of every British reader of both novels. As Dickens masked Preston-
Manchester as 'Coketown' she masks the conurbation as
'Milton-Northern' (i.e. 'a northern mill town').

North and South obliquely alludes to Preston and to the
Oxford religious controversies of the time in discreet
but—for the wideawake reader of the 1850s—transparent
codes. Both Dickens and Gaskell are doing, in these 'problem novels', what fiction, in an expert's hands, does very
effectively—writing about 'the problem' without directly
naming it, but in such a way that it does not have to be
named. It is analogous to what in gunnery is, I believe,
called 'aiming off'—having your shells land a little to
the side of the target. It is clear that this 'aiming off' was
deliberate on Gaskell's part in the matter of Mr Hale's

doubts. When she began writing, Dickens specifically warned his author to play down Mr Hale's religious doubts:

This is the place [in the narrative] where we agreed that there should be a great condensation, and a considerable compression, where Mr Hale states his doubts to Margaret . . . What I would recommend—and did recommend—is, to make the scene between Margaret and her father relative to his leaving the church and their destination being Milton-Northern, as short as you can find it in your heart to make it.[5]

Dickens gives as the reasons for this curtailing 'the mechanical necessities of *Household Words*', but this is clearly a pretext. As Easson points out, Dickens 'shied away' from 'doctrinal controversy' in his paper. He did not want a *Nemesis of Faith* and some zealot burning copies of *Household Words*, God forbid! As with Preston, some decent muffling was in order. *Household Words* had a broad-based 'family' readership, as its name implied: the kind of readership which required caution on the perennially divisive and sensitive topics of sex, religion, and politics. He was not imposing a total suppression. A little 'aiming off' would do it.

Mrs Gaskell duly did as tactfully instructed and, in the matter of Mr Hale's doubts, alluded to what she meant, rather than plunging into the religious disputes of the 1840s. Intelligent readers would fill in the blanks without difficulty. What one concludes is that we lose a lot in Victorian fiction by not reading Victorian daily newspapers. With *North and South*, modern readers are in the position of their great-great-grandchildren watching a rerun of *Our Friends in the North* in—say—2098. Without, that is, having followed the 1984 coal strike on the evening television news, or without knowing—from personal and painful acquaintance—what the stresses of the Thatcherite 'enterprise culture' meant for those who lived through it and had their lives turned upside down. Doubtless those future watchers of the television mini-series will, with the advantage of a century's historical hindsight, see the drama more clearly than we do. But that hand-in-glove intimacy with the present, and that precious ability to intuit what the author *means* (but is not directly saying) will be lost.

The Oxford World's Classics *North and South* is edited by Angus Easson, revised by Sally Shuttleworth.

Name Games

An Oxford World's Classics reader, John Cameron, writes to ask if I have noticed that between pages 123 and 147 of *Oliver Twist*

> there are lots of references to Jack Dawkins (the Artful Dodger) and Charley Bates. Bates is referred to variously as Mr Charles Bates, Charley Bates, Charley, and, most equivocally, *Master Bates*. Out of 28 references, he is called 'Master Bates' 7 times. Dawkins, on the other hand, is called Jack Dawkins, John Dawkins, Dodger, Mr Dawkins but never 'Master Dawkins'. Is Dickens having a joke at the expense of his readers, I wonder? Or is this just a figment of my own suspicious mind?

Other suspicious readers and some critics have wondered whether Dickens is making an off-colour joke with 'Master Bates'.[1] There is no doubt that Dickens often uses embedded word-association in the names of his characters. Murdstone and Merdle, for instance, combine the overtones of the French *merde* ('shit') and 'murder'. Murdstone is a stony-hearted murderer; Merdle deals with 'filthy' lucre. 'Uriah Heep' brings with it, every time the name and its owner crop up in *David Copperfield*, a subliminal vision of a heap of ordure ('uria' is defined in the dictionary as 'urine' and 'urea', even less attractively, as 'the solid component of mammalian urine'). Likewise, Carker and 'cack' (a slang term for excrement). Dickens, we may deduce, would not flinch from 'Master Bates— masturbates' on grounds of taste. But the objection to its being deliberate is that the schoolboy joke ('This is Mr and Mrs Bates, and their son Master Bates')—although current from time immemorial—would seem *below* the author of *Oliver Twist*.

Dickens's mastery of the art of nomenclature is most

striking in his creation of new names that carry with
them suggestions that we cannot quite pin down. Of all
the Victorian novelists, he is the most original coiner of
names. The originality has not pleased every reader.
Thackeray observed while *David Copperfield* was still
coming out: 'I quarrel with his [Dickens's] Art in many
respects; which I don't think represents Nature duly; for
instance Micawber appears to me an exaggeration of a
man, as his name is of a name.'[2] Philip Collins once told
me that there are no Scottish names in Dickens, with the
possible exception of the less-than-his-best M'Choakum-
child in *Hard Times* or Mrs MacStinger in *Dombey and
Son*. But 'Micawber' has a certain Scottishness to the ear;
if not the eye, and it is not impossible to hear (if not see) it
as a bastard variant of 'MacIvor' (a prominent and heroic
name in Scott's *Waverley*, and ironically appropriate for
the great Wilkins).

Quilp is—for reasons which are hard to express—
horribly sinister; Gargery is vaguely reassuring; Rosa Bud
is perhaps too obviously virginal (although we may suspect the Blakean worm at work within); Estella is cold,
distant, and starlike ('Stella' would be less so); Biddy is
biddable (but not, alas, to her suitor Pip); Bounderby is a
bounder; Scrooge (with the echo of 'screw') is miserly; and
Cratchit catches, by its onomatopoeia, the weary scratch
of the clerk's pen on paper. Dombey, Dorrit, and Jarndyce
are pregnant with suggestive but ultimately elusive
associations. Sometimes Dickens was prepared to load
the name of a character with private reference: he called
his wicked Jew by an Irish name, because—for reasons
that only a psychoanalyst could fathom—he associated
the merry old gentleman with a young gent, Bob Fagin,
one of his workmates in the blacking factory. He called the
wife- and horse-beating villain of *Great Expectations*,
'Bentley' after the 'Brigand of Burlington Street', the

publisher Richard Bentley, whom he conceived to have robbed him when a young author.

Occasionally a literary echo can be picked up in Dickens. Esther Summerson is, presumably, so-called by allusion to that other famous foundling, Tom Jones, whose father we discover on almost the last page, was called 'Summer'. Hence Tom is Summer's son. The haughty Sir John Chester in *Barnaby Rudge* recalls Lord Chesterfield, whose doctrine of 'manners maketh nobleman' Dickens despised. 'Humouristic' names often figure in the Ben Jonson-loving author's fiction. Hence the paralysed-by-rank Dedlock, and Gradgrind, the grinder out of graduates (although after some thought, Dickens gave him the 'doubting' Christian name Thomas, leaving open a small aperture for future redemption).[3]

I suspect that the 'Master Bates' acoustic pun was accidental, although it may have been unconsciously revolving in Dickens's mind (hence the obsessive seven usages). Richard Altick suspects that Thackeray's 'naughty joke' in *Pendennis* was similarly accidental or unconscious.[4] In that novel, Thackeray called the purest of maiden heroines Laura Bell. This happened to be the name of one of the most notorious courtesans of the mid-Victorian age. Putting it into *Pendennis* would be like John Updike naming the heroine of his next novel 'Heidi Fleiss'. In 1848, however, when Thackeray began serializing his novel, she was not as notorious as she was later to become. It may have been, as the twentieth-century disclaimer routinely puts it, 'entirely coincidental'.

According to Henry James, Thackeray is 'perfect' in the devising of comic, or otherwise meaningful names for his characters. Nowhere is this perfection more evident than in his Bunyan-titled novel *Vanity Fair*. Becky is sharp both by name and by nature. The Scott allusion (to Jewish Rebecca and Saxon Rowena in *Ivanhoe*) carries, as Kathleen Tillotson notes, a slight but tingling racial charge.[5] Amelia recalls Fielding's passively good wife in the eponymous novel. Dobbin is the steady-as-she-goes carthorse who gets there in the end. George Osborne combines the Christian name of the author's abhorred 'first gentleman of Europe', and a buried anagram of 'snob' (Thackeray invented the term, in his great 'snobonomy', *The Snobs of England*, 1846–7).

Thackeray hit his title and main elements of *Vanity Fair's* plot while holidaying at Brighton (the Prince Regent's favourite holiday resort). Brighton and Sussex inspired many of the names. The 'Southdown' family is headed by its sheepishly docile (and plain) Lady Jane. The Crawleys (Crawley is a small town near Brighton) are so named for their hundreds of years of sucking up ('crawling') to those in power. The Crawleys always, however, 'rat' at the wrong time, as Chapter 7, summarizing the family history, makes clear. Dominating this complex of Brighton names is the Marquis of Steyne—with its combination of the grand esplanade and 'stain'—appropriate for this most morally spattered of noblemen.

In his later fiction Thackeray curbed his propensity for meaningful or prophetic names. But Arthur Pendennis ('Pen') is, in his nickname at least, the embodiment of hopeful authorship. It would have pleased Thackeray to think that, a century later, the most powerful society of authors would be called 'PEN'. The young swell, and would-be seducer of women, is called 'Foker' (which may be as near an improper pun as Thackeray would consciously allow himself); the future doctor in *Pendennis* is called 'Huxter' (or 'huckster'). In *Esmond* Rachel is so called because, like her biblical namesake, she must faithfully wait many years and outlive a husband before she can be united with her true love (in Virginia—some hopes!). Beatrix was originally (in the manuscript of the novel) called 'Beatrice'—the young girl worshipped from her fourteenth year, Dante fashion, from afar by the older hero. In Thackeray's next full-length novel, the Newcomes are so called because they are both a *nouveau riche* and an *arriviste* family. By this middle stage of his career Thackeray is more consistently realistic in his naming practices. By the time of his last completed novel, *The Adventures of Philip*, he has adopted the 'muscular school' habit of using ostentatiously democratic surnames: Philip Firmin belongs with Tom Brown, Lance Smith, and Guy Livingstone. Trollope guys the Guy Livingstone fashion in the title of his 1861 novel, *The Struggles of Brown, Jones, and Robinson* (one of his weakest efforts). These manly ('firm') heroes are emblematic of the 'best of Britishness' (see Hughes's eulogy on the 'Browns of England' in the opening chapters of *Tom Brown's Schooldays*). In shorter fiction, to the end of his career Thackeray confected aptly descriptive names. We know, from the moment we hear the name, that Mr Batchelor will not win the girl in *Lovel the Widower* and that Lovel (love-all) will.

Henry James uses Thackeray's mastery in the 'science of names' as a stick with which to beat Trollope's clumsiness.[6] James specifically cites, from *Barchester Towers*, the doctor Mr Rerechild and the Revd Mr Quiverful (with his many children) as examples of Trollope at his most heavy-handed (compare Quiverful, for example, to Thackeray's delightfully philoprogenitive 'the Revd Felix Rabbits'). One could cite in support of James's criticism Trollope's litigious barrister Samuel Dockwrath (in *Orley Farm*), his brewers Bungall and Tappitt (in *Rachel Ray*), his lethal physician Dr Fillgrave (in *Doctor Thorne*), his arch-feminist Baroness Banmann (in *Is he Popenjoy?*), and the breeches-maker Neefit (in *Ralph the Heir*). These, particularly the last, are groan-making.

Nonetheless, even in *Barchester* one can find a bundle of

wittily apposite names. There is Miss Trefoil (an amateur
botanist), 'old Scalpen' (the retired apothecary and tooth-
drawer), farmer Subsoil, and Mr Finnie (the cold-blooded
attorney). Mr Plomacy, although we are never informed of
the fact, must have a first name beginning with 'D'—he is
so unfailingly diplomatic. The peas-in-a-pod doctors, Sir
Lamda Mewnew and Sir Omicron Pie, have their names
made up of the eleventh to sixteenth letters of the Greek
alphabet—a little Hippocratic joke. Mr Arabin's curious
name can be glossed as 'a rabin' (or 'religious teacher'),
and strikes one as just right for the man.

According to James, Trollope's indicative names are
acceptable when they are attached to background characters (like Dickens's generic 'Barnacles'), but they jar
when those characters (as do Neefit and Quiverful) move
to the foreground of the action. 'We can believe in the
name [of Quiverful] as we believe in the [fourteen] children, but we cannot manage the combination,' James concludes.[7] James is aware (as not all modern readers may be)
of the joke in Mr Quiverful's name—the allusion to Psalm
127: 4–5: 'As arrows are in the hand of a mighty man: so
are children of the youth. Happy is the man that hath his
quiver full of them.'

Mrs Proudie, James concedes, is an excellent name. But
is the pronunciation as in 'proud' or 'prude'? Trollope
never tells us, letting both adjectives hover over the proud
and prudish lady. Other felicities can be found in the ranks
of Trollope's principal characters. Augustus Melmotte, in
The Way We Live Now, is imperious, cosmopolitan, and
rootless, like the hero of Maturin's novel *Melmoth the
Wanderer* (there are fainter echoes of the common Jewish
name 'Malamud'). Quintus Slide is a slithery journalist's
name (in *Phineas Finn*) that Thackeray himself might be
proud of. Johnny Eames (the faithful lover in *The Small
House at Allington* and *The Last Chronicle of Barset*) is so

called, I believe, in deference to that favourite Horatian
tag of both Thackeray's and Trollope's:

servetur ad imum
Qualis ab incepto processerit, et sibi constet.[8]

Eames is faithful to Lily Dale *ad imum* ('to the last'). But
why, one wonders, did Trollope pick up that obnoxious
Thackeray name for his most admirably dogged hero,
Josiah Crawley (in *The Last Chronicle of Barset*)? The
Revd Mr Crawley is no crawler, but it may be that bowing
the knee to proud bishops called Proudie sticks in his
craw. The obnoxious Thackerayan tinge in 'Crawley' is
none the less disturbing, as is the Shakespearian tinge of
'Shylock' in Sherlock Holmes.

Trollope is responsible for the funniest joke by an
author about his own name in Victorian fiction. Apropos
of Obadiah Slope, in *Barchester Towers*, the narrator
notes that the clergyman may be descended from 'that
eminent physician who assisted at the birth of Mr T.
Shandy' (I. 25). Trollope here refers to an unsavoury
episode in the early chapters of Sterne's *The Life and
Opinions of Tristram Shandy*. In Volume II, chapter 9 of
Sterne's narrative, the 'man-midwife', Dr Slop, is introduced, accompanied by a maladroit servant, Obadiah.
Slop is short, fat, and 'a Papist'. The name alludes to
his besmirched appearance (he is introduced, having just
fallen in the mud). Many chapters and much salacious
detail is devoted to the subsequent delivery of the hero
at Dr Slop's 'obstetrick hand'. 'For euphony' an 'e' has
been added to 'Slop(e)' we are told. The euphonious 'e'
introduces an overtone of both 'slippery' and 'trimmer'.
Mr Slope is no Catholic, but an evangelical Protestant.
As David Skilton has noted, the remark about other
great men having added an 'e' to their surname 'for
euphony' evidently refers to Trollop(e)'s own surname.[9]

It's amusingly sly. Trollope, especially at school, must have
put up with much badinage. ('Hey, Anthony! Is your
mother a trollop?')

George Eliot's names are frequently 'loaded' with literary or other implications. 'Adam Bede' incarnates Adamic
rural strength and venerable Christian integrity. Hetty
Sorrel's surname recalls a bitter (forbidden) fruit. 'Hetty'
throws back the echo 'petty' and 'pretty'. In *Middlemarch*
Mr Brooke babbles—especially after two glasses of sherry.
Unfortunately, his name is bequeathed for part of the book
to his niece Dorothea, who does not babble, although
Celia may be said to do so. Lydgate's fall is like the fall of
the princes about whom John Lydgate wrote. Edward
Casaubon's name has tantalized generations of commentators with its apparently over-determined allusion to the
seventeenth-century French scholar; Isaac Casaubon.
Ladislaw (originally pronounced 'Ladislav') is the slave of
ladies. Gwendolen Harleth, the heroine of *Daniel Deronda*,
is a woman who sells her body to a man she does not love.
Her surname evokes Richardson's Clarissa Harlowe, and
through her, 'harlot',

Elizabeth Gaskell has a good ear for a naturalistic
sounding name, but an odd preference for the '-on' suffix:
as in Jem Wilson and John Barton (in *Mary Barton*), Mr
and Mrs Thornton (in *North and South*), Ruth Hilton and
Mr Benson (in *Ruth*), Sylvia Robson (in *Sylvia's Lovers*),
and Molly Gibson and her father Mr Gibson (in *Wives and
Daughters*). Mrs Gaskell's maiden name was Stevenson.
The Brontës, as David Lodge has noted, have a tendency
towards powerfully elemental names: Jane Eyre (air),
Helen Burns (fire), St John Rivers (water), Lucy Snowe
(frozen water), Heathcliff (heath and cliff), Robert Gerard
Moore (moor), Helstone (stone).[10]

Wilkie Collins usually invents names with no superficially obvious loadings. An exception is the right-hearted

Walter Hartright in Collins's *The Woman in White*. Like the
wavering Waverley in Scott's novel, or the *toujours l'audace*
Lady Audley in Mrs Braddon's sensation novel, Walter's
character is encapsulated in his Dudley Dogood name. More
to my taste are Collins's out-and-out surrealistic names, such
as the tract-dropping Drusilla Clack in *The Moonstone* or
Ozias Midwinter, the Creole hero of *Armadale* (a novel which
is remarkable for having five characters called Allan
Armadale).

Thomas Hardy typically flavours his names with
regional associations, but occasionally adds tinctures
from other sources. In *Tess of the d'Urbervilles: A Pure
Woman*, his 'pure man' is called 'Angel Clare' and plays a
harp, which may be an allusion too far. 'Durbeyfield' has,
to my ear, a meaningful echo of 'dirty-field'. An exception
to Hardy's usual realism where names are concerned is
Far from the Madding Crowd, in which the oak-like hero is
called 'Gabriel Oak', the flashy soldier who abducts the
beautiful woman 'Sergeant Troy' (provoking a little war by
so doing), and the woman who is lusted after by three men
'Bathsheba'. And did any Victorian novelist come up with
a better name for a flirt than 'Fancy Day' (in *Under the
Greenwood Tree*)?

Names have values embodied in them. They carry baggage. It is noticeable, for example, that characters named
after middle-sized (particularly northern) English towns
are invariably strong people in Victorian fiction, although
not always nice: see, for example, Edward Rochester (*Jane
Eyre*), George Warrington (*Pendennis*), Stephen Blackpool
(*Hard Times*), John Halifax (*John Halifax, Gentleman*),
and Arthur Huntingdon (*The Tenant of Wildfell Hall*).
Villains are rarely called Frank (an exception is the utter
cad Frank Levison in *East Lynne*). 'Fred', on the other
hand, seems to bring with it associations of weakness: as
in Fred Vincy (*Middlemarch*) and Fred Neville (*An Eye for*

an Eye), two of the weakest-kneed heroes to be found in
the novel of the period. Latin names in Trollope's fiction
(see Adolphus Crosbie, Undecimus Scott, Augustus Melmotte, and the Revd Joseph Emilius) are invariably dubious. His elder brother was called Adolphus, and—'a student of Draco'—beat Anthony mercilessly when they were
boys at school together. Jasper is not a reassuring name,
and from its overtones alone I deduce that John Jasper did
indeed murder Edwin Drood. It could, however, be a case
of 'give a dog a bad name and hang him'.

Charles Dickens · *A Tale of Two Cities*

———

Where does Sydney Carton get his chloroform?

———

Before Sydney Carton can do the far better thing than he has ever done he is obliged (rather ignobly) to disable his double, Charles Darnay, with an anaesthetic and have him smuggled insensibly out of Revolutionary France to the safety of England. Carton's plan is complicated by the fact that, in reprisal for the Evremonde crimes (testified to, unwillingly, by his father-in law, Dr Manette), Charles has been sentenced to death. The young aristo is being held in the impregnable 'black prison of the Conciergerie' (p. 428), closely guarded by fanatic sentinels, until—in a few hours—Madame Guillotine does her bloody work and there is one Evremonde the less.

Carton lays his plot with care. First he pays a call on a sinister Parisian apothecary:

traversing with the decided step of one who remembered the way well, several dark and dirty streets—much dirtier than usual, for the best public thoroughfares remained uncleansed in those times of terror—he stopped at a chemist's shop, which the owner was closing with his own hands. A small, dim, crooked shop, kept in a tortuous, up-hill thoroughfare, by a small, dim, crooked man. (p. 386)

Carton gives the crooked chemist a prescription which he has written himself. '"Whew!" the chemist whistled, as he read it. "Hi! hi! hi!".' (That 'Whew!', incidentally, strikes one as un-Gallic.) As he fills the prescription in 'certain small packets' the chemist accompanies it with a warning:

'You will be careful to keep them separate, citizen? You know the consequences of mixing them.' 'Perfectly,' Carton answers, in what we take to be flawless French. The second, and more dangerous part of the plan follows. Carton has recognized the turnkey at the Conciergerie as a former Old Bailey spy, Barsad (he is also, by fantastic coincidence, Miss Pross's scapegrace brother Solomon). Armed with this information, Carton is able to blackmail Barsad to smuggle him into Darnay's solitary cell on his day of doom.

As the Oxford World's Classics notes point out, condemned prisoners were allowed to write a 'last' letter—a privilege equivalent to the English prisoner's 'hearty' last breakfast. It is on this pretext that Carton comes to the jail. Once in the cell, by sheer peremptoriness the young lawyer cajoles a mystified Darnay to change outer clothes, cravat, and boots with him and to shake out his hair from its 'queue', to look more like his (Sydney Carton's). Darnay does as he is told; without having the faintest idea, apparently, what purpose his visitor has in mind with these instructions. Fear has paralysed him. 'The prisoner was like a young child in his hands' (p. 433), as the narrative records.

Their outer dress exchanged, Carton instructs Darnay to take down a letter to his (Carton's) dictation. Meanwhile, the Englishman stands over the sitting prisoner, 'with his hand in his breast'. 'What is it in your hand?' Darnay asks. Carton does not answer but merely commands 'Write on.' The words he dictates seem of little significance. But while uttering them, Carton's hand 'slowly and softly moved down close to the writer's face'. Darnay breaks off from writing, with a 'vacant' look; 'What vapour is that?' he asks. 'Vapour?' Carton echoes. 'Something that crossed me' (p. 435), Darnay says. It was nothing, he is told. An increasingly distracted Darnay writes on—

his breathing becoming heavier. Again Carton's hand crosses 'slowly and softly' across the other man's face. Darnay's writing deteriorates into 'unintelligible signs' and, 'within a minute or so, he was stretched insensible on the ground' (p. 435).

Darnay uses the term 'vapour', which indicates fumes rising off a liquid, as opposed to wholly airborne 'gas'. We assume that Carton is administering some narcotic. We may also note that, whatever it is, it works extremely fast—a couple of minutes is all it takes—and is practically odourless. Carton now puts on the remainder of the prisoner's clothes and summons Barsad to take out the insensible young Frenchman—who will, of course, be mistaken for a fainted Sydney Carton by any suspicious guard. It was too much for the young man. Carton instructs Barsad that the unconscious Darnay be taken to Mr Lorry and given 'no restorative but air'. And, he adds, tell Lorry 'to remember my words of last night, and his promise of last night, and drive away!' (p. 436), taking Darnay and Lucie to safety in England.

A swarm of questions hover round this scene. First, how does Sydney Carton know so much about dubious French apothecaries and the dubious chemical substances they purvey? The clue is given in an early exchange with Stryver. The two lawyers were schoolboys together at Shrewsbury. Since those days, Carton ruefully observes, 'you have fallen into your rank, and I have fallen into mine. Even when we were fellow-students in the Student-Quarter of Paris, picking up French, and French law and other French crumbs that we didn't get much good of, you were always somewhere, and I was always—nowhere' (p. 105).

This period of study in Paris explains how it is that Carton can speak the language well enough to pass for a Frenchman (the chemist calls him 'Citizen'). And, we assume, among the 'crumbs' the two young dogs picked up was a knowledge of illicit pharmacology. Students don't change much. Carton 'remembers' the chemist's location well because he went there often as a young man. In passing, we may be curious as to why—alongside the obvious drugs a licentious law student might want ('recreational' substances, and nostrums for venereal disease)—Carton should have made himself so knowledgeable about 'Mickey Finns', or 'knockout drops', as they are called in pulp fiction.

The overriding question is—what is this unnamed 'vapour', a couple of whiffs of which renders Darnay rapidly unconscious—but not life-threateningly so? The Oxford World's Classics notes tentatively suggest that it is 'Sulphuric ether'. This was one of the varieties of 'laughing gas' that became commonly used in the mid-nineteenth century (the other was nitrous oxide). Andrew Sanders's note is on the right lines, but chemically wrong. The substance Carton uses is quite clearly chloroform.

Reference either to ether or chloroform, would, of course, have been entirely appropriate for the 1859–60 period in which *A Tale of Two Cities* was written and published, but entirely inappropriate to the French Revolutionary period in which the narrative is set. The history of 'inhalation anaesthetics' in the mid-nineteenth century is a matter of medical-historical record. In 1846 it was successfully demonstrated in America, by an American dentist called Morton, that sulphuric ether could be used to anaesthetize patients undergoing operations. Hitherto the only anaesthetic available to surgeons or dentists was mesmerism. Enthusiasts believed in it, many (particularly those about to undergo radical surgery) were sceptical. There could be no doubt that ether, properly applied, rendered the subject wholly unconscious, deadened the pain of operation, and represented little risk to recovery.

Morton's discovery was picked up by the English medical establishment in late 1846 and triggered what has been called an 'Ethereal Epidemic'.[1] Although ether (and chloroform) had been around for some time as compounds, and their properties recorded, the realization that they could be safely used for surgery was one of the most exciting medical breakthroughs of the century.

In the first six months of 1847 the *Lancet* published 112 articles on 'ether anaesthesia'. The Scottish physician James Simpson made a worldwide reputation, and earned himself a knighthood and a place in the *DNB* as an advocate of the ether-anaesthetic technique in the late 1840s. Exciting breakthrough though it was, ether had some shortcomings as an ideal inhalation-anaesthetic. As a 'laughing gas', it was widely abused and popularly associated with 'drunkenness', in much the same way that aerosol-based nitrous oxide and ether-based glue are today. For the physician ether was difficult, being a gas, to administer. Effectively, it could only be done with the full co-operation of the patient, either through a mask or by breathing in from a beaker with a covering over the head.

There were obvious difficulties with delirious patients, infant patients, or patients thrashing about in pain. These problems were remedied with the innovation of chloroform. Chloroform could be easily produced, in liquid form, by the mixture of various agents (hence the 'several packets' which the chemist gives to Sydney Carton). It could be stored, ready for use, as a stable, room-temperature, 'ponderous' liquid. A few drops on cloth (the amount could be accurately measured) would suffice, as it vaporized, to render the patient unconscious. All that was required by way of co-operation was that the subject should breathe. In addition to being easier to administer, chloroform was extremely efficient and produced controllable unconsciousness quicker than sulphuric ether. Nor did it have any attractions for the drug-abuser. No one was tempted to take chloroform for kicks. Nor can chloroform be abused as a sedative, or as a means of suicide.

Dr John Snow publicly demonstrated the efficacy of chloroform to his fellow professionals in November 1847. They were persuaded of its superiority. By the end of the decade, as Alison Winter reports, chloroform had entirely replaced sulphuric ether as the inhalation-anaesthetic of choice. Chloroform was publicized to the British middle classes in the most effective way, when Snow used it in the delivery of two of Queen Victoria's children in April 1853 and April 1857. It was now an anaesthetic with a royal warrant. Snow died in 1858, and in the same year his great posthumous work, *Chloroform and other Anaesthetics*, was published.

Dickens's journals took a keen interest in the chloroform phenomenon. There were three articles in *Household Words* in the years leading up to *A Tale of Two Cities*: 'Some Account of Chloroform', by Percival Leigh (10 May 1851); 'Chloroform', by Henry Morley (23 April 1853); and 'Chloroform', by William Overend Priestley—one of Simpson's assistants—on the eve of publication of Dickens's novel (12 February 1859). Priestley's article hailed the drug ('this cup of Lethe') as a medical advance as momentous as Harvey's discovery of the circulation of the blood and Jenner's invention of vaccination. Dickens must have edited the article.

It seems incontrovertible that Dickens was thinking of chloroform in the Conciergerie scene in *A Tale of Two Cities*, written 1858–9, although he prudently doesn't identify Carton's drug by name. We are led to suppose that Carton has prepared the mixture before coming to the prison, secreting it on his person in a small pocket-flask, or as lint wrapped in greased paper. While leaning over Darnay, he passes the open flask (or uncovered lint) in front of his unsuspecting victim's face. A couple of passes does it. The vapour does its work, as efficiently as it doubtless did on Queen Victoria.

Although it is not named, every Victorian reader of 1859–60, bombarded as the public had been with descriptions of the new wonder drug, would have known what Dickens was writing about in this scene. One concludes that Sydney Carton should really have studied medicine rather than law. He is fully sixty years ahead of the British medical establishment. This use of chloroform—a drug not used as an inhalation-anaesthetic until 1847—seems, on the face of it, wildly anachronistic. It is equivalent to Jude Fawley and Sue Bridehead sharing a joint, or Tess Durbeyfield dropping some acid with her fellow milkmaids.

Novelists of the late 1850s and early 1860s were, however, entranced by the plot opportunities which chloroform offered, and be hanged to any anachronism. Thackeray in *Philip* (1860) similarly uses the drug to engineer a dramatic climax to his novel. As it happened, Thackeray was very interested in chloroform for personal reasons. He was considering an operation to relieve the stricture of the urethra which had tormented him for years. Without anaesthetic, such an operation would be hideously painful. In 1860 he published an article, 'Under Chloroform', in the *Cornhill Magazine* (of which he was the editor), in which he clearly outlines the surgical benefits of the anaesthetic.

Philip was first serialized in *Cornhill*. The novel's last section is set in the 1840s. Dr Firmin, the hero's worthless father, has been packed off to America, from where he sends back a number of products with which he hopes to make his fortune. They include, among other quite plainly crazy inventions, 'a cask of petroleum from Virginia' (that will never catch on!), and a small flask of chloroform ('this was what Dr Firmin chose to call his discovery'.

Rather surprisingly, Thackeray seems to imply that the name of the drug originated with one of his fictional personages). The 'Little Nurse'—a good woman who was seduced by Firmin years earlier—takes possession of this bottle of chloroform, and is instructed by her mentor, Dr Goodenough, how to use it.[2]

As it happens, she does not use it for medicinal ends. Instead, she employs it to knock out a villainous defrocked clergyman who is blackmailing the hero, Philip, with a money order on which Dr Firmin has forged his son's signature. While he is dozy from drink, the 'Little Nurse' passes a cloth, on which she has dropped some liquid chloroform, in front of his face. When he is 'under' she steals the bill, and Philip is safe. I would guess that Thackeray, as even great novelists are prone to do, 'borrowed' this chloroforming from *A Tale of Two Cities*, published a few months earlier. Thackeray, however, knew—when he wasn't changing history for fictional purposes—that what had been imported from America in 1846 was not chloroform but sulphuric ether. He also knew that the use of chloroform as an inhalation-anaesthetic had been pioneered not by a quack like Dr Firmin, but by the eminently (indeed royally) respectable British physician, Dr John Snow. Thackeray therefore added the following editorial footnote to the letter in which Dr Firmin announces his 'discovery' of what he calls 'chloroform':

'*Ether* was first employed, I believe, in America; and I hope the reader will excuse the substitution of Chloroform in this instance.—W.M.T.'[3]

One does forgive the author of *Philip* because it would have been impractical for the Little Nurse to have administered a gas like ether. Chloroform was required. Thackeray admits his anachronism, and craves the reader's indulgence, which is readily granted. On his part, Dickens

Judith and Holofernes

fudges the issue (and avoids the necessity of an embarrassing footnote) by never actually mentioning chloroform, although every wide-awake reader of 1859 would have realized what Carton had in his breast pocket.

In his 1859 novel, *The Woman in White*, set in 1851, Wilkie Collins also draws on the chloroform mania (the novel followed on *A Tale of Two Cities* as the lead serial in *All the Year Round*). In the crisis of Collins's narrative, at Blackwater Park, Count Fosco engineers the dismissal of the family physician Mr Dawson and takes personal charge of the neurasthenic Laura and the delirious Marian. Collins makes the point that Fosco has a 'vast knowledge of chemistry' and is well up with medical innovation in the 1850s. As she later recalls, Fosco contrived to render Laura senseless, in order to abduct her to his hideaway in St John's Wood, where vile things will be done to her. He does so by offering her a restorative, as (typically) she turns faint on being told that Marian is not to accompany her:

she hastily took the bottle of salts from Count Fosco, and smelt at it. Her head became giddy on the instant. The Count caught the bottle as it dropped out of her hand; and the last impression of which she was conscious was that he held it to her nostrils again. (p. 435)

It is clear that Fosco has spiked the smelling-salts with chloroform, although the drug's name is not mentioned. It is not, as in *A Tale of Two Cities* and *Philip*, an outright anachronism, although one does rather wonder at the Count's being so far ahead of the Queen's physician in these matters.

Does Dickens have any warrant for chloroform's being available to his hero in France in 1793, some fifty-four years before it was available to Dr Snow? A very small warrant. As the *OED* indicates, 'chloroform' was originally a French word and was current in French usage as early as the 1830s. If the word circulated in earlier decades in France, why should not the anaesthetic itself? It is a straw, but it is something on which to build narrative plausibility.

Postscript: What is Carton doing in France?

There is an incidental puzzle in *A Tale of Two Cities* which Kenneth Fielding points out. How do all the English nationals and sympathizers—Lorry, Lucie, Manette, Carton—have free right of entrance to and departure from France, a country with which England is at war? After a period of great turbulence, hostilities broke out between the two countries in January 1793. It is clear from internal references (to such things as the king's death in December of that year, see pp. 259–60, and Andrew Sanders's chronology of historical events in the Oxford World's Classics edition) that the climax of the novel is taking place in the last months of 1793.

The free passage of these English visitors in wartime France can be explained by a historical oddity in the history of passports. They were introduced to allow nationals privileged entrance to and exit from countries at war with each other and to control such aliens while they were within the borders. Passports did not serve, as they do today, to enable civilians unhindered passage during time of peace. Until the twentieth century passports were largely dispensed with during times of peace and normality. It is clear from his last conversations with Lorry that Carton is in possession of a certain 'certificate' which enables him 'at any time to pass the barrier [of the city of Paris] and the frontier'. There is some slightly mystifying conversation about these 'papers', but they are, evidently, 'letters of introduction'. This system of monitoring aliens was in the process of being superseded by strict passport controls, which required registration with the authorities. The new passport system was introduced by the Revolutionary government, culminating in the statute of September 1797. Doubtless, as a prudent man of law, Carton had letters of introduction drawn up with the authorities before coming to France, but has caught wind of sinister changes in the offing.[4]

The Oxford World's Classics *A Tale of two Cities* is edited by Andrew Sanders. The Oxford World's Classics *The Woman in White* is edited by John Sutherland.

==

Why doesn't Laura tell her own story?

==

The Woman in White opens with Walter Hartright's startlingly original declaration of how the subsequent narrative will be laid out:

> As the Judge might once have heard it, so the Reader shall hear it now. No circumstance of importance, from the beginning to the end of the disclosure, shall be related on hearsay evidence. When the writer of these introductory lines (Walter Hartright by name) happens to be more closely connected than others with the incidents to be recorded, he will describe them in his own person. When his experience fails, he will retire from the position of narrator; and his task will be continued, from the point at which he has left it off, by other persons who can speak to the circumstances under notice from their own knowledge, just as clearly and positively as he has spoken before them. (p. 5)

Wilkie Collins's reportage style of narration was to be central in the evolution of the 'Sensation Novel', and its influence can still be felt as far afield as contemporary docufiction. *The Woman in White* is, in terms of its narrative technique, one of the most innovative novels of the nineteenth century.

As Hartright arranges the evidence, there are ten narrators or 'witnesses'. Hartright himself and Marian Halcombe tell the main lines of the story. Their account is supported by testimony from: Count Ottavio Baldassore Fosco; Vincent Gilmore (the Fairlie solicitor); Frederick Fairlie, Esq. of Limmeridge House; Eliza Michelson, housekeeper at Blackwater Park; Hester Pinhorn, cook in the service of Count Fosco; Alfred Goodricke (the doctor who signed the death certificate of 'Laura'; Jane Gould (who laid out the body); and Mrs Catherick (mother of the 'Woman in White').

As the critic David Grylls has pointed out to me, one witness's evidence is mysteriously missing—and that the most important person of all. Laura Fairlie (subsequently Laura Glyde, and Laura Hartright) is not called on. Why? It's a damaging omission, since the abduction of Laura, and the theft of her identity, is at the heart of the story. She is, needless to say, the person 'more closely connected than others with the incidents' that make up *The Woman in White*. It is true that after her rescue from the asylum Laura is traumatized. But by the end of the narrative (the period in which Walter is putting together his account) she is alert and wholly *compos mentis*. Yet with her alone, the reader has to be satisfied with 'hearsay evidence'.

Dr Grylls suggests that the mysterious silence of Laura can be linked to sexual *pudeur*. Her experiences as wife to the degenerate Glyde are held back from the respectable reader, lest they offend like undraped piano legs in the drawing-room. A useful way of testing this hypothesis is through the 1997 television adaptation of *The Woman in White*—a dramatization which wilfully reinserted the sexual explicitness which, the scriptwriters assumed, Collins had been reluctantly obliged to leave out in deference to his stuffy Victorian age.

The dramatization confined itself to two ninety-minute segments and necessarily streamlined the three-volume novel narrative. Blackwater Park was merged with Limmeridge. The encounter with the woman in white on Hampstead Heath (which Dickens thought one of the two best scenes in literature) was sacrificed. A host of secondary characters were dropped. Regrettably, the end of Fosco (stretched out on the Paris morgue slab, like a cod in a fishmonger's) was dropped. The heroines were made not half-sisters but sisters (Marian Halcombe became 'Marian Fairlie'). This was a pity, since Collins's main point in making them half-sisters was to open the way to Walter's being able to marry Marian after the delicate Laura dies, as the reader perceives she soon must. As deceased wife's sister, Marian 'Fairlie' would be forbidden fruit.

Most arresting, however; were the changes that the televisers made to sexual plot and motivation. Sir Percival Glyde was transformed into a monster of depravity. Shortly after marriage, he takes the servant Margaret Porcher as his mistress. And the 'secret' which can ruin him (in the book, it is disinheriting illegitimacy) was changed to paedophilia. Anne Catherick's mother had been mistress to the Fairlie girls' father; Glyde had made 12-year-old Anne Catherick his mistress. Glyde is that most detested of modern criminals, a child-abuser. It was his molestations that drove Anne mad.

In fact, the dates—in so far as we can reconstruct them from Collins's narrative—fit the television scenario rather neatly. The 'prehistory' of *The Woman in White* goes thus. In July 1803 Sir Percival Glyde's parents 'married' (in fact, since his mother, Cecilia Jane Elster, was already married, the union was invalid—this is to be the great 'secret' in the subsequent narrative). The Glyde parents died abroad, at some point between 1825 and New Year 1827. In March 1804 young Percival Glyde was born abroad. Around 1825 Marian Halcombe was born. Her father died soon after. In autumn 1826 Philip Fairlie vacationed at Varneck Hall near Southampton, where he had an affair with a married woman of the lower orders, Mrs Jane Anne Catherick. From this union, in June 1827, Anne Catherick was born, the illegitimate daughter of Mrs Catherick and Philip Fairlie. In 1827 Sir Percival Glyde committed his forgery at Welmingham, falsifying evidence of his parents' 'marriage', to protect his title and inheritance. In the summer of 1827 Philip Fairlie married the widowed Mrs Halcombe. On 27 March 1829 Laura Fairlie was born, the only child of Philip and Mrs Fairlie (formerly Halcombe), and half-sister to Marian. In 1838 Anne Catherick came to school for a brief period at Limmeridge, where she developed her lifelong fixation on Mrs Fairlie. In November 1847 Philip Fairlie died, leaving his daughter Laura and his stepdaughter Marian Halcombe orphans. Before dying, he obtained a promise from Laura that she would marry Percival Glyde. In the interval between his death and Laura's marriage, he left the girls in the care of his younger unmarried brother, Frederick, at Limmeridge. In 1847 Percival Glyde committed Anne Catherick to a private lunatic asylum, from which she escapes to have her midnight meeting with Walter on Hampstead Heath in August 1849. With this wonderful scene the novel proper begins.

It is quite feasible that in 1838–9, when Anne was 12 years old and at Limmeridge, a villainous 34-year-old Sir Percival might have had his evil way with her. And that Glyde might have gone on to blackmail Philip Fairlie with the threat of exposing him as the father of Anne. The price of Glyde's silence?—The hand (and wealth) of Laura when she comes of age. Collins gives not the slightest hint of such a sub-plot, but, as I say, it fits chronologically and has a certain plausibility.

Other aspects of the television characterization of Glyde are implausible. The dalliance with Margaret Porcher, for instance. In the novel, this woman is grossly unappealing. She is the 'largest and the fattest' of the housemaids at Blackwater; with a 'fat shapeless face' (p. 208). She is 'the most awkward, slatternly, and obstinate servant in the house', with an idiotic, slow-witted grin, and great red arms (p. 298). Glyde would need to be degenerate indeed, if Porcher were his taste in sexual diversion.

What do we know about Glyde's 'tastes', and his conduct as a husband? What clues, if any, do we have as to the bedroom activities of Sir Percival and Lady Glyde? There are some tantalizing fragments of evidence in the novel. The letters which Laura sends Marian over the six months of her wedding trip on the Continent notably lack the 'usual moral transformation which is insensibly wrought in a young, fresh, sensitive woman by her marriage . . . it is always Laura Fairlie who has been writing to me for the last six months, and never Lady Glyde' (p. 203). From which we may deduce that the marriage is blank. None the less, when she finally arrives, Marian notes that: 'There is more colour; and more decision and roundness of outline in her face than there used to be; and her figure seems more firmly set, and more sure and easy in all its movements than it was in her maiden days' (p. 213). From which we deduce that, like Tess, Laura is a maiden no more. The marriage *has* been consummated. Miss Fairlie has become Lady Glyde in more than name.

Laura declines to enter into any details on the subject of her marriage, even with Marian (p. 214). None the less, some hints slip through. In the tremendous scene in which Laura refuses to sign the document making over her property, Sir Percival savagely (and in the presence of Marian) accuses his wife of making 'a virtue of necessity by marrying *me*'—by which the swine implies that she did not come to the marriage bed pure (p. 250). This raises some interesting speculations. In a later confidence with Marian, Laura recalls that when they were in Rome, only a few weeks married, Percival used to 'leave me alone at night, to go among the Opera people' (p. 263)—a clear euphemism for courtesans (nothing in Collins's description of Glyde suggests any musical taste).

Percival's dry cough, lean looks, bald head, advanced years (he is 46), and swishing cane suggest a certain bedroom sadism. But the broadest clue we have to the married life of the Glydes is given in the unbuttoned man-to-man talk of Sir Percival and Fosco, smoking, drinking, and chatting late into the night. Collins is obliged to use all his sensationalist's ingenuity to set this scene up so that we (and the women among his readership) may plausibly overhear this conversation. He does so magnificently. Marian literally 'eavesdrops'. First, she is made to strip off her silk gown and the 'white and cumbersome parts of my underclothing' (her petticoats). She then clambers out, with only a thin cloak over her exciting undress, to perch precariously on a windowsill over a verandah under which Glyde and Fosco are talking.

Fosco quizzes Glyde as to the conditions which obstruct their getting hold of her £20,000 fortune. 'In the case of Lady Glyde's death,' Fosco asks:

'what do you get then?'
    'If she leaves no children—'
    'Which she is likely to do?'
    'Which she is not in the least likely to do—'
    'Yes?'
    'Why, then I get her twenty thousand pounds.'
    'Paid down?'
    'Paid down.' (p. 333)

How would adult Victorian readers take 'not in the least likely to'? In one of five ways. They might assume that Glyde was using some form of contraception. Or they might assume that even if Glyde (as would be in character) brutally took his conjugal rights over the honeymoon, he now has no use for his insipid wife. The tender-hearted might assume that the marriage has *never* been consummated; that Laura will, eventually, come to Walter still pure—a white bride (she is, on all the evidence, fertile enough: they have their little Walter within a year of marriage). Cynics and 'men of the world' might assume that the worldly Percival Glyde is (like Walter in *My Secret Life*) sterile as the result of venereal disease (who knows what infections he may have picked up from those Roman 'Opera people'?).

Collins cunningly leaves all these options open. Had Laura been made to speak, that openness would have been compromised. If, like other 'witnesses', she were to give the 'whole truth' as she (alone) knows it, Lady Glyde would have had to say something more tangible about the marriage, and what kind of husband Sir Percival was to her. David Grylls, I think, is right. Laura is silenced to preserve the interesting aura of sexual ambiguity that hovers around her career in the novel. Like the other 'Woman in White', Laura remains a woman of mystery.

The Oxford World's Classics *The Woman in White* is edited by John Sutherland.

_____

Why was Pip not invited to Joe's wedding?

_____

Malcolm Hurwitt writes to ask 'if you are aware of the puzzle which I feel exists in *Great Expectations*? It may be described as "Why was not Pip invited to the Wedding?".' Mr Hurwitt goes on:

At the end of Chapter 57 Pip has decided to go to his old home to propose marriage to Biddy, Joe Gargery's housekeeper. At the end of the first section of Chapter 58 he meets Joe and Biddy and discovers that it is their wedding day. He collapses from the shock. He had not even been informed of it, yet he was Joe's brother-in-law; he was on good terms with them; Joe had recently nursed him through a long and serious illness and had secretly paid off his debts. There had always been a deep and warm affection between Pip and Joe in spite of and perhaps partly because of the strictness of Pip's sister, Joe's first wife. There was no closer relative, yet Pip had not been invited to the wedding nor even told of it. However little fuss Joe and Biddy wanted, it is hard to understand why Pip had not been let in on the secret.

It is, as Mr Hurwitt rightly says, odd; and it gets odder the closer one looks at the episode. After Magwitch's euthanasia, during a 'cold and dusty spring' (p. 453), Pip falls into a 'fever'—the dreaded 'jail-fever', as we apprehend. (The *OED* defines the disease as 'a virulent type of typhus-fever, formerly endemic in closed jails, and frequent in ships and other confined places.') The illness is the last of Magwitch's gifts to Pip, and the most fatal.

Pip has—in the intoxication of his 'expectations'— run up debts of some £123 with a jeweller, and is now summonsed for debt. Two bailiffs call on his rooms in the Temple; either he must pay the money or surrender his person (this is the era before the reform of laws on personal debt). The usual sequence of events was that the debtor would be held in a 'sponging house'—under house arrest, and given a last chance to pay (or 'expunge') his bills. Failing this last chance, he would be carried off to prison. If he settled his account (not necessarily in full), the sponging house would collect its cut.

Were he in health, Pip would presumably go to the house with the bailiffs and shoot off desperate letters to all his friends, requesting aid. But the young man is now too ill to be moved. The arresting officers know jail fever when they see it, and they refrain from carting his insensible body into captivity. As a debtor, of course, there is no question of calling in a doctor (who would pay the guinea fee?). He is left to die or recover as fate pleases.

Pip falls into a delirium in which he evidently remains for several weeks. When he comes round, it is the last day of May. Joe has been taking care of him, he discovers. This 'gentle Christian man' (p. 458) was summoned by letter, from his village home down by the marshes. Who, one wonders, sent the letter telling Joe of Pip's plight? It cannot be Herbert, who has gone off to Egypt with his bride. It cannot be Pip's slatternly, thieving, and illiterate maidservant. It can hardly be the bailiffs who have come to take him away. They would not know Joe's address, nor his relationship to Pip. Conceivably, Pip himself might have babbled out something in his semi-consciousness and later forgotten doing it, but this is unlikely. It must, one assumes, have been either Wemmick or Jaggers who sent the letter to Joe. But the kind-hearted Wemmick would surely not have left Pip to die alone and untended in his apartment. Hard-hearted Jaggers, on the other hand, might feel obliged to contact the 'next of kin' (which Joe is), as a point of professional etiquette but would not trouble himself to attend his former client's bedside at any risk to his own health or legal safety.

One can reconstruct the scene. It is quite plausible that Jaggers would have sent a clerk round to Pip's rooms in the Temple, just to see the lie of the land. The man reported back and Jaggers sent a letter, possibly unsigned, to Joe. Jaggers, of course, would still be nervous about being involved in a prosecution arising from the (clearly felonious) conspiracy to smuggle Magwitch out of the country. He is a cautious lawyer. Jaggers knows everything about Pip; more, in fact, than the young man knows about himself. He would certainly have Joe Gargery's address in his files. If he wrote the letter, Jaggers would also, doubtless, add the detail that Pip was being distrained for debt and precisely how much debt.

This last supposition would clear up another little mystery: namely, how it is that Joe happens to be able to pay the very substantial sum of £123. 'Ready money' is, of course, the only form of payment the bailiffs would accept at this stage of the game. As the receipt he leaves for Pip indicates, Joe paid the debt in full in cash, while in London. The country blacksmith would not, of course, have a bank account in town. Nor would he have one in the country. Like Silas Marner, Joe would keep his savings under a floorboard. Those savings would be made up of the sovereigns, florins, half-crowns, and the smaller silver he received over the years for his smithy work. Unless forewarned, he would not bring this treasure to London with him. It is hard to credit that he has much more than £123 in his life's savings. He may even have had to borrow from Biddy's savings to make up the sum of Pip's jeweller's debt.

As June draws on Pip makes a rapid recovery. Early in the month Joe departs precipitately, leaving a cryptic

letter ('Not wishful to intrude I have departured fur you
are well again dear Pip and will do better without . . . Jo
. . . P. S. Ever the best of friends'). Joe also leaves the
receipt for payment of the jeweller's bill and the bailiff's
costs. 'Down to that moment', Pip ruefully says, 'I had
vainly supposed that my creditor had withdrawn or suspended proceedings until I should be quite recovered. I
had never dreamed of Joe's having paid the money; but,
Joe had paid it, and the receipt was in his name' (p. 466).

It is still June when Pip makes his sudden decision to go
down to the village and propose marriage to Biddy. On his
part Joe must, of course, have known that *he* (Joe Gargery)
was going to be married to Biddy when he came up to
London. He must surely have sent love-letters to his
intended in the country, together with bulletins about
Pip's health and when he expected to 'departure' London.
Banns would have had to be called in the village church.
And it is doubtless to prepare for his imminent wedding
day that Joe has rushed back—without explanation to Pip.
Joe's letter hints that he is not entirely keen that Pip
should follow him. It would, for instance, have been easy to
add a 'coddleshell' or another 'P. S.' saying something like:
'do come and see us soon.'

Joe's conversational exchanges with the convalescent
Pip are hilariously circumlocutory. But, conceivably, he
did try on at least one occasion to broach the subject of
his impending nuptials. On resuming consciousness, after
his long delirium, the first question Pip asks is 'How long,
dear Joe?':

'Which you meantersay, Pip, how long have your illness lasted,
dear old chap?'
'Yes, Joe.'
'It's the end of May, Pip. To-morrow is the first of June.'
'And have you been here all the time, dear Joe?'
'Pretty nigh, old chap. For, as I says to Biddy when the news of

your being ill were brought by letter, which it were brought by the
post and being formerly single he is now married though under-
paid for a deal of walking and shoe-leather, but wealth were not a
object on his part, and marriage were the great wish of his hart—'
(p. 458)

At this point, Pip interrupts, bringing Joe—as he
thinks—back to the point. But, conceivably, 'marriage . . .
the great wish of his hart' *is* Joe's point. It is not the post-
man's marriage that he really wants to talk about so much
as his own imminent union with Biddy. Had his wits been
recovered Pip might have been suspicious about the relationship between Joe and Biddy. Joe's new literacy—his
ability to read and write—argues close intimacy.

Biddy is not (as Mr Hurwitt says) Joe's housekeeper at
this point of the narrative. Alter the death of Mrs Gargery
no housekeeper is required and Joe and Biddy agree that it
would not be respectable for her to stay in the house of an
unmarried man—even a man twenty years older than her.
Nor, until a decent interval elapses, can Joe remarry.
Biddy leaves to take up a post as the village schoolteacher.
There will, of course, be a tied-house with the position.

When Pip comes down to the village, he stays at the Blue
Boar. Everyone at the inn knows about his reduced
'expectations' and he is lodged in a poor room, at the top
of the house. The innkeeper and his staff would, one
imagines, surely know of an impending wedding in their
small community. But, if they know, nothing is said to Pip
about his brother-in-law's big day.

The forge and Joe's house are near the village, but on his
early morning walk Pip does not go there. He returns
instead to his hotel for breakfast, and who should he meet
but Pumblechook. The merchant pompously upbraids Pip
for 'ingratitood'. The two men do not, however, mention
what one would have thought to be matters of more direct
interest. Their mutual assailant Orlick, for instance—now

in custody at the county jail. More curiously, Pumblechook does not mention the wedding, which is, as we later
learn, taking place at that very moment. Joe is a relative
of both Pip and Pumblechook. And Pumblechook does
talk about 'Joseph' at great length. Surely—as a relative, a
neighbour, a village dignitary, and an old family friend—
he would have been invited to the wedding? If not, surely,
his wrath against Joseph's 'ingratitood' would have been
even more virulent than against Pip's. He would certainly
not have kept his peace on the subject. We have to assume
that Pumblechook does not know of the wedding, any
more than Pip does. What is going on?

Pip first calls at the school—which is mysteriously
closed. He arrives at the forge:

Almost fearing, without knowing why, to come in view of the
forge, I saw it at last, and saw that it was closed. No gleam of fire,
no glittering shower of sparks, no roar of bellows; all shut up,
and still.

But, the house was not deserted, and the best parlour seemed
to be in use, for there were white curtains fluttering in its window, and the window was open and gay with flowers. I went softly
towards it, meaning to peep over the flowers, when Joe and Biddy
stood before me, arm in arm.

At first Biddy gave a cry, as if she thought it was my apparition,
but in another moment she was in my embrace. I wept to see
her, and she wept to see me; I, because she looked so fresh and
pleasant; she, because I looked so worn and white.

'But, dear Biddy, how smart you are!'

'Yes, dear Pip.'

'And Joe, how smart *you* are!'

Yes, dear old Pip, old chap.'

I looked at both of them, from one to the other, and then—

'It's my wedding-day,' cried Biddy, in a burst of happiness, 'and
I am married to Joe!' (p. 472)

Evidently Joe and Biddy were married at crack of dawn.
There has been no breakfast, no reception, no wedding

guests. Who were the witnesses? Who was the best man?

Can one make any sense of this perplexing episode? One can dismiss out of hand the usual motive for a hole-in-corner wedding; namely, that Biddy is pregnant (little Pip turns up much later; well beyond the nine-month mark). There is, I think, a more likely explanation. Joe can never have been prosperous, and never less so than at the moment. He has taken two months off work to look after Pip. Clearing Pip's debts may conceivably have put him in debt himself. While in London, he had further financial burdens—squaring the bailiffs, day-to-day living expenses, and the cost of medical attention for Pip. Biddy can only be earning a pittance at the school. What these two good people have done, we apprehend, is to cancel their wedding party (for which they had prudently saved) and had a 'paupers' wedding'. There is no feast, no honeymoon because, having given their all to Pip, they can no longer afford such luxuries. Their marriage contrasts with the sumptuous and sterile party which never was at Satis House. That was an affair with all the trappings of the marriage ceremony but no union, this a union without trappings.

Pip's ignorance of the wedding is a puzzle—but not, I think insoluble, nor deleterious to our respect for Dickens's artistry. Clearly Pip was not invited because there was no party to invite him to. Nor was he told of the wedding, because of the embarrassment of having to explain why there was no party. The money saved up for it had been spent on his jewellers' debts. Why make the young fellow feel even more guilty than he already does?[1]

The Oxford World's Classics *Great Expectations* is edited by Margaret Cardwell with an introduction by Kate Flint.

Should we change the end of The Mill on the Floss?

In *Can Jane Eyre Be Happy?* I drew attention, as have other commentators, to troubling improbabilities in the tremendous watery climax to Eliot's novel. Among other things, I pointed to: (1) the meteorological improbability of a flash flood of the torrential nature which Eliot describes in the low-lying, flat countryside around St Ogg's. As Gordon Haight neatly put it—if all the twenty-five inches of rain that falls on Lincolnshire in a year were to fall in a single night, it would not produce the biblical deluge Eliot portrays at the end of *The Mill on the Floss*; (2) the physical improbability of the large, wooden lump of machinery which rushes down on the flood current to crush Tom and Maggie, 'overtaking' their boat. This is against the laws of hydrodynamics. Large wooden objects do not float faster than smaller objects in the same stream.

These problems were confronted and solved (after a fashion) by the adaptors of Eliot's novel for television. The programme went out on BBC Television on 1 January 1997. Maggie was played by Emily Watson, and the screenplay was done by Hugh Stoddart. Stoddart and his collaborators evidently decided in their story conferences that the climactic flood scenes, as written by George Eliot, were unfilmable—whatever 1990s special-effects magic was drawn on.

It would, of course, have been possible to make a small change to Eliot's narrative by having Tom and Maggie's

'It is coming, Maggie!' Tom said, in a deep hoarse voice, loosing the
oars and clasping her.

boat snag on some obstacle (a submerged tree branch, for example). But there remained other improbabilities and impossibilities—evident in the foregoing illustration from the 'Cabinet' Edition. Why doesn't the boat, as depicted above, tip over? Why isn't the boat moving? Why is the 'wooden machinery' riding so high in the water? The whole thing looks and feels entirely *wrong*.

Although elsewhere faithful to the main lines of Eliot's narrative, Stoddart completely changed the ending. As I saw the TV version (for reasons that will become clear, one has to be rather subjective in one's speculations), there *was* a flood. But it was more a quiet seep of water over low banks, turning the water-meadow outside the Tulliver Mill into a huge, still, millpond. On the mirror-like surface of this pond at midday, as it seemed (the scene in the novel takes place at stormy night, and still-stormy early dawn), Maggie sculled her way to the mill. Tom—from a top window—saw his rescuer and, using the rope with which grain was hoisted to the top of the building, lowered himself down. But he became tangled in the rope and fell into the (glassily still) water. For mysterious reasons, he sank like a stone. Maggie, on impulse, jumped in—converting the episode into what looked like a double suicide. The dramatization ended with an underwater sequence of the two Tullivers, a coiling umbilical rope around them, going to the bottom. Neither seemed to be making any attempt to swim or regain the surface.

In an eerie way it was—if untrue to Eliot—effectively enigmatic. The reviewer in *The Times*, Peter Barnard, was entranced by the scene:

It is one thing to describe in words Maggie trying to rescue Tom but deciding once his life is clearly gone, to die with him. To do so in a television sequence underwater is quite another. But the combination of Graham Teakston's directing, Hugh Stoddart's script, and Emily Watson's ability to make her face act for her achieved that feat and the result was a moment of real dramatic brilliance.[1]

A moment of melodramatic improbability on the page became a moment of 'real dramatic brilliance' on screen. But, even to achieve this 'brilliance', is an adaptor licensed to make changes of this radical kind to Eliot's text?

The main objection one would make to Stoddart's changed ending is that it is manifestly false to Maggie's character, as conceived by her creator. Maggie has, we remember, already contemplated suicide in Bob Jakins's parlour, just before the flood, and rejected it as the solution to her overwhelming problems (it is at this moment that she feels the swirling water round her ankles). Just as the television version takes all the storm out of the flood—making it no more dramatic than a leaking cistern—so it siphons all the life-force out of Maggie in her last moments. When she bravely accepts fate, in the form of the great mass of wooden machinery looming down on them, it is as an acceptance of God's will, and she stands up—as the accused in court stands up to receive sentence. Supinely letting herself sink to the bottom of a pond seems wholly out of character.

Is there any way out of this narrative impasse? I thought not. George Eliot had written herself into a box and all we could do was cavil or sympathize. A solution to the problems of the ending of *The Mill on the Floss* came, however, from an Oxford World's Classics reader, Mr Mark Tatam, of Hall Farm, Gainsborough, Lincolnshire. Mr Tatam's letter to me (dated 4 January 1998) began:

Dear Professor Sutherland, I have been greatly enjoying your book *Can Jane Eyre Be Happy?* I hope you will forgive my presumption in writing to you, not as a literary critic but as a farmer living close to 'St Ogg's' [i.e. Gainsborough]. In the spirit of your own writing, I would like to suggest that George Eliot's hydrodynamics do, if you will excuse the phrase, 'hold water' quite well.

Mr Tatam firmly—and rather chauvinistically—locates the action of George Eliot's novel around Gainsborough, in Lincoinshire (as have other authorities—although I think there is a strong infusion of Coventry, where Eliot was brought up).[2] Historically, the area around Gainsborough has been transformed over the century by the practice of 'warping'—controlled flooding so as to leave a sediment of rich silt on the bordering agricultural land. At the time George Eliot was writing, the land was much lower: 'well below mean sea level' (as Mr Tatam points out). Gainsborough lies alongside the Trent, which is tidal in this region. Mr Tatam goes on:

> You quote Gordon Haight as saying that the necessary rise could not occur 'if the whole twenty-five inch rainfall of Lincolnshire had dropped there in one night'. This is, of course, misleading . . . what if the 'Trent is in flood and then meets an extreme Spring tide coming the other way? A cousin farming on the banks of the Trent nearby assures me that a very powerful backing up action occurs that even now, after vast sums of money have been spent on bank raising and flood defences, can be quite frightening . . . A breach of the Trent bank by both river and tide would have spilled vast quantities of water onto the land twenty or more feet below. The low hills beyond would have stopped the waters from spreading more than a few miles. My cousin assures me that he has seen excavators and straw stacks totally submerged from even minor flood problems, even though the land level is now higher than it was because of the effects of warping. The once-in-sixty years flood proposed by Eliot would certainly cause the rapid and deep flooding she suggests.

Mr Tatam offers a remarkably welcome explanation in so far as it makes more plausible what Eliot herself wrote. Mr Tatam's follow-up explanation for the paradoxical hydrodynamics of the last scene is, I think, even more satisfactory than his suggestions about the plausibility of the flash flood around St Ogg's:

Finally the question of the wooden machinery rushing down on the boat. Whilst this takes a little more reconstructing, it is certainly not impossible. The famous Trent *Aegir* is an example of the odd things that can happen when outflowing river meets incoming tide. Given a massively swollen river, a very high and powerful spring tide, and the effects of the Trent bank bursting and water flooding out onto the land below, massively complex and powerful swirls, eddies, cross-currents and undercurrents can develop. In tidal water the undercurrents may often be going in the opposite direction to the top flow. It would be quite possible for the Tullivers' shallow boat, affected only by the top current, to be swept away by a 'huge mass' being dragged along by the undertow.[3]

Not everyone will agree with Mr Tatam—but his points are extraordinarily well taken. Better than any academic critic I have come across, he reads the ending of *The Mill on the Floss*, through his formidable expertise as a Lincolnshireman, in such a way that Eliot's text *makes sense*. I am glad (even though I have been comprehensively corrected) to have inspired this display of Oxford World's Classics reader power. Should we change the end of *The Mill on the Floss*? Not now, we shouldn't.

Postscript: Is Maggie Tulliver a murderer?

In conversation with me, Dinah Birch, who has written the introduction to the Oxford World's Classics *The Mill on the Floss*, agreed in finding Mr Tatam's *Aegir* thesis plausible, adding that it was additionally satisfying in mirroring Maggie's 'massively complex and powerful swirls' of emotion in these last chapters. This was something entirely missing in the placid 'millpond' climax of the television dramatization.

Dr Birch offered another puzzle. Does Maggie 'murder' Tom? Had she not gone to the Mill—but simply saved herself (or put herself out to save the Jakins family), Tom would presumably have weathered out the flood in sturdy Dorlcote Mill. The building has manifestly survived the great flood of sixty years before and would doubtless survive this one too. Had Maggie not gone to the Mill, had she not induced Tom to get into the boat (instead of herself taking refuge in the Mill), he—and conceivably both of them—would have lived through the deluge. There is, of course, a lot of repressed violence in the sibling relationship, going back to Maggie's 'killing' (by negligence—or was it?) Tom's rabbits, and Tom's sadistic interference with her love-affair with Philip Wakem. At some subconscious level, has Maggie resolved that he (and she) must die? As they go under, is she to be pictured with a stranglehold round him, in the same way that Bradley Headstone takes Rogue Riderhood to the bottom in his 'ring of iron'?

The Oxford World's Classics *The Mill on the Floss* is edited by Gordon Haight, with an introduction by Dinah Birch.

Lewis Carroll · *Alice's Adventures in Wonderland*

How long is Alice in Wonderland for?

The above is a minor puzzle among those in the most puzzle-packed of Victorian narratives, *Alice's Adventures in Wonderland*. The story opens:

Alice was beginning to get very tired of sitting by her sister on the bank, and of having nothing to do: once or twice she had peeped into the book her sister was reading, but it had no pictures or conversations in it, 'and what is the use of a book,' thought Alice, 'without pictures or conversations?'

So she was considering, in her own mind (as well as she could, for the hot day made her feel very sleepy and stupid), whether the pleasure of making a daisy-chain would be worth the trouble of getting up and picking the daisies, when suddenly a White Rabbit with pink eyes ran close by her. (p. 9)

It is, we apprehend, gloriously high summer. The 'hot day', the daisies, and the dress in which Tenniel portrays the little girl confirm this seasonal dating. It would be logical to assume the setting in Carroll's mind was 4 July 1862; the day, that is, when Charles Lutwidge Dodgson took Alice Liddell, and her sisters Lorina and Edith, on the boating trip on the Cherwell. On that day, as literary history records, *Alice's Adventures in Wonderland* was conceived as an entertainment by the maths don for his young guests.

The vegetation which Carroll describes and Tenniel pictures confirms the midsummer setting: the 'great thistle' behind which Alice hides from the puppy, or the harebells around the mushroom on which the caterpillar sits.

Similarly high-summery are the open-air 'mad tea-party', and the roses in bloom, about which the Queen of Hearts is so tyrannical. This, one confidently gathers, is a July–August story.

How, then, does one make sense of the end? In her dream Alice is growing embarrassingly during the peremptory trial presided over by the King and Queen of Hearts. Defying the ordinance that 'all persons more than a mile high should leave the court', she stays on to hear sentence passed:

'Off with her head!' the Queen shouted at the top of her voice. Nobody moved.

'Who cares for *you*?' said Alice, (she had grown to her full size by this time.) 'You're nothing but a pack of cards!'

At this the whole pack rose up into the air, and came flying down upon her; she gave a little scream, half of fright and half of anger, and tried to beat them off, and found herself lying on the bank, with her head in the lap of her sister, who was gently brushing away some dead leaves that had fluttered down from the trees upon her face.

'Wake up, Alice dear!' said her sister. 'Why, what a long sleep you've had!' (pp. 109–10)

After Alice has gone off home, her older sister remains sitting on the bank, thinking about Wonderland. She also foresees 'how this same little sister of hers would, in the after-time, be herself a woman'. How the adult Alice would, at some distant point in time, entertain her own children with her dream of Wonderland, 'and find a pleasure in all their simple joys, remembering her own child-life, and the happy summer days'.

So the story ends, with the phrase 'summer days' that seems so appropriate for all the preceding narrative. All, that is, except for that detail about what it was that woke Alice up: 'some dead leaves that had fluttered down from the trees on to her face.' The leaves of brown, as the song tells us, come fluttering down in September and in the rain.

Alice goes to sleep in midsummer and wakes up in autumn, in the sere and yellow leaf of the year. Her sister's exclamation is apposite: 'Why, what a long sleep you've had!' Rip van Alice, one might think. How can one make sense of this? The most attractive hypothesis is that *Alice* is not just the story of a summer afternoon. It is an allegory of the transitions accompanying puberty: the growing-pains which intervene between a little girl's childhood and her young womanhood. This transition is remarkably rapid in physiological terms: it happens in just a few months. The child grows, as we say, 'overnight'—by which we mean in just a few months. Carroll, it seems, plays with the same kind of metaphorical foreshortening in his story. Alice goes down the rabbit hole a little girl, and comes out—if not an adult woman—a pubescent girl on the brink of womanhood. How long has she been asleep? A few minutes and an epoch.

The Oxford World's Classics *Alice's Adventures in Wonderland* is edited by Roger Lancelyn Green.

Does Dickens know his train signals?

Departing from his normal practice, Dickens offers at the end of the serialized *Our Mutual Friend* a 'Postscript: in lieu of Preface'.[1] This afterword reminds readers of what most of them must have well known—that there almost was no concluding part of the novel. Everything after Chapter 51 was, in a sense, a 'postscript', because thereafter Mr Charles Dickens was living on borrowed time.

Our Mutual Friend was serialized from May 1864 to November 1865. As Dickens recalls:

On Friday the Ninth [of June] in the present year [1865], Mr and Mrs Boffin (in their manuscript dress of receiving Mr and Mrs Lammle at breakfast) were on the South Eastern Railway with me, in a terribly destructive accident. When I had done what I could to help others, I climbed back into my carriage—nearly turned over a viaduct, and caught aslant upon the turn—to extricate the worthy couple. They were much soiled, but otherwise unhurt . . . I remember with devout thankfulness that I can never be much nearer parting company with my readers for ever than I was then, until these shall be written against my life, the two words with which I have this day closed this book:—THE END. (p. 822)

Dickens gives here a vivid thumbnail account of the terrible Staplehurst accident, in which ten less fortunate passengers perished and forty were seriously injured. The 2.38 train from Folkestone to London (Dickens had been in France) crashed at speed on a viaduct under repair. The system of red-flag warnings (it was daylight) had failed.

Dickens's was the only one of seven first-class carriages not to fall off the viaduct. In the above, semi-comic account, Dickens omits to mention his own heroic conduct in aiding the injured and dying. He also omits to mention that, in addition to Mr and Mrs Boffin, his mistress Miss Ellen Ternan and her mother were in the train with him.

The trauma of the Staplehurst accident may well have shortened Dickens's life. It certainly made him nervous about trains. As his son Henry recalled, after Staplehurst, 'I have seen him sometimes in a railway carriage when there was a slight jolt. When that happened he was almost in a state of panic and gripped the seat with both hands.'[2] The Boffin–Lammle breakfast episode Dickens mentions as carrying with him occurs in Book IV Chapter 2 ('The Golden Dustman rises a little').

Oddly enough, there's a railway scene a few chapters earlier in which—as we may think—a terrible rail accident is eerily forecast. It occurs at the end of Book III, Chapter 9. Bella Wilfer and 'the secretary' (John Rokesmith) have come to Betty Higden's pauper's funeral, near Henley on Thames. After her conversation with Lizzie Hexam, in which the two young ladies strike up a friendship, Bella and Rokesmith make their way back to the railway station and the train that will carry them back to London. It is night as they approach the station on foot. From the fact that they can see the signal-lights, they must be coming to the station in the same direction as the train is travelling (i.e. up-line):

The railway, at this point, knowingly shutting a green eye and opening a red one, they had to run for it. As Bella could not run easily so wrapped up, the Secretary had to help her. When she took her opposite place in the carriage corner, the brightness in her face was so charming to behold, that on her exclaiming, 'What beautiful stars and what a glorious night!' the Secretary said 'Yes,' but seemed to prefer to see the night and the stars in the light of her lovely little countenance, to looking out of [the] window.

O boofer lady, fascinating boofer lady! If I were but legally executor of Johnny's will! If I had but the right to pay your legacy and to take your receipt!—Something to this purpose surely mingled with the blast of the train as it cleared the stations, all knowingly shutting up their green eyes and opening their red ones when they prepared to let the boofer lady pass. (pp. 530–1)

One notes the slight, but palpable, differences in Victorian rail travel from ours. Because they wore bulkier clothes than us (particularly crinolined women) and had a baffling array of carriages to choose from (three 'classes', 'ladies only', 'smoking'—i.e. gentlemen only), simply alighting and descending from the train were complex operations and might take some minutes. To warn passengers, Victorian stations had a 'departure bell' (not to be confused with the whistle, which was a signal for the driver). Dickens specifically mentions this bell, in a later railway scene in *Our Mutual Friend*, where Bradley Headstone has his epileptic fit.

Getting on board was, as I have said, a much more fussy business than it was to become in the twentieth century. And once aboard and settled inside the appropriate carriage, the dim, oil-fuelled lights would allow one to see the stars outside (all modern travellers can see by night are their own reflections—the interior being so much brighter than the exterior). Steam engines give a warning blast as they move off or sound a warning toot from their whistles as they thunder through stations.

But one thing has not changed over the last 130 years: red means stop and green means go. How then, should we understand the description of the signals in the above passage? Victorians, of course, did not have the profusion of highway traffic-lights that we have. They did not have

the Highway Code drummed into them as kindergarten
pedestrians. It might be that they, in general, had as little
sense of railway signalling codes as most present-day sea
travellers do of whether red stands for starboard or green
for port.

In the above passage, Dickens clearly describes what
looks like a dangerously wrong sequence. Modern passengers, seeing a red platform signal-light come on, would
assume that there was no need to 'run for it'. The train will
only leave when the light turns to green. That is when you
would run. No driver will drive his train through a red
light. And in Dickens's final sentences, the business of the
railway stations 'all knowingly shutting up their green
eyes and opening their red ones when they prepared to let
the boofer lady pass' would seem to lay the ground for any
number of Staplehursts.

Is Bella's beauty so radiant as to have disoriented the
signals, so they do not know their red from their green? Is
there, perhaps, some play with the symbolism of Othello's
green-eyed monster or Macbeth's bleeding eye of day
which overrides the signalling codes of the Great Western
Railway (which the couple are evidently riding, if they
have been to Henley and back)? However ingenious, it is
hard to make headway here with the traditional literary
associations of red and green.

The most satisfactory explanation of this problem is
given by T. S. Lascelles, in his article 'A Railway Signal
Puzzle in *Our Mutual Friend*'.[3] Lascelles argues that
'Dickens had seen and correctly observed the old time-
interval system of train working'. The explication of how
the 'old time-interval system' worked is complicated, but
basically as follows. This signalling system was developed
before the electric telegraph allowed stations to know that
a train was coming, or what other traffic might be on the
line. All that the managers of the station knew, for certain,

was that a train had arrived when they saw it come in. A technique was thus devised by which, when a train drew in, the green signalling lamp would (by the dropping of a filter over the lens of a bright oil-lamp) turn red. It would remain red for a 'safe' period after the train had departed—say ten minutes. The red signal did not indicate to the driver waiting at the station 'don't go'; it indicated 'we shall ensure no one follows you too closely, so leave at your discretion—but don't wait too long'. The signal-light would not be placed at the head of the platform, but in the middle, where it would be more visible to the majority of passengers and to incoming trains.

What, above all, had to be avoided was an incoming train—particularly a 'through' train—crashing into one which had already halted at the station, or that was still moving slowly out of the station. For this reason the signal-light at the rear-end of the station to the oncoming train, the first light the driver would see, needed to be red as well. And it, like the front light, would stay red for some time after the train ahead left. So when Rokesmith and Bella see the red light, this, as Lascelles points out, is no guarantee that the train in the Henley on Thames station is still waiting—it could be just gone, or about to leave. All that it indicates is that a train is in the vicinity. On modern stations, a green light following a red means a train is coming—stand by. When the time-interval system operated, a green light did not mean a train was coming; 'all it could definitely mean was that the previous train had gone by so many minutes'.

The Lascelles explanation, counterfactual as it seems to us and extremely hard to grasp, is satisfying, although not without some difficulties in the application. As Lascelles notes, Dickens was extraordinarily observant. It must have struck him, however, that in the 1860s the time interval system of signalling was extremely antique. The Great

Western Railway began experimenting with electrical-telegraphic signalling techniques in the late 1830s, and they were universal a decade later. As Lascelles notes: 'as electric telegraphy spread, the "time interval" gave place to the "space" interval and what was called . . . the "block system"', which resulted in the signalling conventions we are familiar with today. If, as Dickens noted, *Our Mutual Friend* was set 'in these very times of ours', the time-interval system would have been a thing of the distant past. As Lascelles points out, the line which Bella and John travel on to Henley on Thames opened in 1857, with up-to-date telegraphic signalling (of the kind familiar to us). The 'time-interval' system had no place on this line. One can make sense of the red-green signalling paradox only by recourse to a chronological paradox: one of Dickens's many time-warp effects. Bella and John are not only travelling at unimpeded speed, they are travelling thirty years in the past.

The Oxford World's Classics *Our Mutual Friend* is edited by Michael Cotsell.

Wilkie Collins · *The Moonstone*

———

Is Franklin Blake a thief and a rapist?

———

The Moonstone has an honoured place in literary history as, to quote no less an authority than T. S. Eliot, 'the first, longest and best of English detective novels'. Many detective novels have been written since Eliot's accolade (offered, it is pleasing to note, in the first World's Classics edition of *The Moonstone*).[1] But Collins's novel still retains the power to delight and to surprise.

The story, a version of the 'locked room mystery', hinges on a jewel theft. A fabulous Indian gem, the Moonstone, is left to Rachel Verinder. So nervous is she on getting possession of it that she keeps it safely secreted in her bedroom suite at night. None the less, it is stolen. The thief must be someone in the household. Sergeant Cuff of Scotland Yard is called in. There is a likely looking clue. Whoever stole the diamond must have brushed against some wet paint on the door to Rachel's boudoir. But the incriminatingly stained garment is never found. Rachel's maid, Rosanna Spearman, is a prime suspect; she has a criminal past. But Rosanna is now a reformed character and her alibi holds up. Cuff declares himself defeated and goes into retirement in Dorking, where he will devote himself to the cultivation of roses.

There are two rather strange *sequelae* to the mystery. Rachel, who seemed to be in love with Franklin, will have nothing more to do with him after the theft. And Rosanna commits suicide, throwing herself into some conveniently

nearby quicksands. But of the diamond, there is no sign.
The denouement, when it comes, very late in the narrative,
is a bombshell. A year later Franklin returns from a trip
'wandering in the East' (still heartbroken) to the grand
Verinder house in Yorkshire. Here he comes by Rosanna's
suicide note. It appears the poor woman loved him—
hopelessly, of course. She discovered Franklin's paint-
stained nightgown on his unmade bed the morning after
the theft and realized that he must have been in her mistress's rooms the night before. Whether to steal gems or
embraces she does not, of course, know. Out of love, she
hides the incriminating article. And out of hopeless love,
she later kills herself.

All this is a mystery to Franklin. He *knows* he was not in
Rachel's boudoir that night. None the less, an even greater
shock awaits him on his reunion with a still-frigid Rachel.
Despite her coolness:

I could resist it no longer—I caught her in my arms, and covered
her face with kisses.
    There was a moment when I thought the kisses were returned
. . . [then] with a cry which was like a cry of horror—with a
strength which I doubt if I could have resisted if I had tried—she
thrust me back from her. I saw merciless anger in her eyes; I saw
merciless contempt on her lips. She looked me over, from head to
foot, as she might have looked at a stranger who had insulted her.
    'You coward!' she said. 'You mean, miserable, heartless coward!'
(p. 380)

What does she mean? She tells him: '*You villain, I saw you
take the Diamond with my own eyes!*' He came into her
boudoir at one o'clock at night and took the gem ('I saw
the gleam of the stone between your finger and thumb',
p. 387). She saw his face, quite clearly. But Franklin still
knows he did not do it. To cut Collins's entertainingly
long story short—Franklin was sleepwalking. Why did his

unconscious self want to 'steal' the jewel? Because he
knew there were dangerous burglars about (the Indians),
and he did not think the diamond safe in Rachel's room.
Another, more villainous occupant of the house, was
observing him and purloined from the 'thief' what Franklin would never know he had stolen. Had Rosanna not
hidden his nightgown Franklin would, of course, have
been arrested by Sergeant Cuff.

The Victorians were fascinated by somnambulism. In
the medical authority which Collins cites on page 433,
John Elliotson's *Human Physiology* (1840), there are a
large number of examples of sleepwalking and sleep-
talking described. But I would guess that Collins was
inspired principally by a report in *The Times*, 18 September 1866, at a period when he was beginning to write *The
Moonstone* (serialized, January–August 1868). Entitled
'Somnambulism Extraordinary', the newspaper story
records that:

At a farmhouse in the vicinity of Guildford, a few evenings ago, a
large roll of butter was brought in at tea. The careful wife proceeded to cut the butter in two in order that one half of it might
only remain on the table. The knife grated upon something in the
centre of the butter, and in the very heart of the lump she found a
gold watch and chain, very carefully rolled up, but not enveloped
in paper or any other covering. At this juncture Sarah B——, the
domestic, entered the room, and uttering a sharp exclamation,
darted off again precipitately. Scarce had the farmer time to
remark upon Sarah's strange conduct than she returned, breathless, with haste and anxiety, ejaculating, 'It's mine, mum! it's
mine!' Mrs—— remembered to have heard Sarah say that she had
been left a gold watch and chain by a deceased relative, that she
was always in terror of losing it, that she did not wear it, as not
suitable for a person in her station of life, and that for safety she
kept it locked up in her box under her clothes. Sarah declared
that she had been in the habit, when under the influence of
strong emotion, of walking in her sleep. On the previous Monday

she had been reading in the newspaper some dreadful tales of burglary with violence. On the same night she had a most vivid dream. She thought the house had been entered by burglars, and that she saw them through a chink in the door enter her master and mistress's room. She tried to scream, but could not, and although very anxious for her master and mistress's welfare, her thoughts seemed to revert in spite of everything to the necessity of saving her watch. At length she dreamed that she hit upon an expedient. She quietly got out of bed, unlocked her box, took out the watch, slipped on her dress, and softly glided down stairs and made her way to the dairy. She there took a roll of butter of the Saturday's making, wound the chain around the watch, and deftly inserted both watch and chain in the very centre of the butter, making up the roll precisely in the form that it was before. She then thought she passed swiftly upstairs, and reached her room unmolested. On inspecting the watch found in the butter, she had no hesitation in declaring that it was hers! Farmer—— and his wife accordingly handed over to Sarah B—— the watch and chain.

Many such stories are to be found in the newspapers and psychological writing of the period. But it was not just the curious pranks that somnambulists got up to which interested Victorians. Much as with Multiple Personality Disorder for us today, the condition raised teasing ethical, moral, and legal questions. Was someone like Franklin a 'thief', or not responsible for his actions? Was the somnambulist an 'automaton' or what some French psychologists called an *automate conscient*?

There was a relevant case, a few years earlier, described in Roger Smith's *Trial by Medicine*:

In 1862, Esther Griggs threw one of her children through a closed window, believing the house to be on fire. A passing policeman stated that she had a nightmare which caused her to try to save her children. Though arrested, she never faced trial as the grand jury did not find a true bill against her, presumably on the ground that she had behaved as an automaton.[2]

So, too, might Franklin claim that he was an automaton, not a conscious agent, when he 'stole' the diamond—although it might be difficult to persuade a jury. There are, however, other rather trickier legal complications. Rosanna's first assumption is that Franklin sneaked into Rachel's bedroom at one o'clock in the morning for a more probable reason than jewel theft ('I shall not tell you in plain words what was the first suspicion that crossed my mind, when I had made that discovery. You would only be angry', p. 353). When he sees Rachel again, after his long travels, despite her clear distaste for him, he cannot help himself: 'I could resist it no longer—I caught her in my arms, and covered her face with kisses' (p. 380). He may on that fateful night have had a strong unconscious urge to protect the diamond. But he has other, stronger, unconscious urges. What would a somnambulant Franklin do if he found himself in the boudoir of an unclothed Rachel? Would he, all unconscious, behave with the propriety of a Victorian gentleman? He doesn't behave like one, even when conscious.

This relates to an oddity in the novel. Why does Rachel not inform on him? There are three possible reasons. She loves him so much, she will protect his grand felony (a felony which robs her grievously). This is unlikely. Less unlikely is that she does not want to have to explain why she did not shriek out the first moment she espied him in her room. Why didn't she? Because she was not intending to offer any resistance to him when he came to her bed, as she thought he must have been meaning to. To have shouted out after he had been in her room for some minutes might give rise to awkward questions.

The third possible reason for Rachel's silence is the most speculative but in many ways the most interesting. Suppose he did make love to a sleepy Rachel—and she acquiesced, rather as Tess acquiesces (as we may assume)

to Alec in Hardy's novel? Then, as he rose, she realized
he was unconscious; then he took the jewel—the other
and less valuable jewel, as we may think. She could not,
in such circumstances, say anything. Even if poor
Rosanna were to go to prison for the crime (as looks quite
likely, for a while). And would Franklin have been, in such
a circumstance, a 'rapist' or merely a lucky somnambulist?

Postscript: Who is the real thief?

Jonathan Grossman writes to say that a student, Beth
Steinberg, working on *The Moonstone*,

wrote a wonderful paper for my Victorian fiction class that might
be thought of as this puzzle: 'How do the Indians get away with
the Moonstone and the murder?' Her brilliantly executed argument revolves around the idea that the Indian explorer
Murthwaite abets their getaway in his (and the novel's) final
letter. This makes good sense because Murthwaite, self-named
'semi-savage', rather sides with the Indians throughout the novel.
Ms Steinberg argues that Murthwaite's letter effectively puts the
British authorities off the scent of the murderers (the British are
after all the law in India) by saying that the three men have gone
their separate ways as mendicant, anonymous pilgrims. This
stymies any further pursuit of the murderers: 'The track of the
doomed men through the ranks of their fellow mortals was
obliterated.'

Like Professor Grossman, I am impressed and half-
convinced by Ms Steinberg's ingenious speculation. More
so since Murthwaite, on the evening that the Moonstone
is stolen, has a longish conversation with the Indians in
their native language. And what is he doing at Frizinghall
anyway?

The Oxford World's Classics *The Moonstone* is edited by Anthea
Trodd.

Elms, limes, or does it matter?

George Eliot's huge canvas in *Middlemarch* allows the author the opportunity for luxuriant scene painting. One location, central to the narrative, is described in loving detail—Mr and Mrs Casaubon's married home. Although—as a beneficed clergyman—he has the Lowick living, Edward Casaubon lets the rectory and lives in the nearby manor-house (inherited on the death of his elder brother).[1] We are given an estate agent's eye-view of Lowick Manor when Dorothea, a bride to be, calls to inspect her future home, on a 'grey but dry November morning', in Chapter 9:

> It had a small park, with a fine old oak here and there, and an avenue of limes towards the south-west front, with a sunk fence between park and pleasure ground, so that from the drawing-room windows the glance swept uninterruptedly along a slope of greensward till the limes ended in a level of corn and pastures, which often seemed to melt into a lake under the setting sun. This was the happy side of the house . . . (p. 71)

It is not entirely clear to the mind's eye, but it seems that a ha-ha has been banked up to hide the public thoroughfare from which one turns down the private avenue of limes to approach the manor house. As one looks out from the windows of the house, the road is invisible. For the person looking out of its windows the prospect gives the impression of a huge estate, rather than a modest country house surrounded by working farms.

On this first visit Dorothea chooses the room that is to be her 'boudoir', or private retiring room. It is upstairs, with a large bow window, and 'looks down the avenue of limes'—due west. Obviously, before the advent of artificial lighting, west-facing rooms were a desirable interior feature, allowing as they did a longer enjoyment of daylight. Candlelit evenings, even in a prosperous household like Lowick, would be dim affairs; and in summer the flames would make the rooms hot and (given the fact that tallow rather than wax would be used for all but special occasions) smelly. The detail is something to which the nineteenth-century reader would be better attuned than we are. So well attuned, indeed, that it would not need pointing out. Our Victorian predecessors would also pick up (as we do not) the joke in Lady Catherine de Bourgh's remark, on visiting the Bennets' house for the first time, that 'This must be a most inconvenient sitting room for the evening, in summer; the windows are full west' (p. 312). Inconvenient because, as a lady somewhat far gone in the vale of years, she would (like Blanche Dubois) prefer to avoid the strong light of day illuminating her features. Candles are so much friendlier.

Dorothea Casaubon's west-facing boudoir and the westward avenue figure recurrently in key scenes in the later narrative. When Ladislaw returns to Middlemarch and informs Dorothea of his intention to take up work with Mr Brooke, Casaubon senses danger. He writes his cold letter of severance, declaring war, as it were, on his young cousin, with Dorothea the prize to the victor. Mr Casaubon dispatches his frigid letter in the morning, after what is evidently a tense night in the marital bedroom (if, that is, Dorothea is sleeping with her husband and not by herself in her boudoir):

Meanwhile Dorothea's mind was innocently at work towards the further embitterment of her husband; dwelling, with a sympathy that grew to agitation, on what Will had told her about his parents and grand-parents. Any private hours in her day were

usually spent in her blue-green boudoir, and she had come to be
very fond of its pallid quaintness. Nothing had been outwardly
altered there; but while the summer had gradually advanced over
the western fields beyond the avenue of elms, the bare room had
gathered within it those memories of an inward life which fill the
air as with a cloud of good or bad angels . . . (p. 367)

One thing has, however, been 'outwardly altered'. The
lime-trees have become elms. Elms and limes are, as trees
go, very different to the eye—at least when in full leaf. One
assumes that when Dorothea made her first visit in grey
November the avenue was leafless and—as often
happens—the trees less easily identified without their
foliage. Even though the elm's is rougher-barked than the
lime's, one trunk looks very like another to all but the
forester's eye. Now it is verdant summer.

This explanation, however, is dashed by the next appearance of the avenue. It is another crisis in Dorothea's life.
She is now a widow, and has taken the painful decision to
renounce Will, whom she now realizes she loves:

One morning, about eleven, Dorothea was seated in her boudoir
with a map of the land attached to the manor and other papers
before her . . . She had not yet applied herself to her work, but
was seated with her hands folded on her lap, looking out along
the avenue of limes to the distant fields. Every leaf was at rest in
the sunshine, the familiar scene was changeless, and seemed to
represent the prospect of her life . . . (p. 532)

'Changeless'? The limes which became elms are limes once
more.

The final appearance of the westward prospect is one of
the most admired and familiar moments of the novel. After
her long night-time vigil, Dorothea, as dawn breaks,
resolves to dedicate herself to a life of duty, now truly
understood and stripped of all girlish idealism:

It had taken long for her to come to that question, and there was
light piercing into the room. She opened her curtains, and looked

out towards the bit of road that lay in view, with fields beyond, outside the entrance-gates. On the road there was a man with a bundle on his back and a woman carrying her baby; in the field she could see figures moving—perhaps the shepherd with his dog. Far off in the bending sky was the pearly light; and she felt the largeness of the world and the manifold wakings of men to labour and endurance. She was a part of that involuntary palpitating life, and could neither look out on it from her luxurious shelter as a mere spectator, nor hide her eyes in selfish complaining. (p. 776)

It is a high point, perhaps the highest point, in Eliot's novel. But, playing the part of the 'mere spectator', the reader may wonder about the topography of the scene Dorothea looks out on. She is, as before, looking westwards (whether from her boudoir, or the marital bedroom is not clear)—although 'pearly light' suggests an easterly prospect towards the sunrise. The avenue of limes or elms has disappeared. And the road, which was previously concealed by the ha-ha, has reappeared. Or possibly, it is just the gap where the ha-ha is broken to allow the turn-in from the road. It would be only ten yards or so, and it is hard to think of the family being visible for more than a glimpsed second or two.

If Coleridge, half way through 'This lime-tree Bower my Prison', referred to the embowering tree as an elm, it would be troubling. Eliot's lime/elm variations are almost invisible in the narrative backdrop. But, once perceived, they unsettle us. Readers will have their own responses, and some may opt for a 'silent emendation' of 'elms' to 'limes' on page 367. No editor, as far as I know, has done it—for the likely reason that no editor has noticed (the anomaly was pointed out to me by the Eliot scholar Margaret Harris, and was pointed out to her by a sharp-eyed undergraduate). For me, the elm–lime confusion 'humanizes' a narrator who might otherwise seem divinely infallible. I like to see George Eliot make tiny mistakes (which, frankly, matter not a jot in themselves) because it makes her a little more like me and less like the Oracle at Delphi.

Can one ascertain what trees *really* border the avenue? English elm (*Ulmus procera*) is most commonly a hedging tree. In the early nineteenth century (when *Middlemarch* is set) landowners encouraged their tenant farmers to plant them, and reserved the timber rights as an eventual cash crop. Elm is not favoured as a decorative border tree for park avenues, because of its tendency to throw out lots of suckers. The small-leaved lime (*Tilia cordata*) or linden (it has no connection with the citrus fruit) was commonly used for avenues in the early nineteenth century. A lime-bordered avenue is prominent, for example, at Donwell Abbey in *Emma*, as the company saunter through Mr Knightley's grounds in mid-June:

It was hot; and after walking some time over the gardens in a scattered, dispersed way, scarcely any three together, they insensibly followed one another to the delicious shade of a broad short avenue of limes, which stretching beyond the garden at an equal distance from the river, seemed the finish of the pleasure grounds. (p. 325)

Lime grows quickly, is handsome looking, and can be readily clipped or pollarded. The wood is of little use for timber (although it does, apparently, have some use for sculpting or carving). My guess is that Lowick Manor's avenue is bordered by limes, and there is a stand of elms beyond in the farmer's 'westward fields'. Dorothea's eye has momentarily confused the two.

The Oxford World's Classics *Middlemarch* is edited by David Carroll, with an introduction by Felicia Bonaparte. The Oxford World's Classics *Emma* is edited by James Kinsley, with an introduction by Terry Castle.

Anthony Trollope · *The Way We Live Now*

How criminal is Melmotte and when is he criminalized?

Novelists, from Henry Fielding to Jeffrey Archer, are perennially fascinate by great swindlers—the most adventurous of criminals. For the Victorians, the most notorious such 'buccaneer' was John Sadleir (1814–56). One of the few financier-criminals (along with Robert Maxwell) to earn an entry in the *DNB*, the Irish-born Sadleir rose to fame, power, and high political office on the immense bubble of speculative wealth created by his fraudulent banking activities. When the Tipperary Bank collapsed in February 1856, Sadleir was found to have embezzled £200,000 of its funds and to have ruined legions of widows and children. A couple of days later his body was found on Hampstead Heath, alongside a phial of prussic acid.

Sadleir's meteoric rise, Luciferian fall, and dramatic self-destruction inspired Merdle in *Little Dorrit*, the swindler hero in Charles Lever's *Davenport Dunn* (1859), and—at least partly—Melmotte in *The Way We Live Now* (not least, in regard to the prussic acid). How criminal is Augustus Melmotte? Simply persuading fools (even foolish widows) to part with their money is not necessarily felonious. There is one born every minute, and if the Sadleirs, Merdles, Maxwells, and Melmottes of the world do not fleece them someone else will. Is Anthony Trollope's villain a confidence trickster, or something more serious? Is he a rogue, or an 'arch-criminal'? The question, if one tries to balance all the available evidence, is a lot trickier than it may seem.

The central issue is Pickering Park. Following the tangled career of this property through the long length of *The Way We Live Now* clarifies what is, I think, a significant change of intention by Trollope during the three-months' composition of his novel. Close examination of this issue also highlights that familiar feature of his writing methods—a reluctance to go back and change what he had earlier written. For Trollope, once on paper the narrative was marble. If subsequent problems in consistency or logic arose, Trollope relied on running repair work—a kind of narrative jury-rigging. He did it well and one would not want to catch him out. But uncovering this kind of repair work increases one's respect for his peculiarly fluent genius.

We are introduced to Pickering Park in Chapter 13. A possession of the Longestaffes, it is, like the family's other, and larger, Suffolk property, Caversham, and their town-house in Bruton Street, 'encumbered'. The Longestaffes are 'old' gentry whose income comes from land and they are hard up in these modern times, when big money is made by gambling in the city. Mr Adolphus Longestaffe is keen to sell Pickering so that he can 'disembarrass' Caversham, where his family live (when they are in the country) and where he is squire.

The *nouveau riche* Mr Melmotte is keen to buy (or at least acquire) Pickering as a dowry for his daughter Marie, with which to bribe Lord Nidderdale—his prospective marital target. As the father-in-law of a belted lord, the great financier's campaign to conquer English high society will be usefully advanced. Melmotte is, of course, rather less than keen to pay for Pickering Park, unless he has to. But, keen or not, Mr Adolphus Longestaffe cannot sell the property to Melmotte without the express consent of his

son and heir, the dissolute Adolphus ('Dolly')—an habitué
of the Beargarden Club. Nor, on his part, can Dolly sell
without the consent of his father, who has a life interest
in the estate. Their minds must meet. As Mr Longestaffe
ruefully tells Melmotte, Dolly 'never does do anything that
I wish' (i. 115). Their minds will not meet. There is an
impasse on Pickering Park and the matter is dropped. But,
to raise a few thousands, Mr Longestaffe gives Augustus
Melmotte the title deeds to the London house (in Bruton
Street, as we later learn). What Melmotte subsequently
does with these deeds we never learn (unless I have missed
the detail).

This transaction with the Bruton Street deeds takes
place in mid-April. In mid-June it seems that Dolly has
been brought round on the other matter. More specifically,
he has bargained with his father that, after the outstanding £30,000 mortgage debt on Pickering Park is paid off, he
should receive, cash down, half of the balance, namely
£25,000. Mr Longestaffe's fond hope was that the whole
£50,000 should be applied to Caversham's debt. In course
of time Dolly will reap the benefits when he inherits
Caversham. But Dolly wants 'ready' ('rhino', as they call it
at the Beargarden).

In Chapter 35 (published some six months after Chapter
13 in the novel's serial run) we learn that a paragraph has
appeared in the London newspapers, 'telling the world
that Mr Melmotte had bought Pickering Park, the magnificent Sussex property of Adolphus Longestaffe, Esq., of
Caversham'. And so it was, the narrator confirms: 'the
father and son, who never had agreed before, and who now
had come to no agreement in the presence of each other,
had each considered that their affairs would be safe in the
hands of so great a man as Mr Melmotte, and had been
brought to terms' (i. 325). The awkward phraseology of
'no agreement in the presence of each other' sticks in

the mind. The business was conducted by correspondence or through an intermediary, we assume. It is not, however, a detail we linger on. A lot is happening at this point in the book.

Augustus Melmotte now takes over Pickering Park as its new owner. Masons and carpenters, 'by the dozen' move in. Ten chapters later (Chapter 45), we are vouchsafed some extra details:

Pickering had been purchased and the title-deeds made over to Mr. Melmotte; but the £80,000 had not been paid,—had not been absolutely paid, though of course Mr. Melmotte's note assenting to the terms was security sufficient for any reasonable man. The property had been mortgaged, though not heavily, and Mr. Melmotte had no doubt satisfied the mortgagee; but there was still a sum of £50,000 to come, of which Dolly was to have one half . . . (i. 422–3)

There is a significant new twist in the account of the earlier negotiations for the sale. Although it was said earlier that the arrangements had been made without the parties meeting, now we are told that Dolly 'had actually gone down to Caversham to arrange the terms with his father'. However one reads it, the versions are contradictory— though again all this is on the level of background detail and can be comfortably overlooked. Of course, if we think about it, the Longestaffes in their meeting at Caversham have discussed the disposition of the title deeds, on which joint assent, by writing, was strictly required. Dolly is now reported to have been very happy with the 'arrangement' he made with his father at Caversham, so long as he gets his £25,000 (the next day, he fondly hopes). All this takes place in the period between mid-June and early July—the zenith of 'Melmotte's glory'. It is a crowded month for the 'great financier'. On 8 July he is to host a magnificent banquet for the Emperor of China, and two days later he will

be elected member of Parliament for Westminster. A fortnight later—after a fall like Lucifer's—he will kill himself, leaving behind a faint aroma of almonds and some
unbelievably vast debts.

In Chapter 45 we are told that Mr Longestaffe has 'let his
[Bruton Street] house for a month [i.e. mid-June to mid-
July] to the great financier' (i. 421). This is the first we have
heard of the arrangement—which is to be of vital narrative significance. One deduces, although one is not told,
that Mr Melmotte has taken over the Longestaffe house as
a temporary refuge from the works being carried out in his
Grosvenor Square mansion in preparation for the Emperor
of China banquet. None the less, despite the chaotic
remodelling going on around them, the Melmottes manifestly continue living in Grosvenor Square, right up to the
eve of the banquet. It is from Grosvenor Square, for
example, that Marie makes her ill-fated elopement with
Felix. After the banquet, the Melmottes seem to have
moved lock, stock, and barrel into the Bruton Street house.
It is there that Melmotte beats his daughter, and it is in the
Bruton Street study that he finally poisons himself.

The whole question of the move of residence is
blurred—and not made any clearer by the reader's (but
not Trollope's, apparently) recollection of those Bruton
Street title deeds. There is, legally, no need for Melmotte
to rent Bruton Street; it is his to do as he likes with. A new
phase in the Pickering saga begins in Chapter 58, where
Dolly—enraged by the fact that he has not yet received so
much as a ten-pound note—recruits a sharp lawyer, Mr
Squercum, to pursue his interest. At this point in the narrative (during the early days of July) the idea is introduced
that Melmotte has committed 'forgery' to gain possession
of Pickering Park. Forged what? Why should he have had
to forge anything? Rumours claim he has forged title
deeds—which is clearly absurd tittle-tattle. Subsequently,

it emerges that he is thought to have forged Dolly's letter, assenting (in mid-June) to the making over of the title deeds of Pickering Park, directed to Mr Longestaffe's dilatory lawyers, Slow and Bideawhile. This is later confirmed by the narrator, in Chapter 73, shortly before Melmotte kills himself.

It is not, as presented by Trollope, an easy morsel of information for the reader to swallow. Melmotte, we are asked to believe, forged Dolly's signature to a blank letter of assent, which he found in a drawer, in mid-June, in a desk used by Mr Longestaffe, in Bruton Street, in a study which contained two desks, the other of which was reserved for Mr Melmotte's use, in which he (on his part) keeps documents so confidential that he is obliged to eat them before doing away with himself. He evidently also keeps a handy phial of prussic acid in the desk drawer. Mr Longestaffe, of course, being the owner of the house and the two desks, would have a master-key to the receptacle of the great financier's darkest secrets

At this point, scepticism crowds in. The tissue of narrative invention is so flimsy that one can poke holes in it at almost any point. Is it conceivable that Dolly and his father, coming to their meeting of minds at Caversham in mid-June (long before we are told the son has his own lawyer—an afterthought) would not have touched on the business of the deeds? Would not their handing over or holding the deeds back have been a central part of any 'arrangement'? The notion that Slow and Bideawhile would not have notified Dolly of the transfer of these documents (representing £80,000 of his inheritance) is similarly incredible. A witnessed statement would have been required for the title deeds and property to be passed over. Melmotte could not have paid off the mortgage holder; were he not the titled owner.

On his part, Dolly cannot sign away his property with a

casual, unwitnessed, letter. Nor would lawyers as respectable as Slow and Bideawhile fail to keep their client
informed of what they were doing with a stream of
missives—among which would be their bill, detailing the
transfer of the deeds. This business with the forged letter
is supposed to have taken place in mid-June, at the time of
the newspaper announcement. But Dolly is clearly aware,
in Chapter 35, that the deeds *have* been made over. Melmotte's workmen would hardly have descended on the
place, nor could the mortgagee have been paid off by Melmotte, otherwise. All that worried Dolly at that point was
not that the deeds had gone but that his £25,000 was slow
in coming.

The business about the blank letter, left conveniently in
Melmotte's temporary residence (at a time when he was
not residing there), is highly implausible, as is the account
of the financier's housing generally. Melmotte would
surely have kept confidential documents locked in his safe
in Abchurch Lane, or in Grosvenor Square—not in a study
shared with someone whom he was criminally defrauding.
And what—before the sale of Pickering Park was in
prospect—was Mr Longestaffe doing with a blank lawyer's
letter of consent (naming Melmotte as purchaser) in his
desk drawer in Bruton Street? Is he perhaps a clairvoyant?

Trollope gets round this problem very awkwardly.
Retroactively (in Chapter 45) he has Melmotte living simultaneously in Bruton Street and Grosvenor Square, from
mid-June onwards. And, in order to get Longestaffe (or his
current business correspondence) into Bruton Street—a
house we were told in Chapter 35 that he has entirely
vacated—Trollope tells us (in Chapter 73) that Mr Longestaffe has been given *carte blanche* to use this study
whenever he wishes: 'Oh dear yes! Mr. Longestaffe could
come whenever he pleased. He, Melmotte, always left the
house at ten and never returned till six. The ladies would

never enter that room. The servants were to regard Mr. Longestaffe quite as master of the house as far as that room was concerned' (ii. 118).

We never actually see Longestaffe occupying Bruton Street while the Melmottes occupy it—but we are to assume he *did*—inconvenient as such an arrangement would be to all parties. Convenience, of course, is hardly served by there being two desks in the shared study. Mr Melmotte has the key for one, and Mr Longestaffe the key to the other. And in *his* desk, Mr Longestaffe secretes the unsigned lawyer's letter. And then, with no other motive than curiosity, Mr Melmotte forces the lock—breaking it in the process—and discovers—to his immense convenience—the blank letter awaiting only his forged addition.

One could go on poking holes, but the improbabilities are legion. One recalls one of Trollope's aphorisms in the novel: 'A liar has many points in his favour,—but he has this against him, that unless he devote more time to the management of his lies than life will generally allow, he cannot make them tally' (ii. 254–5). So too with narrators who try to change their plots as they go along. To make the late stages of the novel's narrative tally with the earlier, Trollope has to convince us that Dolly and his father are criminally negligent of their property, that lawyers do not answer letters or draw up contracts, that both Melmotte and Mr Longestaffe contrive to live in two places at once and conduct their very personal business matters in the same office, leaving sensitive documents for each other to happen on. That, just on the off-chance of finding something valuable, Melmotte takes a jemmy to his landlord's furniture.

What happened? Trollope's notes for the novel offer a clue. In his early scheme, Trollope clearly meant Melmotte to be a great confidence trickster—less a villain than a

682 Anthony Trollope

swindler who plays on the gullibility of the English public; a kind of Volpone *de nos jours*. Subsequently—around the middle of his composition—a darker and more feloniously criminal conception of the 'great financier' emerged. In a chapter plan for the novel, as it was evolving, it is clear that Trollope was toying with the idea of climaxing the book with a great trial—Melmotte in the dock at the Old Bailey for forgery.[1] This was to happen around Chapters 71–7. But after projecting this end for the novel, Trollope decided instead on suicide. The evidence is that he began seriously to think of this turn of plot around Chapter 45. He added, as he went along, details that would make the forgery retrospectively plausible—beginning with the lease, and ending with the business of the two desks in the shared study. In a novel less crowded with distracting incident than *The Way We Live Now*, the improbabilities might have protruded fatally. As it is, the reader has so much else to think about that Trollope's fumble passes unnoticed, or if noticed, not dwelt upon.

The Oxford World's Classics The *Way We Live Now* is edited by John Sutherland.

====

Jules Verne and the English Sunday

====

Verne's most famous story has a wonderful narrative 'gimmick'. Phileas Fogg lays a bet with his fellow Reform Club members that he can—using the latest transport systems (as advertised in the *Daily Telegraph*)—circumnavigate the globe in 'eighty days or less; in nineteen hundred and twenty hours, or a hundred and fifteen thousand two hundred minutes' (p. 20). He will leave England on 2 October, and return on—or before—'Saturday the 21st of December, 1872', at a quarter-to-nine. This narrative idea was supposedly inspired by the advertising material of Thomas Cook, catering for the first generation of world 'tourists'.

The story which Verne builds on the 'eighty days' gimmick is wonderfully entertaining. And it ends with a fine *coup de théâtre*. By dint of ingenuity, lavish outlay of money, pluck, and sheer will, Phileas and his comic, but omnicompetent 'man', Passepartout, make it back to England in the nick of time. But at this moment Phileas is falsely arrested for bank-robbery (like tourism, one of the modern world's new growth industries).

He misses the deadline by minutes. To console himself he decides that he will marry the Oriental beauty, Aouda. Passepartout is sent out to arrange things with the clergyman. Then, the following day—again with only minutes to spare—Passepartout rushes back to Fogg's grand mansion in Savile Row. It is, he announces, a day earlier than they think:

Three minutes later [Passepartout] was back in Savile Row, staggering, completely out of breath, into Mr Fogg's room.

He couldn't speak.

'But what's the matter?'

'Master's . . .' spluttered Passepartout, '. . . wedding . . . impossible.'

'Impossible?'

'Impossible . . . tomorrow.'

'But why?'

'Tomorrow . . . Sunday!'

'Monday,' said Mr Fogg.

'No . . . Today . . . Saturday.'

'Saturday? Impossible!'

'Yes, YES, YES!' screamed Passepartout. 'Your calculations were a day out! We arrived 24 hours early. But there are only ten minutes left!' (p. 200)

The two men rush the 576 yards to the Reform Club, arriving breathless but just under the wire, as the club clock pendulum beats the sixtieth second, marking the deadline.

As the editor of the Oxford World's Classics edition points out, Jules Verne is engagingly slapdash about the fine detail of his narrative. He mixes up East and West, left and right, and there are many chronological and geographical slips. And striking at the heart of the plot is the business about the 'phantom day'. Fogg, that is, does not undertake to go round the world in '80 days'; but 'within' 80 days—in 79 days, that is. It is an analogous confusion to that currently raging about the new millennium: as pedants love to point out, it will not start on 1 January 2000, but on 1 January 2001—long after all the celebrations have ended and the site at Greenwich is once more a rubbish dump.

Verne's wonderful idea (at least for readers on this side of the Channel) is damaged by another implausibility, attributable to a Gallic incomprehension of the English 'weekend'. Arrived and detained by the police at Liverpool, Fogg dashes to the station and orders a special train to London.

There were several high-speed engines with steam up. But given the traffic arrangements, the special train couldn't leave the station until three o'clock.

At 3 p.m., Phileas Fogg, having mentioned to the driver a certain bonus to be won, was heading for London together with the young woman and his faithful servant.

Liverpool to London had to be covered in five and a half hours: perfectly possible when the line is clear all the way. But there were unavoidable delays—and when the gentleman got to the terminus, 8.50 was striking on all the clocks of London.

Having completed his journey round the world, Phileas Fogg had arrived five minutes late.

He had lost. (p. 191)

He must also have lost a large part of his formidable powers of observation if he cannot tell the difference between Friday night and Saturday night, at a London railway station. Nor have noticed that the Saturday train service differs from that of other days of the week. Fogg, we remember, is a man whose 'sole pastimes were reading the newspapers and playing whist'. Obviously no papers have come to his notice on his six hours' train journey.

Most improbable is that, during the hours of daylight the next day, Fogg should be under the illusion that it is Sunday. Even if the papers were not delivered, the sounds (or lack of them) from the street outside would surely have alerted him. In Britain in 1872 Saturday was not as distinctively different from Friday as it was to become in the twentieth century, with the extension of the English weekend and the five-day working week. But Sunday— oppressed by the iron pieties of the Lord's Day Observance Society—was uniquely grim. Fogg and Passepartout would have to be deaf, dumb, and blind not to notice the graveyard stillness of the English Sunday. Or not, in this case, to notice that it was *not* Sunday, but bustling Saturday, with open shops (Savile Row then, as now, was the Mecca of English gentleman's tailoring), busy places of entertainment, postal deliveries (banned on Sunday by the LDOS), and hectic traffic.

This is an implausibility which would, I think, tend to slip by the French reader (it would have been easily remedied, had Verne noticed it, by having the eightieth day fall midweek). The implausibility will, increasingly, slip by the British reader after the 1990s, with the innovation of Sunday Trading, and the homogenization of the British week. But for those older readers who can remember the full awfulness of the Victorian Sunday, a phenomenon which lasted well into the last decades of the twentieth century, the ending of Verne's romance will always ring false.

The Oxford World's Classics *Around the World in Eighty Days* is translated and edited by William Butcher.

What happens to Jim's family?

The most discussed anomaly in *Huckleberry Finn's* narrative has been satisfactorily explained away by modern critical commentary. In Chapter 8, Huck meets up with his fellow runaway, the slave Jim, on Jackson's Island. Jim explains why it is he has run away. He overheard Miss Watson, his owner, planning to sell him in New Orleans, for $800, 'and lit out mighty quick, I tell you' (p. 41). He has hidden on the island, waiting for a raft to carry him downriver. He intends to go some twenty-five miles downstream, then hide on the Illinois side of the Mississippi. That is, he will go south, not north or east.

The question is, why doesn't Jim just go across into Illinois, which is not a slave state, only a few hundred yards from Jackson's Island where he and Huck are hiding? Why go further into the dangerous south? The question is picked up by Huck in Chapter 20, throwing his new companions the 'Duke' and the 'Dauphin', off the trail:

They asked us considerable many questions; wanted to know what we covered up the raft that way for, and laid by in the day-time instead of running—was Jim a runaway nigger? Says I—

'Goodness sakes, would a runaway rigger run *south*?'

No, they allowed he wouldn't. (p. 116)

It looks, on the face of it, like a lapse of logic. Rather as if Liza, in *Uncle Tom's Cabin*, instead of crossing the ice-floes to the other side of the Ohio had decided to float down on one, further into the slave-owning territory she is trying to escape. But, as commentators have made clear, Jim's decision is a wise one on closer inspection. The western part of Ohio, bordering the Mississippi, was notoriously dangerous for runaway slaves. They might be captured by bounty hunters, who did a thriving trade in returning runaways (illegal as the business was). They could be held as indentured labourers for a year until reclaimed; and even then be returned.

The safest strategy, which Jim has evidently worked out, is to drift south to Cairo, then go north (as best he can) on the upstream tributary and get deep into Ohio, where the underground railway is established and he can travel on to freedom. Of course, events intervene when he and Huck arrive at Cairo and this plan is foiled. But it is, none the less, the best plan and, we may assume, no blunder on Mark Twain's part.

There is another problem which is less tractable. In Chapter 16 we learn that Jim is not—as the reader previously was led to believe—a single man. The raft is approaching Cairo. Jim is excited, because he sees this city as his jumping-off place for freedom. Huck is increasingly gloomy at the thought that he is abetting in the robbery of Miss Watson, assisting the escape of $800-worth of her property:

I got to feeling so mean and so miserable I most wished I was dead. I fidgeted up and down the raft, abusing myself to myself, and Jim was fidgeting up and down past me. We neither of us could keep still. Every time he danced around and says, 'Dah's Cairo!' it went through me like a shot, and I thought if it *was* Cairo I reckoned I would die of miserableness.

Jim talked out loud all the time while I was talking to myself. He was saying how the first thing he would do when he got to a free State he would go to saving up money and never spend a single cent, and when he got enough he would buy his wife, which was owned on a farm close to where Miss Watson lived and then they would both work to buy the two children, and if their master wouldn't sell them, they'd get an Ab'litionist to go and steal them.

It most froze me to hear such talk. He wouldn't ever dared to talk such talk in his life before. Just see what a difference it made in him the minute he judged was about free. It was according to the old saying, 'Give a nigger an inch and he'll take an ell.' (p. 82)

We learn a little more about Jim's family in Chapter 23. His children are called Elizabeth and Johnny. He gives a pathetic description of how, after 'Lizabeth recovered from the scarlet fever, he slapped her for not paying attention to him. Then he discovered, the disease had made her deaf:

'Oh, Huck, I bust out a-cryin' en grab her up in my arms, en say, "Oh, do po' little thing! de Lord God Almighty fogive po' ole Jim, kaze he never gwyne to fogive hisself as long's he live!" Oh she was plumb deef en dumb, Huck, plumb deef and dumb—en I'd ben a-treat'n her so!' (p. 142)

It is, arguably, the most moving section of the novel.

Nothing more is said of Jim's family. In 'Chapter the Last' Jim discovers he is free, is taken from his chains, 'given all he wanted to eat, and a good time ... and Tom give Jim forty dollars for being prisoner'. No mule is forthcoming, but

Jim was pleased most to death, and busted out, and says:

'*Dah*, now Huck, what I tell you?—what I tell you up dah on Jackson islan'? I *tole* you I got a hairy breas', en what's de sign un it, en I *tole* you I ben rich wunst, en gwineter be rich *agin*.' (p. 261)

Jim's former richness was the possession of $14, as we recall. He is now $36 better off. His estimated value is $800. How is he going to buy his wife and children? The narrative ignores this question, in its wrap-up of events. The novel ends with Huck's deterinination to 'light out for the territory ahead of the rest, because Aunt Sally she's going to adopt me and sivilize me, and I can't stand it. I been there before.' So the novel ends. And what of Jim, his wife, 'Lizabeth, and Johnny? Obviously Jim will never have the wherewithal to buy them. Huck might loan or give him the money from his $6,000 treasure; which would make a nice romantic ending. It is, as best we can guess, the late 1840s or early 1850s.[1] If Jim can wait fifteen years, the Civil War will unite his family (the romantic Tom will be fighting for the South, realistic Huck for the North). His best hope, probably, is some 'Ab'litionist'.

There is currently much discussion about the propriety of suppressing *Huckleberry Finn* on the grounds of its profuse (and disquieting) use of the N—— word'. Personally I can tolerate this evidently accurate depiction of the callous vernacular of the place and period more easily than Twain's indifference (and the anaesthetized indifference his narrative induces in us, its readers) to Jim's still-enslaved family

The Oxford World's Classics *Huckleberry Finn* is edited by Emory Elliott.

What English novel is Anna reading?

If Tolstoy's novel *Anna Karenina* had ended a fifth of the way through, at the end of Chapter 29, we would have a bittersweet short story with a happy ending. In this chapter Anna is returning from Moscow to her home, her beloved son Seriozha, and her less-than-beloved husband, Alexei, in Saint Petersburg. She has been in the capital to sort out the marriage problems of her hapless sister-in-law, Dolly

In Moscow, Anna has fallen under the spell of the dashing cavalry officer, Count Vronsky. But she has not surrendered to temptation. She is still a virtuous wife and matron. By no means entirely happy: but virtuous.

She now travels back to St Petersburg by train, at night, accompanied by her maid, Annushka. 'Well, that's all over, thank Heaven!' Anna thinks as she enters her 'dimly lit' carriage: 'Thank Heaven, tomorrow I shall see Seriozha and Alex Alexandrovich again and my good accustomed life will go on as of old':

With the same preoccupied mind she had had all that day, Anna prepared with pleasure and great deliberation for the journey. With her deft little hands she unlocked her red bag, took out a small pillow which she placed against her knees, and locked the bag again; then she carefully wrapped up her feet and sat down comfortably. An invalid lady was already going to bed. Two other ladies began talking to Anna. One, a fat old woman, while wrapping up her feet, remarked upon the heating of the carriage. Anna said a few words in answer, but not foreseeing anything interesting from the conversation asked her maid to get out her reading-lamp, fixed it to the arm of her seat, and took a paper-knife and an English novel from her handbag. At first she could not read. For a while the bustle of people moving about disturbed her, and when the train had finally started it was impossible not to listen to the noises; then there was the snow, beating against the window on her left, to which it stuck, and the sight of the guard, who passed through the carriage closely wrapped up and covered with snow on one side; also the conversation about the awful snow-storm which was raging outside distracted her attention. And so it went on and on: the same jolting and knocking, the same beating of the snow on the window-pane, the same rapid changes from steaming heat to cold, and back again to heat, the gleam of the same faces through the semi-darkness, and the same voices,—but at last Anna began to read and to follow what she read. Annushka was already dozing, her broad hands, with a hole in one of the gloves, holding the red bag on her lap. Anna read and understood, but it was unpleasant to read, that is to say, to follow the reflection of other people's lives. She was too eager to live herself. When she read how the heroine of the novel nursed a sick man, she wanted to move about the sick-room with noiseless footsteps; when she read of a member of Parliament making a speech, she wished to make that speech; when she read how Lady Mary rode to hounds, teased her sister-in-law, and astonished everybody by her boldness—she wanted to do it herself. But there was nothing to be done, so she forced herself to read, while her little hand played with the smooth paper-knife.

The hero of the novel had nearly attained to his English happiness of a baronetcy and an estate, and Anna wanted to go to the estate with him, when she suddenly felt that he must have been ashamed, and that she was ashamed of the same thing,—but what was she ashamed of? 'What am I ashamed of?' she asked herself with indignant surprise. She put down her book, leaned back, and clasped the paper-knife tightly in both hands. There was nothing to be ashamed of. (pp. 99–100)

It's a wonderfully evoked scene—familiar to anyone who has travelled through the night by train, yet strange, in many of its physical details, to a non-Russian reader (how should we visualize that movable 'reading lamp', for example, hung on the arm of Anna's seat?). Vladimir Nabokov, when a lecturer at Cornell University, used to give a whole lecture to his American undergraduates based on this passage. 'Any ass can assimilate the main points of Tolstoy's attitude toward adultery,' Nabokov asserted, 'but in order to enjoy Tolstoy's art the good reader must wish to visualize, for instance, the arrangement of a railway carriage on the Moscow–Petersburg train as it was a hundred years ago.'[1]

The passage is shot through with omens—trains will not be lucky for Anna. But the attention of the English-speaking reader will be particularly drawn to the 'English novel' whose pages Anna is cutting and reading. We are given precise and detailed descriptions of its narrative. What, then, is it? Surely we can identify it by title? A. N. Wilson, in his life of Tolstoy, is in no doubt that Anna has in her hands a novel by Anthony Trollope.[2] Tolstoy wrote *Anna Karenina* between 1873 and 1878, and it is known that during this period he read and admired Trollope's equally massive novel of parliamentary life, *The Prime Minister*. That novel, published in England in June 1876 (although it cannot have been translated into Russian until a few months later), had a momentous influence on *Anna Karenina*. Trollope's narrative climaxes, brilliantly, with the suicide of the villainous Ferdinand Lopez, in front of a speeding train. There are other such deaths in Victorian fiction (notably Carker's in *Dombey and Son*). But it is likely that the climax of Tolstoy's novel—Anna's self-immolation at Nizhny railway station—is directly indebted to *The Prime Minister*.

There is, however, no scene in *The Prime Minister* in which Lopez makes a speech in Parliament. That episode seems to belong to an earlier Trollope novel, *Phineas Finn, the Irish Member* (1869), whose narrative revolves around the hero's initial failure to make a good maiden speech to the House, and his eventual success in doing so. And the business about Lady Mary riding to hounds and teasing her sister-in-law seems to allude to still another Trollope novel, *Is he Popenjoy?* (1878), where the spirited heroine, Lady Mary Germain (née Gresley), outrages her husband's straitlaced sisters by dancing and hunting. Mary Germain's husband, however, attains his Englishman's idea of happiness not in the form of a 'baronetcy and an estate', but the unexpected legacy of a marquisate and an estate. Tolstoy's 'baronetcy' seems to be a recollection of Trollope's *The Claverings* (1867), in which the hero, Harry, unexpectedly inherits a baronetcy, an estate (and some of the attendant guilt which Tolstoy mentions) when his distant cousins are drowned sailing. As for the business of the heroine nursing a sick man—that would seem to be an allusion to a quite different novel— Charlotte Yonge's sensational best-seller of 1853 *The Heir of Redclyffe*, in which the baronet hero, Guy, is nursed on his lingering deathbed by his young wife Amy. They are on their honeymoon in Italy and Guy dies an exemplary Christian death.

What, then, is Tolstoy aiming at with this mélange of bits and pieces of English fiction? What the Russian writer is doing, I suggest, is something rather chauvinistic. It was Virginia Woolf who claimed that there was only one 'adult' novel written in Victorian England— *Middlemarch* (a novel that Tolstoy seems not to have read). The mass of English Victorian novels, particularly with their sugar-stick endings and generally optimistic view of life, were essentially *juvenile*, Woolf thought. Henry James made much the same point when he talked, at the end of the century, of the tyranny of the young reader over the adult novelist.

The point that Tolstoy makes is, I think, that Anna is

not reading an English novel so much as 'English fiction'—with all its falsities and its childish addiction to 'happiness', particularly happy endings. To paraphrase the famous opening of *Anna Karenina*, all happy novels are alike, so it does not really matter *which* particular English novel the heroine is reading. What Anna is reading, we apprehend, is a generic English novel—a novel that never existed, but which typifies the genre. And to represent the quintessence of English fiction Tolstoy amalgamates a variety of works by that most English of English novelists, Anthony Trollope, the 'Chronicler of Barsetshire', with a dash of Miss Yonge. He, Count Leo Tolstoy, will write a different kind of novel: one that is harder, sadder, more realistic—Russian, in a word. A novel that does not succumb to the debilitating 'English idea'. 'Expect no pernicious "English happiness" in this Russian novel,' is the implicit warning.

What English novel, then, is Anna Karenina reading? All of them and none of them.

The Oxford World's Classics *Anna Karenina* is translated by Louise and Aylmer Maude, with an introduction and notes by Gareth Jones.

Thomas Hardy · *The Mayor of Casterbridge*

Why are there no public conveniences in Casterbridge?

The furmity-woman is Michael Henchard's albatross, or the equivalent of Macbeth's witches. Whenever she appears on the scene, bad things happen to the Mayor of Casterbridge. It is at the furmity-woman's marquee that her rum-laced drink drives Henchard to the wild act of selling his wife Susan and his daughter Elizabeth-Jane for five guineas—precipitating the long series of events which will, twenty-two years later, lead to his final disgrace and wretched extinction.

Henchard first meets this ominous figure at the Weydon-Priors annual fair (located as Weyhill in Hampshire). The date of the encounter is around 1828 (a period of historical significance—the main part of the narrative pivots around the mid-1840s repeal of the Corn Laws; as the story opens, Wessex is still enjoying its protected prosperity as the granary of England). The fair, as a harvest festival with distant pagan origins, takes place in the hot mid-September (the fifteenth, as we can work out from Henchard's great oath the next day). Its main attractions are 'peep-shows, toy-stands, wax-works, inspired monsters, disinterested medical men, who travelled for the public good, thimble-riggers, nick-nack vendors, and readers of Fate' (p. 8). Liquid refreshments are also on offer.

On her first appearance the furmity-woman is thriving, if unappetizing. She is in her physical prime and at the zenith of her fortunes:

A haggish creature of about fifty presided, in a white apron, which, as it threw an air of respectability over her as far as it extended, was made so wide as to reach nearly round her waist. She slowly stirred the contents of the pot. The dull scrape of her large spoon was audible throughout the tent as she thus kept from burning the mixture of corn in the grain, flour, milk, raisins, currants, and what not, that composed the antiquated slop in which she dealt. (pp. 8–9)

The antiquated slop is a traditional rural beverage. Otherwise known as 'furmenty', its liquid base is wheat boiled in milk. In its unadulterated form, furmity is non-alcoholic. But, of course, the furmity-woman is lacing her drink with strong liquor. As she later admits, she is a 'land smuggler'. Her rum and brandy will be contraband bought from sea smugglers. We should assume that, in addition to her fairground business—which is nomadic and takes her all round Wessex, she sells smuggled liquor to the inns and public houses on her circuit. We do not know what town she comes from, and where she has her base; probably it is on the coast, somewhere like Portsmouth.[1] As the century progresses, more rigorously imposed licensing laws, and a more efficient customs and excise, will ruin her. Like Michael Henchard in his palmy Casterbridge days, hers is a prosperity whose days are numbered. The future is with the licensed marquee at the Weydon-Priors fair, selling 'Good Home-brewed Beer, Ale and Cider'. Its canvas has a pure, 'milk-hued' aspect. The furmity-seller's large tent has an appropriately soiled canvas. Hardy wants us to recall Hogarth's Gin Lane and Beer Street.

After his terrible deed, Michael Henchard wakes up in the melancholy depths of remorseful hangover. His first thought is, 'Did I tell my name to anybody last night, or didn't I tell my name?' (p. 18): He decides he didn't (this seems to have been the case; nor did Susan divulge her married name to onlookers). Henchard then swears his terrible abstinence oath, and goes off to 'far distant' Casterbridge.

Eighteen years later, to the day, Susan and Elizabeth-Jane return to Weydon-Priors. They find the fair 'considerably dwindled' (p. 22). So too has the business of the furmity-seller dwindled. She is now 'an old woman haggard, wrinkled, and almost in rags . . . now tentless, dirty, owning no tables or benches, and having scarce any customers except two small whitey-brown boys' (p. 23). The furmity-seller vouchsafes some details of her personal history to the two ladies:

'I've stood in this fair-ground maid, wife, and widow these nine and thirty year, and in that time have known what it was to do business with the richest stomachs in the land! Ma'am, you'd hardly believe that I was once the owner of a great pavilion tent that was the attraction of the fair. Nobody could come—nobody could go, without having a dish of Mrs. Goodenough's furmity.' (p. 24)

She even, as she says, 'knowed the taste of the coarse shameless females'—which suggests that in addition to being a bootlegger, Mrs Goodenough may have dabbled in abortion (an overdose of strong liquor and a hot bath was a favoured remedy for young girls in trouble).

More to the point, can she remember the wife-sale eighteen years ago? Only very dimly, it transpires. She now has no clear mental picture of Michael Henchard, beyond his workman's corduroy and hay-trusser's tools. But she does vaguely recall that he came back to the next year's fair (i.e. seventeen years' since), 'and told me quite private-like that if a woman ever asked for him,' she was to say 'he had gone to—where?—Casterbridge' (p. 25).

Two years pass—with immense personal and professional consequences for Michael Henchard, corn factor and Mayor of Casterbridge. In Chapter 28, with his business collapsing around his ears, Henchard goes to take the

chair at petty sessions. He is a magistrate by virtue of his
late mayorship. There is only one case to be heard, that of
'an old woman of mottled countenance' and greasy
clothes—'The steeped aspect of a woman as a whole showed
her to be no native of the country-side or even of a country
town' (p. 199). She has drifted in to Casterbridge as so much
vagrant refuse from a conurbation like Bristol, we gather.

The court proceedings open with the comedy of the
constable Stubberd's Dogberry-like malapropisms:

'She is charged, sir, with the offence of disorderly female and
nuisance,' whispered Stubberd.
   'Where did she do that?' said the other magistrate.
   'By the church Sir, of all the horrible places in the world!—I
caught her in the act, your worship.' (p. 199)

It emerges from Stubberd's circuitous testimony that 'at
twenty five minutes past eleven, b. m., on the night of the
fifth instinct, Hannah Dominy,' he found the old lady
relieving herself in a gutter. She was observed 'wambling'
(staggering) and, as the constable came up to her with his
lantern 'she committed the nuisance and insulted me'. Her
insult, as he reports it, was 'Put away that dee lantern'.
Then she added—'Dost hear, old turmit-head? Put away
that dee lantern.' It is that 'turmit-head' that gets her
arrested. Had she been properly meek, she would probably
have been told to 'move on', with the customary 'warning'.
And it is already clear that Stubberd was fabricating his
evidence ('fitting her up') when he earlier claimed that it
was *after* he approached her with his lantern that she
(provocatively) committed her nuisance. Clearly she was
discreetly relieving herself in the dark, over a gutter, and
was disturbed by the officious Stubberd throwing his light
on her.

Once in court, the hag shows that she has her wits about
her. She runs rings round Stubberd and the magistrate.

Then, with her eyes 'twinkling', she recounts, in malicious detail, the Weydon Fair episode. Henchard is publicly unmasked as a wife-seller, and completes his shame with a manly, but suicidal, confession: ''tis true . . . 'Tis as true as the light.' A few more details add to the tableau of Henchard's downfall. There is a crowd gathered in court because, it emerges, 'the old furmity dealer had mysteriously hinted . . . that she knew a queer thing or two about their great local man Mr. Henchard, if she chose to tell it' (p. 202).

A number of puzzling questions arise from this scene. Why has the furmity-woman just now come to Casterbridge, a town which, self-evidently, has always been off her circuit? Where has she been in the interval? How is it that she can now recognize Michael Henchard, when her memory was so blurred in conversation with Susan a couple of years before? Most intriguingly, why has she been arrested in the first place? Was her offence so rank? Casterbridge is a market town, as we are continually reminded. Livestock are regularly driven through its streets. In the very next chapter (29) there is a description of how, 'in the latter quarter of each year', vast herds of cattle are herded through Casterbridge (this leads to the fine episode in which Henchard saves Lucetta and Elizabeth from a runaway bull). On routine market days, 'any inviting recess in front of a house [is] utilized by pig-dealers as a pen for their stock' (p. 61). These herds, styes, and flocks—not to mention the town's innumerable horses—will deposit hundredweights of dung in the public thoroughfares every day and tons of it on market days.

Judging by Stubberd, Casterbridge's municipal employees are not paragons of efficiency. Street-sweeping will not take place more than once a week, if that often. The nostrils of the town's citizens must be inured to the pervasive stench. Why should an old woman at midnight in a deserted back alley adding a few drops to the Niagara of urine that flows through Casterbridge gutters cause such a pother? And what *should* the old lady, caught short, have done? Where are the 'public conveniences'?

The arrest seems, on the face of it, excessively officious. There was, of course, a wave of 'respectability' sweeping over mid-Victorian Britain. Society was becoming stricter and more 'decent' by the year. And then, of course, there is the imminent visit of the 'royal personage' (Hardy's recollection of Prince Albert's passing through Dorchester in July 1847). When royalty comes, lavatories and what goes on in them are hidden away—except for that gleaming and virginal facility reserved for royal use. It may be that, like the luckless vagrants in any city where the Olympics are due to be held, the furmity woman is the victim of a 'crackdown'. She chose the wrong time to commit her nuisance.

Most significantly, there was at mid-century a new wave of 'sanitary' legislation directed at the 'cleanliness' of the British population—the Municipal Corporations Act of 1835; the Public Health Act of 1848; the Public Baths and Wash Houses Act of 1846. Central to the court scene in *The Mayor of Casterbridge* is the Nuisances Removal Act of 1846. The legal euphemism 'nuisance' (like 'public convenience', 'spending a penny') became the material of music-hall jokes for a century after. The furmity-woman is, evidently, one of the first victims of the 1846 Act.

Legislation was, however, more effective in setting up machinery for the prohibition of 'public nuisance' than the 'conveniences' to eliminate the nuisance. What, in 1847, could the furmity-woman have done, other than use an alley to empty her drink-distended bladder? The only public lavatory in Casterbridge, or towns like it, would be at the railway station.[2] And those 'conveniences' would probably be nothing more than a slate-backed row of stand-up urinals for travelling males (or those who went to the expense of buying a 'platform ticket'). There was, as it happened, great resistance to 'public conveniences' for ladies, well into the late Victorian period. The respectable residents of Camden, as late as 1880, opposed a *chalet de toilette et de necessité* (of a kind available to Parisian ladies) on the grounds that 'it would have a tendency to diminish that innate sense of modesty so much admired in our countrywomen'.

One of the great attractions of the new department stores which sprang up in great cities in the later decades of the nineteenth century was that they were 'convenient' for lady shoppers. As Alison Adburgham notes, in *Shops and Shopping*:

The department stores, with their variety of ready-made clothes and accessories at reasonable prices, played an important part in the emancipation of women. One could go to town for a day and get everything done in one store; and more and more the stores in London and the big cities set out to attract shoppers from a distance by offering auxiliary non-selling services such as restaurants, banking facilities, and exhibitions—and cloakrooms. These last were particularly appreciated. The Ladies' Lavatory Company opened its first establishment at Oxford Circus in 1884, but there were few such facilities, and one feared to be observed using them.[3]

The Mayor of Casterbridge (serialized January–May 1886) was being written in the immediate aftermath of the setting up of the inaugural convenience at Oxford Circus. It would be many years, one imagines, before the Ladies' Lavatory Company reached Dorset.

It may well be that the fashion for the incredibly cumbersome crinoline enjoyed its long vogue, from the 1850s onward, partly because of the freedom which, paradoxically, it offered wearers. In her life of Havelock Ellis, Phyllis Grosskurth records how, as a 12-year-old child, the great sexologist was directed towards his later researches by a traumatic experience. He was walking in the London Zoo with his mother. She bade him wait a second while she stood motionless, with a serene expression on her face. When they went along their way (she lifting her skirts slightly) he looked back to see a faintly steaming puddle.[4] The vogue for gusset-less, 'free-trade' underwear probably also had its origin less in the sexual promiscuity of Victorian ladies, than in their need for clandestine relief while in public. Had the furmity-seller been wearing a crinoline and the appropriate underthings, she could have relieved herself in Casterbridge high street at midday, and suffered no persecution whatsoever beyond a lift of the cap from the passing Stubberd. But neither a *chalet de necessité* nor the camouflage of crinoline are available to Mrs Goodenough, only the dark and handy gutter.

The Oxford World's Classics *The Mayor of Casterbridge* is edited by Dale Kramer.

A. Conan Doyle · *'A Scandal in Bohemia'*

Cabinets and detectives

The Sherlock Holmes mania—which shows little sign of abating a century on—took off not with the first full-length novel (*A Study in Scarlet*, 1887), but with the series of six short stories that began in the *Strand Magazine* in July 1891 and were later collected as *The Adventures of Sherlock Holmes* (1892). The first story, 'A Scandal in Bohemia', lays down what was to be Doyle's favourite narrative formula in these short tales. It is March 1888. Dr Watson (now a married man) finds himself in the vicinity of 221B Baker Street and drops in on his bachelor friend. Holmes is discovered in his usual cocaine-alleviated state of ennui. He delivers himself of some bracing Holmesian maxims. 'You see, but you do not observe,' he tells his dull *fidus Achates*; how many steps, for example, are there from the hall to the room where they are sitting? Seventeen, as Watson has a thousand times seen and never observed.

A visitor is expected. Of course Watson ('my Boswell') must stay. The client is a sumptuously dressed, masked, middle-European who introduces himself as 'Count von Kramm'. Holmes effortlessly penetrates the incognito. It is, of course, 'Wilhelm Gottsreich Sigismond von Ormstein, Grand Duke of Cassel-Felstein, and hereditary King of Bohemia'.

The King, it seems, is to be married. But, 'Some five years ago, during a lengthy visit to Warsaw, I made the acquaintance of the well-known adventuress Irene Adler'. Holmes looks her up in his files:

'Hum! Born in New Jersey in the year 1858. Contralto hum! La Scala, hum! Prima donna Imperial Opera of Warsaw—Yes! Retired from operatic stage—ha! Living in London—quite so!' (p. 12)

The King is 'entangled'. There was no secret marriage and no legal papers or certificates. There are some letters, whose importance Holmes airily dismisses ('Forgery') even though they are on the King's private notepaper ('Stolen'). The King can easily lie his way out of these embarrassments.

What Holmes does not dismiss is a photograph. 'We were both in it,' the King confesses. 'Oh, dear! That is very bad! Your Majesty has indeed committed an indiscretion' (p. 13), the detective agrees. Adler will not sell the incriminating photograph. Five attempts have been made to steal it by thieves in the King's pay. According to the King, it is her intention to 'ruin' him by sending the photograph to his intended, the Scandinavian Princess Clotilde, on the day on which their betrothal is publicly announced. 'She [Clotilde] is . . . the very soul of delicacy. A shadow of a doubt as to my conduct would bring the matter to an end' (p. 14).

The game is afoot. Holmes requires only two more pieces of information:

'And mademoiselle's address?' he asked.

'Is Briony Lodge, Serpentine Avenue, St John's Wood.'

Holmes took a note of it. 'One other question,' said he. 'Was the photograph a cabinet?'

'It was.'

'Then, good-night, your Majesty, and I trust that we shall soon have some good news for you.' (p. 15)

By judicious espionage (in tramp's attire) Holmes discovers that Miss Adler has a regular visitor to her villa, a young lawyer called Godfrey Norton. He subsequently discovers the whereabouts of the photograph by a cunning

ruse. Disguised as an elderly clergyman, he has himself
attacked in Serpentine Avenue by hired accomplices. He is
brought into the sitting-room of Briony Lodge by the compassionate and unwitting Miss Adler. Watson, meanwhile,
has been charged to throw a smoke-bomb through the
window. Thinking the house on fire, Irene Adler rushes to
the secret hiding-place of the photograph. It is revealed to
be 'in a recess behind a sliding panel just above the bell-
pull' (p. 25), in the sitting-room.

The next day the King, Holmes, and Watson go to Briony
Lodge. But Adler is gone. In the secret compartment is an
innocuous publicity photograph of herself and a letter to
Mr Sherlock Holmes. She has penetrated his disguise and
his ruse. She has married young Mr Norton and
decamped:

As to the photograph, your client may rest in peace. I love and am
loved by a better man than he. The King may do what he will
without hindrance from one whom he has cruelly wronged. I keep
it only to safeguard myself, and to preserve a weapon which will
always secure me from any steps which he might care to take in
the future. (p. 28)

All the payment Holmes requires from the King is the
photograph which Adler has left of herself. And, as
Watson notes, 'when he speaks of Irene Adler, or when he
refers to her photograph, it is always under the honourable
title of *the* woman' (p. 29).

There are obviously some missing pieces in the puzzle.
How long has the 'entanglement' been going on? It seems
that since her prima donna role in Warsaw, five years ago,
Adler has not worked in opera. Who has paid for her villa
in fashionable St John's Wood? Not the impecunious lawyer Mr Norton, surely. What is the 'cruel wrong' that the
King has done her? Why does he tell Holmes that she
intends to 'ruin' him, when it is clear from her letter that
she has no such intention?

We must assume that the King has not told the whole truth. It is he, of course, who has been keeping her in the St John's Wood villa (the traditional hiding-place for expensive mistresses, as the Oxford World's Classics notes point out). An arranged marriage has been made for him. She has clandestinely fallen in love with another. Clearly she has demanded a vast sum, by way of severance payment. It is to forestall further exactions that the King wants his photograph back. But, evidently, she has had enough from him to start a new life, under a new name, in a new place (this, surely, is the import of Watson's reference to her in the first paragraph as 'the late Irene Adler'). If he gets the picture back, Adler clearly fears, the King will have her and her lover assassinated. 'Cruel wrong' suggests that some such attempt may already have been made.

As Holmes will surely have realized, when love goes sour parties rarely tell the full truth. All's fair. But most enigmatic is—what exactly does the photograph show? We never know what 'scandalous' image has been captured on that 'cabinet' picture. Doyle had, shortly before writing his story, met Oscar Wilde and his (Doyle's) publisher had, a few months earlier, published *The Picture of Dorian Gray*—the story of another mysterious and scandalous portrait.

Why does Holmes ask if the photograph is a 'cabinet'? As the notes to the Oxford World's Classics edition explain, 'cabinets' took over in 1866 from the *carte de visite* photographs, which had themselves become a craze around 1860. '*Carte*' pictures of celebrities were collected by the general public. As Brian Coe puts it in his book, *The Birth of Photography*:

Photographers vied with one another to photograph the famous and infamous, supplying from stock pictures of royalty, artists, churchmen, writers, actors and actresses, politicians and even well-known courtesans. Some photographs ran into editions of thousands, especially pictures of the English Royal Family.[1]

The cabinet was 'similar in presentation and appearance to the *carte* but much bigger, about four inches by five and a half. The cabinet photograph was a more suitable size for quality portraiture, a dozen cabinets usually cost almost two guineas' (p. 36).

One's first suspicion is that Holmes's question ('Was the photograph a cabinet?') was astute and that the King's answer ('It was') was disingenuous. A cabinet photograph produced by a commercial studio (as they all were) would not be a single object to be hidden behind a sliding panel. Cabinets were produced in bulk and circulated in the public domain. The King would not have to burgle the villa in St John's Wood, but also the shop in Oxford Street, and any number of other houses which had come by the cabinet.

What kind of picture was it, then? At the period in which 'A Scandal in Bohemia' is set (1888) there was a craze for what were called 'detective cameras'. To quote Coe again:

From the early 1880s so-called 'detective' cameras were disguised as or hidden in parcels, opera glasses, bags, hats, walking-stick handles and many other forms. Some, like the popular Stirn 'Secret' or waistcoat camera, were worn concealed under clothing.[2]

The blackmailing potential of photographs had been evident from the earliest days of the technology. In 1869, for example, a secret camera was set up on Derby Day, to take photographs of gentlemen visiting the races with ladies other than their wives. But detective photographs brought a whole new range of possibilities. What seems likely is that the photograph in question was not, as the King claims, an innocuous 'cabinet'—something that would exist in numerous copies, either actual or *inpotentia* (the studio photographer would have stored the original plate on his premises). What would such a picture show? A posed couple. Studio protocol would forbid any intimate closeness between the sitters. Not even Princess Clotilde could take exception.

The photograph which has caused the King so much alarm (alarm sufficient for Irene Adler to anticipate assassination) was, in all probability, a much more dangerous snap taken with a Stirn, or some such detective camera. We do not know what it showed—but something more exciting than two frozenly rigid, ceremonially dressed adults alongside an aspidistra. Given the fact that detective cameras performed badly in interiors, possibly a snap of the King furtively entering the villa. The cabinet–detective distinction would explain the implicit joke in the photograph which Adler leaves to be found in the recess behind the bell-pull. It shows her 'in evening dress' and is, evidently, a genuine 'cabinet', in a cabinet, no less.

The Oxford World's Classics *The Adventures of Sherlock Holmes* is edited by Richard Lancelyn Green.

Why isn't everyone a vampire?

Readers of a perverse turn of mind will have wondered at the epidemiology of vampirism as it is described in Stoker's *Dracula*, and as it is displayed in the numerous film adaptations. The crucially puzzling passage is found in one of Van Helsing's incidental lectures to his friends the Harkers and Lucy Westenra's fiancé, Arthur. They are steeling themselves for the stake-through-the-heart operation which will 'save' (by truly 'killing') Lucy—Dracula's first English victim, as we understand (what, one wonders, happened to the crew of the *Demeter*, the vessel which brought the count to England?). To uninformed observers, Lucy has been dead and buried a week. But she has risen from her grave to suck the blood of children playing at dusk (it is late September, the days are short) on Hampstead Heath. Her little victims know her as the 'Bloofer Lady'. Van Helsing knows her as one of the grisly army of the Un-Dead.

They have earlier confronted the 'thing that was Lucy' on her nightly ramble round the heath. When she tries to kiss her husband ('Come to me, Arthur', p. 211), the doctor violently intervenes, physically preventing any embrace. After the thing has retired to its tomb, Van Helsing enlightens his friends as to the nature of their fearful antagonist, in his rapid but flawed English:

Before we do anything, let me tell you this; it is out of the lore and experience of the ancients and of all those who have studied the powers of the Un-Dead. When they become such, there comes with the change the curse of immortality; they cannot die, but must go on age after age adding new victims and multiplying the evils of the world; *for all that die from the preying of the Un-Dead become themselves Un-Dead, and prey on their kind. And so the circle goes on ever widening, like as the ripples from a stone thrown in the water.* Friend Arthur, if you had met that kiss which you know of before poor Lucy die; or again, last night when you open your arms to her, you would in time, when you had died, have become *nosferatu*, as they call it in Eastern Europe, and would all time make more of those Un-Deads that so have filled us with horror. (p. 214; my emphasis)

The doctor goes on to explain that so will the little children who have been bitten by Lucy become *nosferatu* when they die. None the less, if they can contrive to render the Un-Dead Lucy truly dead *before* the children die, 'the tiny wounds of the throats disappear, and they go back to their plays unknowing ever of what has been'.

The problem lies in Van Helsing's use of the term 'multiplying'. One need only be moderately numerate to realize that increase will very soon vampirize the whole population of the world—probably around the 1 billion mark at this period of history. Vlad Dracula, king of fifteenth-century Wallachia, evidently became the first of the Un-Dead in the fifteenth century (his transformation is vividly evoked in the prelude to the Francis Ford Coppola film; it occurs when he returns from battle to discover that his wife has committed suicide). It takes only a week for Lucy to stir from her grave and start vampirizing the children of Hampstead.

Let us assume that each vampire infects one victim a year, and that this victim dies during the course of the year to become, in turn, a vampire. Since they are immortal, each vampire will form the centre of an annually expanding circle, each of which will become the centre of his or her own circle. The circle will widen at the rate of 2^{n-1}. In year one (say, 1500) there is one new vampire;

in 1501, two; in 1502, 4; in 1503, 8; and so, by the simple process of exponential increase, there will be 1,024 *new* vampires in 1510. And, since they never die, the numbers are swollen cumulatively. Within thirty-one years the vampire population will have reached 2 billion. By 1897, the presumable date of Stoker's novel, the numbers are incalculably vast. In fact, so vast that they will probably have collapsed to nil. Long since everyone will have been vampirized; there will be no more food-supply (no more 'live' people with human blood, that is, for the 'Un-Dead' to suck). Dracula and his kind will die out. And with them, the human race.

In the films, such uncomfortable calculations and consequences are brushed away in a gothic surge of horror. Forget the numbers, ignore the algebraic projections, look at the fangs. There have, however, been a number of science fiction narratives which have played with the Van Helsing paradox—notably Richard Matheson's witty *I am Legend* (filmed, disastrously, as *The Omega Man*, with Charlton Heston, in 1971). In Matheson's novel the whole human race has become vampires except for the hero— who lives in a state of Crusoe-like isolation and siege. The day is his, the night is theirs. The twist is that vampires (now the 'moral majority') have become normal and he is the 'leper' or the 'unclean one'—a judgement which eventually he himself comes to accept.

Stoker, dimly worried that the mathematics of vampirism invalidate his story, falls back on a number of makeshift get-outs. At a late point in the narrative Van Helsing implies that strictly imposed immigration laws will do the trick, and keep the vampire horde out of England (historically the late 1890s were the period in which such legislation was actually being introduced, culminating in the Alien Control Bill of 1905). Transylvania, Van Helsing explains, is a 'barren land—barren of peoples'. This shortage of Transylvanians has, effectively, kept the population of vampires down. Britain, however, is 'a new land where life of man teems till they are like the multitude of standing corn.' Having used up the meagre demographic resources of his own 'barren' country Count Dracula, an illegal and undesirable immigrant if there ever was one, intends to ravage Albion's pure and teeming human stock.

This explanation for the venerable, 400-year-old vampire population of Transylvania being so numerically insignificant is, however, contradicted by Van Helsing's earlier rhapsodies on the subject:

For, let me tell you, he is known everywhere that men have been. In old Greece, in old Rome; he flourish in Germany all over, in France, in India, even in the Chersonese [Thrace]; and in China, so far from us in all ways, there even is he, and the peoples fear him at this day. He have follow the wake of the berserker Icelander, the devil-begotten Hun, the Slav, the Saxon, the Magyar. (p. 239)

Vampires, we are to believe, have been everywhere at all periods of recorded history (although Van Helsing's 'follow' gives him a possible let-out). They are not, that is, restricted to a barren tract of Transylvania.

How has England managed to stay inviolate to this point in history? More so if vampires have 'followed the wake' of the invading Saxon? And how has the explosion in numbers across national boundaries been contained at the English Channel? Bram Stoker has one last desperate try at the problem. It is clear, in the last stages of the action, that Mina is a very special kind of victim. As a mark (literally) of her singularity, she has taken part in a gruesome blood-exchange ceremony with the count. It is a scene with disturbing sexual undertones. Having sucked blood from her neck, as she recalls:

he pulled open his shirt, and with his long sharp nails opened a vein in his breast. When the blood began to spurt out, he took my hands in one of his, holding them tight, and with the other seized my neck and pressed my mouth to the wound, so that I must either suffocate or swallow some of the—Oh, my God! my God! what have I done? (p. 288)

It is a good question. It seems that, by taking back the blood which he earlier took from her, she has become one of a privileged caste of living victims—one who seems to have some of the powers of the Un-Dead while still alive. Mina manifestly has superhuman powers—a radar-like apprehension of where Dracula is, for example. She is 'unclean'—the Christian cross burns her skin like acid. Her teeth have become sharper, and she looks—from some angles—vampiric.

There is, one deduces, an inner élite of 'super vampires' who circulate Dracula's sacramental blood among themselves—true communicants in the horrible sect, and Mina is now one of them. It is only this small coterie which is immortal, we may speculate.[1] The bulk of their victims are disposable nourishment—a kind of human blood-bank to be discarded when exhausted. Unfortunately, Stoker does not give us any clear warrant for this speculation, nor does he (as far as I can see) work it plausibly into his narrative.

The Dracula paradox touches on what was, for the nineteenth century, a strange mystery about actual epidemics. How and why did they burn out? Cholera, for instance, smallpox, and venereal disease infected large tracts of the population, often very quickly. Why did their infectious spread ever stop? Why did not, over the course of time, one catch these diseases? And, if they were fatal, die from them? Why did not every epidemic become, literally (as no disease ever truly has been) a pandemic? The nineteenth century developed a number of causative theories for the finite nature of epidemic disease. For the faithful, the hand of God (as with Job's plague of boils) was the remote reason for the starting, cresting, and stopping of disease. There were predisposing causes (heredity—which could predispose to resistance or infection), and immediate causes (polluted water supplies). Darwinists believed that disease was a mechanism for separating the weak from the strong, building up 'resistance'.

Epidemiologists also drew on the same image as Van Helsing—that of the widening ripples from a pebble thrown in a pond. With the dispersion of energy, as the ripple enlarges it becomes weaker. So, it was believed, did the virus (literally 'poison') lose its virulence.[2] And through exposure, the host population might become stronger, develop strategies of resistance.

But Stoker—through the inextinguishably gabby Van Helsing—specifically contradicts this 'widening ripple' thesis where vampirism is concerned: 'The *nosferatu* do not die like the bee when he sting once. He is only stronger, have yet more power to work evil' (p. 237). With vampires, the wider their circles spread the stronger, rather than weaker, they grow. Unlike King Cholera, the more victims he kills, the more irresistible Dracula becomes.

There seems to be only one way out of this narrative cul-de-sac—although Bram Stoker does not, as far as I know, turn to it. As the ur-vampire—the source of all subsequent infection—when Dracula is beheaded all the 'grim and grisly ranks of the Un-Dead' should die with him, as the whole body dies when the head is destroyed. This is the implied 'happy ending' when Jonathan Harker and Mina make their journey to Dracula's old lair, seven years later:

In the summer of this year we made a journey to Transylvania, and went over the old ground which was, and is, to us so full of vivid and terrible memories. It was almost impossible to believe that the things which we had seen with our own eyes and heard with our own ears were living truths. Every trace of all that had been was blotted out. (p. 378)

Every trace? We know that Van Helsing has disposed of those lady vampires who slavered, seven years earlier, over Jonathan's neck. But what has happened to Dracula's legion other victims over the last 400 years? Are they not roaming around Transylvania? Perhaps Stoker shrewdly foresaw that he would need to leave open the door for an infinite number of sequels. You can kill them, but the Un-Dead will never die.

The Oxford World's Classics *Dracula* is edited by Maud Ellmann.

Notes

Is Heathcliff a Murderer?

Mansfield Park

1. Edward Said, *Culture and Imperialism* (London, 1993).

2. Kotzebue's play, 'The Natural Son' was first produced in England, translated as *Lovers' Vows*, 1798–1800. Mrs Inchbald's translation (which is presumably what is used by the amateur troupe at Mansfield Park) is printed as a supplement to R. W. Chapman's edition of the novel, in *The Novels of Jane Austen*, 5 vols. (Oxford, 1934). *Mansfield Park* is volume 3 in the set.

3. According to Chapman, the composition of *Mansfield Park* was begun 'about February 1811' and finished 'soon after June 1813'.

4. The World's Classics edition of Thomas Hughes's *Tom Brown's Schooldays* is edited by Andrew Sanders.

5. In an appendix on the chronology of the novel, Chapman deduces (from internal evidence) that Austen used almanacs of 1808–9 in order to arrange day-to-day, month-to-month events and episodes in the novel. But she did not necessarily identify the *historical* period as that year. Chapman sees the question of historical dating as ultimately unfixable: 'As to the "dramatic" date of the story, the indications are slight. It is probably hopeless to seek to identify the "strange business" in America. Many strange things happened in those years. The *Quarterly Review* was first published in 1809 (and therefore could not have been read at Sotherton in 1808). Crabbe's *Tales* (1812) are mentioned. A state of war is implied throughout, and there is no mention of foreign travel, except Sir Thomas's perilous voyage' (p. 556).

6. See chapter 13 of Lockhart's *Memoirs of the Life of Sir Walter Scott, Bart.* (London, 1836, much reprinted) describing Scott's removal to the small farm of Ashestiel, and the advantageous economic arrangement it represented.

7. *Mansfield Park*, Stephen Fender and J. A. Sutherland, Audio Learning Tapes (London, 1974).

8. For the role of evangelicalism in *Mansfield Park* see Marilyn Butler, *Jane Austen and the War of Ideas* (Oxford, 1975), 219–49;

and the same writer's essay 'History, Politics, and Religion' in (ed.) J. David Grey, *The Jane Austen Handbook* (London, 1986). Professor Butler convincingly argues that the evangelicals of the early nineteenth century are not to be confused with the lower-class evangelicals of the Victorian period; 'During the war against France and against "revolutionary principles", pressure for a renewed commitment to religious and moral principle was not so much petit bourgeois as characteristic of the gentry' (p. 204).

9. The whole business of 'Slavery and the Chronology of *Mansfield Park*' was revived in a lively article by Brian Southam in the *TLS* ('The Silence of the Bertrams'), 17 Feb. 1995. The key assumption in Southam's argument is that the 1812 publication of Crabbe's *Tales* and the information that Sir Bertram returns in October enables us to 'pinpoint the course of events'. The chronology Southam deduces is as follows: 'Sir Thomas and Tom leave for Antigua about October 1810; Tom returns about September 1811; Sir Thomas writes home, April 1812; Fanny in possession of Crabbe's *Tales*, published September 1812; Sir Thomas returns, late October 1812; Edmund turns to Fanny, summer 1813' (p. 13). Southam correlates this schedule of events with the evolution of the slave trade, following the Abolition Act of 1807. Convincing as Southam's argument is, I remain somewhat sceptical that Jane Austen would expect her readers to register September 1812 as the publication date of Crabbe's *Tales* (much of his poetry has an earlier publication date), and the detail may have been as loosely installed in her mind as in those of the bulk of her readers, who would simply recall the volume as a 'recent' publication. It may also be, as I argue above, that '*Tales*' should be read as the less precisely dateable 'tales'.

Waverley

1. *The Letters of Sir Walter Scott*, ed. Sir Herbert Grierson (London, 1932–7), iii. 478–9.

2. John Hill Burton, *The History of Scotland from the Revolution to the Extinction of the Last Jacobite Insurrection, 1698–1748*, 2 vols. (London, 1853), ii. 463.

3. See chapter 7 of Lockhart's *Life of Scott*.

Emma

1. These essays of Scott's are conveniently collected in Ioan Williams (ed.), *Sir Walter Scott on Novelists and Fiction* (London, 1968).

2. See Edgar Johnson, *Sir Walter Scott: The Great Unknown*, 2 vols. (London, 1970), ii. 1084.

3. See the World's Classics edition of *King Solomon's Mines*, edited by Dennis Butts, p. 332.

4. See the World's Classics edition of *The Swiss Family Robinson*, edited by John Seelye, pp. 25, 332.

5. R. W. Chapman (ed.), *Emma* (London, 1933), 493.

6. Presenting to the mind's eye a montage of the year's passing season was a favourite device of William Cowper, a poet Austen is known to have read. See for instance vi. 140–60 of *The Task*, 'But let the months go round, a few short months . . .'

Frankenstein

1. One text reprinted in World's Classics (eds. James Kinsley and M. K. Joseph) is the revised, 1831 'third edition'. The other from which I have taken quotations, is 'the 1818 text', edited by Marilyn Butler. Substantive changes between the 1818 and revised 1831 texts are noted in Appendix B of Professor Butler's edition.

2. T. J. Hogg, *The Life of Percy Bysshe Shelley* (London, 1858), i. 70–1.

3. Maurice Hindle (ed.), *Frankenstein* (Harmondsworth, 1988), p. xxi.

4. See Steven E. Forry, *Hideous Progeny: Dramatizations of Frankenstein, from Mary Shelley to the Present* (Philadelphia, 1990), p. ix. Forry detects three phases in the successive dramatizations of the story: (1) 1823–32 (which saw fifteen versions) were years of 'transformation and proliferation' during which 'the myth was mutated for popular consumption'; (2) 1832–1900 were 'years of diffusion', in which the myth was spread into the general Anglo-American consciousness; (3) 1900–30 were 'years of transition', as the stage-generated versions of *Frankenstein* were gradually displaced by imagery derived from the cinema. For the changing cultural fortunes of Victor Frankenstein and his monster (frequently the two were confused) in the hundred years following 1818, see Chris Baldick, *In Frankenstein's Shadow* (Oxford, 1987).

5. Edison's *Frankenstein* was presumed lost, but a print was recovered in the 1980s. See Forry, *Hideous Progeny*, 80.

6. Ibid. 85.

7. *Mary Shelley's Frankenstein*, Leonore Felisher, based on a screenplay by Steph Lady and Frank Darabont, from the novel by Mary Shelley, with an afterword by Kenneth Branagh (New York, 1994), 307.

8. Lightning had only recently been identified as an electrical phenomenon by Benjamin Franklin. See the experiment described on p. 24 of *Frankenstein* and the note to it on p. 255.

9. The role of Fritz goes back to the most successful of the early stage adaptations, *Presumption, or the Fate of Frankenstein* (1823), by Richard Brinsley Peake. The play is usefully reprinted in the Everyman edition of *Frankenstein*, ed. Paddy Lyons (London, 1994).

10. The significance of the changes which Mary Shelley made between the 1818 and 1831 texts is examined by Marilyn Butler in 'The First *Frankenstein* and Radical Science', *TLS* (9 Apr. 1993), 12–14. Professor Butler explains the relevance of the first edition to the 'celebrated publicly staged debate of 1814–19 between two professors at London's College of Surgeons [John Abernethy and William Lawrence] on the origins and nature of life, now known as the vitalist debate' (p. 12). Mary Shelley toned down her opinions in the 1831 revised text of *Frankenstein*. See also the appendices and introduction to Professor Butler's World's Classics edition of the novel.

11. Ellen Moers, 'Female Gothic', in *New York Review of Books* (21 Mar. 1974), reprinted in G. Levine and U. Knoepflmacher (eds.), *The Endurance of Frankenstein* (Berkeley: California, 1979), 77–87.

12. For a survey of recent feminist argument and discussion on the novel see Catherine Gallagher and Elizabeth Young, 'Feminism and *Frankenstein*: A Short History of American Feminist Criticism', *The Journal of Contemporary Thought*, 1 (Jan. 1991), 97–109. An influential reading along this line is found in Anne K. Mellor, *Mary Shelley: Her Life, her Fiction, her Monsters* (Berkeley: California, 1988). According to Mellor: 'From a feminist viewpoint, *Frankenstein* is a book about what happens when a man tries to have a baby without a woman'. See also Sandra M. Gilbert's and Susan Gubar's *The Madwoman in the Attic* (New

York, 1979) which reads *Frankenstein* as an Eve-myth. A good selection and discussion of feminist readings of the novel is given in the endmatter of Lyons's Everyman edition.

Oliver Twist

1. Jonathan Grossman, in a forthcoming article in *Dickens Studies Annual*, points out that this is the first time Oliver refers to Fagin as 'The Jew'—a fact of which he seems previously to have been unaware.

2. Bayley's essay, 'Things as they are', is to be found in John Gross and Gabriel Pearson (eds.), *Dickens and the Twentieth Century* (London, 1962), 49–64.

3. J. Hillis Miller, *Dickens: The World of his Novels* (Cambridge: Mass., 1958).

4. Colin Williamson, 'Two Missing Links in *Oliver Twist*', Nineteenth-Century Fiction, 22 (Dec. 1967), 225–34.

5. See Alison Winter; 'Mesmerism and Popular Culture in early Victorian England', *History of Science*, 32 (1994), 317–43. Kaplan discusses the O'Key connection at length in *Dickens and Mesmerism*, 34–44.

6. Kathleen Tillotson (ed.), *Oliver Twist* (Oxford, 1966), 392. Thackeray, who illustrated his own serial novels, frequently ran into difficulties supplying designs sufficiently ahead of time for the engraver. See the 'Commentary on Illustrations' by Nicholas Pickwoad, in *Vanity Fair*, ed. P. L. Shillingsburg (London and New York, 1989), 643–4. Shillingsburg gives further examples in his companion edition of *Pendennis* (London and New York, 1990), 'Writing and Publishing *Pendennis*', 375–98.

7. That Dickens altered his plan of *Oliver Twist* as he went along is convincingly argued by Burton M. Wheeler, 'The Text and Plan of *Oliver Twist*', Dickens Studies Annual, 12 (1983), 41–61. Wheeler notes particularly that 'the conspiracy between Monks and Fagin does not bear close scrutiny' (p. 56) and that this section of the novel bears witness of being improvised from one instalment to the next.

8. See *The Letters of Charles Dickens, vol. 1, 1820–39*, ed. Madeline House and Graham Storey (Oxford, 1965), 403, 461.

Martin Chuzzlewit

1. George Eliot's schedule for these events is to be found, with some alterations and later changes of mind, in her 'Quarry for *Middlemarch*', A. T. Kitchel (ed.) (Los Angeles, 1950), 45–6. As Kitchel's transcription shows it was, for instance, Eliot's original intention to have Dorothea marry as early as 1827.

2. I examine this topic in 'The Handling of Time in *Vanity Fair*', Anglia, 89 (1971), 349–56.

3. See P. D. Edwards, 'Trollope's Chronology in *The Way We Live Now*', Notes and Queries, 214 (1969), 214–16.

4. See Bert Hornback, 'Anthony Trollope and the Calendar of 1872: The Chronology of *The Way We Live Now*', Notes and Queries, 208 (1963), 454–8. Peter Edwards's article in *N&Q*, cited above, specifically refutes Hornback's thesis.

5. Dickens is also vague about historical dating. In *Martin Chuzzlewit* (London, 1985, Unwin Critical Library), 35, Sylvère Monod notes the contradiction of the world of coaching around Salisbury and the steam-driven vessels on which Martin and Mark travel to and in America.

6. Monod makes the point that errors and awkwardness in the narrative construction of *Martin Chuzzlewit* are at least partly to be attributed to the novelist's artistic inexperience (see p. 141). Monod cites as examples of loose threads in the story such things as Pecksniff's loss of all his fortune before Tigg has any reasonable chance of acquiring it (p. 81).

Wuthering Heights

1. Heathcliff's complicated legal manœuvre is explained in Appendix VI, 'Land Law and Inheritance', by E. F. J. Tucker, in *Wuthering Heights*, ed. Hilda Marsden and Ian Jack (Oxford, 1976), 497–9. Tucker assumes there may have been same 'dishonesty' and collusion between Heathcliff and Mr Green, the Gimmerton attorney, in alienating Hindley so entirely from his inheritance. As Tucker points out, Green evidently 'misinforms' Edgar Linton as to the state of the law, so as to favour Heathcliff's claims. Bribery is implied.

Jane Eyre

1. See Michael Mason's note to this episode in his Penguin Classics edition of *Jane Eyre* (1995). Mason quotes George Troup, reviewing the novel in *Tait's Edinburgh Review* (May 1848): 'the voice has not got a telegraphic communication direct to the ear at fifty miles distance, although intelligence by the magnetic wire may travel hundreds and thousands "in no time".'

2. On her visit to London in June 1850 Thackeray made a point of introducing Charlotte Brontë to Catherine Crowe, 'the reciter of ghost stories'. It would be interesting to know how the two ladies got on. See Clement Shorter (ed.), *The Brontës' Life and Letters*, 2 vols. (London, 1908), ii. 94, 147.

3. Winter is drawing on a report by John Elliotson in his journal of mesmeric science, *Zoist*, 2 (1844–5), 477–529, 'Reports of Various Trials of the Clairvoyance of Alexis Didier Last Summer in London'.

4. The connection was via Charlotte's father, Patrick. See Juliet Barker, *The Brontës* (London, 1994), 401, 511.

5. See the *Athenaeum* (30 Nov., 14 Dec., 21 Dec., 1844), 1093–4; 1117–18; 1173–4.

Vanity Fair

1. Keith Hollingsworth in *The Newgate Novel* (Detroit, 1963), 212–15, argues that *Vanity Fair* is, in its last pages, emulating the Newgate Novel. Hollingsworth accepts that 'Rebecca murders Joseph Sedley' and that she does it by poison, presumably arsenic, the poison of choice for murderesses in the 1840s (p. 212).

Henry Esmond

1. Gordon S. Haight (ed.), *The George Eliot Letters*, 9 vols. (London, 1954–78), ii. 67.

2. See, for instance, S. J. Kunitz and Howard Haycraft, *British Authors before 1800* (New York, 1952), 391–2: 'Coleridge, Charles Lamb and Leigh Hunt all admired *Peter Wilkins*, and Southey wrote that the winged people of the book "are the most beautiful creatures of imagination that were ever devised." Paltock's book (dedicated to Elizabeth, Countess Northumberland, presumed to be the prototype of his heroine) ran through four editions before

1800 and at least sixteen later. A musical pantomime based on the book was produced in 1800 and a play in 1827.'

3. Thackeray began his reading for the 'English Humourists' in December 1850. The first series of lectures were delivered in London, 22 May–3 July 1851. Composition of *Henry Esmond* began in August 1851. He delivered lectures around the UK over the following year. The novel was published in October 1852, on the eve of Thackeray's departure to lecture on the English Humourists in America.

4. See G. N. Ray, *Thackeray: The Uses of Adversity* (New York, 1955), 1–3. Thackeray's actual injunction to his daughters was 'Mind, no biography!'

Bleak House

1. 'Mud-pusher' was a slang term for crossing-sweepers in the Victorian period. See J. Redding Ware, *Passing English of the Victorian Era: A Dictionary of Heterodox English, Slang, and Phrase* (London, 1909), 178.

2. F. S. Schwarzbach, *Dickens and the City* (London, 1979), 124.

3. Norman Gash, *Robert Surtees and Early Victorian Society* (Oxford, 1993), 48–9. On the question of 'little commercial value' that Gash mentions, Susan Shatto, in her *Companion to Bleak House* (London, 1988) cites from Mayhew the fact that 'great quantities of mud were collected daily and carted off to manure barges, the owners of which sold each load for £5 to £6' (p. 23). Mayhew estimated that four-fifths of the gathered-up street dirt was horse droppings and cattle dung, and around 100 tons of the substance was deposited on the London streets every working day.

4. H. Mayhew, *London Labour and the London Poor* (London, 1851, repr. and enlarged, 1861), ii. 465. The long section on crossing-sweepers extends to ii. 507.

5. Harvey P. Sucksmith disputes Gill's assertion in 'The Dust Heaps in *Our Mutual Friend*', Essays in Criticism, 23 (1973), 206–12.

6. See the World's Classics edition of *Middlemarch*, ed. David Carroll, 72, 74.

Villette

1. See, for instance, Terry Eagleton, *Myths of Power: A Marxist Study of the Brontës* (London, 1975), 92; Janet Gezari, *Charlotte*

Brontë and Defensive Conduct: The Author and the Body at Risk (Philadelphia, 1992), 167–70.

2. Kate Millett notes that had Paul returned to claim his bride, 'we should never have heard from her'—Madame Emanuel, in other words, could not have written *Villette.* Brenda Silver astutely notes: 'Lucy's life does not end with Paul's; the observant reader will have noted that the school clearly continues to prosper and that Lucy, by the time she begins her narrative, knows the West End of London as well as her beloved City . . . She has survived the destruction of the romantic fantasy and grown into another reality.' Millett's and Silver's essays are printed in *Critical Essays on Charlotte Brontë*, ed. Barbara Timm Gates (Boston, 1990); see particularly 263, 303.

3. Carol Hanbury Mackay (ed.), *The Two Thackerays: Anne Thackeray Ritchie's Centenary Biographical Introductions to the Works of William Makepeace Thackeray*, 2 vols. (New York, 1988), i. 385.

4. Guinevere Griest, *Mudie's Circulating Library and the Victorian Novel* (Bloomington: Indiana, 1970), i. 21.

Adam Bede

1. *Victorian Studies* (Sept. 1970), 83–9.

2. Sedgwick's essay, which was originally a paper delivered at the MLA annual convention, is printed in *Critical Inquiry*, 17: 4 (Summer 1991), 818–37.

3. Although modern readers frequently complain that Hetty's pregnancy is invisible, Victorians felt that it was obtruded—by precise dating references—too forcibly on the reader. See, for instance, the *Saturday Review* (26 Feb. 1859): 'The author of *Adam Bede* has given in his adhesion to a very curious practice that we consider most objectionable. It is that of dating and discussing the several stages that precede the birth of a child. We seem to be threatened with a literature of pregnancy'. The review is reprinted in *George Eliot: The Critical Heritage*, (ed.), David Carroll, (London, 1971), 73–6.

4. See the chapter 'Effie's phantom pregnancy', above.

The Woman in White

1. Kenneth Robinson, *Wilkie Collins: A Biography* (London, 1951), 149.

2. Nuel P. Davis, *The Life of Wilkie Collins* (Urbana: Illinois, 1956), 216.

3. The review is reprinted in Norman Page (ed.), *Wilkie Collins: The Critical Heritage* (London, 1974), 102–3.

4. Ibid. 124.

5. Ibid. 95.

6. This anomaly in the novel's chronology is noted by W. M. Kendrick, 'The Sensationalism of *The Woman in White*', Nineteenth-Century Fiction, 32: 1 (June 1977), 18–35 (see particularly 23) and by Andrew Gasson '*The Woman in White*: A Chronological Study', *Wilkie Collins Society Journal*, 2 (1982), 12–13.

7. J. G. Millais, *The Life and Letters of John Everett Millais* (London, 1899), 278–9.

Pendennis, A Dark Night's Work, Rachel Ray

1. The text was published in the first serial instalment of the novel, April 1836. The footnote was added for the 'Cheap' 1847 reissue of the novelist's works. See the World's Classics *Pickwick Papers*, 726–7.

2. See *Rob Roy*, chap. 21. For other chronological anomalies see the Everyman edition of *Rob Roy*, ed. J. A. Sutherland (London, 1995).

3. For instance: (1) Pen's visit to Vauxhall in Number 15, where Simpson—who retired in the mid-1830s—still presides; (2) the rage for 'silver fork' novels, which Thackeray pointedly recalls as a foible of 'that time' (p. 525); (3) London excitement at the performance of Taglioni in *The Sylphide* in the early 1830s (p. 478); (4) the huge box-office success of Bulwer's play, *The Lady of Lyons*, in 1838.

4. See J. A. Sutherland, 'Dickens, Reade, and *Hard Cash*', Dickensian, 405, 81, 1 (Spring 1985), 9–10.

5. For a closely examined survey of the composition of *A Dark Night's Work* see J. G. Sharps, *Mrs Gaskell's Observation and Invention* (Arundel, 1970), 353–4.

6. For further minor dating errors in the narrative see ibid. 360. Sharps concludes with something of an understatement, 'Mrs Gaskell's chronology was not especially accurate'.

7. In Ellinor's Italian trip, Mrs Gaskell is recalling her own trip to Rome, Feb.–May 1857. As with her heroine, she was recalled to

England in distressing circumstances. Having made an unhurried return to Paris on 26 May, Mrs Gaskell was met with the news that publication of *The Life of Charlotte Brontë* had been suspended, on grounds of libel. She rushed back to London, in a state of extreme anxiety—all of which is mirrored in the account of Ellinor's return to save Dixon's life. See Winifred Gérin, *Elizabeth Gaskell* (Oxford, 1976), 187–8.

8. The first edition of the World's Classics *Rachel Ray* (1988) had as its cover illustration one of Millais's unused illustrations for the novel, showing Rachel dressed in an extravagant crinoline of 1860s vintage.

Phineas Finn

1. See *TLS* (1944), 156, 192, 372.

2. See Simon Raven, 'The Writing of "The Pallisers"', *The Listener*, 91 (1974), 66–8.

3. Stephen Wall, in *Trollope: Living with Character* (London, 1988), notes that the last-page marriage between Phineas and Mary 'verges on the perfunctory'. It is best read, Wall suggests, as 'an action of Phineas's Irish self' (p. 149).

Middlemarch

1. It is feasible that Farebrother is simply retailing vulgar Middlemarch gossip here (as the narrative earlier suggests), assuming that all pawnbrokers are Jewish. Since Dunkirk attends the same fundamentalist Christian church as Bulstrode he would have to be an apostate as well as Jewish. If the 'grafting of the Jew pawnbroker' is accepted as true it may be taken to have consequences in the text. Bernard Semmel, in *George Eliot and the Politics of National Inheritance* (New York 1994), 97–8, suggests that Ladislaw's revulsion at Bulstrode's offer to make amends may reflect his horror at discovering his unsuspected Jewish ancestry. Semmel, who accepts that Dunkirk was Jewish (and Ladislaw therefore partly Jewish), further suggests that the characterization of Will may owe something to Eliot's conception of Disraeli, who in 1830 would be about the same age as her hero.

2. *Middlemarch*, ed. R. D. Ashton (Harmondsworth, 1994), p. xxi.

3. R. D. Ashton, *G. H. Lewes* (Oxford, 1990), 10–11.

The Way We Live Now

1. See, for instance, Noel Annan's downright statement in his introduction to the Trollope Society edition of *The Way We Live Now* (London, 1992): 'Melmotte is a Jew and the upper class characters say, as they would in those days in real life, plenty of disagreeable things about Jews' (p. xiv). Bryan Cheyette, in *Constructions of 'The Jew' in English Literature and Society, 1875–1945* (Cambridge, 1993), is more discriminating. Cheyette sees Melmotte as emblematic of a 'fixed racial Jewishness' without being himself clearly Jewish. Cheyette notes a number of learned commentators who have misled themselves as to Melmotte's being Jewish (see p. 39).

The Prime Minister

1. See J. A. Sutherland, *The Longman Companion to Victorian Fiction* (London, 1989), 511.

2. Victorian railways were very dangerous by today's standards. The *Annual Register, 1875* (London, 1876), 236, reports that, in 1874, 1,424 passengers were killed and 5,041 injured.

Is he Popenjoy?

1. See *The Annual Register, 1875* (London, 1876), 13.

2. See his letter of 10 March 1875, *The Letters of Anthony Trollope*, ed. N. John Hall (Berkeley, 1983), ii. 653.

The Portrait of a Lady

1. Dorothea Krook, 'Two Problems in *The Portrait of a Lady*', in *The Ordeal of Consciousness in Henry James* (New York, 1962), 357.

2. The Hutton review is usefully reprinted in Roger Gard (ed.), *Henry James: The Critical Heritage* (London, 1968), 93–6.

3. See *The Portrait of a Lady* (World's Classics edition), 628.

4. A selection from Hutton's reviews of the serial and collected *Middlemarch* is given in David Carroll (ed.), *George Eliot: The Critical Heritage* (London, 1971), 286–313.

5. See Robert Tener and Malcolm Woodfield, *A Victorian Spectator: The Uncollected Writings of R. H. Hutton* (Bristol, 1990), 30.

6. See G. S. Haight, *George Eliot: A Biography* (London, 1968). A more hostile depiction of the social pressures on 'Mr and Mrs

Lewes' is given by Marghanita Laski, *George Eliot and her World* (London, 1973), 98: 'the Leweses, if they had not come to believe they were somehow or other married, at least began to forget they were not. In 1873, Lewes felt able to tell a correspondent that he had lived with his mother till he married his "Dorothea".'

Dr Jekyll and Mr Hyde

1. There have been 'at least 69 films' of Stevenson's novella, of which the 1941 Spencer Tracy version is the most famous, and Rouben Mamoulian's 1932 version (starring Fredric March) is regarded as the finest achievement artistically. See V. W. Wexman's essay, 'Horrors of the Body' in William Veeder and Gordon Hirsch (eds.), *Dr Jekyll and Mr Hyde after One Hundred Years* (Chicago, 1988), 283–307. This volume has many illustrations from book versions of the story over the years and stills from dramatic and film adaptations.

The Master of Ballantrae

1. See Mary Lascelles, *The Story-Teller Retrieves the Past* (Oxford, 1980), 70 and the RLS essay on 'The Genesis of *The Master of Ballantrae*', reprinted in the 'Vailima' edition of *The Works of Robert Louis Stevenson* (London, 1922), xiv. 15–19.

The Picture of Dorian Gray

1. p. vii. See Karl Beckson (ed.), *Oscar Wilde: The Critical Heritage* (London, 1970), 67–86, for a representative selection of reviews of *Dorian Gray*. Beckson summarizes the novel's extraordinarily hostile reception on 7–12.

Tess of the d'Urbervilles

1. See *Thomas Hardy: The Critical Heritage*, ed. R. G. Cox (London, 1970), 217–18.

2. Ibid. 212.

3. Tony Tanner, 'Colour and Movement in *Tess of the d'Urbervilles*', *Critical Quarterly*, 10 (Autumn 1968); repr. in R. P. Draper (ed.), *Hardy: The Tragic Novels* (London, 1975), 182–208. The passage quoted comes on 205.

4. *The 1890s*, ed. G. A. Cevasco (New York, 1993).

5. Ian Gregor, *The Great Web* (London, 1974), 182.

6. *Tess of the d'Urbervilles*, ed. James Gibson (London, 1994), 411.

7. Ibid. 417.

The Speckled Band

1. The story was first published in the *Strand*, Feb. 1892. It is recorded as being the author's own favourite among his works.

2. See *The Annotated Sherlock Holmes*, ed. W. S. Baring-Gould, 2 vols. (New York, 1967), i. 263–6. In a sceptical appendix on 'the deadliest snake in India' the editor concludes that there is no such reptile as an 'Indian swamp adder', and no known snake could kill a human victim in ten seconds, as does Roylott's reptilian assassin. The most satisfactory explanation is that the thing in question is half Gila monster and half Indian cobra. It would be impossible for a snake to clamber up a bell-rope as is claimed in the story, 'for snakes do not climb as many think—by twining themselves around an object; they climb by wedging their bodies into any crannies and interstices, taking advantage of every irregularity or protrusion upon which a loop of the body may be hooked' (i. 265).

3. The point is made in *The Annotated Sherlock Holmes*, i. 249.

4. The Roylott misnaming, which is found in the original *Strand* publication of 'The Speckled Band', has unfortunately been corrected in the World's Classics edition. There is a possibility that the 'error' (if that is what it is) arose from the fact that in the original manuscript of the story, 'Helen Stoner is Helen Roylott, and Dr Roylott is her father' (*The Annotated Sherlock Holmes*, i. 246). I would prefer to see it as a subtlety deliberately introduced by the author. A facsimile of the original Feb. 1892 *Strand* text of 'The Speckled Band' may be found in the Wordsworth Classics edition of *The Adventures of Sherlock Holmes* (London, 1992), 213–29. The 'Miss Roylott' comment is on 219.

Jude the Obscure

1. Kate Millett, *Sexual Politics* (New York, 1969), 130.

Weir of Hermiston

1. 'A Hanging', in *The Collected Essays, Journalism and Letters of George Orwell*, ed. Sonia Orwell and Ian Angus, 4 vols. (London, 1968), i. 45.

The Invisible Man

1. Harris Wilson, *Arnold Bennett and H. G. Wells: A Record* (Urbana: Illinois, 1960), 34–5.

2. This point is made by Jack Williamson, in *H. G. Wells, Critic of Progress* (Baltimore, 1973), 85–6.

Dracula

1. Paul Barber, *Vampire, Burials and Death* (New Haven: Conn., 1988).

2. For a survey of invasion fantasies in the 1890s as reflected in fiction, see I. F. Clarke, *Voices Prophesying War, 1763–1984* (London, 1966).

Kim

1. In Kipling's case, puberty did not bring any great change in his stature. As Kingsley Amis notes: 'Physically, Rudyard Kipling was a small man' and never exceeded five feet six inches in height. See Kingsley Amis, *Rudyard Kipling and his World* (London, 1975), 9.

2. Rudyard Kipling, *Something of Myself* (New York, 1937), 3.

Can Jane Eyre be Happy?

Robinson Crusoe

1. Giving Robinson shoes, boots, or moccasins is a very common error, although specifically contradicted by the 1719 illustration, which follows the text closely. See Fig. 1.

2. Stith Thompson's *Motif Index of Folk Literature* (Copenhagen, 1955), contains many entries on the motif of the devil—and sometimes angels—leaving single footprints in rock or soil.

Fanny Hill

1. When, in the 1940s, it was learned that the Cambridge teacher and critic F. R. Leavis was in the habit of referring to James Joyce's *Ulysses* in his classes, he was visited and warned by the police.

2. *Fanny Hill* was prosecuted and banned by London magistrates in the early 1960s. The ban was never formally lifted, although later

in the decade Cleland's novel drifted back into print. See J. A. Sutherland, *Offensive Literature* (London, 1982), ch. 3.

3. Joss Lutz Marsh, 'Good Mrs Brown's Connections: Sexuality and Story-telling in Dealings with the Firm of Dombey and Son', *English Literary History*, 58: 2 (Summer 1991), 405–26.

4. See the episode with the sailor in vol. ii, in which Mrs Cole specifically warns Fanny against the dangers of disease ('the risk to my health in being so open-legg'd and free of my flesh', p. 142).

5. Peter Fryer, *The Birth Controllers* (London, 1965), chs. 1–2.

Tristram Shandy

1. Barbara Hardy, 'A Mistake in *Tristram Shandy*', *Notes and Queries*, 207 (1962), 261.

2. On the question of fifth-of-a-second measurements, see David S. Landes, *Revolution in Time: Clocks and the Making of the Modern World* (Cambridge, Mass., 1983), p. 130: 'The growing importance of small unities of time led to the invention in the 1740s of center-seconds watches—that is watches whose second hands ran off the center arbor and tracked the circumference of the dial . . . These watches were customarily fitted with a stop lever, which allowed the user to freeze the result, the better to make his count . . . By 1770 the logic of this pursuit of ever finer time measurement led to the appearance of the first center-seconds watches with fractions of seconds marked on the dial; the earliest I have seen show fifths. Who cared about fifths of seconds in those days?' Laurence Sterne evidently did.

3. H. K. Russell, '*Tristram Shandy* and the Techniques of the Novel', *Studies in Philology*, 42 (1945), 589.

Mansfield Park

1. Tony Tanner, *TLS*, 25 June 1995.

2. The full text reads: 'She had not time for such cares. She was a woman who spent her days in sitting nicely dressed on a sofa, doing some long piece of needlework, of little use and no beauty, thinking more of her pug than her children' (pp. 16–17). Conceivably, it could be the needlework which is of 'little use and no beauty', but I prefer to think Austen meant Lady Bertram.

3. I discuss this question, which remains somewhat ambiguous, in *Is Heathcliff a Murderer?* (Oxford, 1996), 5–9.

Emma

1. *The Review of English Studies*, NS 45: 177 (1994), 70–5.

2. The excellent education Jane has received is described on pp. 145–6 of the World's Classics edition.

Oliver Twist, Great Expectations

1. As many commentators note, there is ambiguity about the historical setting of *Oliver Twist*, and some perplexing pockets of anachronism. The Bow Street Runners who come to the Maylie household, for example, would have been abolished and replaced by modern policemen, around the same time that the Bloody Code was abolished in 1829. In chapter 9, Oliver overhears the Jew musing about five 'fine fellows' who have gone to the gallows— for robbery, one assumes—and never 'peached' on him. They too would seem to be victims of the pre-1829 Bloody Code. It is arguable that we are to assume the execution of Fagin to take place in one of these pockets of anachronism, in the mid-1820s, a decade before other sections of the narrative.

2. As Angus Wilson sardonically notes in his Penguin Classics edition of *Oliver Twist* the murder of a London tart by her ponce cannot have been all that rare an event in the London underworld of the 1830s.

3. Oddly enough, in *Sikes and Nancy*, the 'reading version' of *Oliver Twist*, Dickens altered the episode, so Nancy does indicate Sikes by surname. See the World's Classics edition *Sikes and Nancy and Other Public Readings*, edited by Philip Collins.

4. Philip Collins, *Dickens and Crime* (London, 1964), 281.

5. *Great Expectations* (Everyman Paperback, ed. R. Gilmour, London, 1992), 442.

Jane Eyre

1. For the popularity of the Bluebeard story in the nineteenth century, see Juliet McMaster, 'Bluebeard at Breakfast', *Dickens Studies Annual*, 8 (1981), 197–230.

2. See Sherrill E. Grace, 'Courting Bluebeard with Bartok, Atwood, and Fowles: Modern Treatment of the Bluebeard Theme', *The Journal of Modern Literature*, 11: 2 (July 1984), 245–62.

3. The 'Sister Anne on the Battlements scene' in the Bluebeard

story is alluded to in Jane's visit to the towers of Thornfield Hall with Mrs Fairfax, pp. 111–12.

4. See J. A. Sutherland, *Victorian Novelists, Publishers and Readers* (London, 1995), 55–86.

5. As Michael Mason points out, in his Penguin Classics edition of *Jane Eyre* (Harmondsworth, 1996, p. viii), there is confusion as to whether Bertha is confined on the second or the third floor. She is no madwoman in an attic, or locked in a tower (as the 1944 film suggests).

6. See, for example, the allusions to Byron's *The Corsair* (1814) by the Ingram party (p. 189 of the World's Classics edition).

Shirley

1. According to her nephew, James Austen-Leigh, Jane Austen 'took a kind of parental interest in the beings who she had created, and did not dismiss them from her mind when she had finished her last chapter'. Of *Emma*'s characters she told him 'that Mr Woodhouse survived his daughter's marriage, and kept her and Mr Knightley from settling at Donwell, about two years' (James E. Austen-Leigh, *Memoir of Jane Austen* (1871), ed. R. W. Chapman, Oxford (1926), 157).

2. See Joan Stevens, *Mary Taylor: Friend of Charlotte Brontë: Letters from New Zealand and Elsewhere* (New York, 1972).

3. Juliet Barker, *TLS*, 31 May 1996.

4. The British circulating libraries united to boycott three-deckers in 1893–4. See Guinevere E. Griest, *Mudie's Circulating Library* (Bloomington, Ind., 1970), 95.

Barchester Towers

1. As R. H. Super surmises, on 17 Feb. 1855. See *The Chronicler of Barsetshire* (Ann Arbor, 1988), 79.

2. *The Letters of Anthony Trollope*, ed. N. John Hall (Stanford, Calif., 1983), i. 40.

3. The Revd Quiverful has been carefully introduced (on p. 56) and we may expect that if his lover's ambitions are thwarted, Mr Slope will switch his patronage to the other candidate for the wardenship.

4. Between 3 May and 13 June 1855 Trollope travelled in Italy with his wife, meeting his brother Thomas in Venice. This excursion to

Italy evidently inspired the Stanhope family. There is one previous mention of Mr Stanhope but it is slight and rather out of character (see for instance 'the unique collection of butterflies for which he is so famous'; there is no subsequent allusion to Mr Stanhope being an amateur entomologist; nor is any mention made in this first appearance of his extraordinary family).

Adam Bede

1. Robert Hughes, *The Fatal Shore* (1986; repr. London, 1987), 244–5.

The Mill on the Floss

1. Henry James, 'The Novels of George Eliot', *Atlantic Monthly* (Oct. 1866), repr. *The Mill on the Floss* (Norton Critical Edition, ed. Carol T. Christ, New York, 1994), 465.

2. Ibid. 480.

3. F. R. Leavis, *The Great Tradition* (London, 1948), 24.

4. An exception is Gordon S. Haight, whose appendix 'A' on the geography of *The Mill on the Floss* in the Clarendon edition of the novel (Oxford, 1980, 463–7) I draw on in this chapter.

5. Ibid. 466.

Great Expectations, The Coral Island

1. 'Universal struggle' is an allusion to the third chapter of Darwin's just published *Origin of Species*. K. J. Fielding informs me that Dickens had the second edition of Darwin's work, published in January 1860. Dickens first makes mention of *Great Expectations* in August of that year.

2. I would guess that like most early and mid-nineteenth-century authors Eliot and Dickens were not much good in the water. There were a few exceptions. Walter Scott, for example, seems to have been a good swimmer. Like Byron (another good swimmer), he was disabled, and had courses of 'water treatment' at the seaside inflicted on him in childhood which probably accounts for his proficiency.

3. Ben Franklin, as his autobiography informs us, was inordinately proud of his ability to swim, and saw it as something extraordinary in the mid-eighteenth century. See the World's Classics edition, *Autobiography and Other Writings*, edited by Ormond Seavey.

4. The most commented-on error in *The Coral Island* (see the notes to chapter 4, p. 340).

Armadale

1. In his epilogue Collins claims that 'the end of the story' was sketched in a notebook in spring 1864—a period when he was recuperating his health in Rome. R. D. Altick, *The Presence of the Present* (Columbus, Ohio, 1991), 86–7, suspects that Collins in fact got the details from the *Times* report, cited below: as do I. See note on the text, *Armadale*, ed. J. Sutherland (Penguin Classics, 1995).

2. See the chapter on *The Woman in White* in *Is Heathcliff a Murderer?*, pp. 117–22, for Collins's apprehensions about being caught out by *The Times*.

Felix Holt, the Radical

1. For the early history of World's Classics see Peter Sutcliffe, *The Oxford University Press* (Oxford, 1978), 140–5.

2. See the Lynton Lamb illustration to *Robinson Crusoe* in the first chapter.

3. The World's Classics edition *of Felix Holt, the Radical* follows the Clarendon text.

Ralph the Heir

1. See appendix 1, in the World's Classics *Ralph the Heir*, on 'Shilly Shally'.

2. See my chapter on *Barchester Towers*, above.

Daniel Deronda

1. Kenneth Newton, 'Daniel Deronda and Circumcision', *Essays in Criticism*, 31: 4 (1981), 313–27.

2. Ibid. 313.

3. Gordon S. Haight, *George Eliot* (Oxford, 1968), 470–1.

4. Richard Owen, *The Life of Richard Owen*, 2 vols. (London, 1894), i. 231–2.

5. Rosemary Ashton, *G. H. Lewes* (Oxford, 1991), 11.

6. See the entry on 'Circumcision' in the 11th edition of the *Encyclopaedia Britannica* (1910), vi. 390.

7. It is not just Victorian novelists who were inhibited where circumcision is concerned. In her first Lord Peter Wimsey novel, *Whose Body?* (1923), Dorothy Sayers conceived a vivid opening scene. A naked body is found in a bath-tub in Battersea. It is assumed to be that of a Jewish millionaire. Wimsey comes in, and instantly detects it is not said millionaire. How does he know?— in the manuscript, apparently, Sayers used non-circumcision as the tell-tale evidence which keen-eyed Lord Peter immediately perceived. Sayers's publishers demanded she take the scene out. She made the crucial evidence 'dirty fingernails' instead.

8. Female opposition to the ritual of circumcision boiled up in 1995–6, following the broadcast of Victor Schonfeld's Channel 4 programme, *'It's a Boy!'*. In the furore that followed, largely conducted in the *Jewish Chronicle*, it emerged that a number of defiant Jewish mothers were, on principle, refusing to have their children circumcised.

9. Gordon Haight, *George Eliot* (London, 1968), 40.

The Woodlanders

1. Michael Millgate, *Thomas Hardy: a Biography* (London, 1971; repr. 1994), 245–6.

2. David Lodge, *The Woodlanders* (Macmillan: London, 1974), 392.

3. Thomas Hardy had doubts about the propriety of this phrase; see Dale Kramer's notes to the World's Classics edition of *The Woodlanders*, p. 388.

The Yellow Wall-Paper

1. See, for instance, Dr Mandelet in *The Awakening*, ch. 22. Gilman was treated by Silas Weir Mitchell and the heroine in *The Yellow Wall-Paper* is threatened with 'Weir Mitchell in the fall'. The neurologist-novelist also appears in William Dean Howells's *The Shadow of a Dream* (1890).

2. Jennie is called Jane in the last paragraphs of the novel, which may be an allusion to *Jane Eyre*.

The Sea-Wolf

1. See, for instance, the business of the Bible on board the *Ghost*. Early in the narrative, when the mate drinks himself to death, it is specifically said that there is no 'Bible or prayer-book on

board' (p. 20). Later (p. 96), Wolf Larsen is found reading a Bible. Cloudsley Johns (who read the MS for London) pointed out the error, and the author made the necessary correction about a Bible being found in the dead mate's gear.

2. There is another episode, late in the action, when Larsen again shows these god-like powers. Completely blind, on board the *Ghost*, he deduces the hero's silent presence, despite the fact that Humphrey is thought to be drowned.

The Good Soldier

1. Eugene Goodheart, 'What Dowell knew: A Reading of *The Good Soldier*', *Antaeus*, 56 (Spring 1986), 70.

2. Thomas Moser, in the World's Classics edition of *The Good Soldier*, gives a full account of the story's anachronisms.

3. Martin Stannard (ed.), *The Good Soldier* (Norton Critical Edition, New York, 1991), p. xi.

4. Vincent Cheng, 'A Chronology of *The Good Soldier*', *ELN* 24 (Sept. 1986), repr. in Stannard, 385.

5. J. F. Kermode, 'Novels: Recognition and Deception', *Critical Inquiry*, 1: 1 (Sept. 1974), repr. in Stannard, 336.

6. *LRB* 20 June 1996.

7. The editor of the World's Classics *The Good Soldier*, Thomas Moser, also briefly raises this possibility, only to pass it by as implausible.

8. Max Saunders, *Ford Madox Ford* (Oxford, 1996), i. 422.

9. It is possible to date this episode as 1897, but I follow Cheng in preferring 1895.

Mrs Dalloway

1. The novel began as the short story, 'Mrs Dalloway in Bond Street', which is occupied only with the morning expedition.

2. In 'Mrs Dalloway in Bond Street' the time is given specifically as 'eleven o'clock'. See *The Complete Shorter Fiction of Virginia Woolf*, ed. Susan Dick (London, 1985), 146.

Who Betrays Elizabeth Bennet?

Moll Flanders

1. See Ian Watt, *The Rise of the Novel* (Berkeley, Calif., 1957), 100.

2. Ibid. 99.

3. George Orwell, *Nineteen Eighty-Four* (New York, 1949), 91–3.

4. There is a complicated 'double-time scheme' reading of Defoe's fiction which has been advanced by some critics. John Mullen discusses the issue in the introduction to his Oxford World's Classics edition of Defoe's novel *Roxana* (Oxford, 1996), 341–2.

Tom Jones

1. Coleridge's reported ejaculation (in conversation) was: 'What a master of composition Fielding was! Upon my word, I think the *Oedipus Tyrannus*, the *Alchemist*, and *Tom Jones*, the three most perfect plots ever planned' (quoted in Ian Watt, *The Rise of the Novel*, 269).

Pride and Prejudice

1. Kathleen Glancy was kind enough to read this chapter in proof. 'Your explanation is most ingenious', she concedes. But Miss Glancy is 'not wholly convinced. Charlotte may very well have scores to settle with some members of the Bennet family … Elizabeth, though, was the person whose friendship Charlotte valued most in the world and except for one unguarded reaction to the news of Charlotte's engagement—and Charlotte was *expecting* that—says and does nothing unkind to her. Would one careless remark be enough to rankle to the extent of making Charlotte want to ruin Elizabeth's chances of making a brilliant match?' Miss Glancy is not, as she says, 'wholly convinced'. On the other hand she sportingly offers a conjecture that 'might add weight to your theory. Mr Collins's letter to Mr Bennet, after his warning against Elizabeth's supposed engagement, goes on about his dear Charlotte's situation and expectation of an olive branch. Pregnancy can lead to mood swings and irrational behaviour, and it is easy to imagine that the thought of Lady Catherine dispensing advice on prenatal care and the rearing of the child and the awful possibility that it would resemble its father might prey on Charlotte's mind and cause her subconsciously to

blame Elizabeth for her predicament. After all, if Elizabeth had accepted Mr Collins Charlotte wouldn't be pregnant by him.'

Mansfield Park

1. Deirdre Le Faye, 'What was the History of Fanny Price's Mother?', Jane Austen Society *Report* for 1982 (pp. 213–15 of the *Collected Reports*, Vol. III, 1976–85).

2. For the vexed question of the date of the action of *Mansfield Park* see J. Sutherland, *Is Heathcliff a Murderer?* (London, 1996), 1–9.

3. Miss Le Faye makes enlightening comments on this chapter which she was kind enough to read in proof. On Mrs Norris's first name, Miss Le Faye notes: 'I think it was Dr [R. W.] Chapman who pointed out that as Mrs Norris is godmother to nasty little Betsy Price, it is probable that Mrs N.'s Christian name was Elizabeth'. This is neat and plausible. On the question of the sisters' 'portions' Miss Le Faye suggests that 'Miss Maria Ward may have had a separate fortune, from a godmother or grandmother perhaps. Or possibly the three sisters did each have £7,000—but Miss Ward was already too venomous and scared suitors off, perhaps? Maybe Miss Frances lost hers by making an unsuitable marriage?' On the runaway Bertram daughters, Miss Le Faye notes discriminatingly that 'in fact, both Maria *and* Julia Bertram elope—but Julia's is more literally the elopement, as she and Yates flee together to get married at Gretna Green, which was the classic form of elopement. Maria more correctly speaking *runs away* with Henry Crawford, knowing full well that marriage would not be possible for several years at least, while the ecclesiastical and civil divorce proceedings trundled on their ways.' Miss Le Faye picks up, as I did not, that Lieutenant Price is 'disabled for active service' (p. 3). But, as she points out, 'we don't see or hear of the loss of a limb; and he certainly does not seem to suffer from tuberculosis or cancer; and is certainly capable of continuing to beget children. Does he have a bad rupture, perhaps? Or possibly some form of arthritis or rheumatism which might stiffen his arms and legs and so make it impossible to climb ladders, etc., aboard a ship? or to hold a gun to fire volleys? Bearing in mind that Nelson was perfectly able to continue an active career with only one arm and one eye, what can be wrong with Lieut. P. that he too can't serve actively?' All I can suggest is that 'disabled' here means not that Lieutenant Price is physically impaired, but

that with the lull in the war there is no active service for him to perform; 'disabled' means 'unable'. I am aware this is a feeble retort to Miss Le Faye's witty conjectures. She reserves her most vigorous protest for my suggestion that Lieutenant Price is an abusive parent. 'He *comes home* to drink his rum and water— doesn't stay out boozing with the boys till all hours. And at home, he sits down *and reads the newspaper*—perfectly domesticated! Makes no complaint about his wife's incompetent housekeep-ing—doesn't go out with the town tarts but begets an honest and healthy and goodlooking family. Admittedly he has no interest in Fanny when she returns to the fold, but then neither has her own mother—and he does give her a "cordial hug" on the first evening at least . . . *Not* a brutal and harsh father!' Here I feel on stronger ground. Lieutenant Price's first entry into the action is with an oath and a kick for Fanny's band-box (p. 345). And, a couple of pages later, we are told that Fanny 'could not respect her parents, as she had hoped. On her father her confidence had not been sanguine, but he was more negligent of his family, his habits were worse, and his manners coarser, than she had been prepared for . . . he swore and he drank, he was dirty and gross' (p. 354). I can't think of another character in Jane Austen's fiction who attracts this kind of censure. Given the prevailing decency of her fictional world, one can read a lot into those jarring words, 'dirty and gross'. On the other hand Miss Le Faye is clearly right to point out that there is no evidence of physical violence. Would a contemporary social worker worry about the condition of the younger Price children? Miss Le Faye's comments leave me in two minds about what Fanny's father must have been like to share a small house with.

Emma

1. In *Is Heathcliff a Murderer?* I committed an error of my own by confusing the Donwell outing with that to Box Hill, as a number of readers pointed out.

2. Constable's paintings and sketches are reproduced in *The Early Paintings and Drawings of John Constable*, ed. Graham Reynolds (New Haven, 1996) and *The Later Paintings of John Constable*, ed. Graham Reynolds (New Haven, 1984).

3. Euan Nisbet, 'In Retrospect', *Nature* (10 July 1997), 9.

Rob Roy

1. Notably Philip Gosse, see Edmund Gosse's *Father and Son* (London, 1907).

2. See J. Sutherland, *The Life of Walter Scott* (Oxford, 1995), 205.

3. The bridge shown in this illustration is that which Scott mentions in his 'Advertisement' to the first edition of *Rob Roy*, dated 1 December 1817: 'in point of minute accuracy, it may be stated that the bridge over the Forth, or rather the Avondhu (or Black River) near the hamlet of Aberfoil, had not an existence thirty years ago.' Frank and Nicol Jarvie cross this as-yet-non-existent bridge in 1715. On 27 May 1997 a news item appeared in the *Daily Telegraph* announcing that the inn at Aberfoil 'used by Rob Roy is up for sale . . . it is unlikely to survive as a drinking den, as planning permission has been granted to convert it into a house with a small extension'.

Frankenstein

1. In addition to Gothic 'shockers', one can cite D. H. Lawrence's rewriting of the Gospel story, *The Man Who Died* (London, 1931).

Oliver Twist

1. *Can Jane Eyre Be Happy?* (Oxford, 1997), 54 (300 in the present volume).

2. In *Can Jane Eyre Be Happy?*, pp. 54–5, I noted that Fagin was based on the historical fence, Ikey Solomons. Philip Collins made this link earlier in his authoritative *Dickens and Crime* (London, 1962). The connection was contradicted by J. J. Tobias in *Prince of Fences: The Life of Ikey Solomons* (London, 1974), 147–50. Philip Collins accepts the correction in the preface to the third edition of his book, and courteously wrote correcting the perpetuated error in my book.

Vanity Fair

1. 'De Finibus', in *Roundabout Papers*, the 'Oxford' edition of the works of Thackeray, ed. George Saintsbury, 17 vols. (London, 1908), xvii. 593.

2. Thackeray's chapter title was probably inspired by Charles Lever's military novel, *Tom Burke of Ours* (London, 1843).

3. See the explanatory notes to the Oxford World's Classics edition of *Vanity Fair*, p. 892.

Wuthering Heights

1. *Is Heathcliff a Murderer?*, 57.

2. See Keith Hollingsworth in *The Newgate Novel 1830–1847* (Detroit, 1963).

3. Edward Bulwer-Lytton, *Eugene Aram* (1834, repr. London, 1887), 57 (my emphasis).

4. Ibid. p. x (my emphasis).

5. Elizabeth Gaskell kept a diary of her daughter's baby years, to present to the young woman in later life. It makes a number of references to teething. See *Private Voices: The Diaries of Elizabeth Gaskell and Sophia Holland*, ed. J. A. V. Chapple and Anita Wilson (Keele, 1997).

6. Quoted by G. M. Young in *Victorian England: Portrait of an Age* (1936, repr. New York, 1964), 24.

7. J. Menzies Campbell, *Dentistry Then and Now* (Glasgow, 1963), 61.

Dombey and Son

1. John Woodforde, *The Strange History of False Teeth* (London, 1968), 1–3.

2. For the reasons for supposing the woodcut 'suppressed' (because it too much resembled the Lawrence portrait of the Marquis of Hartford) or merely dropped because the block was damaged see the Oxford World's Classics notes to *Vanity Fair*, p. 928.

3. Woodforde, 61–2.

4. *The Virginians* (1859, repr. Boston, 1896), i. 244–5.

5. Woodforde, 38.

David Copperfield

1. Andrew Lewis informs me that baptismal names sufficed for legal purposes until 1837, so Miss Trotwood can rename David 'Trotwood Copperfield' (after the symbolically baptismal act of washing him, as soon as he arrives at Dover). A more puzzling question is whether she can 'adopt' him, as she tells Wicklow without some legal form of deed. Has she 'adopted' Mr Dick as well? Mr Lewis comments: 'Can DC be adopted by Betsey? The

answer is no. Adoption was not possible in England until 1926 (before then it would have created havoc with primogeniture in succession to land). Dickens is careful to say at first that she and Mr Dick become his guardians. This is a purely informal arrangement (though it mirrors a formal legal institution of guardian appointed by the court). He later uses the term "adopt" for the relationship but this has no legal significance—the language is merely borrowed from those legal systems (like the old Roman) which had a system of adoption.'

2. The notes to the Oxford World's Classics edition of *David Copperfield* point out that these grounds for annulment were repealed in 1823. Andrew Lewis notes that Benjamin's ruse 'would not amount to falsification of the register, a capital offence under Lord Hardwicke's Marriage Act. (This 1753 Act made recording the marriage in a register a prerequisite to validity.) This dodge ceased to be possible after 1823 (4 Geo. IV c. 76).'

3. Andrew Lewis, who was kind enough to read this chapter in proof, made a number of corrections (which I have silently and gratefully incorporated) and concluded his letter in a spirit of friendly scepticism: 'I have a difficulty with John Rokesmith/Harmon's child. She is Rokesmith and unquestionably legitimate, until the truth gets out and she changes her name: there is certainly no need for a remarriage of her parents! Can you take more? Laura and Walter could not, as you say, have been married by banns in less than three weeks, but they could, under the terms of the 1836 Marriage Act have been married by licence from a registrar in less than a fortnight.' This, I assume, is what happened. But I remain curious as to what name Laura gave the Registrar.

Ruth

1. Mrs Twinn, who read this chapter in proof, thinks that 'this final sentence of Chapter 4 is the crucial one. Ruth is active here. She got into the carriage and the way Gaskell uses the verb "drove" implies that Ruth did the driving. (Of course she did not.) That is, Ruth is being made to be made responsible for her own destiny to some extent. It is a subtlety of which Gaskell is a past master.' Mrs Twinn is inclined to see Ruth as more the author of her own misfortune than I am. The novel, I think, leaves space for both interpretations.

2. Mrs Twinn, who has thought deeply about this question, per-

ceives a radical confusion in the author's conception of the 'absent' London episode: 'In Gaskell's mind Ruth and Bellingham did not travel to London at all. However, in the novel, they went to London; (a) because as you rightly comment it would have been the natural route from East Anglia. Close study of the Betts map of 1838 demonstrates that it might have been possible to find a cross-country route but unlikely because of the state of the roads—Bellingham's carriage would have required the better turnpike roads which would have taken them to London; (b) because London provided the right image for Ruth's "deflowering". I believe Gaskell's perception of London was associated with the image of "Babylon". Also Bellingham probably rented a house in London, as was usual amongst the gentry of the time, although I agree he would have been unlikely to have taken Ruth there. I think the choice of London would have been an appropriate and recognisable signal to readers of the events which took place there.' I find Mrs Twinn's reconstruction very persuasive.

Henry Esmond

1. See the Penguin Classics *The History of Henry Esmond*, ed. Michael Greenfield and John Sutherland (London, 1970).

2. For the pressures under which Thackeray wrote, revised, and corrected the proofs of the novel see *The History of Henry Esmond*, ed. Edgar F. Harden (London and New York, 1989), 'Textual Introduction', 406–24.

Bleak House

1. See F. S. Schwarzbach, 'The Fever of *Bleak House*', *English Language Notes*, 20 (Mar.–June 1983), 21–7.

2. F. S. Schwarzbach, 'Deadly Stains: Lady Dedlock's Death', *Dickens Quarterly*, 4 (Sept. 1987), 160–5.

3. It is curious that Lady Dedlock has to enquire where Hawdon is buried. As we are told in Chap. 16, she has already visited his resting-place and (as Professor Schwarzbach suggests) has caught smallpox there.

4. When she paid her earlier visit to Hawdon's grave, Jo 'silently notices how white and small her hand is, and what a jolly servant she must be to wear such sparkling rings' (p. 243).

5. Susan Shatto, 'Lady Dedlock and the Plot of *Bleak House*', *Dickens Quarterly*, 5 (Dec. 1988), 185–91.

North and South

1. I am indebted to Frances Twinn for this suggestion.

2. In an interesting article, 'A Crisis of Liberalism in *North and South*' in *Gaskell Journal*, 10 (1996) 42–52, Andrew Sanders argues that Frederick's struggle is central to the novel, which articulates an essentially political assertion about 'liberalism', a movement which was emerging out of Manchester radicalism in the 1850s.

3. Angus Easson, 'Mr Hale's Doubts in *North and South*', *Review of English Studies* (Feb. 1980), 30–40.

4. This summary is taken from J. Sutherland, *The Longman Companion to Victorian Fiction* (London, 1988), 458.

5. *The Letters of Charles Dickens*, ed. Graham Storey, Kathleen Tillotson, and Angus Easson (London, 1993), vii. 402.

Name Games

1. Most recently by William A. Cohen in *Sex Scandal: The Private Parts of Victorian Fiction* (Durham: NC, 1996).

2. Thackeray made the comment in a letter of 6 May 1851 to the critic David Masson. See *The Letters and Private Papers of William Makepeace Thackeray*, ed. G. N. Ray (1945, repr. New York, 1980), ii. 772.

3. For Dickens's uncertainty about the Christian name of Gradgrind see the Oxford World's Classics edition of *Hard Times*, ed. Paul Schlicke, p. 400.

4. Richard D. Altick, *The Presence of the Present: Topics of the Day in the Victorian Novel* (Columbus, Oh., 1991), 539–40.

5. Kathleen Tillotson, *Novels of the Eighteen-Forties* (Oxford, 1954), 236.

6. James's remarks were originally published in his obituary essay on Trollope in the *Century Magazine*, July 1883. The essay is reprinted in *Anthony Trollope: The Critical Heritage*, ed. Donald Smalley (London, 1969), 525–45.

7. Ibid. 537.

8. The Latin, from Horace's *Ars Poetica*, 126–7, means: 'As it unfolded from the beginning, so let it remain till the end.' It is quoted on the title page of Thackeray's *Henry Esmond* and in Chap. 8 of Trollope's *An Autobiography*. See the Oxford World's Classics edition, p. 139.

9. See the Everyman edition of *Barchester Towers*, ed. David Skilton and Hugh Osborne (London, 1994), 462.

10. David Lodge, 'Fire and Eyre: Charlotte Brontë's War of Earthly Elements', in *The Language of Fiction* (London, 1966), 114–43.

A Tale of Two Cities

1. See Alison Winter *Mesmerism: Powers of Mind in Victorian Britain* (Chicago, 1998), 163–86.

2. Dr Goodenough, who is very sceptical about chloroform, was based on John Elliotson, a good friend of both Thackeray and Dickens. Elliotson, as the country's foremost practitioner of mesmerism, was scathing about ether and chloroform as anaesthetics, advocating mesmerism as the better option. Thackeray reflects Elliotson's scepticism in his depiction of Goodenough and possibly his (Thackeray's) own hesitation about having an operation on his obstructed urethra, something that he was still putting off at the time of his death in December 1863.

3. *Philip* (1860, repr. Boston, 1896), iii. 41.

4. I am indebted in these remarks about passports to John Torpey's 'Passports and the Development of Immigration Controls in the North Atlantic World during the Long Nineteenth Century', conference paper, American Historical Association, Jan. 1998.

Great Expectations

1. Malcolm Hurwitt, who read this chapter in proof, comments: 'As a lawyer I appreciate the way in which the evidence has been unearthed and collated. The only doubt I have relates to the last paragraph: if Pip was kept in ignorance of the wedding to save him from embarrassment it was only putting off the evil day; he would be bound to discover it sometime. Perhaps Joe and Biddy reckoned that passage of time would lessen the sting of the disclosure of Joe's financial sacrifice.' Mr Hurwitt's speculation is shrewd, I think.

The Mill on the Floss

1. Peter Barnard, *The Times*, Thurs. 2 Jan. 1997, p. 39.

2. Beryl Gray, in her Everyman edition of *The Mill on the Floss* (London, 1996), offers an instructive appendix: 'Gainsborough and St Ogg's', pp. 476–80.

3. Gray mentions the *Aegir*, ibid., p. 477, and observes that Eliot mentions it in the early chapter, 'Tom Comes Home'.

Our Mutual Friend

1. Dickens alludes to Scott's 'A Postscript which should have been a Preface' in *Waverley* (1814).

2. Peter Ackroyd, *Dickens* (London, 1990), 963.

3. T. S. Lascelles, 'A Railway Signal Puzzle in *Our Mutual Friend*', *The Dickensian*, 45 (1949), 213–16.

The Moonstone

1. T. S. Eliot, introduction to the World's Classics *The Moonstone* (Oxford, 1928), p. v.

2. Roger Smith, *Trial by Medicine: Insanity and Responsibility in Victorian Trials* (Edinburgh, 1981), 98.

Middlemarch

1. For the tangled genealogy of the Casaubon family see *Is Heathcliff a Murderer?*, pp. 146–55.

The Way we Live Now

1. See P. D. Edwards, 'Trollope Changes his Mind: The Death of Melmotte in *The Way we Live Now*', *Nineteenth-Century Fiction*, 18 (1963), 89–91.

Huckleberry Finn

1. On the title page Twain declares: '*Scene*: The Mississippi Valley. *Time*: Forty to Fifty Years Ago.' Given a publication date of 1884 this suggests a historical setting of 1834–44. But Tom Sawyer's references to Jim's being incarcerated in 'Castle Deef' suggest a later date. Dumas's *The Count of Monte Cristo* was published in France in 1844–5 and could hardly have percolated through as juvenile reading in the Mississippi Valley until a few years later.

Anna Karenina

1. Brian Boyd, *Vladimir Nabokov: The American Years* (Princeton, 1991), 175.

2. A. N. Wilson, *Tolstoy* (London, 1988), 274.

The Mayor of Casterbridge

1. The notes to the Oxford World's Classics edition suggest she must be a townee, see p. 380.

2. Whether there is a railway station at Casterbridge at the time of the novel's action is a nice question, see p. 391.

3. Alison Adburgham, *Shops and Shopping* (1964, repr. London 1981), 231.

4. Phyllis Grosskurth, *Havelock Ellis* (New York, 1980), 17. After relieving herself Mrs Ellis told her son, 'I did not mean you to see that'.

'A Scandal in Bohemia'

1. Brian Coe, *The Birth of Photography* (London, 1989), 35.

2. Ibid. 48.

Dracula

1. This seems to be the line adopted in Anne Rice's very successful series of modern vampire stories.

2. See Margaret Palling, *Cholera, Fever and English Medicine, 1825–1865* (Oxford, 1978).